TRAVELS
IN
WESTERN INDIA

TRAVELS

IN

WESTERN INDIA,

EMBRACING

A VISIT

TO

THE SACRED MOUNTS OF THE JAINS,

AND THE MOST

CELEBRATED SHRINES OF HINDU FAITH

BETWEEN

RAJPOOTANA AND THE INDUS:

WITH AN

ACCOUNT OF THE ANCIENT CITY OF NEHRWALLA

JAMES TOD

GYAN

Published by

Gyan Publishing House
5, Ansari Road
Daryaganj, New Delhi-110002
Phone: 011-47034999, 9811692060
E-mail: books@gyanbooks.com

Distribution Network
gyanbooks.com
India, USA, Canada, UK, Australia

ISBN: 978-93-6920-748-0 (HB)

First Published, 1839

2nd Impression 2025

Printed at: Gyan Press, Delhi.

TRAVELS IN WESTERN INDIA
Author: JAMES TOD

TRAVELS

WESTERN INDIA.

[illegible] del. from a sketch by M.rs Col. Hunter Blair. W. F. Starling sculp.

INTERIOR OF A TEMPLE, AT DAILWARRA, ON ABOO.

TRAVELS

IN

WESTERN INDIA,

EMBRACING

A VISIT

TO

THE SACRED MOUNTS OF THE JAINS,

AND THE MOST

CELEBRATED SHRINES OF HINDU FAITH

BETWEEN

RAJPOOTANA AND THE INDUS;

WITH AN

ACCOUNT OF THE ANCIENT CITY OF NEHRWALLA

BY

THE LATE LIEUTENANT-COLONEL JAMES TOD,

AUTHOR OF "ANNALS OF RAJAST'HAN."

LONDON:

WM. H. ALLEN AND CO., 7, LEADENHALL STREET.

1839.

TO

MRS. COLONEL WILLIAM HUNTER BLAIR.

MY DEAR MADAM:

UNDER whose name and auspices can I present this work to the Public with more advantage to it and to its Author than yours? My motives in dedicating it to you are two-fold—gratitude and inclination. The Public, so greatly indebted to your exquisite pencil for its illustration, can appreciate the former; but the other could be understood only by one who, like me, has been followed into the heart of the Hindoo Olympus by an adventurous Countrywoman, who has the taste to admire and the skill to delineate the beauties it contains. It would have been sufficient to command my homage that you had been at Aboo; but you have done more—you have brought Aboo to England.

I am,

MY DEAR MADAM,

Faithfully and truly your's,

JAMES TOD.

ADVERTISEMENT.

Although the publication of this work has been unavoidably delayed for a considerable period, the manuscript was left by the Author in a state almost complete: a few unimportant omissions in the Appendix it has been found impossible to supply. Except that the work has been deprived of the benefit it would have received from the Author's last revision, it is essentially in the exact state in which he would have given it to the world. A variety of hints occur amongst his papers of topics which he intended to treat of in the Preface to this book; but it would be presumptuous in any other to make such use of such materials.* By the delay, an additional

* The following fragment may be here introduced, as singularly illustrative of the feelings and motives of the Author:—"Custom has taught us to dread the ordeal of a second appearance before the public; but I feel no alarm; on the contrary, fortified by the encouragement I have received, I send forth this as a companion of the other great *tomes* produced by the same motive and nurtured under the same circumstances. Were this new candidate a work of imagination, I might labour under some apprehension; but the materials are the same as those, to the arrangement, as well as to the accumulation, of which I devoted all the energies which God has granted me. Heart and soul did I labour for the one, and with the same idolatrous affection for the subject have I given up every pursuit, every thought, to this, in the hope of making the Rajpoots known by their works. The scene is removed; but I linger awhile in the skirts of Rajpootana, to lead my reader into the hardly less interesting region of Saurashtra, and to the mounts, as sacred to the monotheistic Jain as were Gerazim or Sinai to the Israelite."

interest has been imparted to the subject of the work, by the flood of light which is now pouring upon the antiquities of Western India —the Girnar inscriptions, in particular, being now in a course of interpretation by the Asiatic Society of Bengal, whose learned secretary, Mr. James Prinsep, has already discovered the name of "Antiochus the Greek," and that of one of the Ptolemies of Egypt, recorded in them.

The reader will find a few discordancies in the spelling of proper names, such as *Nehrwalla* and *Nehrwaleh*; but this has been unavoidable. Native writers are not exact: Mr. Colebrooke has remarked of the Rajpoot MSS., that "the orthography of names of persons and places, purporting to represent the pronunciation, is not uniform in manuscripts of the vernacular language."

CONTENTS.

CHAPTER I.

CHAPTER II.

CHAPTER III.

CONTENTS.

CHAPTER IV.

CHAPTER V.

CHAPTER VI.

CHAPTER VII.

CHAPTER VIII.

CHAPTER IX.

CHAPTER X.

CHAPTER XI.

CHAPTER XII.

CHAPTER XIII.

CHAPTER XIV.

CHAPTER XIX.

CHAPTER XX.

CHAPTER XXI.

CHAPTER XXII.

CHAPTER XXIII.

ORDER OF THE PLATES.

MEMOIR OF THE AUTHOR.

If the world be, as Gibbon remarks, "always curious to know th(history of those who have left behind them any image of their minds," it: curiosity must be stronger, as well as more natural, when a posthumou: work is offered to its notice.

Lieutenant-Colonel James Tod was the second son of Mr. James Tod,* anc was born at Islington, on the 20th March 1782. His original destination wa: a mercantile life; but his inclination (which would have led him to choos(the Navy) rebelled against the drudgery of the counting-house, and hi: uncle, Mr. Patrick Heatly, having, in 1798, procured for him a Cadetshi] ii

* Colonel Tod's father (the eldest child of Henry Tod and Janet Monteith, born 26th Octobe 1745) was a native of Scotland, and descended from an ancient family, one of whose ancestors John Tod, having rescued the children of Robert the Bruce, who were captives in England, wa created by the King's own hand a knight banneret, with permission to bear the crest of a fo: rampant (*Tod* being the name of a fox in Scotland), and the motto "Vigilantia," which is stil borne by the family. Mr. Tod married at New York, 4th November 1779, Miss Mary Heatly, th daughter of Mr. Andrew Heatly, of Lanarkshire, who settled at Newport, Rhode Island, America where he married Mary, the daughter of Suetonius Grant, of Bellwadden, who had left Inver ness in 1725, and settled as a merchant at Newport, Rhode Island; he died there 27th Septembe 1744, having been killed by an explosion of gunpowder. Mr. Heatly (who was likewise the fathe of the late Mr. Patrick Heatly, of the Bengal Civil Service) is characterized, in an inscription to hi memory in the burial-ground at Newport, as "the truest gentleman and the most honourabl merchant that has visited this state." Suetonius Grant, who was the son of Donald Grant, o Dalvey, and of Marjorie Stewart, of the family of the Barons of Kinmeachley, county of Banf succeede

in the East-India Company's service, he was sent to the Royal Military Academy, Woolwich, where a limited number of Cadets were educated before the establishment of the Company's Institution at Addiscombe; and proceeded to Bengal in March 1799. His commission in the 2d European Regiment was dated January 9th, 1800. He then volunteered for the Molucca Islands,* was transferred to the Marines, and served in that capacity on board the *Mornington:* so that he knew, by experience, every variety of a soldier's life. On the 29th May 1800, he was appointed a Lieutenant in the 14th Regiment of Native Infantry; and afterwards "ran the gauntlet," as he expresses it, "from Calcutta to Huridwar." An officer (Lieut.-Col. Wm. Nicholl), who served with him in the 14th Regiment, describes Colonel Tod at that time (1800) as "a youth of an amiable disposition, beloved by all his brother-officers, and exhibiting the promise which his talents afterwards realized."

In 1801, when stationed at Delhi, he was selected by Government, in consequence of his skill and acquirements as an engineer, to conduct a survey of an ancient canal in the neighbourhood of that city. In 1805, Mr. Græme Mercer,

succeeded on the death of his grandfather (both his parents having died whilst he was an infant) to the baronetcy; but being then intent on settling as a merchant in the "New World," as America was then called, he negociated the sale of his title to his cousin, Mr. Alexander Grant, an eminent merchant in London, and proceeded to Long Island, New York. Here he became acquainted with Mr. Thomas Tollemache, or Talmage (Tammage, as the name is pronounced in America), a member of the Dysart family, who had an estate at East Hampton, on Long Island, where he died in 1769, at the age of ninety. The grandfather of this gentleman, a Puritan, had quitted England in the latter end of the Protectorate of Oliver Cromwell. Suetonius Grant married Temperance, the daughter of this Mr. Talmage, and had a son, who threatened to claim the baronetcy; but, leaving no heir (his wife and only child dying at Newport), the title remains in the family of Sir Alexander Grant. The Talmages of New York are a highly respectable family, one member being a General in the army of the United States, another a Judge.

Mrs. Tod, the grand-daughter of Sir Suetonius Grant and the mother of Col. Tod (a lady remarkable for her intellectual accomplishments and for the vigour of her understanding), still survives, at a great age.

* The expedition to the Moluccas seems to have been that planned by Lord Wellesley, and ordered to rendezvous at Trincomalee, but which was not carried into execution.

Mercer, a friend of his uncle, then about to proceed to the Court of Dowlut Rao Sindia as Envoy and Resident, in consequence of a wish expressed by Lieut. Tod, whose honourable and independent character he knew, obtained permission from the Government for the young officer to join his escort; and thus an avenue was opened to a career of usefulness and honour, and his zeal and talents took every possible advantage of it.

On their march from Agra, through the southern part of Jeypore to Oodeypore,—a country which had been but little traversed by Europeans,—Mr. Mercer states that Lieut. Tod "applied himself with much earnestness to making a survey of the route, and with imperfect instruments, by perseverance and the *perfervidum ingenium Scotorum*, which he possessed in a high degree, in spite of very indifferent health, he performed his task in a manner, which better means, and increased knowledge of practical and theoretical surveying, could afterwards, I believe, but little, if at all, improve." It is a sufficient proof of the ignorance which then prevailed respecting the geography of Rajpootana, that the position of the two capitals, Oodeypore and Cheetore, was, in the best maps, precisely reversed; Cheetore being placed S.E. of Oodeypore, instead of E.N.E.

When, in the spring of 1806, the embassy reached the Court of Sindia, it was encamped amidst the ruins of Méwar, the Mahratta chief having forced the passes to the Rana's capital. Lieut. Tod undertook to supply the deficiencies in our knowledge of the geography of this country; and he has publicly asserted, and no one has disputed the correctness of the assertion, that "every map, without exception, printed since that period, has its foundations, as regards Central and Western India, in his labours." The course he pursued in this great undertaking he has described in the paper, on the Geography of Rajast'han, prefixed to its *Annals*.

A portion of the route had been surveyed, and points laid down from celestial observations, with considerable accuracy, by Dr. Wm. Hunter, who accompanied Colonel Palmer in 1791; and this route was made the basis

 of

of the survey, which embraced all the extreme points of Central India*—Agra, Nirwar, Dutteah, Jhansi, Bhopal, Sarungpoor, Oojein, and back by Kotah, Boondi, Rampoora, Biana, to Agra. From Rampoora, where Hunter ceased to be a guide, the new survey commenced, to Oodeypore, from whence the Mahratta army marched past Cheetore, and through the centre of Malwa, crossing in detail all the grand streams flowing from the Vindhya range, seven hundred miles, to the Bundlekhund frontier, at Kemlassa.

In 1807, the Mahratta army having undertaken the siege of Rahtgurh, Lieut. Tod, aware of the time wasted in such operations, determined to avail himself of the delay, and push through an untrodden and disorganized country. With a small guard, he proceeded along the banks of the Betwa to Chanderi,† and westward to Kotah, tracing the course of all the streams from the south, and the points of junction of the most important, continuing his route to Agra. This undertaking he accomplished (being then only twenty-five years of age) at great personal risk, meeting with many romantic adventures, and being more than once an object of plunder. On his return to the Mahratta camp, finding he had still time at his disposal, he set out upon a new journey, proceeding westward by Bhawulpore to Jeypore, Tonk, &c. to Saugur—a journey of one thousand miles, the camp, on his return, being nearly where he left it.

With Sindia's ambulatory court he moved throughout this region, constantly occupied in surveying, till 1812, when it became stationary at Gwalior; and he then formed his plans for obtaining a knowledge of those countries into which he could not personally penetrate.

He despatched two parties for geographical and topographical discovery. The

* It may be observed, that the term "Central India" was first applied by Col. Tod to these tracts, in 1815, in the map he presented to the Marquess of Hastings.

† Speaking of Chanderi, in the *Annals* (i. 138), he says, "I was the first European who traversed this wild country, in 1807, not without some hazard. It was then independent; but three years after, it fell a prey to Sindia."

The first proceeded west by Oodeypore, through Guzerat, Saurashtra, Cutch, Luckput, Hyderabad, Tatta, Seewan, Khyrpore, and Bekher, crossing and recrossing the Indus, and returned by the desert of Oomrasoomra, through Jessulmér, Marwar, and Jeypore, joining him in the camp, then at Nirwar. The other party was sent to the desert south of the Sutlej. The conductors of both expeditions were natives, selected and trained by himself, well-informed, fearless, enterprizing, and imbued with his own zeal in the cause of science. " From these remote regions," he says, " the best-informed native inhabitants were, by persuasion and recompense, conducted to me, and I could at all times, in the Mahratta camp at Gwalior, from 1812 to 1817, have provided a native of the valley of the Indus, the deserts of Dhat and Oomrasoomra, or any of the states of Rajast'han." Elsewhere he says: " Though I never penetrated personally further into the heart of the Indian desert than Mundore, the ancient capital of Maroost'hali, the old castle of Hissar, on its N.E. frontier, and Aboo, Nehrwalla, and Bhooj, to the W., my parties of discovery have traversed it in every direction, adding to their journals of routes living testimonies of their accuracy, and bringing to me natives of every *t'hul* * from Bhutnair to Omurkote, and from Aboo to Arore. The journals of all these routes, with others from Central and Western India, form eleven moderate-sized folio volumes."† These materials were accumulated with a disregard of pecuniary sacrifices, as well as of health and toil, which evinced the ardour of his zeal and the sincerity of his views. " During the period I remained in the Residency," observes Mr. Mercer, " he continued to take advantage of every opportunity in his power to enlarge his knowledge of the geography of the country; and the greatest part of his allowances was, I am confident, expended in paying agents sent to various quarters to collect topographical information. His personal labour for the purpose was also unceasing; and instead of stimulating his exertions, I was sometimes obliged to endeavour

* *T'huls* are bare and arid tracts, contradistinguished from *rooê*, ' jungle desert.'

† *Annals*, ii. 289.

endeavour to restrain them, as incompatible with a state of health which, from rheumatic affection, frequently disabled him from taking even common exercise."

He was rarely satisfied with the result obtained by one set of his parties, but made the information gained by one a basis for the instructions given to others, who went over the same ground with additional advantages. Thus, in a few years, he had filled several volumes with lines of routes; and having fixed the positions of many frontier and intermediate lines, a general outline was constructed, wherein all the information was laid down, and he then determined to test its accuracy by recommencing the survey trigonometrically; and this he accomplished by despatching his parties afresh, who, from fixed positions, as centres, collected every radiating route to all the towns within twenty miles. "By such means," he observes, "did I work my way in these unknown tracts."

These details, which are given almost in Colonel Tod's own words, may, perhaps, appear unnecessarily minute; but they show the extent and the value of the resources he possessed, and the important services they enabled him to render in the Pindarry campaign.

Mr. Mercer left India in 1810, and was succeeded in the Residency at Sindia's court, then at Nirwar, by Mr. Richard Strachey, who had become acquainted with Lieut. Tod ten years before, at Delhi. In October 1813, he was promoted to the rank of Captain, and to the command of the escort; and a short time previous to Mr. Strachey's quitting the court, in October 1815, Captain Tod was nominated to the civil post of Second Assistant to the Resident. During all this time, Mr. Strachey states, he was engaged in collecting geographical materials, relating chiefly to the countries between the Indus and Bundlekhund, the Jumna and the Nerbudda. "My official duties," that gentleman says, "having constant reference to these countries, I derived great advantage from his geographical knowledge of that extensive tract. He was ever ready to communicate the information he had acquired,

and

and which, at that important period, proved most useful: it was well appreciated by Government."

The state of Rajpootana at this time is forcibly depicted in his great work. The Mahrattas, who first crossed the Chumbul in 1735, soon formed establishments in Malwa, and passing the Nerbudda in swarms, intermingling in and fomenting the quarrels of the different states, lending aid sometimes to one and sometimes to another, at length gained a permanent footing in Rajast'han. The weak Mahomed Shah, of Delhi, had surrendered to them the *chout'h*, or 'fourth' of his revenue, and this grant formed the ground of their exactions here as well as elsewhere. Their leader, Bajeerao, appeared in Méwar, and the Rana was compelled to conclude a treaty, whereby he bound himself to pay an annual tribute to the three great Mahratta leaders, which remained in force about ten years, till it suited the convenience of the invaders to augment their demands. In imitation of the wretched policy of inferior states, the Rana employed Holkar in one of his quarrels (paying him nearly one million sterling), and from this time (1750) the Mahrattas gained a firm hold of Rajast'han, which became the theatre of their mutual conflicts, as well as of predatory spoliation and intestine civil strife, till the Pindarry and Mahratta war, and the treaties concluded with the British Government in 1817-18. The devastations of these locusts, in little more than half a century, are described in impassioned and glowing language in the *Annals of Rajast'han.* Their abstractions of territory, from 1770 to 1775, as pledges for contributions, satisfied their cupidity till 1792, when the civil disorders of Rajpootana brought the great Madhajee Sindia to Cheetore, and his lieutenant, Umbajee, is supposed to have extorted two millions sterling from Méwar alone, when it was assigned to the tender mercies of his deputies. Ravaged alternately by the rival armies of Holkar and Sindia, which were let loose to prey and fatten on this devoted land, their passions inflamed by occasional defeat, and their appetite stimulated by unbounded license, Rajpootana was rapidly transforming into a desert. "It would require," says Colonel Tod,

Tod, " a pen powerful as the pencil of Salvator Rosa to paint the horrors which filled up the succeeding ten years (after 1805), and of which the Author was an eye-witness, destined to follow in the train of rapine, and to view, in the traces of Mahratta camps, the desolation and political annihilation of all the central states of India, several of which had aided the British in their early struggles for dominion, but were now allowed to fall without a helping hand."—" In the spring of 1806, when the embassy entered the once-fertile Méwar, nothing but ruin met the eye—deserted towns, roofless houses, and uncultured plains. Wherever the Mahrattas encamped, annihilation was ensured—it was a habit: twenty-four hours sufficed to give to the most flourishing spot the aspect of a desert. The march of destruction was always to be traced for days afterwards by burning villages and destroyed cultivation."—"Méwar was rapidly approaching dissolution, and every sign of civilization fast disappearing: fields laid waste, cities in ruins, inhabitants exiled, chieftains demoralized, the prince and his family destitute of common comforts."*

The warm and sensitive feelings of the young soldier appear to have been deeply wounded by the sad spectacle of a fine country, whose martial races exhibited the rudiments of virtues which even tyranny could not eradicate, consigned to the hands of the oppressor. He was present at the interview, in June 1806, between the Rana of Méwar, Bheem Sing, and Dowlut Rao Sindia, at the shrine of Eklinga, about six miles from Oodeypore, during the memorable transactions which ended in the inhuman sacrifice of the Rana's daughter, Kishna Komari, " the Flower of Rajast'han," the whole of which dreadful drama was acted before his eyes. The appearance of the Rana, the descendant of the ancient sovereigns of India, now at the mercy of a peasant's son, produced a lasting impression upon him. Sindia, in order to increase his importance in the eyes of the Rana, had invited the British Envoy and his suite to be present on this occasion. " I well remember," observes Mr. Mercer,

* *Annals,* i. 458 469-70.

cer, the Envoy, "the enthusiasm he (Lieut. Tod) evinced when he was introduced to the Rana of Oodeypore, at a conference to which we accompanied Dowlut Rao Sindia. The appearance of the Rana and his attendants, the ancient nobility of Hindust'han, was certainly highly impressive; and although I had been previously present at almost every court in India, I was much struck with the aspect and demeanour of a family which had been entitled to the appellation of 'Kings of the Hindus' before the Musulman conquest." It is plain from what Colonel Tod states, when referring to this interview, in his Annals of Méwar, that it was at this moment he first conceived the idea of that benevolent scheme for the regeneration of Rajast'han, of which he became so prominent an instrument: "The impression made upon the Author, upon this occasion," he says, "by the miseries and the noble appearance of this 'descendant of a hundred kings,' was never allowed to weaken, but kindled an enthusiastic desire for the restoration of his fallen condition, and stimulated his perseverance to obtain that knowledge by which alone he might be enabled to benefit him. It was a long dream, but, after ten years of anxious hope, he had the gratification of being instrumental in snatching the family from destruction, and subsequently of raising the country to comparative prosperity."*

At this period, the Anglo-Indian Government, under Lord Minto, had, in conformity with its pacific, or rather timid, policy, determined to refrain from all interference with the internal arrangements of these states, and its Envoy was compelled to be a passive spectator of the havoc around him. In 1817, however, the resolution of Marquess Hastings, to put down the Pindarries (a community of organized robbers, the offspring of a diseased state of society), which involved him in an extensive war with the Mahrattas, their protectors, in one short but active campaign, overthrew that vast predatory system under which Rajast'han had

* *Annals*, i. 461.

had so long groaned. That country and the states surrounding it became the scene of our military operations, and now the knowledge and experience acquired by Captain Tod, at so much risk and cost, were of inappreciable value. There were no maps of these parts; the geography, statistics, and military topography of Central and Western India were unknown; and our commanders, who had to track, unaided by an adverse population, the swift-moving Pindarries to their haunts and recesses by devious routes, and through secret passes, would have been constantly at fault, and must have been ultimately foiled, but for the forethought, sagacity, industry, and public spirit of a young subaltern, "the sole individual in India who had any personal or acquired knowledge of the seat of war."

An abstract of a short sketch or summary, in his own hand-writing, of his services at this critical period, will show how much Colonel Tod contributed to the success of that brilliant and decisive campaign.

When the operations against the Pindarries commenced, he commanded two companies of infantry and half a troop of cavalry, for the protection of the Residency at Sindia's Court. In 1814-15, he had sent in a Memoir of the rise, progress, and existing condition of the Pindarries. This he followed up by a map of all these regions, with an account of their geographical, political, and physical history,* together with a general plan for the subjugation of those marauders, which was closely followed in the actual campaign. As the face of affairs changed, he sent in another restricted plan, with a minute map of the countries north of the Nerbudda, to which he strongly urged that the campaign should be confined. For these communications he received the hearty thanks of Lord Hastings, and copies of the maps were transmitted to the head-quarters of every General of division in the field. The last of these documents

* A specimen of the fulness of these disquisitions may be seen in the Annals of Ambér or Jeypore, given in the *Annals of Rajast'han* (ii. 345), which is nearly the same as he communicated to the Government.

documents which reached his lordship was deemed of so much importance (as he informed Captain Tod), that he despatched copies by express to Sir Thomas Hislop, commanding the army of the south.

Having prepared these valuable materials for the scheme of the campaign, he volunteered his personal services to any of the divisions in the field, which were accepted by Lord Hastings, who said, "I have always had an eye on you for service on this important occasion." At first, it was intended to attach him to Major Gen. Sir D. Ochterlony's division; but his general knowledge, it was thought, would be more usefully applied by placing him at Rowtah,* in Harouti, a situation central to all the divisions, whereby he became the pivot of movement and intelligence: "Indeed," he observes, "I may say that I guided the movements of all the divisions of the army north of the Nerbudda, *viz.* those of Generals Donkin, Marshall, Adams, and Browne." The value of his services was acknowledged in repeated thanks from Lord Hastings and every General in the field.

Having learned that a body of Pindarries, under Kureem Khan's son, had taken refuge in the recesses of the Caly Sinde, thirty miles from his own position, he added 250 matchlocks (Kotah auxiliaries) to thirty-two firelocks of his own men (who had volunteered with him from the 25th N. I.), and despatched them to beat up the enemy's camp, of 1,500 men, telling them "not to return till they had done something." The auxiliaries hung back; but the little band of thirty-two, intent on the admonition of their commander, did not hesitate to attack the enemy, whom they dispersed, killing 100 or 150. The moral effect of this exploit was wonderful. Not a single Pindarry had been hitherto molested, even by our allies; but next day, the spoils of the discomfited party—cattle, elephants, camels, and

* In his Personal Narrative (*Annals*, ii. 700), when he records his encamping on this spot, in the journey to Kotah, in 1820, he says: "Rowtah is hallowed by recollections the most inspiriting: it was on this very ground I took up my position throughout the campaign of 1817-18, in the very centre of movement of all the armies, friendly and hostile."

and valuable booty—were captured, and brought to the camp of the Regent of Kotah, who sent the whole to Captain Tod, at whose suggestion it was sold, and a bridge of twenty arches over a torrent leading from the high road east of Kotah was built with the proceeds. This trophy was named, at the instance of Captain Tod, " Hastings' Bridge." Lord Hastings was so pleased with this exploit (which was not the only one of the kind), that he declared " it was worthy of a medal," and the men concerned in it were rewarded with extra pay.

After the destruction of the grand horde of Pindarries, under Kureem Khan, Captain Tod prepared a Circular Memorandum, proposing a combined movement for the destruction of the other grand horde, under Chetoo, which he addressed to every General commanding a division north of the Nerbudda, *viz.* Sir Thos. Hislop, Sir Wm. Grant Keir, Sir R. Donkin, and Colonel Adams, which gained him the special thanks of Lord Hastings. The plan was not acted upon, though the movements of the enemy were precisely those which had been anticipated in it and provided against. The Assist.-Adj. General with Colonel Adams' division, in writing to Captain Tod in his own and his Commander's name, said of this Circular, " rest assured that no officer but yourself could have penned it."*

The information and the intelligence which he was thus enabled to contribute so opportunely for his country's service, were mostly derived from a system organized, at his own private expense, for the collection of geographical, statistical, and archæological knowledge, wholly foreign to his official duties. Every day, during this campaign, he had from ten to twenty written reports, from whence he extracted bulletins, which he sent to the head-quarters of every division. The Marquess Hastings, at the close of the war, spoke of his services

* Singular enough, this Circular became a document of some importance in the discussions respecting the Deccan booty. Col. Tod had proposed in it to make himself " the pivot of the operations which must destroy Chetoo ;" and it was relied upon strongly by Lord Hastings' counsel, to show that he was considered as Commander-in-Chief of both armies.

services in the highest terms, as having "materially contributed to its success:" adding that "testimonials highly creditable had been received from every General in the field to his services in the guidance of the operations."

Nor were these services of a diplomatic and political nature merely; they partook essentially of a military character. Upon this point, a Memorandum, drawn up by Colonel Tod and found amongst his papers, is decisive:

"If calling out the whole disposable military resources of Kotah was a political act, their application was purely military; and if, by my knowledge of the character of the individual (Zalim Sing), I was enabled to wield his incalculable resources for our purposes, it was my military knowledge of the country alone which could render perfect this diplomatic attainment. Here was a chief, the wisest and most powerful in Central India, whose country was in the heart of operations, and the only one which contained resources of any kind; but he remembered the injuries his aid to us in Lord Lake's wars had inflicted on him, and our abandonment of him to Holkar's anger, when it suited our policy, under Lord Cornwallis. Some skill, it will be conceded, was required to overcome such recollections; yet did I, in five days after my arrival, not only overcome them, but prevail upon him to place his military resources under my *sole* control.

"My first application of them was to despatch to Sir J. Malcolm's aid (he had just crossed the Nerbudda into the heart of our enemies, who, had they possessed the least energy, should have destroyed his weak corps) a regiment called 'the Royals,' one thousand strong, with four guns, and a corps of three hundred good horse. These remained with Sir John throughout the campaign, and were eminently distinguished, especially in the escalade and capture of one of the enemy's forts. 2*ndly.* I distributed corps at the different passes, several of whom had affairs with the enemy. 3*dly.* When hostilities commenced with Holkar, in one short week I took military possession of every district of Holkar's, from the Boondi mountains

to

to the field of battle at Mahidpore. To each of these detachments I gave an English union, which, within that short space, was planted in every fortified town and post, and allegiance (demanded by proclamation) yielded to the British Government. Nothing but a military knowledge of the country and its application could have obtained such results.

"All these duties were essentially military, though intermixed with diplomacy. Even my most diplomatic duties involved the exercise of a military judgment, and their correctness could be tested only by military results. For example—the negociations with Holkar's government, immediately preceding hostilities, were entrusted to me. The juncture was most delicate. This Court had tendered an application for protective alliance, and I was authorized to employ the right grand division of the army, under General Sir Rufane Donkin, to give the Court that protection which would enable it to conclude its measures in security. Scarcely had this trust been reposed in me, and but a few days after I had taken up my central position, when the Peshwa and the Bhonslah broke the alliance with us, and I discovered agents of the Peshwa having bills of exchange to induce Holkar's government to declare for his master. At such a moment, it being far better to have declared foes than pretended allies, I despatched an express, through my agent, to the Regent Baê, acquainting her with my knowledge of such duplicity, and adding that, if in thirty-six hours she did not publicly proclaim her alliance with my Government, call for the assistance she required, expel the Peshwa's agents, and attack a body of Pindarries, then close to her camp, as a proof of good intentions, I would consider her Government amongst the foes of my own; and my agent had orders to quit her Court at the expiration of that period. He did so;—the step was one of great responsibility, and I felt the weight of it; but an express from Lord Hastings soon relieved me of this by gratifying comments on my conduct. I may add that, on withdrawing my agent, I sent duplicate despatches to Sir John Malcolm,

colm, and gave my opinion, 'that any delay in attacking Holkar's camp was merely a question of expediency, of which he was best judge.' Unfortunately, he renewed the negociation I had thrown up, in a pacific tone, which, in the first instance, incurred the serious displeasure of Lord Hastings, and shortly afterwards, the most wanton insults and attacks on his camp-suttlers, until the action of Mahidpore.

"Out of this arose another diplomatic measure, which was again mixed with military tactics. The Kotah Regent, who had been wavering between us, and the entire native force of India,—his old friends,—I determined to secure by the partition of Holkar's territory; and immediately that I foresaw hostilities to be unavoidable with this power, I recommended to Lord Hastings to promise to the Regent the sovereignty of four rich districts, rented by him from Holkar. The suggestion was highly approved, and I had a *carte blanche* as to the time and manner of making the offer; with power to make the grant under my own seal, which would be hereafter confirmed. Every effect I had anticipated followed: present interest banished all apprehension for the future; and I made an act, which, as he said, would 'for ever blacken his face' amongst his old friends, the touchstone of the Regent's good faith: *viz.* the capture and delivery to me of all the wives and children of the great Pindarry leaders, whom I had discovered in concealment near his fortress of Gogeaun. This acted like a charm: their moral strength was dissolved, and from that hour their chiefs came in and were deported from the scenes of their intrigues. By this act, the Regent had for ever severed himself from the Pindarries; while his acceptance of the four districts, and the military possession of them, and all the other districts of Holkar, for ever disunited him from the politics of that Court and the whole Mahratta nation.

"In each of these measures—of the last importance at this crisis—military combinations were so involved with diplomacy that it would be difficult to separate

separate them: it is easily seen that not only the one might not have been conceived, but would have been poorly executed, without the other.

"Other measures and responsibilities which I incurred were still more decidedly military.—When Sir T. Hislop retrograded in his advance north of the Nerbudda, the Peshwa having broken the alliance, the Bombay Government detained its advanced army under General Sir W. Grant Keir, to whom was assigned an important position in the general chain of operations against the Pindarries. At this moment, General Sir John Malcolm had actually crossed, at the head of one weak division of the army of the south, unsupported; and the whole plan of the campaign was changed by the movement of General Sir T. Hislop, so that the Pindarry war was rendered secondary. Judging, however, that the Commander-in-Chief would not desire any change in the operations chalked out, from the Peshwa's revolt, and fearing the result to Sir John Malcolm's division, without support, I took upon me to send an express despatch to General Sir W. Grant Keir, pointing out all these things, and stating my confidence that Lord Hastings would be pleased if he marched with all rapidity into Mêwar, and took a position in the vicinity of Oojein. This was a purely military question. General Sir W. Grant Keir was 350 miles from me; but I had laid and kept up a regular and rapid communication, in the midst of enemies, even with his camp. A copy of this despatch was sent express to Marquess Hastings: again I deprecated the responsibility I had assumed, and again received the expression of his high approbation and thanks for having done so. General Sir T. Browne not only moved as I directed, but had some of my principal guides to conduct him in the enterprise which ended in the destruction of the corps under Roshun Beg."

Rajpootana being now redeemed from the grasp of the spoiler, it was of essential importance to its interests, as well as to those of British India, in order to prevent a renewal of the predatory system, and to interpose a

barrier

barrier between our territories and the strong natural frontier of India, that these newly settled states should be united in one grand confederation; and they were accordingly invited to accept the protective alliance of the British. With a single exception, Jeypore, which demurred for a few months, they eagerly embraced the invitation; and in a few weeks all Rajpootana was allied to Britain, by compacts of one uniform character, securing to them external protection and internal independence, in return for an acknowledgment of our supremacy, and the annual payment of a portion of the revenue. These treaties were signed in December 1817 and January 1818, and in February Captain Tod (then Political Assistant to the Resident at Gwalior) was appointed by the Governor-General (a pretty sure criterion of the value attached to his services) his Political Agent to the Western Rajpoot states.

Clothed with this ample authority, he applied himself to the arduous task of endeavouring to repair the ravages of foreign invaders who still lingered in some of the fortresses, to heal the deeper wounds inflicted by intestine feuds, and to reconstruct the frame-work of society in the disorganized states of Rajast'han. The undertaking would have appalled any man but one who was already familiar with the intricate mazes of Rajpoot politics, who had studied the institutions, the character, and the prejudices of the people, and was well skilled in their popular literature;* who could debate any difficult question with them in their own dialect, on their own maxims and principles; above all, whose temperament was sanguine, whose energy was irrepressible, and whose views were direct and disinterested.

Proceeding

* In a MS. note for a translation of the Rajpoot poet, Chand or Chund, Col. Tod says, "I lived familiarly amongst these people and imbibed their sentiments, and although they might not reach to our standard of excellence, the deterioration was endurable from the knowledge of what they had been ere corrupted by tyranny and oppression. When I say I lived six years amongst them, and twice that time in their vicinity, the surprise will only be that I know so little. I do not pretend to any critical knowledge of the language of these poems; but I had one advantage, which such knowledge could not give me—a power of conversing in it, not with elegance, but with fluency, and its tropes and metaphors were matter of colloquial common-place."

Proceeding to the scene of his new and important functions, in his journey to Oodeypore from Jehajpoor, 140 miles, only two thinly-peopled towns were seen which acknowledged the Rana's authority. All was desolate: even the traces of human footsteps were effaced. "The babool and gigantic reed, which harboured the boar and the tiger, grew upon the highways, and every rising ground disclosed a mass of ruins. Bhilwara, the commercial *entrepôt* of Rajpootana, which ten years before contained 6,000 families, shewed not a vestige of life: all was silent in her streets; no living thing was seen, except a solitary dog, that fled in dismay from his lurking place in the temple, scared at the unaccustomed sight of man." This is an image of desolation scarcely to be paralleled by any which a poet's fertile fancy could suggest, to express the combined ravages of war, famine, and pestilence.

"Such," observes Colonel Tod, in his Annals of Méwar, after a deplorable picture of the condition of the country in 1818, "was the chaos from which order was to be evoked. But the elements of prosperity, though scattered, were not extinct; and recollections of the past, deeply engraven in the national mind, became available to reanimate their moral and physical existence. To call these forth demanded only the exertion of moral interference, and every other was rejected. The lawless freebooter, and even the savage Bhil, felt awed at the agency of a power never seen." The instruments, with which the Agent was to work out this moral regeneration, were by no means adapted for that purpose. The Rana, though amiable, was weak, unsteady, and passive to female influence. Amongst the ministers, "there appeared no talent, no authority, no honesty." In a short period, however, the firm, conciliatory, and skilful measures of the British Agent changed the aspect of affairs. The refractory nobles were induced by his mediation to forego their resentments and come to the capital; the Rana, who, in 1818, had not fifty horse to attend him, found his authority recognized and his retinue swelled by his feudal nobles; the exiled population were restored to their *bapota*, their "father land," and agriculture and trade began to revive

and

and flourish. Within eight months after the execution of the treaties, above three hundred deserted towns and villages were reinhabited, and lands, which for many years had been untouched by the plough, were broken up. Foreign merchants and bankers, relying on the pledges of the British Agent, came to the country and fixed their factors in every town. The restrictions on external commerce were removed, transit duties abolished, the frontier customs reduced, the products of the imposts, notwithstanding these reductions,—to the astonishment of the ministers, who could not comprehend a result so incongruous with their narrow calculations,—in a few years exceeding the highest amount that had ever been known. The once deserted Bhilwara, in 1822, contained 3,000 houses, and an entire new street was erected, inhabited by merchants and bankers, as well as citizens. The number of houses in Oodeypore, which in 1818 was 3,500, in 1822 was 10,000 : the fiscal revenue, which in 1818 yielded Rs. 40,000 (about £4,000), in 1821 had reached upwards of ten lakhs (about £100,000).

To describe in minute detail the reforms effected by Colonel Tod in this and the other states placed under his charge, and which produced these beneficial results, would extend this Memoir to an inconvenient length. They are recorded by himself in his great work, with a manly indifference to the charge of egotism (from which weakness, in its vulgar form, no man was more exempt*) from those who cannot distinguish between the self-adulation of a superficial mind, and the satisfaction which, in a generous and noble nature, springs from the consciousness of having, with the purest motives and at many a painful sacrifice, conferred a lasting benefit upon large masses of the human race.

The sentiments of the people themselves afford the least equivocal evidence of the value of his services; and these sentiments have found a public organ in the late Bishop Heber, who visited Rajpootana two years after Colonel Tod had left it. "All the provinces of Méwar," says the Prelate, "were, for a considerable time after their connexion with the British Government, under the administration of Captain Tod, whose name appears to be held in a degree of

* "No one," says an intimate friend, "could weigh more modestly his pretensions than Col. T."

of affection and respect, by all the upper and middling classes of society, highly honourable to him, and sufficient to rescue these poor people from the often-repeated charge of ingratitude. At Dabla, and in our subsequent stages, we were continually asked by the cutwals, &c. after 'Tod Sahib,' whether his health was better since his return to England, and whether there was any chance of their seeing him again? On being told it was not likely, they all expressed much regret; saying that the country had never known quiet till he came among them, and that every body, whether rich or poor, except thieves and Pindarries, loved him. He, in fact, Dr. Smith told me, loved the people of this country, and understood their language and manners in a very unusual degree. At Bhilwara, every one was full of Captain Tod's praise. The place had been entirely ruined by Jumsheed Khan, and deserted by all its inhabitants, when Captain Tod persuaded the Rana to adopt measures for encouraging the owners of land to return, and foreign merchants to settle. He himself drew up a code of regulations for them; obtained them an immunity from taxes for a certain number of years, and sent them patterns of different articles of English manufacture for their imitation. He also gave money liberally to the beautifying their town. In short, as one of the merchants, who called on me, said, 'it ought to be called Tod-gunge; but there is no need, for we shall never forget him.' Such praise as this, from people who had no further hopes of seeing or receiving any benefit from him, is indeed of sterling value."* The fact is, that Bhilwara

* "Narrative of a Journey through the Upper Provinces of India in 1824-5," &c. Vol. II., p. 42. The Bishop adds, "His misfortune was that, in consequence of favouring the native princes so much, the government of Calcutta were led to suspect him of corruption, and consequently to narrow his powers and associate other officers with him in his trust, till he was disgusted and resigned his place. They are now, I believe, well satisfied that their suspicions were groundless." If this be a correct representation of the matter, it conveys a very serious imputation upon the Bengal Government, which must have adopted and acted upon a suspicion without the slightest ground. It does not appear that even the native servants of Col. Tod were obnoxious to the charge of venality, which the Bishop brings against those of Sir David Ochterlony, who found his name placed by his own moonshee, without his knowledge, as a pensioner to the amount of £1,200 a year, on the civil list of the poor old King of Delhi!

wara was actually called "Tod-gunge," which name was, however, suppressed at the earnest entreaty of Colonel Tod himself, who wished that the Rana should have the merit of every beneficial act, contenting himself with the secret praise which his own heart bestowed.

In February 1819, the state of Marwar was placed under his agency, in addition to Méwar, Jessulmér, Kotah, Boondi, and Sirohi; and in October of that year he proceeded to Jodpore, the capital of Marwar, where he conferred with its sovereign, Raja Maun, a man of very singular qualities, whose character Colonel Tod has developed with great ability in his Personal Narrative.* The demoniacal spirit of revenge which actuated this prince, appears to have disappointed the hopes and expectations of the Agent.† He visited Ajmér, and in December returned to the valley of Oodeypore.

In January 1820, he set out on another expedition to the Hara states of Kotah and Boondi. The former of these two states was under the actual rule of the Regent, Zalim Sing, a remarkable personage, whom Colonel Tod has aptly termed the "Nestor of Rajast'han." His shrewd sagacity is apparent from two circumstances,—first, that his "eagle eye" saw at once the virtue of compliance with the invitation of the British Government to conclude a protective alliance, and the grace of yielding quickly (Kotah having been the first state which formed a connexion with us); secondly, that he foretold that, "at a day not distant, but one emblem of power (the British) would be recognized throughout India." The history, measures, and political and moral character of this very remarkable man form the subject of some of the most interesting chapters in the Annals of this state.

With the Rao Raja of Boondi, Bishen Sing, Colonel Tod had contracted a friendship, and he gives an animated description of the joy which his appearance excited in the capital, where the generous interposition of Britain, which had

* *Annals*, i. 713.

† The recent conduct of Raja Maun seems, from the latest advices from India, likely to embroil him with the British Government.

had restored Boondi to independence, was felt and acknowledged by prince, chiefs, and people.

On leaving the capital, the party began to sink under the influence of this destructive climate. At Jehajpore, which they reached on the 28th September, Colonel Tod was attacked by fever and ague. Fancying a cake of *mukhi* flour, he had not eaten two mouthfuls before he experienced extraordinary symptoms. "My head," he says, "seemed expanding to an enormous size, as if it alone would have filled the tent; my tongue and lips felt tight and swollen; and although I underwent no alarm, nor suffered the slightest loss of sense, I deemed it the prelude to one of those violent attacks which have assailed me for several years past and brought me to the verge of death. I begged Captain Waugh* to leave me; but he had scarcely gone before a constriction of the throat came on, and I thought all was over. I rose up, however, and grasped the tent-pole, when my relative entered with the surgeon. I beckoned them not to disturb my thoughts; instead of which, they thrust some ether and compounds down my throat, which operated with magical celerity. I vomited violently; the constriction ceased; I sunk on my pallet, and about two in the morning, I awoke, bathed in perspiration and without a remnant of the disease." There was reason to believe (and the surgeon was of opinion), that this was the effect of poison administered in the cake. Three or four times he had been reduced to the brink of the grave since he commenced his harassing duties in Méwar.

As they proceeded, the climate threatened to destroy the whole of the party. Ensign Cary died; Captain Waugh narrowly escaped the same fate from the Kotah fever and Guinea-worm; and Colonel Tod, when he reached Mandelgurh, in addition to fever and ague, had a diseased spleen, which did not, however, suspend his attention to business. Stretched on his *charpae* (pallet), almost dead with inanition, with some three score leeches of enormous

* Captain Waugh, the commander of the escort, was Colonel Tod's kinsman.

mous size on his left side, he noted down the oral reports of the Bhomias and Patels of the district, who filled his tent and remained in groups outside.

He returned to Méwar in October 1820;* but nature now began to warn him in a tone not to be misunderstood. His once robust form was reduced to a mere wreck; and Dr. Duncan, the medical officer of the Agency, assured him that he must die if he stayed in the country six months more. In the spring of 1821, he determined to proceed to his native land, and only waited the termination of the monsoon to execute this design; but in July, he received an express from Boondi, announcing the sudden death, by cholera,† of his estimable friend the Rao Raja, from whom he had parted but a few months previously, who, in his last moments, nominated Colonel Tod guardian of his infant son, and charged him to watch over his welfare and that of Boondi. The formal letter of the minister was accompanied by one from the Rani, the mother of the young prince, from whom also (or in his name) he had a few lines, both seconding the bequest of the dying Raja, and reminding him of the dangers of a minority, and of the elements of mischief by which they were surrounded.

On the 24th July 1821, in the midst of the monsoon, he set out for Harouti. Having to pass through Bhilwara, his reception was enthusiastic. The entire population, headed by the chief merchants, and preceded by damsels with the *kullus*, or water-jar, advanced a mile to meet and conduct him to a place, now full of life and activity, which a few years before was tenanted only by a famished dog. "I passed," he says, "through the main street, surrounded by its wealthy occupants, who had suspended over the projecting

* This year, when the rupture with Sinde took place, he drew up and transmitted to Lord Hastings a plan for marching a force through the desert. He was at that time in communication with Meer Sohrab, the Governor of Upper Sinde.

† The spasmodic cholera morbus, called in these parts *murri*, or 'the death,' it is well known, made its appearance in British India at the commencement of the war of 1817, and was at this time (1821) wasting these regions. We owe to the researches of Col. Tod, in the archives of the Rajpoot princes, the knowledge of the fact, that this terrific scourge is no new disease, having ravaged India nearly two centuries ago, and often since. In 1661, it swept off numbers in Méwar.

projecting awnings the most costly silks, brocades, and other finery, to do honour to one they esteemed their benefactor. As my tent would not contain a tenth of the visitors, I had its walls removed. Every moment I expected to see it fall upon us, for there were hundreds of hands at each rope, swinging it in every direction in their eagerness to see what was going on within between the *Saheb* and the *Punchaet* of both sects, Oswal and Mahesri, or Jain and Vishnuvé. We talked over many plans for the future benefit of the town, of further reducing the duties, and giving additional freedom to the transit trade. My good friends having no inclination to retire, I sent for the presents and the *utr-pán*, and they departed with a thousand blessings and prayers for the perpetuity of our *raj*."* He has often spoken of the gratification he experienced on this occasion, which was calculated to leave an indelible impression upon a heart like his.

On arriving at Boondi, where he received all the attentions which the most delicate friendship could dictate (even to the sprinkling of his path with holy-water by a Brahman, to prevent the approach of evil), the *ráj-tilac*, or ceremony of inauguration of the young Rao Raja, Ram Sing, took place, on a lucky day, the 3d of Sawun. This imposing ceremony is picturesquely described in the last Personal Narrative, at the close of the *Annals*. The British Agent placed the young prince of the Haras on the *gadi*, or throne, and dipping the middle finger of the right hand into an unction composed of sandal-wood powder and aromatic oils, presented by the officiating priest, he made the *tilac*, or mark of inauguration, upon the prince's forehead, girding on the sword and congratulating the new sovereign of Boondi in the name of the British Government. The Agent, then, conformably to the will of the late prince, and to the injunctions of the queen-mother, entirely reformed the offices of the chief functionaries, providing a system of checks on the receipts and disbursements of the revenue, making no material innovations, and displacing or displeasing no one. At the next *durbar*, by request of the Rani, he

* *Annals*, ii., 690.

he pointed out to the chiefs, before they were dismissed to their estates, the line of their duty and the necessity of conforming to the old laws of the state. Although the festival of the *Rakhi** had not arrived, the mother of the young prince sent Captain Tod, by the hands of the family priest, the bracelet of adoption as her brother, which made his young ward thenceforth his nephew. He had received the *rakhi* from, and become the "bracelet-bound brother" of, two other queens, the Ranís of Oodeypore and Kotah, besides the maiden sister of the Rana, and many ladies of chiefs of rank: these, he observes, were all the treasures he brought away. He had afterwards the honour of a personal conversation with the princess mother (a curtain being interposed between them) on the affairs of the state and the welfare of her "Lalji." After a fortnight spent at Boondi, and having given a right tone to the Government, he took his leave, reminding the Bohora, or chief minister, by a metaphor full of intelligence to a Hindu, that if the administration was conducted upon just principles, "the lotus would once more blossom on the waters of the lake."

Captain Tod returned by way of Kotah, which he found to be very far from enjoying the tranquillity of its sister state of Harouti, Boondi. Here, therefore, fresh toils and vexations awaited him. The three months of August, September, and October 1821, he describes as the most harassing of his existence: "civil war, deaths of friends and relations, cholera raging, and all of us worn out with perpetual attacks of fever, ague, anxiety, and fatigue." But even these physical ills were trivial compared with the moral evils which it was his duty to remedy or mitigate. His offices were well appreciated by the blind and aged Regent, Zalim Sing, then in his eighty-second year, "whose orbless eyes," says Colonel Tod, "were filled with tears, and as I pressed

* The Festival of the Bracelet (*rakhi*) is one of the few occasions on which an intercourse of a most delicate nature is established between the fair sex and the cavaliers of Rajast'han. By the present of a bracelet, the Rajpoot dame bestows upon a favoured individual the title of "adopted brother;" scandal itself never suggesting any other tie between the lady and her defender, or *rakhi-bund-bhae*, 'bracelet-bound brother.'—See *Annals*, i. 312, 581.

pressed his palsied hands, which were extended over me, the power of utterance entirely deserted him."

At Rowtah (the scene of his labours in the Pindarry war) he determined to make a tour through Upper Malwa. Traversing the fatal pass of Mokundarra, he came upon the magnificent ruins of Barolli (situated on the tract named Puchail, or the flat between the Chumbul and the Pass), of which he has given exquisite graphic delineations, with descriptions that will tempt many a visitor of taste to those desecrated and mouldering relics, which attest the refinement of Hindu art at a date anterior to tradition. The *choolis*, or whirlpools, of the Chumbul, the fragments of ancient grandeur at Gunga-bhéva, and the caves of Dhoomnar, successively arrested the attention of the enthusiastic traveller, and of these remains, (some of which, it is said, have already disappeared under that powerful solvent, the climate, aided by the more destructive hand of man,) drawings were made, engravings from which adorn the *Annals*. The admiration which these specimens of architecture inspired, was increased by a discovery of the extensive ruins of the ancient city of Chandravati, the rich and gorgeous workmanship displayed in which may be ranked amongst the most finished productions of the chisel. The elaborate carving of the flowers and foliage Col. Tod considers "perfect." The tracery and other ornaments of one of the shrines, he says, "no artist in Europe could surpass." Apprehensive that the English public might be sceptical as to the fidelity of the engravings, he deposited the original drawings with his bookseller, in order that it might be seen that the engraver, so far from improving them, had scarcely done them justice. Chandravati is a city of the Pramara race, situated at the western face of the stupendous Aravulli chain; its ruins had long been the haunt of wild beasts, and from its ready-formed materials the city of Ahmedabad arose. Colonel Tod had an inscription in his possession, six hundred years old, which mentioned Chandravati, but it was of little interest till he discovered its site and ruins. It is also referred to in the *Bhoja Charitra*. At Bijolli and Mynál, he discovered other "architectural wonders," which he has also perpetuated by the pencil and graver.

Ere he reached the valley of Oodeypore, he met with a serious accident, which had nearly cost him his life. On the 24th February 1822, he was proceeding to restore to the chief of Beygoo, the head of the Meghawuts, his territory, of which the family had been deprived by the fraud and force of the Mahrattas for nearly half a century. The "sons of Kala Megh" had assembled from all quarters to honour the event, and to welcome their benefactor. The old castle of Beygoo has a remarkably wide moat, across which there is a wooden bridge, leading to an arched gate-way. Colonel Tod's *mahout* (elephant-driver) warned him that there was not space to admit of his elephant and howdah; but a preceding elephant having passed through, he was desired to drive on. The animal, from some cause, at this critical moment, became alarmed, and darted forward. Colonel Tod, as he approached the gate-way, perceived it was too low, and expecting instant destruction, planting his feet firmly against the howdah and his fore-arms against the gate-way, by a desperate effort of strength, burst out the back of the howdah, and dropped from the elephant senseless on the bridge below. He was sadly bruised, but not seriously injured. The sympathy of the Rawut and his chiefs, which made them almost prisoners beside his pallet, would have amply consoled him for an accident which partly arose from his own want of caution; but two days after, going to fulfil his mission, what was his astonishment to see the noble gate-way, the work of Kala Megh, reduced to a heap of ruins, through which he was conducted to the palace situated on a terrace, in front of which was the little court of Beygoo! On expostulating with the Rawut for his rash destruction of the gate-way, he declared, that "he never could have looked upon it with complacency, since it had nearly deprived of life one who had given life to them."* These are people who are said to be "without gratitude!"

After

* *Annals*, ii. 574.—In a letter to a friend, when in England, Colonel Tod refers to the inicdent, in a manner which shows how sensibly he felt this noble tribute of grateful respect: "—— I had the principle of life strong within me. It appears now a dream. But a week before, I was knocked off my elephant in going to restore to the chief of the Meghawuts twenty-seven villages, alienated for

After a visit to Cheetore, the ancient capital of Méwar (of whose architectural remains he has given specimens), he returned to Oodeypore in March 1822.

He had now been twenty-two years in India, eighteen of which were spent amongst the Western Rajpoots; the last five in the capacity of political agent to the Governor-general. His public duties and his extensive geographical and statistical researches—alone sufficient to engross an ordinary mind—were not the only objects which had occupied his studies; he employed the facilities of his post, and of his connexions with the native princes, to obtain an insight into the political history, the science, and the literature of the Rajpoots; and the result brought to light a vast body of genuine Hindu history, reaching to a remote period, disproving a notion which had been adopted even by the best Eastern scholars. Before the successful researches of Colonel Tod, no dogma was more generally acknowledged, than that the Hindus had no native history; though it was naturally and pointedly asked, "If the Hindus have no history, where did the Mahomedans discover the facts which are recorded by Abulfazil?" The course pursued by Colonel Tod, in exploring the historical works of the Rajpoots, is described in the Introduction to the first volume of his *Annals of Rajast'han*. He appears to have had unrestricted access not only to the archives of the princes, but to the immense libraries* of the Jain sect (of which his *guru*, or preceptor, was a learned member), which appear to have escaped the scrutiny of the Mahomedans, from whence he was permitted to bring away MSS. of considerable value: these are deposited in the library of the Royal Asiatic Society. The Rana of Méwar allowed him to borrow from his

for forty-five years, which I recovered from the fangs of the Mahrattas. The animal ran off, crossing the wooden bridge of the moat, and the arch, being too low, carried me fairly off. That I was not crushed is a miracle. *That night, the triumphal arch of the Meghawuts was levelled to the ground.* These are the men without gratitude! It was worth a broken limb, yet I escaped with bruises."

* In page 235 of this work will be seen an account of the literary treasures of the Jains.

his archives those sacred volumes, the ***Puránas***, from whence he deduced the genealogy of the Rajpoot tribes. Raja Maun, of Marwar, a man of literary taste, and remarkably well read, had copies made for him of the principal histories of his family, which are likewise deposited in the Society's library.* The " Book of the Johyas," a race of Jits, occupying one of the districts of Bikanér (amongst whom some traditions of Alexander the Great are preserved), was sent him by the prime minister of Jessulmér. Amongst other valuable historical works obtained by him in the country may be mentioned the poems of Chund, the Rajpoot Homer (or rather Ossian), of which Colonel Tod possessed the most complete copy extant, and which are esteemed authentic history; and various *Charitras*, particularly the ***Komarpál Charitra***, or history of Anhulwara, from whence he has incorporated copious extracts into this work. No subsidiary aids were neglected; he was indefatigable in his search for inscriptions, grants, coins, and other similar records, which are the most irrefragable of historical documents. In the course of these researches, he discovered (on his homeward journey), at Puttun Somnath, on the coast of Saurashtra, an inscription, in the Devanagari character, which not only fixed the era of the Balhara kings of Nehrwalla, but disclosed a peculiar era, the Balabhi Samvat.† His skill in decyphering dates concealed, or rather secured from sophistication, in the cryptographic form,‡ was of great advantage at a time when the art was by no means extensively known even amongst the pundits of India. " Many inscriptions," he observes,§ " have been passed by me as useless from their not containing the date

* A description of these Rahtore records is given in the *Annals* (ii. 2); one of them is the *Rasa Rao Rutna*, in which the heroic deeds of prince Rutna, of Rutlam, are " wreathed in immortal rhyme."

† The inscription is given in the Appendix to the *Annals*, vol. ii. The dates are of the following four eras: year of the Hejira, 662=year of Vicrama, 1,320=year of Balabhi, 945=year of Siva Singha Samvat, 151. The date in our era is 1264.

‡ An example of these cryptographic dates may be seen in p. 375 of this work

§ *Asiatic Journal*, vol. xxii. p. 14.

date in numerals, nor was it until the last years of my researches that my *Yati* (preceptor), through the medium of the primate, and some more learned of his sect (the Jain), solved this difficulty, as well as the enigmatical character of several of these inscriptions." Colonel Tod was the first to make known in Europe this peculiar system, which has since been fully developed by M. von Schlegel, M. Csoma de Koros, and Mr. James Prinsep.

Nor were his archæological investigations exclusively limited to purely Hindu antiquities. His discoveries of Bactrian and Indo-Grecian coins, of which he accumulated a considerable number,* and his learned and accurate illustrations of them, initiated the study of a branch of numismatic science which has since produced important results.

The biography of Colonel Tod is now taken up in the work which is in the hands of the reader, wherein he relates the cause of his quitting India, the reason why, notwithstanding the reduced state of his health, instead of proceeding directly to the nearest sea-port, he commenced a circuitous journey of discovery (the motives to which are highly characteristic of his inextinguishable zeal in the cause of science), the scenes and objects he met with, and the incidents which attended this journey. It will be sufficient to say, that he bade farewell to the capital of Méwar on the 1st June 1822, arrived at Bombay on the 14th January 1823, and in the following month embarked for England.

A long interval of uninterrupted tranquillity and repose should have been allowed to repair the wear which body and mind had undergone during so many years of excitement in an enfeebling climate; but his generous purpose was incomplete until he had imparted to the world the knowledge he had gained, and until he had made "his Rajpoots," as he affectionately termed them, known to the people of Europe. Instead of carefully nursing his health, he applied himself eagerly to the arrangement of the immense mass of materials he had accumulated† for his meditated work, which demanded incessant toil and

* These he bequeathed by will to the Royal Asiatic Society.

† His collections of MSS., coins, and antiquities, the most valuable of which were presented to

and study. The consequence of thus over-taxing his physical powers was, that, in 1825, his labours were interrupted by an attack of the same character as that which, ten years later, terminated his valuable life.

Just before his arrival in England, the Royal Asiatic Society had been formed (March 1823); Colonel Tod immediately enrolled himself amongst its members, and was subsequently appointed librarian, which office he retained as long as his health permitted. In May 1824, a paper was read by him before the Society, being a translation, with comments, of a Sanscrit inscription (a copy of which accompanied the paper), relative to the last Hindu king of Delhi. This inscription he obtained at Hánsí Hissár (situated about 126 miles N.N.W. from Delhi), when he left his post at Sindia's court, on a visit to his friend, the late James Lumsdaine. The object of the inscription is to commemorate a victory gained by Pirthi-raj or Prithwirája, the renowned Chohan sovereign of Hindust'han (in the ruins of whose palace it was found), over the race of Doda (A.D. 1168), by his vassal chiefs Kilhan and Hamir, names of great celebrity in the contests of that period. This paper is made the vehicle of much learned elucidation of the history of Western India, and illustration of the character of the people, then new to European scholars. The slab containing this inscription Colonel Tod transmitted to Lord Hastings, in 1818; but its fate is not known.

In June of the same year, he presented to the Society three copper plates, containing grants, found by him at Oojein, in 1812, and an inscription upon marble, at Madhucarghar, discovered in his last tour in Central India, in 1822. They all relate to the same family, the Pramara dynasty, whose period they fix, as well as an important era in the history and literature of India. These inscriptions, which were re-translated by Mr. Colebrooke, are, like the preceding, illuminated with a glow of learning.

His

to the India House or the Royal Asiatic Society, were subjected to heavy duties and charges in this country, and there is amongst his papers a list of these articles, with the charges upon them paid by him, amounting to £72, headed, in his hand-writing, "Encouragement to Oriental Literature."

His account of Greek, Parthian, and Hindu medals, found in India, read before the Society in June 1825, is one of the most valuable papers recorded in its Transactions. It was accompanied by fac-simile engravings (executed at his own expense) of several medals, and in particular of two, which filled up a chasm in the numismatic series of the Greek kings of Bactria, namely, Apollodotus and Menander, the former of which is not included by Bayer in his lists of the kings of Bactria, and was only known from the mention made of him by Arrian. Colonel Tod, in explaining how and where he found these valuable coins, relates that, for the last twelve years of his residence in India, the collecting of coins, as an auxiliary to history, was one of his pursuits; that, in the rainy season, he employed persons at Mathura and other old cities, to collect all that were brought to light by the action of the water, while tearing up old foundations and levelling mouldering walls. "In this manner," he says, "I accumulated about twenty thousand coins, of all denominations; among which there may not be above one hundred calculated to excite interest, and perhaps not above one-third of that number to be considered of value: but among them there are an Apollodotus and a Menander, besides some rare medals of a Parthian dynasty, probably yet unknown to history."*

This paper attracted much attention on the continent of Europe, and a paper upon the subject of these coins, by Mr. A. W. von Schlegel, was read before the Asiatic Society of Paris.† Since that time, and probably in consequence of this discovery, a powerful impulse has been given to the collection of these coins in Western India and Affghanistan, which are now obtained

* In the *Annals* (i. 40), he states that he found the Apollodotus, in 1814, when he discovered a remnant of the ancient city of Soorpoor, the capital of the Surseni of Alexander's historians. "The plains of India," he observes, "retain yet many ancient cities, from whose ruins somewhat may be gleaned to add a mite to knowledge."

† "Observations on the Bactrian and Indo-Scythic coins discovered by Col. Tod."—*Journal Asiatique* for November 1828.

obtained in considerable numbers, and the fortunate and skilful discovery by Mr. James Prinsep, the secretary of the Asiatic Society of Bengal, of the key to the characters, whence it appears that the legends are in a dialect or modification of the Sanscrit, has opened a new train of investigation into the connected history of the East and West, which, as already remarked, has led to important historical results.

The other papers submitted by him to the Society are the following:—An Account of the Religious Establishments of Méwar (read in 1828), which was afterwards incorporated in the *Annals of Rajast'han;* Remarks on certain Sculptures in the Cave Temples in Ellora (read also in 1828); Observations on a Gold Ring, of Hindu fabrication, found at Montrose, in Scotland; and a Comparison of the Hindu and Theban Hercules, illustrated by an ancient Hindu Intaglio (both read in 1830). The ring, which is the subject of the last paper but one, was dug up on the Fort Hill, near Montrose; it was purchased by the late Miss Erskine of Dun, as it was supposed to bear the supporters of the arms of that family (two griffins), and was duly considered as a family relic. The Countess of Cassilis having shown it to Colonel Fitzclarence (now Earl of Munster), he instantly recognized its Hindu character; and forwarding it, with Lady Cassilis' permission, to Colonel Tod, requested he would offer to the Society "such observations on the discovery of so extraordinary a relic in so unlooked-for a quarter as his extensive information respecting the history and antiquities of India might suggest." Colonel Tod has demonstrated that this mystic amulet represents the symbol of the sun-god, Bal-nat'h, around which is wreathed a serpent *guardant,* with two bulls, as supporters; or the powers of creative nature in unison, typified in the miniature Lingam and Yoni—"in short, a graven image of that primeval worship which prevailed amongst the nations of antiquity." He considers that it belonged to some pious devotee, who, desirous never to lose sight of the object of his adoration, wore it as a talisman on the thumb.

The liberal and generous spirit by which he was actuated, did not allow him to stint his communications to the scientific bodies of his own country; he diffused his information with true cosmopolitic ardour over the world. Whilst at Milan, in 1827, six weeks after his marriage, labouring then under a distressing asthma, the result of an inflammation of the chest, which left him scarcely power to write, or voice to dictate, he composed (without either books or references of any kind at command), and forwarded to the Asiatic Society of Paris, a paper, which was inserted in their Journal,* entitled "De l'Origine Asiatique de quelques-unes des Anciennes Tribus de l'Europe, établies sur les Rivages de la Mer Baltique, surtout les Su, Suedi, Suiones, Asi, Yeuts, Jats, ou Gètes-Goths, &c." In 1828, he presented to the same Society six rolls of inscriptions from Western India, of which a report was made by M. Burnouf, who recommended that they should be lithographed and circulated through France and Germany.

His regimental promotion, which had been hitherto retarded, now acquired an accelerated impulse. On the 1st May 1824, he attained the rank of major; and on the 2d June 1826, that of lieutenant-colonel, being transferred to the 2d European Regiment, the very corps in which he commenced his military career. His state of health, however, rendered a return to India, though much desired by his friends in Rajpootana, unadvisable, and on the 28th June 1825, he retired from the service.

In 1829, appeared the first volume of his *Annals of Rajast'han*, which created a strong sensation amongst Oriental scholars at home and abroad. It had, however, to contend against a formidable impediment to its popularity with general readers; for it was not only a volume of history,† but the history of

* *Journal Asiatique* for May 1827.

† At the very time when Col. Tod was bringing this volume before the British public, Sir N. H. Nicholas was writing (1830) his "Observations on the State of Historical Literature," wherein he declares that scarcely any work of an historical nature, which had been published for the last ten years, had paid its expenses; and that "not a single publisher in London, at this moment, will risk the cost of paper and print upon a volume illustrative of history, however interesting or important it may be."

of a country which, till the appearance of Sir John Malcolm's *Memoir of Central India* (and he scarcely touched the confines of Rajpootana) was almost entirely unknown. The name of the Author was not at this time sufficiently familiar to the public in Europe, or even to the British community in India, to impart that species of currency to his writings, from which many books derive their chief saleable value. "His course," says an intimate friend of Colonel Tod, "was such as to lead him but little into European society in India, and his attachments were much concentrated in the native society around him." The work offered so few attractions to London publishers, that he was compelled to take upon himself, which he did with alacrity, all the risk and cost of bringing it out, and the plates and printing of this large and very expensive work occasioned no slight drain upon a very moderate fortune. Profit, however, was not his aim, nor even fame in its ordinary sense; his impelling motive was the discharge of what he terms, in his Dedication to the King, "a paramount duty;" a desire to make known to the world "an ancient and interesting race." Nevertheless, in spite of these obstacles, and the high price of the work, it has gradually taken a station in the permanent literature of the country. Our periodical vehicles of criticism pronounced the most favourable sentence upon it; on the Continent of Europe it has extorted the warmest eulogiums from veterans in Oriental studies; and in British India, where its value can, perhaps, be best appreciated, it is regarded as a standard work. Principal Mill, one of our first Sanscrit scholars, and amongst the most successful investigators of ancient Hindu history, characterizes the *Annals* as "a most valuable and elaborate contribution to Oriental and general literature." It is, in fact, the mine from whence ephemeral writers still draw their information respecting Western India, increasing knowledge of these parts having confirmed the accuracy and fidelity of its details. The second and concluding volume appeared in the early part of 1832.

g 2 The

The interest inherent in this mass of genuine original history, many parts of which possess the fascinations of an elaborate fiction; the heroic attributes of the actors and incidents recorded in it; the highly curious and exact pictures of Hindu society which it exhibits; the exquisite delineations of local scenery and of ancient cities and edifices from which the veil of oblivion has been withdrawn after the lapse of ages; the erudition displayed in the archæological disquisitions; the ease and liveliness of the Personal Narratives; the Ossianic character of the extracts translated from the native chronicles, and the lustrous qualities of the Author's own style, which, though its purity may be occasionally adulterated with a few of the vices of Oriental composition, rises in some passages into the highest strain of fervid eloquence—conspire to invest the *Annals of Rajast'han* with extraordinary attractions to those who dare venture upon the perusal of so large a work. The enthusiasm of the author, who is the historian of some remarkable events in recent Rajpoot history, of which he was an eye-witness and in some of them an agent, has, moreover, infused into the narrative a portion of his own feelings, and incorporated with it many of the adventures of his own life. If this be a violation of the rigid laws of historical composition (though it is expressly declared by the Author, in the Introduction to the first volume, that "it never was his intention to treat the subject in the severe style of history, which would have excluded many details useful to the politician as well as to the curious student"), the reader finds some compensation in the vivacity and fidelity which are thus given to the narrative, and in the distinct picture it presents of the character and virtues of the narrator.

The only portions of this great work which have experienced anything like censure are those of a speculative character, namely, the curious Dissertation on the Feudal System of the Rajpoots, and the passages wherein the Author shows too visible a leaning towards hypotheses identifying persons, as well as customs, manners, and superstitions, in the East and the West, often

on

on the slender basis of etymological affinities. But most of these speculations are offered as conjectural, all of them being ingenious and plausible, and some probably true. The rash conclusions of Major Wilford, and even of Sir William Jones, in the infancy of our knowledge of Hindu literature, had the natural and necessary effect, from the constitution of the human mind, of causing prejudice to oscillate in an opposite direction, and all the demonstrations derived from recent discoveries in the coins of Bactria, the topes of Affghanistan, and the rock-records of Hindust'han, which have at length yielded their secrets to the perseverance and skill of European scholars (some of which seem to justify the boldest conjectures of Colonel Tod),* have scarcely cured the obstinate scepticism as to an original connexion between the Eastern and Western nations, notwithstanding the obvious grammatical affinities which their dialects present, and the well-established fact of an intercourse between them in very early times.

The hypothesis of an identity between the feudal systems of Europe and of Rajpootana is, indeed, founded upon better indicia than verbal resemblances. But, as it was observed in a critique† on the *Annals*, "the tenure of land on condition of military service, which is a simple and an obvious expedient in order to provide for public defence, must every where produce incidents more or less alike." The idea of a feudal system in the East had been conceived by learned writers antecedent to Colonel Tod, though he has the merit of having fortified conjecture by practical evidence.‡ There are, however,

* When the industry of European collectors began to be directed to the search for coins in India, and to produce such valuable results, Col. Tod, in writing to a friend, who communicated them, says, "The numismatic discoveries are grand and delightful; they fulfil in extent and value all I anticipated, and so often have expressed. Do you observe the confirmation of my observation, that the Persian Gulf and Mesopotamia were the places *ever* for Bactrian medals, contained in my letter from Rome?"

† *Edinburgh Review*, for October 1830.

‡ Richardson, in the learned Dissertation prefixed to his Persian and Arabic Dictionary, expressly ascribes to the Feudal System an Eastern origin. "In Persia, Tartary, India, and other

ever, two very important marks of distinction between the respective systems. In the East, especially in Rajast'han, the king has no title to the soil, nor any right whatever over the land, beyond the revenue which accrues from it. In our feudal system, however, it was an essential principle that the king was the universal lord and original proprietor of all the lands in the kingdom, which were derived from him and held of him. Again: under our feudal system, the villein or cultivator could acquire no property, and if he purchased any land, the lord could enter upon it, and take it to his own use; whereas, in Rajast'han, the ryot, or cultivator, is the actual proprietor of the soil.

On the 16th November 1826, Colonel Tod married the daughter of Dr. Clutterbuck, a physician of considerable eminence in London. The state of his health (as well as that of his lady) induced them to travel over various parts of the Continent. In one of these journeys, passing through Savoy, he paid a visit to the Count de Boigne, the celebrated General of Sindia, before whose disciplined battalions the rude valour of the Rajpoots was of little avail, and four thousand of them fell martyrs to liberty on the field of Mairta, in 1790. Colonel Tod spent two delightful days with this veteran, at his princely residence, in his native vale of Chambéri.

In these journeys, and in his occasional sojourn in England, he was never idle, but devoted his time, fortune, and health, to literary pursuits. His mind, fraught with the stores of Eastern learning, and with the fruits of his personal knowledge and experience, was ever teeming with projects for communicating them to the world, of which many traces are to be found amongst

Eastern countries," he says, "the whole details of government, from the most ancient time down to the present hour, can hardly be defined by any other description. The rise and progress of our Feudal System is marked; it was an exotic plant, and it has of consequence engaged the attention of our ablest antiquaries; but in the East, it is indigenous, universal, and immemorial, and the Eastern historians have never dreamt of investigating its source, more than the origin of regal government." Pp. xlii. and xliii.

amongst his papers. He planned, and partly executed, a translation of the poems of Chund,* for which undertaking no one could possess equal qualifications; and the specimen from the fifth book, which he printed for private circulation, illuminated by notes containing a prodigious effusion of varied historical knowledge, leaving no expression of his author obscure or unintelligible, excites a keen regret that he did not live to complete the design.†

The chief object of his later labours was the work now before the reader, to which he dedicated the principal part of the winter of 1834, whilst at Rome; and, perhaps, to these exertions, which were unremitted, when he was not disabled by actual suffering, his premature death may be mainly attributed. He had resided in Italy during part of 1834 and 1835, in the hope of conquering a complaint in his chest, and he returned to England on the

* Of Chund, or Chand, called Trí-cála, from his supposed prophetic spirit, Col. Tod has given some scattered notices in various parts of his writings. He flourished at the close of the twelfth century. He was the companion and bard of Pirthi-raj, the last Chohan Emperor of Delhi. His work, consisting of sixty-nine books, comprising 100,000 stanzas, though dedicated to the exploits of Pirthi-raj, is a universal chronicle of the period when he wrote. The wars of this martial sovereign, his alliances, his numerous and powerful tributaries, their abodes and their pedigrees, which are recorded in the poem of Chund, make this work invaluable for its historical and geographical memoranda, as well as for its details respecting mythology and its pictures of manners. "To read this poet well," observes Col. Tod, "is a sure road to honour, and my own *guru* was allowed to excel therein. As he read, I rapidly translated about 30,000 stanzas. Familiar with the dialects in which it is written, I have fancied that I seized occasionally the poet's spirit; but it were presumption to suppose that I embodied all his brilliancy, or fully comprehended the depth of all his allusions. But I knew for whom he wrote. The most familiar of his images and sentiments I heard daily from the mouths of those around me, the descendants of the men whose deeds he rehearses: I was enabled thus to seize his meaning where one more skilled in poetic lore might have failed." Of the dialect in which the poem is written, he says (in a MS. note):—"We may assign as a parallel to the variation of the provincial dialects the same difference as exists in that of Languedoc and Provence, which bears the same analogy to the parent Roman as do the Bakhas, or dialects, of Méwar and Vrij to the Sanscrit."

† This specimen, which is an episode, entitled "The Vow of Sunjogta," translated into a kind of Ossianic rhythm, has been since published in the *Asiatic Journal*, vol. xxv.

the 3d September. Whilst on a visit to his mother, in Hampshire, he wrote the concluding chapters of the work, which was complete, except a few notes and the Appendix. He had purchased a town residence in the Regent's Park, and came up to London on the 14th November, in full spirits at the idea of putting his work to press, and of settling down into a permanent residence in the metropolis. The visible improvement in his appearance and feelings gave sanguine hopes of his entire restoration to health. On Monday, the 16th November 1835—the anniversary of his marriage nine years previously—whilst transacting business at his bankers, Messrs. Robarts and Company, Lombard Street, he was seized with apoplexy; after the first fifteen minutes, he lay speechless and without consciousness for twenty-seven hours, and expired on the 17th November, at the age of fifty-three.

In person Colonel Tod was, perhaps, rather above the middle size; his frame had the appearance of having been robust, and was still vigorous. His countenance was open and cheerful, his features were expressive, and in the discussion of literary or scientific subjects, especially relating to India and to Rajpootana, they were lighted up with extraordinary animation. His general knowledge was various; his writings indicate a very wide range of inquiry, more particularly in the branches of learning connected with history, embracing Western as well as Eastern authors. With the Sanscrit and learned languages of the East he was not, perhaps, so intimately acquainted as with the Western dialects of India, which were the vehicles of oral communication and the depositaries of the history and science of Rajpootana. The prominent qualities of his character were indomitable energy; zeal bordering upon enthusiasm; decision and perseverance; inflexible integrity, and an independence of spirit, which made him jealous even to irritability of wrong or encroachment. These qualities were tempered by great kindness of disposition, warmth of affection, amenity of manners, frankness and sincerity: few men have so much transparency of heart with so little of the weakness which is one of its ordinary incidents. After administering the affairs

affairs of kingdoms, with almost boundless authority,—for the discretion of a political agent in India is extensive,—neither the indulgence of power, nor the vexation of harassing duties, nor the inroads of disease, could sour his temper, or change the radical virtues of his character; he was to the last the amiable person his brother officers found him, when a subaltern of eighteen, in the 14th regiment of Native Infantry.

A better instrument for working out the political regeneration of such a country as Rajpootanac ould not have been discovered than a man constituted like Colonel Tod, whose feelings and qualities, in many points, coalesced with those of the people; a community of sentiment was thus established between them, which inspired confidence on one side, and gave a great moral influence on the other. It has been remarked by the ablest of our Anglo-Indian statesmen (and the remark does not require the sanction of local experience, since it is founded in human nature itself), that no European can be an acceptable or useful functionary amongst the Hindus, who is not familiar with their language, manners, and institutions, and disposed to mix with them upon equal and social terms. Prejudices on either side, which are the chief barriers to improvement, will then disappear; the natives of India will more readily adopt our views, when they perceive that they are suggested by a deep and sincere interest in their welfare; and on the other hand, as Sir Thomas Munro has justly observed, "those who have lived longest amongst the natives (and this is a strong argument in their favour) have usually thought the most highly of them."* "Never mixing with the natives, an European is ignorant of their real character, which he, therefore, despises," says another profound observer, Mr. Colebrooke; "when they meet, it is with fear on one side,

* Gleig's Life of Sir Thomas Munro, vol. ii. p. 12. Mr. Chaplin, Commissioner of the Deccan, who was for more than twenty years in close contact with the natives of India, declared to the Committee of the Commons on East-India Affairs, in 1831, that the more he saw of the natives, the better was his opinion of them, and that "they will bear an advantageous comparison with the natives of any country in the world."

side, and arrogance on the other." The hold he obtained upon the affection and attachment of the people, from the prince to the peasant, was the grand secret of Colonel Tod's success, which affords a great practical lesson to the rulers of British India.

A striking proof of the moral power which his knowledge of the native character gave him, and of its utility in critical emergencies, is seen in the following anecdote, which has been recorded by himself.* At the termination of the campaign of 1817-18, General Donkin's division (the right) was directed to clear Méwar of the enemy, and had invested the strong hill-fortress of Komulmér, the garrison of which could not be brought to surrender. Colonel Tod (the Political Agent), being made acquainted with the position of affairs, came to the spot, and determined to try the effect of a parley. In spite of the general's dissuasives, he offered to meet, unattended, the sirdars half-way between the British post and the fort. They consented; four of the sirdars sat down with him on a rock, and in half an hour all was arranged, namely, that the garrison should have their arrears of pay, and the British be put in possession of the first gate next morning. At sunrise, Colonel Tod moved down with the troops, Colonel Casement at their head. The sum to be paid was about Rs. 40,000 (£4,000); Colonel Casement had only Rs. 11,000; but the Political Agent had a native banker with him, who made out a bill of exchange for the balance, which was accepted, and the fort was evacuated just as an engineer officer arrived to report on the practicability of the siege of a place 25,000 feet above the plains, which were without shelter, there being but one face of attack, the approach to which was over an exposed causeway. The engineer (Major Macleod) declared that he could not have had a gun in position for six weeks.†

Some

* *Asiatic Journal,* vol. xvi. p. 264.

† To show "how perfectly simple was the method he adopted, and how perfectly tractable these people are when led through the medium of their feelings and prejudices," he describes the mode

Some surprise was felt by the friends of Colonel Tod,* that, in the distribution of honours from the Crown amongst the officers of the East-India Company, his name should have been overlooked. His services were never undervalued, but, on the contrary, were always handsomely acknowledged by the Court of Directors; and his experience and judgment in respect to the politics of Western India were appealed to by the Government during the inquiries which preceded the adjustment of the great India question. The admirable paper on this subject, drawn up by him, and which is printed in the Appendix to the Minutes of Evidence taken before the Committee of the House of Commons on East-India Affairs, is specially noticed in their final Report of 1833. There were, however, technical difficulties in the way of his claims, which, though not insuperable, had he been of a temper to solicit what he perhaps esteemed his due, were suffered to weigh with those who dispensed the favours of the Crown. It was intimated to Colonel Tod, as an excuse for the non-insertion of his name on those occasions, that such distinctions were not conferred on individuals who had retired from active employment, and who had not been officially gazetted for military services. His remarks on

of negociation:—"The prelude to the argument was on indifferent subjects, for even in the midst of hostilities there is no deficiency of the courtesies of life among them. My first question was on the *wuttun* of each of the sirdars, a matter of interest to every human being. They were all Mooslem; two of them from Rohilcund. With these I talked of their native land, of their towns, which I had visited, of the gallant Hafiz Rhamut. The others had served Sindia—we had mutual acquaintances in that camp; and in ten minutes thus passed, sundry moral links of sympathy made us no longer strangers. Confidence once awakened, the main object was discussed; and I soon convinced them that it was their interest, and no disgrace, to surrender Komulmér. I pointed out to them the difficulty of their position, so different from what it might have been even a few weeks back, when they could have had both friends and supplies from the Marwar territory; adding, that I had now only to address the chiefs in the plains below to block up every avenue; and that they well knew they had created abundant enemies there as well as in Méwar, who would bar all safe retreat: for which, however, I pledged myself, if they surrendered."

* "It seems strange," writes a friend of Colonel Tod, "that one who had done so much for the arts and literature, and so much in his military and diplomatic capacities, should have received no honour from his Sovereign; but he was a man who could not stoop to solicit what he felt to be his due."

on the futility of these reasons show that he was somewhat hurt at his exclusion.

But although such a token of his Sovereign's approbation would have been prized by Colonel Tod, the permanent distinction he had acquired in the deep-seated gratitude of a noble-minded nation, amongst whom his memory is cherished with fondness, and will be perpetuated by future generations, more than consoled him for the loss of these fugitive honours. Whatever be the fate of Rajast'han, the praise of having raised it from ruin to prosperity, from anarchy to peace—of having been its benevolent ruler and its enlightened historian—of having earned the love of all but thieves and Pindarries, and provoked the groundless suspicion of a jealous Government, through the unwonted equity and mildness of his administration—this praise, which will associate the name of Tod with the names of Duncan, Cleveland, and the few real "friends of India," cannot be withheld from him, and no prouder heir-loom could descend to his family.

Colonel Tod left two sons and a daughter.

TRAVELS

IN

WESTERN INDIA.

CHAPTER I.

INTRODUCTION.

Motives for the present Journey.—Reasons for the Author's leaving India.—Sentiments of respect and regard of the native Princes towards the Author.—His proposed route to Bombay.

THOSE who have looked into the Annals of Rajast'han, could make an easy transition from the close of that work to the commencement of this, without needing any prefatory or introductory observations. It would, however, be treating the reader too unceremoniously, perhaps, if, even assuming that he transferred his attention immediately from one work to the other, I should say nothing of my motives for this last journey; nor would it be decorous towards the reader, if I did not offer some apology for the frequency with which, in the present work, the pronoun *I* is obtruded upon him.

In a narrative of personal travels, it would be extremely embarrassing to the relator if he were compelled to shun fastidiously, upon all occasions, the mention of himself. The perpetual periphrasis would betray an affectation more displeasing than the natural and simple style of narrative, which can only be offensive where it is unnecessarily employed: further, the reader of personal adventures must desire to be acquainted with as much, at least, of the personal history of the relator, as will familiarize him with the circumstances of his connexion with the individual scenes he describes, especially where, as in the present instance, that connexion affords a guarantee for the fidelity of the descriptions. I shall, therefore, without scruple, and without anticipating a charge of vanity, speak of myself and my concerns with as little restraint as if I were speaking of another person.

At the period of commencing this, to me, the most interesting of all my journies, I had completed the term of my banishment, twenty-two years, and nearly another, since I first left England; eighteen of which had been spent among the Rajpoot tribes of Western India—the last five in the capacity of Political Agent to Government; having, as such, the sole control over five of its principalities, namely, Méwar, Marwar, Jessulmér, Kotah, and Boondí, besides the little state of Sirohi. My health was so worn out by the laborious and incessant duties of so extensive a charge (which afterwards gave sufficient employment to four distinct agents), that it would have been impossible for me to get through another season. Occupied from twelve to fourteen hours daily, amidst surrounding broils and discords, visited every alternate day with excruciating head-ache, and doomed to severe abstinence, though without intermission of toil, the only wonder to my medical friends was, that I escaped this ordeal, and outlived such constant persecution. Nothing, I believe, but the conviction that I was benefiting thousands by my exertions, could have enabled me to surmount it; but sentence of departure pressed, and with no little

bitterness

bitterness I was compelled to turn my back upon the land of my adoption, where I would willingly have laid my bones.

If ever there be a time in which there is a "joy in grief," it is when the sorrow you create or feel springs from a sense of good done. Providence had placed me in a situation to dispense benefits, not to individuals but to petty kingdoms. It would not become me to speak of the expressions of gratitude from princes and nobles for their restoration from poverty to affluence, from intestine feuds to political tranquillity; but the epithet of *baba*, or 'father,' conferred by the peasantry, may be appealed to as an unexceptionable criterion of the nature of my services.

A fortnight had been spent in preparations, and in order that I might experience less interruption from visitors, I retired to the Suhailea-ca-bari, a delightful villa belonging to the Hara Queen, about a mile north of the capital, the pleasant groves and lakes of which I have elsewhere described. The Rana, when he came for the last time with his court to 'grant me leave,' was amused at seeing me surrounded with workmen employed in making cases for statues, inscriptions, minerals, manuscripts, &c. It was a painful interview to all parties. Till this period, not a chief present had throughout his life ever laid his head upon his pillow without being prepared to be roused from his sleep by the cry of "the enemy is at the gate:" some ancient foeman, who had come to 'balance the feud,' or marauding mountaineer or forest Bhil, who had emptied his cow-pens. All these sources of anxiety were now at an end; the predatory Mahratta, the ruthless Pat'han, the kinsman-foe *(weri)*, and border-plunderer, whether the son of the mountain *(Mairote)* or of the forest *(Vaniputra)*, were all restrained by fear, or their swords turned into plough-

 shares;

shares; and the lordly chief could now indulge his natural indolence, or enjoy his noon-dose of opiate, without dread of hostile interruption. To some, these halcyon days brought no content. We had amongst us spirits to whom "quiet was a hell." Such were Hamira, the chief of Badeswar, and the 'mountain lion' (Bahar Sing.) The latter, with many others, had good excuse for dissatisfaction, the greater portion of his hereditary fields being now held by the Mahrattas, and it was a part of his creed never to rest until this was redeemed.

The severing of such ties could not but produce a pang on both sides; it is a libel upon our nature to suppose what, in the plenitude of arrogance, is too often proclaimed, that no virtue can dwell under a complexion a few shades darker than our own. On this occasion, instead of his usual good-humoured and always instructive loquacity, the Rana was silent and thoughtful, and what he did utter was in abrupt sentences, with frequent repetitions of "Remember, I give you leave only for three years. *Ruma dohae!* (by Rama!) I will send and fetch you if you remain longer." But the expression which pleased me most was a powerful appeal to the assembled chiefs: "He has served me five years, raised the country from ruin, and does not take even a pinch of the soil of Méwar along with him *(ek chookti bei Méwar ca Mat'hi sung nahyn lea játa)*." He was right; but having only the example of the Mahratta lieutenants before them, they could not comprehend how it was possible that the stranger could disinterestedly perform all the onerous duties of a minister of revenue and finance. Herein consists the grand secret of European superiority, which with temper and courtesy can never fail to command unlimited influence and respect at a native, and especially a Rajpoot court. No human being is more alive to the abstract beauties of morality than the Rajpoot;

poot; and if he cannot through habit practise it himself, he may be guided by a thread by one who does.

After sitting a couple of hours, it became necessary to take leave, and the parting gifts were produced. At length, the Rana made an effort, and bidding me be careful of my health for his sake, his steed was summoned; and telling him to consider my cousin, Capt. Waugh, as myself, adieux were exchanged with rapidity and pain. Several of the chiefs lingered behind, to have a last word, especially the fat lord of B'heendir, who afforded a conspicuous instance of what disinterested plain-dealing will effect with a Rajpoot. From this chieftain, when I mediated between the nobles and their sovereign, no less than thirty towns and villages were taken, which, during the troubles, he had contrived to hold in addition to his *putta* or grant; and it was this chief who, during that painful and most delicate task attending a reciprocal restoration of lands, which the feuds and frauds of more than half a century had made objects of contention, observed to me: "Do not expect too much, for if Bhagwan (the Almighty) himself were to make the attempt, he would find it impossible to restore order in Méwar."

I could expatiate longer upon these topics, the retrospect of which is delightful to me; but more than enough has perhaps already been said. It may, however, be requisite to explain why, in the reduced condition of my health, instead of going directly to the nearest sea-port for embarkation for Europe, I commenced a long and arduous journey of discovery. These researches, which present to the mind of the inactive an employment at once fatiguing and dangerous, were to me recreations from the toils of public business; and often, when compelled to fly for a few days from the capital and its cares, in

pursuit

pursuit of health, I used to pitch my tent either in the grove, in the gorge of some valley, or at the outlet of the Bairis from its noble reservoir, the Oody-sagur, or perhaps isolate myself entirely in one of the fairy islets of the Péshola lake; where, with my manuscripts, the old Gurú, or the poet Chund, I passed the time in luxury with Pirthiraj and the heroes of past days. Such being my disposition, and with objects at hand which for years had dazzled my fancy, I could not hesitate for an instant whether I should hazard a little more for their attainment, or proceed direct to Bombay. I had traversed the united floods of the Ganges and Brahmaputra,

"O'er whose expanse scarce dare the muse take wing;"

had wandered where the Ganges and Yamuna break through their rock-bound barriers, and had long set my heart upon a visit to the 'father of rivers,' the *Abba-sin* or Indus, to tread the Delta of this most classical of the many noble streams of India. But this was the ultimate object: the secondary, intervening ones were of vast interest to me. First, I determined to cross the alpine Aravulli, in my route to the Olympus of India, the celebrated Aboo, in one of the lines of its greatest breadth, either through the independent Bhil communities of Ogunah Panurwa, or by the more intricate region, the source of the Bunas river, said to be the highest point of this grand mountainous range. Secondly, to descend its northern declivity to Marwar, and skirting this magnificent hem of the desert, penetrate by Sirohi to Aboo. Various reasons combined to recommend the latter course, in preference to an object of no small interest, that of visiting those aboriginal communities, which have long been isolated, geographically and politically, from all other societies. So far back as 1808, one of

my

my parties had traversed these tracts, and brought me accounts of their primitive and independent condition, which made me eager to visit them. It was in this impervious region that the arrow from a quiver of a deceased son of the forest, given by his widow, served my messenger as a passport through its otherwise inaccessible vallies. In exchange, however, I was to see the defiles where the Ranas circumvented and destroyed their Mogul oppressors; the sources of the Bunas; and at the pass of Sadri, near that by which I intended to debouch into the plains, the celebrated Jain temple of Rainpoor. At the same time, I despatched a party, on whose intelligence and sagacity I could rely, to traverse the other route, and meet me at Aboo. These objects, which had found a daily place in my meditations for many years, were at length within my grasp. Well do I recollect when, for the first time, in 1806, Aboo had a niche in my map. I was then in search of the source of the Bunas river, which we had more than once crossed in our route to Sindia's camp in that year; when, to my inquiries as to its fountains, I was told, "they were far away amongst the hills towards Aboo:"—and where was Aboo? "thirty coss westward from Oodipoor, towards Sinde." Down went Aboo with the Bunas on my map; and this first step made, I gradually attained its source, the summit of Aboo, and, within a few hours' sail, the Indus itself.

Between these points, the first and the last of my present journey, I had chalked out many intermediate objects of the deepest interest. After the passage of the Aravulli, and the exploration of Aboo, my intention was to discover what remained of the ancient Nehrvalla, the Tyre of Western India; thence to trace the site of Balabhi, for the purpose of verifying the traditions of the Rana's family. As this would

lead

lead me by the Gulf of Cambay to the shores of the Saurashtra peninsula, I resolved to effect, if possible, a visit to the sacred mounts of the Jains, the cradle and still the stronghold of their faith; *viz.* Palit'hana and Girnar; and to conclude my pilgrimage in the Syria of India by a visit to the shrine of its Baal and that of Krishna, at Dwarica, the Land's End *(juggut coont)* of the Hindus. Thence, by the Pirates' Isle, Bét, cross the Gulf of Cutch, make an excursion to Bhooj, the capital of the Jharéjas, return to the grand mart, Mandavie, sail on to the eastern arm of the Indus, and visit the last shrines of Hinduism at its embouchure with the ocean.

All this I accomplished, save the last object, which seventeen hours of fair wind would have effected; but for ample reasons, which will appear in the sequel, I was obliged to stretch my sail across the ocean to Bombay, instead of coasting to the terminating scene of Alexander's exploits in India. With this previous exposition, I shall now request my reader to strike his tent, and begin his march with me from Oodipoor.

CHAPTER II.

Departure from Oodipoor.—Enter the pass to Gogoonda.—Aspect of the country.—Gassyar.—Asylum of Krishna.—Discharge of servants.—Improvement of the climate.—Temple of the Buroonie pass.—Geology of the Hills.—Gogoonda.—Revenue.—Cultivation.—Chief of Gogoonda.—Matrimonial connexion between the houses of Oodipoor and Gogoonda.—Effects of unequal alliances in Rajpootana.—The Rao of Kotario.—Saimur.—Aspect and climate of the Aravulli.—Plants.—Agriculture.—Character of the mountain Rajpoots.—Chiefs of villages.—Their traditionary tales.—Dress.—Habitations.—Sources of the Bunas.—Legend of the river.—Western declivity of the Aravulli.—Magnificence of the pass.—Vegetation.—Fruits.

It was on the 1st of June, 1822, that I bade farewell to the capital of the Seesodias. The morning was brilliant; the thermometer, even at the early hour of five, standing at 96°, the medium temperature at morning and evening for the last few days at the villa :—Bar. 27° 90′.

As we skirted the hills on our left, to gain the entrance of the valley which was to conduct us to Gassyar, I feasted my eyes, for the last time, on each well-known object. In the foreground, immediately to my right, peeping through the thick foliage, appeared the spire of the village temple, near the villa, with the little pointed arched bridge over the rivulet, along whose banks I used to wander in the early morning, followed by myriads of the finny tribe, which had become quite familiar, from my habit of feeding them.* A little further, the cupolas of the

* This may appear strange to some persons, but it is well known to all who have been in India, that fish in sacred tanks will feed from the hand; and I have elsewhere mentioned, that in the Mahanaddy, where it is three miles broad, the fish will follow for miles for a little burnt rice. I have the merit of being teacher to those in the valley. I have also mentioned, I think, the mode of taking the fish in the rainy season, by poisoning the waters with noxious weeds, when the fish, floating to the surface, are taken by the hand, or killed with sticks; a process which alike prevailed amongst the Americans (*Robertson*, vol. ii. p. 113); and in Abyssinia (*Bruce*, vol. 1.)

the Baidla chieftain's castle, embowered in a deep grove of date trees; beyond, the well-known cleft in the rock, which indicated the pass leading by Dailwarra to the plains, and by which I entered, eighteen years before, a young Sub., in the train of the embassy, and twelve years later, as Political Agent: the whole backed by the towering peak of Rata-Mata, and the many noble pinnacles which diversify in the most picturesque manner the outline of this fine valley.

At the distance of a mile and a half from our villa, we reached the gorge of the pass which leads to Gogoonda, and which, taking an abrupt sweep to the left, shut us out from the valley, and led us upon land untrodden by the European. For some distance, we pursued our route, over broken ground, with very little ascent, the hills on each side being covered with the prickly *thoor* (*cactus*) to the summit, which served as underwood to scattered trees of no great growth.

As, after a long halt, both men and cattle get tender in the feet, it is bad policy to make a long march. We halted at Gassyar, only six miles from the capital. From the entrance of the valley, the ascent became gradual, and our position was some hundred feet above the level of Oodipoor. Though I felt inclined to term the entrance to Gassyar, the eastern hill of the Aravulli, I believe that, properly, we must only regard the valley of Oodipoor as a fertile oasis within its rock-bound barriers, the chains which encircle and mingle in every way with the loftier portion of the mountain. Gassyar is an inconsiderable village, but obtained much celebrity from being chosen as the retreat of the god of Nath-dwarra, during the days of evil, when neither Mahratta nor Pat'han respected the Apollo of India, who, on being driven from his proper shrine on the Yamuna, by Aurungzebe, found refuge with the King of all the Rajpoots. It was the father of the

the present high priest, at the recommendation of Zalim Sing of Kotah, and with the assent of the Rana, who conveyed the god from Nathdwarra to this retreat, which was strongly fortified by a wall with towers thrown across the valley, for whose defence the regent furnished two companies of infantry. These embattled walls lend a very picturesque appearance to this wild spot, which possesses some fine foliage, amongst which I observed an elegant and majestic shrub, having a rich crimson berry, about the size and appearance of that of the arbutus. It was called *akolia.*

I had, however, little time for observation, being followed by the minister, several chiefs, and a crowd of others, who escorted me thus far on my journey. My cavalcade and equipage came straggling in throughout the morning: the camels evidently not relishing in these rugged paths their burthen of mutilated divinities and inscriptions. Though the sun was broiling hot, we enjoyed the novelty of our position, and had the breakfast-table spread under the shade of a fine tamarind tree. But, let the lovers of Hyson imagine my consternation when, on sipping the infusion, the only panacea for my ills, I found that the whole stock was perfumed with an overpowering aroma. In the hurry of packing, my domestic had stowed away a bottle of cajeputi oil in the very core of my magazine of tea, and the cork having escaped, the precious extract, which cost me two gold mohurs the bottle, was mixed with the yet more precious herb.

This was a day of labour, and so checquered with mingled pain and pleasure, that it was difficult to say which predominated. It was at once a painful and pleasing task to pay off and reward the long and faithful services of domestics, several of whom had grown grey in following my steps, from my thoughtless subaltern days to the moment of my retirement. It is a practical reply to those who can find no gratitude or fidelity under a dark skin, that I have yet met with none who have served long in India, and lived to return to their own country, who did not draw comparisons in the highest degree favourable to the Asiatic, in regard to all the higher qualities as well as the subordinate—honesty—sobriety—fidelity, and respect.

June 2d. Near Gogoonda.—Another short march through a country, every step in which discovered rugged and picturesque grandeur. The barometer at sunset, 27° 25′, denoted that we were climbing, and the thermometer, 82°, or thirteen degrees below its range in the valley, afforded an agreeable proof of improved climate within the space of twelve miles. We had rain yesterday, with the wind from the west; and to day it veered to the south-west, between which points are the prevailing winds of this season. About midway, as we abruptly entered the Buroonie pass, its little temple came in sight—the sole indication that man abided in these wilds, which Nature, as if in a moment of freak, had done much to diversify; for, amidst their rugged acclivities, there was no want of foliage, over which the tufted *kujoor*, or date, and the graceful *tal*, or palmyra, lifted their airy forms, indicating that there was no deficiency of water in this alpine tract. Wherever the mountains were laid bare, they shewed their granitic formation, while the base of the valleys exhibited slate of every form and colour, from the massive compact dark blue, to the schistose dark brown and aquamarine, the predominant colour about Gogoonda, the roofs of its houses presenting a singular appearance, from being covered with this sea-green slate, of which the chief temple was entirely composed—its blocks being of this material. The loftier peaks of the mountains, which rose many hundred feet above the level of our route, were

chiefly

chiefly of rose-coloured granite, sometimes presenting a vitreous appearance, sparkling in the sun.

Gogoonda is a town of some consequence in this region, being one of the sixteen great fiefs of Méwar. The estate is nominally Rs. 50,000 annual revenue; but as it is necessary, in the phrase of these regions, to expend a rupee in order to make one, in other words, to lay out both skill and capital, in order to secure a return, in both of which points the nobles of this country have been, from many concurrent causes, sadly deficient, the Gogoonda fief has not realized more than a tithe of this sum for many years past. The prevailing mode of cultivation in these mountainous tracts is, by embanking, terracing, and damming; but this region has for centuries been the scene of strife, as well as under Mahratta domination. The chieftain of Gogoonda is a J'hala Rajpoot, a tribe peculiar to the Saura peninsula. It would be unfair to take the present incumbent as a specimen of the great vassals of Méwar, even in these degenerate days, as he is, without exception, one of the meanest of mortals;—stunted in growth, dark and ill-favoured, weak in intellect as in body, he might be supposed a specimen of the *Vanmanoos*, or Man of the Woods, to whom the gift of speech had been imparted; for his lineaments assimilate more to those of the long-armed race than any I have ever seen. Moreover, to complete the picture of deformity, the few teeth, which the use of metallic poisons had left him, were black, and bound together by gold wire. The envenomed tongue of slander, which penetrates even to the recesses of the Aravulli, has ascribed this anomalous physiognomy to a son of the forest—the Vana-putra Bhil; but let us repudiate the scandal: for, as Chund says, "The child of a crow must be a crow."* Now the

* Ferdousi, in his satire upon Mahmoud, says, "a raven's egg can produce nothing but a raven."

the heir of Gogoonda being a perfect contrast to his father in limb and feature, the father is not "the son of a crow," and his personal deformity must be ascribed to a freak of nature. I have elsewhere explained the reasons* which compelled the Ranas of Méwar, who boast their descent from the deified Rama, to renounce all matrimonial connexion with the other noble Rajpoot princes, from the moment that the latter debased the purity of Hindu blood by alliance with the Islamite sovereigns of India. Accordingly, as the laws of propinquity do not admit of intermarriage with their own nobility, the Ranas enrolled amongst them a proportion of foreign Rajpoots, of the Chohan, Rahtore, and J'hala tribes, through whom the line of their founder, Bappa Rawul, was carried on; and who, on receiving wives from amongst the Ranas' daughters, obtained an importance which wealth could never confer, and they consequently claimed equality of rank with the lesser independent princes of India. The mother of the present Rana was a daughter of the Gogoonda house; a woman of an intrepid and masculine understanding, and whose personal attractions, if we judge by her son, must have been eminent; for the Rana's family is esteemed the handsomest in Rajpootana. The present heir, now Rana Jowan Sing, has been stamped by Nature with the outward impress of sovereignty. The niece of that Ranee is the mother of the chieftain of Saloombra, the premier noble of Méwar, which connects him with his sovereign by a double tie. The female issue of this connexion may be wedded to the Chohan noble of Baidla, or the Rahtore of Ganora—two of the Sixteen; and the daughters of such marriage may be espoused by the sovereign: and thus the blood of the great founder of the race is transfused by indirect channels into the original current, carrying with it that scarcely less

* Annals of Rajast'han, vol. I. p. 335.

less noble, the Chohan, Rahtore, and Chawura, from the descendants of the kings of Dehli, Kanouj, and Anhulwarra. The following anecdote at once exemplifies the dangerous effects of these unequal alliances, and the mischiefs resulting from polygamy. In the ANNALS, I have given an example of the former, in the case of the chieftain of Sadri, who was betrothed to a daughter of his sovereign; whilst the chronicles teem with instances of the evils of polygamy, engendering disputes and appeals, which the love of authority too frequently encourages; and where, as in the instance about to be related, the sovereign is weak enough to lend his countenance to the females, over whom he ought to claim no authority after they have acknowledged a lawful lord: the consequence is lamentable.

The Chohan chief of Kotario, one of the Sixteen, a lineal descendant of the last Hindu emperor of Dehli, had espoused two wives, one from the Suktawut house of Bheendir, the other a branch of the royal family, being one of the daughters of a Ranawut chief, who, by courtesy, are styled *babas*, or infantas. But as love is not inspired by the accident of birth, and the daughter of Bheendir added the virtue of obedience to other qualities required in a Rajpoot household, she became the favourite, to the mortification of the nobler wife. Both had male offspring, but the inheritance of Kotario was the right, by birth, of the son of the fair Suktawutni, who was, accordingly, received and caressed by all. Unhappily, however, this pledge of affection sickened and died, and the bereaved mother scrupled not to attribute the loss to her rival's designs to secure the succession to her own son, and openly accused her of having instigated the *dakunie*, or witch, to "eat the liver" of her child. Where such superstition reigns with unlimited sway, a doating husband would give easy credence to the suspicions

suspicions of his favourite wife, which estranged him still more from her rival. The high-born dame resented this, and, through her father, made application for the restitution of connubial rights to their common sovereign, the Rana, with such a colouring as suited their purpose of obtaining revenge for the grossest insult one Rajpoot can offer to another. The Rao,—for such is the title of the Kotario chief,—had already enemies at his sovereign's court, and those chiefly of his own kin and tribe; for, as he observed, the Chohan (his tribe) was the most accursed of all the Rajpoot races—no man could look on his brother's prosperity without envy. The Rana was made to believe that this unhappy father, who had lost one son, contemplated the destruction of the other, the offspring of the neglected wife, in order to avenge the favourite, who suggested the deed.

Unhappily, infanticide, arising out of the complex connubial ties of the Rajpoots, is too common to have created surprise or doubt, and the supposed intention was eagerly assumed by the Rana as a pretext for commencing a series of persecutions against the last scion of a long line of heroes. The tenure of the foreign vassalage of this court is termed *kala-putta*, or, black grant; meaning that it is resumable, in contradistinction to the ancient indigenous *puttaets*, whom the oppressions practised on the Kotario chief would have driven into rebellion: but his estate was isolated in the very heart of the country, and his means of opposition were already exhausted in perpetual contests with the roving Mahrattas.

It was this chief who, on returning from his tour of duty at his sovereign's court, at a time when loyalty durst not shew its front in Méwar, with his little band of twenty-five horse, was suddenly surrounded by the Mahrattas and called upon to surrender; whereupon the Rao,

dismounting,

dismounting, at one blow hamstrung his own horse, and calling to his vassals to imitate his example, with their gallant steeds bleeding around them, stood with sword and shield on their defence. As plunder, more than glory, was the object in those days, the predatory Southron cared not to assail those from whom, if successful, he could merely obtain cold steel, and they wisely left the Rao and his band to regain the castle of Kotario on foot.

The family of the Kotario chief formerly possessed the estate of Chandwar, near Agra, of which they were deprived by Secunder Lodi, who demanded a daughter of the chief and met with a refusal. The then possessor, Rao Manikchund, emigrated with his family to Guzzerat, and was well received by Mozuffer Shah, who appointed him to command on the Kathi frontier. In an engagement with the Kathis, he was severely wounded, and taken from the field by the king in person. His son, Dulput, acting as an auxiliary to the Rawul of Dongersau, was defeated and killed. He was succeeded by his son, Sungram Sing, who accompanied Bahadur Shah, of Guzzerat, against Cheetore, when Humayoon came to the Rana's assistance. It was at this period that the Chohan, who had 2,000 horse and 1,500 foot, with thirty-five elephants in his train, was prevailed upon by the Rana (Oody Sing) to remain in Méwar. The conditions attached to this engagement were, that the Chohan should accompany the Rana only when he took the field; that he should not act under an inferior; that he should make his obeisance only once a week; and that his rank should be equal to that of the highest chiefs of the Seesodia family.

The Rana, about the period of my joining his court, had sent the Zubtee to sequestrate the only two remaining townships of Kotario which afforded the Rao means of subsistence, the others being laid waste by the incursions of the general enemy. He had assigned them to the surviving child, who, being the son of one of the infantas, was, by courtesy, his nephew, and whom he considered, from this assumed treachery of the parent, as his ward. But the Rana having, with the assent of his nobles, made me general umpire and arbitrator in all disputes between Southron and vassal, the case of Kotario came under my adjudication. I was interested for the lineal representative of Kan-Rae, the generalissimo and uncle of the last Chohan emperor of Dehli, whose armies he led against the 'Sultan of the North,' and whose glory is exalted even by the Islamite historian; for it was Kan-Rae (written by Ferishta *Kandirai*) who propelled his steed against Shabud-in, at the head of his cuirassiers, and but for his armour of proof, the prince would have had his pretensions to the throne of Dehli for ever sealed by that chieftain's lance. "Is the descendant of Kan-Rae to be at the mercy of the back-biter who has poisoned the sovereign's ear? My poverty is my foe, for I have nothing left to bribe those around the *Huzoor* ('presence'), to shield me from injustice!" This forcible appeal, the personal demeanour of the Rao, and, above all, the abstract justice of his case, were irresistible, and I told him to be of good cheer, for that I would willingly be his vakeel with his sovereign.

That day, I sought the presence of the 'Sun of the Hindus,' whom I found, however, prejudiced; but I reminded the Rana of the services of the Chohan, at times when those now basking in the beams of his favour durst not, or at least did not, shew their faces; and urged him to mete out the same measure of grace to the Rao that Providence had shewn to himself. There was nothing of obduracy in the Rana's character, and if there was a single good point in that of the client, it

was

was readily admitted by him. On this occasion, our conference concluded with the assurance, on the Rana's part, that if the Rao would overcome his dislike to his Bhanaij,* and introduce him to the Durbar, he would shew every proper attention to his interests in return. I lost no time in telling the Rao, that compliance with the wish of the prince was his duty, and the road to favour. The struggle was evidently a bitter one, and evinced that he participated in the suspicions of his now childless and favourite wife; and although he promised compliance, as he said, from gratitude to me, his delays and excuses appeared interminable. At one time, he had the small-pox; at another, he pleaded that his poverty disabled him from carrying his wife and family to the capital; that it would bring her kindred to visit her, when entertainments with gifts must follow, and that he had neither funds nor credit. Although there was truth in all he advanced, his reasons were inadmissible, in competition with his sovereign's wishes, on the fulfilment of which his own welfare depended. He confessed the abstract force of my argument, but, while he acknowledged the obligations of duty, he denied the right of the prince to interfere in his domestic affairs. "If I yield on this point," said he, "I shall be a slave in my own house:—far better that I should go to ruin!" adding, that his personal enemies were desirous to get rid of him, and wished to force him to retire on a pension to Nathdwarra, and make way for his son. I pledged myself that this should not be, if he acted up to his prince's demands. All points were at length conceded, and in a few days I had the satisfaction of seeing presented to him a fresh grant of Kotario, in which the sequestrated townships were included. The boy

* *Bhanaij,* or *Bhanja,* is a nephew by the female side, and *Bhateeja* by the male.

boy was introduced to me, exhibiting a fine specimen of the Rajpoot youth of Méwar, before indolence and opium had exerted their influence. Could these drawbacks be removed, I should not despair of this descendant of Kan-Rae doing honour to the race from which he sprung.

Adieu, however, to these topics! We have now done with the J'hala of Gogoonda and the Chohan of Kotario. May their descendants prove worthy of the many noble examples which could be adduced to corroborate their claims to the admiration of the good and great of all climes!

June 3d. SAIMUR.—This is about the highest point of the cultivated portion of the Aravulli, though peak on peak darts up around us in every direction. At 2 P. M., the barometer was 27° 38′—the thermometer 82°. At sunset, the former was 27° 32′, the latter 76°—the summer heat of England in the dog-days of the tropic of India. What a climate, compared with the valley of the capital, where it had stood at 95°, both at sunrise and setting, when we started on this journey! In a transport of delight and short-sightedness, I threw away my tatties, of which I had abundant reason to repent, as the sequel will show.

We had showers in the evening, with the wind from the south-west. The interest of my journey over this alpine region increased at each step; every thing was novel in nature and her works, animal and vegetable. We had heard that the almond and peach-trees flourished in these wilds, and to an extent so considerable, that the kernel of the fruit, which they call the *aroo-badam*, or almond-peach, formed an article of exportation. We had seen them in the valley of Komulmér and in the pass of Dailwarra, though we had supposed the peach to be cultivated, and had some doubts regarding it, this having so long been

the

the abode of the Mahratta chiefs, until we saw some which were growing self-planted from amongst the interstices of the stone facing of a well. In to-day's march we observed several. Expressing my surprise, I was told they were more abundant in the valleys of Komulmér, which are said to produce many curious and useful indigenous plants; and, besides a crab-apple, the *saloo* or *saloo-misri*, which is either the arrow-root of our pharmacopœia, or a plant which yields a farinaceous substance of the same kind. It was described to me not as a root, but as a *bel* or creeper, sending forth spurs or clusters, like fingers on the hand. They, however, could not, or did not attempt to prepare it for use. Whether they meant to liken it to the clustered pods of the bean, I do not recollect; if so, it is probably the same as the *calamus*, described by Diodorus Siculus, and found in Ceylon.* I wrote my kinsman, Capt. Waugh, whom I left in charge at the capital, to procure some of it, and named the village, *i. e.* Kurria, in the alpine district of Komulmér, where the wild grape (*dhak*), and the wild apple, as well as the *saloo-misri*, were produced.†

If the true definition of *alp* be an upland, or mountainous pasture-land, this magnificent region well merits the epithet of alpine; for, amidst its towering rocks and numerous rivulets, there was not only abundance of fine pasture, but arable land, of which a considerable quantity was under the plough, preparing for maize, wheat, barley, and even sugar-cane. If the operations of agricultural industry are ever pleasant

* He says: "plenty of calamus is produced there, whose fruit has the appearance of white vetches. When gathered, they steep it in hot water till it swells to the size of a pigeon's egg; then rub it in their hands into a dough, knead and bake it into delicious bread."—(*Diod. Sic.* book ii. c. 4.)

† This note will, I trust, be made available hereafter for the purpose of much varied knowledge, by that zealous botanist, Dr. Royle, author of "Illustrations of the Botany and other Branches of the Natural History of the Himalayan Mountains."

pleasant to behold, they are especially so in these mountainous recesses, where the forest has been levelled to make way for the plough. But here was an additional source of interest to the contemplative mind, in finding the Rajpoot mountaineer, descendant of the ancient princes of the land, in the full enjoyment of all his native dignity, lofty in mien, strong in limb, and independent in soul; and, though eating his bread by the sweat of his brow, losing not an iota of the remembrance of his high descent: the sword and shield being as familiar to his hand, as to his indolent brethren of the plains; his life being a scene of warlike defence against the lawless surrounding tribes, the Mair, Mheena, and Bhil. All the *thakoors*, or chiefs of villages, collected round me to-day, to proffer their services, and several remained in and about my tents the whole day, regaling me with the traditions of past times,—how their ancestors had defended to the death each pass in the vicinity, "when the cloud of war rolled from the north," and the Toork had resolved on the subjugation of their prince; or inroads of their marauding neighbours; or classic stories, which immortalized each peak or dell.

One spot they pointed out, dusky and deeply wooded, which backed the sources of the Bunas, and to which the hero Pertap was oft-times indebted for shelter when hard pressed by his relentless foeman. To this, as to many other of his retreats, they give the name of *rana-paj*, or footsteps of the Rana. In listening to these exhilarating narrations, or in trying my skill with the *kumpta*, or bamboo bow, and arrows a full yard long, the day was soon spent. The garb of these mountain lords was very different from that of the plains, and harmonized with the scenery around. As the Dussanoh chieftain advanced, we might have fancied him an antique Greek, saving the turban. His loose

chadur

chadur, or mantle, was tied in a knot on the left shoulder, leaving the breast and arms free; while a cloth was wrapped round his loins, in length and form corresponding to the kilt. In his hand he held the bow, while the quiver depended from his shoulder. This is the usual dress of the hills, and which I found extending to Sirohi. Some of the more polished wear this robe over loose trousers; but this is an innovation on the ancient garb. The construction of their villages is in unison with the simplicity of their costume, the dwellings being of a circular form, with conical thatched roofs; and, when grouped in small hamlets, perched for security half-way up a peak, and shaded by neem trees, their appearance is highly picturesque. Occasionally, as at Pudzaroh, the village temple with its spire gives dignity and effect to the scene. As I passed, its blind chief was led out to meet me; and here I beheld a striking contrast between the tolerant Rajpoot and the fierce, bigotted Islamite, whose *eedga*, or place of worship, the mark of conquest, was left unscathed, though within sight of the half-demolished shrine of Pudzaroh.

Another of my enjoyments this day was the discovery of the long-looked for sources of the Bunas river; a stream which, whether regarded in respect to magnitude or to utility, is one of the most important in Rajwarra. To me, who had traced its course through many a region to its confluence with the Chumbul, the discovery of the fountain-head could not fail to suggest those pleasurable, though complex and indescribable sensations, which the source of a great river always excites. It lay about five miles to the south-west of my encampment on the highest point of the table-land, and was joined by many smaller rills, as they poured their shallow but crystal waters over their rocky beds. If the Rajpoot "lord of the mountain and the flood" offers

offers a resemblance to the ancient Gaul in outward costume and the superficial points of character, the analogy is further preserved with respect to the legends of romance, which their imaginations identify with every visible object. Unfortunately, I confided to my memory alone a very pretty traditionary legend attached to the source of the Vanasi, the more classic name of this Naiad of the Aravulli. The pith of it is, that she was a chaste shepherdess, who, while disporting in the waters of this natural fountain, espied, to her horror, an intruder gazing upon her charms. A stranger to the delicacy of the lover of Musidora, he could not say,—

> "Bathe on, unseen but by the eye of love;"

and as, in all probability, the art of writing was unknown to the invader, he was obliged to come forward *in propriâ personâ.* Be this as it may, she prayed to the guardian divinity of the fountain to shield her from his gaze. The prayer was heard; the waters rose and covered the Bhilni, who was thus metamorphosed into the crystal stream, the Vanasi, or 'Hope *(asi)* of the Forest *(vana)*:'—a most appropriate appellation for the genius of the stream, the life and soul of the inhabitants of this rock-bound abode. Her subsequent course, which I have traced through all her meanderings, from the cradle to her union with the Chermutti (the classic appellation of the Chumbul, a male stream), is not less interesting; and, were this a convenient place, I would invite the reader to an excursion along her banks for full three hundred miles. At one lonely and lovely spot, amidst the covert of wood and rock, before she gains the plain, the legend says, a hand sometimes appears above the waters.* We should next overtake her coquetting

* In the "Annals," I describe this spot in the journey to Komulmér; where the fable goes, that the hand of the genius of the stream used often to be seen above the water, until a barbarian *Toork* threw a piece of the sacred kine for it to grasp.

coquetting about the shrine of Kanya, at Nathdwarra; but in vain she seeks to reach the hallowed fane of Radha's lover; whether at her command, or raised by the rival Gopis, a rocky barrier intervenes; and the 'Hope of the Aravulli,' frustrated in her design upon the Apollo of the Yamuna, darts rapidly across the plains of Méwar, in quest of society amongst the Dryads and Naiads of the Pathar. Another stream, bearing the same name, takes it rise in the same elevated spot, and, pursuing its course over the western declivity of the mountain, sweeps by the eastern base of Aboo, and thence, by the once-celebrated city of Chandravati, traverses the woods of Koliwarra, and is finally engulphed in the *Run*, or salt-marsh, at the head of the Kutch gulf.

June 4th. Camp in the Nulla, or Pass. At ten A. M., the thermometer was 86°; barometer 28° 12′. At 1, P. M., thermometer 93°, barometer 28° 8′. At 6, P. M., thermometer 92°. and barometer 28°. This morning we commenced our journey over the western declivity of the Aravulli, leading to the "Land of Death," the sandy plains of Maroo. From the point of descent, until we cleared the hills, the pass *(nal)*,* though its sinuosities were very trifling, was full twenty-two miles in length, and twenty times more difficult than that of Komulmér,† by which we last year entered Marwar; but, like it, amply repaying the toil,—if toil it can be called, where the mind is in one tumult of excitement, from the varied magnificence of Nature's works. As

* The term *nala* is applied to a mountain-stream, from *nal*, 'a defile,' indicating that the course of a stream always presents some mode of penetrating into mountainous regions. *Nal* also means 'a tube,' whence the warlike *nal-gola*, a kind of arquebuss; a ball propelled by whatever force from a tube; a term used by the old martial poets of India for a warlike engine, long before gunpowder was known in Europe.

† See Annals of Rajast'han, vol. i. p. 676.

As it would have been impossible to make this in one march, without distressing both men and cattle, we halted midway, in a lovely wild spot, in the very heart of the defile, but affording sufficient room for my little camp, on the bank of a crystal stream, which, rising near the sources of the Vanas, precipitates itself over the western face, and traversing the finest districts of Marwar, falls into the Loony, or Salt River, near J'halore. Although it occasionally expands into these charming little spots, this pass may be described as one continuous defile, frequently contracting to very narrow dimensions, and in one place presenting a gorge so confined, and this for a mile and a half in length, that it might be defended by a handful of men against a host, who would have no apprehension of their flanks being turned, blocked in as they would be by deep forests and other defiles on all sides. The first sight of this superb region discovers to us the secret of the long successful resistance of its princes against the tyranny of the Islamite oppressor. All was grand in this region—lovely and wild, as if destined by nature to be the haunt of her favourite progeny, and where human passions should never intrude to disturb the harmony of the scene. The sky was cloudless; the notes of cuckoos were heard responding to each other from amidst the deep foliage, while the *cuckroos*, or jungle-fowl, were crowing their matinals, as the sun illumined the groves of bamboo which sheltered them; and groups of the grey partridge, nestled in the trees, vied with the ring-doves in expressions of delight, as the sun cleared the alpine cliffs and darted his fervent rays amongst them. Others of the feathered tribe, not belonging to the plains, were flying about, while the woodpecker's note was heard reverberating from the hard surface on which he plied the power of his bill. Fruits and flowers of various kinds and colours invited the inha-

bitants

bitants of the forest, whether biped, quadruped, feathered, or the industrious bee, who here could sip the sweetest of sweets from the *chaméli*, or jasmine, both white and yellow, which climbed the giant foliage; the *ca'mb'ir* and *ca'noa*, whose clustering purple and white flowers resemble the lilac; while the almond-scented *kinĕr*, or oleander, covered the banks of the stream, on whose margin abundantly flourished the *arund (ricinus*, or *palma Christi)*, and willow. There were likewise many beautiful plants less aspiring than the climbing *chaméli* and *jambolia*, but worthy of notice, especially one resembling the hyacinth. Of fruits, besides an occasional *aroo-badam*,* or almond-peach, there was the *anjer*, or wild fig (not the *gootur* fig, whose fruit issues, instead of from the branches, direct from the stem); the *sureefa*, or custard-apple; the *khutoom*, a kind of wild grape; the *rae-goonda*, also called *laiswa*, a glutinous fruit about the size of a walnut, and the *taindoo*, or fruit of the ebony tree, which is abundant here. These and many other objects, affording attraction to the botanist and zoologist, passed us in review. The honey produced from such a congregation of sweets far excels that of the Isle of Bourbon or Narbonne, the latter of which I have since tasted at the fountain-head, and the former fresh from the isle.†

The day was far too short for my inquiries, or to satisfy those of my insatiably

* Botanists imagine the peach to be the cultivated almond; an assumption which appears to be borne out by this double term.

† I have yet some of the Aravulli honey, preserving nearly all its pristine flavour, ten years after its collection. This may, perhaps, be accounted for by its having undergone no manipulation or igneous process; it being allowed to drop from the comb into baskets lined with plantain-leaves, from which it was poured into bottles, and well corked. I brought twenty bottles to England, which I distributed amongst my friends, who acknowledged its superiority over all the European kinds. There were two sorts: the one colourless, from the upland; the other of a slight brown tint, from the mango-blossom of the lower range.

insatiably curious native friends, whose society contributed not a little to the interest of this picturesque scene. As the night began to close around us, I dismissed them to their homes, with a promise to write to the Rana in their behalf; for they complained loudly that the Minister, aware of their fealty at all seasons and under all provocations, sent his emissaries to levy contributions, notwithstanding this was prohibited since the new era set in.

CHAPTER III.

Grateful attention of the Author's attendants.—Narrowness of the pass.—Cairn.—Forays of the Meenas.—Power of the Bhils.—Their habits, manners, origin, and language.—Wild Bhils.—Anecdote.—Aborigines of India.—Superstitions of the Bhils.—Fidelity of the Bhils to their religion and country.—Causes of their change of character.—*Sirna*, or sanctuary.—The Saloombra chief and his vassal, the murderer of some Bhils.—Execution of Bhil plunderers.—The Sariahs.—Their habits and manners.

June 5th.—Veejipoor, or Beejapoor.—The night passed without any alarm from the inhabitants of the forest, quadruped or biped; but what was my surprise, on issuing from my tent to give the order of march, to see groups of my faithful Rajpoots standing to their arms around the embers of their night-fires! they had been watching to defend me from the Bhil or the bear while I slept. On expressing my regret that they had not retired to their respective villages, after leave-taking the preceding evening, a multitude of tongues hastened to deliver the same sentiment. "*Eh Marajah!* this is the last service we can render you—the service of the heart (*mun-ca-chakri*), for all you have done for us." Will it still be said that there is even no term for gratitude in these regions? Were this assertion true, which it is not, here is the *act* without the *profession.* What can equal such spontaneous homage to one who in a few hours was to quit them for ever! Equally strong were the expressions of gratitude from the man of wealth in the city, and the cultivator at his plough. But let us continue our journey through the remainder of the pass, into the burning plains of Maroo.

Yesterday, the entrance of the pass was decorated with a rude statue to to Nain-Mata, whose name it bears; and, shortly afterwards, when we began to descend, we attained a point which, forming a neck or barrier across the *Nal*, becomes the head of another, or, at least, furnishes another term to the superabundant nomenclature of these wilds, and the remainder of this was dedicated to Seetla-Mata, protector of infancy, and especially when visited by that scourge, the small-pox, called *seetla*. We reached this point at 9 A. M.; thermometer 82°, barometer 28° 25′. A little in advance, where the gorge contracts to the smallest dimensions, and for some distance, at an angle of 45° with the horizon, the surface is rugged, broken, and requiring all the care of the camel-drivers and the sagacity of the elephant to thread their way without danger to themselves and their burdens, more than once displaced by the boughs of trees. Here we passed a cairn of loose stones, marking the spot where the nephew of Pudzaroh had been slain in the rescue of his cattle "driven by the Meenas of Ootwun," who, in order to avoid pursuit, left the pathway of the *Nal*, and, taking a sweep through the woods to the left, came out upon the head of a smaller diverging branch of the pass, hoping by this stratagem to elude the chase. The boldness and dexterity of the attempt merited success. The point of divergence from the main pass to this branch is by a perpendicular scarp of full twenty feet, over which a rivulet precipitates itself in the rainy season, and has hewn for itself a path, by which they essayed to escape. The old adage, of "one fool makes many," may be strictly applied to the mountain cattle in these alpine tracts, who are as wild and active as colts, and, wherever one goes, the rest follow. The Meenas, reckoning on this propensity, when they reached the precipice, plunged their daggers into the leading beeve and threw him over, when, serving at once as a guide and a break-fall, the others took the leap. But, notwithstanding this

this skilful and daring act, they were overtaken, and several fell on both sides, and amongst them, as mentioned, the nephew of Pudzaroh, some of whose kindred accompanied me to see me across the border.

To those who love to hear of such feuds, or the legends of the nobler strife of past days, each valley and defile is a book teeming with records ; and were I not afraid of taxing too severely the patience and time of my reader, I would relate the raids of the Meenas of Ootwun among the cow-pens of the Aravulli ; or those of the more distant Bhils of Chappun, in conjunction with their more civilized brethren of Ogunah, Panurwa, and Meerpoor. But even a brief history of the Meenas* alone would occupy too much space, while that of the Bhils has perhaps been already sufficiently elucidated.† I have, moreover, slightly touched, in a short geographical sketch of these regions, on the independent Bhil communities, full of interest, from their manners, traditions, and insulated position.

I have stated that my intention was to have penetrated to Aboo by these towns ; but I deem the interest likely to be excited by the route I have chosen superior. When I say insulated, I mean in a geographical and political point of view. Surrounded by lofty mountains, defended by numerous defiles and forests, almost impervious to bodies of troops, they enjoy a life of perfect independence, subject alone to their own chiefs, who, if congregated, it is affirmed, could assemble "fifteen thousand bows" for the defence of their passes. The names of the

* I intend this to form the subject-matter of a paper for the Transactions of the Royal Asiatic Society. [This is one of the many valuable memoirs of which the lamented death of the Author has deprived the public.]

† Vide Transactions of the Royal Asiatic Society, vol. i. p. 65, for an extended account of this tribe, by the late Sir John Malcolm.

the principal towns of this association of semi-indigenous brotherhood, are Panurwa, Ogunah, Joora-meer-poor, Jowas, Sumaija, Madri, Ozah, Adiwasa, Beroti, Novagong, &c. &c., whose chieftains, deriding their aboriginal descent, as Vanaputras, or Lords of the Forest, claim a mixed parentage and Rajpoot blood. The chief of Panurwa is lord paramount of the whole, and all attend him on the military festival of the Dusserah. He takes the august title of Rana, and has no less than twelve hundred townships *(poora)* and hamlets *(poorwa)* under his immediate sway, of which many are doubtless very insignificant, the majority being in one large valley, several coss in area, in which wheat, gram, or vetches, yams *(rutaroo)*, turmeric *(puldi)*, and the esculent root called *arvi*, somewhat resembling the Jerusalem artichoke, are abundantly grown. They even export superfluous produce to the neighbouring states. The wild peach and pomegranate, indigenous to these hills, are cultivated successfully, both at Ogunah and Panurwa. The next in rank is the chief of Ogunah—his name Lall Sing, who, with the title of Rawul, acknowledges himself to be the vassal of Panurwa, having sixty townships and hamlets in his grant. Ogunah, which is full twenty miles from Panurwa, is called Little Nat'hdwarra, and contains much wealth, as does Meerpoor. The expelled *purdhan*, or minister, of the Gogoonda chief, now fills the same office with the Bhomia Bhil of Ogunah. They are very partial to the use of this epithet, which identifies them with the soil *(bhom)*, making them in fact the autochthones. The Panurwa Rana has his little court, in imitation of *the* Rana, at which I am told the greatest etiquette prevails, and that he exacts as much deference from the numerous bowmen who constitute his vassalage. The Panurwa, Ogunah, and subordinates, call themselves of Pramara blood, and intermarry with the Bhomias of Joora-meer-poor

poor, Jowas, Madri, who claim descent from the Chohan race of Rajpoots. Joora and Meer-poor, which are always conjoined in name, though five miles asunder, are situated in the tract called Nayr, touching the Eedur frontier, and embrace no less than nine hundred of these scattered hamlets in their scope. Joora was only about twelve miles from my position at Saimur, and it was about eight further to Ogunah, but the route lay through an impenetrable wild. Ogunah was the same distance from Gogoonda, having the Rana's post of Sooruj-gurh intermediate, his boundary and frontier garrison, to overawe these independents, or claim their support if requisite. There is little doubt that in ancient days these "children of the forest" all professed obedience to the king of the Hindus; and the excellent service which they performed, when the honour of his house was so often perilled against the Mogul, merited the highest gratitude, to which feeling in part, but still more to their inability to compel obedience, they owe their independence. Nor can they be assailed with impunity. A dispute arose between the Rajpoot chief of Jerole, the frontier post between Oodipoor and Ogunah, and the Bhil of Ogunah, who had led his vassals against it; but not one returned to tell the tale. In revenge, Jodaram led his cavaliers, all clad in quilted mail, when thousands of bowmen collected; but though only twenty-five horse, the Rajpoots charged the dense mass, defeated them with slaughter, and entering the town, made good their retreat with booty which yielded twelve thousand rupees. The tract called Khuruk, of which Jowas is the capital, touches Dongerpoor and Saloombra, whose chiefs are at constant enmity with their inhabitants. Environed by lofty hills, covered with deep forests, chiefly of bamboo and *dhak*, *(butea frondosa)*, successful invasion is impracticable with numbers, and a few would be cut off, unless they took them by surprise. Death

 is

is the lot of any who dare to cut a tree in the paths of outlet. Fire-arms are only used by the chiefs and head-men; the national weapon being the *kumpta* or bamboo bow, having the bowstring *(chulla)* from a thin slip of its elastic bark. Each quiver contains sixty barbed arrows, a yard long. Although they claim descent from every race of Rajpoot, and prefix the tribe, as Chohan-Bhil, Gehlote-Bhil, Pramar-Bhil, &c. &c., their origin is best evinced in the gods they worship and their prejudices as to food. They will eat of nothing white in colour, as a white sheep or goat; and their grand adjuration is, "By the white ram!" These prejudices, however, belong only to those who affect to call themselves *Oojla*, or pure Bhils; and, if we may judge by the freedom from prejudice of the greater number, few are entitled to the distinction of 'pure.' In fact, we may assert that they are still demi-savage, as they are assuredly an aboriginal race, whether we regard their superstitions, their habits, or their language; for, although the latter contains much of Sanscrit derivation, their vocables are distinct. I advance this, however, more from the report of their neighbours than from personal investigation—a Bhil vocabulary remaining amongst my desiderata. Had I explored the haunts described above, I should certainly have made some acquisitions of this kind, as well as gained a more extended knowledge of their habits, amongst the Lares and Penates, the 'white ram,' and *aswa-mukhi*, or horse's head (the grand symbols of adoration), at their own firesides. This study will amply repay those who are desirous to read the book of nature under every aspect; and the inquirer will be surprised and gratified to prove the truth of the old axiom, "extremes meet." Here, in the abodes of savage uneducated nature, he would form an acquaintance with the virtues of truth, hospitality, and that proud distinction, gradually disappearing from the European codes, which

which provides a sanctuary for the refugee. If a Bhil pledges protection, he will sacrifice his life to redeem his word; if the traveller through his passes pay the customary toll, his property and person are secure; and any insult or injury by another will be avenged. The pass-word, *Maula-ca-sirna* or the Sanctuary of Maula, or whatever other name the protector may bear, would be a safeguard from one end of the community to the other; and if his protector did not furnish him with a guide, an arrow from his quiver would answer the purpose, and be equally recognised with the ambassador's signet of any court in Christendom. Nor would he, like the mountain Afghan, perform the rites of hospitality while under the eye of the Penates, yet hesitate not to plunder its object so soon as he had passed a decent distance from his roof.

The historian of America observes, that "nations which depend upon hunting are in a great measure strangers to the idea of property; and with the natives of those regions, the forest or hunting-grounds were the property of the tribe." The Bhil is a step in advance in the scale of civilization, their hunting-grounds being separated into individual portions, as the following anecdote, which I noted down many years ago, will attest. The Bhils of the most desolate and unfrequented wilds of Méwar and the Nerbudda to this day lead a life little short of that of nature, and with the exception of a few articles of luxury, resulting from the discovery of fire, as roasted vermin and distilled waters, are not more civilized than the Esquimaux on the verge of the Polar Basin, to whom a piece of putrid blubber is not less a delicacy than a roasted guana or jackall to the Bhil. These are delicacies to the Vanaputra table, supplied by the spontaneous and abundant fruits of the forest, such as nourished the forefathers of the heroes of Marathon and Thermopylæ; but our Bhil has a more varied and palatable repast than their

 acorn

acorn dinner, *viz.*, the ebony, tamarind, mango, and many other fruits, besides the seeds of various wild grapes, and esculent roots : though he is not always permitted to apply these to his own use, free from the claims of other dwellers in the forest, the bear and the monkey. But now to our anecdote. "Go," says the father Bhil to the suitor for his daughter's hand,—"I resign yonder mountains as her *daeja* (dower), nor shall I henceforth within its bounds entrap hare or fox, pluck its fruits or roots, or its branches or leaves for fuel. All are yours." The bear does not, however, so readily relinquish his share, but will fight for the possession of his darling Mhowa tree. A young Bhil had fallen asleep beside his basket, filled with its fruit, either intended for the family dessert, or to be converted into *aruc* ('essence'—the whiskey of the East), when a bear, in his rounds, roused him, somewhat rudely, from his slumbers, and prepared apparently to make his repast on the Bhil, who escaped much lacerated from his embrace. Such an infraction of sylvan polity was not to be borne by the father Bhil, who sallied forth with bow and arrow to avenge the insult. He found the bear feasting on the scene of aggression, slew him, and carried his skin to a neighbouring chief, to whom his fealty was due ; and on telling the story, thus concluded his harangue : "There is the hide of the offender ; it is hard that brothers of the forest cannot live on terms of friendship :—but he began the war."

"If," as observed by the celebrated Goguet (vol. I., p. 78), "there has always been a great conformity between the ordinary food of men and their sacrifices, who have always offered to the gods a part of those things which were the chief support of their own lives, as in the first ages, herbs, fruits and plants, and at length animals, when they became their ordinary food ;" the legitimate inference would be, that human sacrifices

sacrifices and cannibalism were co-existent; but although we have on record that the Hindu, as well as the ancient Briton, offered human sacrifices to the Destroyer, we have no authority for the belief that the votaries either of the Celtic Belenus or Hindu Bal participated in such food to their gods. It is true that we might cite the brutalized Aghori as a proof of still existing cannibalism; but he would only prove the exception to the rule. Yet, though this proof of the last stage of human degradation be wanting,—the very lowest dweller in these forests,—we may not resist the suspicion that the stomach which does not revolt at making its repast on an offal-feeding jackall, hideous guana, or half-putrid kine, would not find the transition to a human limb very objectionable.

At no period in the comprehensive range of Hindu tradition, is there a time discoverable at which the natives of India were ignorant of the element of fire, and its domestic uses; and yet it must have been a discovery with them as with the other nations of the earth. Who, however, would imagine that fire could be a discovery, when nature teems with it, whether in the coruscations of the heavens, those *Jowala Mukhis* (literally, 'mouths of flame,'—volcanos), which rend the bosom of the earth, or the innumerable *Seeta coondas*, or hot-wells, scattered over her surface? and though the story of Columbus and the egg may present itself to the mind, when we moralize on the subject,

> " ———— so simple seemed it found,
> " Which yet unfound, most would have thought impossible."

it is no less true, that the mode of obtaining it for artificial purposes was a discovery, and, to the feeders on acorns, of the most important nature.

We

We need not revert to the pages of Pliny and Plutarch for proofs of nations being without the use of this apparently indispensable element; for we have abundant instances of it in the more modern history of the world, amongst the African and American tribes, and in the Isles of the Atlantic: for instance, the Marian Isles, discovered by Magellan, in 1521, "whose inhabitants took it for an animal which fed on trees and wood, and felt alarm for their safety."* Nay, Bruce, whose veracity has been established beyond the reach of malice, by the first of modern travellers, the enterprizing Burckhardt, asserts that people about the sources of the Nile were ignorant of its application, or, as Burke would have said, had not attained the degree of reason which distinguishes a roasting animal. Our aborigines of India, the Bhil, Koli, and Goand, had, doubtless, found the art of cooking their food at a very early period, having a natural tinder-box and flint in every bamboo grove, and having only to watch, during a high wind, the emission of flame from the friction of these natives of the hills, to obtain a supply more than sufficient of the devouring element: their sylvan retreats being often burnt over their heads. I have witnessed the magnificent spectacle of a forest of bamboo blazing, crackling, and exploding, said to be self-ignited; and although any hard wood will yield fire by friction, the silicious coating† of the bamboo makes it by far the most ready instrument of *Agni*, whom the universal Hindu nation, the learned Brahmin, the warlike Rajpoot, as well as the half-savage Vanaputra, worship as a divinity.

A thorough

* Goguet, vol. i. p. 73.

† The substance found in the pith of the bamboo, and termed *tabasheer*, and used by the Hindus medicinally, is pure silex, and would appear to be the internal flowing of the sap, which there coagulates and hardens.

A thorough study of the uncivilized tribes of India, the Bhil, Koli, Goand, Meena, Mair, would disclose important links in the physical history of man ; even in those enumerated, the most powerful distinctions, as well in form and lineament, as in habits and superstitious rites, the result of example or locality, would be observed ; and though all alike bear the impress of originality, yet their respective characteristics are so dissimilar, that we should reject the idea of their common descent from one great family. There is not a greater difference between the squat, flat-nosed, Tartarian-visaged Esquimaux, and the ancient noble Mohican savage, than between the Bhil of Méwar and the Khole of Sirgoojur ; nor are the habits of the dweller on the verge of the Polar sea more distinct from those of the migratory races of the Missouri, than are those of our forest *indigènes* from the more locomotive Rajpoot. If man had sprung, like a fungus, from the earth, it might be said these were the uncultivated mushrooms of India, fixed, as the rocks and trees of their mountain wilds, to the spot which gave them birth. This entire want of the organ of locomotion, and an unconquerable indolence of character, which seems to possess no portion of that hardiness which can brave the dangers of migration, forbid all idea of their foreign origin, and would rather incline us to the Monboddo theory, that they are an improvement of the tribe with tails. I do not reckon that their raids from their jungle abodes, in search of plunder, supply any argument against the innate principle of locality. The Bhil returns to it as truly as does the needle to the north ; nor could the idea enter his mind of seeking other regions for a domicile. Their very names imply this principle :—*Vanaputra*, 'child of the forest ;' *Mairote*, 'born of the mountain,'—*Goind*, apparently a compound of *Gopa* and *Indra*, 'lord of the cave :' *Pal-Indra*, 'lord of the pass.'

pass.' In like manner, *Kol*, signifying 'mountaineer', from *Ko*, 'a mountain,' which, though less commonly used than the Sanscrit word *Gir*, is beyond a doubt a primitive root with the Indo-Scythic nation.

The Bhils, having no order of priesthood, have recourse to the Guru of the Bullaes, one of the most debased of the Sudra classes. On the occasion of any nuptial ceremony, this Guru decks himself in the sacerdotal thread of the Brahmin, whose appellation he assumes with the badge, though he partakes both of the food which is dressed and of the cup, which flows freely. A scene of riot follows every such rite, and a general fray is the never-failing *finale*. Whatever *daeja* or dower is given with the bride, the bridegroom invariably presents the father with a buffalo, twelve rupees, and two bottles of liquor, to defray the marriage-feast. On a birth, the same self-created Brahmin names the child, generally after the genius presiding over the day of its birth: *Boodh*, if born on Wednesday, from *Boodh-war*, or the day of Mercury; or *Boodhia* if a female. On this event, as well as on deaths, there is another very important character called in to take part in the ceremony, the *Camra*, or minstrel, of whom there is one in every large village. His garb is that of the Jogi ascetic, and as it is necessary he should be initiated in the mystical doctrines of the sectarian Kabri, he is indifferently named Kamra Jogi, or Kabri Punti. On births, accompanied by his wife, he takes his position with his guitar before the door, first placing a small figure of a horse beside the threshold. He then commences a hymn, propitiating Seetla Mata, the protectress of infants, who is much dreaded by all the wild tribes, his wife blending her voice with his, and beating time with the cymbals. A large *d'hol*, or alarm-drum, is kept in every village, which by a peculiar beat announces such an event to the neighbours, who, according to their ability

ability and inclination, present gifts to the parents of the new comer. On deaths, a monotonous beating summons the neighbours, each of whom brings in his hand a seer of grain. Close by the door of the deceased, the minstrel takes his post, the image of the horse and an earthen jar of water being placed beside him. Each relation and visitor, on approaching, takes some of the water in the palm of his hand, which he sprinkles over the image, invoking the name of the deceased, and presenting the measure of grain to the minstrel. Why such reverence is shown to the emblem of the horse, I have been unable to learn—unless it be as the symbol of the sun, adored by all classes—but nothing is undertaken without it.

I have elsewhere mentioned,* that the Rajpoot tribes are conquerors, and that the birthright of all the intricate regions of India belonged to these aboriginal tribes, traces of whose importance in their ancient fortified abodes are by no means uncommon, and so late as a century ago, one of these lords of the soil had eight hundred horse in his train, besides bowmen. Their chief warriors were styled *Sawant*, and, as a distinguishing badge, wore a waistband of small brass bells. They never went to battle but encased in armour, and to look behind was a capital crime, and entailed loss of title, which went to the nearest of kin, or if there were none, the most worthy was elected Sawant. During the lengthened anarchy which afflicted these regions, and tore asunder all the bonds of fealty or affection that held societies together in these complicated abodes, the Bhil had often sealed his fidelity with his blood. In those exterminating conflicts waged between the Ranas and the Emperors of Dehli, the former were indebted to these children of the forest for

* Annals of Rajast'han, vol. ii. p. 2, *et scq.*

for their own preservation, and what is yet more dear to a Rajpoot, that of their wives and daughters from the hands of a foe whose touch was pollution. We have represented them, while the immortal Pertap was confronting his inexorable foe, bearing these his treasures at one time to the mines of Jawura, or when these no longer proved a safe concealment, threading their way through passes unknown but to themselves; nor will it be forgotten that in more recent times, when the capital was besieged by the great Sindiah, its protracted defence was in a great measure due to the Bhils, who conveyed supplies to the besieged across the lake. But the heart-stirring days which kindled a tumult in the bosom of the Bhils, as well as in that of his lordly superior, being exchanged for inglorious inactivity and all the vices springing from poverty and oppression, is it to be wondered at that the children of the forest degenerated with their superiors; or that, being oppressed instead of fostered, they should pilfer where they once protected, hate where they honoured, despise where they dreaded? Such was the change of sentiment which I found in full activity, when, in 1817-18, I became a mediator between them, and a reclaimer of their rights. I have stated how my Brahmin envoy made treaties with 750 townships and villages in the mountains of the west, and that these simple treaties, invoking the sun to witness, or attested by the symbol of the plough, the dagger, or bow and arrow, tantamount to the vow of the cavalier of the west, "May my stirrups fail me!" were religiously fulfilled; peace, good order, and the seeds of industry were established, until these Rajpoot superiors, taking advantage of my absence, in some places renewed their old exactions, and in others cruelly balanced some ancient feud. Such was the atrocious case of Kaba, a considerable community about ten miles west of the capital, two of whose inhabitants were barbarously

rously murdered by a vassal of the Saloombra chief; and, as if in defiance of the sovereign, within the walls of the city, at the public well, and in the face of open day. The question involved a ticklish point, that of *sirna* or sanctuary, and this with the premier noble of Méwar; but there was only one of two courses to pursue: either to set at nought the pledge of protection given by the Rana, and guaranteed by the envoy to the British government, or to disregard the right of sanctuary of the Saloombra chief. There could be no hesitation; instant search was made, but in vain. Under shadow of the night, the culprit escaped from the city; but, in spite of every attempt at concealment, I traced him through many doublings to the Saloombra dominions. I requested the chief to call upon me, and at once invited him to choose between the effects of his sovereign's displeasure, together with the termination of our friendship, or to 'break the Sirna' (*sirna toorna*) with the murderer, whom he might place in the hands of justice in the way least likely to violate his feelings, or the prejudices which none better knew than himself how much I respected. He talked of abandoning his fief and withdrawing to Benares, and, as an ancestor, who preferred his honour to his land, had done before him, of gaining his bread by the manufacture of horsewhips, for that his "face would be blackened" among his brethren if he surrendered him. This and much more of eloquent and manly remonstrance, with the denial on oath of all foreknowledge of the deed and all participation in it, was concluded by his saying, he would punish his vassal in any manner commanded by his sovereign. The negociation closed with a compromise: the culprit was to be dismissed from Saloombra, and desired to seek sanctuary elsewhere; and whilst in quest of this, was to be pounced upon by a party of the Rana's people. This salvo for his honour

being

being acceded to, the murderer was brought to the capital: but such is the force of habit, as regards this privilege of sanctuary, which even forms a stipulation in the grants of some estates, that, in announcing the arrival of the culprit, the Rana, or rather his advisers, endeavoured to throw on me the odium of the transaction. While, however, I supported the cause of his government, I was unwilling needlessly to invest with an odious character the British representative, and therefore replied, that there could be no occasion to consult me on a point in which the personal dignity of the Rana was to be maintained. I heard no more until the following day, when the murderer had suffered the extreme penalty of blood for blood, but with a barbarous and unnecessary severity. He was placed vertically in a pit and covered with earth, his head alone remaining exposed to the sun; and having during the day died, by anticipation, a hundred deaths, his skull was smashed by a mallet. A few years back, the Rana must have submitted to the indignity; and would as soon have thought of bearding the tiger in his den as of breaking the Sirna of a much less powerful chief than Saloombra. After this retaliation, the Rana propitiated the community of Kaba by sending for the representatives of the murdered Bhils, and gratifying them with turbans and silver *kurras* or wrist-strings, which did more than an army to secure their fidelity.

But alas! for the poor Vanaputras, whose friends are few, and who, being considered as outcasts from society, are likened to the sons of Esau! a more grievous example was subsequently forced upon us, and this occurred unfortunately about the end of my career amongst them. My repeated absence from Oodipoor, in the countries of the Rahtores and Haras, gave too many opportunities to the enemies of those poor people to stir them up to acts of violence; and without a constant

and

and local surveillance, it was impossible to distinguish their return to lawless habits from their obedience to provocation. Various were the insidious methods adopted by their Rajpoot superiors to tempt them to aggression; and unhappily their natural propensities led them too easily into the snare; whether to plunder the traveller, or to molest the camp-followers with the British cantonment at Neemuch, while cutting wood and bamboos in their forests. I had frequent representations from the gallant Colonel Ludlow, then commanding that camp, regarding these obstructions; and, at length, the still bolder step of plundering one of these parties and retiring with their spoils to the jungles, compelled me to apply to the Rana for his permission that our own troops might punish the offence. Armed with his authority, a party was equipped under command of Lieut. Hepburn, who conducted it with such caution, that he took the village completely by surprise, made prisoners about thirty of the offenders, who were not only recognized by the parties aggrieved, but whose huts furnished proofs of the plunder. Unfortunately, instead of using the discretion demanded by the nature of the service, Lieut. H., to the no small embarrassment of Colonel L. and myself, conveyed his prisoners to the cantonment. Through me, the result was reported to the Rana, and it being imperative to check such audacity, Colonel Ludlow was instructed to select five or six of the ringleaders, who were delivered over to a confidential officer of the Rana, by whom sentence of death was carried into execution by hanging them at different posts along the frontier, the scene of their depredations. Five of them suffered, the sixth being respited by the Rana's officer on account of his youth, and at my request pardoned. He was afterwards brought to thank me for his life, when he promised never more to join in such raids. He was about nineteen; of of middle stature, slim, but well-formed; complexion, a clear shining dark bronze, eyes and hair jet black, and an expression of ingenuousness, which, as far as might be judged while he was yet under the influence of fear and the novelty of his situation, indicated the entire absence of vice. It was long before I ceased to feel the pain arising from this act of necessary severity, more especially when it was pleaded in justification, that the parties were more bent on foraging for the Bhilnis than for bamboos. Except for murder, I never would inflict death: fines to the very limit of ability, and restitution of property, act far more powerfully as punishments.

With the great Bhil family, I would not hesitate to class the Saireas, inhabiting the mountains that separate Malwa and Harouti, and all those complicated ranges which, running from the verge of the table-land of Malwa, through Chandéri and Nurwur, terminate, some branches in Gohud, while others merge into the masses of Boondelcund, anciently peopled by the tribe of Sarja, now extinct, but in all probability the Saireas of Central India. Amongst the thirty-six royal tribes of Rajpoots, one is called the *Sari-aspa*, contracted *Saria*, of whom we have inscriptions of a very remote date, indicative of their consequence amongst the ancient races of India. Whether this degraded tribe (*Saria*) may be descended illegitimately from these, it is useless to enquire. The Aspa or Aswa race is decidedly of Indo-Scythic origin, the first (*aspa*) being the Persian, the latter (*aswa*) the Sanscrit term for 'horse,' and were the Saireas illegitimately descended from them, it might account for the introduction of the horse into their ceremonies. I have elsewhere remarked the habit, amongst the old tribes of Central Asia, of assuming the names of quadrupeds. Thus, besides the *Aspa* or 'horse', we have the *Noomries* or 'foxes', a great branch of the Getæ or Jits of Transoxiana, and

and the *Varahas*, or ' hogs', of Mooltan and the Upper Indus. But the habit of distinguishing families by epithets derived from objects in the animal or vegetable creation has prevailed in every land, and many a name, which receives our homage from blending phonetic dignity with historical recollections, traces its origin to some humble and often ludicrous incident; as that watch-word of chivalry, *Plantagenet,* derived from the lowly broom. Besides these, the horse, fox, and hog tribes of the Indus and Oxus, we have the hares (*Seesodias,* properly Sussodias), the *Cuchwahas,* from the *Cusha*-grass, with many others.

Whatever be the descent of the Saireas of the plateau of Central India, they have the same distinguishing moral and physical properties as the Bhils, though without the bad qualities which mark the most degraded of this tribe in the west. The Sairea has no prejudices, and will eat of any thing, but cats and dogs: whence this aversion, or whether it extends to their brethren of the west and south, I am ignorant. They subsist chiefly by hunting, and are most expert in the art, which they exercise on all the inhabitants of the forest, from the majestic nil-gae and the savage boar, to the timid hare, their *entremets* being abundant from foxes, jackalls, snakes, guanas, lizards: nothing is rejected save the animals which man has domesticated. The wild fruits, as the *taindoo,* the *cheraonji,* the *aônla,* the *imli, i. e.* the ebony fruit, and the tamarind, they gather, and either use themselves or barter for grain. They dig in the earth for various roots applicable to mechanical arts; as that termed *coli-cundo* from which starch is made, and the fibrous roots of the cusha-grass, which they make into brushes, both indispensable to the cloth-weaver. They are likewise the wood-cutters of these parts, and in this occupation collect the various gums required in medicine or manufactures. They have, moreover, an art peculiar

peculiar to themselves, of making ropes and twine from the macerated epidermis and roots of various trees, especially that of the *kesoola*, of which they recognise two kinds; also from the root termed *bukhora*. Whether the fibrous portions of the bark are mixed with the roots, I feel uncertain, though my notes would imply it; the mass being reduced to a mucilage, from which fibres are drawn of great delicacy and length, dried in the shade, and afterwards twisted into ropes of any dimensions. They gather a small fruit, called *bahera* or *hurra*, abounding in the Shah-bad hills, and used by the dyers to give a yellow ground; and a nut (*reeta*) used in bleaching, and which forms a substitute for soap. In Harouti,—and these details apply chiefly to the Saireas of this region,—they collect the fruit of the *mhowa*, of which they make a spirit resembling whisky, and at the risk of their necks, they climb the scarped rocks and rob the bees of their produce. Occasionally, they bring a few patches into cultivation, if loosening the scanty soil with an iron spud, and dropping the seeds therein, may thus be termed. When their little harvest, chiefly of Indian corn and maize, is ripening, they move to it with their families, gathering it for consumption even in its green state, until expended.

Of the moral habits of these people we may speak favourably: to use the phraseology of the person* from whose intimate knowledge of them I obtained much information, "they are so susceptible of gratitude, that

* Futteh, one of my Dhak Jemadars, whose name I mention in the "Annals," and who converted these people into most useful relays on the line of post. It was almost entirely by the means of these wild tribes that I kept up a communication between Bombay and the Provinces on the Ganges, at the period when to my other duties I added that of Postmaster in Sindia's camp; and in 1815, I was enabled to convey to Marquess Hastings, then at Ferrukabad on the Ganges, an important overland despatch in the short space of nine days from Bombay. This, it will be recollected, is a distance of more than nine hundred miles, and through countries in which neither the British Government, their allies, or enemies, had any control.

that it is a proverbial expression in these regions, 'once give a meal to a Sairea, and he will remember it to the end of his days.'" Amongst the hills of Nirwur, Sheopoor, and those skirting the left bank of the Chumbul, are found numbers of these children of nature, whose first wish is to be left to the unmolested enjoyment of the spontaneous gifts of the great mother; but this is not permitted, the poor forester being deemed of no more value in the scale of creation than the boar or fox on which he preys; nor is his name ever mentioned by his lordly superior except as the *Pat'hal pootra*, 'child of hell,' or by other degrading epithets. I might add that there are some distinctions of feature, though none of complexion, between the more northerly Bhil and those of the western regions; the former have the lips more protruding, and are generally stout, fat, and with prominent bellies. In these traits they bear a stronger resemblance to the inhabitants of Choota-Nagpoor and Sirgooja, than to the Bhils of Méwar, though less strongly marked than the Khole of Sirgooja, who looks as if he were a connecting link between the negro and the genuine Oojla Bhil.

CHAPTER IV.

Beejipoor.—View of the Aravulli.—Unfavourable state of the season.—Temple of Rayn-poorji.—Coins.—Ancient towns.—Respect paid by the Rana towards the Jain priesthood.—Bhyâd of Beejipoor.—Correspondence between the religious rites of Syria and of the Saura Peninsula.—Sun-worship.—Birgong.—Meena towns.—Anecdote of a Meena feud.—Great heat.—Different effects of the same degree of heat on the frame.—Buhee.—Sarohi, Capital of the Deora Rajpoots.—Temple of Siva.—Indo-Getic Customs of the Chohans.—Condition of the principality of Sarohi. Its enfranchisement from dependence upon Marwar effected by the Author.—Beneficial results of the measure.—Policy to be pursued towards the native princes of India.—Want of a Code of Laws for British India.—Geography of Sarohi.—Reports of the Rajpoots by early travellers.—Interview with the Rao.—Description of the Capital.—Statistics.—Early history of the Deoras.

It was nearly noon when I cleared the pass of Seetla Mata, and as the bluff head of Mount Aboo opened upon me, my heart beat with joy as, with the Sage of Syracuse, I exclaimed, *Eureeka!* Half an hour more brought me to my tents at Beejipoor,—thermometer 98°, barometer 28° 60′, shewing a difference of about five hundred feet in elevation between the plains of Méwar and those of Marwar, skirting the Aravulli on either side, the desert being the most elevated. At 3 P.M., the barometer was 28° 50′, and thermometer 102°,—the rains collecting in the west, and the hot winds blowing a sirocco over the desert. I lamented my folly in throwing away my refrigerators, as I looked back from the arid sand, on which my tent was pitched, to those lofty and delightful regions I had quitted. The prospect was indeed magnificent, and infinitely more imposing than any part of the gradual ascent from Méwar. Here I had a full view of the precipitous face of the noble Aravulli; its towering and ever-varied pinnacles of gneiss, its dark indented recesses, lined with forest and underwood, through which stole many a crystal rivulet from its alpine cradle, to refresh

refresh the inhabitants of Maroost'huli. But the heat had been unusually great, and little rain having fallen this year, some of these Naiads had altogether abandoned their sandy beds. Had public duty permitted, I should have started at least a fortnight earlier; for the clouds of the *choota-bursât*, or introductory monsoon, are congregating fast, and I fear may frustrate much of my design. Already am I compelled to forego one object, which induced a preference of this route to that through the Bhil forest, *viz.* the temple of Rayn-poorji, in the Sadri Nal, one of those clefts in the ribs of the Aravulli, accessible only to foot-passengers; and although within view, I dare not attempt it, being in the direction diametrically opposed to that in which the many objects of my journey lay. This is perplexing, for had I at all questioned my ability to examine this stupendous pile, I should have visited it two years ago, when passing from Oodipoor to Jodpoor. It is an object left, with many others, for the future traveller, who, although he may not discover in it the exquisite proportions of the more ancient temples of Komulmér and Ajmér, nor the sculptures of Barolli and Aboo, will find much of solid grandeur.

I had sent my scouts in advance to the Jain town of Balli, to which the inhabitants of Balabhi, the ancient capital of Saurashtra, fled when assailed by Indo-Scythic invaders in the fifth century. They collected many curious coins, some of that Indo-Scythic stamp, having a princely head on one side and an altar on the reverse, the epigraph being in those occult characters of which I have already given some account;* others likewise of a very singular nature, having on the obverse a kind of hieroglyphic (if we may use the term) combined into the form of a warrior

* See Transactions Royal Asiat. Soc., vol. i. p. 338 and Plate I. No. I.

warrior on horseback, lance in hand; or the sacred bull in a kneeling posture, and on the reverse Sanscrit characters containing the name of a Rajpoot prince, but neither date, tribe, nor country.* Of the same apparent age, and also with the Devanagari character, was a third kind, having the name and titles of a Hindu sovereign on one side, and those of the great Mahmoud on the reverse, doubtless re-struck by the Ghisnivi monarch in the mint of his camp, as a token of conquest, in like manner as the republicans of France placed the Goddess of Liberty on the reverse of the currency of Louis XVI. I could have desired time to explore personally the ancient towns of this tract, the contiguity of which to the Aravulli afforded their people shelter when driven from the more exposed kingdoms of Anhulwarra and Saurashtra, overrun at various times by Greeks, Parthians, and Huns. It was from Balli I obtained one of the most important historical rolls relative to the history of the Ranas of Méwar, and, strange to say, the Juti who gave it to me still held the honorary distinction of Guru to the kings of Méwar, after a lapse of thirteen centuries. Although the Rajpoot is tolerant, in matters of faith, and the present Rana especially so, his behaviour towards those who held the Jain persuasion was always marked by peculiar regard, a sentiment which cannot be accounted for by their religious or social consequence, but arises out of a traditional knowledge of some vital services they had rendered his ancestry in very remote times, probably on the destruction of Balabhi. I recollect well, when some matter of importance to a Jain was agitated, and the minister urged that he held some property, the right of the crown, without warrant, he was cut short by the remark that he should not be molested, for

* See Transactions Royal Asiat. Soc., vol. i. p. 338 and Plate I. Nos. 2 and 3.

for that the Rana's ancestry were under obligations to this sect, which neither he nor his descendants could ever repay. From this feeling, as well as from a spirit of toleration, whenever a high priest of the Jains passes through Oodipoor on his way to visit his flocks in the desert, the Rana advances to welcome and escort him to his capital. Of the immunities and charters granted to them I have spoken at length in the 'Annals.'

Beejipoor is divided into four portions, held by Rajpoots, termed the *Bhyâd* or brotherhood of Nana Bera, the head of whom resides at Nana. They are descendants of the immortal Rana Pertap, and have the customary appellation of *Babas* or infants, and hold equal rank with the chief of Sunwar at the Rana's court. With the traitorous acquisition of the rich province of Godwar, which includes Balli and all this tract, by the princes of Marwar, this allegiance has been severed, and these 'children of Pertap' are now vassals of Jodpoor: but while they fulfil all their obligations to the new power, if asked to whom their *ân* or allegiance is due, it will be seen how easily Rajpoot casuistry can reconcile service to two masters. I had a visit from the only representative of the Hero of Rajasthan who was at home, and who, though he had adopted the garb of Marwar, had lost in heart and noble bearing none of the marks of his illustrious descent. Excepting the prince, heir to the throne, I know no finer specimen of royal progeny than the petty chief of Beejipoor ('the City of Victory') : tall enough for dignity, and strong without bulk, while his fair and intelligent countenance and graceful demeanour would render him conspicuous in any court. We conversed more on the past than the present, and he was not displeased at finding me more deeply versed in the history of his race than himself.

June 6th.—Birgong.—The line of march lay parallel to the Aravulli,

sometimes

sometimes touching its diverging ribs, which looked gigantic in the early morning, before the sun had travelled over them and variegated their sable garb with tints of gold. We crossed a small stream, called the Jooé Nullah, which is of some political importance, being the boundary between the provinces of Godwar and Sarohi. We likewise crossed the Sukri river, which continues its course by the fortress of Jhalore, and falls into the Looni, or salt river. Near where I crossed it, I visited a small temple, dedicated to Balpoor-Siva, or Siva of the city of Bal; in front of the mythic emblem of the god was the *vahan* or courser, the bull in brass, at one time, apparently, the sole object of worship of the Saura peninsula; a land which, there can hardly be a doubt, was in communication with the shores of the Red Sea, Egypt, and Palestine, in the earliest periods of history, probably long before Hiram and the mariners of Tyre were carriers to the wise king of Jerusalem. What are Bal and the brazen calf, to which especial honours were paid on the "fifteenth of the month," but the Bâl-eswar and bull (*nanda*) of India; (the Osiris and Mnvis of Egypt), whose sacred day is the black *Amavus*, also the fifteenth of the month, when the rays of the sun cease to illuminate the face of the moon? Balpoor, or the city of Bal, is therefore the same as the Balbec or Heliopolis of Syria; coincidences in name, rites, and symbols, all denoting one universal natural religion, namely, the worship of the sun, and his type the bull, emblematic of fertility and production. Whence the origin of this wide-spread idolatry, whether in the plains of the Euphrates, the Oxus, or the Ganges, in the peninsula of Mount Sinai or that of the Sauras, it would be vain to enquire; but it is far from improbable that the "sweet cane of a far country,"* which Solomon tells us was not indigenous to Syria

* Jer. VI. 20.

Syria or Egypt, may, as well as some of the architectural details of his temple, have come from this Syria of India.

But to return to Birgong and the banks of the Bhao-Bunas, for such is the name of the streamlet, whether from being the wedded or would-be lord of the fair Bunas, the legend sayeth not. The centre of the majestic Aboo bore south, 25° west, distant twenty-four miles; from this the peaks of the Aravulli, which, by the aid of my telescope, I brought within view, appeared highest about Sadri and Roopnigurh. Komulmér appeared depressed below both of these, but all the inhabitants agreed that the peak of Jirga near Saimur, in the heart of the upland, is in a clear day seen overtopping all the rest. I had also distinct bearings of several of the chief haunts of the Meena brigands, so long the terror of these regions, dwelling amongst clusters of hills, which may be considered offsets of the Aravulli, and which, from being covered with forest, are very difficult of access: they are termed *Mewassoh,* or fastnesses of the Meenas. The principal towns in these are Ootwun, bearing S. S. 25° W. 12 miles, Kolur S. 10° E. 6 miles, Radour S. 30° W. 10 miles, Rewarro N. 65° W. 12 miles; and last not least, Machal, due west 13 miles. Each of these Meena towns would afford ample materials for the romance-writer, in the history of their raids and internal feuds, or contests with the Rajpoot chiefs their neighbours. To-day I heard one which, related circumstantially, might form the subject of a drama. It was between the Meenas of Ootwun and the Rajpoots of Pirai. Constantly engaged in warfare, and generally prepared for the midnight attacks of the mountaineer, the Rajpoots of the latter village, on one of their gala days, had omitted the usual precaution, although they "had Meena blood on their swords," having but a short while before surprised the Mewassoh, fired the village, and carried off captive

the

the mother of the Mukhia, or head of Ootwun, whom they lodged in the frontier garrison of Jodpoor. This hostage had put the Rajpoots off their guard; but either from some private communication with her kindred, or from indignation at her captivity, the Meena matron, determined that she would be no bar to their revenge, enfranchised herself with a dose of poison. Meanwhile, her son, at the head of his bowmen, as soon as the enemy had retired, collected his brethren of Machal and Radva, repairing first to the hill of Kolur, the point of rendezvous and preparation by augury for these raids. The omen was favourable,—"the arrows fell inwards, point to point,"—and as there was yet enough of night to execute their purpose before the festivities of Pirai were over, they sallied forth. The surprise was complete, and forty-six Rajpoots were sacrificed to the manes of the Mother of Ootwun.

When I reached my tents, at 10 A.M. this morning, the thermometer ranged 96°; at 2 P.M. it reached 108° in the tent; at 5 P.M., with rain-clouds collecting to the westward, 88°, and at 7 P.M. 86°, while the oscillations of the barometer, at these respective hours, were 28-77, 28-73, 28-65, and 28-70. This 108° is the highest range in the shade I ever noted of the thermometer, with the least diurnal variation; though, whether owing to the equability of temperature, which sustained the animal circulation in corresponding uniformity, I never suffered less from extreme heat. Yet, if I looked across the expanded plains, the arid soil appeared as if emitting colourless flames, and as I steadied the barometers, suspended in their tripod-stands, the brass-work was painful to the touch. Although this degree of heat would appear intolerable to "the cold in clime" and "cold in blood," the external air, though some 25° warmer than within the tent, was not beyond endurance, and

and I have since felt infinitely more oppressed on an English summer day than in the dog-days of India on the verge of the desert. I would not draw a comparison between an autumnal day at Naples, for, while under such influence I penned these observations, I could barely crawl up the shady side of the Strada di Toledo, in the month of October, two years afterwards, although in tolerable health. I leave the physiologist to discover the cause of these inconsistencies of sensation, merely recording the effect of the intense heat, which, like many other evils, political as well as personal, brings bane and antidote together. At 108° and even much lower, the pores are all opened, and the system is in perpetual thaw and dissolution, and were the vapour thus extricated, condensed and made to re-act upon the calico covering, no other refrigerator would be required. But when the thermometer is at the freezing point at day-break, and from 90° to 100° two hours after the sun has passed the meridian, in the tent, and 130° when exposed to his rays, what frame can stand this? I have, however, stood such alternations; but when I look back to those days, enumerate the companions who have growled or laughed with me, and consider where they are gone, I find it difficult to verify my assertions: just two out of twenty are living!—and but one—that one myself—spared to retire to his native land. I subjoin the list as a curiosity, but alas, it is the common fate of most who go to India.*

June 7th.—Buhee.—Our route to-day was over an uniform flat, distance

* Rámgurh, a local battalion. Col. Broughton, Major Ruffsage, Lieut. and Adj. Higott, Lieut. Broughton, Drs. Laidlaw and Limond, all dead. 20th or Marine Regt. Lieut.-Col. Maclean, Major Yule, Capts. Mainwaring, Weston, Porteous, Sealy, Lieut. Manly, all dead. Lieuts. Tod, Murray, survivors in 1833. Macpherson, son of the translator of Ossian, dead. Montague, left India for Europe at an early period of service. Macnaughten, dead. Artillery. Capt. Graham, dead.

distance twelve miles and a half. Three miles from Birgong we again crossed the Sukri, and passed, at Pawori, a thanah, or military post, of Jodpoor, stationed to overawe the Meenas. At seven miles we passed within a mile of Posaleo, another celebrated community within the Sarohi territory, whose prince has established therein a military post since he came under the protection of the British Government. Buhee, like Birgong, possesses no local interest; but both villages are creeping into prosperity, after many years of dilapidation from the exactions of the state on one hand, and the raids of the depredators on the other. Aboo lay between S. 10° E. and S. 20° W., about thirteen coss or twenty-five miles distant, and the Mewassohs of Ootwun and Machal, the former S. 20° E., the latter N. 20° W. Several of these banditti leaders, of Ootwun, Machal, and Posaleo, came to visit me, and promised entirely to abandon their hereditary pursuits. They are an athletic, agile race, and with their bamboo bows, quiver, and dagger in the girdle, form no indifferent subject for the pencil. Several Deora Rajpoots also visited me here, armed like the Meena. We had a trial of skill, and by some good luck I sent an arrow several yards beyond the Deora. A yell of applause was sent forth by the Meenas, but I took care not to risk my reputation by a second attempt. The change of costume was marked, not only in the tie of the turban, but in the enormous trowsers, or still stranger substitute, the kilt-like equipment of the Deoras, whose favourite lock, nourished with *l'huile du jasmin*, was trained over the cheek. Thermometer to-day at 9 A.M., 3 and 5 P.M., ranged respectively 86°, 99°, and 96°, and the barometer 28° 80′, 28° 77′, and 28° 75′; the second barometer, but in which I did not confide, being 14° lower.

June 8th.—Sarohi.—Twelve miles and a half. Every step of the way was

was through a diminutive forest, chiefly of the useful and tenacious *dhow*, or the evergreen *peloo*. At the seventh mile we crossed the Ootwun range of hills, and passed through the valley in which lays the capital of the Deoras. One mile farther on, we passed the ruins of a fortress, built by Koombho, Rana of Oodipoor, when driven from Komulmér by the Ghorian King of Malwa. At this point, we approached the shrine of Sarnéswar, around which are congregated the mausolea of the princes and chieftains of Sarohi. The original object of attraction is a *coonda*, or fountain, whose waters are efficacious in cutaneous diseases: and this, as are most of the thermal springs of India, was dedicated to Siva. The temple has a vaulted roof, supported by columns; the shape of the dome is peculiar to this region, being the section of an egg, the smaller portion placed perpendicularly on the longer axis. Within is the phallic emblem of the god; and without, a ponderous trident, full twelve feet in height, and said to be a combination of the seven metals. Two elephants, carved in stone, guard the entrance, and the whole is surrounded by a fortified wall, erected by the Islamite King of Mandoo, who is reported to have been cured of a leprous disease, called *kosa*, by bathing in the fountain. Miracle or no miracle, that the use of the waters is beneficial, is sufficiently attested by his having repaired and endowed the temple, in spite of the prohibition of the prophet. The present type of the "Lord of the Bull," is not the original, which, together with an ancient inscription, was carried to Méwar and inaugurated into a new temple. The cenotaphs of the Deoras are very curious, both in their architectural form and details, and what is unusual, each has its separate inscription; that of the father of the present prince has a miniature shrine within the mausoleum, beside which is a small equestrian statue of the deceased; but that of

 Rao

Rao Guj is the most conspicuous, having four Satis, besides a train of his vassal Rajpoots, represented in basso-relievo on the internal altar,—they are armed with sword and shield. This affords another proof of the Indo-Getic descent of the Chohan race, converted, as has been already shewn, to Brahminism.

My approach to Sarohi, the capital of the Deoras, was hailed by the song of joy, sung by some of the handsomest women I had seen in India, beating time upon brass cymbals of a peculiar form. They preceded the Rao with all his chivalry, who advanced to conduct me to the city, through which I passed, and encamped half a mile southward.

Aboo, which increased in grandeur as we approached, bore S. 10° E. to S. 25° W.; the thermometer at 9 A.M., 3 and 6 P.M., being 86°, 98°, 92°; the barometer 28° 75′, 28° 70′, and 28° 75′.

June 9th.—Sarohi.—This morning at 8 A.M. noon, 3 and 5 P.M., the barometer stood 28° 75′, 28° 77′, 28° 75′, and 28° 70′, the thermometer being 84°, 95°, 92°, and 92°, at the respective hours. After mid-day, I got some new tatties, which cooled me some degrees. Halted for the purpose of devoting one day to personal observation of the condition of this principality, which, though one of the smallest, is not the least renowned of Rajpootana. It possessed peculiar claims to my regard, its political relations having been entirely under my management since the general pacification in 1817-18, and its independence, both political and social, having been preserved, entirely through my exertions, from the specious pretensions of her powerful neighbour, the Raja of Marwar, who claimed her as a tributary. These claims were so well supported by argument and documentary evidence, as to obtain credence with the functionary who was then the medium of the political relations of

Marwar

Marwar with the British Government, and they had nearly obtained the sanction of the Governor-General, Marquess Hastings. It was on this occasion, as on several others, that some historical knowledge of the complicated international politics of these regions, enabled me to unravel the perplexities of the case, and save the lands of the Deoras from the relentless tribute-collectors of their powerful opponent.

Deora is the tribe of the Sarohi princes and the subordinate aristocracy. It is a branch of that noblest of Rajpoot blood, the Chohan, whose cradle is said to be on the summit of Aboo, whence they spread over the regions skirting the Aravulli to Ajmér, establishing many minor principalities, as Nadole, Jhalore, and others, long before the Rahtores of Jodpoor had set foot in Maroo, but were yet enjoying all the pomp of royalty in the splendid city of Kanouj. Sarohi, Aboo, and Chandravati, then appertained to the Pramara race; nor was it until the thirteenth century that the uncle of Kana Deo, prince of Jhalore, treacherously obtained possession of the former with its dependencies, by the slaughter of the Pramaras. The city, now the residence of the Deora princes, is comparatively of modern date, the ancient Sarohi lying behind a second range of mountains; but this I had not time to visit.

But to return to our politics. The envoys of Jodpoor advanced their right to tribute and service from the time of Raja Abhi Sing, which claims I met with counter-proofs from their own annals, shewing that, although the quotas of Sarohi had served under the princes of Jodpoor, it was as Viceroys of the empire, not as Rajas of Marwar; and that, in the wars of Guzzerat, where the Deora sword was second to none, it was under the imperial banner that they fought with Abhi Sing as generalissimo. These were distinctions in political casuistry for which they were unprepared, but as a corollary, they then adduced the services

actually

actually performed by the chieftain of Neemaj, the first of the Sarohi nobles. This argument was met by the reply that there were traitors and time-servers in every state, as none better knew than the Raja of Jodpoor, and that Sarohi, being too reduced in power to punish or protect her vassalage, was no exception to the rule. Moreover, Neemaj, being exposed on the borders of Marwar, was at the mercy of its enemies : but more than all, this chief being already *primus inter pares*, whom " one step higher would make highest," looked to the aid of Jodpoor to attain this. When they found their documents would not bear out their claims for tributary service, they tried the pecuniary part, presenting a schedule of unconnected levies made by predatory incursions as time and opportunity served ; but no continuous, regular, conditional payment, nor written stipulation to legalise lawless inroads, chiefly by the provincial governors acting for themselves, appeared to substantiate this plea. They did produce one deed, it is true, signed by the elder brother of the present prince, admitting, on certain conditions, his subordinacy to Jodpoor ; but they warily omitted to state the position of the prince when this document was drawn up, namely, that he was a captive, in the power of his would-be lord-paramount, having been kidnapped while in the act of conveying his father's ashes to the Ganges. Most wisely, most justly, then, did the Deora feudality regard this deed, extorted by so unworthy an expedient, as so much waste paper ; nor was there a single rupee voluntarily remitted to the Jodpoor treasury on this account.

When every other argument failed, they set up one of some validity, *viz.* that, as Sarohi could not control or chastise her depredators, from whose inroads they suffered, this power ought to be in their hands, and they further supported the demand by instancing a recent outrage, in which

which the bands of Ootwun and Machal had made an incursion into Marwar, when loss of life and property ensued. The case was well authenticated, and made an impression on the conservators of order: but when the wholesome maxim "*audi alteram partem*" was enforced, not only were the Meena subjects of Jodpoor found to have united in this raid, but the provocation to have originated with Marwar. Moreover, it was pertinently asked by the envoy of Sarohi, if the raids of our Meenas, whom we cannot all at once control, afford pretexts for the troops of Jodpoor to enter our territory and there establish posts (which was actually done), what reply will the Raja of Marwar give to the British Government for the enormities committed by the hill tribes under his dominion against all his neighbours? All these arguments, though managed with great skill and subtlety, were unavailing when confronted with the truth; and I finally placed the independence of Sarohi beyond the reach of fate, obtaining for myself, in lieu, the hatred of the prince of Jodpoor, his varlet ministers and envoys, with the doubtful gratitude of the Deoras, whose lands were yet the scene of division and discontent. The desire of Marquess Hastings, however, to conciliate all conflicting interests, inclined him to soothe the wounded pride of Raja Maun, whose attempts to establish supremacy over the Deoras were thus frustrated. To this end, at a very early period of the discussion, I had suggested that he should be invited to submit a schedule of his tributary collections for the last ten years, the average amount of which was to be henceforth annually paid to him through the British Government. While I submitted this to my Government, as a test of the justice of his claims, I knew that I was neither overburdening the finances of Sarohi, nor trenching upon their independence. It fully answered the end. Raja Maun could prove no continuous exactions, and

and though in every other respect very unlike angel visitors, they had, like these, at long intervals, exacted contributions, but always *au bout du fusil.* For a few thousand rupees, annually paid to the British Government by Sarohi, who, however, protested against being a party to its ultimate disposition, which might otherwise at some future period again have involved her independence, she was enfranchised for ever from the claims of Marwar, and now looks to the British Government alone.

To the extent of his means, the young Rao has done his best to fulfil his obligations. The Meena tribes have been restrained; posts are established in the fastnesses, passports are given to the merchants, artizans, and cultivators, to return to the country, with a guarantee against exaction and promises of encouragement. The town, which had been almost a ruin in the wilderness, is again becoming peopled; and the merchant who, three or four years ago, would literally have entered a den of thieves in entering Sarohi, has opened his *dokân* or store, and to the utter astonishment of the inhabitants and the curious, the Meena who may dare to shew his face in the streets, and who was wont, in common with the bear and tiger, to prowl about the grass-covered walks, now sees heaps of merchandize and money in the bazaar, which by some irresistible, and to him inexplicable cause, he is withheld from seizing. I have already, in the 'Annals', given a similar picture, on a larger scale, in the account of Bhilwarra; but a miniature of the same lineaments of peace amidst the dwellings of the Meena mountaineer, or his Suzerain, the Deora Rajpoot, whose joint pursuits have been for ages assimilated to those of the tigers of their hills and forests, cannot fail to afford interest to those who care to speculate upon such strange incidents in the history and operations of human passions. I may take this

this opportunity to remark, that it behoves us to exercise the utmost forbearance in the work of amelioration amongst races thus placed by Providence under our protection; and should there even be an occasional out-break, let us never forget that we are too powerful to need being unmerciful, and that our chastisements should be attempered to the end in view. Unhappily for the various tribes placed under the ægis of Britain, there is too little of mercy blended with punishment; and the rod of justice, when uplifted, is apt to kill at once where it strikes. Our eastern legislators seem not to remember, that the natural propensities of man gain the mastery over his political or social duties, and to deem no penalty too severe for deviation from the paths of perfect obedience. This feeling is, perhaps, inseparable from the nature of our rule, styled as it is "the government of the sword," and ephemeral in every part of the machinery, from the Governor-General to the lowest agent; though the controlling power at home is not obnoxious to the same reproach, but provides new measures with new men. The exercise of their functions by the executive body is too uncertain and transitory to enable each or either of them to observe the gradual workings of important changes. Each is breathless to obtain as much applause as possible in a limited sphere of action, in conducting the portion of the machine entrusted to his guidance, and whatever internal force impedes its equable movement, must at once be annihilated. Perhaps this is ordained for wise purposes, and the want of continuity of plan in the conquerors, together with the civilisation we are gradually imparting to the conquered, may at length lead to their emancipation from thraldom, both mental and political. By some, this is avowed to be the end-all of their measures; but if such enlarged philanthropic views be in truth indulged, the means are most inaptly computed.

 We

We dare not say " our yoke is easy," while our tribute is galling, and our imposts on our immediate subjects are heavy and impoverishing. Gainsay it who may, every fiscal and financial enactment of our Government is framed, not with a view to better them, but to fill our own treasury. It is curious to see men who recognise the beauty of honesty and truth in their individual capacities, as members of society, throw aside all these considerations when discussing the benefits which India derives from our rule. To hear them eulogize the single-heartedness and benevolence displayed towards its people, one would be apt to fancy these favoured spots an Utopia. When Rome, the mother of nations, conquered and colonised the most remote regions of Europe, she introduced her arts, made the conquered the instruments of Government, and left monuments of her power and her sway, in works of grandeur and utility, many of which still survive to attest her power. What has Britain done in this way? what portion of the millions of gold extorted from the industry of her Indian subjects, has she applied to their benefit? where are the bridges, the public roads, the places of recreation, such as were raised by Trajan or Hadrian? where are the shaded walks, the caravanserais, the wells, or reservoirs, made by our predecessors, the intolerant and oppressive Mahomedans, during their sway in Hindustan? Let the holders of India Stock in London answer these questions!

I may conclude these reflections with one more, obviously exemplifying the real nature of our government of the sword. Although far advanced into the second century of our sway, no Justinian has yet appeared to condense into a simple form those vast, accumulating, and crude materials called "Regulations." Is it that the period of one, or at most two lustres, accorded to our ephemeral governors, is too limited

limited for its accomplishment; or does the pusillanimous maxim, "a little knowledge is a dangerous thing," operate to prevent it? Let us hope that this anomaly in our administration may be removed, and that vanity, if no better feeling, may stimulate some future vicegerent to immortalize himself by the formation of a legal code, which may be at once adapted to the comprehension and guidance of the people, and a fitting record of our supremacy when the Atlantic shall roll between us and the governed.

The difficulty of framing a code of laws which may be applicable to the condition of the complicated masses under our rule, may be urged in palliation of its total omission; but this plea cannot be deemed valid in the absence of all experiment with the extensive provinces adjacent to the seat of Government, as laws framed for these could always be modified to meet a further extension of territory. As regards our tributary or subsidiary connections, the political treaties must necessarily form the basis of our relations and conduct with them; but even these might be reduced to something like uniformity, and instead of the eccentric movements now given by individual will, be made to harmonize with one general design.*

But to proceed in our sketch of the Deora principality, which is not much

* In the spirit of these remarks, (which were penned many years ago) are the following observations from the luminous and masterly speech of Mr. Macaulay, on the India question, which I only perused when the MS. of this work was nearly ready for the press:—"I believe that no country ever "stood so much in need of a code of laws as India.—It is time that the magistrate should know what "law he is to administer, that the subject should know under what law he is to live."—"Much, I "am persuaded, may be done to assimilate the different systems of law, without wounding those "feelings (of religion and caste). But whether we assimilate those systems or not, let us ascertain "them, let us digest them. We propose no rash innovation; we wish to give no shock to the preju-"dices of any part of our subjects. Our principle is simply this,—uniformity where you can have "it,—diversity where you must have it,—but in all cases, certainty."

much larger than one of our medium-sized English counties, being about seventy miles in length, and fifty in breadth. Although the greater portion of this surface is mountain, and the more level part, being the frontier* of the desert, more or less sandy, there are in the former many fertile vallies, and the latter produces abundant crops of maize, wheat, and barley. It is intersected in every direction by streams flowing from the Aravulli, or from its own majestic Aboo. Its boundaries will be best understood by reference to the map : to the east it is fenced by the Aravulli, to the north and west by Godwar and Jhalore, the western districts of Marwar, and on the south by the chieftainship of Palunpoor, now under the protection of the British Government. During the empire, and while Guzzerat formed one of its richest satrapies, Sarohi was locally of some importance, being a place of halt for the commercial caravans passing from the maritime provinces to the metropolis and other great cities of India. Accordingly, it is noticed by all the early travellers, Herbert, Olearius, Della Valle, Bernier, Thevenot, and verily without good report, for "the Razpoots" appear to have adopted, at the period of their visits, all the habits of rapine of their Meena subordinates, plundering indiscriminately all who fell in their way. The provocation they received was unknown to these travellers, who could thus make neither distinction nor allowance ; they did not know that the stranger reaped what they sowed, and hence the strife that ensued between the vassalage of these regions and the myrmidons of Mogul viceroys, whose main principle was to get money when and how they could. This, added to the incessant aggressions of the princes of

* May not the name of this country be derived from its position at the head (*Sir*) of the desert (*rohi*)?

of Marwar, who attained greatness by subserviency to the kings, an example which Sarohi long disdained to follow, tended to foster a state of half-savage but lofty independence. Some addition to this local importance was derived from her princes being the guardians of the sacred Aboo, whose shrines attracted pilgrims of the Jain faith from all parts of India. Strange to say, none of these travellers appear to have attempted to gain access to the temples, although their celebrity could not have been unknown to them.

On the second day's halt, I interchanged visits and gifts with the Rao, who mustered all his vassals for the occasion: there had not been so grand a convocation of Deoras, to do their prince honour, within any one's remembrance. As the *tosha-khaneh* (wardrobe) of the descendant of Manik Rae was not overstocked, I had a pleasure in presenting him with gifts befitting my Government to bestow; and without much charge to it, the jewels, garniture, &c. being the last gift to myself from the Rana of Méwar: an elephant, a horse, both richly caparisoned, a pearl necklace with jewelled pendant, a brilliant *sirpêsha* or aigrette for the turban, with the proper number of shields (the Rajpoot tray) of shawls, brocades, muslins, turbans, scarfs, &c., besides some articles, more rare to him, of European fabric. In the afternoon, I returned his visit, when he advanced half-way to my tents, with all his court, to escort me to the palace. There, after a long discourse on the advantages and necessity of order, the sole return my Government demanded for its protection, and for having rescued them from the fangs of their enemies, his gifts were produced. I touched them, in token of acceptance, observing that they would be taken at some future period, when his finances might better enable him to offer them. They were returned to his scanty wardrobe. This procedure is quite in

accordance

accordance with custom in the East, non-acceptance, under such circumstances, never being construed into insult. The Rao, Seo Sing, was a young man of about twenty-seven, stout, but rather short, and of fair and not unpleasing aspect, though his countenance was not indicative of very great intellect. He possesses bravery, the natural inheritance of every Chohan, but has little experience in matters of government, his life having hitherto passed in repelling the Meena and Kholi raids, those of his more dangerous neighbours of Jodpoor, or the treasonable pretensions of the first of his nobles, the chief of Neemaj. The palace still bore testimony to the hostility of this vassal, who entered it by storm, and with his lance shivered to atoms the splendid mirrors and other ornaments which adorned the hall of audience. On another occasion, this insolent traitor, supported by Jodpoor, led an army against his sovereign, and while he hoped to supplant his prince, the Rahtore sought to supplant both. Already had works been constructed which entirely commanded the town, when, fortunately, the league of 1807 compelled an abrupt abandonment of the design. Sarohi is extensive; the houses are good and built of brick, but still more than half untenanted; water is within twenty to thirty cubits of the surface. The mahl or palace is on the declivity of a gentle eminence, but has nothing to boast in architectural beauty. Aboo is the natural fortress of the Deoras, but, like Cheetore, as a place of residence, it is *tilâk* or accursed, since the death of Rao Maun, who was there poisoned.

Sarohi affords one of many instances which might be adduced, that the "divine right" of princes, whether or not they fulfil their obligations, is not recognised in Rajpootana more than elsewhere, despite the authority of Menu. Their power, which is absolute, while they uphold the laws and customs, as regards the rights of their kin and vassalage,

is

is frequently overturned when flagrant violations of either occur. The elder brother of the reigning prince of the Deoras was formally deposed by a convocation of the nobles and principal inhabitants, over whom he exerted the most infamous tyranny, extending even to the virtue of their females. Moreover, he was never forgiven for signing away Deora independence when kidnapped and carried to Jodpoor, as related above. Being declared unworthy to reign, he was condemned to perpetual captivity, and the present prince, Seo Sing, installed in his place. Nothing can better illustrate the morality and kindly feelings of this young man than his granting every indulgence to his captive brother, treating with scorn the pusillanimous advice, to prevent a re-action by the usual method in Asia, where death follows deposal.

The fiscal revenues of Sarohi may, with the continuance of tranquillity, reach three or even four lacs of rupees annually, and the fiefs of the vassals half as much more. Of these, the greater chiefs are five in number, namely, Neemaj, Jawala, Paria, Kalindri, and Boaria; lying within fourteen to twenty miles of the capital. In productions, Sarohi can boast of the fine marbles of Aboo, and of its sword-blades, as famed among the Rajpoots as those of Damascus among the Persians and Turks. Mounted on a gallant Kattiwar charger, his lance in hand, and *sirohi* (the sword being so termed) by his side, the Deora is "*sans peur.*"

I had intended to give the genealogy of the Deoras *ab origine*; but considering that, whatever pains I had taken to unravel this knotty subject, it would not awaken the interest of the English reader, I thought it better to suppress it; and the more, that whatever requires to be known of their ancestry, from the time of Manik Rae, prince of Ajmér, the cotemporary of Haroun and Charlemagne, is already detailed in the 'Annals,'

'Annals;' and all prior thereto is of the usual fabulous stuff which chokes the fountain-head of every history, whether Greek, Roman, Persian, or Rajpoot, as the following prelude from the mystic page of their bard attests:—"The pedigree of the Deoras dates from the golden "age *(satya yug)*, when human life was prolonged to a hundred thou- "sand years, when man's stature was twenty cubits, and swans were "endowed with speech." Nor do the subsequent periods of her career contain much to which we should attach the term historical. Wars, intestine feuds, gallant deeds, cruel oppressions, dark assassinations, would in turn claim the attention of the romance-writer, but would have little charm for the philosophical mind; while the repetition of "improper names," as some will call those of my heroes, would weary those who read only for diversion. From such sources, however, the bard has culled instances of brilliant achievement, mingled with satirical and familiar anecdote, which he has chronicled for the example and amusement of their posterity, making them in some cases the foundation of popular tales. Of these I possess a collection of nearly four hundred, which, if translated, would perhpas afford the best portraits of Rajpoot manners.

CHAPTER V.

Maireoh.—Jain temples.—Palrie.—Reach the skirts of Aboo.—Preparations for its ascent.—Journey up the mountain.—Shrine of Ganésa.—The Rahtis, or Mountaineers.—Geological formation of the lower part of the mountain.—Ascent to the Saints' Pinnacle.—Prospect from the summit.—*Pudda-ca,* or Impress of the foot of Data-Briga and Rama-Nanda.—Seeta ascetic.—Cave-dwellings.—Extensive view.—Descent from the summit.—Achil-éswar.—The brutal Aghori.—Self-entombment of one.—Incongruities of Hindu superstition.—Rules of Jain architecture.—Agni-Coonda, or Fire-fountain.—Temples.—Shrine of Achil-éswar described.—Act of sacrilege of Mahomed Beyra, of Ahmedabad.—Statue of Narayana.—Inscription.—Mausoleum of Rao Maun.—Statue of Adipala.—Ruins of Achilgurh.—Jain temple.—View from the watch-tower.—Statues.—Interview with the Rao.—Journey to Dailwara.

June 10th.—Maireoh.—Eleven miles and a half, little more than ten in direct distance, having had to cross and re-cross the range. The first five miles lay through a fine valley, long a stranger to the plough, and now covered with jungle. At the end of the first mile, we crossed a small but nameless stream, at the village of Palrie, and at the fourth, another called the Jhamp (or leap), falling from the summit of Aboo, and which, passing the residence of the Kalindri chief, flows into the Sukri, and with it joins the Loony. At the fifth mile, we traversed the valley to the range on our right, at the southern extremity of which lay the village of Sindurh. Here the eastern declivity of Aboo bore S. 35° E. and the two considerable villages of Damtah and Net-torah S. E. and E., each about five miles distant. Hitherto the direction of our route was S. 50° W.; for the next three miles we deviated to S. 15° W., when we re-crossed the Sarohi range at the village of Hamirpoor, under which is an insulated rock, having at one end a columnar-shaped mass, of considerable elevation, bearing the appearance of a tower, and called *Pahar*, or '*the* hill,' whence our place

of

of encampment, Maireoh, was nearly three miles distant. This village, which lays in a cluster of hills, has claim to some antiquity, and contains no less than five Jain temples. It is divided into three allotments, of which one is fiscal, the second is granted to a Deora vassal, and the third to a *Charun* or bard. The huge mass of Aboo now extended from S. 70° E. to S. 15° W.

	8 A.M.	Noon.	3 P.M.	6 P.M.
Bar.	28° 71′	28° 71′	28° 65′	28° 62′.
Therm.	86°	94°	98°	94°.

JUNE 11th.—PALRIE.—Seven miles six furlongs; the first four in the direction of S. 55° W., when we reached the village of Sunwaira, whence the extreme superior points of Aboo bore from S. 85° E. to S., and its loftiest peak, the Guru Sikra, S. E. Two miles more brought us to the village of Seeroria, under the lower range, where we crossed another stream. Thence, after two miles due south, we arrived at our place of halt, Palrie, having a rivulet of the same name on its northern side, flowing, like the former, from the clefts of Aboo, whose extremities ranged between N. 70° E. and S. 5° E. The Guru Sikra, S. 70° E., reckoned two coss or about five miles distant. At eight A.M., one, three, and six P.M., barometer 28° 75′, 28° 70′, 28° 65′, 28° 65′; thermometer 86°, 96°, 98°, 92. My second barometer, on which I placed less dependance, at six P.M. stood at 28° 43′, shewing a difference of range of 22′, which subsequent observation renders worthy of remark, as I found my confidence was placed in the least worthy.

At length, we reached the skirt of the gigantic Aboo, and encamped on the fringe of his garment. To exist for twenty-four hours in such a position, contemplating the steeps we were to climb, required an exercise of patience. The day was passed in preparation for scaling the

the Hindu Olympus, an enterprise not to be attempted without invoking the aid of *Boodh*, or Wisdom. The Rao sent forty sturdy mountaineers to transport me with my party to the summit. They were furnished with two vehicles, called *Indra-vahana*, or celestial cars, consisting of a couple of long bamboo poles, from the centre of which was suspended a small seat about a foot square, by help of which alone the indolent or infirm pilgrim could attain the " Mount of Wisdom." Not being in robust health, I was far from sorry to see such aid at hand ; the other was appropriated to my Guru, who was determined to accompany me on my pilgrimage to all the shrines of his faith. Thus the day passed in conversing with the children of Arbudha, or gazing on the gigantic object, till the shades of night threw a mysterious darkness around it. The jackal had set up his howl, and the fox his shrill bark, denoting their time for preying on the defenceless dwellers in the forest, and with such music, almost unheeded from its frequency, I took to my pallet to prepare for an alert on the morrow.

June 12th.—" There are two palaces, Umeer" (Ambér), " and " Jeipoor, surpassing all which I have seen of the Kremlin, or heard " of the Alhambra ; a third, Jodpoor, is said to be equal to either ; and " the Jain temples of Aboo, on the verge of the western desert, are " said to rank above them all." Such is the report of Bishop Heber, who has the merit of being the first to render Indian topics palatable to the British public. Let us proceed to verify his declaration.

At four in the morning, all was bustle in my little camp. In half an hour I was on horseback, the Guru and barometers by my side, and followed by my mountain train, with the celestial cars and terrestrial camp-baskets, containing such provender as would not offend the eye either of Brahmin or Jain. A few of my Hindu Sipahis, Brahmin and

 Rajpoot,

Rajpoot, accompanied me, partly for my protection, but chiefly that they might worship Wisdom in his *sanctum*. We were a full hour winding our way through the labyrinth of forest which environs the mount, to the point of ascent, where, suspending my barometers on their tripods, I noted 28° 55′, or ten seconds lower than the minimum range of the flats. At six A.M. precisely, we made the first step *en avant*, and at twenty minutes past seven, attained the shrine of Ganésa, the guardian of the ascent, called the Ganés' ghaut: we had a tremendous tug before we gained this halting-place, where we lingered a quarter of an hour to take breath and contemplate our achievement. The Rahtis (for thus are termed the rustic dwellers on Aboo), as well as my Sipahis, were glad to moisten their parched lips from the *Ganés-coonda*, or Fountain of Wisdom, a small source close to the shrine, though the waters were sulphureous and bitter as those of Asphaltites. It was curious to see the elastic spring of these sturdy mountaineers, as they stepped from one rock to another, frequently over chasms many yards deep, the well-balanced car yielding to every inequality of step; but my ancient instructor complained bitterly of the agility of these sure-footed creatures, who heeded not his appeals for mercy to his half-dislocated bones, but, on the contrary, jocularly remarked that the carriage was like the path to Heaven, not intended to be easy. The Rahtis style themselves Rajpoots, and the majority of those with me were of the Pramara tribe, the rest Chohans and Puriharas, but not a single Solankhi, or we should have had representatives of the four Agnicŭla races, who, according to the mythos, claim their origin from the Fire-fount *(agni-coonda)* of Aboo, having been there created when the Dytes or Titans waged war against Siva to expel his worshippers from this his Olympus. The Rahtis bear more resemblance to the

Vanaputra

Vanaputra than to the dignified Rajpoot, which may possibly be ascribed to their situation amidst mists, and to impoverished fare, and, during the rains, unwholesome water. But, in all probability, they are of mixed blood, like many of the mountain and forest tribes, who all arrogate Rajpoot descent, preferring to bastardize their origin rather than acknowledge themselves of pure Sudra extraction. Clumps of bamboo and the thorny *thoor (cactus)*,—the latter is the peculiar characteristic of the Aravulli,—were abundant, but no lofty trees marked the ascent. A stream, whose impetuous current had channelled itself a bed in the mountain, disclosed the formation of this to be gneiss, in which the proportions of feld-spar and quartz greatly varied, being sometimes in equal combination, and at others, in irregular crystals a full inch long, of rose-coloured feld-spar, interspersed in the predominating quartz. Massive veins of compact blue slate are observable in different parts, and fragments of marble (abounding in the *Kuchala Nal*, or fissure), of various hues, as well as slate of every description, strewed the bed of the stream now parched up by the intense heat. During our halt, many jokes were passed between the "Moon of Intellect,"—such was the significant appellation of my Guru,—and myself, on the position of Gunésa amidst the cliffs of this pathless ascent. His station would have been more characteristic at the outset, where he might have determined the propriety of the undertaking; but the most difficult being mastered, the votary would rather have invoked Asapurna, divine Hope, to cheer him onwards. Imagination dwelt upon the mythos of the Hindus, which had created a type for every attribute of divinity, each having its peculiar shrine, hymns, priests, and offerings, thus converting the land into one grand Pantheon, and therewith a nation of priests, who enthralled the minds, while they drained

drained the purses, of their votaries. Of the creation of Gánesa, his duties as janitor to the supreme, and the import of his name *gana-esa* (chief of the inferior divinities, the Jins or Genii of the Persian mythos), I have spoken in the 'Annals.' The adoption, for this emblem of wisdom, of the head of an elephant, requires no explanation; but why they have selected a rat for his companion, unless as an antithesis, it is difficult to comprehend. The Greeks gave Minerva an owl, which, at all events, wears the aspect of wisdom; but the sagacious attributes of the rat are unknown,—save to the politician.

Having refreshed our wearied limbs, we proceeded on our route, and at ten A.M. reached the lowest point of the plateau, making several intermediate halts. My barometers this morning evinced symptoms of plethora, especially that to which I had pinned my faith: this, at the shrine of Ganésa, stood at 27° 65′, shewing only one degree of elevation, or six hundred feet, above the level of the plains of Maroo; while, judging by my eye, we appeared elevated above the table-land of the Aravulli. This was still more apparent when we had gained the crest of the mountain, when the mercury stood at 27° 35′, only 30′ for nearly two hours of ascent. The thermometer, 77°, full 15° below what it would have been on the plains at the same hour, afforded a truer indication of the height. In descending from the Aravulli to Marwar, two years before, the mercury had escaped and left me in doubt as to the comparative elevation of the regions skirting this range, though I afterwards proved that the plains of Marwar are full five hundred feet higher than those of Méwar: before quitting Oodipoor, therefore, on the present occasion, I had taken the precaution of re-filling both tubes, first purifying the mercury, and guarding against the disjunction of continuity, and proving their accuracy by bringing the

the elevation of the column to the precise point it occupied previous to the injury. But let us proceed to the Saint's Pinnacle, which towers over all the other diminished peaks, forming, as it were, a radiated coronet on the head of Arbudha.

The path lay through a little forest of the *Karounda*, the *Kantee*, and a variety of shrubs rich in flower and fruit at the same time. The first-mentioned was large, as the cultivated kind in Hindostan, and apparently at this time in perfection. We protracted the halt, in order to enjoy the delicious repast, doubly welcome from the fatigue and thirst attending our exertions. The *Kantee*, which was new to me, though a pleasant and beautiful little fruit, wanted the refreshing subacid of the *Karounda*. Midway, we passed through Oreah, one of the twelve hamlets which decorate the summit of Aboo, whose wonders became every instant more fully developed, while peaks of the most fantastic forms towered from amidst noble foliage. The golden *Champá*,—

"Strong Champá, rich in odorous gold,"—*

and many other rarities of the vegetable creation, adorned our path; but being yet more abundant in other parts of the mountain, they will be noticed in the general recapitulation of the productions of Aboo.

The sun had reached his meridian career when we attained the summit of the Guru Sikra, the loftiest of the peaks of Aboo, where European foot had never trod. Although presenting externally scarcely any sensible elevation above the crest of the mountain, as we approached

* Hymn to Camdeo, by Sir Wm. Jones. He observes, in his Indian Botany, that "the strong aromatic scent of the gold-coloured Champá, or Champaca (*Michelia*), is thought offensive to the bees, who are never seen on its blossoms; but their elegant appearance in the black hair of the Indian women is mentioned by Rumphius, and both facts have supplied the Sanscrit poets with elegant allusions."

approached through the plains of Marwar, it towered full seven hundred feet above the level of its plateau; still my sluggish barometer only indicated 15′ of elevation, being 27° 10′, while the thermometer, exposed to the sun in the dog-days of India, and within the tropic, fell to 72°, and proved the better guide. A strong chilling wind blew from the south, to avoid whose influence, the cautious mountaineers, coiling themselves in their black *comlis* (blankets), lay prostrate on the ground, sheltered behind a projecting rock. The picture was equally grand and novel: masses of cloud floated under our feet, through which the sun occasionally darted a ray, as if to prevent our being dazzled with too much glory. A small circular platform, having a low parapet wall on the outer side, crowned the giddy height. On one side was a cavern, about twenty feet square, within which is a block of granite, bearing the impress of the feet of Data Briga (an incarnation of Vishnu), the grand object of the pilgrim's attainment, and in another corner are the *pudda-ca* (or footsteps) of Rama Nanda, the great apostle of the Seeta Ascetics. In this gloomy abode dwells a disciple of the order, who rings a bell on the approach of a stranger, continuing the uproar till an offering induces silence. The staffs of pilgrims were heaped in piles around the footsteps of the saint, as memorials of their successful intrepidity. Caves innumerable were seen in various parts of the mountain, indicative of a Troglodyte population in former ages; and there were many curious orbicular holes, which could only be compared to the effect of cannon-shot. I patiently awaited the termination of the struggle between the powers of light and darkness, in conversation with the recluse. He told me that, during the *Bursât*, or rainy season, when the atmosphere is cleared of all impurities, the citadel of Jodpoor, and the desert plain, as far as Balotra

Balotra on the Loony, were visible. It was some time before I could test this assertion, though, during occasional outbreaks of the sun, we discerned the rich valley termed Bheetril, extending to Sarohi; and nearly twenty miles to the east, the far-famed shrine of Ambá-Bhavani, amongst the cloud-capped peaks of the Aravulli. At length, however, Surya burst forth in all his majesty, and chasing away the sable masses, the eye swept over the desert, until vision was lost in the blending of the dark blue vault with the dusky arid soil. All that was required to form the sublime was at hand; and silence confirmed the charm. If the eye, diverted from the vast abyss beneath, turned but half a circle to the right, it rested on the remains of the castle of the Pramars, whose dusky walls refused to reflect the sun-beams; while the slender palmyra, as if in mockery of their decay, fluttered its ensign-like leaves amidst the ruined courts of a race who once deemed their sway eternal. A little further to the right rose the clustering domes of Dailwarra, backed by noble woods, and buttressed on all sides by fantastic pinnacles, shooting like needles from the crest of the plateau, on whose surface were seen meandering several rills, pursuing their devious course over the precipitous faces of the mountain. All was contrast—the blue sky and sandy plain, the marble fanes and humble wigwam, the stately woods and rugged rocks. In spite of the cold blast, it required an effort to withdraw from the state of contemplative indolence which overcomes one amidst such scenes, where, as if brought into the immediate presence of the Creator of such grandeur, the mind feels oppressed with its own insignificance. Even on my retinue it had the same overpowering influence; they gazed on the scene, without uttering a remark on the novelty of their position. But reflection at length warned me that it was time to

 retrace

retrace our steps: besides the necessity of making observations on the towns within view, there were certain indications of something more solid than karoonda berries being required to fortify the inner man, after efforts of strength from four in the morning until one P.M., and our place of halt and refreshment was yet two miles distant.

Although the descent was easy, we did not reach Achil-éswar until three P.M.; the barometer 27° 25′, and thermometer 78° in the open air. At four P.M., the mercury had risen to 82°, rather an unusual change of temperature at this period of the day. The barometer also evinced an unusual oscillation of 5′ in the same space, being now 27° 20′. At half past five, it was 27° 17′, and the thermometer 78°. Our path lay through the same scented groves, nature scattering her bounties with a lavish hand; yet had the superstitions of man intruded, and converted a spot fit for the parents of the human race in their primitive innocence, into an abode of demons, where man degraded himself to the level of the brute.

I had often witnessed, and more frequently read of, the revolting practices of numbers of the countless inhabitants of India, the slaves of a knavish hierarchy; but it was reserved for me this day to discover the extent to which the debasement of man could be carried without the intervention of priestcraft, and which, happily, was too far below the attributes of human nature to be erected into a system. I allude to the Aghori, who finds a place in the interminable nomenclature of Hindu sectarian classification. I may style this outcast of human nature the jackal of his species; but even this midnight reveller amidst graves and impurities is cleanly in his habits compared with the Aghori. The brute would turn away from putrefaction, and refuse to prey on the dead of his own kind; not so the Aghori, by

whom

whom a dead man or a dead dog is viewed with equal indifference, or rather appetite, and, disgusting as is the relation, he does not hesitate to feed on the excretions of nature. I had heard that such wretches did exist, not only in the sacred Aboo, but amidst the impenetrable recesses of the other mounts dedicated to the Jain faith, in the peninsula of the Sauras. The illustrious D'Anville speaks of them as "*une espèce de monstre*," whose existence he doubted, though quoting from his veracious countryman, Thévenot. He says: "Thévenot dit avoir vu dans les habitans de ce lieu, un caractère de hardiesse et d'insolence tout extraordinaire, en sorte qu'on soit obligé d'être armé en passant chez eux; apprenant, en même temps, qu'ils étoient peu auparavant de ceux qu'on appeloit *Merdi-coura*, ou mangeurs d'hommes.* Ce qui prouve que le fait n'est pas avancé légèrement par notre voyageur, c'est que le terme de *Merdi-coura*, qu'il ne parait pas avoir connu autrement que par cette rencontre, se retrouve dans la haute antiquité."†

It is a curious fact, as D'Anville adds, that this "*espèce de bête*," this *Merdi-cour*, or properly *Merdi-khor*, should have been noticed by Pliny, Aristotle, and Ctesias, under nearly the same name, *Marti-chora*, giving its synonym in their own language, Ανθροποφάγος, for *Merdi-khor* is a Persian compound from *merd*, 'man,' and *khoordun*, 'to eat.' Three facts are deducible from this etymology of the Greek writers; first, that this brutalized sect is of ancient date; secondly, that the Persians must have had an intimate intercourse with these regions in early times;

* "Les habitans de ce bourg (Debca) estoient autrefois de ceux qu'on nommoit *Merdi-Coura*, ou Antropofages, mangeurs d'hommes; et il n'y a pas grand nombre d'années qu'on y vendoit encore de la chair humaine dans le marché."—*Voyages de M. de Thévenot; Paris*, 1684.

† Antiq. Géograph. de l'Inde, p. 96.

times; and thirdly, that the western historians must have had more recourse to Persian authorities than we at present are aware of.* I passed the *gopha* or cave of the most celebrated of these monsters of the present age, who was long the object of terror and loathing to Aboo and its neighbourhood. His name was Futteh Poori, who, after having "embowelled," to an advanced age, whatever came in his way, took the extraordinary resolution of immuring himself in his cell. The commands of maniacs generally meet with ready obedience, and as he was regarded by many in this light, his desire was implicitly fulfilled. The mouth of the cave was built up, and will remain so until some mummy-hunting Frank shall re-open it, or till phrenology form a part of the modern education of a Hindu; when, doubtless, the organ of destruction on the cranium of Futteh Poori will exhibit a high state of development. I was informed that there was still a considerable number of these wretches inhabiting the caverns of the mountain, from which they seldom emerged to open day, but prowled about in search of fruits, or whatever food the Rahtis conveyed to the paths they frequented. One of the Deora chiefs told me that, a very short time since, when conveying the body of his brother to be burnt, one of these monsters crossed the path of the funeral procession, and begged to have the corpse, saying that it "would make excellent *chatni*," or condiment. He added, that they were not actually accused of killing people.†

It

* A fourth might be added—the close affinity which it proves between the modern and the ancient Persian tongues, in the identity of the meaning of the names.

† The head-quarters of the caste are at Burputra (Baroda), and there still exists on the old site a temple dedicated to the patroness of the order, Aghor-éswar Mata, represented as "Lean Famine," devouring all. Her votaries are brought into the compendious class of ascetics, of whom they are the

It was strange to meet with the cave of a cannibal, if not within the precincts, in the immediate vicinity, of the shrines of Jainism, whose first tenet is, " thou shall not kill,"—not man alone, but the smallest sentient being: presenting another anomaly in the history of Hindu superstition, which recognises the grossest incongruities. The orthodox, whether followers of Siva or Vishnu, seem to consider their respective tenets too stable to fear the contact of other creeds; and even the Jain Unitarian, while he professes devotion to " the Spirit" alone, does not refuse the homage of a reverence to the symbol of " Wisdom," to the beneficent Anapoorna or Ceres, or the universal " Destroyer." Sects and creeds have no martyrs; no relics of saints are required to keep their respective votaries fixed to the principles in which they were born; and the ignorant, the superstitious, the timid, or the humane, may supply food even to the basest of his species, the horrid Aghori. In this tremendous Pantheon, no one is called to account for actions not affecting society.

Between the hamlet of Oreah and the shrine of Achil-éswar we found a group of small temples, the most conspicuous of which was dedicated to the " God of the Bull," Nand-éswar. It afforded corroboration of a fact hitherto unestablished, namely, that their architectural rules

the most degraded, beyond all controversy; they eat whatever falls in their way, raw or dressed, flesh or vegetables, and drink whatever is at hand, spirits, or their own urine.

Marco Polo speaks of a class of magicians who are akin to our Aghoris. " The Astrologers, who practise the diabolical art of magic, are natives of Cashmere and Thibet. They exhibit themselves in a filthy and indecent character; they suffer their faces to remain uncleaned by washing, their hair uncombed, being in a squalid style. Moreover, they are addicted to this horrible and beastly practice—when any culprit is condemned to death, they carry off the body, dress it with fire, and devour it."—*Marsden's Marco Polo*, p. 252.

The Ethiopian Troglodytes of Herodotus seem to have been very similar to them: " their food is lizards, serpents, and other reptiles; their language like the screaming of bats."—*Melp.*, p. 341.

rules were unchangeable, and that in the general form and details, each divinity had its peculiar style. This temple is in all respects the counterpart of those to Ganga-bheo,* at the falls of the Chumbul, and that on the Bairis, near Oodipoor. Its simple yet solid construction, the external pilasters with almost Doric capitals, were of the same mould, and one would have imagined of the same age and by the same chisel. There was only one inscription, importing that Bheem-deo Solankhi, lord of Anhulwarra, repaired the shrine.

At three P.M., after ten hours and a half of toil, we bivouacked in a grove between the mausoleum of Rao Maun and the Agni-coonda. I was indebted to the civilities of a pilgrim merchant of the Jain faith, who compelled me to accept the use of a small tent, saying he preferred the open air, and that if I did not use it, it would remain empty. "All hail! ye small sweet courtesies of life!" I shall forget myself when I forget these white spots in my chequered career. The offer was, indeed, most welcome, for I dreaded the night-dews, and nothing but the excitement, which lent a giant's force to my frame, could have enabled me to get through this day's labour.

While the camp-baskets were unlocking, I could not resist taking a peep at the fire-fount and the shrine of Achil-éswar, one of the most renowned in the fabulous annals of the Hindus. The Man-agni-coonda is about nine hundred feet long by two hundred and forty in breadth, excavated in the solid rock, and lined with solid masonry of immensely large bricks. An insulated mass of rock has been left in the centre of the coond, on which are the ruins of a shrine to Mata, the universal mother. On the crest of the northern face of the coond is a group of small

* Vide Annals of Rajast'han, vol. ii. p. 716.

small temples dedicated to the Pandu brothers, but, like the former, a mass of ruins. On the western side is the shrine of Achil-éswar, the tutelary divinity of Aboo. There is nothing striking as to magnitude, and still less as to decoration, in this, but it possesses a massive simplicity which guarantees its antiquity. It occupies the centre of a quadrangle, surrounded by smaller fanes, alike primitive in form, and built of blocks of blue slate. But it is the object of worship which confers celebrity, being nothing less than the great toe of the devil, for so we must translate *Patal-éswar*, the Lord of Hell. On entering, the eye is attracted by a statue of the mountain nymph, Méra, the wife of this multiform divinity, which, at first sight, appears to be the object of adoration; and it is only on stooping to look into a deep fissure of the rock, termed the *Brimh-khar*, that the bright nail of Siva is visible, which has attracted homage from myriads of votaries from the remotest ages. In front of the temple is a brass bull, of colossal size, bearing the marks of violence on his flanks, the hammer of the barbarian having penetrated them in search of treasure. Mahomed Beyra, Padsha or king of Ahmedabad, has the credit of this sacrilege; but whether it was rewarded by the discovery of any secret hoard, is not told: though the legend details the manifestation of Siva's wrath upon the "barbarian king" for the ill-treatment of his favourite. In descending from Aboo, after the reduction of Achilgurh, his banners "fanned by Conquest's crimson wing," confusion waited on them from an unlooked-for source. A legion of bees, issuing from their pinnacled retreats, attacked and pursued the invaders even to Jhalore. To commemorate this victory over the spoiler, the name of *Bhomar-t'hál*, or 'Bees' Valley,' was given to the spot. A temple was erected, and from the captured arms thrown away in their flight, a vast *tridanta*

(trident)

(trident) was formed, and placed in front of the divinity who thus avenged the insult to Nanda.

On the outside of one of the smaller shrines which surround the chief temple, lays a statue, Narayana, floating on Sehes-nag, the thousand-headed hydra, on the waters of Chaos, and who, whenever he awakes from his slumber, will be astonished to find himself "high and dry." Upon my remarking to the high priest, that the "Preserver" seemed to have indifferent accommodation, he coolly replied, "I wanted a place for chúnám;" and on looking into the desecrated fane, I found it filled with lime, made from the marble with which the hill abounds; but I have little doubt that the priest would not have hesitated to calcine the war-shell of the god also, had it answered his purpose. Here all honour is paid to the lord of Patal, and the angelic host are subordinate to the powers of darkness. This fact alone would determine the antiquity of the worship, fear being, amongst all uncivilized nations, predominant over love. On quitting the temple, the eye rests on a number of rude pillars at the gate, bearing the *tilac*, or maledictory inscription, each having the figure of the ass *(gadda)* carved thereon. Surrounding the shrine are some noble trees, among which the mango is conspicuous; amidst its branches the vine, untouched by the pruning-knife, was interlaced, bearing a good-sized grape, yet unripe: they told me it was indigenous to the mountain. The *champa*, *chameli*, *seoti*, *mogra*, and various other plants, blossomed luxuriantly around. There was no inscription in the temple of Achil-éswar, but I copied one from the adjacent reservoir.

On the same side as this temple, and on the very verge of the Agnicoonda, is the mausoleum of Rao Maun of Sarohi, who fell a victim to poison while in one of the Jain temples, where they point out a spot in the marble stained by the poison which he voided. His body was burnt near the shrine of his patron deity, when five queens accompanied him to Yamaloca, the realm of the Indian Pluto. Their effigies are carved on a small altar erected in the centre of the monument, which is a simple cupola supported by columns. They are represented with folded hands and eyes cast down, supplicating that their atonement may be received in expiation of the sins of their lord, that he may be released from the grasp of Yama, and admitted to Vaicoonta, the paradise of the Hindu, a most comfortable *viaticum* for the last hours of a vindictive, cruel, and drunken Rajpoot, for such is the character of Rao Maun. On the east side of the fire-fountain, the remains of a temple sacred to the founder of his race, the first of the Pramaras, strewed the ground. The statue, however, of Adipala is firm upon its pedestal, and intact, and was to me an object of far greater interest than anything I had previously viewed. Here was a type of ancient days, of antique costume, and early realities. It is of white marble, about five feet in height, and, with the exception of the sculptured figures on the column of Barolli, the finest piece of sculpture I met with in India. He is in the act of slaying with an arrow the Hindu Bucentaur, Bhynsasūra, a buffalo-headed monster, of Titanian brood, who used to drink during the night the sacred waters of the fire-fountain, to guard which the Pramara was created. The arrow has just sped, and the marks of his unerring aim and muscular arm were visible in the wounds of three of these, having penetrated through all impediments and integuments to boot. The original representatives of the monsters must have been destroyed, for these are coarsely fashioned of blue slate, having nothing to indicate their fabulous attributes. The right hand of the Pramara, still close to the ear, denotes determination of purpose; the arm is free and flexible,

 of

of good proportions, the turn of wrist admirably managed, but the fingers are perhaps too much curved; the limbs are well-proportioned, and the whole attitude is graceful. Some fanatic has broken a portion of the bow, which is not of *dhunoos*, or bamboo, but of the more classic buffalo-horn, whose relaxed *chulla*, or bow-string, denotes more than ordinary attention to propriety of action. The head is bold and well set, with only its natural covering, and the sole vestment is a kilt-like drapery, reaching to the middle of the thigh, in fashion like that still worn by the mountaineers of the Aravulli, with a belt or waist-band, in which the dagger is placed. A triple string of pearls, with bracelets and anklets, attest the rank of this representative of the first Pramara. There was an inscription on the plinth of the pedestal, but some bigot had effaced the most material part, the Samvat or era; it runs thus: "Samvat——[the month] Phâlgân (in spring) and Thursday the 13th, Crishnapateh, or enlightened half of the moon, Sri- - râs, king paramount; seated on the regal cushion of Achilgurh, the Pramara Sri Dharaburz* repaired the temple of Achil-éswar." The inscription from the shrine of Kunkul-éswar (*vide* App. No. I.) gives us the era of Dharaburz, *viz.* S. 1265, or A.D. 1209; but I have no idea who the paramount sovereign was, whose name terminates with the syllable *ras*. The Pramaras of this period, who possessed the three famed cities, Chandravati, Aboo, and Sarohi, in their contracted principality,

* This name may possibly be derived from the metaphor of the Rajpoot bards, who liken the quick-descending blows of the sword to a cascade, termed *d'hara*; while *burz* may be a repetition of the same idea, from *bursna*, 'to rain;' "the sword rains" on the head of a foe, being a common phraseology with Hindu poets. Or it may refer to his being a branch of the Pramars of *Dhar*, the ancient capital of Central India. Dharaburz merited the metaphorical appellation, for his Sirohi literally "rained" upon the heads of the barbarians on their conquest of India. Ferishta lauds the energy and intrepidity of this prince of Aboo, under the name of Daraparais, which has puzzled all the readers of Hindu-Mahomedan history, but which, we see, was not wide of the original.

principality, were tributary to the kings of Anhulwarra; but there is no name with such a termination in the annals of this state at that epoch. The execution of the statue forbids the idea that it could have been sculptured at the period of the inscription, or we might suppose it to have been erected by Dharaburz to the memory of the first of his race, himself being the last who enjoyed independence in Aboo. But the arts were already in decay in his time,* and it is probable, therefore, that he merely availed himself of this monument to commemorate his act of repairing the shrine. The Hindu bard, who is apt sometimes to draw inferences to suit his purpose, ascribes his loss of kingdom, not to political, but moral causes, namely, the impiety already recorded, of attempting to fathom the mysteries of Achil-éswar. There was something so attractive to the imagination in this ancient piece of sculpture, and in the whole fable connecting the Pramara with this Olympus of the Hindus, that I felt a powerful inclination to remove the statue from its perilous post on the crest of the fire-fount. But better thoughts interposed. It was the cradle of his race, and the scene of their regeneration through the fiery ordeal. No other position could furnish so appropriate a resting-place. I recollected, too, the anathema of Lord Byron on the plunderer of the Parthenon:

> "What! shall it e'er be said by British tongue,
> Albion was happy in Athena's tears?
> Though in thy name the slaves her bosom wrung,
> Tell not the deed to blushing Europe's ears;
> The Ocean Queen, the free Britannia, bears
> The last poor plunder from a bleeding land:
> Yes she, whose generous aid her name endears,
> Tore down those remnants with a harpy's hand,
> Which envious Eld forbore, and tyrants left to stand."

May no unhallowed hand hereafter displace Adipal! The

* This assertion involves a seeming paradox, but the Jain temples executed at this period, however splendid in their details, contain no single figure of such exquisite proportions.

The fable regarding Achil-éswar is inseparably connected with the history of Aboo and the creation of the Agni-vansa to fight the battles of Siva against the Dytes, who banished his rites from this his favorite mount. It is a less refined fable than the Grecian, of the Titans waging war with Jupiter, but the outline is the same. Having already described this in the 'Annals,' I merely subjoin, for the information of the curious in mythology, that relating to the origin of Arbudha itself.

"In the golden age of man's simplicity, this spot was in high favour with Siva and the millions who peopled the Hindu Pantheon, who frequently assembled here in person. Here the Moonis or sages, of whom Vashishta was head, and the representative of Siva, passed their time in austerities and prayers, living on milk and the spontaneous fruits of the earth. At that time there was no mount; all was level to the Aravulli. There was, however, an abyss, or *coonda*, of unfathomable depth, into which the cow which supplied the sage having fallen, she was miraculously floated out by a rise of the waters. The Mooni, desirous to prevent a recurrence of the accident, wafted a prayer to Siva, then dwelling amidst the glaciers of Kylas. He heard the invocation, and calling the sons of Himaleh to him, he demanded, who would make a voluntary sacrifice and become an exile from their ice-bound abode. The youngest son of Himachil offered to fulfil the behest; but he was lame and could not travel, whereupon the mountain serpent, Tacshac, volunteered to transport him upon his back. In this manner they journied together to the Holy Land, where dwelt the Mooni Vashist. Having explained the purport of their errand, in obedience to the command of the sage, the son of Himachil leapt into the void, but his friend, Tacshac, refusing to quit him,

wound

wound his indented folds around him, and retained him in his embrace. For this sacrifice they stipulated that their names conjoined should henceforward designate the rock, thence called Arbudha, from *ar*, 'mountain,' and *budha*, 'wisdom,' typified by the serpent. But this ample fragment of the father of mountains, either did not suffice to fill the chasm, or the snake, repenting of his change of place, made such writhings that Vashishta again had recourse to the divinity to still its motion. Siva then, from the depths of Patal, extended his limb through the earth's centre, until the toe became apparent on the summit of the mountain. The vibration ceased, the mountain became immoveable *(achil)*, and over the toe of the god *(éswar)* was erected the fane."

If this fable be deemed worthy of interpretation, I would say that the cow, which is typical of the earth, in falling into the abyss, represented the iniquities of man, and the Dytes, who disturbed the rites of the worshippers of Siva, are the irreligious sectarians. The son of Himachil, who filled up the void, may signify a northern colony, whose conversion by Vashishta originated the fable of the creation of the Agni-vansa, said to have sprung from the Agni-coond, over which the temple of Achil-éswar is raised.

The fissure of the rock is covered with a silver plate furnished by the Deora chiefs, of a form emblematic of Sacti, and it is related that an impious Bhil, not having the fear of Patal before his eyes, stole the precious metal. He had not, however, proceeded a mile from the spot, when he was struck blind. Repentance following punishment, he suspended the object of his avarice on a tree, and it being found, his sight, for this act of penitence, was restored. The emblem was purified by *agni* (fire), re-cast, and replaced over the fissure. There

There is a record of still more daring impiety in one whose especial duty it was to guard the shrine. The Pramara chief of Aboo and Chandravati, having determined to verify the legend of the Brimh-khar being *áthar*, or unfathomable, constructed an aqueduct from the adjacent fountain to the temple, and for six months did the water flow incessantly into the chasm without any visible effect. For this attempt to penetrate the mystery of Achil-éswar, the Pramar was driven from the throne of Chandravati, he being the last of his race.

June 13th.—At six A.M. I quitted the Agni-coonda for Achilgurh, whose ruined towers were buried in the dense masses of cloud that surrounded us. The thermometer at the point of ascent was 66°, barometer 27° 12′, and at eight A.M. on the summit, barometer 26° 97′, and thermometer 64°. I entered this once regal abode through the Hanuman portal, which is composed of two noble towers, built with huge blocks of granite, black with the rude blasts of some thousand winters. The towers had been connected at top by a guard-room, and the gate served as the entrance to the lower fort, whose dilapidated walls were discoverable up the irregular ascent. Another portal, called the Champa-pol, from a noble champa-tree growing close to it, but which was formerly denominated the 'Gate of Wisdom,' conducted to the inner fortress. The first object that strikes the view, on passing the latter gate, is the Jain temple to Parswanat'h, erected at the sole expense of a banker of Mandoo, and at this time under repair. Its columns are of the same character as those of the ancient shrine of Ajmér. The upper fortress is attributed to Rana Koombho, when driven from the "eighty-four castles" of Méwar; but he merely repaired this, the Donjon of Achilgurh, which, with the inferior works, is of the most remote antiquity. These were the ruins of a granary, called

ANCIENT FORT OF ACHILGURH, ON ABOO.

London, Published by W. H. Allen & Co.

called the Bindâr of Koombho Rana, coated within with a very strong cement: the roof had fallen in. Close on the left is the Mahl or palace of Oka Ranee, his queen, so designated from being of Oka-Mundala, near the Land's End of the Hindus. A small lake in the keep is called Sawun-Bhadoon, and well merits the names of the two chief months of the monsoon, for, in the middle of June, it is yet full of water. On the most elevated knoll, to the east, are the remains of an alarum-tower of the Pramaras; from this point, the eye, occasionally piercing the swift-scudding clouds, had glimpses of the ruined altars and palaces of the brave race, who, on the spot whence I surveyed them, had fought and bled in their defence. I thought of Lakshun, the wise and chivalrous brother of the fair Echinie (wife of the last of the Chohans), whose name is recorded with that of his sovereign on the pillar of Delhi. The name of Lakshun may not perish. The Rajpoot of every tribe, after a lapse of seven centuries, yet pays it homage; and the stranger from the west, alike an admirer of heroic achievement, under whatever clime or lineaments, seeks to perpetuate the memory of one whose worth has been transmitted in the song of the bard (Chund), and is still recalled by these moss-covered ruins.

In such a position, one may well repeat, with the first of our own antiquaries, "Who can stand among the ruins of the mouldering pile "without a heaving of the heart? How many reverend histories attach "to the dark green stones you tread upon, the broken scutcheon and "dark ivy mantling over it, where once the banner hung! What "sublime objects for the eye of contemplation, what temples for "thought, these roofless palaces, from whence we come out humbled "and yet hopeful, in charity with the dead and the living!"

As the sun dispelled the watery darkness which enveloped us, the

landscape

landscape of this magic realm was to the last degree imposing, every change of position unfolding some new object. First, the Jain shrines of Dailwarra (bearing S. 80° W. six miles distant), backed by the peak of Arbudha Mata; the Guru Sikra (N. 15° E. four miles); with many other pinnacles scattered over the summit of this fairy land, each with its name and its legend. After three hours' excursion, the excessive cold (the thermometer having sunk to 64°) compelled me to quit my elevated abode, where, as my guide metaphorically said, "the feud between Indra and the mountain was one of ancient date." On the descent, I paid my homage to the representative of one of the worthies of Méwar, an equestrian brass statue of Rana Koombho, who, within these walls, had often stood the brunt of war. Besides this were also statues of his son Rana Mokul and his grandson Oody Rana, the latter of whom "tarnished the glory of a hundred kings." I turned from the image of the recreant, of whom his heroic grandson, Sanga, the opponent of Baber, said that, had Oody Sing never lived, the Toork had never subjugated Rajast'han. There was a fourth statue, of the domestic priest *(Purohit)* of Koombho Rana, which eclipses all the others in magnitude. The cause of this distinction I could not learn, but it might possibly be owing to some act of bravery, for the brahmins occasionally wield the sword as well the Rajpoot. It was pleasing to witness the homage still rendered, within these now desecrated walls, to departed worth; prayers are made, and daily oblations of saffron brought to the defender of Achilgurh, and these not by any of his descendants, who are ignorant of this deed, but by others utterly unconnected with him, actuated by the traditional record of his glory or greatness. The humble straw shed which covers these effigies, conveys a finer lesson to the mind than if they were enshrined in marble.

Here,

Here every thing is Jain, and the shrine dedicated to Vrishabdeva* is well worthy of notice, from its containing no fewer than twelve immense images to this, the first of the twenty-four pontiffs who attained the honours of apotheosis. They are said to weigh many thousand maunds, and to be a compound of all the metals. Near the base of the inner fort, on the left hand, on leaving it, is another temple dedicated to Parswanat'h, whose statue it contains. This was erected or repaired by the celebrated Komarpal, King of Anhulwarra, the patron of the sect, and disciple of Hemachundra, a potent name among the Jains. The external sculpture is curious, but the execution has no pretensions to elegance. At one P.M., at the foot of Achilgurh, the barometer was 27° 4′, the thermometer 78°; at three P.M., barometer 26° 95′, thermometer 78°; at eleven A.M. on the same day, having sent a trusty and intelligent servant to mark the position of the mercury, on the summit of the Guru Sikra, the result was, barometer 26° 86′, and thermometer 68°; on which difference from the former observation we shall remark hereafter.

In the cooler part of the day, as I was prowling about my bivouac, the sound of Rajpoot military music met my ear, and shortly after, the *cortège* of the Deora Prince appeared, in all the pomp and circumstance of state,—banners flying, drums beating, trumpets sounding,—advancing towards the mango grove environing the shrine of his patron Achil-és. The animation of this scene contrasted well with the stillness of nature; the ruined castle of the Pramaras recalling the day,

——— "When

* Vrishabdeva, vulgarly Brishabdeo, has the same meaning as the Nand-éswar of the Sivites, the bull being the effigy of both. In order to distinguish the particular pontiff to whom any Jain shrine is consecrated, it is only requisite to look on the pedestal for the symbol, as the bull, the serpent, the lion, &c. &c., each having his peculiar emblem.

——— "When they were young and proud,
Banners on high and battles pass'd below;
But they who fought are in a bloody shroud,
And those which waved are shredless dust ere now,
And the bleak battlements shall bear no future blow."

Rao Sheo Sing (who was the Lord of Aboo as well as of Sarohi) had signified his intention to repeat his visit; but I wished to spare him and his followers so fatiguing a journey, and to save myself from interruption. This, however, proved unavailing, and my reveries were soon interrupted by his messenger announcing the Rao's desire to see me. On reaching the grove, I found his vassals ranged in two lines, between which I passed, his Highness advancing to greet me, when, having gone through the paternal hug with him and his chiefs, he insisted that I should share the royal cushion; an honour I courteously declined. Upon this, he observed, that he could neither measure his gratitude by speech or personal attention to one who had saved him and his country from affliction; but he added, like a true Chohan, that rather than humiliate himself by submission to Jodpoor, he would associate with the Bhil amidst his native wilds. I liked him better on this occasion; he was less embarrassed, and, with the pure air of his own Aboo, he seemed to enjoy ease and freedom of speech. We conversed on various topics, besides those affecting his own and his country's welfare: such as cherishing his subjects, abolishing all *corvées*, protecting merchants, coercing the lawless tribes and subjecting them to orderly habits. Then, adverting to the history of his ancestry, we dwelt on the exploits of the famous Soortan, who, far excelling our Canute in arrogance, "shot his arrows at the sun for daring to incommode him." At length we parted, with many injunctions

on

on both sides; on his part, that I would not forget him nor neglect my health, which was dear to him; on mine, that he would be true to himself. A general salutation followed from all assembled, with a deep rolling hum, which expressed much from all hearts, and a flourish of cymbals and trumpets. Having made my *adieux*, as the Rao and his chivalry wound down the steep of Aboo, I turned to take a last look at the shrine of Achilésa, and to visit my friend the high priest, amongst whose *chēlas* or disciples I was now enrolled. I presented the accustomed pecuniary offering to the Gosaen.

It was late in the afternoon when I left the Agni-coond, and the interesting objects in its precincts, for Dailwarra, which I did not reach until dusk. The road lay through a succession of rugged descents, and being very unwell from a cold caught amidst the clouds of Achilgurh, I was forced to call the Swerga Vahana, or celestial car, to my aid. Near the termination of this journey, we made the *dētour* of a small lake, whose banks abounded with the *kinēr*, or oleander, and the white dog-rose; while, from an umbrageous peepul, the Kamérie* poured forth his monotonous but pleasing notes, amidst the stillness of a lovely scene, where the last tints of sunset illuminated the dark hues of the surrounding woods.

Passed the night in a ruined building attached to the temple, and rose from my pallet in a high fever, and unable to articulate, the mind having overstrained the body: but there yet remained much to be done, for this sacred spot is a concentration of wonders. I was about to visit the temples alluded to by Bishop Heber, and of which

* This appellation of the cuckoo is derived from Kama, the God of Love, whose emblems are peculiarly appropriate, being a bow and arrow composed of roses and jessamine, and other flowers in which the Hindu poet allows no thorn to lurk.

which he had heard through my communications to a friend in Calcutta, who published them ten years ago in one of the periodicals. The discovery was my own: to Aboo I first assigned a local habitation and a name, when all these regions were a *terra incognita* to my countrymen; and if I am somewhat jealous of my rights in this matter, it is the sole recompense for the toils I have gone through, and no small deterioration of health as well as of purse.

CHAPTER VI.

Dailwarra.—Temple of Vrishabdeva.—Its history.—Its description.—Ceremonies in the temple.—Inscriptions.—Temple of Parswanath.—Its architecture and description.—Reflections on these splendid remains.—Hamlets of Aboo.—Fruits and vegetables of the mountain.—Temple of Arbudha-Mata.—Cave-dwellings.—Lake of Naki-taloo.—Peril of the last descent.—The Gao-mukh.—Temple of Vasishta.—Worship of the Mooni.—Inscriptions.—Cenotaph of Dhar Pramar.—Temple of Patal-éswar.—Statues.—Reflections.—Elevation of Aboo.—Defects of the Author's barometer.—Aspect of the soil.—Passage of the forest.—Attack of Hornets.—Circumference of Aboo.—Analogy between the physical phenomena of Aboo and Sinai.—Severe effects of the ascent on the Author's health.

June 14th.—Dailwarra.—At seven A.M. at noon, and at four P.M., the barometer stood at 27°, 27° 5′, and 27° 5′, the thermometer being at the respective hours 72°, 86°, 90°. It is evident, from the inequality of variation, that the barometer on which I have been depending is most unfaithful, bearing no relation to the state of the thermometer. But a truce, for the present, to these technicalities. Let the reader discard his shoes, and prepare to enter with me the sacred fanes of Dailwarra. This is a contraction of Dewulwarra, 'the place or region of temples,' a term aptly applied to the site of this numerous group, from which I select two of the most remarkable.

The reader will be pleased to consider himself at the entrance of the shrine sacred to Vrishabdeva, the first of the Jains. Beyond controversy this is the most superb of all the temples of India, and there is not an edifice besides the Taj Mahl that can approach to it. The pen is incompetent to describe the exuberant beauties of this proud monument of the Jains, raised by one of the richest of their votaries (by whose name, and not that of the pontiff enshrined within, it is still designated),

designated), and which continues to attract pilgrims from every region of India. Bimul Sah,* whose work has immortalized him, was a merchant of Anhulwarra, at one time the Tyre of India, and the ancient stronghold of the Jain faith. It was, however, towards the close of her long career of renown, that these two edifices were erected, and happily for these votaries of Jainism, who, to use the words of the bard, "exchanged their perishable wealth for an immortal name," for hardly were the fabrics reared, when the metropolis of Western India was sacked, its merchants driven forth, and their riches transferred to the Northern Invader. Previous to their erection, the immediate spot was occupied by the orthodox divinities, Siva and Vishnu, whose ministers would not tolerate the approach of any of the sectarian enemies of their faith; but the Sahoos of Nehrwalla, giving this the preference over any other site on the surface of Aboo, determined to try the effect of gold on the sovereign, or, as they allegorically say, "Lacshmi herself entered into the scheme, to gain a victory for their faith." The bribe was high; they offered to cover as much ground as they required for their purpose with silver coin,—a temptation too powerful for the Pramara to withstand,—and, despite the anathema of the priests of Bal-Siva and Vishnu, he took the lacs of the Jain merchants. The name of the prince is not mentioned, but the date of the temples shews him to be the same sacrilegious Dharaburz, who attempted to inundate the Khar of Sacti. The merchants were not ungrateful to Lacshmi, whom they enshrined in a niche on the right hand of the entrance.

The temple of Vrishabdeva stands isolated in the centre of a quadrangular

* *Sah, Sahoo, Sahoocar,* are different terms for a merchant, vulgò *Soucar.*

rangular court, the length of which, from east to west, is about one hundred and eighty feet, and the breadth one hundred feet. Along its internal faces are ranges of cells, nineteen on the larger, and ten on each of the smaller sides, each cell being of uniform dimensions. A double-colonnaded piazza, elevated on a terrace, rising four steps above the level of the court, passes all round in front of the cells, the inter-columniations being the breadth of these; each, besides its four columns, having two pilasters to correspond therewith and the partition walls of the cells, the roofs of which are flat. In each cell, opposite to the door of entrance, is an elevated altar, on which is placed the image of some one of the twenty-four Jin-éswars. Architraves, passing from each pair of columns and resting on the corresponding pilasters, constitute a separate vestibule to each cell, and this is rendered the more distinct by every compartment between the four columns having either a vaulted or flat roof. The whole is of pure white marble, every column, dome, and altar varying in form and ornament, the richness and delicacy of execution being indescribable. Each of the fifty-eight cells merits an entire day's study, and a first-rate pencil to delineate it. It is asserted that each separate cell was added by wealthy individuals, of various cities and countries, professing the Jain faith, which may account for the great diversity of style and ornament, while the harmony and symmetry of the whole attest that one master-mind must have planned and executed it, except at the south-west angle, where some dissimilarity prevails. The altars are of a chaste and simple design, while money, labour, skill, and taste, have been lavished on the details of the colonnade, wherein each of the columnar rules of Jain architecture has its example. Each cell contains its statue dedicated to the particular object of worship of the person at

whose

whose expense it was raised, and inscriptions recording the period of erection are carved on the inner lintel of every doorway.

We now descend to the tesselated marble pavement in the area, crossing which we reach the Sowa-munduff, fronting the shrine of Vrishabdeva. It may be well, in the first instance, to explain the meaning of this term *(munduff)* in Hindu architecture, which belongs more to the Sivite than to the Jain style, and was perhaps borrowed from the former. The munduff may be either square or circular, and its roof, whether vaulted or pyramidal, is generally supported by open columns. In the Sivite shrine it contains the symbolic bull, while the appropriate representative, the lingam, occupies the interior cella. Whoever has noticed the ichnographic plan of the temple of Jupiter Serapis at Puzzuoli, will be tolerably familiar with a Sivite shrine. With the Jain, the munduff contains no object of adoration, and serves merely for the votaries to prepare themselves and their offerings. The one in question has a hemispherical vault of twenty-four feet diameter, supported by columns of proportional height. As these are ranged in a quadrangle, ponderous architraves are thrown across, excluding the corner columns, thus making the dome rise from an octagonal base. This is only perceptible from the inside; externally it appears an ovate spheroid, but obtained from an horizontal, not a radiating pressure. Each pair of columns is connected by a *torun*, or triumphal arch, of peculiar but very elegant form, and of most elaborate workmanship. On the east, north, and south sides, intervening columns unite the munduff with those of the piazza, and thus conjoined, they fill up one entire side of the area. The roofs, either domed or flat, which cover these intervening columns, and surround the larger vault, rivet attention. In their surfaces are sculptured innumerable incidents from their

various

various epics, the *Ramayana*, the *Mahabarat*, &c., thus whimsically blending the unitarian and polytheistic sects; while Kanya, in the Ras-Mandola, is represented encircled by the Gopis, relieved by festoons of foliage, flowers, and fruit. While the eye detects a want of ease in the figures of the animals, the most fastidious critic could not find fault with the copies from inanimate nature. The flowing lines and graceful pendant flowers could not be surpassed by the work of any chisel in Europe.

A small flight of steps conducts from the munduff to the shrine of Vrishabdeva. This consists of three parts, a colonnaded piazza, an internal vestibule, and thirdly, the sanctum of the object of homage. Here the mind is diverted from the contemplation of art, by the various paraphernalia of worship. The first thing I noticed, on entering, were two marble slabs, on one of which a devotee was employed in preparing an unction of saffron, as an offering to Kesaria-Nath, the familiar appellation of the god, from *kesar*, ‘saffron’, which, after prayer, purification, and incense-burning, the votary places before him. As I entered this large chamber, I observed through the *chiaroscuro* of ghee-illuminated candelabras, whose dim light contended with day, my Samaritan friend, who had lent me his tent, absorbed in devotion, before the image of the god. He was stripped, excepting the cloth round his loins; in one hand he swung a censer, in which gum benzoin and other incense was burning, while a bandage passed round his head, covering his mouth, that his impure breath might not offend the divinity, or, while employed in this devotional office, entail a curse by the destruction of an insect. He saw and recognised me, but was too abstracted to suffer his thoughts to be diverted fiom his occupation, and there was a benign and religious

 tranquillity

tranquillity in his countenance, which said that all was right within. There were some statues in the vestibule, and large brass bells to toll the hour of worship; and on one side there stood a huge iron chest, containing things savouring of *mrit-loca* of this nether sphere. In the sanctum, raised on a high altar, was a colossal statue of Vrishabdeva, in the usual sitting posture, and composed of *heft-dhal*, or the seven metals; the eyes were of crystal, and there was a precious gem, or *tika*, in the centre of his forehead. He was canopied by a rich web of gold brocade, and censers filled with incense were burning before him. But the lover of the arts would soon turn away from the contemplation of the deity of this splendid edifice; for although of tolerable execution, considering its ponderous size, it is despicable when contrasted with the rich specimens around. The same sentence must be passed on the statues in the vestibule, which do not at all harmonize with the purity of taste in the other ornaments. My admiration, which had advanced in an accelerated ratio until I approached the cella, here came to a dead halt; and what with the fumes of the incense, the glare from ill-fed candelabras, the impure atmosphere, and the abominable physiognomy of this Kesar of the Jains, I felt as if I were in Yama-loca, in presence of Rhadamanthus. My curiosity being satisfied, I escaped into the region of pure air and pure art, where my equanimity was soon restored; but the painful sensation excited by the dazzling light from the rays of a vertical sun, reflected from the marble pavement, drove me for shelter into the piazza.

The merchant of Anhulwarra has immortalized his name, and testified his gratitude to Bhavani, by enshrining her on the right hand of Vrishabdeva, in the south-west corner of the quadrangle, making her cell larger and more elevated than the rest; while in the adjoining cell

is

is the statue of the twenty-second and most celebrated Jinéswar, Ném Nât'h, also called Arish-Nemi, or 'black.' The statue, which is colossal, and in keeping with his name and complexion, is carved out of a block of marble from the quarries of Dongerpoor. On leaving the quadrangular court, we pass to a square chamber with numerous columns supporting a low roof, at the entrance of which, and facing Vrishabdeva, is an equestrian statue of the founder, rather larger than life, with his nephew seated behind him, while over his head is raised the *chattrie*, or parasol, emblematic of nobility. The old merchant is rather clumsily fashioned, and crowned with a thing resembling a cacique tiara: his nephew is handing to him something like a field-marshal's truncheon, most likely a roll of account regarding the edifice. Surrounding the Prince of Merchants are ten figures, seated on as many elephants, each, with the rider, being six feet in height: they are of marble, and tolerably executed. Local tradition says, these are the effigies of the kings of the twelve great European nations, whom Bimul Sah, by the influence of gold, brought to swear that this work of his hands, and its divinity, should ever be respected by them. This story, which is not peculiarly flattering to European vanity, has descended through centuries, and like all the legends of the place, finds implicit credence with the true believer, the extent of whose faith may be inferred from the fact, that they had never even counted the number of potentates who had left their thrones to fulfil Bimul Sah's behest. On my observing to them that there were only ten, unless they included the merchant and his nephew in the list of "barbarian kings," they were not a little astonished; and when, moreover, I pointed out that these ten infidels had each four arms, they were still more at a loss; but as they agreed that they could not be kings,

 who

who had only one pair, they thus excluded the merchants from the barbarian association. By the morning, a new legend was got up, and the "twelve kings" were converted into the *kootum*, or family of the Sah, *i. e.* brothers, nephews, sons-in-law, &c. I proposed another solution, namely, that it might be a mythological allusion to the origin of the Sah's ancestry, which was of the Rajpoot tribe of Chohan, whose divinity was four-armed, and that the introduction of the Sah in the centre of the group, was probably an act of piety performed by one of his family. *Bhagwan janna*, 'God knows,' was the calm reply to the suggestion. Whatever the origin, it was indifferent to the iconoclastic Toork, who had indignantly smashed the four royal arms, leaving merely the stumps to shew that "such things were." Immediately behind the equestrian statue of the founder, is a column, several feet high, of three compartments, gracefully tapering as it rises from a circular base, consisting of three marble steps. It is sculptured with innumerable minute niches, each containing a figure of the Jinéswar, in the customary contemplative attitude. This column is a common appendage of Jain temples: I am inclined to rank with it the celebrated Cootub Minar at Dehli, imagining that the Islamite architects have only fluted the latter, in order to remove the obnoxious images. Of this class also, is a column on the summit of Cheetore, nearly eighty feet in height, similarly decorated with images, and covered by an open cupola supported by pillars. I copied and translated several inscriptions, one of which contained a *tilac* of inhibition of Koombho Rana, who, when driven from Méwar, raised the banner of the Sun on the long abandoned battlements of the Pramaras. Every stone teems with historical data, but it requires a wide acquaintance with the past to apply them.

I could

I could have consumed a month in surveying the works of the princely merchant, but time pressed, and other objects of equal importance awaited me.—Passing through a court, a flight of steps conducts to the rival temple, dedicated to Parswanat'h, the twenty-third and most popular of the Jinéswars. This shrine was erected by the brothers Tej Pal and Bussunt Pal, likewise merchants of the Jain persuasion, who inhabited the city of Chandravati during the sway of Dharaburz, and when Bheem Deo was paramount sovereign of Western India. The design and execution of this shrine and all its accessories are on the model of the preceding, which, however, as a whole, it surpasses. It has more simple majesty, the fluted columns sustaining the munduff are loftier, and the vaulted interior is fully equal to the other in richness of sculpture, and superior to it in the execution, which is more free and in finer taste. The span of the dome is two feet more in diameter than the other, being twenty-six feet; the ponderous architraves of marble, fifteen feet long and of solidity proportioned to their length and the superincumbent weight. The peristyle corresponds precisely with that already described, and, like it, is united by an intervening range of columns to the quadrangle. It is impossible to give a distinct idea of the richness and variety of the bassi-relievi either of the principal dome or the minor ones which surround it. We must not, however, overlook a singular ornament pendant from the larger vault, the delineation of which defies the pen, and would tax to the utmost the pencil of the most patient artist. Although it has some analogy to the corbeille of a gothic cathedral, there is nothing in the most florid style of gothic architecture that can be compared with this in richness. Its form is cylindrical, about three feet in length, and where it drops from the ceiling,

ceiling, it appears like a cluster of the half-disclosed lotus, whose cups are so thin, so transparent, and so accurately wrought, that it fixes the eye in admiration. The dome is divided into concentric compartments, by richly sculptured cordons, each intervening space being filled with elaborate and elegant devices. In one compartment, a bacchanalian group seems to indicate the season of the year when, all nature rejoicing, the man of wealth abandons all thought of Lacshmi (the goddess of riches) for the verdant Vassanti or spring, in allusion probably to the name of the founder, Bussunt Pal, which signifies 'fostered by the spring.' In the other divisions are rich festoons, in high relief, of flowers, fruits, and birds, down to the last, which contains figures of warriors, each standing on a projecting pedestal, in various attitudes, some holding the sword or sceptre: these may represent the kings of Anhulwarra. The *torun* divides our admiration with the vault. It appears as if spouted forth from the mouths of two marine monsters, whose heads project from the capitals of the columns supporting the arch. But it is vain to attempt a verbal description of this, and we must quit the munduff for the shrine. On ascending the steps, we enter the vestibule, on each side of which is a *tauk* or niche, partly sunk in the wall, and partly projecting from it. The base is in the form of an altar, over which, small and very chaste columns support an exquisitely designed canopy. Though plain, nothing can surpass the execution; not an unequal line or uneven surface is perceptible. All is so finely chiselled, that it appears as if moulded of wax, the edges, semi-transparent, not being a quarter of a line in thickness. These niches are said to have cost a lac and a quarter of rupees, or about twelve thousand pounds. Such was the wealth of individuals in those days! At present, a whole year's

revenue

revenue of the kingdom of Anhulwarra would not suffice for the erection of one of these shrines. In the sanctum appears the statue of Parswa, whose symbol is the serpent. Here we have the same incidents of worship, saffron-offerings, candelabras fed with ghee, benzoin incense, crystal eyes, emerald *tika*, and the same subordinate ill-favoured brass images around him.

Let us proceed to the court environing the shrine. The area of the quadrangle is about the same size as the other, or perhaps rather larger. Its double-colonnaded piazza is equally striking as a whole, but the columns are more simple, and the vaulted compartments equally rich and of bolder execution. Amidst the complicated sculptures of these vaulted roofs (no less than ninety in number), of satyrs, gods, demi-gods, and heroes, there were ships; indicating that the wealth of the founders was derived from maritime commerce, at a period when the proud city of Anhulwarra, and her prouder kings, the Bâlhâraés, basked in the full sunshine of prosperity, their ships visiting all the adjacent kingdoms, and diffusing the products over the entire Hindu land. While my eye rested with delight on these Argosies of the Hindus, it was gratified by finding, amidst details often too mystical for a western intellect, something that savoured of a more classical Pantheon. Here, amidst a mingled crew, appeared the Greek Pan, his lower extremities goat-like, with a reed in his mouth. To the east, the intercolumniations of the piazza have been built up, and in the centre is a procession of elephants, with their riders, drums. and caparisons, each cut from a single block of marble, of tolerable execution, and about four feet high. Fronting this is a column, similar to that noticed in the other temple, rising from a circular base. The various cells, their altars and their occupants, and the different Jinéswars

(each

(each about four feet high), in the usual sitting posture, are objects eminently worthy of admiration.

But it would be tedious to particularize the varied riches of these shrines; still less would it be desirable to repeat a vague and indistinct outline of the architectural details of the minor temples which surround these glories of Aboo; although each is entitled to notice, and, in point of magnitude, they surpass those described. That, for instance, which still retains the name of its founder, the merchant, Bheenia Sah, is totally different in style from the rest, being four stories high, and resembling the temple in the Sadri Pass. The brazen image of the Jinéswar is said to weigh 1,440 maunds, or 108,000 pounds. It rises in high relief from a huge brazen screen, like a pulpit in form, divided into compartments occupied by the subordinate Pontiffs, men, and animals, the whole evidently cast from one mould. Several other statues, said to be composed of the seven metals, are ranged on either side this object of homage.

We shall conclude as we began, with Bishop Heber's remark, that what he had seen of the palaces of Jeipoor surpassed both the Kremlin and Alhambra; and that what he had not seen, the Jain temples of Aboo on the verge of the western desert, might rank above them all,—a remark which I have confirmed, and I repeat, that, taken as a whole, and considering the vast sums expended upon these temples, the skill and labour employed upon them, the Taj Mahl at Agra is the only edifice which may rank above them, though even this is a matter of taste, the objects being as dissimilar in character as the Parthenon and St. Peter's. The principal features, however, are not mere solidity and vastness; their merits consist in the proportions, the endless variety and richness of the sculpture; the extended colonnaded piazzas and vaulted roofs suggesting

suggesting ideas, not only of unbounded wealth in the founders, but of high refinement in the arts. The most fastidious admirer of chaste design need not apprehend that his taste would be shocked by the accumulation of details, or that the minuteness of ornament would detract from the massive dignity of the whole; on the contrary, in these instances, the breaking into parts is by no means detrimental to the general harmony. When we reflect that all this magnificence is found on the summit of an isolated mountain on the verge of the desert, now inhabited by a few simple and half-civilized people, the association cannot fail to enhance our impressions of wonder. It is difficult to assign a reason for the forbearance of the intolerant Islamite towards these shrines, save their being Unitarian: they may be said to have had an almost miraculous escape, and they were fortunately out of reach of the illiterate Mahratta, and his follower, the barbarous Pat'han.

The day was far spent before I had seen half the beauties of Dailwarra; already the soft tints of evening were beginning to veil the landscape, and the feathered tribe, at their vespers, warned me that it was time to commence my pilgrimage to the shrine of Vashishta, still five miles distant. This excursion revealed to me by far the most interesting portion of the table-land of Aboo. There is more of cultivation, the inhabitants are more numerous, the streams and foliage more abundant; here and there a verdant carpet decked the ground, while some new wonder, natural or artificial, appeared at every step. The kamérie, as usual unseen, uttered its welcome note, and the strong, clear voice of the blackbird issued from a dark coppice, whence stole a limpid brook, all serving to remind me of the almost forgotten land to which I was about returning. Every patch where corn could grow was

 diligently

diligently tilled, and in this short space I passed four of the twelve hamlets of Aboo. These were in harmony with the scene; the habitations neat and comfortable, circular in form like wigwams, and coated with clay washed with a light ochre colour. On the margin of each running brook, was the *Aret*, or Egyptian wheel for irrigation, and as the water lies close to the surface, the excavations were not required to be deep. The boundaries of these arable fields, chiefly of the prickly *thoor* or *cactus*, were clustered with the white dog-rose, here called *khooja*, with which was intermingled the kind called *seoti*, (sacred to Seo or Siva), much cultivated in the gardens of India. The pomegranate was literally growing out of a knoll of granite, where there was scarcely any soil beyond the decomposed surface of the rock. The apricot or nectarine appeared occasionally, covered with fruit, but being yet quite green, it seems probable that it will never ripen. They also brought grapes, which, from their size, I should have deemed cultivated. These, as well as the citron, which I did not see, but which they pointed out in a deep valley, are claimed amongst the indigenous products of Aboo. The mango was abundant, and a rich and elegant parasite, with a beautiful pendant blue and white flower, resembling the *lobelia*, found root in its moss-covered branches. This parasite is called *ambatri* (from *amba*, mango,) by the mountaineers, with whom it appeared to be an especial favorite, as I observed that, whenever it grew within reach, it was plucked and " wreath'd in their dark locks" and their turbans. The trees generally, from the extreme humidity, are covered with a vesture of grass and moss, and at Achil gurh, the lofty *cajoor* or date tree was coated to the uppermost branch. It is from this deposit that the parasites spring. Of flowers there was a profusion: amongst them were the *chaméli* or jasmine, and all the varieties

F. Meadows, del. from a sketch by Mrs. Col. Hunter Blair. W. E. Starling, sculp.

THE DUBBY TALAO.

London, Published by W. H. Allen & Co. 1838.

varieties of the *goolabas*, or balsam, as common as thistles. The golden *champa*, the largest of the flowering trees, rarely met with in the plains, and which, like the aloe, is said to flower but once in a century, was seen at every hundred yards, laden with blossoms and filling the air with perfume. In short, it was

> " A blending of all beauties, streams and dells,
> " Fruit, foliage, crag, wood, cornfield, mountain, vine,
> " And chiefless castles, breathing stern farewells
> " From gray, but leafy walls, where Ruin greenly dwells."

About a mile from Dailwarra, and more than half-way up a lofty peak, upon the verge of a deep cleft in the rock, stands the temple of the tutelary goddess of Aboo, (called by the more refined, Arbudha-Mata, ' the Mother of the Mount of Wisdom,) half hid amongst luxuriant foliage. A streamlet issues from the cleft, and, after many windings, precipitates itself over the eastern face of the mountain, through the Kairlie pass, and, with several other rills, proceeds to join the Bunas, which here flows close to the skirt of the mountain. We passed the fragments of several ancient temples, dwellings, and caverns, where the Troglodyte sages of the golden age spun out their existence in adoration of the ' Great One.' One grotto, in a shady recess, looked so tempting, that, with some addition to the indigenous productions, a man might pass a summer even cheerfully there, though something would be required to qualify the water, which has a very strong mineral taste. At a little distance we saw the Nuki-talao, a beautiful lake, about four hundred yards in length, which merited a day of itself; but time pressed, and I was forced to content myself with a glance *en passant*. Those who have seen the lakc three miles above Andernach, on the Rhine, have beheld its counterpart. It is surrounded by rocks, wooded to the margin, while the water-fowls skim its surface unheeding and unheeded by man: for on this sacred hill, neither the fowler's gun, or fisher's net, is known; "thou shalt not kill" being the supreme command, and the penalty of disobedience, death. Its waters are said to be fathomless, but I observed no traces of volcanic scoriæ.

After two or three abrupt descents, I reached the summit of the last, leading to the shrine of Vashishta. I was totally unprepared for the scene, or should have taken more daylight to view it. Here I abandoned my car, in which fatigue had forced me to seek refuge. A tremendous abyss was before us, and the only mode of descent was over dislocated fragments of rock, while but a narrow ledge was between us and perdition. My old Guru, who was a little in advance, had come to a dead halt. Amused at the novelty of his position, he was holding forth to the mountain guides, but though conversant with all the dialects, he failed to make them comprehend him. At length, they caught the drift of his main question, "Where should he go if by chance he slipped?" to which they simply replied, "Oh Bapji (Sire), you would go a great way." This is the wildest scene on the surface of Aboo. About half-way down, while frowned upon by the impending crags, one still looks into the dread abyss below, studded with magnificent foliage, the *jamun*, tamarind, &c. &c., and wrapped in impenetrable gloom. The face of the mountain, from the valley upwards, was further obscured by masses of cloud, and we almost groped our way by the last glimmerings of light, guided by the alarum-drum of the monastery, whose deep rolling sounds contended with the rush of waters, which, issuing from the Gao Mukh (Cow's Mouth) above, were received in a fountain beneath. The effect altogether was

sublime.

sublime. One false step, and what were man, so vain of his powers? At length, our loud "halloo" was heard, and torches appeared through the palpable obscure, by the glare of which we descried the sacred fane, and the ascetic disciples passing to and fro to aid the descent of the pilgrims. Salvator Rosa would have selected the scene for a *chef-d'œuvre* of his pencil. On reaching the Gao Mukh, we halted a few seconds to take breath, and soon after attained the little plantain grove, where I found a *pal*, or open tent, pitched for my reception. Although desperately fatigued, curiosity would allow me no respite till I had seen the shrine of Vashishta. The temple is a small plain edifice, and though of remote antiquity, has been so often repaired, that little of the original structure remains. In a sanctum, at the further extremity, the head alone of the deified *Mooni*, or sage, appeared through his vestments. It is of black marble, and occupies a low altar. The whole was lighted up, and the brethren were chaunting a hymn in praise of Vashishta. Being in boots, I stood outside the threshold, listening with interest to the conclusion of their well-modulated strain. The ancient Guru, or Abbot, a tall spare figure, was seated on a black antelope's hide within the portico, and formed a striking contrast to his sleek, well-fed disciples, looking as if he really mortified the flesh. His hair was clotted, his body smeared with ashes, and he was too abstracted to notice external objects. The ceremony was impressive, and when it concluded, all his disciples approached, and in turn made the *dhandote*, or prostration, bowing lowly, their head touching the feet of the Guru. On retiring, they congregated in small groupes round their fires (which the chill damp air rendered very necessary), lounging on the floor of the ample *Dhermsala*. I placed my offering, through the hands of my own Guru, at the feet of this ancient ascetic,

and

and left the contented monastics rolling about the floor; for though their bodies were covered with ashes, it was evident from their plump appearance, that their penance was not severe. Had they inhabited the plains below, with the thermometer 135°, there might have been some merit in sitting round a penitential fire; but here, at a temperature 70°, perched amidst the clouds, it was a luxury.*

Setting my Guru to copy some inscriptions, which covered two large black marble tablets on each side the threshold of the temple, and of which a translation is given in the Appendix, I surveyed the inclosure by torch-light. The first object is of deep interest, being the cenotaph of the last of the Pramaras, separated by a slight passage from the temple. It consists of an ovate-formed cupola, supported by columns, with an altar beneath, on which stands a statue of the Pramar, turning in an attitude of supplication to the Mooni. It is of brass, about three feet and a half in height, and had attracted the notice of the Islamite, who had smitten it with an axe in the thigh, in search of treasure. From the inscription, it would appear that the Mooni turned a deaf ear to the entreaties of Dharaburz, whose twofold offence against the divinities of Aboo has been already related. He was the last of his race who ruled on the sacred hill, but tradition still respects the name of Dhar Pramar, as he is familiarly called by the mountaineers, and the annals of his foes attest the patriotic valour of the vanquisher of the emperor Kootub-u-din; nor was it until the reign of Altumsh, that he succumbed to the whole power of the empire, aided by the Chohans of Nadole, of whom a branch, the Deora, succeeded to the patrimony of the Pramars. These inscriptions embody the patent of the first

Deora

* One of the penances of the Jogi ascetic, is to be seated between four fires in the hottest months of the year, to which he continually adds fuel with a pair of large tongs.

Deora prince, confirming the lands and privileges granted by his predecessors and adding new ones from himself.

At the southern extremity of the area, is a small temple, consecrated to Patal-éswar, the Pluto of the Hindus, and which is placed several steps below the level of the court; but there was nothing to excite attention in the abode of his Satanic majesty, whose statue, surrounded by some of the *Dii minores*, was dimly visible by the light of a single *cheragh*, or lamp.

Upon an altar canopied by the vault of Heaven, are placed a number of divinities, whose temporal dwellings have gone to decay. The image of one of these, Sham-nath, or the black god of the Yamuna, is remarkably well-executed, as are two marble pilasters, about two feet high, divided into compartments containing small figures in relief, which, had they been designed as Sileni, would be pronounced excellent. In the centre of the area are two allegorical figures, reported to be Nandi-Vardana, the son of Himachil, seated on the back of his friend, the Serpent, who, it will be remembered, conducted this halting scion of the Hircanian cliffs, to fill up the chasm made by the bolt *(bajra)* of Indra. Near this are several highly-sculptured sacrificial stones of Satis, brought from the ruins of Chandravati.

Having seen whatever possessed interest within the precincts of the ancient sage, Vashishta, I retired to my tent, after sixteen hours of physical and mental excitement, exhausted by fever, cold, and fatigue; and though a cup of green tea was *imrit* (nectar), it did not contribute to "steep my senses in forgetfulness." All the spirits of Aboo seemed unchained; the rude blast rushed down from every crag, sweeping amongst the lofty foliage or the humbler plantain grove, whose broad leaves rattled like a thousand banners,

ners, to which was superadded the unceasing monotony of falling waters. But even through this chaos of sounds, the voices of the ascetic brethren were heard, addressing, in one united and not inharmonious strain of adoration, the "Universal Father." This exercise of devotion, in the mountain solitude, inspired the most tranquillizing sensations, and recalled to my mind the words of Rana Raj Sing of Méwar: "Whether the voice of the Islamite from the mosque, or the bell of the Hindu which tolls to prayer, it is to the same divine object." It is in such positions that the heart feels all the sweet influences of superior protection,—an impression never yielded up in after-life,—teaching us to abstract ourselves from the every-day bent of human pursuits, and to cleave a path, which, while broad enough for all social enjoyments, shall not be considered the end-all of existence. This is not solitude, but converse with Nature amidst the sublimest of her works. In this mood, my mind reverted to the description of night in the *Ramáyana*, the most ancient profane poem in existence, and composed by the sage, Valmika, who was the spiritual guide of Rama. It was customary for the kings and chieftains of old (a practice not yet renounced) to visit these sages in their cells, in order to imbibe moral instruction for the guidance of themselves and their families; and it was on the occasion of Rama and Lakshmun, the two sons of Raghoo, being at the hermitage of Valmika, when he set before them the exploits of their fathers, commanding them to sing them, that the following beautiful invocation occurs:

"Peace be to thee! resign thyself to sleep, and may nothing prevent thy repose, O son of Raghoo! all the trees are motionless, the beasts and birds are wrapped (in silence), and the face of nature is overspread with nocturnal darkness. Evening has receded by slow degrees,

and

and the constellations and this field of stars, resplendently shine as though the sky were covered with eyes. The expeller of the darkness of the world is risen, by its light, rejoicing the mind of animated nature."*

Amidst such reflections, I fell asleep, and was awakened by the same chorus, but whether in homage to the Mooni, Pluto, or some more benign divinity, I did not inquire. At seven in the morning, the monastery was still shrouded in mist, the prevalence of which renders it, though dressed in perpetual verdure, a bleak and dreary abode. I strolled into the garden, wrested from the mountain brow, and containing a few simple roots and vegetables, trusting that the sun might dispel the gloom and give me another view of the scene, but in vain.

The temple is well endowed, and the zeal of the pilgrims supplies all the wants of its inmates. Rao Sheo Sing, of Sarohi, recently expended ten thousand rupees in repairing it, and had also consecrated a golden chalice to Doorga Devi, the Cybele of Aboo; but the Rana of Burrur, pretending to have a dispensation from the goddess to partake of all her offerings, removed the gift of the Deora prince, and actually pleaded this privilege in defence of the sacrilegious burglary.

June 15th.—The barometer on which I most relied was broken on leaving Achil-éswar, where the difference between it and the remaining one amounted to no less than 1° 40′, the broken one being 26° 95′, and the other 25° 55′. At the shrine of Vashishta, the last stood at 26° 20′, thermometer 72°; the true height, therefore, of Aboo, must remain a desideratum until I reach the shore of the ocean, or be otherwise

* Book I. sec. 30, Carey and Marshman's Translation, 1808.

wise able to test its accuracy. The elevation, however, as thus indicated, accords with my own rough estimate, formed from the time occupied in ascent, the judgment of the eye, and the extent of vision over the surrounding region.

At eight A.M., commenced my descent amidst shoals of clouds. Our path was over a gradual declivity, frequently interrupted for several hundred yards by trees, which had been felled by the Rahtis for purposes of cultivation. An iron spud, with which they make a hole in the ground for the seed (chiefly of maize), is the sole substitute for the plough. There was abundance of the fruit called in Hindustan *falsa*, and the *karounda* accompanied us for about a third of the descent, and then suddenly disappeared. This spot may, therefore, be considered on the same level with that where I first met them on ascending, and where the plethoric barometer stood at 27° 35′. Many bulbous roots were shooting forth, and I was told that in a fortnight hence, when the rains shall have fairly commenced, the ground will be enamelled with flowers.

At eleven A.M., we reached the tank at the foot of the mountain, where I had ordered my people to meet me; but neither man nor horse was to be seen, and I was indebted to the civility of the Girwur chief, who furnished me with two of his own horses. On one I mounted my old Guru, and on the other a lame domestic, while I retained the celestial car to traverse the woods to Girwur, our place of halt, four miles distant. In passing through the tangled forest, which I have already described as fringing the base of Aboo, my little escort experienced the same fate as the barbarian king of Guzzerat. A legion of hornets, from some lofty *kor* trees, so called from the leprous-like *(koira)* bark, descending with furious impetuosity, fastened on every individual.

individual. *Sauve qui peut!* was the order of the day. The old Guru, like Johnny Gilpin, ventured to put his heels to his steed, his white vestments streaming like a meteor to the troubled air; the soldier threw away his firelock to facilitate his escape; the celestial car and its occupant were abandoned, and but for the charity of a domestic, who threw his *chudder* or mantle over me, I should have suffered doubly, being too ill to save myself by flight. Partly from this panoply, partly owing, as the Rahtis said, to my offerings to Achil-éswar, I remained unscathed. While waiting till the hum of our foes receded in the direction of pursuit, the lame domestic passed at full gallop on the Thakoor's mare, albeit big with foal, roaring out "*Ali Mudit!*" "For the aid of Ali!" The baker passed without either scarf or turban, and I was obliged to send back a pallet to bring in a Sipahi, who was so severely stung as to be unable to move.

At noon, we reached Girwur, where I found my tents just arrived from Palrie. The barometer now stood at 28° 60′, and as at Palrie, (the base of the point of ascent) this same instrument was 28° 50′, a value is at once stamped upon its results.

I have elsewhere mentioned that the natives estimate the external circumference of Aboo at from twenty to twenty-five coss, or forty to fifty miles. Of the approximation of this to the truth, the following rough sketch, founded on a direction I took from the highest peak, the Guru Sikar or Sikra, north, to the shrine of Vashishta, or rather to the tank at the base of its descent, will give a tolerable notion: it pretends not to exactitude. The general direction of this line is S.S.W., and with all its sinuosities and elevations, is estimated at eleven coss, or twenty-two miles; but we must add two coss, or four miles, more for the abrupt descent, were it practicable, from the Saint's Pinnacle to the plain,

plain, which would make the span of the mountain, with these inflexions, thirteen coss, or twenty-six miles, and this, *minus* a third, might give the direct horizontal distance, at the base, of seventeen miles, which would produce the maximum estimated circumference: but this I consider too much. Perhaps we might form a more correct estimate by calculating from the line contained between the Guru Sikra N., and the shrine of Vashishta S., considering these stations as the *terre-pleine* of Aboo. This line is eight estimated coss, or sixteen miles, including inflexions and inequalities of surface, but certainly not more than twelve miles in direct distance. With these extreme diameters of twelve and seventeen, we have a mean of about fifteen miles, or forty-five miles for the circumference, which is also the mean of the native computation.

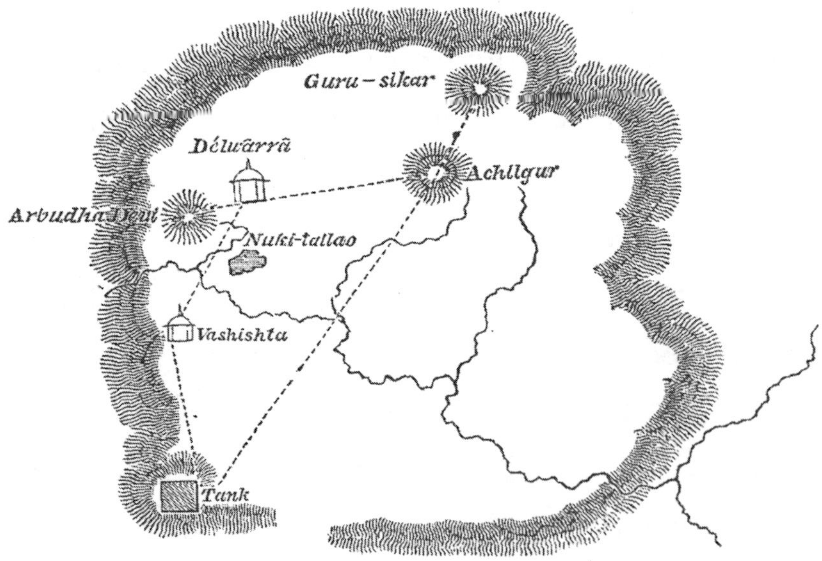

There is a singular analogy in some of the phenomena of nature between this sacred hill of the Hindus and one connected with the belief of the Christian, Mount Sinai, which, although four degrees more to the north, presents nearly the same variations of temperature, with the same results in the vegetable kingdom. The first of modern travellers,

travellers, the ingenuous and intrepid Burckhardt, was on the summit of Mount Sinai at the same period of the year that I was on Mount Aboo,—*i. e.* the middle of June. He says the thermometer at the base ranged from 100° to 110°, while the summit enjoyed the summer heat of England, 76°. With me, it ranged from 95° to 108° at the base, and on the summit from 64° to 76°. "The apricot, which ripens at Cairo at the end of April, was not," he says, "eatable on Mount Sinai in the middle of June:" a perfect coincidence with the state of the same indigenous fruit on Aboo, whose botany would appear to afford even a greater variety than the Mosaic Mount. Burckhardt does not record the height of Sinai,* but we may judge of it from the temperature, and the snow which covers its top in winter, a phenomenon never witnessed in India south of the Himalaya.

Now that my pilgrimage to Arbudha is over,† I feel content; it is one of my desiderata accomplished; but there is another in store, Chandravati, which I fear I must relinquish, and rest satisfied with being its discoverer. Aboo has completely demolished me; the fever raging, my face and hands prodigiously swollen and inflamed from a vertical sun, whose power was intensely felt through an atmosphere quite keen when his beams were withdrawn. The European traveller should mistrust his physical powers on this seductive mount, when cool, refreshing air tempts him to exertion, from which he eventually suffers. Moreover, none should approach it who cannot command more

* [The elevation of Mount Sinai is 7,952 E. feet.]

† I brought away a work called the *Aboo Mahatma* (a term applied to all the books relating to sacred places), which explains the rituals to be practised, interspersed with notices of princes who had either endowed or repaired its shrines, and of the "eight thousand various plants" found on its surface. This work, a fine specimen of caligraphy, is in Pracrit (if I recollect rightly), having an interlinear Sanscrit interpretation; but I had no leisure, when my Yuti tutor was with me, to examine its contents. It is now in the museum of the Royal Asiatic Society.

more time than I had, for a month at least is requisite merely to contemplate its precious and wonderful stores. A topographical map, views of its varied landscapes, plans, elevations, and sections of its shrines, and, if possible, casts of some of their details, sketches of the princes who have ruled, of its mythology, and varied superstitions, together with an account of its zoology, mineralogy, and botany, would form a work of no common interest.

This *opus magnum* we leave to the future traveller and lover of nature and the arts, whom we would, however, apostrophize in the words of the bard, whose muse would have found ample scope in these regions :

> Let such approach this consecrated land,
> And pass in peace along the magic waste,
> But spare its relics—let no busy hand
> Deface the scenes, already how defaced !
> Not for such purpose were these altars plac'd:
> Revere the remnants, nations once rever'd :
> So may our country's name be undisgrac'd.

Temple on Aboo.

REMAINS OF A BRAHMINICAL TEMPLE AT CHANDRAVARTI.

London, Published by W. H. Allen & Cº [illegible]

CHAPTER VII.

Girwur.—Chandravati.—Dilapidation of its relics.—Discovered by the Author.—Inscription.—Epochs of Chandravati.—Description of the ruined city.—Baories.—Coins.—Journal of Mrs. Blair.—Journey resumed.—Desertion of ancient roads.—Character of marauding tribes in the time of early European travellers.—Mountainous range.—Sarotra.—Return to the plains.—Cheerasani.—Palhanpoor.—Dewan of the district.—Antiquities of Palhanpoor.—Major Miles.—Sidpoor.—Ruins of the Roodra-Mala, a temple to Siva.—Inscriptions.

Girwur.—June 16th.—Heavy masses of clouds, congregating from the rainy quarter, indicate that the monsoon is at hand, and that I must push on, lest the swollen streams obstruct my passage to Baroda. With grief I renounce Chandravati, and the reader must rest satisfied with some slight details regarding it.

Chandravati, or, as it is pronounced, *Chandrôati*, to which, denoting it to be a fortified city, the word *Nagri* is added, bears S.E., and is ten miles distant, from Girwur, in which fief it is situated, and in the principality of Sarohi. Although indebted to the chief of Girwur for much civility and information, I cannot view with any antiquarian charity the dilapidator and salesman of what Time and the ruthless Toork have spared of its relics. Yet this sentiment is, perhaps, a false one, for it is already excluded from the haunt of man, and but for the cupidity of its owner, who derives a petty annuity from the sale of its remains, the link which connects it with the past might be lost. Nature herself, so prolific in these regions, is rapidly covering the glories of the Pramaras with an impenetrable veil. The silence of desolation reigns amongst these magnificent shrines, and the once populous streets, which religion and commerce united to fill with wealthy

wealthy votaries, are now occupied by the tiger and the bear, or the scarcely more civilized Bhil. With the destruction of Chandravati, the route of commerce was changed, and but for straggling passages in ancient books or inscriptions, it would not have left a record in the desert. The first intimation I had of it was from the *Bhoj Cheritra*,* in which it is related, that when Raja Bhoj was driven from the throne of Dhar by some northern invader, he fled to Chandravati, from which we may infer that it was then a fief of Dhar. Still my attempt to discover its position was long futile, chiefly, as I afterwards found, from the corruption of its name to Chundaôli. At length, one of my parties, roaming for inscriptions, discovered a clue to it on a reservoir at the village of Chaupi, in the chieftainship of Korabur, on the southern side of the Aravulli. This inscription, which mentions the international wars waged by the Gehlote princes of Cheetore, the Solankhis of Anhulwarra, the Pramaras of Chandravati, and the Chohans of Nadole, remarks, when touching the genealogy of the latter tribe: "Ari Sing had two sons, mighty warriors, Kanya and "Beetyuc; both fell in the battle of Chandravati-Nagri, fighting with "Sri-bhavan-gûpta. Sri-bhavan-gûpta had two sons, Bhima Sing and "Sri-loca Sing. In the heart of the dwelling of pleasure of Visala-"deva, Haradri, Kurrun, and Moolraj, did Bhima Sing, inflicting "wounds on mighty warriors, receive his death. His brother, Sri-loca, "attempting to gain the city of Sasra-Arjuna (now Chooli-Mahaswur, "on the Nerbudda), was killed on the field of battle at Bamunst'hali, "by his foeman Somaverma, prince of Malwa." A great deal follows before we reach the founder of the reservoir, whose date is S. 132 —the concluding

* Cited by me, in a paper printed in the *Transactions* of the Royal Asiatic Society, vol. I. p. 223, to settle the period of Raja Bhoj.

concluding cypher being obliterated, say S. 1325, or A.D. 1269. The allusion, however, to the battle of Chandravati, is about a century earlier, as is demonstrated by inscriptions of some of the actors there mentioned, *i. e.* Ari Sing Chohan, and Somaverma Pramara; the first of which I obtained at Nadole, the other in Haravati. Thus, from the history of Raja Bhoj we have two epochs of that of Chandravati; the first being in the seventh, the other in the twelfth century. How much earlier than the first it may have existed, we have only tradition to enable us to judge. We have likewise a third period, *i. e.*, the fifteenth century, when it was sacrificed to give life to the city of Ahmed, the new capital of Western India. I have detailed in the 'Annals' the rise of the dynasty which founded Ahmedabad, erected out of the ruins of Chandravati, and which not only eclipsed it, but also Anhulwarra, the more ancient capital of Guzzerat; but the city of Ahmed, whose architectural beauties proclaim the design and workmanship of the Hindu artist, is rapidly going to decay. When Ahmed, the grandson of the apostate Jaka,—better known in history under his Islamite name of Wujeh-ol-moolk,—determined to immortalize himself by a new capital, the site he chose was the residence of a community of Bhils, whose marauding exploits were the terror of the country; in order to commemorate whose extirpation, he disregarded its local disadvantages, and the city rose upon an uninteresting, unhealthy, low flat, on the banks of the Sahermaty. Not content with transporting the materials of Chandravati, he resolved that its soul as well as body should migrate—that the population should follow the spoils of the temples and the dwellings.* But the Jain votary, the soul of Chandravati, when placed between

* This general migration was once attempted by a still more magnificent madman than Ahmed—Mahmoud the Ghilji—who resolved that Dehli should take root on the Vindya Hills; but Mandoo and Ahmedabad shared the like fate.

between the Holies of his faith, Mounts Aboo and Arasinni, languished on the banks of the Sahermaty, and, like the banished Hebrew of old, wept by its waters, as he contemplated the gorgeous mosques erected from the shrines of his ancient abode.

But to return to Chandravati and its site. A little better than half-way to it from Girwur, and in the S.E. direction, is the village of Mahole, said to have been a suburb of the city, and at which stood one of its gates. The Bunas river passes Mahole and flows under the ruined city, which probably stretched along its banks. A low ridge, running southward from the base of Aboo, is crossed before reaching the village, and the route is through one continuous forest, where it was impossible for my baggage to penetrate. The city itself is now overgrown with jungle; its fountains and wells choked up, its temples destroyed, and the remains daily dilapidated by the Girwur chief, who sells the marble materials to any who have taste and money to buy them. Chandravati stands midway between the shrines of Amba-bhavani and Taringi on the one hand, and Aboo on the other; the former being fifteen miles east, the other the same distance west. They are almost equally attractive, and, like Aboo, are equally sacred to both Jain and Sivite. If we may credit tradition, this city was more ancient than Dhar, being the metropolis of Western India when the Pramar was paramount lord, to whom the *Nokoti Maroo-ca*, or 'Nine Castles' of the desert, were the grand subordinate fiefs. These are enumerated in a stanza elsewhere given,* shewing that the sway of this tribe extended from the Sutledge to the Nerbudda, and in which Dhar is mentioned as one of these fiefs. Although, as before stated, the word *Nagri* shews that Chandravati was a fortified city, yet the castle of Aboo must

* See 'Annals,' vol. i. p. 760.

MARBLE PILLARS AT CHANDRAVATI.

London, Published by W. H. Allen & Co. 1839.

must have been its stronghold in emergency; and however ineligible its position may now appear as a commercial mart, we must on the other hand remember that religion and traffic are twin-sisters in the East, and that every place of pilgrimage is a place of trade, and being in the centre of several, and little out of the route which served to convey the maritime commerce of both peninsulas over India, this must have ensured its prosperity. Were proof of it required, we have only to look at the work of the merchant-brothers on Aboo. The date of this shrine, S. 1287 or A.D. 1231, forty years after the subjugation of Northern India by the Islamite, strikingly attests the magnitude of its wealth, the power of its princes, and the yet undecayed condition of the arts. It is evident, however, notwithstanding the inscription says "the umbrella of the godlike Dharaburz alone shaded Chandravati," that he acknowledged the paramount sovereignty of Anhulwarra, from which dependance his ancestor, Jaita, had been snatched, and gave his allegiance with his daughter "the wise Echinie," to Pirthi Raj, the last Rajpoot monarch of Dehli.* That the Pramaras did not long preserve independence after Dharaburz, is evident from an inscription found at the shrine of Vashishta, recording the conquest of Aboo by Kanir-deo Chohan, prince of Jhalore, and containing the following singular adjuration: that should the Pramar regain his birthright, his religious grant should be perpetuated to the shrine, under the penalty of sixty thousand years' residence in hell. There is no date to this, but as his

* One of the sixty-nine books of the last of the bards, Chund, is devoted to the war for the restoration of the independence of Aboo and Chandravati, subjugated by Bhima, sovereign of Anhulpoor, and which ended in his defeat and death. Jaita, who had his dominions restored, became one of the most renowned of the hundred and eight Sawunts or leaders, and his son, Lacshan, eventually became Premier to the Chohan.

his son, Beerum-deo, was driven from Jhalore by Alla-u-din in S. 1347, or A.D. 1291, it is probable that Kanir-deo wrested Aboo from Preladum, the son of Dharaburz. At all events, it was a transitory acquisition; for the Deora Annals state that it was Rao Loombho who made a final conquest of Aboo and Chandravati; of the former in S. 1352, or A.D. 1296; of the latter in S. 1359, or A.D. 1303. The battle which transferred the sovereignty of the Pramaras to the Deoras was fought at the village of Baraillee, where Merhutungi, son of Aggun Sén, fell with seven hundred of his kindred. Between these periods, however, the Chohans had been gradually reducing the inferior fiefs of the Pramaras, each conquest giving birth to a new branch, and many of these being made without the aid of their Suzerain, their descendants are disposed to pay but a scanty obedience to his representative; such are the chieftains of Madar, Girwur, &c.

But however interesting such details may be to the investigator of Hindu antiquities, the general reader can scarcely participate in this feeling. I shall, therefore, take leave of ancient Chandravati, which, on the foundation of Sarohi by Rao Subboo, in S. 1461, or A.D. 1405, as well as Ahmedabad, fell into utter decay. I sent a party to the ruins, from whose report I might better judge than from the gossip of my Deora friends, for whom these relics have no charms. Their accounts only the more excited my desire to visit one of the most important of my discoveries, which I rank with Arore on the Indus, Soorpoora on the Jumna, Barolli on the Chumbul, Chandrabhaga in Harouti, and many other long forgotten names. They spoke in raptures of the temples, and *Baoris*, or reservoirs, yet remaining; of

> Columns strewn on the waste sand,
> And statues fall'n and cleft,
> Heap'd like a host in battle overthrown,

which

which remain to immortalize the pencil of some future traveller. It is a curious fact, that sacred architecture alone remains in India to indicate the past state of this art. There are scarcely any vestiges of civil architecture, except in Cheetore; but wherever they do exist, they are at once apparent, from the walls having a *talus*, or external slope, like the Egyptian. We may include in the domestic structures, those useful and ornamental excavations called *baoris*, which serve both as reservoirs and abodes in the hot season. Some of these are on a gigantic scale, and may be described generally as circular pits, from twenty to fifty feet in diameter, and of depth proportionate to the springs. Suites of chambers, story below story, approached by a staircase, surround them from the surface to the water's edge, which, in hot weather, form delightful retreats for the chiefs and their families. Unless the internal slopes are prominent and walled with cyclopean masses, the external pressure, conjoined with the ever-springing vegetation so destructive to edifices in India, reduces them, in the course of a few centuries, to ruin. It is rarely that the treasuries of the modern princes permit them to indulge in such luxuries. The sole exception within my knowledge, is the Boondéla prince of Dutteah, who has constructed one both solid and capacious.

My exploring party likewise found among the ruins three antique coins of the Pramaras, on one of which the legend is visible. And here I check my own dull chronicle of the past, to enliven my page with an extract from the journal of the friend to whose pencil my work is indebted for its chief attractions. The world will look upon the monuments of past ages with redoubled interest, when it learns that no traces of them longer exist. The dilapidator of Girwur, whom I have already anathematized, has "done his worst," and the domed shrine of

Siva

Siva and those magnificent toruns, or arches, of the Unitarian Jain, have been despoiled, sold, and converted into lime, probably to cement some structure ignoble as the spoiler.

"The ruins of Chundrawuttee, which was anciently the capital of the Pramar Rajahs, are situated about twelve miles from the foot of the Aboo mountain, on the banks of the Bunass, and in a fine well-wooded country. The city is said to be mentioned in ancient legendary tales and poems, but until the beginning of the year 1824, when this view was taken, it had never been visited by Europeans, to whom it was scarcely known even by tradition, and its past history is lost, except some particulars in the possession of Colonel Tod. The city, to judge from the fragments of marble and stone strewn over an extensive plain, must have been of considerable size, and its pretensions to great refinement and riches, may be admitted from the beautiful specimens still remaining of its marble edifices, of which twenty of different sizes were discovered when the spot was first visited by his Excellency Sir Charles Colville and his party in January 1824. The one here represented is Brahminical, and adorned with rich sculptured figures and ornaments in high relief, those of the human form being nearly statues, and only attached to the building sufficiently for their own support. They are executed with a degree of excellence scarcely equalled in Indian sculpture, and which would not in some instances disgrace more cultivated artists. Of these images there are one hundred and thirty eight. The smallest are two feet high and placed in niches of the most elegant workmanship. The principal figures are a Triad, or three-headed statue, with a female seated on his knee, sitting on a car, with a large goose in front:—Siva with twenty arms:—the same with a buffalo on his left, the right foot raised and resting on a small figure,

TEMPLE AT CHANDRAVATI.

figure, resembling Garud: a figure of Death with twenty arms, one holding a human head by the hair; a victim lying beneath, and a nymph on each side; one seems drinking the blood falling from the head, the other devouring a human hand:—with many others, surrounded by different attributes and in various postures: but the most admirable are the dancing nymphs, with garlands and musical instruments, many being extremely graceful and well executed. This building is entirely formed of white marble, and the prominent parts have retained their lustre; but those which recede are become dark from the influence of weather and atmosphere, adding to, rather than diminishing, the effect of the rich carving.

"The interior of the temple and centre dome is highly finished; but the roof and exterior of the domes have lost their outer coating of marble. The pillars in the foreground of the drawing appear to have been part of a colonnade, which once surrounded the temple: they are of marble, which material is strewn over the adjacent ground in great profusion, and columns, statues, cornices, and slabs, are tossed in heaps all around.

And many a proud
Cotemporary pile the Wilderness
Environs with her solitary waste,
Where mortal visits rarely—save the step
Of Eastern Bandit over the deep wild
Tracking the Beast of Deserts."

June 16th.—Sarotra.—Being sufficiently recovered from my fatigues, and laden with all that tradition and the Scalds of Sarohi could supply, I struck my tents. At ten A.M., the thermometer 86°, barometer 28° 90′, distance ten miles, general direction S.S.W. The road lay through a deep forest, consisting chiefly of *Dho* trees, and although quite practicable for foot-passengers and oxen, I was obliged to send

on

on men with hatchets, to clear the way for the larger animals. No better proof can be given of the abandoned condition of this country, once the highway of commerce between the sea-ports and Northern India, than this relapse of civilization into a state of nature. Here, with all the wonders of Aboo, Taringi, and Chandravati around us, the one fallen, the other fast sinking into decay, we can speculate upon the Hindu doctrine of the destruction of worlds, and the passions of their lordly inhabitants. These roads, once crowded with caravans of commerce and of pilgrims, or resounding to the tramp of the war-horse, were now little trodden, save by the foot of the savage Koli, who finds shelter amidst his own indigenous woods and rocks. This tract was celebrated, in the first days of European travel, for the loose, marauding habits of the *Razbouts*, as well as the Kolis, whose manners, as detailed by Thévenot and Olearius, prove that the *morale* of my Deora friends is not worse now than in the days of Shah Jehan.*

Four miles from Girwur, we crossed a rivulet, called the Kalairè, which has its source in a small lake, named Moongt'hal, four miles west of the first mentioned town. On our right, bearing due west and four miles distant, rose a lofty three-peaked mountain, on which is a temple dedicated to Aya-Mata, also called Isani, the tutelary divinity of the Kolis. This, and the effigy of the horse, are the only objects of adoration among this aboriginal race.† This Tricuta, or triple-pinnacled

* "Nous rencontrâmes une *Caffila*, ou caravane, de marchands Benjans, qui nous dirent, qu'ils avoient été attaquez par deux cens voleurs Razbouts, qui les avoient contraints de se rançonner de cent *ropias*, et que nous devions nous tenir sur nos gardes; parceque, le jour précedent, ils 'en avoient vû cent autres, qui, ayant appris d'eux ce qu'ils avoient payé à leurs camarades, ne leur avoient rien dit, et s'etoient contentez d'emmener un de leurs bœufs; mais qu'ils alloient joindre les prémiers, et qu'ils ne manqueroient pas de nous attaquer."—*Olearius*, vol. i. liv. 1, 113.

† This is the first time I ever saw a personification of Mother Earth; such is Isáni, from *Isa*, 'goddess,' and *Awani*, 'earth,' the universal nurse-mother, (*aya-mata*). Whether the worship of the

pinnacled hill, is the commencement of a range which runs westward to Deesa and Dantiwarra, and, though superficially unconnected with it, no doubt has a subterranean union, as well as the more prominent ridge on the left, crossed midway between Girwur and Chandravati, and which afterwards, though broken, shews some fine picturesque and primitive peaks rising as it were out of impervious woods, which form a foreground; while the giant Aravulli, towering in the eastern horizon, fills up the distance, having a fine valley between, fifteen miles in breadth, watered by the Bunas. It is from this point, where crowned with the shrines of Arisinni and Taringi, that the Aravulli sweeps away to the south, encircling Poloh and Eedur, and with more or less continuity and elevation, to the Nerbudda, which severs it from the Indian Apennines, the Koncan chain, terminating at the bridge of Rama. I omitted to mention that this broken ridge on the left ceases at Dantal, twenty miles distant, the residence of a chief of the Rajpoot race, called Burrur, with the title of Rana. This tribe is said to be originally from the valley of Sinde, and the legend says that his ancestry were conveyed thence by Bhavani herself, from whom he has license to divide with her all offerings of gold and silver made at any of her shrines. This is the chief who abstracted the golden chalice from the temple of Arbudha Devi; and here was another charge against him, of having laid impious hands on a cup presented by the chieftain of Daroo to the Cybele of Arasinni. If his origin was Sinde, his ancestors must have been transplanted many centuries ago, though the terrific Devi still has a shrine and worshippers far west of the Indus, on the shores of Mekran.

At

the horse is typical of the sun, "the swiftest of created, representing the swiftest of uncreated objects," I know not; but in this they resemble the other forest tribes, the Bhils and Séryas.

At the village of Kuraitur, midway between Girwur and Sarotra, we crossed the Bunas, which, emerging for a moment from the coverts of the forest, passes on to Sarotra, where we encamped on her banks. The forest was alive with wild-fowl crowing in all directions, and the cuckoo accompanied us as far south as Cheerasani: the Kolis call this bird *sûk'hi*, or 'ease-giving'—perhaps as expressive as Kaméri, 'the bird of love.' In the valley of Oodipoor, and on the plateau about Kotah, they apply other epithets to this bird, alike indicative of its being sacred to Cama-deva. The psychologist cannot fail to be surprised at finding a metaphorical language and allegorical allusions of the most sentimental cast amongst these uncivilized denizens of the mountain and forest, whose occupations are so incongruous. Sarotra is in Koliwara, and is the head of a small talook or tithing. The language changed rapidly. At Sarohi we could make ourselves understood, but here with great difficulty, and only on the commonest subjects. These are the descendants of the Koli friends of Bernier, who will pursue the same mode of life until the axe is laid to their forest, which is as old as Isáni herself. Chandravati is reckoned eight coss, and Dantah thirteen, from hence. The shrine of Vashishta bore N. 25° E., and the triple-peaked hill from N. 25° to 35° E.

June 17th.—Cheerasani.—Direction S. S.W., distance eleven miles and a half. Here our eyes were again blessed with a sight of the plains. For the first seven miles, the road was through the same deep forest, at the termination of which a village had been recently established by the chief of Palhanpoor. Two miles further, we crossed a stream, called the *Balaram balla*, or rivulet, flowing from the Aravulli, and which joins the Bunas four miles below a small temple dedicated to Bala-rama, whence its name. Here ceased the forest, through which

we

we had marched from the skirt of Aboo, a distance of twenty-five miles. The broken ridge, described in yesterday's route as occasionally rising into lofty peaks, still preserved the same character, and ran parallel to our route, at the distance of four to five miles, as did the Isáni range, diverging in a S.W. line to Dantiwarra. Towards the end of this day's march, the sandy nature of the soil increased, and the plants underwent a corresponding change. In lieu of the lofty *dho* and the variegated *kesoola*, of whose leaves they form cups and platters by means of rivets of grass, we had the babool *(mimosa arabica)*, the evergreen *peloo*, and the *khureel*, all inhabitants of the desert. At every step the sand augmented. The declivity of the country throughout this march was apparent to the eye, and was confirmed by the barometer, which at noon stood at 28° 80′, and the thermometer 96°. From a knoll near Cheerasani, I took my last bearing of Aboo, N.N.E.

June 18th.—Palhanpoor.—Direction S.S.W. distance nine miles. This town is the head of a small independent district, which is now under the protection of the British Government, in the presidency of Bombay. Half-way, its chief, or as he is styled, *Dewan*, did me the honour of a greeting, and with great courtesy conducted me to his city, where he saw me safely lodged under the hospitable roof of Major Miles, the resident agent, through whose judicious superintendence the town was rapidly rising to prosperity. The Dewan is a Mahomedan, and his ancestors held Jhalore and other dependencies, alike ephemeral, in grant from the kings of Guzzerat, whence they were expelled by the Rahtores. The Dewan is a young man of promise, of great propriety of demeanour, and all about him indicated comfort and respectability. His retainers are chiefly Sindies, holding lands for service. Palhanpoor is walled, and said to contain six thousand habitations. It was an ancient appanage of Chandravati, and claims especial notice from having been founded by Pal Pramara, whose name it bears and whose statue it contains. The respect paid to him, however, is rather of an equivocal character, as he is nearly imbedded in a heap of lime, amassed for the repairs of the shrine which shelters him. Whether this statue originally belonged to Palhanpoor, or was brought from Chandravati, I know not; but it is of far inferior stamp to the slayer of the Bucentaur on Aboo, though the general costume and character are the same. It is either very antique or very modern; but the appearance certainly does not authorize the latter conclusion. Palhanpoor also boasts of being the birth-place of that beacon-light amongst the Balhara kings, the great Sid-Rae. If she has a title to this distinction, his mother, the wife of Raja Kurrun, must have been travelling elsewhere with her precious burthen, to pay her vows, than to the shrine of the Hindu Cybele, west of the Indus, as stated in the history of Komarpal; but more of this hereafter.

I remained all this day and the next with Major Miles, and have seldom passed eight and forty hours more agreeably; for in him I not only found a courteous and friendly brother-officer, but one whose mind was imbued with the same taste and pursuits as my own. We had much to talk over and to compare, and our general conclusions as to the character of the dynasties of ancient days were the same. It was gratifying to find in the wilderness one pursuing similar avocations with myself. I gave the Major the strongest proof I could of my esteem, in a duplicate of the Bactrian medal of Apollodotus, which I obtained either from the ruins of the ancient Avinti, or from the sacred lake at Ajmér.

SIDPOOR.

SIDPOOR.—JUNE 20th.—In the infancy of our geography of India, the illustrious D'Anville said of this city, "*ville qui tire son nom des Shites, ou toiles peintes, qui s'y fabriquent;*" but it boasts of a more dignified etymology, being called after its patron, the Balhara prince, Sid-Rae. By some he is supposed to be the founder, but there is every reason to believe that he was only the renovator, of this place, the position of which on the Sarasvati, flowing from the shrine of Amba-bhavani, is well-chosen. Here are the remains of what in past ages must have been one of the grandest efforts of Hindu architecture, a temple dedicated to Siva, and termed Roodra-Mala, or 'the chaplet of Roodra,' the god of battle; but so disjointed are the fragments, that it is difficult to imagine what it may have been as a whole. They are chiefly portions of porticoes, one of which tradition names the prostyle of the munduff, or vaulted mansion occupied by the bull, companion of Roodra, whose *sanctum* was converted into a mosque. It is said to have been a rectangular building, five stories in height, and if we may judge from one portion yet remaining, this could not have been less than one hundred feet. This portion is a mass of two stories, each supported by four columns, and the columns of a third story, preserving, without any entablature, their perfect perpendicularity:

> Self-poised, the top-stone seems to rock,
> But ages past have seen it mock
> The winter's storm or earthquake's shock,

which have levelled the glories of its more modern neighbour, the city of Ahmed.* The pencil of my friend and fellow academical, the Honourable

* The minarets of its finest mosque, called the shaking minars, from the vibratory motion which could be given by any individual on their summit, were, with many other splendid objects, thrown down by earthquakes, and would scarcely have been known but for the pencil of Captain Grindlay, who has preserved them in his interesting work, 'The Scenery and Costumes of Western India.'

Honourable Lincoln Stanhope, enables me to give this singular remnant to the public. It is built of a coarse sand-stone, containing much small granulated quartz, and the sculpture is like the edifice and the material, bold but rough. I found two inscriptions, from one of which I learned that it was commenced by Raja Moolraj (the founder of the Solankhi dynasty of Anhulwarra), in S. 998 (A.D. 942), and from the other that it was finished by Sid-Raj. The following is the translation: "In Samvat 1202 (A.D. 1146), the fourth of the month "of Mâg, the obscure half of the moon, know that the Solankhi Sid "completed the Roodra-Mala, and with pure mind performed worship "to Siva, thereby leaving a name in the world."

A couplet records its destruction by All-u-din :—"In S. 1353 (A.D. "1297), came the barbarian Alla: the Roodra-Mala he levelled, "carrying destruction amongst the lords of men." This is the very year, according to Ferishta, of the conquest of Guzzerat, and the massacre of its prince Kurrun, erroneously called 'the Gohil' by that historian; but even this remorseless tyrant, whose *nom de guerre* was *Khoni*, or 'the sanguinary,' appears to have been actuated by some compunctious visitings, when he spared so much of this splendid temple of idolatry. Besides these fragments of inscriptions, my scouts obtained me the acquaintance of Sankla, the chronologist, who was crammed with tradition, and who spouted a volume of antiquarian metrical lore, of which the following is a sample:—"The temple to "Roodra had 1,600 columns: 121 statues to Roodra, each in its sepa- "rate cella: 121 golden pinnacles (*cullus*): 1,800 smaller statues of "other divinities: 7,212 resting-places in and about the temple: "125,000 carved screens: and of other *pootlis* or images, namely, of "heralds bearing flags, heroes, demigods, mortals, or animals, thou-

"sands

" sands and tens of thousands." But every-where tradition says, that Sid-Rae expended " fourteen millions of pieces of gold" upon it, though the value of each piece is not specified. The chief fragment of this once superb monument is enclosed and half-hidden by the huts of Koli weavers, who one of these days may have their fragile habitations as well as their own heads broken by some of Roodra's skulls falling amongst them;* for although the foundations are on a rock, I have found that the earthquake of 1819, which was felt throughout all Western India, threw down two of the loftiest columns. The only good view which can be obtained of the ruins, is from the interior of these sheds, which form but an indifferent foreground to the picture.

* The chaplet (*mala*) of Roodra, a name of Siva, as the ensanguined god of battle, is composed of human crania,—the drinking-cups of the Rajpoot heroes of past days.

Gateway of the Fort of Unchulgurh, top of Aboo.

CHAPTER VIII.

KINGDOM OF NEHRWALEH.

Nehrwaleh, the ancient capital of Western India.—Its site discovered by the Author.—Inferiority of the Arabian to the Greek geographers of ancient India.—Errors in respect to the position of Nehrwaleh, or Anhulwarra.—Mistake of Gosselin, and probable accuracy of Herodotus.—Annals of ancient Anhulwarra, the Tyre of India.—Origin of the title 'Balhara.'—Sun-worship.—Remains of the city of Balabhi.—Change of capital from Balabhi to Anhulwarra.—The *Komarpal Cheritra,* or chronicle of Anhulwarra.—Extracts therefrom —Synchronisms.—Proofs that historical works are not unknown in India.—Traditional foundation of Anhulpoor.—Revolutions in India at this epoch.—Sudden magnificence of the city.—List of its princes.—Balhara coin.—Relation of the Mahomedan travellers in the ninth century.

Notwithstanding the immense strides which geography has made since the days of the illustrious D'Anville, and my no less illustrious countryman, Rennell, the position of Nehrwaleh, the ancient capital of Western India, was still amongst the desiderata until, in 1822, I discovered, in one of the suburbs of modern Puttun, and touching the ruined Acropolis of the Balhara kings, the name which to this day had puzzled the most celebrated geographers, ancient and modern. The name of this suburb is *Anurwarra,* and in the more correct orthography of the annals of its dynasties, Anhulwarra, whence the very slight corruption of *Nehelvarê, Nehewaleh,* or, as in Edrisi, *Nahroara.* How many able heads have been at work upon this name—Greek, Arabian, French, English, German,—exemplifying the adage, that even the errors of the learned are wise! All have at least concentrated their scattered rays upon the illustrious dynasties which ruled in this hidden capital, and were known throughout the East as the Balhara, or more correctly

correctly Balha-raes, 'exalted kings.' When we contrast the lucid intelligence, slight as it is, on oriental subjects, which guided the pens of Justin, Strabo, and Arrian,* with the crude, incomprehensible details of the Arabian travellers, many centuries later, we are at a loss to account for the discrepancies of the latter; for while the position traced by the first writers is scarcely liable to doubt, that assigned by the Arabians is so vague as to apply equally to any part of the kingdom, so much so as to raise a question in my mind as to the existence of such travellers, the more especially that, as far as regards that portion with which I am acquainted, the world would have lost nothing had their account never seen the light. The translator of these "Arabian travellers of the ninth century," the Abbé Renaudot, in a long prefatory discourse, attacks every wayfarer in the paths of Arabian literature, from Greaves, the translator of Abulféda, to honest Sir John Chardin, not even sparing the learned Hyde; but, excepting some slight phonetic resemblance in the names of towns, with the mention of the silver currency, both of which facts they might have obtained from any common sailor, without quitting their own "happy" shores, the whole appears apocryphal; at all events, so equivocal is the production as far as regards "the Balhara kings of Moharmi al Adar, or of those who have their ears bored," that the literary world would not have lost an iota of knowledge had the "*Relations anciennes*" of M. Renaudot never appeared. The commentators, Arabian and European, after wasting a great deal of ingenious conjecture, have done little to illuminate this darkness. Following Ulug Beg, the princely astronomer of Samarcand,

* Author of the Periplus, and who resided at Baroach, or, as he called it, Barugaza, as a commercial agent, in the second century of our era; Baroach was within the Balhara sovereignty.

cand, they fix the site of Anhulwarra in 22° north latitude, thus bringing it into the Gulf of Cambay, and making this, the sea-port, the ancient capital itself, whose actual position is 23° 48′ north, and longitude 27° 10′ east. How different is the notice given by El Edrisi, in the twelfth century! It is true he has said little, but that little is accurate as regards the extent of the Balhara kingdom, its riches, commerce, and religion, and confirms all my own previously conceived opinions on these points.

Happily—perhaps unhappily for many—the time is past which admitted of literary fraud, or when the loose or corrupt text of a credulous authority, such as Herodotus, could illumine the pages of such men as Gosselin with brilliant nothings. This justly celebrated geographer pours forth all the vials of his wrath upon the father of Indian geography, our own Rennell, for daring even to suppose that the *Padeens,* Ichthyophagists or Anthropophagists of the Indus, could have been allowed a habitation on the fair Ganges; and in the excess of charity for his error, supposes he must have been led into the mistake by the word *Paddar,* ("meaning the Ganges in Sanscrit,") for which he complacently quotes Pomponius Mela as his authority! Seizing the old geographical error, that a river named Paddar issued from the hills at Ajmér and flowed into the Gulf of Cutch, he deems it proof demonstrative that there only should be found the Padeens of Herodotus, and sneers at our countryman for the "*idée bizarre de chercher à confondre les Padeens avec les Gangarides.*"* It is amusing to see scholars quarrelling about the shadow of a shade; there is no Paddar flowing from Ajmér into the Cutch Gulf, and the Salt River, or Loony, which thence has its source and flows into the great Runn, or

* "*Recherches sur la Géographie des Anciens,*" par Gosselin.

or salt marsh overflowed by the Indus, has no Padeens on its banks. As Herodotus does describe his Padeens as hunters, and eating raw flesh, it is most probable he had heard of the class termed *Pardis*, the hunters and fowlers to this day of India, but whose abode, like their occupation, is unrestricted.*

I now proceed to illustrate the state of the kingdom of Anhulwarra from its own Annals, with something of its present condition, from personal observation.

Of the ancient Nehrwaleh, which D'Anville had set his heart upon discovering, we may say, as did the Jewish prophet of old, " and they " shall weep for thee in bitterness of heart, and lament over thee; " saying, 'What city is like Tyre?'" Anhulwarra was the Tyre of India, though not a sea-port, her port being that of Cambay; neither is it improbable that ancient Tyre did contribute to the varied commerce of this city, through which ramified the produce of Africa and Arabia from the remotest times; nor that the mariners of Hiram, the ally and carrier of Solomon, may have found their way to the land of the Sauras—the Syria of India.

Previously to furnishing extracts from the *Komár-pál Charitra*, a historical work, which sketches the dynasties that ruled over Anhulwarra, it may be as well to ascend to a more remote period, in order to trace the origin of the title, *Balhara*, assumed by its successive sovereigns. Amongst the earliest of the tribes which conquered a settlement in the peninsula of Saurashtra (the most interesting region in

* We are gravely informed by the same author (p. 222), that the Syrastrene has its name from a small village called Syrastra, "*vers le fond du Golfe de Cutch;*" and again, vol. iii. p. 224, where a similarity of sound sufficed to establish a fact, that, "*Dunga se reconnoit avec une simple transposition de deux lettres dans le petit village de Gundar.*"

in all India) was the Balla, by some authorities stated to be a branch of the great Indu-vansa, and hence termed Bali-ca-pútrá, and said to have been originally from Balica-des,* or Balk, the Bactria of the Greeks. Whatever truth there may be in this tradition, it is powerfully corroborated by the Bardic title bestowed on the chiefs of this race, *i. e.* "*Tatta Mooltan ca Rae.*" Another authority asserts that Balla was the son of Lava (pronounced *Lao*), eldest son of Rama; that he conquered the ancient city of Dhaûk, also known as Moongy-patun, capital of the region, or division of the peninsula, called Bâlâ-khetra; that in process of time they founded the city of Balabhi, and assumed the title of Bala-râé; that they were consequently of the race of Surya, not Indu: and of this stock are the Ranas of Méwar. The present chief of Dhaûk, who, when I passed, was in confinement, is a Balla. The Balla pays adoration almost exclusively to the Sun, and it is only in Saurashtra that temples to this orb abound;† so that religion, tradition as regards their descent, and personal appearance, all indicate an Indo-scythic origin for this race, and in order to conceal their barbarian *(mletcha)* extraction, the fable of their birth from Rama may have been devised. The city of Balabhi, written *Wulleh* in the maps, and now an inconsiderable village, was said to be twelve coss, or fifteen miles, in circumference. From its foundations, gigantic bricks, from one and a half to two feet in length, are still dug; but of this hereafter. Enough has been said to trace the origin of the Balhara of the Arabian travellers,

* Its former importance is still recognised in its epithet of Um-ul-Belad, the 'mother of cities,' as we are informed by Mr. Elphinstone.

† There is a Sun-temple at Baroda, dedicated to Surya Narayana; the object of worship of the prime minister of the Guicowar, who is of the Purvoe caste, descended, I believe, from the ancient Guebre. There is also, if I mistake not, a Sun-temple at Benares.

travellers, the Baleokouras of Ptolemy; for, even in the second century, it had claims to the attention of the royal geographer of Egypt.

We shall at once commence our extracts from the *Komár-pál Charitra*, which will introduce the change of dynasty and capital, when the Chaura or Saura succeeded to the Balla, and transferred the *gádi* from Balabhi to Anhulwarra. This work, consisting of thirty-eight thousand slocas or stanzas, the original of which is in Sanscrit, was composed by Sailug Soor Acharya, a celebrated teacher of the Jains, in the reign of the prince whose name it bears, who ruled from A.D. 1143 to 1166, and whose life it is chiefly intended to illustrate.* In order, however, to connect the history of the dynasty to which he belongs, the Solankhi, with the Chaura, which preceded, the author commences with the establishment of the latter in S. 802 (A.D. 746), the epoch of the foundation of Anhulwarra, passing over very succinctly the princes prior to his own, and what he does insert is from the *Vans Raj Charitra*, or history of the founder of Anhulwarra, a work whose existence I ascertained, and only through a mistake, failed to obtain a copy of it. I shall neither follow the order in which it is written, nor give it *verbatim*, but take such extracts as suffice to develope the past greatness of this kingdom, commencing with a chronological table of its dynasties, with a few comments on such of the princes whose actions were remarkable. I am too well aware, that such details can afford little

* There is a version of this work in the dialect of Guzzerat, and it was a copy of this, obtained from the Rana's library at Oodipoor, written in S. 1492 (A.D. 1436), which I first translated. It was evidently from this version that Abulfazil composed his sketch of the ancient history of Guzzerat, and furnished his list of its dynasties. Subsequently I obtained from the library at Anhulwarra a transcript of the Sanscrit original, which, by the aid of my Jain Yuti, I likewise translated, and which proved the fidelity of the Guzzerati version. Both editions I presented to the Royal Asiatic Society.

little general interest; and they are therefore more especially addressed to those who continue blindly to assert that the Hindus had no such thing as historical works of any kind.

DYNASTIES OF ANHULWARRA.

FIRST.—CHAORA, CHAWURA, OR SAURA DYNASTY.

Names of Princes.	Date of Installation.		Length of each Reign.	Remarks.
	Samvat.	A.D.		
Bunsraj	802	746	50	The chronicle says, "he ruled fifty years and lived sixty."
Joograj	852	796	35	
Kheemraj	887	831	25	First Arabian traveller (A.H. 237, A.D. 851), and second (A.H. 254, A.D. 868.)
Boerji	912	856	29	
Birsing	941	885	25	
Rutnadit	966	919	15	
Samunt	981	925	7	Reigned till S. 988, or A.D. 932.
			186	

SECOND.—SOLANKHI DYNASTY.

Names of Princes.	Samvat.	A.D.	Length of each Reign.	Remarks.
Moolraj	988	932	56	Commenced the monument of Sidpoor.
Cháond, or Chamund	1044	988	13	Conquered by Mahmood A.H. 416, or S. 1064 according to Abulfazil.
Balli Rao, or Ballabi Sén	1057	1001	½	Mahmood placed on the throne one of the Ancient Rajas, perhaps this Ballabi.
Doorlub, or Nahr-rao	1057	1001	11½	Cotemporary with Moonj of Dhar, father of Bhoj, whom he visited on resigning his throne to Bhímdeo.
Bhímdeo	1069	1013	42	Confederacy of the Hindu princes against the Moslems, in A.D. 1044.
Kurrun	1111	1055	29	Subjugated the Kolis and Bhils.
Sidraj Jey-sing	1140	1084	49	
Komár-pál	1189	1133	33	
Chonipál, Aji-pál, or Jeipál	1222	1166	3	Cotemporary with Jey Sing of Canooj.
Bhola Bhímdeo	1225	1169	3	Antagonist of Pirthi-raj of Delhi.
Ballo Mooldeo	1228	1172	21	Reigned till S. 1249, or A.D. 1193.
			261	

THIRD.—BHAGAILA DYNASTY, still called Chalook in Inscriptions.

Names of Princes.	Date of Installation.		Length of each Reign.	REMARKS.
	Samvat.	A.D.		
Beesildeo	1249	1193	15	
Bhímdeo	1264	1208	42	Aboo inscriptions.
Arjundeo	1306	1250	23	Somnath inscriptions.
Sarungdeo	1329	1273	21	
Gehlá Kurrundeo	1350	1294	3	Ended S. 1354, or A D. 1298; according to Ferishta, a year earlier.
			104	

The two first dynasties are exclusively from the *Komár-pál Charitra*, which work terminates with Komár-pál; the concluding names of this dynasty, as well as that which follows, are from two sources: first, from the genealogies of the bard of the Solankhi chieftains, descended from that line, and now dwelling in Méwar; and secondly, from a miscellany of genealogical, geographical, and historical matter, in the western dialect, obtained from a Jain priest.* Moreover, I have tested the chronological accuracy of these royal lines by a series of inscriptions, collected during twenty years' research, which, with transcripts from the annals of other families, establish a tissue of synchronical evidence, such as few Oriental histories may claim. These will be briefly noticed as we advance. We may remark *en passant*, that the sage Abulfazil did not pronounce *ex cathedrâ*, like our own critics, that the Hindus had nothing approaching to history. He begins his "Summary of the kings of Guzzerat" thus: "*In the books of the Hindus it is* "*written,*

* This contains a chronological list of all the dynasties of Anhulwarra, an account of the source and course of the *western* Bunas river, and various matters highly interesting to the antiquary.

"*written*, that in the year S. 802 of the era of Bikramajit, correspond-"ing with A.H. 154,* Bans Raj was the first king who made Guzzerat "an independent monarchy." He proceeds with the details, which vary in some degree from the *Charitra*, though it is evident the original source is the same.

Now, if from the foundation of Anhulwarra, in S. 802 (A.D. 746), to its destruction by Alla-u-din in S. 1354 (A.D. 1298), we can establish an unbroken chain of princes, cotemporary with Charlemagne, the Caliph Haroun, and the Saxon Heptarchs, down to the Plantagenet John, shall we still be told that the Hindus have nothing even approaching to history? If it be meant that the philosophy of history is not intermingled with the narrative of events, *à la bonne heure*; but, because the Jain monk, in the year S. 1220, did not deem it necessary to draw deductions from the facts which led to Komár-pál's assumption of the crown of the Balharas, are we, therefore, entitled to say, these facts do not belong to history? Look to the Saxon, the Ulster, and the French chronicles of this period—the foundation of the superstructures of Hume, Hallam, Vernet, &c.,—are they materially more copious or philosophical? Let us, then, abandon this assumption, which serves only to palliate the apathy of those whose researches are restricted to a contracted sphere of observation, and which, if not controverted, would quench the spirit of discovery. I repeat that we must examine the Jain libraries of Jessulmér and Anhulwarra, and the numerous private collections of princes and chiefs in Rajpootana, before

* Abulfazil's comparative chronology (or that of his translator) is here at fault. A.D. 802 — 56 = 746; but A.H. 154 is A.D. 771; making a difference of 25 years. We shall of course follow the Hindu date only, which gives S. 802 = A.D. 746, for the foundation of Anhulwarra, and the chronology of its dynasties.

before we indulge such unprofitable conjectures. Meanwhile, we proceed with the Chronicle of Anhulwarra.

"In Guzzerat, there is a tract called Budyar, of which Panchasra is the capital. Thence one day, as Sailug Soor Acharya was walking in the wood, in search of omens, he found a child in a mantle, suspended from a tree, and close by a female, who proved to be its mother. On being questioned, she said she was the widowed queen of the king of Guzzerat, whose capital had been sacked and her lord slain by an invader; that she had escaped from the massacre and had brought forth the infant in the forest. On hearing this, the Acharya gave the child the title of *Bunsraj*, or correctly *Vanaraja*, signifying 'forest-king.' When arrived at man's estate, he associated with Soorapal of Maolah, a celebrated robber, and plundered the revenues going to Kalian. By this means, he raised troops, and established himself in a territory, where he erected a city, the site of which was determined by a cow-herd, named Anhul, after whom he called it *Anhulpoor*, or *Anhulnyr*."*

Before we proceed, it may be as well to mention what the Miscellany and the Bardic traditions relate concerning this epoch in the annals of Guzzerat. The former work states that "Vansraj was the posthumous son of Jusraj Chaora, prince of Saurashtra, whose capital cities were Deobunder,† on the western shore of the peninsula, and Puttun Somnath; that, in consequence of the piracies of the Chaora princes, especially towards the vessels of Bengal, the sea rose and overwhelmed the former city, in which catastrophe all were involved save Soonderupa, the mother of Vansraj, who was forewarned of the danger by Varuna,

* *Nyr* is the Pracrit for *Nagara*, 'a fortified city.'

† The port (*bunder*) of Deo or Diva, 'the island,' written *Diu* by the Portuguese.

Varuna, the genius of the waters." Tradition, while it recognises this event, and adopts this parentage of Bunsraj, affirms that his father, Jusraj, and all his race, were slain by a foreign invader, and that the infant, in gratitude to the Jain priest who saved his life, cherished the sect and embraced his faith. Though some such event may have occurred to Deobunder, I much more incline to adopt the tradition, supported also by the books of the bards, that it was sacked by some foreign invader. I have elsewhere related that there was an unusual stir amongst all the Hindu monarchies at this period; that revolution, dethronement, and creation of new dynasties and tribes, were taking place all over India. It was at this precise time, that Ajmér was attacked, and the Chohan prince, Manikpâl, slain by a foe from Sinde, according to the Chohan Chronicle. At this epoch, also, Bappa (called likewise Balla) Rawul, whose ancestors fled from Balabhi, obtained Cheetore, which he defended from a foreign invader for his uncle the Mori. At this exact era, the ancient Indraprest'ha, or Dehli, was re-founded by the Tuar line of princes; the Pramara sovereign, Bhoj, was driven from Dhar, and, as stated in the *Bhoj Charitra*, by a northern invader, and forced to seek shelter in Chandravati; the Chalook or Solankhi princes were driven from Sooroh-Bhadra, on the Ganges, and established themselves at Kalian, in Malabar; the Yadu-Bhattis were driven across the Sutledge from Salthanpoor, in Panchalica, and forced to fix themselves in Maroost'hali, the Indian desert; and even at Gowal-coond (Golconda) was felt the dire influence of the same destructive foe, who might well be typified, in these books, as the 'Magician of the North,' the 'demon (*danoo*) from Gujlibund,' &c. &c. All these dates and events correspond with the first appearance of Islam, bringing in its train myriads of Indo-scythic tribes,

tribes, whose only objects of worship were the sun, their horse, and the sword, and who were ready to adopt any faith or sect; and authorise us to conclude it was at this time that the Cattis crossed the Runn, in their passage from Mooltan, and established themselves in the region of the Sauras,* where their influence became so predominant, that the name of *Catti-war* superseded the ancient appellation of Saurashtra. Let those who will, still deny the locomotive habits of the ancient Hindu; but they cannot dispute the changes that must have resulted from these incessant irruptions, both before and after Alexander's time. Even if the Indus had been an *attuc*† to those *intra*, it was not so to the plundering hordes *extra*, Imaus; hence, in this small peninsula, specimens of many of the ancient northern tribes may yet be found. But to proceed.

After the foundation of Anhulwarra by Bunsraj, there follows the account of the city, which seems to start into magnificence at once. Whether the hieratic scribe drew its picture as it then existed under his own eyes, or represented it as it was under the founder, we can only conjecture. It is impossible, however, that the splendour and prosperity described by him, could have been the growth of a single reign, although the facility for peopling a new city in these regions of revolution is wonderful. But if the Acharya is correct, we can only come

* It is not unlikely that the term *Chaora*, the tribe of the first dynasty of Anhulwarra, is a mere corruption of *Saura*; the *ch* and *s* are perpetually interchanging. The Mahrattas cannot pronounce the *ch*; with them *Cheeto* is *Seeto*, &c. The Saura princes of Deo and Somnath, in all likelihood, gave their name to the peninsula of Guzzerat.

† *Attuc* means 'a barrier;' a name bestowed upon the Indus in modern times, when the Hindu, from difference of faith, became exclusive. But notwithstanding Menu tells us that Hinduism was established in Central Asia, our *Savans* in Indian literature made the Indus as complete an *attuc* to their researches as the Hindus did to their faith.

come to the conclusion that the fugitive Chaora prince merely transferred his capital from Deva-puttun to Anhulpoor; and we may add from authority, that the dispersed subjects of the devastated Balabhi flocked in to augment the population of this new capital of the Balla-Raes. It is not impossible that a city did already exist, which Bunsraj augmented,—an hypothesis supported in some measure by the Annals of Méwar, which state that when Bappa (whose ancestors, be it remembered, were in remote times sovereigns of Balabhi), the founder of the Gehlote dynasty, was firmly fixed in Cheetore, he marched an army to reinstate his nephew, the Chaora prince, in the territory of his ancestors; from which we may also infer, that the Chaora princes of Deva-puttun were subordinate to Balabhi. S. 796 (A.D. 740) is the period assigned for this intervention in the Méwar Annals.* The Chronicle continues: "Anhulpoor was twelve coss† (or fifteen miles) in circuit, within which were many temples and colleges; eighty-four *chaoks*, or squares; eighty-four bazaars, or market-places, with mints for gold and silver coin. Each class had its separate *mohilla*, or quarter, as had each description of merchandise, *i. e. hati-dhant*, or elephants' teeth, silks, purples, diamonds, pearls, &c. &c.,—each had its separate *chaok*.‡ There was one bazaar for *shraufs*, or money-changers; one for perfumes and unguents; one for physicians; one for artizans; one for goldsmiths, and another for silversmiths; there were distinct *mohillas* for navigators, for bards, and for genealogists. The eighteen *burrun* or castes inhabited the city. All were happy together. The palace

* *Vide* 'Annals of Rajast'han,' vol. i. p. 227.

† In Guzzerat they estimate the coss by the lowing of kine (*gao*), which in a still day may be heard at the distance of a mile and a quarter. Thus twelve coss is *baragao*.

‡ Best explained by the Italian *piazza*.

palace groaned with a multitude of separate buildings, for the armoury, for elephants, horses and chariots, for the public accountants and officers of state. Each kind of goods had its separate *mandavie*, or mart, where the duties of export, import, and sale, were collected: as for spices, fruits, drugs, camphor, metals, and every thing costly of home or foreign growth. *It is a place of universal commerce!* The daily amount of duties was one lac of *takhas.** If you ask for water, they give you milk. There are many Jain temples, and on the banks of a lake is a shrine to Seheslinga Mahadeo. The population delights to saunter amidst the groves of *champa*, *poonaj*, *thal* (palmyra), *jambu* (rose-apple), *chundun* (sandal-wood), mangoe, &c. &c., with every variegated *vela*, or creeper, and fountains whose waters are *imrit.* Here discussions (*badha*) take place on the *Vedas*, carrying instruction to the listener. There are plenty of *Boharas*,† and in Birgong there are also many. There is no want of *Birterans* (Yutis, or Jain priests) or of merchants, true to their word and skilled in commerce; and many schools for the *Byakurn* (literally, grammar-schools). Anhulwarra is a *Nir-Samudra* (sea of men). If you can measure the waters of the ocean, then may you attempt to count the number of souls.‡ The

* A copper coin, varying in value, but, at the general rate, about twenty to the rupee, which would give five thousand rupees, daily, as the import duties of Anhulwarra alone; or, annually, eighteen lacs, equal to two hundred and twenty-five thousand pounds; which in comparative value, even in the present day, would equal a million. If to this we add the import and export duties of her eighty-four ports, we need not marvel at the accounts which the early Arabian travellers give of the magnificence of this city.

† The money-lenders to the artizan and the husbandman throughout India, who receive written pledges for the fruits of their industry; somewhat analogous to the *Métayer* of the old French system.

‡ The chronicler interweaves the following exaggerated anecdote, in proof of the dense population: "One day, a woman had lost her husband. She went to her prince and related her "misfortune.

The army is numerous, nor is there any lack of bell-bearing elephants. Sailug Soora made the *tika* of installation on the forehead of Bunsraj, who erected the temple to Parswanath, whose religion he followed. This was in S. 802. Vansraj ruled fifty years and lived sixty."

With this short introduction, the Chronicle, satisfied with a bare genealogical list of the Chaora kings, successors to Vansraj, proceeds, without comment, to the change of dynasty, which introduces his subject, Komar-pâl, to whom the work is especially devoted. We shall, however, make a few remarks upon other names from cotemporary authorities.

Joograj succeeded to the founder in S. 852 (A.D. 796), and ruled thirty-five years.

Kheemraj succeeded, S. 887 (A.D. 831), and died in S. 912 (A.D. 856), having ruled twenty-five years. It was towards the close of this prince's reign that the first of the Arabian travellers visited the kingdom of Anhulwarra, *i. e.* in A.H. 237, corresponding with A.D. 851, while the second visited it seventeen years later, or in A.H. 254 (A.D. 868), in the reign of his successor,

Boerji, who succeeded in S. 912 (A.D. 856), and died S. 941 (A.D. 885), having ruled twenty-nine years.

Without attempting to apportion the information respectively furnished by these Arabian travellers, who have not even mentioned the names of the princes ruling at the epochs of their visit, we may avail

misfortune. He ordered the heralds to proclaim throughout Puttun, that whoever went by the name of Ranoh, the blind of one eye, should appear at the grand *Chabootra,* or altar of justice; when lo! nine hundred and ninety-nine persons blind of one eye, and each bearing the name of Ranoh, appeared. The disconsolate wife went through the ranks, and yet her husband was not there; nor was he found until a second proclamation was issued."

avail ourselves of their joint testimony, as far as it goes, in corroboration of the Chronicle, on the greatness of the kings of Anhulwarra: "This Balhara is the most illustrious prince in all the Indies, and all the other kings there, though each is master and independent in his kingdom, acknowledge in him this prerogative and pre-eminence: When he sends ambassadors to them, they receive them with extraordinary honours, because of the respect they bear him. This king makes magnificent presents, after the manner of the Arabs, and has horses and elephants in very great numbers and great treasures in money. He has of those pieces of silver, Tartarian drachmas, which weigh half a drachm more than the Arabesque drachm. They are coined with the die of the prince, and bear the year of his reign from the last of his predecessor. They compute not their years from the era of Mahomed, as do the Arabs, but only by the years of their kings. Most of these princes have lived a long time, and many of them have reigned above fifty years; and those of the country believe that the length of their lives, and of their reigns, is granted them in recompense for their kindness to the Arabs. In truth, there are no princes more heartily affectionate to the Arabs, and their subjects profess the same friendship for us.

"Balhara is an appellation common to all these kings, as was Cosroes and some others, and is not a proper name. The country, which owes obedience to this prince, begins on the coast of the province called Kamkam, and reaches by land to the confines of China. He is surrounded by the dominions of many kings, who are at war with him, and yet he never marches against them. One of these kings is the king of Haraz, who has very numerous forces, and is stronger in horse than all the other princes of the Indies, and who has a greater a greater aversion to Mahomedism. His dominions are upon a promontory, where are much riches, many camels, and other cattle. The inhabitants here traffic with silver they wade for,* and they say there are mines of the same on the continent. These kingdoms border upon the lands of a king called Rahmi, who is at war with the king of Haraz, and with the Balhara also. This prince is not much esteemed either for his birth or the antiquity of his kingdom ; but his forces are more numerous than those of the Balhara. In the same country, they make cotton garments in so extraordinary a manner, that no where else are the like to be seen. Shells are current in this country, and serve for small money, notwithstanding they have gold and silver, wood, aloes, and sable-skins, of which they make the furniture of saddles and houses."

We may remark upon this description, first, of the title *Balhara*, that it was derived from Ballâ-câ-Raê, whose ancient capital was Balabhipoor, on whose site Ptolemy has placed a Byzantium. Secondly, on the "Tartarian drachmas" of silver,† of which I have one, with the effigy of the prince on one side, and the obverse covered with the incognate character of the Jains, surrounding a Pyreum. Thirdly, on the great duration of the reigns ; these travellers were in Puttun during the reigns of the third and fourth princes, and the mention of "many" might puzzle us, were they otherwise exact or intelligible : but we may easily imagine, with their imperfect knowledge of the Guzzerati dialect, that from the reign of Vansraj of half a century, and that of his successor of thirty-five years, they might deem themselves entitled

* Hence the name of *Roopavati,* in the Peninsula, from *roopa*, 'silver.'

† The translator guards us against supposing them to be *Tartarian,* saying they are the coin of the country, and spelling the word with a *Th.*

entitled to use this word; or, as I have already said, there was only a transfer of capital from Deva-puttun, the reigns of the princes, anterior to this event, may possibly have authorized the remark. The priestly chronicler, Sailug, did not go further back than the inauguration of Vansraj in Nehrwalla. Fourthly, as to the geography of the travellers, the translator remarks: "the situation of all these places is so very doubtful, that we can hardly even guess at them." There is, however, no doubt that the ignorance of the translator, which he charges to his predecessors, in his Preface, has gone far to render utterly unintelligible what was already obscure, and which the utmost local knowledge of these regions, as well as an acquaintance with their books and traditions, cannot clear up. Every one knows, that the slightest error in the position of the *nooktas*, or points,* in Arabic and Persian, completely mystifies all proper names, of which we could append a few notable instances, to shew how much a new translation is required of this work.

The limits assigned for the kingdom of the Balharas, from the Concan (the Kamkam of the travellers) to the borders of China, would have been perfectly applicable if the "*Relations*" had been composed in the next dynasty, when Sid Raj held sway over eighteen kingdoms, and his successor, Komár-pál, "conquered to the Himalaya mountains, raising his banner even in the city of Salpoora," the ancient capital of Panchalica. We must, however, dispute entirely this extent of dominion at this period: for the Solankhis then ruled the Concan, and

* *Ex. gr.* p. 87: "In the Indies there are certain men called *Bicar*, who go all their lifetime naked." Who would recognise *Fakir* in *Bicar*? a mistake arising from misplaced or deficient punctuation. This error is copied *verbatim* by St. Croix, as editor of that curious work, the fabricated *Ezour Vedam*, composed by Robertus di Nobili.

and cotemporary annals inform us of their independent neighbours.* Of the king of Haraz, the greatest of the foes of Balhara, or of the king called Rahmi, not much esteemed for his birth, with both of whom he was at war, we can conjecture who they were, and the translator, in his annotations, gives us wide scope for this, when he says, "the kingdom of Geraz or Haraj must be somewhere on the continent between Cape Comorin and China." The appellation of *Gújerat* is derived from the tribe of Gújur, one of the indigenous Soodra tribes of India; but whether any principality, founded by this race, then existed, we know not, and it would appear that the travellers were ignorant of its application to the region which formed the best part of the sovereignty of the Balharas. I have imagined that this king of Haraz might be the Hara prince of Gowalcoond, a great branch of the Chohans of Ajmér, who were always at war with the Balla-Raes. This supposition would suit well with his contiguity to the king of low birth, Rahmi, whom I conjecture to be Ram Pramar, of Telingana, who at one time possessed the title of universal potentate. The fine cotton garments, mentioned as made in his territory, would strengthen this opinion; for these, with the muslins (*sindonis*) and purple cloths of Boorhanpoor, were renowned even in Rome, and formed the great articles of commerce, according to the author of the *Periplus*. Shells or cowries, which they mention, were, and are still, every-where current, and even the seed of the date is to this day used along the coast in these regions.

"The kingdom of Kaschbin," described as a desert country full of mountains, must be Cutch-bhooj, and we might be tempted to suppose "that

* We have a conspicuous instance, at p. 87, of the ignorance of "the travellers" on the political geography of India, where they call "Kanouge, a great city in the kingdom of Gozar," meaning Guzzerat.

"that the small and poor kingdom of Hitrunje" was the chieftainship of Satringa-Palit'hana,* still famous. After discussing the geographical position of "Nehelwareh, a city, which, according to the tables of Nasir-u-din and Ulug Beg, is in 102° 30′ longitude, and latitude 22° north, and therefore neither can have been Calicut, Cochin, nor Visiapoor;"—the commentator adds, that the Balhara "translated himself to Calicut for the convenience of the pepper-trade; it is, therefore, probable that, before he went to Calicut, he resided somewhere in Guzzerat:" and he quotes the Portuguese author, John de Barros, "who had seen the books of the country, who says he had been invested with the authority of emperor, or king of kings, over all the Indian princes." It will be seen presently that an intimate relationship subsisted between the Balharas of Anhulwarra and the princes of the Concan, whose capital was Kalian, and whose possessions eventually merged into one great kingdom, although not in the time of these travellers. It is also a curious fact, and which may account for the introduction of the name of Calicut, that the *Nyr*, or fortified city of Anhulwarra, was called, and is still recognised as, *Kali-kote*, or 'Castle of Kali,' in ignorance of which, the annotator has thought it necessary to send the Balhara sovereigns into the heart of the peninsula of India, to gather pepper! I shall conclude these remarks with a curious piece of intelligence from the Annotations (p. 24), for which no authority is cited: "The commendations our authors bestow on the Balhara, for being kind to the Arabs, suit very naturally with these princes, the last of whom, Sarama Payrimal, became a Mahomedan and ended his days at Mecca."†

* The *S*, as I have elsewhere remarked, is the Ṣhibboleth of these regions. Salim Sing is pronounced *Halim Hing*, forming a compound of 'cress' and 'assafœtida'!

† See Wilson's *Mackenzie Collection*, vol. i. p. xcvii.

CHAPTER IX.

History of Anhulwarra continued.—The Solankhi princes of Kalian.—Change of dynasty of the princes of Anhulwarra.—Synchronisms.—Importance of Kalian.—Confusion of Mahomedan writers.—List of princes of Anhulwarra continued.—Sidraj.—Succession of a Chohan prince to the regal chair of the Chalucas.—Countries subject to the dominion of the Balhara.—Actions of Komár-pál.—Confirmation of the *Charitra,* as to the extent and splendour of Anhulwarra.—The country of the Lar.—Komár-pál the supporter of Buddhism.—He apostatizes to Islamism.—Ajipal.

We shall pass over the intermediate princes from those who occupied the throne of Anhulwarra, when this city was visited by the Arabian travellers, to the period of Samunt, the last of the dynasty founded by Vansraj, and introduce the Solankhi line of cotemporaneous princes ruling at Kalian, the capital of the Concan, who displaced the Chaoras in Anhulwarra, after they had held it one hundred and eighty-six years. For this purpose, we must take a leaf from the chronology of the Solankhis, as given me by the representative, the chief of Roopnagurh (now a vassal of Méwar), whose bard, the hereditary scion of the *Vates* of Anhulwarra, still "holds the books" of his ancestry.* As the bard is to tell his own story, we must indulge him with the usual fabulous commencement of all royal lines. He disputes

* We may append the *Gotra,* or genealogical text of the race, in their own tongue. Its translation would afford no satisfaction to the general reader, but there may be, of those who dip into this book, "two or one" who may prize it in its own Doric dialect:

"*Madwani Sac'ha—Bardwaj gotra—Gur'h Lokote—Khâr nekâs—Sarasvatí nadì—Sham Véda—Kupliman-déva — Kurdimân Rikheswar — Teen-purwar-Zinové— Súrí-pâna-ca-Ch'hatto — Gaopal-oopas — Gya-nekâs — Kewnj-Dévi — Maipâl-Putra.*" This Maipal, styled *Putra,* was adopted among the *Penates* of the Solankhis for his heroism in the field of Nairanòh. He was the third son of Raja Boerdeo, who married the daughter of the Chohan prince of Sambhur; and it was in defence of the maternal house against an irruption of the Islamite that he fell. Each great family commemorates

disputes the birth of his princes from the fire-fount of Aboo, and says that "when Brimha had finished the work of creation, he repaired to the Ganges to perform ablutions, and at the Sooroh ghaut (ford) of that sacred stream, he created the Chaluca from a blade of the holy *d'hoob* grass, the which, holding in the palm *(chaloo)* of his hand, and pronouncing the life-giving incantation *(Sujevan-mantri)*, a mortal had birth, hence called the *Brimha-Chaluca*, and *Solankhi* from the place. Here they erected their capital, also called *Sooroo*, whence a name of the Ganges, *Sooroo**-*bhadra*; and here they ruled throughout the *Treta* and *Dwapur*, or gold and silver ages." The reader will estimate this extract at its worth, while the geographer obtains at least the origin of one old capital, which was celebrated so late as the last Chohan emperor of Dehli, and which is still a place of religious resort. We learn also from the *Gotra*, or genealogical text of the tribe, that their origin is northern, *i. e.* from Lokote, an ancient city of Panchalica (the Punjab), on their expulsion from which, they established Sooroh on the Ganges. But without further adverting to the fabulous period of their history, we will set our feet on the *terra firma* of the Bard. "In the seventh century of Vicrama, two brothers, Raj and Beeja, left the Ganges for Guzzerat. The former married the daughter of the Chaora king of Patun, whose issue, in the course of time, ascended that throne, and from Vansraj to Kurrun, expelled by Secunder Khuni, was five hundred and fifty-two years." So much

commemorates some similar event. In like manner, Lot Putra, son of Manik Rae of Ajmér, who fell on the first onslaught of Islam, is placed among the household gods of the Chohans. *Putra* in this sense invariably means a 'stripling,' or one who has not yet attained manhood.

* They still give this name to the dry bed of the river at Khas-gunge, past which the Ganges formerly flowed. I am not quite sure whether this ancient town is not the Sooroh of the Solankhis. Boerdeo was the cotemporary of Manik Rae, which affords another valuable synchronism.

much for the Bard of the Solankhis of Thoda and Roopnagurh. We now return to the authority of the *Charitra.*

"Of Chaluca race was Raja Boerdeo, king of Kanyacubja (Canouj). From his seat of government, Callian-Cuttuc, he came and conquered Guzzerat, slew its king, and, leaving his garrisons there, returned to Callian.* Boer-rae had a daughter, named Milandevi, who was married to the Chohan king of Ajmér, and from whom in the fifteenth generation was Komár-pál," whose name this book bears.

"Boer-rae had a son, Kurrun, whose son was Chandradit; his son was Somadit, and his Bhomadit, who had three sons, *viz.* Ur or Ar, Dhitac, and Abhirama. Ur went to Patun, to worship at the shrine of Soméswar (Somnat'h), and married Liladevi, daughter of Raja Samunt. This princess died in child-birth, but the infant was cut from the womb, and being in the *Mula-nacshitra* (the sun in Libra), the astrologers gave him the name of Moolraj. Raja Samunt Chaora, having no male issue, during his lifetime made over the kingdom of Anhulwarra to Moolraj, but repenting, was about to resume it, when his nephew put him to death. There are seven things without gratitude: a daughter's husband, a scorpion, a tiger, wine, a fool, a sister's son *(Bhanaij)*, and a king. Each is incapable of estimating benefits."

Before proceeding further with the chronicle of the Balhara, we may, at this point, which transfers its crown from the dynasty of the Chaora to the Chaluca or Solankhi, place in juxtaposition the collateral dynasties of each.

CHALUC

* The chronicle of the Solankhi bard places a prince of the name of Indra-dowan amongst the princes of Callian, and states that he founded the temple of Juggernauth, and the suburb, or *Poori*, called after himself, Indra-poori. The latter fact may be true, and he may have repaired, but he could not have founded, the temple.

Chaluc Kings of Callian.	Chaora Kings of Anhulwarra.
1. Boerji	1. Vansraj (A.D. 746 to A.D. 796).
2. Kurrun.	2. Joograj.
3. Chandradit.	3. Kheemraj.
4. Somadit.	4. Boerji.
5. Bhomadit.	5. Birsing.
6. Ur. Dhitac. Abhirama	6. Rutnadit.
	7. Samunt.
married .... Liladevi	daughter of Samunt.

issue

Moolrâj,

whence commenced the second dynasty of Anhulwarra.

Although both these authorities coincide very well, there is some discrepancy in the outset, the bardic chronicle saying that the two Chaluc brothers, Raj and Beeja, left the city of Sooroh in the seventh century, while the *Charitra* at once commences with Boer-rae, king of Canouj, who invaded Guzzerat, slew its king, and returned, not to Canouj, but to Callian, on the Malabar coast. It is well not to pass over the possibility that this may be the conqueror who drove the Chaoras from their more ancient seats of Deva-puttun and Somnath, for acts of piracy admitted in the old chronicle; and this would agree with the Bard's date, the seventh century, for the migration from Sooroh, in the kingdom of Canouj, and establishment at Callian. This supposition derives added weight from the anecdote relating the first exploit of Vansraj, the founder of Puttun, in associating himself with robbers, and plundering the revenues going to Callian. An inscription of the Mackenzie Collection, translated by Mr. Colebrooke, and inserted in the *Asiat. Res.* vol. ix. p. 435, but hitherto without any application,

application, proved of great value to me in confirmation of these opinions, and in corroborating the truth of the manuscript authorities, which record the foundation of the dynasty more than one thousand years ago. It is of the fourth prince, Somadit, and gives his tribe, Chaluca, and his capital, Callian. It runs thus: "For ever be propitious to Someswara,* &c. &c.; a distinguished personage of the noble race, the ornament of the Chaluca tribe, &c. &c., who reigns in the city Calyan, &c." Were there no instance but this, it would suffice to shew the importance of recording all inscriptions, and this is only one of many which have rewarded and encouraged my research.

Callian, or Kalian, was a city of great importance, commercial and political, at a very early period. It is frequently noticed by Arrian, in the *Periplus*, from whose work we may infer that it was a fief of *Baleokouras*, or the Balhara sovereigns of Balabhi, in the second century, and its extent is attested by the ruins described by Orme in his "Fragments."

The transactions of these early periods have attracted the notice of several Mahomedan writers, but their imperfect intelligence has only tended to darken the subject. Abulfazil, unable to disentangle these perplexities, extends the kingdom of Canouj to the shores of the ocean, and Masoudi, who wrote in the tenth century an account of these regions, talks of the "kingdom of Bouroh" as the same as the kingdom of Canouj, an error which can be explained by his ignorance of the name of Boer-rae, the prince of Callian, the emigrant from Sooroh in the kingdom of Canouj, which former city appears to have disputed the palm of greatness with the latter, and was then probably the

* It is scarcely necessary to explain that *Someswara* and *Somadit* have the same signification, 'the Sun, or lord of the Moon.'

the seat of its sovereigns; in fact, Sooroh, according to Persian or Arabic orthography, would require but a point under the *S* to be Booroh. According to the Arabian travellers, there were four supreme monarchies in India at the period of their visit, and they only assign the fourth magnitude to that of the Balharas, whose power they nevertheless magnify beyond all belief, making his army amount to half a million of men. Abulfazil's statement of the power of Canouj at that period is equally remote from truth; for, instead of extending from the Ganges to the shores of the ocean, the potent principalities of Ajmér, Cheetore, and Dhar, intervened even between Canouj and Anhulwarra, whose international wars and marriages even at these periods are recorded. But to proceed with the new dynasty of the Chaluca.

Moolraj ascended the *gâdi* of Anhulwarra in S. 988 (A.D. 932). His reign, like that of the founder of the Chaoras, was of great length, being fifty-six years, and if we take the Miscellany before mentioned as our authority, we should have to add two more. He carried his arms westward to the valley of the Indus, and fought with its prince, a Rajpoot; and he laid the foundations of the temple of Roodra-Mala, which we have elsewhere described.

Chaond or Chamund (erroneously written *Jamund* by Abulfazil) Rao succeeded in S. 1044 (A.D. 988). He ruled only thirteen years, and the conclusion of his reign was most eventful to him, as well as to all India. It was in S. 1064, or A.D. 1008 (A.H. 416, A.D. 1025, according to the Islamite historian), that the Ghiznivite king, Mahmoud, invaded Anhulwarra, throwing down its battlements, and casting the materials of its temples into the trenches surrounding its walls; that, after a six months' repose in Puttun, the conqueror sought out,

 and

and placed upon its throne, one of the ancient line of monarchs, called by the uncouth name of Dabschelim, who, being said to be the son of the prince of Deo and Somnath, was evidently of the Chaora tribe, which, according to inscriptions there found by me, did hold their patrimonial possessions in Anhulwarra so late as in the twelfth and fourteenth centuries. In my edition of Ferishta, he is called Babshelim, with the epithet *Mor Taj*, and this approximates to the Ballirao or Ballabisén* of the Chronicle, the successor of Chamund, and as this authority only allots him six months' sway, he can be no other than the interloper Dabschelim. The epithet *Mor Taj*, which is a duplicate expression in the Hindu and Persian languages, each meaning 'head,' 'chief,' 'crown,' induces me to conjecture that it may be a corruption of *Chaor Taj*, or chief of the Chaoras. Such is the inadequacy of the Persian language for the expression of proper names, that, as already remarked, a point misplaced may completely disguise them. The reader may consult Ferishta and Abulfazil for the disasters which befel Anhulwarra, and the romantic account of the dangers of Mahmoud's army in his retreat to Ghizni, where his guides led him through the desert in revenge for his atrocities on Somnath and the other celebrated shrines in this land.

Doorlub, or Nahr-rao, succeeded in S. 1057 (A.D. 1001), and had reigned eleven years and a half, when his conscience suggested to him the care of his soul. He abdicated, and placing his son on the throne, retired to Gya: a practice by no means uncommon amongst the Rajpoot princes of ancient days. Doorlub was the cotemporary of Raja Moonj of Dhar (the father of the celebrated Bhoj), and we learn

* Abulfazil has given his version also of this name, of which the translator of the *Ayeen Akbery* makes *Beysir*; and D'Herbelot, following the Arabians, styles this the *Dabschalimat* race.

learn from the *Bhoj Charitra*, that the abdicated king paid Moonj a visit on his route to Gya, by whom he was recommended to resume the *gádi*, advice which was subsequently resented by the son.

Bheem Deo succeeded in S. 1069 (A.D. 1013), a name celebrated in the cotemporaneous annals of the Rajpoots. He had a long and not inglorious reign of forty-two years, during which, the Islamites made repeated irruptions into the north of India, and it was during the reign of Modud, the fourth in succession to Mahmoud, that the Hindus made a grand effort to shake off the yoke which oppressed them. The celebrated Chohan king of Ajmér, Besuldeo, (the Visaladeva of the Jyt-khumbo, or pillar of victory, at Dehli,) headed this confederacy in S. 1100 (A.D. 1044). The king of Anhulwarra was invited, with the other princes of the land, who had chosen Besuldeo as generalissimo on this the last united stand which they made for their religion and liberties; but the ancient jealousies between the rival houses of Ajmér and Anhulwarra prevented him from obeying the call, and his refusal subsequently produced a war between these states, which forms the subject of one of the sixty-nine books of the poet Chund. Besuldeo proceeded at the head of the allied troops from triumph to triumph, till the Punjab itself was cleared of their enemies; and it was on this victory, as recorded on the pillar of Dehli, that from the Vindhya even to the Himachil, the barbarian was expelled, when the region of Aryaverta became once more the 'land of virtue.' Chund says, "the oath of allegiance *(ân)* was sent from Ghizni, demanding tribute, when the lord of Sacambhari issued his firmans to call in his vassals. Then came the array *(bhâr)* of Mundore and Bhatnair, with the chiefs of Tatta and Mooltan. The clans of Untervéd* repaired

* The lands lying between (*unter*) the Jumna and Ganges.

repaired to his standard. All came but the Chaluca, who trusted to the shade of his own sword for independence." The rival armies met at Sojut, in Marwar, when the Solankhi was defeated. He retired upon Jhalore, which appears to have been the frontier-post between him and his rival's dominion; but he was compelled to relinquish it, and was pursued by the victor even to Girnar, in the heart of the peninsula. Having reinforced his army, the Chaluca prince sent his ambassadors to the Chohan, already in retreat to his own country, demanding his reasons for this unwarrantable invasion, and asserting his perfect equality with him, while, in reply to his demands, he said "the only tribute should be the sword, whose fragments he might collect if he were again worsted in fight." Besuldeo, with the usual courtesy of a Rajpoot, not only gave him a chance of redeeming himself, but dismissed all his prisoners, and returned all the spoils, that he might, as says the bard, "have something to win back." "The Chohan formed his army in circular array *(chacra)*, and soon had two thousand Solankhis fallen," when the Bal-ca-rae headed a band in person and broke it. "Then the sword made pilgrimage in a river of blood." The rivals engaged hand to hand, and both were wounded. Night alone separated the combatants. The next day, a treaty was made, in which the Chaluca agreed to give his daughter in marriage to Besul, and in remembrance of the battle, a city was to be erected on the spot, bearing the Chohan's name. The town of Beesul Nugger, still existing, proves the fidelity of the Chronicle. Throughout this account given by the bard, the sovereign of Anhulwarra is mentioned solely by his title, Bal-ca-rae; but in the *Hamir-rasa*, a work relating the exploits of Hamir, the Chohan prince of Rinthumbor, and which recedes to his ancestry, the bard alludes to this battle, stating that Besuldeo

Besuldeo took prince Kurrun (son of Raja Bheem) prisoner. Raja Bheem had two wives, *viz.* Beekul-devi, and Oodimati. The first bore him a son named Kheemraj; the other had a son called

KURRUN, one of the most renowned Rajpoots who ever sat upon a throne, and who succeeded his father, in prejudice of his elder brother, in S. 1111 (A.D. 1055). Amongst his many exploits, he completely subjugated the Koli and Bhil tribes, slaying Assa-bhil, styled the *Pillipati*, lord of one hundred thousand bowmen. He rased his city, and founded on its site the city called after himself, Kurnavati,* of whose position we are ignorant. The Chronicle likewise states that he banished the seven *Diddas* (the letter *d*) from the land, *viz. dind, dand, dhomb'h, dhakun, dur, damb'h,* and *doobha;* or exactions, violence, *jongleurs* (which term denotes, at once, itinerant minstrels and jugglers), witches, alarm, impostors, and depression. He erected a superb temple to Nemnat'h, on the summit of Revatachil, in addition to the fifty-two already there existing, and which was called after him, Kurrun Vihar. He espoused Milandévi, daughter of Ari-cesar, lord of the Carnatic, who bore him the celebrated Sid-raj, the glory of Anhulwarra. It is related that when the daughter of this Lion of the Carnatic† reached Anhulwarra, she was so ill-favoured, that Kurrun positively refused to give his hand to her, and it was only in obedience to

* We frequently meet with notices of the great power of the aboriginal tribes at this period, and there are many ancient sites of fortresses and cities appertaining to this race which are well worthy of being explored.

† See *Asiatic Res.* vol. xvi. for notices of this prince; also the Mackenzie Collection. *Cesar* or *Késar*, 'a lion,' is by no means an uncommon epithet with the Rajpoot kings of past days, and it is synonymous with the more common appellation of *Sing'h* or *Sing,* the affix indiscriminately of all Rajpoots. Whether from this Sanscrit term for the king of the forest is derived the Persian *Kaesar,* the *Czar* of the Russians, and the Roman *Cesar,* we leave to etymologists to determine.

to his mother's prayers, and to prevent the bride committing suicide, that he at length complied; but it is added, that for years he did not cohabit with her, until, as related, the unwearied manifestation of her good qualities not only conquered his aversion, but won his esteem and affection. Kurrun ruled twenty-nine years, and was succeeded by his son,

Sid-raj Jey Sing, in S. 1140 (A.D. 1084), under whose reign of half a century, Anhulwarra attained its utmost splendour. He held sway over eighteen distinct kingdoms, either by inheritance or conquest, and was justly entitled to the appellation conferred on him in the *Charitra*, of "the most mighty of all the princes of his time." As the names of these countries will appear in the reign of his successor, where they will be synchronically connected with the affairs of other states, we shall hasten on with the chronicler to the next reign, that of Komár-pál, to which the foregoing succinct analysis merely serves as a preface. I shall follow nearly his own version.

"The mighty Sid-raj,* the conqueror and king of eighteen regions, had no offspring, which took from his riches and power all value. He convened the brahmins, astrologers, and soothsayers, and offered whatever man can covet for an heir. At length, to the demand of who should succeed if Heaven did not grant his desire, one of the seers replied, it was decreed that the son of the chief of Dytulli should succeed.

* There is a curious anecdote in illustration of the name *Sid*. His mother (who in the original Sanscrit is called the daughter of Ari-cesar, and in the dialect Gya-césar, the one meaning the 'lion of Ari,' the other the 'invincible lion,') was said to have been twelve years *enceinte*, during which she suffered such extreme torture, that she set out to end her days in the ocean at Dwarica. On her journey she encountered a Sid or Dervésh, to whom she confided her intention, but through his prayers she was safely delivered of a boy, whom, in gratitude for his mediation, she named Sid-raj.

succeed. At this the prince was wroth, and sending forthwith an army, Dytulli was attacked, the Chohan chief slain, whose son, Komár-pál, with difficulty escaped the general slaughter, and found refuge and concealment with his brother-in-law, Krishundeo, who dwelt in Patun. But here, from the rank of his relation, who was one of the ministers of Jey Sing, he could not expect to remain long undiscovered, and he fled to the house of a potter, where he remained some time, and afterwards, in various disguises, contrived to live even within the walls of Patun, at one time associating with mendicants. He even regained his birth-place, Dytulli, but once more was nearly taken, when again a friendly potter saved him by hiding him in a brick-kiln. He now determined to try Oojein, and had reached the port of Cambayet, when, famished with hunger, and oppressed by fatigue, he fell asleep under a tree. At this time, the celebrated Hemacharya was proceeding with his pupils to the neighbouring woods. He awoke the youth, and perceiving that he was no ordinary person, admitted him amongst the Jaïn youths, his scholars. Here the Acharya cast his horoscope, which foretold his future greatness; but the spies of Sid-raj at length discovered him, when, trusting to the garb of a Jogi, he in safety gained Baroach. A banya, or merchant, of Cambayet, who understood the language of birds, was the companion of his flight. Just as they reached the port, the Devi bird of omen perched on the ball (*cullus*) of a temple, uttering two distinct notes, which the banya interpreted as dominion over both Hindu and Toork. Once more his retreat was discovered, and he fled to Kooloo-nagar. Here a celebrated Jogi taught him an incantation (*muntri*), which was to reveal his future fate, but which, to have any power, must be recited seated on a dead body. He obeyed, and such was the potency of the spell, that the

the dead spoke, declaring that in five years he should be king of Guzzerat. Thence, in his Jogi garb, he went to Kanteepoor, in the country of Kalian-karica,* and hence again to Oojein, where he sought refuge in the famed shrine of Kalka-devi,† where a serpent *(serpa)* addressed him as prince of Guzzerat." He then travelled to Cheetore, and after visiting and describing all the shrines, there is a long dissertation on the founding of this ancient metropolis of Central India by Chitrung-gud.‡ Thence he continued his wanderings to Canouj, Kasi or Benares, Rajgraha, and Sampoo,—all renowned in the history of Buddhism. At the last of these cities, in Chinese Tartary, he describes a wealthy seit or banker, called Jugroo, who in the famine of S. 1172 served out crores upon crores to the princes of the land. Amongst those enumerated as having benefited by the bounty of the merchant, was Hamira of Sinde.§ Komár-pál continued his wanderings, the narrative of which does not contain much useful information, until S. 1189 (A.D. 1133), when the end of Sid-raj approached, of whom it is related that, calling his ministers, Krishun-deo and Kamideo, he made them lay their hands on his neck, bidding them swear never to place Komár-pál upon the throne; but while they were hastening to obey, he expired. A relative of the deceased king, of

* This, in another part of the work, is called 'Kalian Cuttac'—the discovery of Kanteepoor would settle this geographical point.

† This temple, of the most remote antiquity, still exists. Kalka is a female personification of time.

‡ This is likewise in accordance with the local traditions, which make Chitrung Mori the founder of Cheetore.

§ This simple fact is of great importance; by supplying the date of this prince's reign, during which, according to the traditional couplet, the desert stream called Caggar or Kankra was dried up. See 'Annals of Rajast'han,' vol. ii. p. 294.

of Solankhi race, was raised to the *gádi*, but, proving a fool, was as promptly deposed. The moment the tidings reached Komár-pál, who was still amongst the mountains of Thibet,* he repaired to Patun, where he found all classes worshipping the *paduca*, or impression of the footsteps, of the deceased, in such veneration was his memory held. The great officers of the Court, perplexed about a successor to the throne, adopted the same expedient as obtained the Persian crown for Darius; but the Rajpoot nobles, instead of a horse, selected the more regal and sagacious elephant, to discover a fitting ruler for the eighteen kingdoms dependant on Anhulwarra. A *gurra* or jar of water was placed in the trunk of the elephant,† and it was agreed that that individual should be their king on whom the representative of Ganesa should discharge its contents. All was amazement when the animal overturned the *gurra* upon the head of a mendicant Jogi, who was instantly led to the *gádi* "on the black fourth of the month *Megsir*, S. 1189." This Jogi was the disguised prince

* There is no doubt that it was a community of religious belief that procured Komár-pál shelter in the mountains of the north. The characters in use amongst the monasteries of Thibet are the simplest modification of those in Buddhist or Jain inscriptions found in Central and Western India. But although the Buddhists of Thibet occasionally visit the holy mounts of their common faith in Saurashtra, it is hazarding too much to say that this religion was thence transported to the north.

† In all probability, the *great* actor in this scene had been well drilled for the occasion, and the scheme preconcerted by the brother-in-law of Komár-pál. It was very easy to prepare this sagacious animal, by parading him through the street and rewarding him with a few pieces of sugar-cane when he made the ablution over some proxy of the prince. The stratagem which gave regality to Darius was said, in like manner, to have been preconcerted, by tying a mare to the outskirt of his camp, a secret confided to the *ominous* steed, who, when loosened, set off neighing to join her—a *ruse* imitated with equal success, though with a less brilliant result, by my friend Edward Blunt, in our donkey sweepstakes at Agra. He trained his by making him follow a horse with a corn-bag tied to his tail, the contents of which were awarded him on reaching the winning-post. On the day of action, the soundness of this practice was proved, and the recollection of the bribe at the goal won his master the sweepstakes.

prince Komár-pál. "When the relative of Sid-raj was placed upon the *gádi*, the assembled nobles enquired how he would govern the eighteen regions left by Jey Sing; his reply was, 'according to your counsel and instructions;' but when Komár-pál, now seated on the throne, was called upon to answer the same question, he started on his feet, and grasped his sword. Shouts of admiration filled the hall, and all felt assured that he was a fitting successor to Sid-raj." Here follows an account of the inauguration, which it is unnecessary to insert, and which, with the wanderings of Komár-pál, occupies a great portion of the thirty-eight thousand slocas of the *Charitra*.

Before we proceed further with this prince, however, we must revert to some details which regard the era of his predecessor, whose name and exploits are recorded in the poetic annals of every state in Rajpootana existing at that period.

The bard Chund alludes to his wars against the monarchs of Canouj, when "he washed his blade in the Ganges," and to the alliance between the princes of Méwar and Ajmér to check his aim at universal conquest. This is likewise recorded on more durable monuments than Palmyra leaves,—on inscriptions in stone from sites of towns whose very names are forgotten. He married the daughter of Irno Raja, who held seven hundred villages under the prince of Cheetore. This grand fief was on the Pat'har, or highland on the eastern skirt of Méwar; its capital was Mynal (elsewhere fully described),* amongst whose ruins I discovered an inscription proving this alliance. Another most important inscription, relating to the Pramar dynasty of Chandra-

vati,

* See 'Annals of Rajast'han,' vol. ii. p. 746. Another inscription was found amidst the ruins of Mynal, which appeals to the "gate of Balabhi" as a testimony of the greatness of the princes of Méwar, themselves the ancient Balharaes.

vati, informs us that Irno Raja was likewise a cotemporary with Komár-pál. It runs thus: "In the battle between Komár-pál and Irno-deva, Lakshun-pál gathered from the field of battle the fruit of immortality."

In the Sanscrit edition of this *Charitra*, it is mentioned that Sid-raj fought the Pramar princes of Dhar, and after many years of brave defence, captured it and its prince, Nirvarma. I have already settled by a series of cotemporaneous inscriptions and MSS. the era of this prince, the son of Udyadit, and to these I must refer the curious,* merely adding that they afford with this notice in the *Charitra* another valuable synchronism. The celebrated Jugdeo Pramara, the actions of whose life fill a small volume, resided twelve years in sanctuary with Sid-raj at Patun. We learn that Yasúvarma, son of Udyadit, had two sons, Rindhawul by a Bhâgéla princess, and Jugdeo by a Solankhâni Ranee of Patun. The former obtained Dhar, and after his death, by the instrumentality of Sid-raj, Jugdeo succeeded him.

In the same small volume, regarding Jugdeo, it is mentioned that Sid-raj married a daughter of Phoolji Jharéjah of Cutch, better known to tradition as Lakha Phoolani, one of the Desert kings, who flourished at the end of the twelfth century of Vicrama, and whose marauding exploits have signalized him in all the chronicles of his neighbours.

The annals of Jessulmér mention that its prince, Lanja Beeji-rae, married a daughter of Sid-raj Jey Sing, and although no date is assigned to this event, we can easily approximate thereto. Doosaj, the grandfather of Lanja, mounted the throne of Lodorva† in S. 1100, and Jessul, the grandson of Beeji-rae, founded Jessulmér in S. 1212, the

* See *Trans. R. A. S.*, vol. i. p. 207.

† This city, now in ruins, and formerly the capital of the Desert princes of Jessulmér, I have to enumerate amongst my discoveries.

the intermediate term being adopted for the accession of Beeji-rae, proves another satisfactory synchronism. The Bhatti annals shew the mother of this prince advising her son, in consequence of his marriage with the daughter of Sid-raj, "to defend the gates of Patun against the northern barbarians." We might multiply these synchronisms, but the preceding will suffice to prove the general accuracy of the genealogies of the *Charitras*.*

KOMAR-PAL, as already stated, commenced his reign in S. 1189 (A.D. 1133). His first act was to call around him all those who had shielded him in his adversity. Hemacharya was brought from his seclusion at Baroach, and honoured with the title of Guru, or spiritual guide, exchanging his duties, as preceptor of Jain youth in the philosophy and language of Buddhism, for the more responsible office of chief civil minister to the king; while Krishundeo, who was the first to afford shelter to the fugitive prince, was constituted the chief military councillor, with the control of all the vassal chiefs, of whom seventy-two are designated as composing this council. The *Charitra* proceeds with an account of the pedigree of Komár-pál, with the various tribes, and an enumeration of the eighteen kingdoms dependent on Anhulwarra. Komár-pál was not of the same tribe as Sid-raj, but a Chohan, descended from the kings of Ajmér. "In Guzzerat is a town called Dytulli, in which dwelt Tribhawun-pál, chief of twelve townships. By a Ranee of Cashmere† he had three sons and two daughters, *viz.* Komár-pál, Muhi-pál, and Krit-pál, Pemuldevi, and Dewuldevi. His family

* Amongst the numerous inscriptions in the ancient character of the Jains that I have amassed, there is one of Sid-raj, which, with many others, remains undecyphered.

† We find frequent mention of these matrimonial alliances between those Rajpoot princes who followed the Buddhist doctrines, and the princes of Cashmere, which would indicate a community of creed.

family was the most exalted of the thirty-six tribes," of which a catalogue is subjoined, concluding with the following stanza :

> "Of all these the greatest is the Chohan,
> Of which tribe is Komar-Narind,
> Like the sun in heaven,
> Like the swan in Mansurwar,
> Who made the Chaluc house resplendent."

We may here make a reflection on the succession of a Chohan chief to the regal chair of the Chalucas, without changing the name of the dynasty ; a procedure which demonstrates two facts, illustrating the principle of the Rajpoot monarchy, proving it to be at once elective and adoptive, though the exercise of the first right is only had recourse to on emergent occasions. But of the absolute privilege being reposed in the great feudal vassals of these states, we could record many instances, where, in case of any personal defect in the heir-apparent, another branch of the family has been elected by them, and adopted by the monarch at their desire ; though I recollect no other instance in which a chief of another tribe was installed, without altogether changing the dynasty. Notwithstanding Komár-pál did "not bind round his head the turban of Sid-raj" (the symbol of adoption), during the lifetime of that prince, having now become a Chaluc, it was his duty to forget he had ever had other father than this monarch ; and so entirely is this identity recognised, that the Solankhi bard, in his list of the tribes, does not even allude to his ever having been other than a Chaluca. "Of all these tribes, the chief is the Chaluca, whose ornament is Komár-pál, whose Guru is Hemacharya, the sun and moon of mankind."

We now proceed to the names of the eighteen countries subject to the dominion of the Balhara at this period, embracing so wide a range, that,

that, but for confirmation by inscriptions, we might be inclined to treat it as an empty boast of the chronicler; yet, strange to say, this account, written in the twelfth century, accords perfectly with that given in the eighth by the Arabian travellers, since this rule literally did extend from the shores of the Indian peninsula to the base of the Himalaya mountains. "Guzzerat, Carnatica, Malwa, Maroo-dés, Soorut, (Saurashtra,) Sindhu, Concan, Sewaluc, Rushtra-dés, Bhansber, Lardés, Sunkuldés, Cutchdés, Jhalindir, Méwar, Deepucdés, Ootch, Bunbér, Kaerdés, Bheerâk; besides fourteen other regions, within whose boundaries *no animal life was taken.*" Then follows an account of his establishments; but the amount of his army exceeds belief, even supposing his power to have been absolute over the countries described: eleven hundred elephants, fifty thousand war chariots, eight lacs or eight hundred thousand foot soldiers, and eleven lacs or eleven hundred thousand horse, an aggregate far exceeding all that Xerxes ever brought against Greece. The copyist may have added a cipher to each, but even then the amount would exceed probability, in spite of the almost universal power of the Balhara sovereigns at this period, although Arabian visitors of the eighth, tenth, and twelfth centuries, attest their vast numerical array.

Komár-pál had sixteen queens, seventy-two great councillors and leaders of his armies. He divided Anhulwarra into twelve districts, placing a chief magistrate over each. He expelled the tribe of Lar from his kingdom. He made war on his brother-in-law, Poorunpál of Sacambhari, whose kingdom he invaded, making him prisoner. He attacked Samar-és, the lord of Soorut, whom he subjugated.* In S. 1211

* Perhaps this is the Sarama, surnamed Perimal, *i. e.* of the Pramara tribe (p. 163), mentioned by Renaudot, who turned Mooslem and ended his days at Mecca.

1211 (A.D. 1155), he erected the gilt dome of *the* temple,* and with foreign tribute defrayed the expense of excavating the steps which led up to the sacred mount, Girnar, and it is stated that he had many battles with the Islamite invaders, probably by the route of Sinde. Komár-pál is styled in the *Charitra* " the pillar of Jain faith," which, as it deprecates the destruction of animal life, is not a fitting creed for a Rajpoot, and still less was it desirable to have had a minister of this persuasion at the head of affairs.

Returning from the war in Sacambhari, in the rainy season, the sacrifice of animal life† was so great, that he made a vow, probably at the suggestion of Hemacharya, never again to undertake a war at that period of the year. To shew the extent to which this principle was carried, it is related that he sent a letter, with his portrait in an attitude of supplication, to Jey Sing, monarch of Canouj, entreating him to put a stop to the slaughter of animals in his kingdom, a request which, being backed by two millions of gold coin, and two thousand chosen steeds, met with a ready acquiescence from the Rahtore, though we know he had it not in his power to abide by the agreement. His enemies failed not to avail themselves of this infatuation, and the bard states, in the genealogies of the Solankhis, that the kingdom of Patun was overturned, from the Jain religion prohibiting the shedding of blood. In the words of the *Charitra*: " The Khan of Ghizni attacked him,

* As it is only styled *the* temple, we may imagine it to be the grand Sun-temple of Puttun Somnath.

† When I was in Marwar, in 1820, the discontented soldiery complained that while they were starving, the dogs were fed by hundreds by the ministers of the Jain faith. To this same spurious feeling may be attributed the destruction of Anhulwarra. It is a curious but little known fact, that almost all the mercantile communities, especially the Oswâl, consisting of one hundred thousand families, are descended from the Solankhi Rajpoots of Anhulwarra, and it is from this class of laymen (the Oswâl), strange to say, that the successors to the Jain hierarchs are selected.

him, but his astrologer, who would not let him fight in the monsoon, by the aid of magic, conveyed the invading general in his bed to the palace of the Chaluc king, between whom and the khan great friendship arose." The Hindu chroniclers seldom take the trouble to give a proper name where a title will suffice, and we have no record in the Islamite histories of any invasion from Ghizni within the period of this reign, so that we cannot identify this attack except with the expelled prince Jellaloodin, to whose invasion of Sinde and assault of the Raja of Omerkote, allusion is made both by Hindu and Mooslem authorities. But this magical nonsense is merely an invention, to shew that Patun was captured. The end of the story is even more eventful. Komár-pál's friendship with the Mooslem ripened into a love of his doctrines, in which Hemacharya set him an example, and, like whom, he might have died a convert to them, had not poison carried him off in the thirty-third year of his reign. His son and successor, Ajipal, was suspected of this deed, and the reason assigned is, that, when the prince found it had been administered to him, he sent for an antidote made from some kind of shell *(seep)*, which Ajipal, however, had taken care to remove. Hemacharya had died the year before, and although they attempted to conceal or slur over this remarkable apostasy in one of the greatest Acharyas of the Jains, by placing it to the score of insanity, "nothing but 'Allah, Allah,' passed his lips." But the most irrefragable proof of his conversion was in his remains being committed to the earth. This celebrated character died in S. 1221. He was born in S. 1145. We conclude the reign of this prince in the words of the *Charitra*: "In S. 1222 (A.D. 1166) Komár-pál became a ghost. He left this world poisoned by his successor, Ajipal."

We

We shall now comment on the curious and diversified information contained in the narrative of this prince's reign, and from various authorities confirm the general accuracy of the *Charitra.* It was during this reign that the celebrated Arabian geographer El-Edrisi visited the kingdom of the Balhara, and from whose work Bayer and D'Anville gleaned much information. Immediately following the quotation already cited, D'Anville continues: "Dans Edrisi on lit NAHROORA, et c'est non-seulement sur la province de l'Inde, que nous connoissons actuellement sous le nom de Guzzerat, mais *sur la ville la plus considérable de tous les royaumes Indiens,* que cette ville a dominé, selon ce géographe. Un monarque respecté de tous les autres souverains de l'Inde, et auquel le titre de *Balahara,* signifiant 'le seigneur,' ou 'roi,' par excellence, étoit réservé, faisoit sa résidence en cette ville. Ptolémée, dans une province de l'Inde qu'il nomme ARIACA, contigue à celle de Larice, que, plus haut, j'ai remarqué être le Guzzerat, plaçant une ville, sous le nom d'Hippocura, en qualité de ville royale du *Baleocur;* la grande affinité de ce titre avec celui de Balahar, jointe à la convenance de région, me persuade que c'est du même potentat qu'il est question." This acute and learned man then draws the following legitimate deduction: "Voilà donc un état Indien, prééminent en dignité, que nous découvrons existant dans le commencement du troisième siècle (*qu.* deuxième?), et dont il est encore mention, comme subsistant, dans un auteur Arabe qui écrivoit dans le douzième:" and he might have added, "to the fifteenth." He concludes with the following important information: "*Edrisi nous instruit que le Balahara est adorateur de Bodda!*"*

Upon this and other information, D'Anville proceeds to discover the

* *Eclaircissemens,* p. 75.

the site of this famed city : " Les géographes orientaux ne s'expliquent pas avec assez de précision sur la situation de la ville royale de Balahar, pour qu'il soit facile de la reconnoître. Selon Ebn-Saïd, elle est située en plaine, à trois journées de la mer, et *Kombaye est son port*, duquel elle tire ce qui lui est nécessaire." These lucid passages, extracted from the Nubian geographer, confirm, in the most satisfactory manner, all that the *Charitra* states respecting the grandeur of Anhulwarra, the power of its kings, and the religion they followed ; and when Edrisi tells us that it was the largest metropolis of all the Indian kingdoms, we no longer hesitate to credit the extent of fifteen miles circuit assigned to it by the author of the *Charitra*, and the necessity for its division into " twelve districts" by Komár-pál. Edrisi likewise adds his testimony to the extent of the power and influence of this prince, observing that " he was respected by all the other sovereigns of India ;" and we have other authority still stronger and more durable to the same point. We might have imagined the list of eighteen regions, over which he spread his arms, to have been apocryphal, like his armies, but for indisputable collateral evidence. The most powerful is obtained from two inscriptions (App. Nos. III. and IV.), one preserved in a temple at Cheetore, the other at the town of Puttun. Here is undeniable proof of his actual conquest of Méwàr, as stated in the *Charitra*, and of his having established his power in the city of Salpoor in the Punjab, and even as far as the Sewaluc mountains, an external range of the Himalaya. From this, the conquest of Jhalinder, Ootch, and Sindhu, all small states, was comparatively easy, and this supports the Arabian geographer, Abulfeda, quoted by Bayer, in his description of Chorasmia (Khwarezm) : " *Terram Khanbalek ab Austro attingunt montes Belhar, qui est rex regum Indiæ.*" By these extracts from the *Charitra*,

Charitra, we are enabled also at once to clear up two long-disputed points regarding the countries of Larice and Ariaca, which Ptolemy makes contiguous to each other. According to him, *it* appears to have been an important division of the Syrastrene, or peninsula of the Sauras. The *Charitra* enumerates *Lar-dés*, or ‘country of the Lar,’ amongst the eighteen regions dependent on Anhulwarra, but for some fault, Komár-pál “chased the tribe of *Lar* from the country.” Ebn-Said settles the point of position, saying that he had met with “authorities which placed the famous temple of Somnath in the country of Lar.”* At all events, this proves that this tribe was so powerful in the time of Ptolemy, as to give its name to a country, and of sufficient strength even in the twelfth century to draw upon it the especial vengeance of the king of Anhulwarra. The remains of this ancient tribe are now only to be discovered in the third or mercantile caste, forming one of the eighty-four great families residing in Maroo, and following the Jain faith. So much for the Larice of the great Egyptian geographer, and the inhabitants of our *Lari-ca-dés*, or ‘country of the Lar.’ As to the province adjoining Larice, which he names *Ariaca*, we have already incidentally introduced it to the reader, and had the learned Wilford always adhered to such expositions as that “On the site of Tagara, the capital of Aria,” he would have been one of the most illustrious scholars who have ever cultivated the study of Hindu antiquities. The occasion of this dissertation upon Tagara and Ariaca, arose out of an inscription discovered when excavating among ruins at Tanna, near Bombay, and which fortunately fell into the hands of General Carnac. They are beyond doubt amongst the most interesting additions to ancient history hitherto found, and it is but justice to Wilford to

* *Eclaircissemens*, p. 69.

to say, that none, since discovered, have found so able an expositor.* I deem myself fortunate in being able to throw additional light on these valuable records, which at the same time illuminate the subject in hand.

These copper-plates, recording a grant of land made in the year A.Sac. 939, or A.V. 1074, corresponding with A.D. 1018, enter as usual into the ancestry of the donor. Stanza fifth shews that Capardin was "chief of the race of Silâra," which is introduced amongst the thirty-six tribes subject to the emperors of Anhulwarra, with the epithet *Raj Tilac*, or 'diadem of kings.' In all probability, it is the same as *Lar*, with the prefix *Si* or *Su*, meaning *par excellence*, and as, even in the days of Ptolemy and Arrian, the adjoining provinces of Larice and Ariaca were subject to the same prince, we may admit the inference without hesitation. The final *a* is superfluous, and put in by the English editor; it is mute, and calculated to mislead when appended to proper names. The eighth stanza says that his grandson "afterwards became the sovereign of Gogni;" in all probability, he had conquered the important city and sea-port of Cambayet, whose ancient name was Garjni or Gajni, and which lay between, connecting Larice and Ariaca. The sixteenth stanza gives the proper name of the grantee in *Aricésar*, which, though very properly translated 'a lion *(césar)* amongst foes *(ari)*,' would have been rendered more correctly 'the lion of Aria,' his country; his proper name, Deva-Raja, being developed in the next sentence, *viz.* "*Aricésar Deva-Raja, king of the race of Silar, sovereign of the city of Tagara,* governs the whole region of Concan, consisting of one thousand four hundred villages and cities," &c. &c. &c., one of which, and an important one, was Tanna, adjoining Mambei

* See *Asiatic Researches,* vol. i. p. 357.

Mambei (Bombay). Quoting from the *Periplus* of Arrian, Wilford says: "*Tagara was the metropolis of a large district called Ariaca, which comprehended the Subah of Arungabad, the Concan, &c.*," (in fact, repeating exactly the words of the inscription); "*for Damaun, Callian, Salsette* (in which was Tanna), *Bombay, &c. belonged to the Raja of Larikeh, or Lar, according to Arrian and Ebn Said*:" precisely the point I had reached through the *Charitra* and native authorities. Wilford continues, still extracting from Arrian: "In speaking of Tagara, he (Arrian) says that the Greeks were prohibited from landing at Callian and other harbours on that coast," which was not formerly the case, as they were freely admitted into the Deccan to send off the goods to the coast, as Callian, Bombay, where they shipped them. He adds, that Baroach (Barugaza) was the only port at which they were allowed to reside for the purpose of trade, by order of Sandanes, Raja of Larikeh or Lar, who commanded all who disobeyed to be captured and sent to Baroach. Probably, this arose from the superior influence of the Roman agents, who, as Wilford remarks, after the conquest of Egypt, monopolized the India trade, and shut up the Red Sea to all strangers. Wilford suggests that the Greeks had attempted to force a settlement at Salsette, to facilitate their conquests in the Deccan, towards which the influence of their brethren of Bactria may have tended. When we reflect that Menander and Apollodotus penetrated into the kingdom of the Συροι, the Sauras, the suggestion is far from improbable. He cites Pliny, Arrian, and Ptolemy, as to the prevalence of piracy in the ports south of Callian, which deterred the Greeks from landing there.

Now, when we unite all these scattered proofs, we see distinctly the same people as in latter days; and singularly enough, the native traditions assert that it was from acts of piratical violence that the Saura or Chaora

Chaora prince of Deva-bunder was driven from Lari-ca-dés. Who, then, was the expeller? Egyptians, Greeks, Romans, who had all in turn monopolized the trade of India, were driven from the Nile and the Red Sea, on which the flag of Islam floated in triumph, when Anhulwarra was re-founded by Vansraj Chaora, in A.D. 746. It must have been, therefore, by the fleets of the great Haroon that this catastrophe was effected, not *Varuna*, the god of the waters. There is no necessity to say more on Komár-pál being the great supporter of the religion of Buddha, a fact attested by the *Charitra*, and corroborated by El-Edrisi, whose valuable information proves that of which there never should have been a doubt, that Jainism and Buddhism are the same, the one being but a modification of the other. But, as I shall conclude this outline of the annals of Anhulwarra with some reflections on its religion, commerce, and maritime relations, we shall finish our remarks on Komár-pál by stating that the Mooslem historians do not record any distinct invasion previous to the eruption under Shahbudin, which sealed the downfal of Hindu supremacy, about twenty years later than the proselytism of Komár-pál and his Guru, Hemacharya. My own preceptor, who traced his spiritual descent from this celebrated Acharya of the Jains, which proved of no small use to me in my researches in Anhulwarra, admitted the truth of the tradition, though the conversion is slurred over by attributing it to the effect of magic, which produced madness, whence we might almost conclude that the conversion of both was forcible. Komár-pál may, therefore, be dismissed with the reflection that he was the greatest prince of his time, and alternately the strongest supporter and the most vehement opponent of the faith he professed, and from which he apostatized to that of Islam.

Ajipal succeeded in S. 1222, A.D. 1166. He is mentioned in the Jessulmér annals, as the competitor in S. 1215 with its prince for the hand of the sister of Rindhawul,* son of Yasúvarma, king of Dhar, and a reference to the Pramar inscription settling the important era of Raja Bhoj,† at once attests the synchronical rectitude of the Solankhi and Bhatti annals. It is by no means clear whether Ajipal was the son as well as successor of Komár-pál. In the genealogies of the Solankhi bard, he is called Chonipál which name also appears in cotemporary inscriptions. The same authority states "that he was the founder of the third or Bâgéla dynasty; and that the astrologers having foretold that Komár-pál would have a son born in *Mula Nacshitra*, who would cause his father's death, he was sent as an offering to the shrine of Bâgéswara Mata, by whom he was not only preserved from destruction, but she herself, in the form of a tigress (*bâg*), suckled the young Solankhi, whence his issue, which spread over the country, obtained the distinctive name of Bâgéla."‡ Like his father, he became a convert to Islamism, and the first act of his reign was the destruction of every temple of religion, orthodox or heterodox, Jain or Brahmin, throughout his dominions. One, however, escaped, the temple on the hill of Taoringi, said to have been built of kugar wood, which they assert is incombustible.§ Ajipal did not long survive his exaltation and three-fold

* The same Annals mention that the Pramara had three daughters, and that, besides Ajipal of Patun, the heir-apparent of Cheetore was there, in the capacity of a suitor, and although to their own prejudice, they honestly give an anecdote illustrating the superiority of the prince of Méwar, who quarrelled with the Bhatti for presuming to drink water from his cup. Here are no less than four cotemporaneous dynasties brought into notice.

† See *Trans. R.A.S.*, vol. i. p. 226.

‡ The princes of Bâghélcund are of this race, and there are many petty chieftainships of this tribe in Guzzerat, as Lunawarra, Mandvie, Mahera, Godra, Dubboye, &c.

§ This shrine, reported to have been once nine stories in height, is said still to exist.

fold guilt of parricide, apostasy, and sacrilege. In a fit of rage, he put out the eye of the successor of Hemacharya, and soon afterwards, falling from his horse, the animal dragged him through the streets till he was killed. Abulfazil states that Komár-pál reigned twenty-three years, and Ajipal eight, but the *Charitra* places them both within the period of thirty years, allotting to Ajipal less than two.

The chronicle concludes in the following manner: "Thus ends the *Charitra*, done into the Guzzerati dialect in S. 1492 (A.D. 1436), and this copy thereof was written in the reign of Akbar. The original history is in Sanscrit, consisting of thirty-eight thousand slocas, composed by Sailug Soor Acharya, and this version in Guzzerati of thirteen thousand."

CHAPTER X.

History of Anhulwarra continued.—Bheemdeo.—His character.—Cause of the war between Anhulwarra and Ajmér.—Battle between Bheem and Pirthi-raj of Delhi.—The former slain.—Conquests of Pirthi-raj in Guzzerat.—Inscriptions.—Mooldeo.—Beesuldeo.—Bheemdeo.—Opulence of Anhulwarra.—Arjundeo.—Sarungdeo.—Kurrundeo the madman.—Invasion of the Mussulmans.—The Balhara sovereignty extinguished.—The Taka race obtain Guzzerat and change the capital.—Name of Anhulwarra degenerates into Puttun.—Value of these historical records.—Enumeration of the results.

Bheemdeo succeeded in S. 1225, or A.D. 1169. In the cotemporaneous annals, he has the distinctive prefix of *Bhola*, which means simpleton, fool, or madman. The Rajpoot annalist, instead of applying numerals to distinguish princes of the same name, has recourse to some characteristic epithet. It is only from the Chohan Annals that we gather anything regarding Bheemdeo, who, if *Bhola*, would have been the third "madman" in succession on the royal cushion of the Balharas, a circumstance sufficient to sink the most powerful monarchy, even had all their predecessors been Solomons. It is not improbable that the copyist may have substituted *Bhola* for *Bala*, as Chund designates him *Bal-ca-rae Chaluc vira*, or the 'Chaluc warrior, lord of [the country of] Bal;' yet if the poet really means thus to characterize him, it must be understood in the sense so peculiarly applicable to the Rajpoot, of arrogance.

Bheem seems rapidly to have repaired the excesses of his predecessors, and, as a valiant warrior, appears to have been in every way worthy of wielding the sceptre of Sid-raj. His wars with Soméswar, the Chohan king of Sacambhari, whom he slew in battle, and subsequently with his son Pirthi-raj, the Rolando of the Rajpoots, are amongst the most interesting episodes of the grand epic of Chund. If these were madness, it was of a lofty description. It would be out of place here to extract largely from the bard, more especially as I hope one day to give a great portion of this poem to the public; but I will cite enough to shew its value, not alone as illustrative of the manners and customs of the Rajpoots of past days, but as an historical chronicle of the period, particularly in what appertains to the subject under discussion. The battles give occasion to describe not only the personal qualities of "the foe of the Chohan," but the resources of his kingdom, and the variety of its tribes, with their leaders, as they assemble under the banners of the Balhara.

"In Goojur-d'hur ruled Bhola-Bheem Bhoing,* whose array of horses, elephants, and chariots, was innumerable. The lustre *(pani)*† of his falchion was bright and deep as the waters of the ocean. To whom shall his uncle, Sarungdeo, be compared? a god in form, whose son Pertap and brothers seven were like lions. The lustre of Rajpoots sparkled in their countenances. Strong they were, and wise as strong, and in the pride of strength they communed with the rolling thunder. When the command of their lord is to oppose a foe, they fall upon him as the lightning of heaven scorches the earth. It was they who slew the Ran, and the lord of the Rans,‡ the powerful Jhala, who resembled a flaming fire. Sarungdeo had gone to the heroes' abode *(Suraloca)* and Pertap had succeeded. With five hundred warriors in their train, each of whom felt himself a hero, the brothers with zeal served

* *Bhoing,* a contraction for *Bho-jung,* an *opma,* or comparison to the serpent.

† Used in the same sense as in speaking of the *water* of a diamond: likewise applied to the temper of the steel.

‡ *Ran* is the title of the head of the Jhala tribe. *Jowala* signifies 'flame,' a *jeu de mots* upon the name of the tribe. Chund abounds with such.

served their prince, and of the seventeen thousand towns of Goojur-d'hur, they were the *calpa-vrisha*,* faithful to their lord, in whose cause they made the mountain-pinnacle to bow its head."

The story goes on to relate an inroad of the mountaineers and foresters upon the plains of Guzzerat of so serious a nature, that the Balhara in person headed the war against them. The marauders were quickly driven back to their savage retreats, and the prince and his chiefs amused themselves by hunting in the woods. But an incident occurred which we must not mar by a partial relation, that of slaying in self-defence the favourite elephant of the king, which act drew upon them his resentment, and the *désvati*, or sentence of banishment. They proceeded to Ajmér, where they were received by the Chohan king with all the observances of international courtesy and hospitality. " He put into their hands a written grant *(putta)*, and gave to each a dress of honour and one hundred horse." They were enrolled amongst the Sawunts, or great leaders of the Chohan, and prosperity was their portion, till one unlucky day, " when the heir of Somésa, like Soméru, seated amidst his warriors, was listening to the deeds of the days of yore ; Pertap's soul was on fire, and as he kindled at the story, his hand was curling his moustache."

To curl the moustache (interpreted as an act of defiance) is a piece of ill-breeding unpardonable in a Rajpoot, especially before a superior. It was noticed by the reckless Kân-rae, the brother of the Chohan king, and uncle to Pirthi-raj, whose armies he led during his minority, and who is immortalized even by Ferishta, under the name of Khandi-rae, for his personal conflict with, and defeat of, the Sultan of Ghizni. The furious Kan-kaka (the *uncle* Kan), misinterpreting the act, felled Pertap

* The fabulous tree in the heaven of Indra, yielding golden fruit.

Pertap to the earth. His (Pertap's) brothers drew their swords to rescue and revenge him. All was confusion: the youthful prince escaped, but the council chamber became a scene of blood and death. The brothers were all laid lifeless, and had the honour of the bard's applause, who probably incited the mischief which he loved. "Renown to the Chaluc who, in a foreign land, was true to the sense of shame. It was evening when Mahadeo completed his chaplet.* The Joginis† had their platters well filled. The Chohan heroes lay in their gore, Kan, like death, stalking in the midst, for with blood did the brother of Soméru irrigate the field of council."

Such was, such often is, the Rajpoot, and so far he well merits the epithets *benda* and *bhola*,—one who would fight for a feather. Yet for this does Chund sound his praise. "Kan is like Bheem in the *Bharat.* Kan is like Rawuna. Kan puts the string in the nostril of the strong."

It was this mad act which occasioned the war between the ancient rivals of Anhulwarra and Ajmér, and cost the lives of both, besides preparing the way for the eventual success of the Islamite. The sentence of outlawry was forgotten; the incident which occasioned it forgiven: "the honour of the Chaluc race was implicated," and nothing but revenge was breathed in Anhulwarra, when the fate of Pertap and his brethren was made known. "The Chaluc Bheem and his warriors heard of the fate of the sons of Sarungdeo: rage inflamed their bodies." A letter was sent to the Chohan declaratory of war for the the Chaluc's murder of kinsmen, which received the laconic reply, that Somésa "would meet him in arms."

The above is a bare outline of the cause of the war. The next *Samya,*

* The chaplet of the god of war consists of human skulls.

† A kind of female harpy—they frequent the field of battle.

Samya, or section of the sixty-nine books, opens with the preparations for battle on both sides, and gives us the names and families of the leaders, and the tribes which assembled under their banners.

"In Goojur-dés reigns Chaluc Bheem, equal to the Bheem of the Pandus. His renown and his rules of government *(Râjnita)* cannot be described by words. But Somésa of Sambhur is a thorn in his heart; night nor day has he rest."

Then follows the proclamation of assembly to his vassal lords, several of whom, as they reach the presence, make speeches.

"Thus to the Ind* of the Chalucs spoke Runingdeo, lord of the Jhalas: 'If such flames of anger devour you, call on the array of the land, that we may fall on the foe with the velocity of the wind; that as the Bhil robs the honied nest, we may plunder this Sambri.' Then spoke Kun, lord of the Catti (Catti Narind), and Runing Rajb'han the mighty, and the warlike Dhawulanga,† lord of Deo, and the Dholara, Soortan; the Mocwanoh leader, Sarung, with the Joonagurh Tatar,‡ whose body is covered with innumerable scars. Amidst his chiefs in council, the Chaluc thus spoke: 'My ancient feud is like a needle in my heart. Yet, what is Sambhur to me? for till I dye the head of its lord, I can know no rest. Is it because he won the fight of Sajut he is called the player in the game of battle? but he is a thorn in my flesh until I meet him in arms.' Then replied the Runing Rao, and the Chaurasima Bhan, and Shamoh, the lord of the men of Sham,§ and

* A contraction of *Indra,* 'lord, or chief.'

† In this epithet, meaning 'the flag of Siva,' we recognise the ancient princes of Deo and Somnath, now tributary to Anhulwarra.

‡ This shews the influence the Mooslem had in this kingdom, being entrusted with this important fortress in the very heart of the peninsula.

§ Are we to understand from this that he had Syrians in his array? Sham is Syria. This was the period of the Crusades, and Shahbudin had Franks incorporated with his army.

and the Catti warrior Thanung, whose mind was deep and *his body fair*,* and strong to support his prince in battle. Birsing the Chohan, who stormed with rage, and would engulph in his wrath the volcano in the ocean. All swear they will so fight that the world shall hear of it."

The march is then described. "The array advances and increases as it moves, like the dark rolling clouds from the mountains of the north. The warriors strong and haughty stride on; in their pride they say, 'where are our equals?' As did the heroes of Râm advance on Lanka, so does the army of the Chaluc advance on the Chohan. The eye is confused in scanning its numbers. But what shall I say of the Sewaroh Amra Sing,† whose face is the index of fidelity to his prince? what of Bhiroo the bard, imbued with lore? what of the Brahmin Leeladur, familiar with the Vedas?‡ what of the fair-faced Charun Dandroopa? These four ministers (*muntris*) accompanied Bheem."

As we have nothing to do with the Chohan hero, we proceed to the close, which was fatal to Soméswar, a result which Chund, with a laudable partiality, attributes to his young hero Pirthi-raj's absence in the north. "The *son of Jey Sing* § is like the star of the north; yet he would not have set his foot on our land had Pirthi-raj been here." Like a true Rajpoot, he pays this marked compliment to his foe: "As

* This is a good picture of the physical qualities of the Catti, the ancient foe of Alexander, for not only are they fairer than those around them, but blue eyes are met with amongst them, indicative of their northern origin.

† Séwara means a priest, among the Jains: but we must not mistake this Amra for the celebrated author of the dictionary, who flourished at the Balhara court several reigns antecedently.

‡ We are not to infer, because a Brahmin was in the councils of the sovereign of Anhulwarra, that he was a worshipper of Siva.

§ Meaning the son of Aji-sing, the last prince. *Jey* means 'victorious,' *Ujya*, 'invincible.'

" As the Chaluc approached, even the inhabitants of Dehli trembled in their abodes. The standard of Sambhur advanced, like the variegated blossoms of spring. Somésa towered amidst the warriors in the red field of fight," which continued six *ghurries*, when, " with fifty mighty chiefs, Somésa drank of the wave of battle. Immortality was gained. Somésa upheld Somésa. The lord of Sambhur lay in the field, while the Chaluc was borne off in his litter. If ever the Chaluc and Chohan meet again, it must be with other chiefs, for no heroes are left. That immortality which the recluse gains after a long life of austerity, Soméswar attained in the twinkling of an eye. The world shouts ' Applause !'—the gods cry ' Alas !' "

In this war we see no diminution of strength in the kings of Anhulwarra, who claimed full sovereignty over the *seventeen thousand towns* of Guzzerat and the peninsula, the quotas from whose extreme points, Jhalawar, Cattiawar, and Deo, are mentioned, and repeated with many others in the sequel. The success of the Chaluc king, however, on this occasion, ultimately proved his destruction. Pirthi-raj, who was destined to be the first and the last Chohan emperor of Dehli, determined to avenge his father, and the forty-first *Samya*, or section, thus opens : " Like a green wound night and day is this Bheem ; a thorn in the heart of the lord of men ; he is devoured with flame, which the blood of his foe alone can extinguish." As he expresses himself, " the feud of my father is still on my head ; each time I taste water it is like drinking my own blood ; yet my enemy is strong." " Yet," (he adds in another place,) " one day I shall take my father from the very entrails of this Bheem."

A most animated description is given of the assemblage of the sixty-four thousand and their leaders, forming the array of the Chohan, the

account

account of which soon reached the Chaluc, who, nothing daunted, prepared to meet the strife. For the sake of the names of these levies we shall briefly cite it, and we must again admire the noble spirit of the hostile bard, who thus speaks of the foe :

"The son of Jey Sing was enraged; the muscles of his frame started from passion; his eyes became inflamed as he called upon his chiefs to prepare for battle. Throughout the land he sent his summons. The lords of men obeyed. Then came two thousand khans, armed with the *khotban.** Then advanced the Bulla of Cutch, in quilted mail, with three thousand horse. With one thousand warriors came the lord of Soret,† and the Kakraicha Kale, bowman of the hideous face, an archer unequalled, for no second arrow is required from his quiver. Then came the Jhala Narind of Jhalawar, and as he advanced, the sun hid his beams. Then Mukroand, the Kaba‡ chief, at whose approach the country fled. Then advanced the barrier of the Cattis, Narind, whose foe must ever be a stranger to repose—with many of less note, whose names to what extent shall I, Chund, relate? Such were the hordes *forming the host of the Chaluca, from his own land of Goojurkhund, and such did the spies of Dehli see assemble, and report to their lord. They said, 'like the rolling thunder does the Chaluc advance: that the bounds of ocean were broken down, whence poured forth a hundred thousand men and a thousand elephants.*"

It is not my intention to say anything of the array of the Chohan, of which Kan Rae, who had also to avenge his past defeat, was made generalissimo on this occasion, as in later days when he defeated Shahbudin,

* A javelin or dart propelled through a tube.

† Soret either means the modern Surat, or else one of the subdivisions of Saurashtra.

‡ A famous thievish tribe in Guzzerat, not yet extinct.

budin, the emblems of royalty, "the *Châor* and *Cheter** waved over the head of Kan. Pirthi-raj himself led the van (*herole*), Nidder Rae the centre, while the rear was commanded by the Pramara."

Another passage, characteristic of the Rajpoot, may be given. As the armies advanced to meet each other, the heralds on either side exchanged defiance from the princes, and as the bards fulfil this important office on warlike occasions, Chund was deputed by his youthful monarch to the Balhara. "Tell the Chaluc, O Chund, I am come for revenge, yet take from me two gifts; one a coloured turban, the other a corset (*kanchali*), and bid him accept either, as his fancy may incline. Say that this world is a dream, and that one of us must fall." Chund, relying on his sacred character, as *d'hool*, or envoy, adds a great deal more of very curious impertinence from himself, to all of which the Chaluc replies with great dignity: "Bheem I am, and like Bheem [of the *Bharat*] I will give you battle. The fate of the father awaits the son"—and in return he sends one of his bards, by name Jugdeo, to Pirthi-raj. His words are not given, but they doubtless were, as the bard says, full of venom (*vis*), for Chund, as the spokesman for his prince, cuts him short with a sarcastic allusion to the unrefined dialect of his country: "Why torment us with this Guzzerati gibberish?" shewing the difference in those days to have been as striking as at present.

The armies meet, and the poet is in his glory. He says, "A noble field was displayed for Chund, the road to Suraloca was soon crowded with travellers, and immortality was extorted." The battle was long and

* The ox-tail and umbrella, not unfrequently placed over some chief of consequence, to divert attention and protect the king from danger: in Shakspeare's description of the battle of Bosworth field, Richmond, in assaulting the gallant usurper, says "Three have already fall'n who wore that crown."

and desperately contested. Many chiefs on both sides, whose names and actions are recorded, had fallen, when the youthful Chohan fought his way to his foeman. "For one *pahar** the sword had rained upon the casque; the armour of heroes was hewn in pieces. Sarasvati† rose with the torrents of blood. The Joginis filled their cups from the stream of the field, and the Palcharas had their cravings appeased. Pirthi-raj espied his foe; he gave his steed the rein. Earth shook with affright. The guardians of the world fled from their posts. The gods trembled. His hand was lifted to the heavens, and when his bow forms a halo, what can escape? Then Siva's meditations were at an end: his chaplet fell from his hands as the Chohan and the Chaluc encountered in fight. Each warrior wields the lightning's flash,‡ and as they met, Pirthi-raj exclaimed, 'O Bheem, thine hour is come!' 'Beware!' said Bheem, 'for I shall send you to Soméswar.' On rushed Pirt'ha, and where the thread adorned the neck of Bheem, there smote the steel, and as he fell, he made the *teeka* in the fore head of Pirthi-raj. Then the gods shouted 'Victory!' and the Apsaras in their heavenly cars cast a shade over the field. When their lord fell, the Chaluc army took flight."

The bard praises the noble bearing of Bheem, of whom he adds: "But he is gone in the chariot of the gods to Seopoor." But it was no easily-gained victory. "Fifteen hundred horse, and fifteen hundred heroes of renown (amongst whom was Jait, the lord of Aboo), besides five thousand of less note, lay mangled on the field." His description of

* A watch, quarter of the day.

† The river which flows past Anhulwarra.

‡ *Beejulsar,* meaning the essence or cream (*sar*) of lightning, a name not unfrequently adopted by a Rajpoot chief for a favourite sword. The Beejulsar of Pirthi-raj was as renowned as the Balisarda of Ariosto.

of the night succeeding the battle, though irrelevant, may be appended for the sake of the metaphors.

"Pirthi-raj had gained the fight. The heroes sounded the shell of victory, though their bodies were covered with glorious wounds. The wrath of the Chohan was extinct, for his father was avenged. The warriors laud each other's deeds. The glory of his warriors is the wealth of Pirthi-raj. They remained that night on the field of battle, attending to the wounded: but the night was long; anxiously they looked for the morning. Night fled—the lotus of morning expanded; the bee, which it enveloped in its shade, took to wing. The stars grew dim—the veil of darkness was rent asunder. The host of Chandrama soon became invisible. The portals of the gods were opened to admit the prayers of mankind. The eyes of the bird of night were again closing. The shells in the divine mansions sounded. The sun commenced his course."

Immediately after this climax, the poet, as if startled into sympathy for those scattered around him, by whom the influence of the beams of the luminary would never more be felt, exclaims: "How many warriors have trod the earth, who have given their bodies to the sword! but the glory of these Chund himself has rehearsed. The world is a dream! whatever it contains will one day yield to destruction. The hearts of men are foolishly fixed on worldly desires; but though death is a butcher *(khaluk)*, the meed of the warrior is the only real wealth, for by the sword's edge alone is immortality obtained:" a doctrine which, fortified by the joys of Suraloca (the heroes' heaven),—a place combining all the luxury of the Mooslem's paradise, diversified with the strife and feasting of the Scandinavians,—is well calculated to foster the devotion of a Rajpoot for his prince and country.

 The

The Chohan king of Dehli and (since his father's death) also of Ajmér followed up his victory, and "conquered the eighty-four sea-ports of the Chaluc." He raised to the throne a prince named Cutchra, to whom he restored ten of these ports, and carried him to Dehli. Who this Cutchra was, I have in vain attempted to discover. The name may denote a branch of the family who held Cutch as a fief, the final syllable marking the genitive case, as *ra*, *ca*, *da*, *cha*, which are touchstones of the dialects.

The year S. 1224 is given in the annals of the Chohans for this invasion of Guzzerat; but in the chronicle of the Solankhi bard, S. 1228 is the period assigned for the death of Bhola Bheem, a discrepancy quite immaterial; so that we have another very satisfactory synchronism, further confirmed by the Hansi inscription, of a most important epoch, when all the Hindu thrones were on the eve of being overturned. The inscription alluded to, which I brought away from the ruins of Pirthi-raj's palace at Hansi, and sent in the same year to Marquess Hastings, to be presented to the Asiatic Society of Calcutta, but which has never since been heard of, was of infinite value, not only as giving the era of the last Hindu emperor of Dehli, but as affording parallel synchronisms with cotemporaneous dynasties. Of these, one instance has been detailed in the war with Anhulwarra. There is another, scarcely of minor importance, settling the era of the great ancestors of the princes of Ambér. Rao Pirjoon was then its prince (of Ambér), and one of the most conspicuous of the great vassals of the Chohan. His name appears in the Hansi inscription, as holding, in conjunction with Hamira, the guardianship of that important frontier fortress. He is likewise mentioned in the battle in which Soméswar, the father of Pirthi-raj, was slain; and a short *samya*,

or

or canto, called the *Pirjoon Samya*, is introduced between this battle and the one we have just related. It gives an account of an incursion made by this leader for the recovery of a plume lost in the field where his monarch fell. The bard records his success, and the re-instatement of this feather in his cap, we may take it for granted, was a metaphorical expression for a successful foray, as Marik-eswar, or Lord Marcher. An account of the inscription alluded to is given in the *Trans.* R.A.S. (vol. i. p. 154), as I had fortunately preserved a copy and translation of the original.

Ballo Mooldeo ascended the throne in S. 1228 (A.D. 1172). Here is another example of the use of a figurative distinctive affix, and it is not a little curious that the first and last of this dynasty should bear the same name, from each being born under the same zodiacal sign. He ruled the kingdom of Anhulwarra twenty-one years, or until S. 1249 (A.D. 1193), an era for ever memorable in the history of the Rajpoots, when the star of Islam shone triumphant over the palaces of Dehli and Canouj, and when the chivalrous Pirthi-raj fought and fell on the banks of the Caggar, and the monarch of Canouj, having lost all, save his honour, was drowned in the Ganges in his flight. But though the great rivals of Anhulwarra were thus disposed of, the shock did not reach 'little *(ballo)* Mooldeo,' who was succeeded by

Beesuldeo Bhagéla. He commenced his reign in S. 1249 (A.D. 1193). Why he should be styled the first of the Bhagéla or Bhagaila dynasty, I never could discover, for the anecdote which caused the change of name is related of the son of Komár-pál, indicating that Mooldeo was first entitled to the appellation. It is, however, a matter of no importance, as all the inscriptions, even after Beesuldeo, continue to use the prior name of the tribe, Chaluc or Solankhi. We have

have not a single fact regarding this prince, who ruled fifteen years.

Bheemdeo succeeded in S. 1264 (A.D. 1208), and ruled no less than forty-two years. Besides this, of itself a very good proof that the arms of Islam, which had already overturned the monarchies of Dehli, Canouj, Cheetore, did not scathe the kingdom of Anhulwarra, we have the testimony of the temples of Cheetore, erected twenty years after the accession of this prince, and by his ministers. All the inscriptions found on Aboo designate him as paramount sovereign, and as the Pramara princes of Chandravati and Aboo had reverted to a state of vassalage under this kingdom, from which they had been temporarily rescued by Pirthi-raj, we may infer that neither westward nor southward had the power of the Balaraes declined. In fact, the Balabhi inscription, recording the "virtue" of Arjundeo, his successor, clearly proves that not only the country of the Lar, but all Saurashtra, was firm in its obedience, though the mariners of Arabia had been permitted to form settlements on the coast. A more striking proof of the riches of Anhulwarra cannot be afforded, for if we take the temples simultaneously erected on mounts Aboo and Taringi, in the city of Chandravati and on the shores of the ocean, as criteria of its prosperity, we might affirm that if she were not in the zenith of her greatness, she could at least not have materially declined. Or if, since the mighty kings, Kurrun and Sid-raj, to whom both history and tradition point as the great ones of the land, she had deteriorated during the reigns of the "three madmen" which concluded the second dynasty of her kings, what must not her resources and magnificence have been in the plenitude of her glory, when even a century afterwards, during which invasion had twice swept the land, she was yet able

able to expend such munificence on these shrines, each of which cost millions, contributed from the redundant coffers of three only of her merchants? well may we exclaim "her merchants were princes!"

Bheemdeo, in conjunction with his brave vassal, Dharaburz, defended himself nobly against the Islamite, defeating the emperor, Kootub-u-din, who was wounded; nor did his successors gain any advantage over Anhulwarra until the reign of the sanguinary Alla, half a century later.

ARJUNDEO succeeded in S. 1306 (A.D. 1250). As he ruled twenty-three years, he in all probability followed the policy of his father, and while he opposed the arms, cultivated the friendship, of the Mahomedans, who were rapidly environing his kingdom. Yet his title of Chaluca Chacraverta (on the Balabhi inscription), or the 'universal Chaluca,' to which is appended, "always victorious," shews no diminution of power. This inscription is a kind of rescript to his admiral, Noor-u-din Feroz, a native of Hormuz, who was chief of the port of Billacul, near Somnath, and to the vassal princes of the Chaora tribe, holding the island and port of Deo, to see certain duties on merchandise appropriated to the repairs of the grand temple of the sun at Somnat'h, of which the Chaoras continued to be *custodes*. This valuable record involves four great points. *First*, that the temple of Somnat'h, or 'lord of the moon,' is the great sun temple of the Sauras, who gave their name to the peninsula, Saurashtra, the Syrastrene of the Greek kings of Bactria, two of whom, Apollodotus and Menander, carried their arms into this very region of the Σύροι.*

Second, that the Chaora or Saura princes of the island of Deo and the holy city of Somnat'h, though subordinate, continued in the fourteenth

* See dissertation upon this subject in *Trans.* R.A.S. vol. i. p. 313.

fourteenth century in possession of this ancient capital, being driven from which, they founded Anhulwarra in A.D. 746.

Third, that the city of Balabhi, whose sovereigns were the Bala-raes, had a Samvat or era of their own, corresponding with the era of Vicrama 375, or A.D. 319.

Fourth, that an Arabian Amir of the port of Hormuz, was admiral* of one of the fleets of Anhulwarra so late as A.D. 1250.

Sarungdeo succeeded in S. 1329 (A.D. 1273). His reign was a long one for these troublous times, being twenty-one years ; but the period was fast approaching when Anhulwarra was to bend her proud neck.

Gehla Kurrundeo succeeded in S. 1350 (A.D. 1294). At this momentous epoch in the fortunes of the Rajpoot kingdoms, when each required the wisdom of a Solomon to direct its superabundant valour, the *gâdi* of Anhulwarra was occupied by a madman or *imbecile*. Such is the import of *Gehla*,—not *Gohil*, as Abulfazil has it, for none of this tribe ever sat upon the cushion of Vansraj. At this time, Khuni or 'the Sanguinary,' the only title by which the Hindus recognise the ferocious Alla-u-din, who was the angel of destruction to every Rajpoot dynasty in India, approached Anhulwarra, where, as in all places, "he saw and overcame." With Gehla Kurrun the sovereignty of the Balharas became extinct, after having subsisted for five hundred and fifty-two years from the foundation of Anhulwarra. Petty chieftains of the last dynasty, the Bhagéla, continued to hold important fiefs in and about the metropolis, but their dependence was sealed, and the proud walls of Kali-kote were levelled with the earth.†

Years

* It may not be generally known that the word *Admiral* is of Arabic extraction, *viz. Amir-al-âb*, 'lord of the waters.'

† The Balharas have left few traces of their greatness. Of the first dynasty, the Chaora, there are

Years after this catastrophe, a new dynasty once more succeeded to the curtailed sceptre of Anhulwarra, in the person of Seharun, of the ancient

are a few estates in Guzzerat, the most extensive of which is rated at a lac of rupees. The next in importance is equal to forty thousand rupees. With all of these the Ranas of Méwar keep up their ancient matrimonial intercourse, esteeming the pure blood of the Chaora in preference to the more affluent houses surrounding them. The mother of the present Rana of Méwar, and his sister, the ill-fated Kishna Komarie, was a daughter of the latter house. The Raja of Rewah, whose country is called Bhagélkund, is a lineal descendant of the first of this dynasty, and they enumerate thirty-two reigns from Bhagji, the founder. Of those descended from the second or Solankhi dynasty, who still remain on their native soil, the Loonawarri chief is the head. Peetapoor and Therâd are both Bhagélas. The Solankhi chiefs of Tonk-Thoda were celebrated in their day; witness their feud with Boondi, related in the "Annals." They are said to be descendants of one of the outlawed brothers of Anhulwarra, the origin of the feud between Bhola Bheem and Pirthi-raj. They acquired the *putta*, or grant, of Ramsir, near Ajmér, and Boerdeo obtained the sister of Pirthi-raj in marriage. In S. 1280, Govind Rae, the third in descent from this alliance, expelled the Goelwal Rajpoots from Thoda, whose ancient name is Taksilla, and which, when I passed it in 1806, presented some fine specimens of architecture. The Thoda Raos consolidated a very snug principality, and were altogether on a footing with their more powerful neighbours. This consisted of Rin-Binai, Uniara, Todri, Jehajpoor, and Mandelgurh. The two latter districts were held as fiefs of Méwar. In Mandelgurh I found, in a dilapidated reservoir, a pair of large slabs, inscribed with the genealogies of these chiefs, in which they are styled (and still recognised by tradition as) the Balnote Solankhi, shewing their affinity (*ote* means 'belonging to') to the father-land. Of the Balnotes of Mandelgurh, the Mircheakhaira and Butwarro chiefs are the representatives, retaining the title of Rao, but possessing only a single village each! Rae Calyan lost Thoda. It was taken by Raja Maun and annexed to Ambér. He assigned to Calyan lands near Newye, to which he moved with all his *bussi*,—a term expressive at once of subjects and household gods,—and where he pitched his tent a town arose, still retaining the name of Bussi; and here the descendant of the Raos of Thoda, heir lineal of the great Sidraj of Anhulwarra, rules over threescore subjects instead of "eighteen kingdoms." The oppression of Meer Khan has reduced the Rao of Bussi to this condition. His kinsman, who held the chieftainship with the title of Rao of Tonk, is not better off. But despite the loss of "many a rood of land," their alliance is not the less sought; the honour of a Rajpoot lies not in his purse, and the great Jey Sing of Ambér took a wife from the impoverished Solankhi of Tonk. The chief of Roopnagurh, in Méwar, is a branch of the Tonk-Thoda family, and more fortunate than the elders. He is said to hold the heir-loom of the war-shell of Sidraj. It was through him that I made acquaintance with the "Chronicler" of the race. Many of the mixed tribes claim descent from the Solankhis of Anhulwarra, as the Gûjers (doubtless the aborigines of Gujerashtra, contracted to *Guzzerat*) of Sonte and Kotario, the Bhils of Ogunah and Panurwa, and those of Mow-Maidanoh in Harouti, the Soonars or goldsmiths of Bonkun, and various other handicraft tribes.

Thus have we traced the once mighty Balharas through all the phases of their fortunes, from the eighth century, when seated on the *gádi* of Anhulwarra, to the nineteenth, when dispersed through the land.

ancient but now extinct race of Taka, but who, in becoming a proselyte to Islam, concealed his name and race under the appellation of Mozuffir. His son was the celebrated Ahmed Shah, who, aspiring to be the founder of a long line of kings, removed the capital of Guzzerat from the banks of the Sarasvati to the Saburmati. With Ahmedabad, raised from the wrecks of the ancient metropolis, and with the fragments transported from Chandravati, the name of Anhulwarra, in process of time, was altogether forgotten; and when the Ahmedshahi kings, and the yet more glorious line of Timoor which succeeded, each in turn to be forgotten, gave place to the Gâéwar (as the name imports, simple cowherd) princes, Ahmedabad was in turn neglected, and Damoji, with all the ambition of a conqueror, raised a new town, or rather new walls round a suburb of the city of Vansraj, but which, instead of Anhulwarra Puttun, the "city or capital of the land of Anhul," was styled simply Puttun.

To some, this meagre chronicle will present little more than a record of ascents to the *gádi*, and descents to the grave; but those who look beneath the surface will observe that it contains hints, allusions, names of things as well as persons,—ideas, in short, which, to those who can follow them out, afford valuable matter for all that is styled the philosophy of history—whether on religion and the singular sects of this period; on commerce, and its probable extent with the nations of antiquity; on the migration of tribes; on the arts, especially of architecture, sculpture, numismatics; on war; on geography, political and physical, and the international intercourse of the Rajpoot princes, during a period of eleven hundred years. Our own historians did not find the philosophical deductions and illustrations which constitute the charm of their works, when diving for truth, in the dark chronicles

chronicles of antiquity: the woof they wove was of divers materials, obtained from many a source, "the fruit and flower of many a province" in the extended domain of history, in which nothing was overlooked that could contribute to their object.

Nor is there wanting in these regions matter applicable to similar purposes, although the staple may be of a quality less likely to stimulate or reward research than that of the country which gave us birth, or the states connected therewith. But, although secondary, the interest to be derived from the pursuit is still of a positive description. To confirm by inscriptions the chronological verity of the *Charitras*, or Annals, and to trace by the aid of the Bardic chronicles the migrations of tribes from higher Asia, as Getes, Turshkas or Tacshacs, Ballas, Ariaspas, Hoons, Cattis, and others* of foreign nomenclature, and their settlement in these regions; to speculate on the varied worship they may have brought from the "father-land," and on the changes this underwent from their partial amalgamation with those they displaced, and to discover what yet remains of ancient habits and institutions, are objects presenting no mean scope to the thinking mind, and facilities for such research exist in the peninsula of the Sauras to an extent surpassing, perhaps, any other field of enquiry in India.

Here is the very cradle of Budhism; this is the land which either gave these sectaries birth, or nurtured and sheltered them on their expulsion or migration from other regions. The province of Syrastrene, or region of the sun-worshipping Sauras, which anciently extended from the Cutch Gulf to the delta of Sinde, was only divided from the fire-worshippers of Aria and Bactriana by the Indus, no *attuc*

to

* For the list of tribes, see *Annals of Rajast'han*, vol. i. p. 81.

to the Budhists, whose traditions affirm that their primates were accustomed to cross it long before the appearance of Islam, to visit their dioceses in the west. What reference the term *Arhya* and *Arhya-punti* (*punti*, 'a path'), used to designate Budhism, may have to Aria, the land of Zerdusht and the Samaneans, we can only conjecture, in like manner as we may speculate on the resemblance of this sect in name, and perhaps in matters of faith, to the Budhist, some of whose last Jineswars, as Parswa, may have been from Aria. The period of this, the twenty-third of their deified pontiffs, was about A.C. 650, when fresh hordes were pouring into India from Western Asia. Even the name evinces an analogy with the ancient Pars, and the Parthic fire-worshipper; and the characters and symbols on the coins and rock-inscriptions of the sacred mounts of the Jains, have no affinity with the Hindu, and are in all probability a modification of the Chaldean, derived either directly, by communication with the Euphrates, or through Aria: a supposition which would be countenanced by some of our cosmogonists, who make these shores the line of route of the Semitic emigrants into India. Further research amidst the wrecks of ancient civilisation and rock-inscriptions, in these unfrequented holy mounts, may yet reveal some secrets.

Of architecture, from the different features hitherto found in the Budhist and Jain temples, we may conclude that, if they did not bring its elements with their religion from Western Asia, what they adopted has been so modified as to have a distinct style, as is seen in their yet existing monuments, of which I have had the pleasure to present to the world the first specimens.

Summary as is the detail of the foreign products imported by the Tyre of India in the eighth century, it affords sufficient ground to

assume

assume the extended and long established commerce which must have obtained these results.

When I say that the *Charitras* and chronicles, aided by coins, inscriptions &c., present matter for even a continuous history of Anhulwarra and its dependencies, it may be asked why I have not attempted such an undertaking. The reply is easy—not satisfied as to my powers for the task, I have preferred blending historical and chronological facts with matters of personal observation, and am content to furnish, as in my former work, materials for the historian. Nevertheless, we may in this place endeavour to unite the severed links which connect the history of the Balhara kings of Western India from a period almost coeval with the era of Christianity.

The contiguous countries of Gujerashtra (*vulgò* Guzzerat) and Saurashtra (the region of the Gujers and Sauras), formed the nucleus of the Balhara sovereignty, and in one or other, according to political contingencies, was placed the metropolis. Of this we can clearly trace three changes of position, and nearly twice that number of dynasties. According to the Annals of Méwar, the first dynasty was formed by their ancestor Keneksén,* of the Surya (*qu.* Chaora) race of princes, from the northern regions, of which Lokote was the capital. Dhauk or Moongy-puttun† was their residence. Thence they founded Balabhi, proved, by the fortunate discovery of the inscription, to have had an era of its own, commencing in A.D. 319. On the destruction of this city—“ where the bells of eighty-four Jain temples summoned the

* The invasion of this prince was about the beginning of the second century of the Christian era. Had it been somewhat earlier, it might have been supposed that he was the Kanaksha of Wilson's chronicle, the *Raj Taringini.*

† Also called Tila-tilpoor Puttun.

the votaries to prayer"—in the fifth century, by an irruption of Parthians, Getes, Huns, or Catti, or a mixture of all these tribes, this branch fled eastward, eventually obtaining Cheetore, when the isle of Deo and Somnath Puttun, in the division termed Larica, became the seat of government. On its destruction, in the middle of the eighth century, Anhulwarra became the metropolis, and this, as recorded, endured until the fourteenth, when the title of Bal-ca-rae became extinct. Besides the collateral testimony of various writers to the greatness of these kings, we have the corroboration of their coins, which I have found amidst ruins in Cutch, and in those of the ancient Oojein. The characters on these are Budhist, a religion intimately and inseparably connected with the Balharas.

To the author of the *Periplus* we are indebted for the first notice of the commercial greatness of these princes, in whose territory he resided, *viz.* at Barygaza, correctly *Brigu-gocha*, the modern Berwuch, or, anglicised, Baroach, which was still one of the "*eighty-four ports*," when the metropolis was removed to Anhulwarra. Ptolemy also mentions the kingdom of Baleokouras, though we can make nothing of Hippocura, which he assigns as the capital: a name, however, which surprises us less than a Byzantium placed by him on the site of Balabhi. Arrian informs us of the piratical habits of the people of Larica, for which, no doubt, they were expelled the country, as mentioned, in the reign of Sid Raj. From the days of Arrian in the second, to the founder of Anhulwarra in the eighth, and to the time of the last of the second dynasty in the tenth century, notwithstanding its inland position, the commerce he describes appears not to have languished; the same products enumerated by the Grecian agent in the second, continued to crowd the

"eighty-

"eighty-four bazars" of this grand mart in the eighth and twelfth centuries. Her position on the Sarasvati, at a point equidistant from the ports in the gulfs of Cutch and Cambay, threw into her lap all the products of Africa, Egypt, and Arabia. Her chief port, Gujna or Cambayet, was not above one hundred miles distant, and that of Mandvie little more. If Antwerp, in the early stages of her prosperity, had "ten thousand carts constantly employed in carrying merchandise from the four hundred ships at one tide under her walls to and from the neighbouring countries," what may we not credit of the Tyre of India, the metropolis at one time of "eighteen kingdoms," which drew her maritime wealth from every port in Asia, and her inland trade even from the mountains of Tartary? facts which filled the minds of the Arabian travellers of the eighth, tenth, and twelfth centuries, with astonishment. Let us compare the chief articles specified by Arrian* as forming the trade between Barygaza and the Red Sea, with those enumerated in the *Charitra*. After the precious stones, as diamonds, pearls, &c., he particularly notes muslins (*sindones*) of the colour of mallows, as being sent down from Ozene. These are the "*Saloos*" of Anhulwarra, which, with purples and silks, had a separate bazar. From *hati-dhant*, or elephants'-teeth, appearing as one of the chief imports to Patun, doubtless from Africa, we may conclude that the same extensive rage for *chooris* or bracelets† existed amongst the fair sex in the earliest ages. Wine being one of the imports, we may hence infer that the Rajpoot of those days was as partial to the '*piala*' as

* See Dr. Vincent's translation of the *Periplus*, pp. 408 and 459.

† These bracelets sometimes cover the arm from the wrist to near the elbow. I have elsewhere given an account of two marble statues built up in the porch of the ancient church of Moissac, near the junction of the Tarn and Garonne, representing females in a perfectly Asiatic costume, and in all probability of the age of the Visigoths, whose capital was Toulouse.

as now. The learned translator of Arrian asks, "Might such be palm or toddy?" To which we reply, neither, for they had abundance at home of the fermented juice of the *jâl*; but the pure grape (perhaps of Shiraz), whose praise is alike sung by Solomon and Hafiz. The seven metals *(heft-dhat)* were found in Anhulwarra, but the tin could be procured nearer home than the Cassiterides, for India had abundance, as the mines of Jawan in Méwar indicate that they have been worked from the earliest ages, and the hills abound in lead, copper, tin, and antimony. The Venerable Bede was possessed of pepper, cinnamon, and frankincense; Dr. Vincent asks, "how such articles, in that age, A.D. 735, found their way to a monk's cell in Britain?"

Precious perfumes and unguents are enumerated by Arrian, and in the *Charitra* they are described as having a separate market in Anhulwarra. Nard, long pepper, myrrh, the onyx,* are also mentioned by Arrian as being sent down from *Minagara, where, he says, "a Parthian potentate resided, who received tribute from Guzzerat.*" All these articles, except the last, are the products of Thibet, and in making this circuitous route, it is evident that the Indus was the direct medium of commercial intercourse. De Guignes mentions an Indo-Scythic irruption in the second century, and Cosmas one of Huns in the sixth century, the first fixing themselves at Minagara, the Saminagur or Tatta of the Delta; the other, higher up. The first was the period of the Yuti or Gete irruption, which I have described in the Yadu Annals,† and to these Indo-Parthic or Indo-Getic invaders, we must attribute some of the host of ancient medals, and perhaps of the rock-

* The onyx has a peculiar and almost superstitious value in the East, and is especially chosen for amulets. Chaplets of this stone are much esteemed.

† See *Annals of Rajast'han,* vol. ii. p. 221.

rock-inscriptions, with their incognate characters, yet abounding in all these regions. The onyx, the *Sulimani Putr (petros)*, or stone of Solomon, is found at Rajpipli, in Guzzerat, as well as all the precious agates. I possess a vase, purchased in Scindia's camp, evidently of Grecian workmanship, and the numerous cameos* of the onyx found in the Punjab, and other relics of Alexander's conquests, attest the abundance at that time.

Silks of various fabrication are also stated by Arrian to have been one of the staple articles of export, and are mentioned in the *Charitra* as occupying one of the eighty-four bazaars in Patun. Doubtless this grand entrepôt of Western India did not confine its selection of these fabrics to the nearer market of Tagara; we have a right to suppose that the great silk marts of Mooltan, Sirhind, and other places in those northerly regions (not yet supplanted in these productions), supplied the Balhara capital. The ancient western writers have generally agreed in placing Serica in the south-eastern provinces of Chinese Tartary. But may we not conjecture that there was no occasion to cross the Caucasus for this silk mart? Sirhind, or Sirica-hind, the 'head' or frontier of India, might have furnished the supply.†

It is far from improbable that, when Arrian wrote, the Punjab was under the dominion of an Indo-Grecian or Indo-Getic prince, since from

* In such numbers were these cameos found in 1803-4, when Lord Lake dictated peace to Holkar from the Altars of Alexander, that the native artists of Muttra and Agra carried on a successful imitation of them for some time, which encouragement might have raised to celebrity. My friend, Edward Blunt, of Kempshot, possesses one of the pure Grecian specimens, where the artist has availed himself of the dark lamina of the onyx, to place a Moor's head in contrast with that of a beautiful female, cut in the white portion of the stone.

† In this same manner, as explained, *Larice* is the contraction of *Larica-dês*, or country of the Lar. *Sir*, 'head,' is the most common term for a political or geographical boundary, and *Sir-ca-hind*, or the frontier of India (proper), might be contracted to *Sirica*.

from the days of Darius, who considered it the richest satrapy of the Persian crown, to the present time, it has been an object of contention. It was on account of the silk trade that the prince termed Porus, sovereign of Oojein, sent an embassy to Augustus, and a letter *written in Greek* shows the footing they had in Central India. This prince being styled Ranæ, Dr. Vincent refers to him as the ancestor of the Ranas of Méwar, and draws the following curious inference. "Now, were it possible to connect the interests of the Ranas, the most powerful of the Rajpoot Rajas, with those of Guzzerat, we might prove that the trade carried on at Barygaza and Nelkunda was of such importance as to make an intercourse necessary between these Indian potentates and the Emperor of Rome: *if an Indian history of these early times should ever be obtained, that possessed a degree of consistence or probability, some light might be thrown on this subject, which at present is mere conjecture and speculation.*" Singularly enough, we can prove that "the interests of the Ranas," the most powerful of the *(then)* Rajpoot princes, were not only "connected with those of Guzzerat," but that they (though not as Ranas) actually governed it as the first Balhara kings, from Keneksén in the second, to Sailaditya in the fifth century, when Balabhi was sacked by Indo-Scythic invaders.

I have elsewhere stated my opinion, that the name of one of the oldest and most powerful tribes of India, namely, the Pramara, pronounced *Powâr* (sovereigns of Oojein and Dhar from the remotest period), gave occasion to the corruption of the name of the tribe to a proper name, both of this prince, the correspondent of Augustus, and of the opponent of Alexander. I can also prove that the supreme title of Rana did belong to this family of Ozene, and is still borne by the deposed prince of Omerkote in the Desert, of the Soda tribe, one of the

the most conspicuous subdivisions of the Pramaras, at one time sovereigns of all Western India from the Sutledge to the ocean. The ancient title of the princes of Méwar was *Rawul*, and that of *Rana* was assumed when they overcame the Rana of Mandore, the capital of Maroodés, in the thirteenth century.

It is unnecessary to pursue further the comparison of the merchandise described by Arrian in the second century as forming the investments for the ports in the Red Sea, and those of the Balhara metropolis, on which Barygaza was dependent; nor does it matter whether that capital was Anhulwarra or Deva-puttun in the region of the Lar, and on the shores of the *Suroi* peninsula;—the family was one. Well might the Arabian travellers expatiate on "the vast empire, the riches, the splendid court, of the monarch reigning in Guzzerat, by the name of Balhara, his capital Nehelwarra." But we may repeat, that this emporium was not the creation of its founder; on the contrary, the fact of its inland position more strongly proves the antiquity of this commerce, and even this disadvantage did not alter the usual channels of traffic which filled her bazars with wealth; on which point I shall draw an important inference from Masoodi, who visited Anhulwarra in the tenth century, about the period of the change of dynasty from Chaora to Chaluca, and who confirms all that his predecessors had advanced on the opulence of the Bal-ca-raes, and the still increasing greatness of Anhulwarra. He gives us a quaint reason for this, and one honourable alike to Hindu toleration and to Mooslem good conduct. "The Moosulmans were much respected, and they had mosques in the city, in which prayers were read five times a day, and they [the people of Anhulwarra, I suppose] ascribed the long life of the Balharas to their prayers." This points to the conclusion of the reign of Moolraj, who occupied the throne fifty-six years, or from the middle to the end of the tenth century. And although, not many years after this, Mahmoud, with his legions of barbarians, carried desolation over the land, destroying the cities, and sweeping away their wealth, from which Gujni* derived its splendour, yet Anhulwarra rose like a phœnix from her ashes; and when El-Edrisi visited it in the twelfth century, towards *the end of the reign* of Sid-raj, and the commencement of that of his successor, Komár-pál, he found the same splendour and superabundant wealth as were recorded by his predecessors in the eighth, ninth, and tenth centuries. No argument is required to show that commercial industry alone could have been the foundation of this, and the sources thereof were not only too numerous and important, but too firmly established, to be cut off by any temporary calamity, even such as the visitation of Mahmoud. One passage from El-Edrisi we may quote as containing much interest; "*Regnum hoc hereditario jure possidetur a regibus suis, qui omnes uno invariabili nomine vocantur Balahara, quod significat Rex Regum. Ad urbem Nahroara multi se conferunt mercatores*† *Moslemanni ad negotiandum;*"‡ and then he goes on to say that the worship of Buddha was the prevalent religion, as already quoted. This *toleration* extended beyond the admission of the *mercatores Moslemanni* into the capital; for a chief of Islam held in fief the important fortress of Joonagurh, in the very heart of the peninsula, while

* The Yadu Rajpoots claim this as one of their ancient cities, founded by Raja Guj. See *Annals of Rajast'han*, vol. ii. p. 222.

† Throughout the sea-coasts of Saurashtra, at Gogo, and Mandavie, are seamen who call themselves Hindus, but who keep entirely distinct from all other classes. Some of them claim a descent from the mariners of the Arabian shores, but still as Hindus. An inquiry into these classes and their peculiarities of dialect (if any), would be interesting.

‡ Ap. Geog. Nub. p. 63.

while a native of Hormuz commanded the fleet, a toleration ultimately attended with ruinous results, as has been explained.

From the foregoing, we shall make one important deduction in this place, the consideration of which may be resumed as we advance into the peninsula of the Sauras, when we have occasion to remark on the religion, the tribes, and the strange characters on rocks and coins, *viz.* that an extensive commerce was maintained between the Rajpoot sovereigns of Western India, and the shores of Arabia, Egypt, and the Red Sea, at periods long anterior to Christianity; and independently of the evidence of Greek and Roman agents being resident amongst the eighty-four ports of the Balharas, in the second century of the Christian era, we are assured on undisputed authority, that the Romans remitted to India annually, a sum equivalent to four hundred thousand pounds, to pay for their investments, and that, in the reign of the Ptolemies, *one hundred and twenty-five sail of India shipping were at one time lying in the ports of Myus, Hormus, and Berenice*; the ports whence Egypt, Syria, and Rome herself, were supplied with the products of India, and whence the pepper of Malabar found its way into the cell of a monk, during the period of the Saxon Heptarchy.

CHAPTER XI.

Remains of Anhulwarra.—Their rapid disappearance.—Four architectural relics only left.—Specimen of the Saracenic arch.—Its invention, Hindu.—Ruins of Anhulwarra applied to the building of Ahmedabad and modern Puttun.—Antiques contained in the new city.—Inscriptions.—The Library.—Saved from the Mahomedans.—Property of the Khartra sect of Jains.—Extent and condition of the library.—Other libraries of the Jains unexplored.—The *Vansraj Charitra.*

The sceptic in scriptural prophecies should repair to the once proud metropolis of the Balharas. He would there just see sufficient of this once magnificent city, with its "eighty-four squares and eighty-four bazars," to mark the facility with which capitals are raised and overthrown. He would discern but one vestige of the lofty circumvallation which enclosed the palace of its Cæsars; of the rest, like the walls of Babylon, there is not one stone left upon another. When desertion commences in the East, there is soon nothing remaining but sacred edifices, and the *baories*, or reservoirs of water.

The first object that attracts the eye, is a fragment of the Kali-kote, or inner city, consisting of two strong bastions, called the towers of Kali, from a small shrine of Time underneath, near one of the principal entrances to the city. From the summit of these towers, the eye can trace the course of the walls, which formed an irregular trapezium of perhaps five miles circuit, around which extended, chiefly to the east and south, the suburbs, to which there may have been an external circumvallation. The following imperfect sketch may suffice to give an idea of the site.

ANHULVARRA PUTTUN.

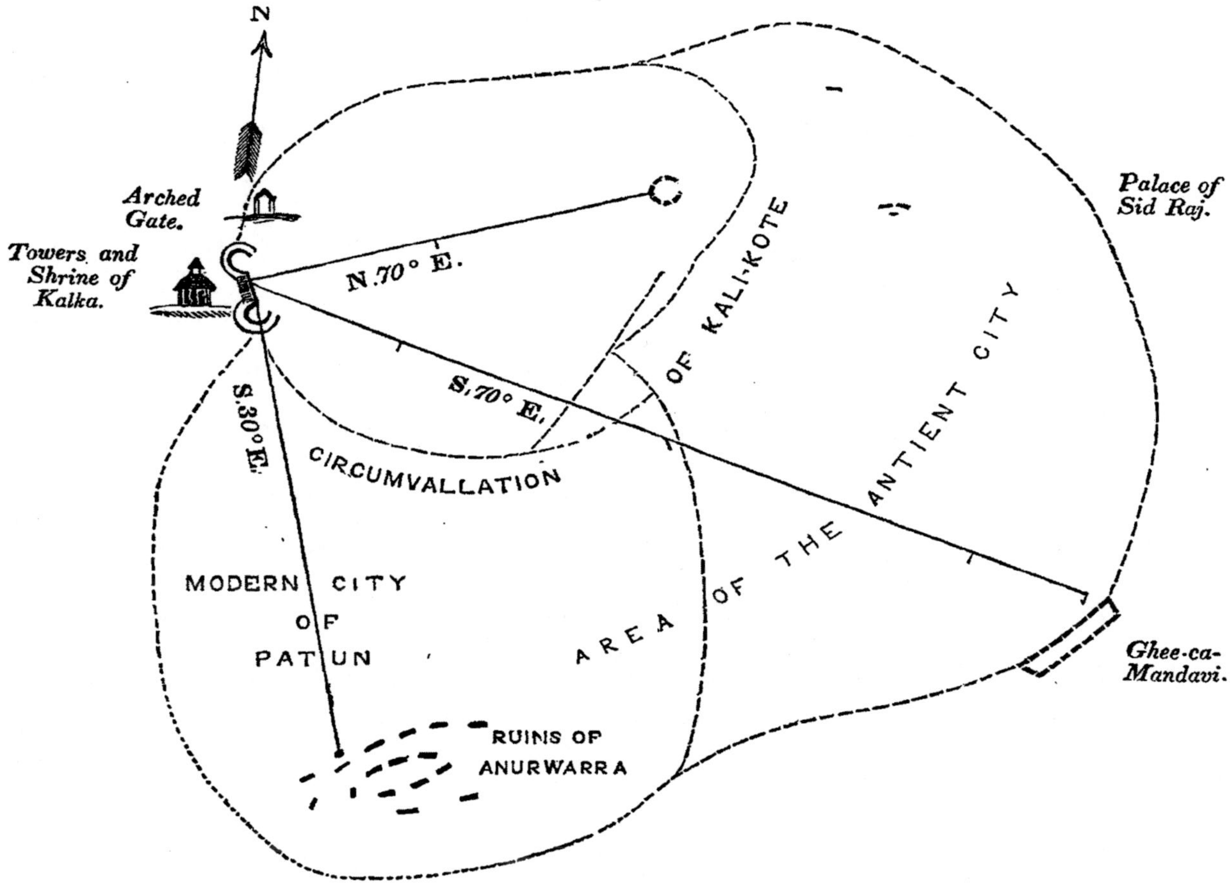

Four relics only are spared of the three dynasties which ruled Anhulwarra; but these, with the aid of the *Charitra* and tradition, sufficiently attest her past greatness. First, the towers of Kali; second, the remains of the old palace of Sid-raj; third, the ruins of one of the eighty-four markets, called the *Ghee-ca-Mandavi*, four miles distant from the towers; and last, not least, the ruins of Anhulwarra itself, two coss, or three miles, from the gate of Kali-kote.

With this discovery, years of anxiety terminated: here, then, is the site of the first city of Vansraj, still locally known; but a few years more, and this will be numbered with the things that were. Damaji Guicowar

Guicowar has the credit of doing more than either time or Toork towards the destruction of Kali-kote; but this may be doubted, for it is well known that the sanguinary Alla not only levelled the walls, but buried the greater part of the temples in their foundations; razed the palaces, and, as the last token of conquest, ploughed up the ground on which they stood with the ass. All is now deserted, and the evergreen *peloo,* which delights in sand, luxuriates amidst the ruins of the Balharas. Kali-kote was elevated considerably above the surrounding country. The remnant of what is still called the palace of Sid-raj, is in the centre of an artificial basin, but the excavation is now barely discernible. There is the ruin of a noble reservoir, from the fragments of which, a new one has been constructed in modern Puttun,* and of a smaller one, bearing the name of the Fountain of Ink, wherein, it is related, the scholars of Hemacharya dipped their pens to write down his *dicta.*

About one hundred and fifty yards from the Towers of Time, stands the skeleton arch of a noble gateway. Were we to take this magnificent relic as a specimen of what the city of Anhul had been, we might at once solve a great problem in architecture; for it is one of the finest outlines of what is termed the Saracenic arch that I ever saw, and could we prove it to be Hindu in origin, we might discover in it the prototype of those in the Alhambra, and the varieties of the pointed style, denominated Gothic, spread over Europe. If, originally, it formed part of the circumvallation raised by Vansraj in A.D. 746, it would

* The accompanying print is from a drawing by Mr. Arthur Malet, whose description is subjoined: "Ruins of a *bowree* (a well with a flight of steps down to it) in the old fort at Puttun. The steps and the galleries have fallen in, and the only part remaining, is one side of the well, finely sculptured, the stones of which probably were taken by the Mussulmans from some Hindu temples; they are covered with figures."

J. Netherclift Lithog.

BOWLEE AT ANHULWARRA PUTTUN.

London. Published by W. H. Allen & Co. 1839.

would be nearly the period of the Alhambra, '*the* edifice,' *par excellence*, raised by Haroun in the kingdom of Granada. I have already given an opinion that, although the Chaora prince established his dynasty at this epoch, it is most improbable that the city could have attained its extent or splendour during his sole reign ; and we may surmise either that Vansraj, when driven from Deobunder for the piratical habits of his family, fled to a secondary metropolis, or that he succeeded to a more ancient dynasty. We know that the Caliphs of Bagdad, who added naval dominion to their wide conquests by land, inherited the exuberant prosperity of a long-established commercial intercourse with India, and that they nationalized whatever they discovered of value in art or science, in every country which they subjected. I have elsewhere* stated, that so early as the eighth century, the arms of Islam were both on the Indus and the Ebro; but where did the Arab learn to turn this arch? Not from the Visigoth in Spain, nor from the architraved edifices of the ancient Greeks or Persians;—not from Tadmor in the desert, nor from Persepolis; neither from Hauran nor from Haleb. Did they then invent and spread it over Europe; or did they acquire the knowledge of it from the Silpi, or architect of the Hindus, who had their Vitruvius before Romulus was born? Of one thing we are confident, that this arch was erected by a Hindu mason, and that its ornaments are pure Hindu, and if the Arabians had anything to do with it, their merit was confined to the design. Can we reasonably concede even so much to probability? We know that the Mooslem never ruled in Patun ; that when the race of Taka obtained Guzzerat, they almost immediately changed the metropolis; nor was it by any means likely, that after Alla, from religious frenzy, had thrown down its

* *Annals of Rajast'han*, vol. i. p. 243.

its mindras and its walls, any prince of Islam would rebuild them for a Hindu to inhabit. The character of this architecture is of a much earlier date, being nearly that of the Ghorian dynasties preceding Alla, which afterwards gradually softened down until it attained the florid embellishments, and effeminate though striking distinctions, of the Mogul. The varied conceptions of the pointed style, in Europe, are much less easy to discriminate than those of the Indo-Saracenic, a term we may be permitted to use, in order to distinguish it from the simple Saracenic, as found in the Western conquests of the Arabians, who, as they and their successors invariably destroyed every edifice of religion, or converted it to the worship of Islam, have left us no means of determining what was purely Hindu. Were any artist, or any curious enquirer, to go to ancient Dehli, and live for a few months amongst the inexhaustible ruins of its various dynasties, he would be enabled to distinguish these with more accuracy from the architecture of the tombs, than from the pages of the historian, each having its character more clearly defined than the styles which we divide into Gothic, Byzantine or Tedesque, Saracenic, and Saxon. We may, I think, claim for the Hindus the invention of the Ogee or contracted arch, of which the pointed horse-shoe arch, as the Saracenic is not unaptly termed, is a modification, as this is the commonest form of their *torun*, the nuptial or triumphal arch. It is at least far more probable that the wealthy and scientific Hindu, whose claims to discoveries in the highest walks of astronomy, algebra, and all the subtleties of metaphysical lore, are placed upon an indisputable foundation, should be the inventor, than the roving Bedouin of the desert.

Before we abandon the arch of Anhulwarra to time and the Guicowar, we we may ask, how has this escaped the general ruin? We can find no motive, but its intrinsic beauty, to account for its solitary towers, with the pure Hindu kankras and embattled parapets, being untouched by Hindu and Toork. I have already said that there remain only the skeleton ribs from the spring to the apex, without a particle of loading; the pilasters supporting these ribs have lost nothing of their perpendicularity, and they are as firmly rivetted to the masonry which supports them, as on the day of erection. They are chaste and well-proportioned to the arch, and the capitals are purely Hindu, being ornamented with chain festoons, having the *Vira-gantha*, or war-bell, the most ancient and general decoration of the columnar architecture of the Jains (of which faith were the Balharas), suspended by a chain between each festoon, like the columns at Barolli.* On each side, and about half-way up the segment of the arch, is the lotos. It is but fair to add, that many of the most celebrated mosques of Ahmedabad have similar ornaments; which, however, would merely prove that the Islamites, in founding the new city of Ahmed from the ruins of Chandravati and Anhulwarra, took from these cities whatever materials suited their purpose.

Why the inhabitants should restrict the name of Anurwarra (as they pronounce it) to that portion of the ruins extending three miles southward of the gateway, I could not learn; and though it would have been more gratifying to discover the *chaok*, or square, appropriated to the Arabian mariners, or that for the purples of Tagara, I was satisfied with finding the Ghee-market, as signally corroborative of the truth of the *Charitra*, which assigns to every article of trade its separate mart.

I am surprised that the city should not have been placed upon the bank

* See *Annals of Rajast'han*, vol. ii. p. 710.

bank of the river Sarsooti, now some distance from it, though I am strongly induced to pronounce that, at least on the north-east, it must have stretched to the stream, and that it included more of modern Puttun than the adherents of the Guicowar are willing to admit. I incline to this opinion, partly from the ancient temples within the walls of the new town, and partly from the magnificent tank (still in excellent preservation) in that quarter, which never would have been excavated had nearly three miles intervened between it and the city. There is another and yet more noble reservoir, called *Munsurwar*, on the Ahmedabad side, now completely dry, to which a legend is attached, importing that it was the work of an *Or*, or brick-maker. Just as it was finished, a quarrel arose between him and his wife, who imprecated a curse upon his work, on which the water exuded as fast as it flowed in. The reader, who has dipped into my former work, may recollect a similar tradition regarding the noble lake at Jhalapatun, also the work of an *Or*. The fact is, though *or* or *ora* is significant of the *caste* of brick-maker, as *khomar* is of that of potter, there was in ancient times a powerful race of this name, kings of Orissa, of whom inscriptions are found in the same incognate character as those in the regions we describe.

From the platform of the tower of Kalka, or Kali, all these objects are distinctly seen, the surrounding plains being very slightly undulated and but thinly wooded. The view is bounded by a distant horizon. To the south, there is much more wood, which serves to diversify this monotonous flatness, further relieved by the minor ranges of Aboo, whose dark summits contrast finely with the clear blue which canopies them. These mountains probably afforded the material with which Anhulwarra was built.

The

The circumvallation of modern Puttun is built half-way up with blocks of stone from the ancient city, and the ambition of Damoji to be its founder has led him to use indiscriminately whatever material was best adapted to the end, whether from the palaces, fountains, or temples of the Balharas. From the slight inspection I was enabled to make, I have no doubt time and labour would be well rewarded in hunting amongst these sculptured fragments for costumes and inscriptions.* The brick wall, which surmounts these more solid foundations, has a very gingerbread-like contrast, evincing that the Guicowar founder has nothing of the Titanic blood of the races reared from the Anhulcoond, or fire-fountain of the Rajpoot Olympus. I had omitted to mention that the towers of Kalka are of brick, and I have made no note of whether they had foundations of stone, though it is most likely they have, for as all these sandy regions† abound in saline ingredients, which corrode and in time undermine all brick walls, it is a matter of necessity to lay their foundations in stone. In fact, from the process visible in all cities whose edifices or walls are of brick, it would be very possible to deduce the age of their erection. The city and walls of Agra afford an example in point, for though little more than two centuries old, not a single wall has its foundation perfect, each presenting, near its level with the ground, according to the strength of the corrosive ingredient, a cancerous crumbling line, shewing that nature, as the Hindu would say, is often at war with art. The shrine of

* I have elsewhere mentioned having made a valuable discovery of the appanage of a Hoon (Hun) prince in Central India, from a diligent inspection of the walls of Bhynsror, which, like most of the ancient cities and sacred edifices of the Hindus, have been often thrown down and rebuilt.

* *Baloo* is a Hindu word for 'sand:' *Bal-ca-dês* would be 'the region of sand;' whence the northern invading tribes, the "Tatta Mooltan ca Rao," on conquest and settlement, might have assumed the epithet of *Balla*.

of Kali, or Destruction, has nothing worthy of remark, save the memorials of her power in the fragments of ancient sculpture which lay around it. Close by is the excavation that served as the 'inkstand of Hemacharya.'

The new city is, however, not devoid of attraction, and contains two objects deserving especial homage: the statue of the founder of Anhulwarra, Vansraj; and the *Pothi-bindar*, or library of the Jains. The former, placed in the temple of Parswa, is of white marble, and about three feet and a half high. Another statue, of smaller dimensions, placed on his right hand, is styled his prime minister, but is more probably intended to represent his preserver, the Acharya. To each an inscription is attached, evidently supplying the place of others destroyed by the great Iconoclast, Alla, whose name is also carved thereon. "Mahraja Sri Khuni Allum Mohumad Padsha—his son (or successor) Sri Allum Feeroz, by whose favour, in the full moon of Kartika, Thursday, (Vrishpatwar)," &c. &c.

"Of Sandera-*gatcha* (sect), in the forest *(vana)* of Panchasra, Sailgun Sura went to seek omens. Under a Mhowa tree, suspended by a *jhola* (swing), was a new-born infant shaded by the tree, which shade remained stationary—from which Sailgun Sura divined his future greatness. He conveyed him, with his mother, to his disciples (*sewuk*), and desired them to foster him, which they did. Being born in the woods, he was named VANSRAJA, and in S. 802 he drew the line of circumvallation of Anhulwarra, and Devichandra Sura Acharya composed the Pratishta to Aleswara* Mahadeva."

The other is as follows: "S. 1352 (A.D. 1296), Friday the 9th of the month Vaisak. He, whose abode is in the East, whose tribe is that of Mor,

* A new title, probably from *Alaya*, or *Alya*, 'a habitation.'

Mor, the son of Nagindra, the son of Kelun, whose son, Asora, obtained from the world the essence of riches, with which, in the temple (*mindra*) of Sriman Mahraja Vansraj, in order that the flowret of the climber of renown might expand, the statue of Asa (Hope) was enshrined by his son Ari-Sing, and the ceremony of installation performed by Devichandra Sura, son of Sailgun Sura Acharya."

These inscriptions are either coeval with the founding of Anhulwarra, or they are copies of such, and the initiatory invocation to the sanguinary Alla on the one, and the date S. 1352, that in which he destroyed the city, on the other, must be considered merely as complimentary to, or imploring the forbearance of, this destructive tyrant. The first contains the outline of the extraordinary birth of the founder, corroborating the *Charitra*; and the second discloses an important fact, namely, that this founder, Vansraj, had the honours of deification, or of apotheosis. In all probability, however, this statue may have been recovered from the shrine dedicated to his manes, which was overturned in the general destruction; or, on the other hand, they may have converted his shrine into a temple to Parswa, in which this votary from the East obtained a niche for his own tutelary divinity, Hope. We cannot easily determine whether this family of the Mor tribe was of the second or third caste, military or mercantile; but as a Rajpoot never talks of riches, or any wealth save that extorted by the sword from his foeman, they were possibly of that great branch of the Rajpoots, which, on becoming proselyte to the Jain doctrine, abandoned, in obedience to its peaceful tenets, the profession of arms for commerce. Each of the Rajpoot tribes, Pramara and Chohan, claims a subdivision called *Mor* or *Mori*, and as Hope is the tutelary goddess of the Chohans, this wealthy individual may have been a merchant of

this

this race, who in his avocation had come to establish a connexion with the grand mart of Western India. "The East" is a term of wide import, but it is generally applied to the provinces we term Bengal Proper, extending to Benares, and he may have been a native of the *Kalikote* of that rich land, corrupted by us to Calcutta.

The veneration of the Jain inhabitants of modern Puttun for the memory of the royal disciple of the great Acharya, continues unabated, and though with Pat-Pramara and Dharaburz, the first and last of that race, he may have been too late for the honours of deification, the Chaora prince receives a portion of the saffron offered to Parswa himself. In this simple fact alone, after the lapse of eleven hundred years, we have the most incontrovertible commentary on the life of the Saura Vansraj, proving that, whatever might have been the faith of his ancestors, whether they were followers of Bal-Siva or simple sun-worshippers, *he* became a disciple of Budha; while, from his not giving his name to the new city, according to universal custom, it would appear conclusive that he was not its original founder.

I may mention that there are several temples in the *Noa-poora*, or new town, though they present nothing particularly worthy of remark. Two are dedicated to Raghu-Nath, and were raised by the potters and goldsmiths. A third to Maha-Lakshmi, the goddess of wealth, was erected by the merchants of the Burr tribe, and is placed near the gate called *Tripolia;* and there is another by the same class to Gordhun-Nath, the Apollo of the Hindus. The Goorjrie gate has a statue of Hanuman, as janitor, and another gate has one to Sidnath-Mahadeva, the tutelary divinity of the mendicant Sids.

We proceed to the other object of interest, the Pothi-bindar, or library, the existence of which was totally unknown until my visit to it.

it. It is contained in subterranean apartments in that quarter of the new town which has appropriately received the name of Anhulwarra. Its position screened it from the lynx-eyed scrutiny of Alla, when he destroyed all that was destructible in this ancient abode. The collection is the property of the Khartra sect, of which the celebrated Amra and Hema were the *Sripooj*, or primates. This sect, called *Khartra*, or the orthodox, (a title conferred by Sid-raj after long theological disputations,) is the most numerous of all the Jain votaries, enumerating at one time no less than eleven hundred disciples, extending from the Indus to Cape Comorin. Though every one, lay or clerical, bearing the name of Khartra, has a property in the library, it is in strict charge of the *Nagar-Seth*, and the *Panch*, or chief magistrate and council of the city, while its immediate superintendence is confided to some Yutis spiritually descended from Hemacharya, the senior of whom has some pretensions to learning. Years before my visit, I had known of its existence from my own Guru, who was equally anxious with myself to place the fact beyond doubt, and on the very day of our arrival, he hastened to "worship the Bindar." Although his venerable appearance was quite enough to make the padlocks fly open, nothing could be done without the *fiat* of the Nagar-Seth. The council was convened, before whom my Yuti produced his *patravali*, or spiritual pedigree, tracing his descent from Hemacharya himself, which acted like a spell, and he was invited to descend and worship the treasures of ages. The catalogue forms a large volume, and I should fear to hazard my own veracity, or that of my Guru, by giving his estimate, from its contents, of the number of books which filled these chambers. They are carefully packed in cases, filled up with the dust of the *Mugd*, or Caggar-wood, an infallible preservative against insects. The old man returned

 to

to me in raptures at what he had seen. But there was a want of correspondence between the catalogue and the contents of the boxes, forty of which he examined in seeking for two works named therein, *i. e.* the *Vansraj Charitra*, and the *Charitra Salivana*, the leader of the Tak or Tacshac horde, which invaded India from the north, overturning the throne of the supreme monarch, Vicrama, and substituting in the south of India the era called *Saca* for that previously used. The excessive closeness of the subterrene atmosphere compelled him to desist from the search, which he did the more readily, as he was promised permission to copy any work he desired on his return. Moreover, he had to follow me twelve miles, for the monsoon had already set in, and with very enfeebled health, I had yet a long journey before me. Had time even admitted of my remaining, I had no copyists with me to employ in this new field of research, and I can only hope, therefore, that my discovery may lead the way to others. Extreme caution and delicacy must, however, be observed in the attempt; the use of anything like power might seal every volume for ever, for the deposit, as before stated, is scrupulously guarded, and only known to the initiated. As they could not have had time to prepare such a receptacle beyond the walls of ancient Puttun, when invaded by Alla, and taking also into consideration the name of Anhulwalla, which this part of the city still bears, we have additional reasons for believing that this portion of the modern city must have been included within the ancient limits.

Books may be borrowed from the library by members of the *gatcha*, who dwell within a certain distance, but they cannot be retained above ten days.

Until we have some insight into the contents of the subterranean "bindar" of Anhulwarra, and a more extended knowledge of the

Oswals

Oswals of Jessulmér, with access to its library, which is equally numerous and probably more select than that of Puttun; above all, until we have formed some acquaintance with the dignitaries of the Jain sect and their learned librarians, we are not in a condition to appreciate the intellectual riches of the Jains, and can only pity the overweening vanity which has prompted the assertion, that the Hindus possess no historical records, and which seeks to quench the spirit of enquiry, by proclaiming such research a vain labour. I may here slightly anticipate my own movements, in order to point out the practicability of profiting by these concealed stores.

Being detained by the monsoon, and extreme bad health, at Baroda, the kindness of the resident, and his influence with one of the ministers of the Guicowar, himself a Jain, induced the latter to write for a copy of the *Vansraj Charitra.* It was promised, and I longed to unravel the early history of this prince's family, which would carry us back to Vicrama and the princes of Balabhi; but alas! when the volume did arrive, either through the negligence of the scribes, or inadvertence in the letter of request, I found they had transcribed the *Komár-pál Charitra*, of which I already had two versions. It was not possible at that time to remedy the error. But among the more important objects of future enquiry, would be a copy of the catalogue itself; for though the titles of works, both of the orthodox and heterodox sects, often have little analogy to their contents, this is not the case with respect to the historical tracts, the *Rasas*, *Charitras*, *Stipasas*, *Mahatmas*, &c. I may also repeat, what cannot be too often stated, in order to stimulate exertion, that I obtained many MSS. from Jessulmér, both on paper and palm-leaves, the latter three, five, and eight centuries old, which still silently adorn the shelves of the

 Royal

Royal Asiatic Society's Library.* The most ancient of these are works on grammar, and of this perhaps our wise men think they know enough. But would it not be worth while to examine works of this antiquity, if only to convince the curious that nothing new is revealed by them? But enough on this head, or, in Indian epistolary phraseology, "what more can I say?"

* One, a copy of the *Harivansa,* is now under translation by an Orientalist of Paris. If the same learned individual would undertake the *Aboo Mahatma,* he would find much of the history of nature and man intermingled, to diversify the dulness of the ritual.

CHAPTER XII.

Journey resumed.—Ahmedabad.—Its architecture.—The ruins of Anhulwarra employed in it — The work of Hindu Silpis.—Comparison of the Islamite and Hindu styles.—Kaira.—Miseries of travelling in the monsoon.— Hon. Col. Stanhope.—Antiquities at Kaira.—Perilous passage of the Myhie river.—A groom drowned.—Baroda.—Sojourn with Mr. Williams, the Resident.—History of Baroda.

THE rains had now (June) fully set in, and we had to pursue our route fetlock-deep in mud. I had one hundred and fifty miles to march before I could reach a place of rest. There was nothing new to detail in moving over this slightly-undulated and sandy plain, studded with the evergreen *khoenie*, a tree of goodly growth, peculiar to Bal-ca-dés, the name of that portion of Guzzerat lying between the Bunas river and Saurashtra. It is, in fact, the southern termination of Marust'hulli, or the great desert: but as there is a good soil beneath this sandy surface, it is admirably calculated for the variety of maize crops and tares, and would be a prolific bed for the potatoe.

Three long marches brought me to the city of Ahmed, the rival of Anhulwarra, and I took up my abode in a beautiful summer palace of the Mozuffur kings, whence I could contemplate their short-lived but brilliant grandeur, in their mosques and madrissas, whose minarets and domes lifted their heads amidst its once populous streets, now the abode of silence and decay. Nothing can more powerfully illustrate the fact, that political greatness must be of gradual growth, and that kingdoms and their capitals, like the human frame, will not be forced, than the state of Ahmedabad, Mandoo, and other cities, where the conqueror

queror has merely left enough to shew that he could hold but an ephemeral existence amongst the *débris* of the indigenous tribes. He must be more deeply imbued with Rajpoot prejudice (I use the word in its liberal sense) even than myself, who, in contemplating the triumphs of architectural art in this city, (some yet nearly intact) does not award the meed of lofty conception to the minds which gave them birth, though we cannot shut our eyes to the combination of incongruous elements, even in the finest structures, especially in the columns and their ornaments, which proclaim their Hindu origin, in spite of the Mooslem's attempt at metamorphosis. Indeed, it is strikingly evident, not only that Chandravati and Anhulwarra have been dilapidated to raise Ahmedabad, but that the work of re-construction has been done by the Hindu Silpi. But, with all their incongruities, we must, nevertheless, admire the perseverance and skill which have surmounted the difficulties of rearing Saracenic superstructures over a Hindu stylobate, without shocking the eye. A more powerful contrast could scarcely be furnished than exists between Mooslem and Hindu architecture;—the one pointed, lofty, airy; the other compact, massive, dignified; and I can imagine, were it put to the vote, that the Islamite style would have the majority of suffrages, especially if association were discarded: though, as with the Grecian and the Gothic, each will ever have its admirers. Viewed as a picture, the dark shades, from the deep-indented masses of the Hindu, give a more solemn aspect, and are more in accordance with the sable sky of a monsoon, laughing to scorn the power of the tempests which play around its pyramidal *sikra* (spire); while the domed mosque and its fairy minarets, towering to the skies, appear most to advantage when nature is at rest, or when the sun-beam from a cloudless vault plays unrestrained on the marble dome or

through

through the painted casement. But the pen is *de trop* where the pencil has already told so much and so well. I recommend all who desire to be acquainted with Hindu-Saracenic architecture, to the work referred to in the note.*

KAIRA.—I was happy to come to an anchor at this place, and to ride out, in such anchorage as I found here, the increasing wrath of the monsoon.

> "Cloud upon cloud is piled along
> The darksome brow of yonder skies, enshrouding
> The face of the bright sun, who, o'er the earth,
> High on his throne of ether erst did reign
> In splendour cloudless, dazzling, and serene.
> The spell of awe hath bound the face of heaven,
> The spell which but the poet's gifted eye
> Can trace, and but his flexile heart can feel,
> Attracted."

Whatever amusement there may be in reading the wanderings of a traveller in India, when "the waters are out," there is not much enjoyment for him, and still less for those about him. A caricaturist would find excellent materials for the exercise of his art in camp during the monsoon, especially in a soil like that of Guzzerat. In the day it is bad enough; first, the attempt to dry the paraphernalia, soaked during the march; then, the endeavour to cook under the canopy of heaven, while *Varuni* and *Agni*, fire and water, are contending for the mastery; camels chewing the cud of reflection; horses with their heads hanging, but shewing a stern front to the pitiless torrent, shaking, not drops of dew from their manes, but buckets full, with every contortion; while the bipeds move about, shivering, silent, and sulky. "*Eh Bhae, my khana kis soorut sa pukasgeh*," exclaims the sepahi, who fears he must rest satisfied with *châbêni*, and that the grateful aroma

* Captain Grindlay's "*Scenery and Costumes of Western India.*"

aroma and simmering sound of the ghee and little Pelion of flour-cakes will not gratify any of his senses to-day, while the more luxurious Pat'han horseman in vain sighs for the flesh-pots of Egypt. If the gods hear their prayers, perhaps Surya is commanded to pierce through the mantle of Indra, and cut short the reign of Varuna; then all issue forth from their corners, chattering, laughing, every hand at work to make dinner while the sun shines. But if the water-god will not yield, and Surya sits in darkness, the Mooslem must rest content with unwrapping from his cloth the cold provender of the preceding day, while the sepahi, whose caste forbids his eating a cold dinner, has no resource but parched peas and water, of which there is no lack. Then all turn in for the night, dreaming of the morrow, and determined to work double tides for lost meals; perhaps their dreams are broken by one loud universal roar of '*Andhi Aya*,' 'the storm is come!' All hands are out without any piping, to hold on, and keep their *pâls* or coverings from falling about their ears. Certes, it is a pleasant thing to be awakened, with one side of the wet kanats, or walls of your tent, splashing against your pallet, and the klassies, or tent-pitchers, roaring out "*Oota Sahib, dera girra jota*," 'get up, Sir, the tent is falling!' You get up and paddle for your slippers in vain, and find that the force of the torrent has broken the embankment raised in the evening, and petty rivulets meander under your bed; thrice happy if the united efforts of your servants and the sepahis, who always come to the rescue, prevent the last crack, by holding on the weather-side, until larger tent-pins, or *bashes*, are driven into the drenched and yielding soil, to supply the place of those which had given way. Meanwhile, water has "done its worst;" your bedding is soaked through, and you have no alternative but to put on your clothes, if they have escaped, and eke out the rest of of the night with your legs on the table; or, if "Nature's soft nurse" has not fled to any crib but yours, to hunt for her under the mattrass, which, if of horse-hair and not too ponderous, may afford you repose, and a comfortable rheumatism in the morning to boot.

Yet, after such a weary night, and a wearier day of aches and pains succeeding, the traveller must be alert; if he meets an old inscription, or ancient temple, want of time, or a world of waters, would be no excuse to the antiquary: as for him who loves to be amused with incident or novelty, you must note it down with all its diversities, and endeavour to cast about for mirth when you have not an atom of it in your composition. For instance, after such a night as this, your horse at the tent-door, housings wet, the road knee-deep in mud, your ears dinned with the disasters of the night, the *tappa*, or fowl-basket, filled with drowned subjects, your favourite steed seized with the gripes, and all the minor miseries that flesh is heir to,—there is but one remedy—march! and let fresh adventures, good or bad, efface the recollection of the past. There is no philosophy like Sancho's, "there is a remedy for every thing but death:" under this consolation, and another favourite apophthegm from his 'budget,' "the longest day has a night," I have acted *literatim*, and have found them worth all the philosophy of all times, whether Sanchya or Platonic.

At Kaira, I found my old friend and fellow-academician (of Bonnycastle's), the Hon. Colonel Lincoln Stanhope, H.M. 17th Dragoons, commanding the station. We had been in communication from his first arrival in India; and during the Pindarrie war, from information one of my subordinate agents had transmitted him from Oojein, he had been enabled, with the advanced squadron of his regiment, to perform one of the most dashing exploits, on a small scale, which these armies of freebooters experienced throughout the contest. As we were returning to Europe about the same time, we had arranged to go overland together, and to pay our respects to the illustrious lady who bears his name, inhabiting the Libanus. But the continuous pressing labours of the last six months had worn both mind and body to such a degree, that I found I should only be a clog to my companion, and with grief I gave up this long-cherished plan, from which I had anticipated some singular results, in contrasting, by local inspection, the religion and architecture of the Hindu, the Egyptian, and the Syrian. I remained a week under my friend's hospitable roof at Kaira, and found myself sufficiently renovated to proceed on my journey.

Even at Kaira, discoveries might be made. The vast mounds and embankments evince the site of some extensive capital, and during my short stay, I added to my collection several silver coins, found amidst the ruins, without inscriptions, but impressed with curious emblems. My friend, Col. S., added two or three to my number. In this way, research, if properly stimulated, might do much in every part of India. But I must repeat what I have often urged, that in numismatics, antiquities in every branch, in the collection of ancient inscriptions or MSS., the English have as yet done next to nothing in exploring ancient India; and when I affirm that, with health and leisure, I could have done ten times more than I have done, and, with increased means, ten times ten, some faith may be placed in my assertion.

Made a tremendous march to get over the Myhie river, every day's contribution adding to its magnitude. I found but one small boat to pass my cavalcade and baggage, and the river was already greatly increased in volume, and flowing with considerable velocity to its

estuary

estuary of Cambay. The only method of passing the horses, which by no possibility could be got into the boat, from its high bulwarks, was by lashing them to the side and ferrying them over. This operation, though the common one, was attended with the risk of strangulation; besides, the afternoon was far advanced, and it would have taken as many hands as I had horses, namely, thirty, to have passed them in detail: moreover, it was pouring torrents of rain, and no supplies were to be had but on the other side. In this dilemma, I turned to the old Rusaldar commanding my party, saying, "what would Secunder Sahib say, if he saw *his* men checked by a stream like this?" It was quite enough: 'strip' was the word, the veteran setting the example. In five minutes, their clothes were bundled into the boat, the old man plunged his mare into the stream, which she took kindly, and, followed by the little troop, buffeting against the current, some trusting to the tails, others to the manes of their steeds, all reached the opposite bank in safety. It was a most anxious moment; the impulse given, there was no checking it: as soldiers, it would have been wrong, and as "Skinner's soldiers," doubly wrong, for they knew what was expected of them. But when I add that the river was about two hundred yards in breadth, very deep, and with a velocity of at least five miles an hour, the act will be acknowledged worthy of applause. The old man evinced a quiet, unaffected intrepidity, and the operation was performed in perfect silence, without hurry or disorder. On reaching the place of encampment, I found one of my grooms missing; not being able to swim, he had given my noble Hae-raj to his assistant. But evening set in, and he did not appear; search was made down the river in vain, and it was reported that, when the train was almost over, he had been seen to plunge in, as if to swim across,—an act of madness,

 especially

especially as he could have waited and passed by the boat. The old adage of the country was too well confirmed by the fate of this poor man: '*Ottura Myhie, Hooa Suhye*,' "you are safe when you have crossed the Myhie;" though this proverb is applied to other dangers, resulting from the lawless habits of the tribes inhabiting the banks, in all its singular course, from its source in the Vindhya hills, to its outlet in the Gulf of Cambay, ten miles distant. One tribe, which dwells on or near its margin, is termed *Myheer*, and is a branch of the aboriginal race of Goand. There is another termed *Mankur*, but their habits are similar, and they possess prejudices which transcend all that belong to the most fastidious and high-caste Brahmin, for a touch of either Hindu or Mooslem defiles them, and renders immediate ablution requisite. They consider the Sanscrit-speaking Brahmin and the Toork alike foreign to them. There is something of originality in this. Amongst the many names given to the Myhie or Muhie, one is *Papasini*, or 'River of Guilt;' another, *Crishna-bhadra*, or 'Black Stream;' which latter may have originated all that has been written on the Paddar falling into this gulf.

The evening was made sad by uneasy sensations regarding the poor Saés, who was a quiet good servant, and had been with me some years.

BARODA.—JUNE .—I was rejoiced to enter this haven of rest, made, by the more than brotherly kindness of the Resident, Mr. Williams, one of unbounded comfort. The roads were impassable to Bombay, and my state of health made me soon yield to his friendly arguments that I should pass the monsoon under his roof. In the mean time, I secured a passage, and as no berth was procurable until the new year, I contemplated with delight the increased feasibility of

my

my desire to penetrate through Saurashtra, a scheme encouraged by my friend, who even promised to accompany me, and aid in the prosecution of my views. The intermediate time was fully occupied in making up for lost ground, translating numerous MSS. and inscriptions, which were to be amalgamated with my sketches of the Rajpoot races, and not a day passed without adding something to my stores.

Baroda itself, though very ancient, presented nothing worthy of research. I did find one inscription in a reservoir, in the ancient Jain arrow-headed character, but the ignorant possessor had defaced it. The ancient name of Baroda is Chandanavati, founded by Chandun, Raja of the Dor tribe of Rajpoots. He is not unknown to legendary lore. By his wife, Muleagri, also a celebrated character, he had two daughters, named Socri and Nila, with whose history I shall not trouble my readers. Like all ancient cities, its name of Chandanavati ('the City of Sandal-wood') was changed to *Veravati*, or 'Abode of Warriors;' and again to *Burpotra*, or 'Leaf of the Bur,' perhaps from some fancied resemblance in its circumvallation to the shape of the leaf of the sacred tree, which Milton describes "broad as Amazonian targe." From this the transition to *Baroda* was simple, and its sovereign lord, the Guicowar, seems inclined to let it rest under its present designation.

CHAPTER XIII.

Departure from Baroda.—Gajna.—Huns.—Cambay.—Its former names.—Legend of the modern name.—Cambay one of the seats of Jain learning.—Library.—Manufactures of Cornelians, &c.—Cross the Gulf.—Gogo.—Inscriptions.—Past and present history of Saurashtra.—Origin of the Saura tribe.—Resemblance between the customs of the Syrians and Sauras.—Establishment of the latter in the Peninsula.—Modern Saurashtra.—Traces of Scythic tribes.—Diversity of races in Saurashtra.—Seat of the Buddhist religion.—Various attractions of the country.—Account of Gogo and Seerum.—Atrocious conduct of the early Portuguese in these parts.—Anecdote of Albuquerque.—Bhaonuggur, capital of the Gohils.—Reception of the chief.—Motley character of his Court.—Portraits of English princes.—Nick-knackery.—Navy of the Gohil chief.—His possessions.—Sketch of the family of the Gohils.—Piracy their principal occupation.—Seehore, a Brahmin colony.—Balabhi, the ancient capital of the Méwar princes.—Ancient fountain and temple of Bheemnath.—Legend.—Place of pilgrimage.

Cambay.—November 4th.—The rains having ceased, and the roads being passable, we marched from Baroda on the 26th October, and crossed the Myhie river at Ometa. It was my intention to have proceeded to the now almost nameless village of Gajna, near the embouchure of the river, a place of this name being celebrated in the annals of the Gehlote princes, when they ruled in the Saura peninsula; but here tradition was mute, and I was told there was nothing to indicate past greatness on either side the estuary. All I could learn was, that Gajna had been formerly inhabited by a powerful community of the Koli tribe, from whom it was captured by the Myrens, a branch of the Bhagéla Rajpoots. Alluvial flats are not favourable to tradition, nor can dynasties be perpetuated by brick-built cities, which soon undergo decomposition in these moist regions. Gajna was the ancient name of a city some miles more towards the head of the estuary than the present Cambay, and it was said to be the seaport of an inland capital,

capital, previous to the existence of the latter. This account is in perfect unison with the Annals of Méwar, which rank Gajna next to Balabhi, the capital of the Bala-Raes. At a small village opposite Ometa, I discovered a few huts of Huns, still existing under the ancient name of Hoon, by which they are known to Hindu history. There are said to be three or four families of them at the village of Trisavi, three coss from Baroda, and although neither feature nor complexion indicate much relation to the Tatar-visaged Hun, we may ascribe the change to climate and admixture of blood, as there is little doubt that they are descended from these invaders, who established a sovereignty on the Indus in the second and sixth centuries of the Christian era, and who became so incorporated with the Rajpoot population, as to obtain a place among the thirty-six royal races of India, together with the Gete, the Cat'hi, and other tribes of the Sacæ from Central Asia, whose descendants still occupy the land of the sun-worshipping Saura or Chaora, no doubt one of the same race. Were we to adopt the term Indo-Getæ, or Indo-Sacæ, for all these exotic races, it would be far more appropriate than the indeterminate designation of Indo-Scythic.

The ancient Cambay, or, as locally termed, Cambayet, now a ruin, three miles from the existing city, was anciently called Papavati, or the 'Sinful City,' with reference to its position, close to the entrance of the Myhie river into the Gulf, the Papasini deriving its name from its dangerous character. This was exchanged, in after-times, for a more euphonous, but alike ephemeral appellation, *viz.* Ameravati, or the 'Immortal City.' Hence it was converted to Bagavati, or the 'Abode of Tigers;' and Trimbavati, the 'City of Copper,' from a notion that its walls were of this material. Its last transition was to Cambayet, or Khumbavati,

Khumbavati, the 'City of the Pillar,' which is thus accounted for. A prince, finding the ancient city no longer fit for a residence, probably from the reception of the waters of the gulf, or an increase of the alluvial deposit of the Myhie, founded the present city, on which occasion he erected a pillar (*S'thamba*, vulgò *Khumb*) to Devi, *the* goddess, on the sea-shore, on which he inscribed a grant of the ancient town, with eighty-four villages, whose resources were to be applied to the maintenance of her shrine, which he placed in the new city. Although no vestige remains of the column, the truth of the story is attested by the existence of a Jain temple dedicated to *S'thamba Parswanat'h*, erected by Sid Raj in the eleventh century, and since converted into a mosque, now forming the only conspicuous object in the town, although presenting a strange mixture of Hindu and Mooslem composition.

The remains of the ancient city are overgrown with jungle, and the sole relics, I was told, are two temples, one to Parswanat'h, and the other to Mahadeva.

The modern city of Cambay presents nothing very interesting to the eye. It is the residence of the descendant of one of the satellites of the Court of Ahmedabad, whose dwelling, yclep'd a palace, he gravely told us, was on the model of that of Sufder Jung at Dehli. As it appeared to satisfy his wishes, it would have been cruel to disturb his complacent conviction, though it was very unlike its boasted prototype. Long anterior to Hemacharya (see p. 175), and down to this day, Cambayet has been renowned as one of the seats of Jain learning, and there are no less than fifty or sixty places of worship of these sectarians within its precincts at the present time. Here, as wherever the Jains are numerous, is a library of considerable importance belonging to the community,

community, and if proper measures were taken to examine its contents, without exciting alarm, something new might be elicited as to their tenets, and the past history of their patrons, for it is from individual biography that we must draw the materials for history. But this can only be effected by great caution and patient inquiry, never by a shew of authority. The best plan of investigation would be to take a Jain priest, as moonshee, one whose *patravali* might trace Hemacharya or Amra amongst his spiritual ancestry; through his means the bolts would fly open. A Brahmin must never be employed: even a Mooslem would have better chance of success.

Cambay still enjoys celebrity for its agates, mocha-stones, cornelians, and all the Chalcedonic and Onyx family, brought from the ruins of Rajpipla, and here worked into every variety of ornament,—cups, boxes, necklaces, handles of daggers, of knives and forks, seals, &c.,—which find a ready sale amongst the European population, who send them as gifts to England. It is a curious fact, that the colour of cornelians is brought out by exposure of the rough mass to heat, when the milky white becomes a yellow, the yellow an orange or brown, and so forth. I purchased many for friends, and could have loitered more time away in the selection, if I had not had more important objects in view; so we merely remained a sufficient length of time to procure boats to transport ourselves, our horses, tents, and baggage, across the gulf to the shores of Saurashtra.

November.—The long muddy beach of Cambay at the reflux, far as the eye can stretch before it rests upon the *Loona-pani*, as our Gangarides term the 'salt water,' was no very pleasing sight to one who was all anxiety to behold the majesty of ocean, after twenty years of absence. It was late when the tide served for embarkation, but the evening set in beautifully, and our pattamar glided gently over the waters until near midnight, when the tide turned. Then "let go the anchor," was the order. I felt as if under a species of enchantment in this scene, so new to me, and both mind and body were renovated by its influence. Captain Shore, who was a fellow-passenger, brought forth his violin, and I my flute, and mounted on the *choppered* poop, under "the sweet influences of the Pleiades," we discoursed most eloquently (as we flattered ourselves) with the Nereids of the gulf.

The morning air blew freshly, and in eighteen hours we came in sight of Peerum Isle, and the range of hills twelve miles inland. We landed at Gogo, where we were obliged to wait a few days until our heavy baggage had made the *détour* of the Runn, at the head of the gulf. The port of Gogo has greatly deteriorated, and is now merely a nursery for seamen, who, in feature, appear a distinct class, partaking much of the Arabian. They are, however, Hindu, and descended from the navigators fostered by the kings of Nehrwalla, in which city an entire square was appropriated to them: they, in return, filling it with the wealth of foreign lands. Still Gogo has a venerable air, and its dusky walls, which must have defended it against the pirates always abounding in these seas, give it an imposing and picturesque aspect. The southern face, with its numerous round towers of unequal height, cannot be less than one thousand two hundred yards in length; yet this is much less than the western side, where the fortifications have been destroyed, apparently undermined by the sea.

Gogo was formerly the residence of the Gohil Rajpoot princes, and in the south-west angle of the town is a smaller castle, which served as their abode. Amongst the few objects to remark, is a *baori*, or reservoir, faced with blocks of stone, the deep-indented annulets on which,

caused

caused by the action of the water, give some notion of its age. The remains of an inscription, in the arrow-headed character, were visible upon it, but this had been replaced by a modern inscription in the Guzzeratti, not above two hundred and fifty years old. It contains the *gadda-ghal* of Rajwarra, or anathema on whomsoever should desecrate the fountain, the offender being desired to look at his parents, a couple of apes *(gadda)*, with rather obscene allusions. We likewise found some Arabic and Persian inscriptions, one of which bore the name of "*Zuffer Khan bin-Wujeh-ool-moolk*, [in the reign of] *Shah ool-Azum, Shems ood-doorica ood-Dín, Sooltan Mozuffer.*" Its date is the 10th Rejib, 777 (A.D. 1375.)

This is an important memorial, especially to any one desirous of attempting a sketch of Ahmedabad, as it shews that Gogo was the first object of ambition to a family which eventually attained considerable splendour. Wujeh-ool-moolk was the apostate chieftain, of the ancient Taka or Indo-Getic race, a brief outline of whose history I have given.* Zuffer Khan, his son, of whom this is a record, was driven from Nagore at the close of the fourteenth century, by Chonda, the Rajpoot sovereign of Mandore, grandfather of Joda, the founder of Jodpoor, the present capital of Marwar.† Zuffer Khan's failure to obtain a settlement amongst the Rajpoots was fortunate, for there success could have been but temporary, and he found a more fitting field for his ambition amidst the dislocated and less warlike materials of the kingdom of Nehrwalla. Sixty-four years later than this record, Ahmed, the son of Zuffer, and grandson of Wujeh-ool-moolk, founded, on the banks of the Sabermati, the new capital called after himself. We are entirely ignorant

* *Annals of Rajast'han*, vol. i. pp. 99, 105.

† *Ibid.* vol. ii. p. 15.

rant of the means by which the ancestor of Ahmed wrested this commercial port from the Gohils, who had retained it since S. 1200, when they were driven from Khérdur, ‘the land of Khér,’ in Maroosthali, upon the irruption of the Rahtores from Canouj. But we shall reserve this matter for a sketch of the Gohil family, which still rules in this region, and has given its name, Gohilwar, to a subdivision of the peninsula of the Sauras. Perhaps, as we have now fairly entered this diversified region, through which my future course will lie, this may be the fittest place for a glance at its past and present history, chiefly as regards the races who have held dominion there.

Saurashtra means the region of the Sauras, an ancient tribe of sun-worshippers, whose origin is lost in the darkness of ages. It is by no means improbable, however, that this was one of the Indo-Getic families of higher Asia, whose redundant population has been constantly radiating in different directions, even from the earliest times of which history affords authentic records, as the names and manners of the remnants of these races, still existing, attest; while the remains of the ancient sun-temples have still their votaries among the Catti, Comani, Ballas, whose physical appearance, notwithstanding the commingling of their blood with the older-established races, vindicates their northern origin.

At what epoch this peninsula was subjected by the Saura race, we are ignorant; but from Justin, Strabo, Ptolemy, and both the Arrians, we can trace their sway to a period coeval with Alexander the Great. The conquests of Menander and Apollodotus in the land of the Συροι, or Sauras, have given rise to much disquisition by the learned Bayer, and the annotators on the French translation of Strabo, who, finding Συρον coupled with Φενικον, were for transferring the Syria of the Indian Sea

Sea to the Syria and Phœnicia of the Mediterranean. It was, however, an easier task for the kings of Bactria, even with the deteriorated remnants of the Phalanx,* to which, no doubt, they drilled their Indo-Getic subjects, to pass from Aria and Arachosia, down the valley of the Indus, into Saurashtra, than to penetrate through the desert lands or hostile tribes which would intervene in their wide march to Syria. In the terms Surastrene and Syrastrene, employed by the ancient authorities to designate our Indian Syria, we have Saurashtra without any variation, and could we master the strange but perfect characters on its old silver coins and rock-inscriptions, we should be enabled to tell, at least, the names of the helmed princes, whose effigies are impressed on the obverse of the fire-altar, and whose profiles proclaim unity of feature with the ancient sun and fire-worshipping Sacæ of Aria.†

It is vain to do more than surmise, that the Saura tribe, thus powerfully marked by ancient writers, and by local traces in their chief emblems of worship, the Sun and the Phallus, may be of the same stock as the Sauromatæ of Herodotus. Certain it is, that the same rites, under the same names, *without variation*, were performed to the same divinities, on the same sacred days, in the Peninsular Syria of India, as in the Syria on the shores of the Mediterranean. But as I have elsewhere enlarged on this, I will only repeat, that the Syrian Bal and Belanus is the Bal-*Nath* (god) of the Sauras, whose grand temple of Somnath is the counterpart of the Syrian Balbec, *Soma-Nath* being merely a figurative appellation of Bal, as the ruler of the lesser orb, *Soma*,

* The *ani*, or wedge, is one of the formations mentioned in the *Sangram-sar*, a treatise on the Rajpoot art of war.

† [Since this was written, and subsequently to the death of the Author, great progress has been made in reading the characters referred to, and the result has been rather to confirm than to destroy these conjectural conclusions.]

Soma, or the moon. Add to the grand object of worship, the Sun, his symbolic representatives, "the pillar raised on every high hill, and the brazen calf under every tree," of the demoralized Israelites, and we have the Lingam, or Phallus, and the Bull Nanda, similarly placed on hills and under trees, especially sacred to these mysteries. Nothing is wanting to complete the picture, but the day set apart by the Syrians for this worship, and followed by the chosen people, "when their hearts were turned away from the Lord;" this was the 15th of every month. Here we have another coincidence with the Sauras and other tribes of India; it was on the day termed *Amavus*, which divides the lunar month into two periods, called *Crishnapacha* and *Sookul-pacha*, when Surya and his satellite appear face to face in the horizon, the one setting, the other rising, in perfect fulness, that the Hindus, like the Sabeans, "threw up their caps at the new moon, and proclaimed a feast."

Whence these minute resemblances? We know perfectly well, that the adoration of the host of heaven is the first element of natural religion, common alike to the inhabitant of the Polar Sea, and to the ancient Gete, who believed in the soul's immortality. But here are peculiarities scarcely to be accounted for without a common origin, or direct intercourse. On this we may by and bye be inclined to hazard some few speculations, as time and place may call them forth.

Saurashtra is mentioned as a subdivision of India in the ancient writings of the Hindus. It occurs in Menu; in the Poorans, especially in the parts touching on cosmography; but it is yet more renowned as the scene of the exploits and death of the deified Crishna, and other leaders of the *Mahabharat.* Although, therefore, we may not venture to assign a date for the establishment of the Saura race in this peninsula,

sula, with such authorities before us, we cannot be wrong in assuming that it must have been some centuries anterior to Alexander the Great, and at least coeval with Saul, or the century before, when the Syro-Phœnician colonies spread in every region. The dynasty which founded Anhulwarra was of the Saura race, inhabiting the sea-coast, whose pursuits were nautical; and there are curious, though unsupported traditions (which will be noted by and bye) of some of the tribes, with their religion, being from the coasts of Arabia and the Red Sea, to which these strange inscriptions would appear to lend a sanction.*

Saurashtra now enjoys no distinction in the political nomenclature of these regions, although so late as Akbar's time, a subdivision of the peninsula still had the appellation, contracted to *Sorat*, of which Joonagurh was the capital, held by a Gehlote prince (of the tribe of the Ranas of Méwar), whose military quota to the empire is stated by Abulfazil; and though three centuries have not elapsed since this period, there is now scarcely a Gehlote in the land. Such is the rapidity with which tribes are extinguished in these countries.

At present, the peninsula is divided into numerous chieftainships, and although the Cattis hold but a small portion, yet by some conventional process, this Indo-Getic tribe has given its name to the entire peninsula, and Cattiwar has completely superseded Saurashtra. There was, however, an intermediate term used to designate it (before the irruption of the Cattis), a term familiar to the author of *Almagestum*, as well as to the Hindu geographers, and this was Lar-dés, from the tribe of Lar, whence the Larica or Larice of the Greeks.

Saurashtra

* The letters *S* and *Ch* undergo constant permutation, according as they are pronounced by an inhabitant of the north or south. Thus the notorious Pindarrie leader, Cheetoo, was always called and written Seetoo by those who followed the Dekhany phonetics.

Saurashtra forms the most important portion of the kingdom of Anhulwarra, nor is there throughout India any region so well calculated to form a compact principality. It is about one hundred and fifty miles in breadth, from Cape Juggut to the Gulf of Cambay, and the same from the small northern Runn, the receptacle of the waters of the Bunas and Sarasvati, to Deobunder, the ancient capital of the Chaoras. It is surrounded by the ocean on every side but the north, where the apices of the two gulfs approximate by means of those vast *aranyas* (corrupted to *runn*), or marshy wastes, leaving but a space of sixty or seventy miles open to invasion. It possesses within itself every variety of soil, with numerous streams flowing from the central range (termed *Paryati* in Hindu geography), towards either coast, these hills affording every description of material for building, and the rivers abounding with fish and their banks with wood. Since the dynasties of Anhulwarra passed away, its various tribes appear to have led a life of nomadic or marauding independence, until the Guicowar princes established feudatory claims over some, and absolute power over other portions of the country. The chief subdivisions are Gohilwar, or the district of the Gohils, on the Gulf of Cambay; Jhalawar, to the north, inhabited by the Jhalas; Noa-nuggur, to the west, by the Jains, a branch of the Jharéjas; Pore-bunder, by the Ballas; Joonagurh, by a Mahomedan chief; with various other minor districts. In the centre of all are the Cat'his, while the Portuguese have for three centuries held Deobunder, the old Chaora capital, now converted into Diu. Besides the tribes originating these divisions of the Peninsula, many others of an equally Scythic character are to be found, as the Camari (now the Jaitwa); the Comani, called a branch of the Catti; the Mac-wahana, who claim to be a branch of the Jhalas; the Jits, or Getes

Getes of Jitwar; and several other original, besides the mixed races of Myreas, Cabas, &c. &c., who will be spoken of as we encounter specimens of each.

In fine, for diversity of races, exotic and indigenous, there is no region in India to be compared with Saurashtra, where they may be seen of all shades, from the fair and sometimes blue-eyed Catti, erect and independent as when his fathers opposed the Macedonian at Mooltan, to the swarthy Bhil, with keen look, the 'offspring of the forest.' Besides this field for the enquirer into the natural history of man, there is one equally wide for investigating the history of all the religions which have swayed the human mind within this sea-girt corner of Asia. Of the religion of Buddha, it will be seen, as we proceed, that of two points, one must be conceded; either, that it originated here, or that this was the region where it took root on importation from Aria. The discussion of this question involves that of the nearly consentaneous worship of Crishna, which, if we are to credit tradition, is an offset from that of Buddha. The antiquary and the architect would find abundant scope for their researches, and new ideas for their studios, in decyphering the cryptographic documents, and in forming hypotheses on the mechanical genius that planned the multiform shrines which have perpetuated the faith of their founders. And lastly, the painter might revel amidst harmonious contrasts, and a diversity of beauty, on the mountain top, or on the margin of the ocean, under a cloudless, dazzling sky, or amidst the almost primeval darkness of the monsoon. He might associate the latter with the shrine of Somnath and the dark rites of Siva, while, on the fane of Radha's lover, he would throw "hues which have words," and tell of youthful loveliness. Or, as he ascends the mountain to the temple of the

 worshipper

worshipper of '*the* Spirit,' whatever characterizes the grand and the simple, in form as well as in colour, would be present to his mind. This is a feeble picture of the attractions of the land through which I now propose to conduct the reader, a land containing subjects for many volumes and many portfolios; but my researches, being limited to a rapid tour, (though with some previous knowledge of the subject,) will oblige me to restrict myself to the most prominent among the many interesting objects of the peninsula of the Sauras.

Let us return to Gogo, which gave its name to the tribe which, at the end of the twelfth century, found an asylum here, when driven from Khérdhur, and which, for the sake of distinction from their more eastern brethren, are termed Gogara Gohil. The now insulated Peerum had precedence of Gogo in the first settlement of the Gohils, at which period, according to tradition, it had not the disadvantage of its present insular position, being connected by a mole with the main land, when in all probability it was the stronghold of the port of Gogo. We have a strong proof, in one of those incidental and pleasing coincidences, perpetually occurring in these closely-connected chronicles, of the priority of Peerum. In the Annals of Méwar, and on the occasion of the ever-memorable catastrophe attending its capture by Alla, in A.D. 1303,* in the enumeration of the chiefs who defended the palladium of Hinduism, mention is made of "the Gohil from Peerum," a place regarding which I could obtain no information when I translated the work, nor until this present time. The chronicle and traditions of the Gohils have preserved the remembrance of this event, which increased the honours of the tribe. Akhi Raj was the name of the Gohil chief, and it was on his return from a pilgrimage to Benares that he lent his sword

* Vide *Annals of Rajast'han,* vol. i. p. 266.

sword to the defence of Cheetore, and fell amongst the crowd of heroes on that disastrous event, having previously received the title of *Rawul* for his services, which continues to be used by his successors. Moreover, his lineal descendant, the present chief, informed me that his ancestor had the still more distinguished honour of receiving in marriage a daughter of Cheetore, her name Soojan Komari; but the virgin-bride became the suttee victim of Alla's success. This anecdote belongs to another part of this work, though it appertains to the name of the ancient city of Peerum, the epithet of the tribe from Gogo, which has to attribute its disasters to the discoveries of Vasco de Gama, and the settlement of his countrymen on these coasts.

"It was in 1532 that Nunna de Canha, governor of the Portuguese interests in India, having failed in his first attempt on Diu, left Antonio de Saldanha, one of his captains, for the express purpose of piracy. They sacked both the coasts of Saurashtra without mercy, burning Gogo, Patam (Puttun Somnath), twelve leagues from Diu, and carrying off their riches."* Five years after this, they murdered in the most treacherous manner their benefactor, Buhadoor, emperor of Guzzerat.† In 1546, Gogo was once more attacked and fired, the inhabitants put to the sword without resistance, and the cattle hamstrung; many other towns, with their shipping, sharing the same fate. These were the first specimens of Christian warfare against the heathen of Hind. Such were the proceedings of a people professing a religion which inculcates, as a primary duty, "Thou shalt love thy neighbour as thyself." The bloody Mahmoud, the diabolical Alla, were satisfied, and instantly granted the boon of protection to the infidel, on his calling

out

* See Churchill's 'Collection of Voyages.'

† See Col. Briggs' 'Ferishta.'

out "*La Illah, Mahomed Rusool Illahi,*" or by taking tribute in lieu of life. It would, perhaps, be fortunate for Christianity, if the historic muse in India were mute, as many have endeavoured to prove her to be, since atrocities like these are alone sufficient to have scared the Hindu from all association with her creed.

Yet, amidst all this crime, there are glimpses of greatness in men and actions, and many curious traits of magnanimity are recorded. One anecdote of Albuquerque is characteristic, not only of the man, but of the manners of those with whom he had to deal. Being in want of an immediate supply of the *primum mobile* to ambition, he coupled his demand upon the city for a loan, with the singular pledge of his moustache, which was enclosed in the letter. This guarantee was the most potent he could offer, and if Lusitanian in its origin, was in perfect keeping with the custom of these regions, where honour and the *mouche* are convertible terms, and stand or fall together.

BHAONUGGUR.—NOVEMBER.—This city, the present capital of the Gohils, is nearly eight miles N.W. of Gogo, and is placed upon a small stream, which falls into the gulf at a few miles distance, whose tides convert it into a good and safe harbour for shipping. The country from Gogo is a dead flat, until you approach the city, when a range of heights intervenes, which screen it from view till you are close upon it; its lofty and roofed towers then appear, shooting up from amidst a grove of mango trees. As we entered the city, there was nothing to call for particular notice, excepting the crowds of wealthy merchants traversing the streets, from whom, as the poet Chund says, "cities derive their beauty;" and in this point of view, Bhaonuggur was certainly beautiful.

This city was founded, or rather re-founded, four generations ago, by

Rawul

Rawul Bhao Sing, chief of Gogo, who gave it his name. Beeji Sing is the appellation of the present chieftain, who courteously advanced more than half-way to Gogo to receive and conduct us to his capital. In a Rajpoot, I always recognise a friend, and my being from the court of *Hindupati*, or the head of the Hindu race, by whom his ancestors were ennobled, if titles could ennoble them, secured me an additional share of courtesy, besides that I should have enjoyed from the society of my friend, Mr. Williams. The few miles we rode together were enlivened by social converse, and ere we made our triumphal entry into the capital, amidst salvos from his ships and ramparts, we had the outline of his history and that of his family, from their expulsion from the "land of Khér," to the present, together with his policy, resources, grievances, friendships, and feuds. My Rajpoot prejudices, however, would not allow me to overlook one grand deviation from the customs of his ancestors, which, as in other matters of far greater import, evinced that the laws of the Rajpoots were not, like those of the Medes, unchangeable. A band of Arab tabors, instead of the Dholi minstrel of his forefathers, chaunted their renown, preceding the Thakoor in the state procession, which altogether presented a singular, though not unpleasing medley. The like incongruities pervaded the *durbar*, when we paid our visit at the palace in the afternoon, and whether of things animate or inanimate, the conclave was the most motley I ever beheld. Arabian and Rajpoot costumes were here commingled, and every thing had a sort of amphibious aspect. The hall of reception was embellished by handsome glass lustres, but these were hoisted by double-blocks, evidently belonging to the dock-yard, and which might have reeved the halyards of a first-rate top-gallant sail. The ceiling was clustered with mirrors as close as they could stow, in which were reflected from

the

the walls portraits of princes, whose memory was associated with every thing English,—among them, George III. and his Queen. As I doffed my hat to the representative of the revered monarch, it did not escape the notice of the lord of the Gohils. The portrait of George III. and of his father, Frederick, Prince of Wales, are by no means uncommon in Rajpootana. The Rana of Oodipoor had one of each, and he was not a little amused when, coming unexpectedly upon them, I made the salutation, so rare in these regions, of uncovering the head; but I remember well, that when the act was explained, he did not lose so good an occasion to testify to those about him, that neither time nor place should ever make a good subject forget "the majesty which hedges in a king." I might have said to him, had it occurred to me at the moment, that this homage to our good old sovereign, especially in a foreign land, was instinctive, and part and parcel of every Englishman's national feeling, born in my time, when the royal birthday was a gala to all the youth of England.

Amongst the varieties of nick-knackery, was a splendid organ, which on one side had its ornamented pipes, and on the other a beautiful piece of mechanism, a musical clock, with scenic representations of a waterfall, and the ocean, on whose margin was depicted the story of Perseus and Andromeda, the former of whom was styled a sea *Rakus*, or demon, about to devour a virgin, who was rescued by a cavalier. This had belonged to the late head of the Mahratta confederacy, and had cost him four thousand pounds; but the Thakoor boasted of having obtained it for a tenth part of that sum, at the sale of the Peshwa's effects. It is from such evidences of mechanical skill that the natives imbibe high notions of our superior attainments. A traveller in the East cannot carry better passports than some of the nursery philosophical

phical apparatus of his native land. I had a magic lantern, with slides, to shew some of the simplest of the celestial phenomena, groups forming constellations, with another set of slides made to order, by Jones, of all the Hindu mythology; others of landscapes, Holbein's Dance of Death, &c. &c.; mirrors of various kinds, distorting objects, elongating or compressing the countenance, with which Scindia nearly frightened one of his chiefs into a fit of illness; chemical tests, which excited especial wonder, and which, in the transformation of colours and substances, appeared to approximate to *the* secret. But the most surprising of all these appliances, was the *Camera Obscura,* the delight of the most refined, and by which even the dying moments of the prince of Oodipoor were soothed. He used to say I brought him *Mun-ca-dowa,* or medicine for the mind, as I sat for hours daily by his pallet, exhibiting these things. On such occasions, he was surrounded by females of the interior, unveiled, of whose name and quality I was ignorant, but it was to be supposed they were only handmaids to the elect.

The youngest child of the chief afterwards produced all his Chinese toys, and we had to admire every thing in turn, which the good-humoured attention of our host rendered no difficult task.

From the durbar of Beeji Sing, we went to visit the port, his grand hobby. A Rajpoot emigrant chief, from the great desert of India, in the capacity of merchant and ship-owner, is a strange compound. We found two vessels, one a snow, pierced for eighteen guns, the other a brig, besides small craft, ketches, and pattamars, all belonging to the Gohil chief. He entered most pathetically into the history of one of his largest vessels, then under condemnation by the Admiralty Court of Bombay, having been seized in conveying a cargo of slaves from Mozambique.

Mozambique. He said it was very hard upon him, who had nothing to do with the trade, whether illicit or otherwise; that he had hired her to a merchant for a specific sum, and all he cared about was the freight. Not having looked into our maritime code, he could not for the life of him see the justice of condemning the ship on account of the illegal acts of the man who owned the cargo. We gave him no hope of a reversal of the decree. The greater portion of his revenue was derived from the port duties, which formerly amounted to seven lacs of rupees, but since we obtained the ports and commercial marts in the neighbourhood, as Dholarra, &c., it has diminished more than one-half; his land revenue is of nearly the same extent, in all amounting to about seven lacs. He told me that eight hundred townships owned his sway within and without the division of Gohilwar, and in fact that he was lord of nearly one-fourth of the peninsula, for, besides his own region, by right of conquest, he held lands in Cattiawar, Jhalawar, and even in the distant Babriawar. But the spirit of conquest is now laid, and the basis of possession is the foundation of order in these days of universal repose.

I shall now present a slight sketch of the family of the Gohils, chiefly with a view to shew that neither time nor place, change of condition or pursuits, can ever make a Rajpoot chieftain forget his ancestry. It is by the itinerant sons of rhyme, who come annually from the ancient land of Khér, that they are reminded of the days of old, for the spirit of poetry and commerce being amongst the antipodes of creation, Sarasvati, the Hindu muse, does not delight in sea-ports and cotton-bales, and I must confess that the chronicles of Bhaonuggur are amongst the most illiterate of the species I have ever encountered. The old capital of the Gohils, in the land of Khér, is, or was, ten miles

west

west from Bhalotra. Sejuk was the chieftain expelled by the Rahtores, and the first emigrant to the land of the Sauras, where he established himself in a new conquest, to which he gave the name of Sejukpoor. His son was Ranji, who added another old township, giving it his own name, Ranpoor. His son, Mocarro, took Bheemaj, Chamaruni, Omralla, Khokra, and the ancient Balli, or Wulleh, all in the tract now known as Gohilwar. He also captured Gogo and Peerum from the Kolis, making the latter his abode. He became a celebrated pirate, and with the gains of his profession he fortified Peerum, and had become so formidable, after the capture of six richly-laden ships, that the king (the legend does not say what king) sent an army against him. Mocarro, whose stature was six cubits, made a brave defence, slaying the king's nephew with his own hand in a sally, nor did he yield till death, and after twenty-five thousand men had fallen. Upon this event, the family was once more dispersed. Doonga, the elder son, remained, however, at Gogo, and Somsi-ji, his brother, went to Nandode, and his descendants rule at Rajpipla to this day.

Doonga had Beejuli, who had Kanji and Ramji. Kanji was killed in battle, defending Gogo against the king, and his son, Sarang, was carried off captive; but a faithful servant gained access to his prison, broke his chains, and carried him to Cheetore, whose sovereign sent him at the head of an army to redeem Gogo, then held by Kanji, his uncle, who, being oppressive, was detested by his subjects. He was deposed, and had the *tuppas* of Palit'hana and Lat'hi, consisting of forty-four villages, assigned to him as a domain. Sarang's son was Seodas; but once more the royal army dispossessed the Gohils of Gogo, and they fled to Khokra and Omralla. Their foe, in all probability, was Wujeh-ool-moolk, whose inscription we have recorded.

 Seodas

Seodas had a son named Jaita, he, one called Ram Sing,—the same who fell in defence of Cheetore, and whose wife, Soojan Komari, burned with him. He left three sons, Sutta, Dewa, and Beera, and from the two latter, two fresh tribes sprung, called Dewana and Beerana Gohils. Sutta had three sons, and to the eldest, Beesul, was assigned the township of Seehore, bestowed in charity on Brahmins, by Moolraj of Anhulwarra; but they fought among themselves in S. 1575 (A.D. 1519), and elected a chief to rule over them. The son of Beesul was Dhoono; his son, Akhiraj, who, having no children, adopted his grand-nephew, Har-brimha, whose son was Akhiraj, whose son was Rutna, whose son was Bhao Sing, who in S. 1779 (A.D. 1723) founded Bhaonuggur, on the site of Joona-Burwar, or ancient Burwar.

Bhao Sing had Akhiraj, and Beesa, who was long a *Barwuttia*, or outlaw; but at length he got Wulleh and Chamaruni in fief. Akhiraj had Bukht Sing, commonly called Atta Bae, whose son, Beejy Sing, is the present chief. His son and heir, Bhao Sing, revives the name of the founder in the fourth generation, and has the management of Balli, the ancient Balabhi, where he resides.

Thus, from the first emigrant from the land of Khér to the present time, there has been a lapse of six hundred and twenty-nine years, and twenty-one generations, averaging twenty-nine years to each, being six years above the general average of the inland princes. If correct, we cannot attribute the increased longevity either to a better atmosphere, or a more peaceful life, for piracy appears to have been the principal occupation of the Gohils, ever since they were driven from their original birthright.

The chief of the Gohils is metaphorically and locally designated *Poorub-ca-Padsha*, or 'King of the East,' restricting the term to the eastern

eastern portion of the peninsula, which is, however, equal to some of the sovereignties of the Saxon Heptarchy, and an empire compared to the "kingdom of Fife." The king of the East is entitled to the character of a courteous, well-bred gentleman. Although only forty-four, he is grandsire to a boy of six. He appeared much gratified by our visit, and we were not less so at the signs of order and industry in every thing about him; and, attached as I am to the ancient customs of these regions, I could not but think them well exchanged for the useful and humanizing civilization attendant upon enlarged commerce.

SEEHORE.—NOVEMBER .—The distance to this town was nine coss. The site of this ancient Brahminical colony, founded in the tenth century by Moolraj, the potent king of Nehrwalla, is most romantic, and the utter contempt of every principle of fortification displayed in its circumvallation, serves to heighten its beauty. Its round towers on every detached peak, connected by low curtains, are commanded by the lofty hills behind. A fine stream runs round the town walls, bordered with trees of considerable magnitude. Seehore boasts of great antiquity, and is associated with much of the legendary lore of past days, besides having been the chief abode of the Gohils between the time of their losing Gogo, and the founding of Bhaonuggur. Its original sanctity arose from a fountain of medicinal virtue, sacred to Gotama (one of the great sages of antiquity), and from the use of whose waters, Moolraj was cured of some inveterate disorder, on which occasion he made a grant of Seehore and its lands to the Brahmins. With them it remained, until internal dissensions arose, ending in a political conflict, when the survivors of these church militants determined to give themselves a master. They made choice of the Gohil of Gogo, but while they invested their new lord with all the rights that regarded the defence and political control of the community, with the exception of sufficient ground for a garden, they reserved all its lands for themselves, and the Gohil, not having yet overcome early prejudices, has not dared to abrogate the *Sasun*, or religious grant of eight centuries' duration, the punishment for which act would be sixty thousand years' residence in hell. The heir-apparent of the Gohil, Bhao Sing, has jurisdiction here, and according to custom, not exclusively Asiatic, is not on good terms with his father, for here, as in more favoured lands, the rising and the setting sun is not worshipped by the same votaries.

Balabhi.—One of the chief inducements for my visiting the "land of the Sauras," was to trace this ancient capital of the princes of Méwar, when driven from the land by the Indo-Getic invaders during the first centuries of the era of Vicrama. The name of this is now Balli, or Wulleh; but it rejoiced my heart, when enquiring of the Gohil chief concerning it, to hear him give its ancient designation in full, *Balabhipoora*, though I was grieved to find that the city, which in former days was eighteen coss (twenty-two miles) in circumference, and in which "the bells of three hundred and sixty Jain temples rang the votaries to prayer," had left not a vestige of its greatness, save the foundation-bricks, which are frequently dug up, upwards of two feet in length, and weighing half a maund, or five and thirty pounds each. Coins of a curious description were likewise often found by the shepherds. As the ruin lay full ten coss to the north of my route to Palit'hana, and the Gohil chief, in whose territory it is, assured me there was absolutely nothing left to interest a visitor, I abandoned my design of proceeding there.

Balabhi continued to be occupied by a descendant of the ancient race

race of Suryavansa princes, until the time of Sid Raj, who expelled him for his oppression to the sacerdotal tribe, on whom, upon the completion of that gigantic temple, the Roodra Mala at Sidpoor, he conferred the city, together with one thousand townships, in *Sasun*, or religious alienation. It continued in possession of the grantees, until internal dissension half exterminated the community, when one of the belligerents bribed the Gohil chief, with the offer of their adversaries' portion of the lands, to come to their aid; since which period, three centuries ago, they have been subject to the Gohils.

An opportunity was reserved, however, till the period of my arrival at the sacred Palit'hana, to make some interesting additions to what I already knew of Balabhi, which amply confirmed all I had recorded of it from the Yutis of Balli and Sandera in Marwar, the descendants of those who were expelled on its sack in S. 300 (A.D. 244). My informants were learned priests of the Jains, who corroborated these facts from books in their possession, as well as from tradition. Both sources afforded them the means of descanting on its celebrity, in antiquity, extent, greatness, and on its having been the cradle of their faith in the earliest periods of their history, when it was ruled by princes of the Surya race. Like myself, they could only surmise the analogy between Surya and Saura, which latter gave its name to the peninsula, and both being so called from being sun-worshippers. My subsequent incidental, but most important discovery, that Balabhi had an era of its own, gave ample confirmation to all that was affirmed regarding it, as did the inscription at Mynal, in Méwar,* which appealed to "the gates of Balabhi" to testify the greatness of its princes, proving that they must have migrated from Balabhi, whose glories

* Vide *Annals of Rajast'han*, vol. ii. p. 217.

glories were at an end when the northern invaders "polluted the fountain of the Sun with the blood of kine."

Still, both books and tradition connect the tribe of Balla with the ancient sovereigns of Balabhi. They state that Keneksén, a descendant of Lava, or Loh (the eldest son of the Surya king of Ajodia, who established himself at Loh-kote, in Panchalica, the modern Punjab), migrated to the peninsula, and fixed his residence at Dhaunk, anciently called Moonjipatun, and that, on the subsequent conquest of the region called Balla-khetra, they assumed the title of Balla Rajpoots. The lord of Balla-khetra would, of course, be Bal-ca-rae, which doubtless originated the epithet, so often noticed, of the Balhara princes. Dhaunk is still occupied by a chieftain of the Balla tribe, which enjoys considerable celebrity within the peninsula; but although they call themselves pure Rajpoots, it is said that they mix their blood with the Catti. The Catti, again, says he is a branch of the Balla, and both tradition and the "byrd of the bard," *viz. Tat'ha, Mooltan-ca-Rao*, place the Catti in the very spot where the Cat'hi opposed Alexander, and near to Loh-kote, the cradle of the race. But we anticipate the narrative.

Not far from Balabhi, there is a spot still sacred to the pilgrim, and connected with the grand national epic, the *Mahabharat*, called Bheemnat'h, where there is a fountain, whose waters, in past days, were of miraculous efficacy, and on whose margin is a temple to Siva, which attracts votaries from all quarters. The origin of this spot is referred to the adventures of the Pandua brothers, and their wanderings in exile amongst the forests of Berat, which tradition places in this very region, and its capital, Beratgurh, is held to be the more modern, but still interesting Dholka, included in Balla-khetra, and affording

affording fresh and almost superabundant testimony to the veracity of the ancient chronicles of Méwar, which state Balabhi, Beratgurh, and Gurh-Gajni, to have been the three chief cities which owned their sway on their expulsion from the "land of the Sauras."

Bheemnat'h derives its name from the Pandua Bheem, and its foundation is ascribed to his affection for his younger brother, Arjoona, who, by the force of a vow, never touched food until he had first made adoration to Siva. But they had wandered several days in the impervious woods of Herimka (in which was Berat), without meeting any symbol of the god, and Arjoona, faint and exhausted, could proceed no farther, when Bheema, retiring to a little distance, discovered a *charwa*, or water-jar. Filling it with water from the stream, he half-buried it in the earth, and placing round it flowers and leaves of plants sacred to Siva, such as the *vela*, the *aka (euphorbium)*, and *dhatura (stramonium)*, he flew to his brother, and, with the zeal of a discoverer, bade him rejoice and worship. Having, by means of this deception, recruited his brother's strength, he was seized with an irresistible impulse to disclose the fraud, and amidst shouts of laughter, told him he had worshipped an old water-jar. His levity so displeased Arjoona, that they were nearly coming to blows, when Bheem, to convince him, with a stroke of his mace broke the *charwa* to pieces, when behold! a rent appeared in the earth, through which a torrent of blood bubbled upwards. Bheem, shocked at his impiety, resolved on self-immolation, and, deaf to the supplications of Arjoona, was proceeding to fulfil his intent, when Siva himself appeared, in the form of an aged ascetic, accepted his repentance, and moreover offered to grant any wish he might frame. Bheem besought the god that the recollection of his impiety might be perpetuated, by having his own

name

name conjoined with that of the divinity he had offended, that the spot might become sacred to future ages; and hence its name of Bheemnat'h.

The object of worship is an emblem of Siva, on the margin of the fountain. Some time ago, according to tradition, the chief priest, intending to raise a temple over the visible type of the deity, was tempted by curiosity to explore its depth in the earth. Thirty feet had been excavated, but no soundings were found; he continued his work, until Siva personally manifested himself, and said that he desired no other shelter than the magnificent Burr (the *ficus religiosa*), whose stately pillared arms, and umbrageous canopy, afforded the most appropriate roof for himself and his votaries. There is a very large establishment maintained by the zeal of the pious, and however Siva may find himself proof against the elements, his followers, resident and non-resident, being made of more penetrable stuff than stone, have deemed it right to have a better protection against them than the stately evergreen. Accordingly, the buildings for the devotees, who come from all parts to this shrine, are considerable. The high priest had, until lately, a stud of one hundred of the choice breed of Cutch and Cattiawar, but he lessened the number one half, by gifts to the bards, a reduction to which economy is said to have been the real motive. Here, as at most of the spots of pilgrimage, the chief priest maintains a *sudda-birl*, or daily distribution of food to all comers, without regard to caste. This *teerut*, or place of pilgrimage, is held in especial veneration by the nomadic Catti. Here, before the ignoble days of peace, ere his lance was turned into a plough-share, he was wont to repair, and bribe Siva to grant success to his intended raid, by the promise of a *tenth* of the anticipated spoil, or if his mare was barren, he intreated the god to make

make her fruitful, dedicating the first-fruit to his service, or, what is the same thing, to the high-priest; but whether the rover fulfilled his votive offering any better than the *kungerin*, or green-seller of Agra, rested with him and his conscience. As the story goes, she had lost her ox or her ass, which carried her vegetables to market, and she sent forth a vow, that if recovered, she would dedicate one-half its value to the neighbouring mosque, or to the poor. The animal was found, but instead of evincing her gratitude, she disturbed the people around her by bitter lamentations. A neighbour kungerin inquired the cause of her grief, and on being told that it was from the necessity of selling her beast, she laughed heartily at her, saying, "if that is all the cause of your sorrow, hold your tongue and keep your heart, for I have often taken in the deity in this way."

Such are the virtues of a pilgrimage to Bheemnat'h, that the mere use of the name is a safe passport every where, and will act as a charm to a traveller, though his route should lay through hostile bands. I shall conclude this notice with the surmise, that this may be the identical Suryacoonda of Balabhi, polluted by the northern invader.

There is no moving in this region without meeting at each step some objects interesting in themselves, or which have become so from association with the mingled history and mythology of past ages.

CHAPTER XIV.

Palit'hana.—The holy land of the Jains.—Mount Satrunja.—Jain pilgrims.—Liberality and intelligence of the Jain sect.—The *Mahatma*.—The five *teerthas* of the Jains.—The *Sikras* of Satrunja.—Personages to whom the edifices on the Mount are dedicated.—Hindu character of the temple of Mecca.—Dates of the erections on Satrunja.—Road from Palit'hana to the mountain.—Ascent.—Shrines and temples.—Temple of Komár-pál.—Shrine of Adnath.—Sad effects of the dissensions of the *garchas*, or sects.—Few ancient relics in the temples.—Bad taste of the ornaments in the temple of Adnath.—Prospect from the temple.—Statue of Adi-Budha-Nathji.—Shrine of Rutna-ghor.—Statue of Adnath.—Analogy between the appellations of the Jain divinities, and those of Siva, and their symbols.—Tomb of Henga Peer.—Descent.—Temple of the sons of Deoki.—Minstrel.—Endowments of the sacred mounts.—Assemblies of pilgrims.—Palit'hana.—Etymology of the name.—Paucity of antiquities.—Love-legend of Sadwaeh and Sawalinga.—Modern history and condition of Palit'hana.

Palit'hana.—November 17th.—I was too unwell to make any observations on the tract intervening between Seehore and this famed spot, the Holy Land of the Jains; although there was nothing known to be worthy of remark there, yet it is next to impossible to pass over fifteen or twenty miles of any part of this territory, without encountering something to reward the toil of an inquisitive traveller, either in the peculiarities of the inhabitants, or local features. I was, besides, too much absorbed in expectation to permit anything not absolutely striking to make an impression on my mind; and never did pilgrim, Jain or Buddhist, approach the sacred Mount Satrunja with more excited feelings than I, a "barbarian" Frank.

I had, however, allowed imagination to outstrip experience, having no right to look for grand discoveries in the lands over which Mahomed and Alla had led their legions, fulfilling the iconoclastic injunctions of Moses, conveyed through the Prophet of Islam; but though

though they ruthlessly defaced whatever militated against the second ordinance of the Decalogue, fortunately, the conversion of the temple into the mosque was held meritorious, and the "*Allah Akbêr*" proclaimed within was a sufficient purification from previous pollution. Moreover, however extensive their demolition of religious edifices, it was beyond the power of these conquerors to destroy the memorials of a sect which, more than any other, depended on tradition for the perpetuity of their tenets.

Palit'hana, 'the dwelling of the Palli,' is situated at the eastern base of Satrunja, the mount sacred to Adnath (the first of the twenty-four hierophants of the Jains), which rises nearly two thousand feet, and is between two and three miles in ascent, taking the sinuosities of the route into account. My researches in this interesting spot were materially aided by an introduction through my own Yuti to some learned priests, now here on a pilgrimage, who gave me much information on points connected with their religion, as well as details concerning the *teerut*, from the *Satrunja Mahatma*, a portion of which work they had with them. I may give this, among other instances, in proof that there exists no barrier to inquiry from those narrow jealousies, which have been so much exaggerated by my countrymen. I have ever found great liberality, and no small portion of intelligence, amongst all of this persuasion, lay or clerical, with whom I have conversed.

Every place of pilgrimage has its *Mahatma*, a work descriptive of the religious rites required from the votary, with which is interwoven much biographical matter, in recording benefactions to the shrine, in repairs, or grants of land, generally perpetuated by inscriptions, besides (as in the *Aboo Mahatma*) some notice of the natural produc-

tions.

tions. "The *Satrunja Mahatma* was composed by Dhuneswar Sur-Acharya, of Balabhi-Nagara, in the year 477, (A.D. 421,) when Raja Silladitya, of Suryavansi race, repaired the temple of Adnath." In this extract, we have a practical example of the advantage of consulting these works, for in this simple record of the date of a book, we have three important historical facts relative to this region. First, the dedication of the hill to Adnath, whose shrine being merely renewed in A.D. 421, allows of our receding at least some centuries for the original erection of the temple; secondly, we have the name and abode of the author, an Acharya of Balabhi; and thirdly, the most important fact, that this prince, Silladitya, was of the Surya race; all confirming, in the most signal manner, the Annals of Méwar. This was the very prince stated therein to have fallen in defending Balabhi from the "barbarian" invaders from Western Asia. This was the second invasion on record prior to Mahomed, the first being in the second century, as mentioned by the author of the *Periplus;* and the third, on the authority of Cosmas, in the sixth century, when the Huns were established in the valley of the Indus. Hence the origin of the Getes or Jits, Hoons, Catti, &c., still discoverable in Saurashtra.

As if to crown my unremitting researches into the history of the most distinguished dynasty of India, and to complete the elucidation of Balabhi, a little further on I discovered the tablet recording that it had an era of its own, instituted a century prior to the composition of this *Mahatma.*

Satrunja is one of the Panj-teert'has, or five places of pilgrimage of the Jains. Of these, three, *viz.* Arbudha, Satrunja, and Girnar, are at hand. The fourth, Samel-sikra, is in the ancient kingdom of Magadha, now Behar, and the fifth, Chandragir, the Silver Mount, also called

Shéscuta,

Shêscuta, or the 'thousand-pinnacled,' lies amidst the snowy regions of the Hindu Kho, or Parbut-put-pamer, the Caucasus and Paropamisus of the Greeks. The Indus was formerly no *Attuc* to the hierarchs of Buddha, and, blending fable and magic (a grand ingredient in their faith) with tradition, they have it written, that "when Jainaditya Sur-Acharya used to visit his flocks west of the Indus, he floated himself across the stream upon his mantle; that, one day, the deity of the waters demanded *dân*, or a propitiatory gift, for passing his domain, when the Acharya cut off and presented his thumb; and that this magic mantle is still preserved, together with *the book, written in strange characters*,* in the temple of Chortaman, at Jessulmér, and the mantle is placed on the shoulders of every pontiff, as the token of inauguration into the chair of Jainadit."

This mount boasts of no less than twenty-one appellations, and one hundred and eight distinct *sikras*, or peaks, uniting it with the sister mount Girnar, which alliance is further traced by the Jain geologist to Aboo and Taringi, by the connecting links of Seehore, Balla, and other eminences, often very low and sometimes subterrene. The following is a selection from the nomenclature.

First. *Sri Satrunjya-teert'hanamina.* The etymology of this name is thus given in the *Mahatma.* In distant ages, Sookh Raja ruled in Palit'hana. By the aid of magic, his younger brother assumed his appearance, and took possession of the royal cushion. The dispossessed prince wandered about the forests, and during twelve years, daily "poured fresh water from the stream on the image of Sidnat'h," who, pleased with his devotion, gave him victory *(jya)* over his foe *(satru)*,

* This Sybilline volume, now a sealed book to all, "is suspended by a chain, and only taken down once a year, to be worshipped and re-placed with a new cover. Its characters are a mystery, and caused blindness to a female Yuti, who endeavoured to master its contents."

(satru), and in gratitude, he enshrined the god upon the mount, hence called Satrunjya. The hill must, therefore, have been originally dedicated to Siva, one of whose chief epithets is Sidnat'h, as lord of the ascetics, a title never given, I believe, to Adnat'h, the first of the Jains.

Pundarie-parvati, or Hill of Pundarie, a favourite disciple of Ádnat'h.

Sri-Sid-khetra-parvati, or Mount of the Holy Land.

Sri-Bimlachil-teert'ha, the Pilgrimage of Purification (from *bimla*, 'purity').

Suragir, Hill of the Gods.

Mahagir, the Great Hill.

Poon-rasa-teert'hanicum, Virtue-bestowing Place of Pilgrimage.

Sri-pati-parvati, Wealth-bestowing Mount (from the goddess Sri, or Lachsmi).

Sri-mookhta-síla, Beatitude-giving Rock.

Sri-prithavi-peeta, Crowning the Earth.

Sri-Patal-mula, whose foundation is in hell.

Surt-Camada-parvati, the Hill which realizes all desires.

To prepare the reader for the architecture of Satrunja, it is proper that he should be introduced to the personages to whom the buildings are dedicated, or whose names they bear, from their having raised them ; we must, therefore, again have recourse to the *Mahatma*, which affords the following extract. "Adnat'h had two sons, Bharat and Bahubala. *Bahubala had the country of Mecca, called Bali-désa*,* and his image was brought thence (from Mecca) by Javur Sah, one hundred

* *Baloo* is 'sandy' in Sanscrit. Baloo-désa would be the Persian Reg-ist'han, or desert, very applicable to Arabia Deserta. Balkh, or Balu-ca-dés, in Hindu geography, may have the same meaning.

hundred years after Vicramaditya, and placed on Satrunja. Thence it was removed to Gogo, where it remained, until the Gohils changed their capital to Bhaonuggur, *where this image now is.* From Bahubala came the race termed Chandravansa, and from his elder brother, Bharat, the race of Surya."

This is one of the most singular passages I ever met with, at once giving an Arabian origin to the religion of Buddha; and, coupled with the fact that Menu and the *Purans* countenance the notion that Bharat was progenitor of the races which spread over Bharatversha, or Bharat-khund (which included the portion of Asia between the Caspian and the Ganges), we have some approximation to ethnographic distinction. *Adnat'h* is a loose term, and may be rendered 'patriarch,' from *ad*, 'first,' or 'progenitor;' and their thus sending two great branches, one apparently direct into India through the Arabian coasts, the other northerly, would indicate the early dispersion of mankind from this admitted centre of radiation, whence might be derived the distinction of Saura or Syria to this peninsula, with its religions, analogous to the Syria of the west; and hence, probably, in like manner, the prominent name of Yavana, or Javana, as recorded by Menu, amongst the Sacas and Getes of the Bharatversha, from their being the offspring of Javan. We may bear this in mind, as we proceed, and especially as we look on the Ethiopic face of "the black Nemi," his curly head, and protruding lips; and at the temple of Crishna at the Land's-end of the Hindu, still containing the older shrine of *Budha-Tri-vicrama.* Again I urge that some attempt be made to master the rock-inscriptions at Girnar.

It has been asserted that Mecca was a Hindu temple, where a paganism, akin to the Hindu, was the worship, and those who have

had

had access to this shrine, Burckhardt among the rest, prove that the black stone, still reverenced by the Islamite, is the *Saligrama* of the Hindu, sacred to the "black divinity, Crishna." We also have the fact placed beyond a doubt, that Hindu pilgrims frequented Mecca from the earliest times, and the colony yet existing at Astrakhan pursue the worship of Vishnu on the banks of the Wolga, as they did in their native land, Mooltan, and are of the same stock as Javur Sah, who was a rich merchant of Cashmere, the period for whose induction of the image of Bahubal into Satrunja, *viz.* one hundred years after Vicrama, would be A.D. 46.

To return. The hill is divided into three portions, called *tooks:* one being named Múlanath; another, the *chaok*, or square, of Sewar Somji, a rich lay-inhabitant of Ahmedabad, who, in S. 1674 (A.D. 1618), repaired the shrines, and surrounded them with a wall, at an enormous expense, for "the sum of eighty-four thousand rupees (nearly ten thousand pounds) was expended in cordage alone, to bring up the materials." The third division is called the *Moodi-ca-took*, after a wealthy corn-merchant of Baroda, who, in like manner, expended immense sums upon it about half a century ago. Within these are the various consecrated objects, ranged according to their antiquity, as follows:

"The first building was erected by Bharat. The next by the eighth in descent from him, Dhundvirya; the third by Isa-Nundra, a *devotâ*, or god; the fourth by Mahindra; the fifth by Brim-indra; the sixth by Bhowur-hatti; the seventh by Sagra Chakravati, an universal potentate; the eighth by Vintra-indra; the ninth by Chandra Jessa; the tenth by Chakra Aeyudâ; the eleventh by Raja Ramachundra; the twelfth by the Pandua brothers; the thirteenth by Javur Sah, a merchant

merchant of Cashmere, one hundred years after Vicramaditya; the fourteenth by Bahirdeo-Mehta, minister of Raja Sid Raj of Anhulwarra; the fifteenth by Sumra Sarung, uncle to the king of Dehli, in S. 1371 (A.D. 1315); the sixteenth by Carmu Dasi, "the slave of good works, minister of Cheetore, in S. 1578 (A.D. 1522.)"

It is added, that Jawur Sah (who transported the image) eventually settled at the ancient city of Madhumavati, now Mhowa, on the coast of Saurashtra.

The road from Palit'hana to the foot of the mount is through an avenue of noble Burr trees, affording a sanctified shade to the vast concourse which flocks to worship. It is spacious, and has at intervals *coondas* and *baories*, fountains and reservoirs of the pure element, excavated by the pious. A flight of steps, cut in the living rock, conducts from the base to the summit, and on either side of these are altars bearing the impress of the feet of some of the most conspicuous of the twenty-four hierarchs, as Adnat'h, Ajitnat'h (to whom Mount Taringi is sacred), Suntnat'h, and Gotama (or Gotamrie, as he is familiarly called), the successor of Mahavira, the last of the twenty-four; but though his name is spread over regions of far greater extent than India, he has not the honours, amounting to deification, enjoyed by his predecessors. A little way up the hill is a *beesama*, or halting-place for the pilgrims, rendered sacred by the *paduca*, or footsteps of Bharat, the eldest son of Adnat'h, and king of Indo-Scythia. Still a little farther, we reach a fountain called *Eetcha*, of excellent water, alike sanctified by the *paduca* of Neminat'h. About four hundred yards beyond, is a second resting-place, with a fountain, excavated by command of Komár-pál, king of Anhulwarra, close to which is a shrine dedicated to Hinglaz Mata, the Hindu Hecate. Thence, and nearly

2 o half

half-way up the hill, is a third *beesamba*, of greater space than any in the ascent, and termed, after its reservoir, the *Silla-Coonda*, having a small garden, and a series of steps to increase the fall of a miniature cascade. This spot is deemed especially holy, from having the *paduca* of Purméswar, a name applied exclusively to the Creator of all. There are many other resting-places, with fountains, and footsteps of various sages of past days. In all the tanks, the water was excellent. After considerable winding, we reached the base of the most elevated peak, which is completely enclosed by an embattled wall, on the eastern tower of which is displayed the white banner of an Islamite saint, called Henja Peer, upon whose intrusion amongst the apostles of the Jains we shall remark hereafter. Leaving this on our right, we wound round the southern face of the mount to the *took*, or space sacred to Adéswara, the road for some distance being walled on each side, until we arrived at the first fortified gateway, called the *Ramapol*, or 'Portal of Rama.' Thence, after passing through four others, over a paved road, bordered on both sides with Neem trees, we reached a little grove of temples, clustering the south-eastern face of the mount. A large fountain, immediately beyond the Ramapol, is dedicated to Koonti, the mother of the Panduas, and tradition says that it was executed at her command, while her sons were exiles in the forest of Virat; but the rock has been rent by some concussion, and this pious memorial of the daughter of Vasdeo is exhausted of its element. The second gateway bears the name of *Sugal-pol*, after a banker of Bengal, in return for his munificent piety, and close to it is a fountain excavated by Nogun, "the first Gohil" of Palit'hana. Here visitors alight and halt, and the pilgrims pursue their devotions at the various spots of worship. The third portal is called the *Waugun-pol*, or 'Tiger-gate,' and

and here is a small statue of Sing-Cesari-Mata, or the 'Lion-born Mother,' the Hindu Cybele. Here also is the *Chaori*, or nuptial-hall, of Neminat'h, of Girnar. Adjacent to this building there is a plain flat stone, having, about three feet above its insertion in the ground, a square hole of fifteen inches diameter, called the *mookt-dwara*, or 'door of bliss,' and whoever can so compress his body as to pass through this ordeal of purity, is sure of beatitude (*mookt*). Few of the sons of Mammon, who "lard the lean earth," can bear this test, unless they greatly mortify the flesh. Strange to say, there is a stone image of a camel, nearly as large as life, in juxtaposition with the 'door of bliss,' and as all these erect stones are termed *sula*, or 'needle,' our scriptural text could not but suggest itself to the mind. At the fourth portal, or *Hatipol*, 'the Elephant's-gate,' is a shrine to another of the most conspicuous of the Jaineswars, *viz.* Parswa, with the cognomen of *Shês-phanu*, or the deity whose canopy is the 'thousand-' (*shês*) 'hooded' (*phanu*) serpent: suggesting another curious analogy to the Egyptian Hermes, whose symbol was the serpent, and one of his names Phanetes.

We next arrive at a temple erected by the famous banker of Bengal, well known to history as Juggut Set'h, or the 'universal merchant,' whose name was synonimous with wealth, at the time the Mahrattas invaded Bengal, and on whom the loss of two crores of rupees, equivalent (taking the value of labour and commodities into consideration) to eight millions sterling, made no sensible impression,—a fact so recent, as to be received without distrust. Another shrine adjoins it, called the *Shesra-stambha*, or 'thousand-columned,' although it has actually but sixty-four columns. Close by is the temple of Komár-pál, which alone contains fifty-two statues. Between this and the fifth portal, are

 two

two fountains, called Suryacoonda and Iswaracoonda, by the former of which is a temple to Siva, and, at a stone's throw, the shrine of a more amiable divinity, Anapurna the Nourisher, the beneficent Ceres.

We now approached the holy of holies, by a considerable flight of steps, leading through an archway, called the portal of Pundarie, which brought us in front of the shrine of Adnat'h. Pundarie, whose gate guards the entrance of the *chowk*, or quadrangular court, was the favourite disciple of the Pontiff, and his abode was the chamber over the gateway. All that is most celebrated for antiquity or sanctity, is contained in this court: but sectarian animosities, the ambition to be regarded as founders, and the bigotry of other creeds, have all conspired to deface the good works which Faith had planted on this holy mount. It is notorious, that sectarian zeal, amongst persons of similar faith, is more destructive than the hatred of those of dissimilar creeds; and here, from the mouths of learned Jains, whose universal law is to "hurt no sentient being," I became acquainted with the fact, that the wars of their two chief sects, the Tup-gacha and Khartra-gacha, did more than the Islamites to destroy all records of the past; for "when the Tup'has had the ascendancy, they tore down the inscribed tablets of the Khartras, and replaced them by their own, which again were broken into fragments, when, during the reign of Sid Raj, the Khartras had power." The separation of these two leading sects took place in the reign of Doorlul Sén, the fourth of the Solankhi kings of Anhulwarra, who ascended the throne A.D. 1011. Such was their mutual bitterness, that many pitched battles took place between them, and, forgetting their first tenet and the sanctity of the mount, they polluted it with each other's blood. Aji-pál of Anhulwarra overthrew all the temples raised by his predecessor, Komár-pál, an an act ascribed by some to the bigotry of his prime minister, but by others, and more in accordance with history, to the fact that this prince had imbibed doctrines altogether opposed to any Hindu sect.

We have no evidence that Mahmoud of Ghizni visited the sacred mounts of the Jains; but it is well attested, that the fury of the "sanguinary Alla" made all sects conceal their gods under-ground, for those they did not hide he destroyed. Many have since been brought to light, but comparatively few of the sculptures of ancient times are now existing. In like manner, the temples suffered, those only escaping which were converted into mosques. The consequence is, that in the Chaok of Adnat'h, although you cannot look around without beholding every where vestiges of antiquity, no entire edifice appears to claim this distinction, as they are for the most part incongruous structures, raised from dilapidated remnants, so that Komár-pál's own temple, from continual deterioration and repair, does not bear any greater signs of antiquity than that recently erected by the wealthy banker.

Although the shrine of Adnat'h is an imposing edifice, it possesses none of the architectural beauty of the shrines of Aboo, either in form or material. The *sanctum* is a large square chamber, with a vaulted roof; a *Sowa-munduff*, or external vestibule, likewise vaulted. The statue of the god, of colossal size, is of pure white marble, and in the usual sitting, contemplative posture, the hands and legs crossed. His symbol, the bull (*Vrishaba*), whence his common appellation, of Vrishabdeva (*vulgò* Ricabdeo), is carved in *basso-relievo* beneath. There is much of that placidity of mien, which is the chief characteristic of all the statues of the Jain hierarchs; but the crystal, or table-diamond eyes, do not improve the expression, any more than the golden

golden collar and bracelets, with which he has been decorated by the tasteless zeal of some modern votary. The effect of the whole is still further injured by the base taste, probably increased or prompted by the vicinity of the Franks, and visits to some of the Portuguese churches at Deo-puttun (Diu): the fane of Adnat'h being decorated with gilded paintings of heavy Dutch-built figures, and cherubim, consisting of fat faces and gilded wings, similar to the emblems in a country church-yard in England. Add to these, a cluster of English lamps, which illuminate the altar, and that the priests are awakened to matins by the iron tongue of a bell from some Portuguese man-of-war, and which bears the name of its founder, Da Costa, and you have some idea of the incongruities of this sanctified abode.

The vestibule contains, besides a marble statue of the bull, an elephant, of small size, of the same material, on which is seated Maru-devi, the mother of Adnat'h, holding in either arm her grandsons, Bharat and Bahubal. There are two tablets at the doorway, bearing inscriptions, but unimportant. One runs thus: "From Chutterkote (Cheetore) Méwar, the merchants Josi Oswal, Beesa, Kurmar Sah, repaired this temple in the time of Buhadoor Shah of Guzzerat, Saturday, S. 1578." The other is the *Varnun*, or eulogy on Adnat'h, the magnificence of his shrine, and the piety of its renovators. On the left hand on entering the area, is a spot peculiarly sacred to all of this faith, where Adnat'h used to sit in adoration of the "One God," when the mountain-top, with no canopy but the sky, was his sole place of worship. A Raen tree still marks the site, and is firmly believed by the faithful to be a never-dying scion of that which shaded the first of their prophets, and which now overshadows his sanctified *paduca*. He could not have selected a spot more calculated to assist the mind's devotion,

devotion, and to elevate it, "through Nature, up to Nature's God." The prospect was sublime, and though clouds obscured the view on the land-side, a beam of the sun burst over the ocean, irradiating the ancient Gopnath and Madhumavati (now Mhowa), on the south-eastern shore of the peninsula. To the west, we had a glimpse of the mount sacred to Neminath, and the noble Girnar; but to the north and east, the gloom restricted us to Seehore, and tracts within twenty miles. We saw the serpentine *(nagavati)* stream shining in mazes at the base of the mount, and darting towards the salt sea, with many smaller rills; and lastly, Palit'hana itself, with its minarets towering through the dense foliage, and its lake east of the town, were lighted by gleams of occasional splendour. Close at hand is a small temple, sacred to his second son, Bahubal, who here shares a great portion of the devotion paid to his father, but no where else in India have I heard of this "lord of Mecca" being an object of adoration. Immediately adjoining, are representations of the other two sacred mounts, without the Land of the Sauras, *viz. Sehêscuta*, or the 'thousand-peaked,' said to be beyond the Indus, and *Samétu-sikra*, in the ancient kingdom of Magadha, now part of Bengal. Near the shrine of Bahubal, is a small image of a *Devi*, or female divinity of the Jains, named Sasan; and, touching the slope, there is another female personification of their faith, called Mata Vehoti, and a shrine erected by the princely merchant of Anhulwarra, not to compare, however, with that he raised on Aboo.

Cells without number run laterally round the faces of the court-wall, each containing some statue, and which serve as places of repose or devotion to the pilgrims who come from all regions to worship the footsteps of Adnat'h. I placed my tripod under the scion of the Raen

tree,

tree, and found the column of mercury stand at 28° 4′, the thermometer at noon being 72°; the former shewing the same elevation as the shrine of Ganésa on Aboo, and that of the elevated valley of Oodipoor.

Notwithstanding the incongruous associations of ship-bells, English lamps, cherubim, and burgomasters, which disfigure and disparage the shrine, he would be a fastidious critic, and but little imbued with the spirit of eld, who could leave *Baba Adam-ca-took*, 'the *took* of Father Adam,' without a sense of satisfaction; albeit, there was little to gratify the historian or the artist. I sought in vain for inscriptions of the olden time in the Pali, or some more cognate character. The oldest I found was of S. 1373, corresponding with A.D. 1317, or twenty years after the death of Alla, the "Avatar of Yama," or God of Hell. On every side are ruins of the most ancient times, from which modern shrines have arisen to commemorate the past.

We must now quit this shrine, and proceed to the next division of the mount, called, after the rich corn-factor of Baroda, *Prem Moodi-ca-took*. Nothing can better exemplify the omnipotence of wealth, than the circumstance that the name of the plebeian Moodi, of but half a century's duration, should extinguish that of the illustrious Sumpriti Raja, who flourished in the second century of Vicrama, and who has left so many superb memorials of his piety, greatness, and good taste, in the temples of Ajmér and Komulmér,* being, moreover, universally recognized by the Jains as the greatest and best of their princes, since Srinica, king of Rajgraha, to the present time, not even excepting the lords of Anhulwarra. I am indebted for this fact to the books of the Acharyas (already mentioned), and local traditions, which

* *Vide* plates in *Annals of Rajast'han*, vol. i. pp. 671 and 779.

which combine the name of Sumpriti with that of the Moodi. This last, however, was worthy of distinction, for he not only repaired and embellished the fallen temples, endowing them with funds for the support of the priests, but encircled them with a strong embattled wall for their defence. No-where are the gods better provided with the means of resistance, and here Adnat'h and his disciples might remain free from all alarm, if they would put faith in the arm of flesh.

A valley divides the peaks, which communicate by a grand flight of steps cut in the rock, and so constructed as to render the ascent as easy as possible to the short-winded sons of wealth. About half-way up stands the statue of Adi-Budha-Nathji, or the 'First Divine Buddha,' of amorphous proportions; and close to it is a fountain, of healing influence, dedicated to Khorea Mata, a form of the Great Mother, who disjointed (says the legend) the bones *(khor)* of the *danoos* and *dytes*, the Titanic brood who infested and defiled all the places of sacrifice and worship in this holy land. This name affords another proof of the identity of the impersonations of Buddha and the Jineswars; indeed, my authorities recognized no difference between Ar-budha and Ad-nat'h, the First Intelligence and First Divinity, though Europeans have contrived to puzzle themselves on the subject. Let them make a pilgrimage to the sacred mounts, and drink conviction at the fountain-head, from existing practice and from the professors of the doctrines.

We soon reached the shrine, bearing the local appellation of Rutnaghor, built of white marble, by the Moodi. Within this are five marble statues of Adnat'h, held to be the original work of the Pandua brothers, each of whom dedicated one to "the first of the Jains;" and a sixth image below is attributed to the piety of their mother, Koonti, who accompanied them in their exile in these lands. Close to the

 door

door of the temple is "the habitation of the five Panduas," which claims a share of regard from pilgrims of every sect, and a little farther on is a fountain called Jinjoo-coond.

Passing through a portal in the embattled wall, we quit the Moodi-took for that of Sewa-Somji, a rich inhabitant of Ahmedabad. His pious munificence has been rewarded by his name being conjoined with the object of worship, whose original temple, which he repaired or re-built, was coeval with the era of Vicrama, nearly nineteen centuries ago. The statue of Adnat'h, designated *Chao-mookhi*, or quadrifrons, is of colossal size, not inferior to that in the chief shrine, which is about eleven feet high. It is related that it cost £8,000 to transport the single block from the quarries of Mokrano, on the eastern frontiers of Marwar; but they needed not to have gone so far for it, as marble, even of a finer grain, abounds in Aboo, as well as in the Aravulli, close at hand. A leaf of the *Satrunja Mahatma* affords the following record of this work: "S. 1675, in the time of Sultan Nasr-o-din Jehangir, Sowae Vizya Raja [universal victor], and the princes Sultan Khoosru and Khoorma. On Saturday, Bysak-sudi the 13th [28th of Bysak], Deoraj and his family, of which were Somji and his wife, Rajuldévi, erected the temple of the Four-faced Adnat'h." This is followed by a long list of Acharyas, which I passed over, until I reached the name of "Jina-Manika-Suri," to which is appended the distinction of having obtained a warrant from the Emperor Akber, embodying the first of boons to his creed, inhibiting the slaughter of animals wherever the Jain faith was practised. It was this scrupulous regard for the religious opinions of all the varied sects within his mighty realm, that procured this monarch the enviable designation of *Juggut Guru*, 'the guardian of mankind,' and which caused him to be

regarded

regarded by the Vishnuvite as an incarnation of Kanya. His son, the unstable Jehangir, eventually confirmed this and all their other privileges, although, while swerving from the tenets of Islam, he wandered amongst the metaphysical sects of the Hindus: on one occasion, he had actually commanded the circumcision of all the priests of the Oswals in his dominions, a fate which was only averted by the tact of an Acharya.

On quitting the *took* of Sewa-Somji, I visited a small shrine of Marudévi, the Mother of Adnat'h, who invariably receives a portion of the homage accorded to her son. There was likewise a small temple to Sunt-nath, the only one of the twenty-four Jain apostles who has a niche on Sid-Achil, sacred to the "First." In this name, one of the many designations of the mount (*a'chil* being a figurative term, meaning 'immoveable'), and in several other appellations of the First Divinity of the Jains, we have an analogy continually presented with that of the Sivites. One of the names of Siva is Sid-nat'h, chief of all ascetics. Adnat'h and Adiswara are commutable, while the most familiar symbolic name of the former, Vrishabdeva, is the synonym of Nandiswara, each meaning 'lord of the bull.' Accordingly, the statues of Adnat'h, or Vrishabdeva, are always to be recognized by his symbol (the bull), carved invariably beneath him; and Iswara, or Siva, is as inseparable from Nanda as Osiris was from Mnevis. Each has probably the same astronomical import, and the only ground for astonishment is how they should be alike found in the Palit'hana of the Indian, as in the Palestine of the Mediterranean Syria—on the Nile, as on the Indus and Ganges—in all which regards the priests of Bâl, or Surya, the Sun-god (whose name and worship in all probability originated the name of Syria in both countries), worshipped in the Tauric type, or the symbolic phallus or lingam, in which the Buddhists and Jains at one time coincided.

We must now descend from the abode of Adnat'h, after this rough sketch of the three *tooks* of his hill. A detail of each separate shrine, or the tradition and fragments of history, which more leisure and better-directed inquiry might detect, could not be expected from my transient visit; but I would recommend to others a more minute research, and to consider what I have done as a mere specimen of what may be effected by a better knowledge of these singular and interesting sectarians.

From the loftiest point we made our exit through a wicket in the wall, the most northern limit of the sacred inclosure, and soon reached that conspicuous mark of Mahomedan intolerance, the tomb of Henga Peer. Our endeavours to discover who this saint was, and when he flourished, were fruitless; ignorance, the parent of bigotry, could give no information beyond the tradition that it was in the time of Ghori Belum, nephew of the king of Dehli, who resided in Palit'hana, and by whom the mosques and eedgas, both inside and outside, were erected. We may, however, gather from the following legend that the "Peer" was in the train of some conqueror of "the Faith." It states that the said "Henga applied his mace to the head of Adnat'h," who, though he could not ward off the blow, "struck the aggressor dead," when he became a *Jin*, or wandering spirit, and so much annoyed the priests at their devotions, that a grand conclave was held, before which the ghost of Henga was summoned to appear, and interrogated as to what could obtain his shade repose. "To lay his bones on this pinnacle of the holy mount," was the reply; and here lies "Henga Peer, who, when living, could control the elements." The Hindus have

have a happy knack at getting up a legend to palliate insults to their faith, to which they could oppose nothing stronger. At present, however, the dervésh attendants on the tomb of their saint have found it requisite to conform to the rules of the place, and never touch food on the rock, nor partake of animal food below.

As we descended, the clouds, which had been congregating for some days, dissolved in gentle showers, cooling the air. The barometer stood at 28° on the summit, and the thermometer at 72° even at the foot of the hill. At a short distance, as we wound our way round the western declivity, we passed the *pallia*, or sepulchral stone, of a sweet-meat-maker, who, as it relates, "sold his life in defence of the sacred mount," when the roving Cattis levied black-mail from the priests of Adnat'h. Further on, we came to the *t'han* of the six sons of Deoki (the mother of Crishna), slain by Kansa, the Herod of India, which fate Crishna only escaped by flight to Dwarica. The temple is hypœthral, consisting simply of columns and entablature, and the representations of the six murdered infants are in black marble. At this point, we encountered a "motley fool," in the shape of an old minstrel. His head was covered with a cap of red cloth, ornamented with mock pearls; he had a doublet of silk, with bells on his legs and castanets in his hand. Beating time with these, and jingling his bells, he sang his old provincial songs—stanzas from the bards of the olden time—with an occasional *varnan*, or eulogistic stave to Adnat'h. Happy in the notice he drew from others, and his self-estimation, he preceded us merrily down the hill until we parted at its base.

Before we take to our tents, or visit Palit'hana, we may add a few words on the endowments of the sacred mount.

The temporalities of Adnat'h are managed by a committee of wealthy

thy lay-votaries from the chief cities, as Ahmedabad, Baroda, Puttun, Surat, &c. These nominate resident and ambulatory agents, who receive the offerings of the devout, carry them to account, and note the disbursements for repairs, daily oblations of frankincense or saffron, the feeding of the sacred pigeons, the animals whose lives have been redeemed from sacrifice, or worn-out kine, which find pension and pasture within the holy precincts. The present resident manager is a native of Méwar. The treasury of the chief shrine is said to be well filled with gold and jewels, and in this *Sat-yug*, or 'golden age' of pacification, its stores must rapidly increase. The predatory Catti, whose roving bands for the last fifty years deterred the wealthy Srawucs, or Jain laity, from visiting this their Palestine, are now known only by name; whereas, in past days, it was a chance that the pilgrim found his journey conclude with a bird's-eye view of the sacred rock from some riever's castle, there to languish until ransomed. But the little kingdom of the ancient Sauras, if governed with the same paternal care as at present,* will again see its rich plains covered with the gifts of Ceres, and the highways will be no longer scenes of jeopardy to those of Adnat'h. On particular festivals, immense bodies of pilgrims pour into the peninsula from every part of India. These congregations are termed *Sungs,* and sometimes amount to twenty thousand. It is not uncommon for some opulent merchant to put himself at the head of all the pilgrims from the region where he dwells, and to dispense subsistence to his poor but pious brethren in the faith, to and from the sacred mount,—a species of charity which has its reward. It is on these occasions that the personal wealth of Adnat'h is displayed and added to, every pilgrim making a gift according to his means. The

* The name of Elphinstone carries with it its own eulogy.

The statue is then laden with massive chains *(sankla)* of gold and silver bracelets, besides golden coin, which flows into the strong box of Adnat'h. Hema Bhye, a rich banker of Ahmedabad, recently presented a crown of massive gold, studded with large sapphires, valued at a sum equivalent to £3,500. There is always a diadem upon his head, its value adapted to the occasion: that in which I saw him was a plain embattled crown, of silver gilt.

But, what will more interest the Frank pilgrim of the West, it is on occasion of these *Sungs*, or assemblies, that the literary riches are brought forth for contemplation, and to receive the homage of the learned doctors (Acharyas), and other wise men amongst the Jains. The name of the most celebrated of all these festivals, which occurs on the 5th of the month Cartic, is in itself complimentary to knowledge, being the *Gyan-Punchamee*, or 'Intellectual Fifth,' when the contents of the Jain libraries throughout India are conveyed in solemn pomp from their hidden retreats to the light of day, cleaned, worshipped, and replaced. The *bindar*, or treasury, whether for literary or worldly wealth, is in the safeguard of Adnat'h himself, adjoining his statue.

PALIT'HANA.—All is sacred ground for several miles round the base of Satrunja, and the abode of the Palli is in contact with the mount. "What's in a name?" I had long indulged the most sanguine expectations, that on the spot where the Palli had perpetuated his name and his faith, I should supply one of the many desiderata regarding this nomadic race, the Galatæ or Kettæ of Indo-Scythia. Let the antiquarian reader guess my mortification, when I had, on authority, an etymology not only utterly destructive of the hypothesis, but one so coarse, so unclassical, as almost to annihilate all my enthusiasm for Palit'hana, Satrunja, Adnat'h, and his disciples. Instead of finding

some

some analogy or affinity with the Philites of Egypt, or the Pales of the Celto-Etruscans, I was referred to a mighty magician, named Padalipta, who used to make aerial excursions from his residence at Brigugacha, (the Barygaza of the Greeks, the modern Baroach,) to the mount of Adnat'h, and the *nom-de-guerre* of this *Vediavan*, or magician, was said to be from smearing (*lipna*) the soles of his feet (*pada*) with a particular ointment, preparatory to a flight. We are thus far constrained to follow the truth of the *Mahatma*, as expounded by the learned Acharyas, puerile and unsatisfactory as is this etymon; but, having sacrificed to candour by this statement, I do not hesitate utterly to reject old Padalipta and his unguents, with whatever magical powers he may have possessed; to deny that his name could have been the foundation for that of this abode of the Palli, who have left traces throughout Western India, in their strange characters and names of cities; and, in short, to assume that it is derived from some grand migration from Central Asia, which brought in its train the elements, at least, of this very religion, here matured into Buddhism or Jainism, and sent back, in its more refined state, to humanize the regions whence it issued.

Palit'hana presents few remains of past ages. There are many *déwuls*, or sacred structures, but none of any antiquity have been left by the worse than Gothic Islamite. The buildings are also chiefly of a free-stone, the decomposed surface of which peels off, to the destruction of inscriptions, though these are most frequently engraved on tablets of compact limestone, or basalt. The town was of much greater extent in former times than at present, comprehending within its walls the mosque, now outside, erected by the Ghori Belum; but in vain I sought for an inscription to guide me to the discovery of the "king's nephew." History acquaints us with none of the race of Ghori who

who ruled in these regions, nor even of any viceroyalty from Dehli. But this, as well as the other Mooslem remains in Palit'hana, gives evidence of the genius and taste of the Hindu architect, even to the *mambar*, or pulpit of the Moollah, which has on either side the *torun* sacred to Siva.

Within the city there is, indeed, one ancient monument, and this is a public *baorie*, or reservoir, consecrated by tradition to the illustrious pair, Sadivaeh and Sawalinga, whose romantic story forms one of the many love-legends of the Hindu, and could we prove this from inscriptions, we should count full eighteen centuries as the least period since its construction. Sadivaeh was the son of the Tacshac Salivahan, vanquisher of Vicrama, the supreme ruler of Hindustan, and whose era, still dominant in Northern India, was fifty-six years anterior to the Christian. At one time it was universal in India, until this chief of the Tacshac, or Takas, invaded and subverted the rule of Vicrama south of the Nerbudda, introducing his own era, which, in its application of *Saca*, gives us another indication of his Scythic or Getic origin. If we credit tradition, their wars terminated in a compromise, by which Salivahan retained Peninsular India, and Vicrama all north of the great line of demarcation, the Nerbudda; and to this day the era in the former region is termed *Saca*, and in the latter *Samvat.* But to return to the legend of the reservoir.

The heroine of the tale, Sawalinga, whose beauty and accomplishments were the theme of eulogy at this period, was of the Jain faith, and the pride and comfort of her father Padama, who was the most opulent merchant of the time, dwelling in Pait'han,* on the Godavery, the

* This is the Tagara of the author of the *Periplus,* which supplied the sindones for the Roman market, a name which I do not hesitate to say is corrupted from Tak-nagara, the city of the Tak, or Takshac.

the metropolis of Salivahan. She had been sought and obtained of her parent, by one of her own faith and rank in life, from the distant city of Parkur, in the southern part of the Marust'hali, or great desert of India, and her future lord had come to Pait'han to claim his betrothed. But alas ! the heart of the fair Sawalinga was not in her own keeping ; she had seen the son of Salivahan ; she loved and was loved, and death would have been preferred to separation from the youth, and exile to the oasis of Parkur. Hitherto their love was pure ; they had grown up in ignorance of their mutual attachment, as pupils of the same Acharya, studying together in the temple of Kalka-devi, the Universal Mother, nor until the fatal day of separation approached, were they aware that the invisible Camadeva (Cupid) had presided at their lessons, and taught them one more easy to acquire, and more difficult to forget, than all that the wisdom of the Acharya could inculcate. But the fatal secret must be told, and Sadivaeh was made acquainted with her destiny even at the altar of Kalka, who had attested their mutual vows that they would live only for each other.

It had been fixed that, on the morning following the nuptial rites, the merchant of Parkur should depart with his bride, visiting, in their route to the desert, all the celebrated shrines of his faith situated in the land of the Sauras. With this she contrived to make her lover acquainted, and appointed a last meeting at the altar of the goddess who had witnessed their mutual pledges of attachment. Sadivaeh repaired to the temple, where the enamoured fair joined him ; but the goddess, indignant at this dereliction in one who was now the wife of another, defeated their design by casting the prince into a deep sleep, from which all the passionate efforts of Sawalinga could not rouse him. Time flew on swift pinions ; she had discovery to dread, but to leave the

the object of her love for the last time, in ignorance that she had been faithful to her promise, was misery. An expedient, a last resource, presented itself; with the expressed juice of the *pân*, she wrote her name in the palm of her lover's hand, and departed. It may be easily supposed that the prince, on awaking from his trance, was in despair. Disguising himself as a mendicant Jogi, with pilgrim's staff, and the antelope hide on his shoulders, he quitted the regal abode of Pait'han in pursuit of his beloved. On reaching Palit'hana, he went to make his ablutions in the ancient *baorie* of the city, and as he bathed, a tablet met his view, on which he read "Remember the vows in the temple of Kalka." No interpreter was needed to decypher these characters, unknown to all "except the eye of love." Joy filled the heart of the heir of Salivahana; he instantly, and with alacrity, grasped his staff, and, full of hope and ardour, renewed his journey towards the desert. The reader must rest content with this portion of the tradition (the remainder having unaccountably escaped my note-book and my memory), or repair to the reservoir of Palit'hana to learn the sequel from the living chroniclers; for though the tablet of Sawalinga has ceased to grace it, as long as the *baorie* shall endure, so long will this tale be handed down from mouth to mouth. India abounds with such narratives, having generally some historical incident for their basis, and familiar alike to the peasant and the prince. But vain was my search for ancient inscriptions,—the ruthless Toork had been before me, and the habit of using inscribed tablets with the other materials of dilapidated edifices in the erection of new ones, both by Hindu and Mooslem, will ever hide much of the past from the eyes of the present generation, or until these in turn fall sacrifices to Time or some other destroyer, when these relics may, perhaps, again see the light.

The modern history of Palit'hana is soon told. It has been possessed by a branch of the Gohil family ever since this tribe settled in Saurashtra, twenty-five generations ago. Its consequence has been considerably augmented within the last sixty or seventy years, by the depopulation of Guriadhar, whose inhabitants fled hither in a body to escape the inroads of the Cattis, and the merciless oppression of the Guicowar government. The name of the present chief is Kanda Bhye; he is about fifty years of age, and enjoys a fair reputation. His little principality consisted of seventy-five townships, including the tything (*tuppa*) of Guriadhar; but all are greatly depopulated and impoverished, partly from the jealous hostility of the senior branch of his family, the Rao of Bhaonuggur, partly from the encroachments of the Catti, or the rapacity of the officers of his Suzerain, the Guicowar. Having been compelled, in accordance with the habits of the times, to entertain a motley crew of mercenary Arabs for his defence, he found, when the reign of peace began, that this precarious source of his protection formed his chief danger, and to save himself from their clamorous threats, reserving an annuity of forty thousand rupees, he mortgaged all his estates, including the pilgrim-tax, to a banker, who advanced the sums necessary to get rid of the turbulent Arabs. How the system works, the facts, collected in a day's halt, afforded not the means of judging. It is manifestly the interest of the renter, who has a ten years' lease, to improve the lands and encourage the prosperity of the cultivator; but the reign of terror has been of such lengthened duration, and the internal policy is so ephemeral in its nature, that they have yet to learn how much their own interests are involved in the welfare of the community. The tax levied by the Gohil chief on the pilgrims was formerly from one to five rupees each, according to their

their means, and the distance they came, but I was told that it is now only one, without regard to circumstances ; but even at this ratio, if the rich always pay for the poor, supposing the *Sungs*, or bands, to amount to from ten to twenty thousand, the town must again flourish. At present, cultivation is scanty in the environs, although the soil is rich, with much of that kind which here, as in Central India, they denominate *mal*, a black friable loam, whence the name of Malwa is derived.

We must not leave Palit'hana without mentioning the clusters of *pallias*, or sepultural stones, at the western gate of the city, and at various other points skirting the base of the sacred mount. These memorials of the chivalrous days of Saurashtra, forcibly strike a wanderer from Upper India, more especially if he have not travelled through Rajpootana, where the *joojurh* (the synonym for *pallia*), which marks the spot where the brave has fallen in defence of his rights, is not uncommon, but here we find them planted thick as grave-stones in an English church-yard. The " short but simple annals," often engraved upon these vestiges of the past, are worthy of attention, and if the traveller fail to extract historic data from them, he may always gain some record of the manners and customs of a people different from any within his knowledge. Even the little allegorical *relievi*, rudely sculptured upon these, afford something more than amusement, denoting, in the absence of inscription, the class in society of the individual. For instance, at the adjoining village of Khyrwa, the effigy of the slain was represented in a car, which of itself bespeaks antiquity, as the war-chariot has long been disused.

I will reserve the little I have to add regarding the Jains, their traditions, theogony, and modern condition, until I have made the pilgrimage

pilgrimage to the 'Mount of purity,' Girnar; even then my remarks will be very succinct, as, independently of the allusions to them inseparable from the preceding pages, my friend Major Miles has anticipated me in most that I had to say, which he has told so fully and so well, that I should only risk repetition by enlarging upon the subject.* Our sources of information being the same, and our views and mode of attaining it similar, the results are necessarily so, and I shall therefore restrict myself to the few points which have come less within the scope of his enquiries.

* *Vide* Trans. Royal Asiatic Society, vol. iii. p. 335.

CHAPTER XV.

Guriadhar.—Aspect of the country.—Damnaggur.—Agriculture.—Akalla.—Pestilential air.—Umrélie.—Region of the Cat'hi.—Manly aspect of the Cat'his.—The provincial chief of Saurashtra.—Apparatus for irrigation.—Mean appearance of the villages.—Magnificent *mirage*.—Deolah.—The chief, a Cat'hi.—Coincidences between the manners of eastern and western tribes.—Anecdote of Jessajee.—A robber turned saint.—Gurreah.—Habits of the Cat'his.—Asylum of the Pandus.—Legend of Koomti.—Statue of Baldeo.—Toolsishama.—Scene of combat between Crishna and the Dyte.—Shrines.—Incorrect geography of our maps of this part.—Dohun.—Geological notices.—Kowrewar.—Pastoral character of this region.—Superiority of the cattle.—Holy Mount Mool-Dwarica.—Soodrapara.—Improvement in the habitations of the peasantry.—Temple of the sun.—Source of the Sirsooti.

Guriadhar.—November.—We marched about seventeen miles to this place, over a fertile tract, as far as regards the capability of the soil, though, except in the vicinity of the villages, there is little cultivation. The plains are gently undulating, sometimes confining the vision within a radius of a few miles, and at others opening the prospect and disclosing Mount Satrunja and its subordinate hills ranging to the southward. The country is but scantily wooded, though a few neem and mango trees, at all the villages, relieve the eye, and the plains are studded with the *babool (Mimosa Arabica)*, which makes up in utility for its want of majesty. Guriadhar has nothing which merits observation, from the causes stated in the preceding chapter, though it is still the head of a *tuppa*, or tything, and the residence of a relative of the chief of Palit'hana.

Damnaggur.—November 19th.—This was a short march of twelve miles. Its being a *Khas talooya*, or royal domain of the Guicowar, accounted for the superior cultivation, owing to the protection afforded to the husbandman. It was in former days a Gohil possession, but had been wrested from that tribe, and now forms a portion of the division of Umrélie. It bore a Hindu appellation anciently, but Damoji, the first southern suzerain of these regions, gave it, *decus et tutamen*, a defence and his name. This is the same prince who fortified the modern Puttun. We saw some patches of magnificent black sugar-cane, and the young *gram* was thriving luxuriantly, as well as the *til*, or sweet-oil plant, and the useful *moong;* but the thin stalks of the autumnal crops of *jowar* and *bajra* afforded evidence that the unusual fall of rain on the continent had equally affected the peninsula of Guzzerat. I observed some very fine fields of cotton, and a novelty to me in agricultural economy, the same field containing a promising crop of the *arend*, or castor-oil plant *(ricinus)*. Water was stated to be within twenty feet of the surface, yet there were no wells or traces of irrigation for wheat, nor have I seen any since we left Gogo, though a finer soil for it could not be found. The deficiency must be attributed to political causes. A small stream flows past the town, and contains a most delicate fish, very like the *gorya* of Upper India, which resembles whiting,

Akalla.—November 20th.—Apprehensive of fatiguing our followers if we made one march to Umrélie, said to be twenty-two miles distant, we determined to divide the journey, but were somewhat annoyed at finding Akalla only nine miles from our last ground, so that we reached our tents at eight A.M., the thermometer being only 68°. This is a small village, situated on a pretty streamlet, called a river in the kingdom of Saurashtra. The soil, surface, and crops, the same as yesterday, but with more commanding views, embracing the whole range, with its grand boundaries, the holy mounts of Girnar and Satrunja, at either extremity, with many intermediate elevations. I passed

passed a small group of hills, on which is placed a shrine dedicated to Khorea Mata, a most unhallowed place of pilgrimage. No ascetic can dwell here for any length of time with impunity, whatever his strength of faith or frame; three months' probation is the utmost limit to endurance in this pestilential spot, although every second or third year the air is said to be purified by a self-ignited fire, which sets the jungle in a blaze. From this we gather that there is some subterrene combustion which occasionally bursts out, while sulphureous agency is always exerted upon the atmosphere. The small town of Sautee is three miles distant.

Umrelie.—November 21st.—Thirteen miles. Roads excellent, and the soil in natural fertility cannot be surpassed, while the cultivation far excels any we have seen in the peninsula. For the last seven miles, the young wheat was springing up luxuriantly, as was the *til*, or oil-plant, but the *gram* was less abundant. The villages, however, had a most impoverished appearance, and their walls of clay must have been a poor defence against the Cat'his.

The town of Umrélie has rather a striking appearance on approaching it, presenting a solid circumvallation, with round towers of good dimensions, enclosing about two thousand houses, with a small stream winding round the northern face. Here the provincial governor resides, it being the chief town of five districts, styled *khâs*, or 'personal demesne,' and consequently in a rather flourishing condition, which has been greatly improved since the general protection extended by the British Government to the tributary vassals of the peninsula. The majestic Girnar continues to develope his fine conical form, and on ascending an eminence, all the *sikras*, or peaks, which link it with Satrunja, were seen sweeping in a bold semicircular curve on our left.

We are now in the very heart of the region of the Cat'hi, which is divided from the land of the Gohils by the Ghagra. This morning I was gratified for the first time by the sight of a genuine Cat'hi, proceeding to the economy of his wheat-fields, which were most industriously irrigated, and, like himself, a fine specimen of purely natural production. His manly form, open countenance, and independent gait, formed a striking contrast to the care-worn peasantry we had left behind, and those throughout Gangetic India. His look denoted that the field was his own, and that courtesy would be more efficacious than force in obtaining the tithe of its produce. Everything was substantial; the bullocks large and well-fed; the ploughmen, all Cat'his, in their peculiar garb, gave us a courteous salutation, and frank replies to whatever questions were put to them, and stood erect, as if they felt themselves of some importance in the scale of humanity.

The Cat'hi, though embued with all the chivalrous pride of the Rajpoot, unlike him, "venerates the plough;" yet even in putting his hand to this implement, it is with an air of conscious dignity, and he is equally ready to enact the part of Cincinnatus, and grasp his lance, which, ere he commences his day's work, he plants firmly in the furrow, as if to say "*gare qui touche*" the field or its owner. To him the transition from eternal strife to monotonous tranquillity cannot but suggest conflicting reflections, and knowing them to be surrounded by ancient foemen and despotic masters, I should be sorry to see a wider disunion between their military and industrious habits: but while ever ready to resist aggression, I would have them learn to appreciate the blessings of peace, and so long as their rights are respected, we may hope that their lawless habits may be controlled without the destruction of that ennobling spirit, which has secured their mental independence from the days of Alexander.

In

In the afternoon, the provincial satrap, by name Govind Rao, paid us a visit, and having conversed for some time, we proceeded together to look at the town, and accompanied him afterwards to his dwelling. The main street of Umrélie is spacious, and thronged with an industrious population. About the centre, there is a *chaok*, or square, whence the streets diverge. In the N.E. angle of an inner circumvallation, is a place of arms, solid, though not extensive, erected under the reign of Damoji, having in front a well-fortified court, in which, under a tiled shed, is placed the Guicowar park of artillery. As we entered the governor's house, we received a salute of five guns. I cannot conceive anything more calculated to surprise the European traveller, than his introduction into the habitation of the satrap of Saurashtra, more especially if fresh from his own land. We were ushered into a hall about fifty feet in length, twenty broad, and somewhat more in height, supported by six columns on each side, connected by arches; the ceiling ornamented with a cornice in good taste, from which were suspended four large lustres in cut glass, the intermediate spaces being filled with rows of globular lamps. Surrounding this spacious saloon, was a verandah, full twenty feet wide, having a sloping roof of painted wood, with similar rows of lamps. At the upper end of the room, chairs were placed for us. Immediately in front, was a *jet-d'eau* in full play, through whose irradiant and mist-like medium, we looked upon a brilliant display of fireworks, let off from the grand court. Verily, we were not a little surprised at this scene from the Arabian Nights, in the heart of this wild region, where but a few years back nothing was heard save the clattering of the moss-trooper's horse, or the report of his matchlock. We sat a full hour in pleasant conversation with our host, a man of courteous manners and good understanding; and after being perfumed with *attur*, and sprinkled with rose-water,

 we

we were *congédiés* with the *pan*-leaf, and its aromatic enclosure, to eat or not as we judged proper.

Deolah.—November 23d.—This proved a long, and to our followers, a tiresome march, being full twenty-seven miles, instead of the ten coss on which we had reckoned. The sun had reached the meridian ere we got to a place of halt, and, to add to our annoyance, we found that Toolsisham, the object which brought us by this route, (instead of going by that which conducts directly to Mount Girnar,) was ten coss farther, instead of six, and, moreover, through intricate paths in the mountains, which will compel us to break it into two marches. This would be nothing, but that time presses, and there are those far hence who already deem me on the deep waters, instead of playing the pilgrim in the wilds of Cat'hiawar. The air to-day was delightfully invigorating until ten A.M., but by the time we reached the tent, the thermometer stood at 90° within. Cultivation in this tract is abundant, and the leathern bucket for irrigation, requiring but one man to apply it, was everywhere in use. Like all the apparatus of industry in these regions, its construction and application are the simplest imaginable, and although throughout India they have something similar, I have not met the precise counterpart of this. I subjoin a sketch of it.

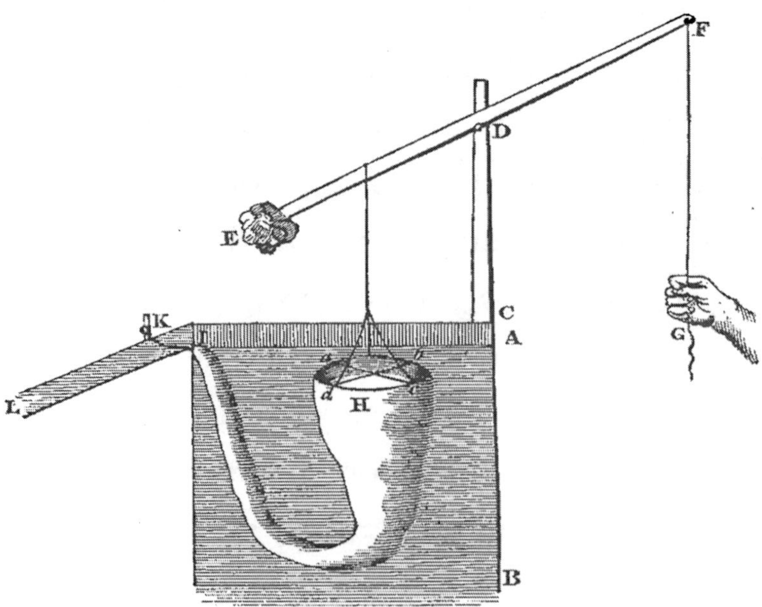

A B. The well.

C D. A pole elevated on the edge of the well.

E F. A transverse pole, moveable on a pivot, *D.*

E. Mass of clay, or stone, to sink the bucket, *H.*

F G. A rope by which the cultivator raises or depresses the bucket.

I H. Flexible leather bucket, open at each mouth, the larger mouth, *H,* about fifteen inches diameter, kept open by a circular iron ring, and two transverse iron bits, as *a, b, c. d.*

K. A peg of wood, driven firmly into the ground, at the edge of the well.

K I. A thong fixing the flexible tube to

K L. A water-course.

The bucket being filled, the action, on elevating the lever *E D F,* brings the main body of the bucket nearer to the cultivator, giving a tension to the thong *K I,* which at the same time brings its mouth into the trough, or water-course, where it remains stationary, and pouring out its contents, as the larger end is raised, until emptied. In like manner, it descends to be refilled by its own weight.

It might easily be adapted to irrigate garden or nursery-grounds, where water is near the surface. That great agriculturist, Zalim Sing of Kotah, who never failed to seek out whatever was useful or economical, copied it.

Eight miles from Umrélie, we crossed the main branch of the Satrunja river, which has its source in the hills south of Girnar, and is the largest I have yet seen in the peninsula. The villages were numerous, but the habitations mean, and the contrast between them and those of Guzzerat, where commerce and agriculture intermingle, is very great. Here there is no trace of commerce but in such towns

as

as Umrélie. The direction of the route to-day was southerly, with Girnar on the right, and Satrunja on the left, about equi-distant, and their diminished hills for the eye to rest on. The grandeur of each was enhanced by their being seen through a magnificent *mirage* in the early morning, when the fantastic and perpetually-changing forms, which the sacred mounts assumed, presented a complete phantasmagoria. At first, a dense black column rested on mount Girnar, gradually expanding to "the Abode of Adnat'h" (Satrunja); a bold sweeping line, embracing about half the circumference of vision. This lurid mass of vapour soon filled up the entire space between the two mounts, and was in powerful contrast with the more transparent medium to the north, in which the towers of Umrélie were reflected, and elevated by this mirror, from their low position, into gigantic height, appearing as if connected with the distant peaks of Seehore. Every moment brought change to Satrunja. From a dark unshapely mass, with precipitous sides, it took a columnar form, then appearing of nearly its natural size, and in a few seconds assuming another disguise, with a huge fragment apparently rent from the side, and parts of the low connecting ridge raised, while the larger mass was depressed. But the most striking effect was when a beam of the sun, rising from the bed of the ocean, darted upwards, lighting up the whole extent, similar to a lake of liquid fire in the midst of chaotic darkness; the light gradually gaining on the vapour until the upper limb of the orb o'ertopp'd the level of the hill on which it had rested, with precisely the effect of a flash of cannon in a dark night. As his power increased, the vapours lost their continuity, and at length broke into a variety of mystic forms, and quickly faded into nothingness. I have witnessed but two of these spectacles superior to this, the one at Hissar,

Hissar, in the north of the Desert, the other in Kotah, both of which I have elsewhere described.*

We commenced the ascent of the ridge, which is a portion of the chain connecting the sacred mounts, at the village of Jair, and having passed over five miles of this wild upland, covered with the t'hoor *(cactus)*, and khajri *(mimosa)*, we reached our place of halt, the small village of Deolah, of little importance save to its possessor. Still it had its diminutive wall of clay, with towers, of which he was as proud as Louis XIV. could have been of Lille. A small mountain-rill of good water completed the exterior of Deolah, whose denizens, few in number, were of the Koombi and Koli tribes; their superior, from whom we had a visit in the evening, being a Cat'hi.

Jessa, or with the more respectful post-fix, Jessajee, was a fair specimen of his race. He said his age was fifty, but had he mown the stubble upon his chin, which was of a full week's growth, his black *mouche* and clear complexion would have allowed a deduction of five good years. After sitting at his ease for some time, indulging, like a true Cat'hi, in the most unrestrained freedom of speech, I turned the conversation to his past life, by asking whether he had not carried the honourable profession of arms to some distance beyond his own sequestered abode. "A mere trifle," replied the moss-trooper, with the greatest nonchalance; "never farther than Bhaonuggur, Puttun, and Jhalawur." If the reader will consult the map, he will find that Jessajee's three points form a triangle, embracing the most remote quarters of the peninsula, east, south, and west; and that a trifle beyond, in either direction, both the horse and his rider must have gone into the sea. On pushing him a little further, by observing that these were very confined limits, and inquiring

* Vide *Annals of Rajast'han*, vol. i. p. 768.

inquiring if he had never tried the northern or continental portion, with the same simplicity of manner and tone, he replied, in his metaphorical diction, "Why, I have driven my lance into the gate of Ahmedabad." I wanted no more; Jessajee, the suzerain of Deolah, and of one dozen subjects, his township covering about as much soil as a good-sized mansion, had, single-handed, insulted the capital of Guzzerat! I was struck by the metaphor, which has since been more strongly impressed upon my mind by reading, amidst the scenes which gave them birth, the exploits of the early tribes who conquered Northern Italy; the identical image, used by the Cat'hi Jessa, being applied by the Longobard Alboin to prove his successful prowess.

From another, of the same race with Alboin, we have nearly the same figure of speech for a similar purpose. When the successor of Rurik, the founder of the empire of the Czars, for the first time crossed the Borysthenes, at the head of eighty thousand men, in a raid against that capital (still the object of ambition), in order to mark the humiliation of the city and his own glory, he "nailed his shield to the gate of Byzantium, on whose emperor he imposed a treaty, sworn to by the Varangian guards of the conqueror on their shields and their arms." In this we have not only the metaphorical record of conquest, but the peculiar form of oath, a form entirely Rajpoot, and a common expression in the mouth of the nomadic Cat'hi. But the Longobardic Alboin, and the Varangian Czar, were both Norman, of the same tribes who peopled the estuaries of the Weser and the Elbe, and were distinguished, even by the first chroniclers of Scandinavia, as the Asi, or Asiatics. Every day is adding fresh proof that a primitive eastern language is plentifully mixed with the Teutonic, which has even obtained the distinctive epithet of Indo-Germanic, while their

ancient

ancient superstitions and customs are parallel: so that, wide as is the separation in country, colour, religion, and manners, between the inhabitants of these regions at the present time, there is not only no impossibility, but no improbability, that the Cat'hi of the Elbe, and the ancestry of the Cat'hi opponents of Alexander, may have migrated from the same regions of Central Asia.

But let us proceed with the sketches of existing manners, in the interesting specimens that come in our way, and return to Jessajee. The present days of ignoble peace are the bane of his repose, and his activity of mind is checked by vague apprehensions of being caught with the javelin in hand in some distant foray, of which he has already had a foretaste, as he related to us with his customary simplicity. He has been reduced from his equestrian state to the superintendence of his serfs in the fields around his dwelling, to which alone he must now trust for support. But to his anecdote. Besides his desultory occupations, Jessa had established his *gras*, or black-mail, on four villages of Gondul, and it was the lesson which the good riever had read to him on this head that first undeceived him as to his influence. Returning quietly to his alpine abode, with the *korees* tied in his *cumerbund*, or girdle, the last *kist*, or instalment of his dues, or more properly extortions, he was beset, dismounted from his mare, the companion of all his travels, and lodged, with base fetters on his limbs, in the castle of Gondul. Jessa's genius did not desert him; an old nail, drawn from some part of his novel abode, answered the purpose of a picklock to his fetters, and awaiting the hour of midnight, he took the chance of breaking his neck by dropping from his prison walls, and luckily escaping unhurt, in a few hours reached a Cat'hi village in safety. As he finished his narration, he complained bitterly of the retention of

 his

his mare, nor can he comprehend on what principle they can retain her, or even justly withhold the *korees*, which, though originally extorted at the point of his javelin, had, from long custom, assumed all the validity of prescriptive right. Jessajee's physiognomy affords an abundant guarantee for his assertion, that he never drew blood, though he "used to frighten the folks to make them part with their *cheetura*," or 'bits of rags,' which signified, in the riever's vocabulary, turbans, scarfs, and such like things; "sometimes a buffalo or cow from Bhaonuggur, a horse, a mare, or any other trifle that might fall in my way." This old bandit has agreed to become our guide through the hills as far as Puttun, and states, what there can be no reason to doubt, that he knows not only every dell in it, but every stone on the road. We shall probably have more anecdotes before we part company.

I may relate another incident illustrative of the manners of these rovers of the peninsula. A Brahmin was holding forth to us on the piety of the Cat'hi proprietor of Charoori, a village of eight thousand rupees' annual rent, which we passed in yesterday's march. Not only had he built and endowed a temple, but distributed to every mendicant Jogi ascetic a blanket and a rupee, besides his liberality to the Brahmins. In short, he was pourtrayed by our informant as a saint. Curiosity tempted me to inquire farther into the history of this isolated man of virtue in the heart of a den of gentlemen-robbers, when he turned out to be one of the most notorious and enterprising of the plundering *bhyad* (frérage) of Cat'hiawar; but, having become too infirm to follow the active duties of his profession in person, he had resigned them to his sons, while he amused his age and calmed his conscience with these devotional pursuits, and in charitable dispensations of his youthful plunder, or the acquisitions of his sons. Thus

in

in every page of history we find the same features in similar periods of civilization. We have only to change the scene to the Guelphic ancestry of our own monarch, speaking of whom, prior to Conrad, in the dark period of the middle ages, the illustrious Gibbon says, "we know little of them, but may fancy that they plundered in their youth, and built churches in their old age."

Force is not the argument likely to eradicate the notions attached to a life such as the Cat'hi's, for not only is there no dishonour affixed to these professional pursuits, amongst "the landed interest" of these countries, but even their lords hold them not in less regard for their past misdeeds, if they ultimately accomplish their conversion, rejoicing more in the surrender of one such restless spirit, than in ninety and nine quiet, regular, tax-paying subjects, who never dreamed of "running the country."

Gurriah.—November 24th.—Marched nearly seven miles over this wild upland scenery, picturesque and interesting in the highest degree. Small rivulets pour their pellucid waters from the dark clefts through well-wooded glens, at every mile of our route, and meander over the table-land, until they find their way to the Satrunja river. Hamlets are seen amidst the dark foliage, at intervals, to shew that man is not wanting in a scene which should be the very paradise of the riever, who may enjoy his *otium* and opium under the umbrageous Burr and Peepul, or superintend the labour of the Koombi serf, as he raises his bread from the patches of cultivation, for where there is soil, it appears as rich as that of the plains below. The summits of hills are seen in the blue distance, and the majestic Girnar, instead of the regular cone which he presented at Umrélie, here discloses five distinct peaks. The approach to Gurriah is a good picture of a Cat'hi chieftain's abode; the square black tower, built of blocks of freestone, with its loop-holes,

 perched

perched on a pointed rock, the hamlet creeping as it were around and below it for protection, the whole embowered in a deep grove of Burr trees, with a crystal stream flowing through it. As I reached this retreat, I found the little camp pitched, and the domestics and followers enjoying their repose after the fatigues of yesterday. To complete the scene, old Jessa, his javelin in hand, and mounted on a neighbour's horse, entered the grove, whence issued at full gallop on a powerful mare, bare-backed, and with merely a rope in her mouth, an athletic figure with a blanket thrown loosely over his shoulders. He made a courteous salaam as he rushed by me at speed. On enquiring of Jessa regarding this apparition, I learned that he was a Balla Rajpoot, proprietor of an adjacent hamlet, in quest of a cow that had strayed. The idea amused me, though it was not a novel exhibition, for it accords with Rajpoot manners every-where. The hamlet over which the Balla claimed sovereignty, contained three subjects, two Kolis and a Koombi. He afterwards came to see us, along with the Bhomia of Jhirrie, of the same tribe. On the faces and forms of both, nature has set the seal of manhood; the one had a long beard, terminating in two peaks; the other was a sturdy youth of twenty-two. Jessajee seemed to know them well; and there is no lack of charity in surmising that they had often, in company, "cried 'stand,' to many a true man." Captain Macmurdo, in his acute observations on the distinctions that characterize the various tribes of the peninsula, draws a line between the Rajpoot and the Cat'hi, which in some situations may be just, but in scenes such as these, when we find them associating for the same lawless objects, it would be refining too much to seek for distinct lineaments: in dress, manners, food, superstitions, and modes thinking, they are one—a shade, a name only divides them.

Toolsisham.—November 25th.—The conventional coss, or estimated distances

distances in the highlands of Saurashtra, differ materially from the continental, or *gao* coss; for instead of the ten or eleven miles, which the seven coss from Gurriah would have given, we came full sixteen; yet did we not weary, nor was it possible for any one, with pretensions to taste, to think of self amidst scenes of such diversified beauty. The first two miles were over a table-land, still somewhat ascending, but on passing between two peaks, which stand as portals on either side, we commenced our descent through upland wilds; nor can I better describe the rest of the journey, than by saying that it was a succession of descents into distinct, well-wooded amphitheatres of limited extent, bounded by irregular peaks of some elevation. From the plains of Umrélie, the ascent to the table-land was gradual, and it is only from the descent, which is abrupt and rapid, that one receives a just idea of the elevation of the mountainous tract connecting the two grand peaks of Satrunja and Girnar. The barometer marked a descent of full five hundred feet in this day's march. The centre of elevation was well marked after leaving Gurriah, by the course of all the streams southward; hitherto they had flowed down the western declivity towards Satrunja. These streams merit more notice in the geography of Saurashtra, from their physical importance. The "black Gurriah" sweeping on our left, through one continuous well-wooded dell, finely contrasted with the milky Rânla, pursuing her course to the sea at Oona, which we crossed and re-crossed four times. I apply this term to the Rânla, because her calcareous bed is no sooner agitated, than the limpid stream becomes of a milky whiteness, indicating that her course is over a limestone formation. From some troopers who had passed over the ground in our campaigns against the Cat'hi, I learned the particular insalubrity of these waters. The plume-like tamarisk

(jhow)

(jhow) hung drooping over the stream in great abundance, and amongst the numerous trees which covered the banks, I recognized the ebony *(taindoo)*, some of considerable size.

My guide through these intricate and interesting regions was mounted on a noble mare, being, as I premised, no less a man than the Cat'hi lord of Gurriah, who beguiled the way with local legends, and never was there a spot better adapted to be the scene of spirit-stirring tales. As we passed a cairn of loose stones, lying on the left of our pathway, and near the river's edge, he very coolly said, "there fell my brother, when the Babrias came to prosecute their feud, and his death balanced an old account." As the old rover passed a log of wood which lay across the path, his mare shyed, when he strapped her unmercifully with a leathern thong. As soon as he had effected his object, I observed, "I thought you Cat'his looked upon your mares as your children, and always treated them kindly:" on which he replied, that it was true, but that his mare knew as well as either he or I did, that it was a log of wood; and then he began to expostulate with her upon her folly, as if she had been endued with reason. His village of Gurriah belongs to Joonagurh, yet the Guicowar has the *chaut'h*, or fourth of his revenue, an abominable tax, and, until done away, the Cat'his never can, and never should, be quiet.

On nearer approach to the object of our pilgrimage, every foot of the way was over classic ground. It was in this savage tract, emphatically called *Herimba Vana*, or 'Wilderness of Herimba,' that the Pandu exiles found shelter when banished from the fair banks of the Yamuna, and although, on the lowest calculation, three thousand years have elapsed since this event, such has been its importance and influence on the universal Hindu mind, that tradition to this day has

consecrated

consecrated every spot where these penalties were mitigated, or their sufferings enhanced. Within two miles of Toolsisham we came to one of these hallowed scenes, the final resting-place of Koomti, the mother of the Pandus, sanctified by an act of filial affection. Here, in their wanderings to elude the spies of their enemies, the mother of the five brothers was overcome with fatigue, and faint from thirst; but there was no water to revive her, when Bheem, smiting the rock with his mace, a spring of water gushed forth; but the pious act proved fatal, for the vital spark and the thirst of Koomti were quenched together. Here the last rites were performed, and a small shrine, which the veneration of subsequent ages has continually renewed, was erected to her memory. A pathway to the left of our route leads to the spot, where the traveller will have pointed out to him the chasm in the rock, whence flows a clear stream, in attestation of the truth of the tradition. It has ever since been held insalubrious, and to this day the *howa-pani*, 'air and water,' are under the ban.

There is another legend attached to the site, and perhaps the more appropriate one. It is said to have been the theatre of combat between Crishna and the Danoo, Toolasie, after whose defeat and death, Crishna, being anxious to lustrate and refresh himself, his kinsman, Baldeo, struck the rock with his ploughshare, when a stream issued through the fissure. The cleft still retains the name of "the furrow of Baldeo," and on close inspection of the statue which the admirers of filial piety had consecrated to the mother of the Pandus, I found it to be a statue of the Indian Hercules, and, to prevent mistake, the name Baladeva was carved upon the pedestal. They were all together, and all were of the same kindred, of *Heri-cula*, or 'race of Heri,' an epithet especially appropriated by Crishna.

TOOLSISHAMA

Toolsishama is a very sanctified spot, and celebrated as the arena of combat between Shama (an epithet synonimous with Crishna, and denoting his 'black' complexion,) and Toola, the demon *(dyte)* of Saurashtra, the terror of all the sacred classes, who, having obtained the boon of invulnerability by any mortal weapon, set the gods themselves at defiance; but he was told to beware of the incarnation of Crishna, which would be fatal to him. And the legend sayeth, that as he lay expiring at the feet of his conqueror, he preferred this last request, that his name might not perish with him; and hence the conjoined names of the victor and vanquished, Tooli-shama, designate the scene of combat. The abode of this Titan is a wild dell, completely enclosed by hills, and may not unaptly be compared to a large bowl, having its sides covered with wood, and at its base a *Seeta-coonda*, or hot-well, the grand object of curiosity. A reservoir has been constructed to retain the waters, which are deemed efficacious in certain complaints. It is eighty feet in length by forty-five in breadth at top, with a flight of steps, which diminishes its base to fifty-five by twenty. I was tempted to bathe in it. The temperature of the water was 21° above that of the external air, and it was disagreeably hot. At this hour, within the tent, the thermometer was 86°, and only 89° outside. After some minutes' immersion in the *coond*, it rose to 110°; but when taken out, it fell almost instantaneously to 76°, and as rapidly recovered the external temperature of 89°.

There is a small and rude temple, dedicated to the black deity, whose image decorates the interior, and presides over these sanatory waters. There are also shrines to the warlike divinities, Siva and Bhiroo, at the entrance of the enclosure. If we accept the local tradition for the origin of the hot spring, it would appear that it did not

exist

exist in the life-time of the giant Toola. Shama, hungry and fatigued after his battle, was awaiting with some impatience the culinary operations of his favourite wife, Rookmani, who with her own fair hands was preparing a mess of rice. But hunger getting the better of temper, he used some phrase which she resented, and overturning the boiling rice, she ran up the hill, leaving her hungry and sulky spouse to "chew the cud of sweet and bitter fancy." As the Gods of Hind, like those of Greece, never get into "hot water" without some consequences resulting from it, the rice-water then spilt became a perennial stream, bestowing sanctity and sanity on all who used it. In proof of the tradition, they appeal to Rookmani, whose enshrined image still looks down upon the Seeta-coonda.

It is a wild sequestered spot, but too confined for a large party, and here, within our bowl, horse, foot, and carts were crowded, creating a din most unsuited to such a solitude. An outlet from the coond allows the superfluous water to drain off, and this is the origin of a small stream, bordered by date and other trees, which meanders through abrupt and broken ridges, presenting some pretensions to the picturesque.

Dohun.—November 26th.—For fifteen miles, we pursued our route over execrable roads, if so they may be called, which roads were none, with all the ruggedness, and none of the beauties, of the scenery in the ascent. Like most mountainous regions, one rejoices in having seen it; but, romantic as it is, one has no desire to repeat the visit. The geography of all this tract is very incorrectly delineated in our maps, and the political divisions and potamology are peculiarly defective; but it is easier to point out errors than to correct them, and my health would not admit of the labour of surveying. Of this I have had enough in my day, but, had I health, I know of no pursuit that would yield me higher gratification than to lay down minutely the natural and political features of this interesting region. At the village of Heteeah, within two miles of Dohun, we cleared the hills. Heteeah is placed between two lovely streams, broad and well-wooded, both of which we crossed; one was the Machandri, on whose clear surface the feathery tamarisk and a species of willow were reflected in great abundance, while it was sufficiently expansive to yield an extensive view of its waters. The water of the Dohun river is esteemed particularly insalubrious, producing dropsy at some seasons to such a degree, that the village belonging to a Koli chief, with several others (depending on Joonagurh), is entirely depopulated by death and desertion. We are here six miles distant from Oona, on the sea-coast.

Kowrewar.—November 27th.—The ten coss of this march proved to be twenty-one miles. What a delightful change to the pastoral district of Nosgair, over whose verdant surface we moved to-day, from the sterile, unwholesome, and mountainous Babriawar, through which we passed from Toolsisham! The first four miles were over an indifferent road, strewed with loose fragments of a pale cellular, or rather vermicular sand-stone, of a very close grain, and containing minute particles of quartz. Wherever the ground was uncovered, the formation appeared of this same substance, presenting wavy lines, as if ploughed through by myriads of serpents. Shortly after entering these pastoral plains, we crossed the Roopni, or 'mirror-like' stream, whose clear and deep waters were confined in a narrow bed, with well-wooded banks. Soon after, we passed over the Sangavari, and another Machandri, near Goreedur. Here is fine exercise for the pencil; the village, surmounted by its castle and quadrangular towers, black with age, seated upon a rock, and overlooking a noble expanse of hill and dale.

On

On one side, the five peaks of Girnar; on the other, the towns upon the sea-coast, whose rocky bound is elevated so as to exclude a view of the ocean. About midway in our journey, we rested between the villages of Jamunwarra and Bheâl, amongst the ruins of a fine old temple, dedicated to Byjnath Mahadeo, placed in a very secluded spot, on the left bank of a small stream. The portico yet stands, and the sanctum, in which is the symbol of the god, is in tolerable preservation; but the munduff, or body of the shrine, is a mass of ruins. There was a ministrant in character with the place, a poor, cadaverous and leprous Jogi, who was drying in the sun the produce of a patch of tobacco. My Rebarri guide threw himself in great fervour before the emblem, and muttered a prayer, most probably a selfish orison, that his cows might yield copious streams of milk. This is called the *Ad-Poshkur*, or 'original' Poshkur, and I learned to-day that there were no less than twelve *teeruts* bearing this appellation.

After twenty-two years' residence in India, I may say that this is the only region of unmixed pastoral character, except Heriana, that I have yet seen, and with pleasure I observed that its occupants partook of the simplicity we attach to this state of existence. The herdsmen, dwelling in these rich and extensive plains, are called *Rebarris*, by which, in Northern India, we generally understand the rearers of, or attendants on, camels. Here the term is restricted to their avocation of graziers, and they form a numerous community, I might even say tribe, for as such they are classed by some of the genealogists, who likewise state that Hoons, or Huns, are intermingled with them. The herds of cattle we saw luxuriating in these fine pastures are not surpassed in shape, beauty, or strength, by any in India, not even in Heriana, where, in the farm of Colonel Skinner, I have seen such

 pictures

pictures of the bovine race, as even from an inexperienced eye claimed all the admiration usually reserved for the nobler horse; and, in fact, their heads had all the symmetry of the Arabian, while the eye (which, even in India, where they are worshipped, is the synonym for stupidity) was full of intelligence, and their limbs were fine and well-formed. Their comparative value may be known by the prices they fetch. Cows sell from ten to fifteen dollars each, and a pair of four-year old (grass four-year) oxen average forty dollars, the currency in which the Rebarris treat for them. As I mentioned the honest simplicity of this race, I may give the instances on which I founded my judgment. My guide, himself a grazier, civil, obliging, and intelligent, refused the silver I offered him, when, having accompanied me fourteen miles, and being in sight of a village, I wished him to return to his own. He even excused himself for doing so, saying that he would most willingly have gone all the way with me, but a favourite buffalo-cow would permit none but himself to milk her; but, added he, pointing to a hut at the village we approached, "you will find my sister's son there, and have only to call him out;" and having made his farewell salaam, and a few steps homewards, he again turned about and begged I would not forget him. I promised I would not, and now have redeemed my promise to the honest peasant of Babriawar. Another I saw, who divided his cake with his comrade, and importuned him to take it all. These facts, and the contented physiognomy (I have always been a disciple of Lavater) of the inhabitants of these plains, have made me jump to the conclusion, that their manners are in accordance with their pursuits. I hallooed to the "sister's son" of my guide, who answered to the call, and came forth from the hamlet of Meeteah; but Kowrewar, the end of our journey, being in sight, I let

let him go back to his work, and proceeded, leaving the square towers, with the memorial *Pallias*, on my right. These towers, placed so as to protect the whole village, have become an important feature in the scenery of this region. They are generally two stories high, or at least have two tiers of loop-holes for matchlocks. Some have flat roofs of clay, while others are unwisely of thatch, which, if fired, would presently unkennel the defenders.

About a mile before Kowrewar, we crossed the finest stream I have yet seen in Saurashtra, called the Singora (and also Nekoomati), pouring its transparent waters in beautiful rapids over a pebbly bed, the banks studded with noble clumps, or rather groves, of the sacred Burr tree. I dismounted, and walked along the margin to our tents, behind which rose the castle of Kowrewar, and a temple of Rinchor is placed upon the stream, which has its source in the chain of hills called *Chirchae*, and flows past the shrine of Roodra Mahadeo, six coss to the north, falling into the sea at the holy mount, Mool-dwarica, which it helps to insulate at high water.

This is all sacred ground to the Hindu, but more especially to the votary of Vishnu, who claims this mount as the primeval *(mool) dwara*, or portal of the divinity, long anterior to the incarnation of Kanya, whose statue, bearing the ignominious epithet of *Rinchor*, or 'deserter from the field of battle,' is here worshipped. It was originally enshrined in the island of Bote, at the mouth of the Gulf of Cutch, whence it was removed 1,400 years ago, and being reputed the "Real Rinchor," the Brahmins have made a good thing of it. He is indebted for a new shrine to the piety of the *Déwan*, or Premier, of the Guicowar, who has also enshrined here a very ancient symbol of Somnath. A great multitude congregates in the Aka-teej, on the third of

the

the month Bysak, to worship both divinities. About twelve coss from this is another place of sanctity, called Gaopati Prag, where a small stream, which bubbles up from a fountain, is dignified by the name of Ganga, or 'the stream,' and here is a temple of Sanyasis, or recluses, who find a livelihood in the faith of the pilgrims who come to purify in its water. Kowrewar has political as well as religious importance, being the head of a *Chourassi*, or district of eighty-four townships.

SOODRAPARA.—NOVEMBER 28th.—Sixteen miles over a very good road and interesting country, while the change from the miserable *jhopras*, or huts of the upland we have just quitted, to the comfortable habitations of the peasantry in the plains of Kowrewar, is very conspicuous; for however delightful it may be to have a gossip with Nature in her russet garb, amidst the tangled thickets, wild rocks, and ever-flowing streams of the highlands of Saurashtra, it is no less pleasant to alternate, and contrast this scene with more of man and civilization. The mind becomes tired of beholding him always in a pugnacious or predatory attitude, and although on our entrance into the plains we saw that the ploughshare had banished the sword, still there was enough of military habits to prevent tameness. The quadrangular tower frowned black defiance over every township of any consequence, and though now untenanted, the reliques of the Mooslem, in mosques and graves, evinced the struggles made against his dominion. We passed several such villages, as Singur, Lodwa, Puchnowra, and Soodrapara itself, whose castle, near the sea-beach, built of masses of hewn stone, is very respectable. The inhabitants were chiefly of the Aheer, Gohil, and Kairea tribes, the first being entirely pastoral; the last, though Rajpoot, as the name implies, now husbandmen by profession, and assuredly the cultivation was excellent.

Between

Between the town and beach of Soodrapara there is a singularly-fashioned temple, dedicated to the sun, in which is a personification of Surya, the divinity once presiding over this fair land, but shorn of his beams, and otherwise so metamorphosed, that it can scarcely come within the meaning of the second article of the Decalogue. As every divinity in the Hindu, as in the Grecian Pantheon, must have a partner of his toils, the *pootli*, or image of Rinadevi, is placed near her lord. Wherever there is a temple to Surya, there is also a coonda, or fountain of the sun, and this has an inscription, but it only tells of the repairs of the temple four hundred years ago. Near it is a temple to No-Doorga, or the 'nine Cybeles,' of whom there are nine small statues; and a short distance east of the temple is another fountain, dedicated to a *Roosi*, or sage of ancient days, called Chowun.

About seven miles to the north is a place called Prachie, which, being the source of the Sirsooti river, is held in high veneration, and attracts crowds of pilgrims. On its bank there is a statue dedicated to Madhu-Rae (the 'Intoxicator'), one of the *roopas*, or forms, of the Indian Apollo, regarding which it is related, that although the stream frequently overflows its banks, to the total submersion of the god, he nevertheless keeps stedfast to his ground. At the same place there is a small shrine to Looteswar, the god of plunder, especially worshipped in these parts. He was called a form of Siva, but I should think more fitly of Budha, or Mercury, who receives great homage, as will be seen by-and-bye, in quality of protector of the pirates, who have infested this coast from the earliest times. *Mĕlas*, or assemblages for prayer and traffic, which always go together in these regions, are frequently held at Prachie, and are attended by Brahmins and Banias from the adjacent towns, as well as by numbers of the 'Independents' from the wild tracts we have quitted.

CHAPTER XVI.

Puttun Somnat'h, or Deva Puttun.—Its celebrity.—Temple of the Sun.—Shrine of Sid-Eswar.—Legend of Kanya.—Place of his death.—Temple of Bheemnat'h.—The Koteswara.—Sculptured cross in a shrine of Mahadeo.—Description of the ancient city.—Original architecture.—Pointed arch.—Temple of Somnat'h described.—Beauty of its site.—Name of Mahmoud, its destroyer, unknown in the city.—MS. "Story of the Fall of Puttun."—Traces of a destruction anterior to Mahmoud's.—Two new eras.—The modern city.

Puttun-Somnat'h.—November 29th.—At length, I obtained a view of this, perhaps the most renowned of all the shrines of India, '*the* city' *par éminence*, more reverentially styled Deva-Puttun, 'the city of the god,' or still more accurately, Deva-Pat'han, 'the chief dwelling of the deity.' The distance from our last ground was seven miles, over a low flat tract, the soil good and well-cultivated. As we approached, we crossed the *Triveni*, or three united streams, *viz.* the Vrijini, the Sarasvati (a name of the Hindu Minerva), and the Hiranya, or 'golden.' The first, flowing through a morass, has little to recommend it; but the others are fine and clear. On crossing the last, the unpinnacled temple of the sun, and the dusky embattled towers of the city, seen amidst the green foliage, carry the mind's eye through the vista of eight centuries, to conquest and Mahmoud. What a host of associations arose to one who had indulged the hope of making a pilgrimage to this the most celebrated shrine connected with Hindu and Mooslem history! Pressing on to the goal, I passed, with mingled prejudice and contempt, the place of sepulture of the Mooslem saint, Abbi-Sah, nor halted for breath, until within the "temple of the sun," deserted, desecrated, a receptacle for kine, the pinnacle, to its spring from

from the *cella*, demolished, and the fragments strewing the ground. There is nothing of immensity, though there is great solidity, in the structure, which is of the order of sacred architecture called *Sikra-bund*, or 'pinnacled,' and with all the details of decoration laid down in the *Silpi-sastra*. The figures are bold in design, the attitudes of some striking, but the material, a coarse gritty sand-stone, does not give great scope or facility to the chisel; yet, as a whole, the edifice is imposing. The jambs and lintel of the entrance-door are of a well-polished yellow-coloured mineral, apparently jasper, though it may be that species of marble akin to the *jaune antique*. The *munduff*, or central dome, is not above sixteen feet in diameter, supported by strong, slightly ornamented columns, having a portico all round, terminated by square pilasters abutting from the external wall. Beyond the *munduff*, there is a domed vestibule, with pillars and pilasters, leading to the *sanctum*, where a globular patch of red paint, placed by the cow-herds, is now the only symbol of the sun-god. The sovereigns of Nehr-walla had repaired the injuries done by Mahmoud; but the spire, again thrown down by the sanguinary Alla, has never been re-erected. North of the temple is the Surya-coonda, excavated from the solid rock. The descent to it is by a steep flight of narrow steps. The water is said to cure the diseases of both body and mind, the term of ablution and probation being one solar revolution, during which, not only faith, but good works must be manifested, in order to make the remedy efficacious. Those who are not in a state of grace, we were gravely told, are detected "by having all the silver they carry with them turned into copper." Hence, it may be inferred, first, that the truly faithful part with all their silver to the priests of Surya ere they taste the waters; and secondly, that the others, who keep their cash about their persons, are made to believe that it is transmuted by their sins, instead of by the sulphureous agency of the water.

From the shrine of the god of light, I descended to that of Sideswar, the god of the monastic orders, obscurely buried in an excavation of the rock, dismal and damp, the low roof supported by a few crumbling columns. One might fancy this the cave of Delphos, though the perceptions of our blind oracle proved far more acute than those of most of his brethren. However rudely executed, all was strictly characteristic of "hell's dark abode." Besides statues of Hinglaz Mata, and Patal-eswar, 'lord of the infernal regions,' there were nine small figures in high relief, carved on the frieze of a miniature shrine, said by the blind minister to be "the images of those who rule the destiny of man." There was a small square court in front of the cave, whose walls have been repaired or constructed out of the ruins of other temples, having fragments of the gods in every attitude. It is shaded by some fine Burr trees, which are sacred to Siva. Although there is nothing attractive here, yet whoever is conversant with mythology will be struck, not only by the classical nature of the cave-temple, but by the perfect contrast it exhibits between the powers of light and darkness, in juxtaposition, and the rapid transition of the votary from the one to the other.

From this cave I proceeded to a spot, deemed by the Hindu the holiest of the holy, where the shepherd-god resigned his breath. We have elsewhere fully entered into the history of this prince of Yadu race, who during his lifetime was deified, and invested with the honours of Vishnu, under the title of Crishna, or Shama (denoting his dark complexion), but more familiarly known as Kanya. In the civil wars of his kinsmen, the Cúrús and Pandus, he sided with the latter, and

and shared their exile. He had then thrown aside his Apollonic character of Múrali, when, by the sounds of his pipe *(múrali)*, he captivated the shepherdesses as he attended the kine in the pastoral Surasén, and had assumed that of Chacradhari, or 'wielder of the discus,'* the most ancient of this Indo-Getic race. But although on this occasion he entered the region of the Sauras as a conqueror, this character was not always preserved; for he had before been compelled to seek shelter there on his flight from the king of Chedi, which obtained him the unenviable epithet of 'Rinchor,' already explained. But whatever name he assumed, he gained fresh votaries, and like those who, with Falstaff, think that "the better part of valour is discretion," the Hindu appears to consider Rinchor a complimentary title, as under this designation they worship him in crowds.† But, I repeat, he now visited the land in company with a few of his kinsmen, the remnant of that tremendous civil conflict which desolated India, to pass the remainder of their days in this insulated nook, the Land's-end of the Hindu, in sorrow and repentance for the blood their ambition had shed, though in defence of their rights. Thus, wandering from one *teerut*, or place of pilgrimage, to another, he, with his friends, Arjuna, Yudishtra (the abdicated paramount sovereign of India), and Baldeo, approached the sacred soil around the shrine of Somnat'h. Having performed his ablutions in the holy *Triveni*, Kanya took shelter from the noon-tide heat under an umbrageous Peepul, and while he slept, a forester Bhil (says the legend), mistaking the *padma*, or lotus-like mark on the sole of his feet, for the eyes of a deer, sped an arrow to the mark. When his kinsmen returned, they found that life was extinct.

* The Sikhs are the only people in India who now make use of this weapon.

† We must except the majority of the *Rajpoots* from the number of these votaries.

extinct. For a long time, Baldeo would not part from the corpse, but at length they gave it sepulture at the point of junction of the three streams. A Peepul sapling, averred to be "a scion of the original tree," marks the spot where the Hindu Apollo expired, and a flight of steps conducts to the bed of the 'golden' Hiranya, for the pilgrim to lustrate himself. This place of purification bears the name of *Swerga-dwara*, or 'door of bliss,' and contends with that of Deva-puttun for superior efficacy in absolving from sin. It is adorned by two beautiful reservoirs, called the *Bhalca* and *Padma*-coondas, the 'dart and lotus fountains.' The former is a dodecahedron, whose diameter is about three hundred feet. The lotus-coond is smaller, having its surface covered with this elegant flower, sacred to Kanya, and whence his most euphonous appellation, Comala, is derived; while on its eastern bank there is a small shrine to Mahadeo. These fountains are peculiarly sacred in the eyes of the followers of the shepherd-god, and were so in Akber's time; for Abulfazil devotes some space to the holy pilgrimages of Peepulsirr and Bhalcateerut (*bhal*, 'a dart'). Mooslem intolerance is strikingly obvious in the erection of a place of prayer touching the consecrated Peepul, and although the government of these regions has now long been under Hindu princes of strong religious zeal, the offensive Musjid remains undisturbed, furnishing a powerful contrast between the amiable endurance of the one, and the bigotry of the other faith.

From this I bent my steps a little farther up the Hiranya, to a temple in honour of Bheemnat'h, an epithet of Siva. The *sikra*, or distinguishing order, is of the kind called *Derah*, or tent-fashioned, its roof being the frustrum of a pyramid, perhaps the most ancient form of temple dedicated to the Destroyer. I should, however, rather speak of of what it has been, than what it is, for a wide-spreading Burr tree has contrived to take root therein, thrusting its branches through the roof, and this will in time destroy the whole, and leave the vault of heaven for its sole canopy. Nor dare the votary touch the tree, it being equally sacred with the temple to all-destroying Time; so it is not without meaning that Siva has adopted the Burr amongst his many devices. I put the question to the officiating priest, arguing, that if he did not destroy the tree, it would ruin the temple, and of two evils why not choose the least? He acknowledged the truth of this, observing, in his metaphorical language, that he "was between a well and a fountain," *i. e.* the horns of a dilemma.

Near this shrine is a multiform symbol of Mahadeva, called Koteswara, meaning 'with a million of lingams.' It is a huge cylinder of red freestone, covered with miniature lingams. It had stood in a temple, of which there is not a vestige left, dedicated to Pap-eswara, or Sin personified. This was the first time I ever heard this member of the boundless Pantheon mentioned. The fair Rookmani, the favourite wife of Kanya, is said not only to have been the high priestess of this temple, but to have erected it. If this be true, it is another proof that Crishna, before his exaltation amongst the gods of Hind, and the enrolment of his followers into a sect, adored the impure orgies of Siva, as well as made homage to Buddha, the protector at once of thieves and learning. The Mooslems appear to have taken especial pains to fulfil the sentence of their law upon this temple of sin, for they have actually not left one stone standing upon another; but why they permitted the emblem itself to escape destruction, I could not learn. The whole story, however, is allegorical, and a very curious allegory it is; and though, like many others, at the first aspect it appears too

puerile

puerile for notice, it supplies food for reflection. But although the root of sin is justly fixed in hell, we cannot see the propriety of making the fair Rookmani, the partner of the deified Yadu (whom they clothe in the varied garb of Apollo, Phœbus, Mercury), the ministrant. Just across the Hiranya is the site of another temple to that orb, "the eye and soul of this great universe," proving the combination of the mythological analogies.

Hence I passed to the *Sungum*, or point of junction of the two smaller streams with the Hiranya, and to the embouchure of their confluent waters with Samudra, or the ocean, where there are a few small *mindras* and *dhermsalas*, shrines and resting-places for the devotee, for whom alone they have any attraction, though we may well conceive the exaltation of feeling in the pilgrim from the continent, who for the first time sees the expansive surge driving back into their confined bed the united Triveni. Having seen these, the accessories, and but the accessories, to the grand object of my pilgrimage, and having, with all the fervour of the most ardent worshipper, made my salutation to Samudra, who was connected with all my earliest associations, to whose mighty voice I had been a stranger for twenty long years, and on whose waters I was soon once more to trust myself, I turned my steps to the shrine of Somnat'h. Midway between the temple of Surya and the portal of the city of Bal, I passed a shrine of Damoodra Mahadeo, which had been thoroughly renovated by Vitul Rao, the Dewan of the Guicowar, whose munificent piety and works of real utility have done honour to himself and his government, and what is very uncommon (not alone in India), the repairs, internal and external, are in unison with the original design. Although worth seeing, it merits no laboured description. I must remark, however, that

that an external canopied niche, where heretofore stood a statue of Sookha Mata, an impersonation of Famine, is now occupied by a large slab bearing a St. Andrew's cross. I never heard of the peregrinations of Scotland's 'Peer' so far east, and am probably not wrong in attributing this to the Portuguese, who once possessed all this coast, and proved greater foes than Mahmoud himself to the ancient glories of Saurashtra. Crosses, however, of many kinds, are not uncommon emblems with the Hindus, especially the Jains, on whose coins and structures I have met with the *Crux ansata* of the Egyptians, another added to the many curious resemblances between their respective objects of worship.

I entered Deva-puttun by the *Suryapol*, or 'portal of the sun.' The walls which environ the city are, in character and material, worthy of the object for which they were raised. They are composed of large square blocks of freestone from the adjacent quarries, and imbibing the moisture of a saline atmosphere, they have acquired a tinge which increases the sable hue of antiquity, while the square towers, constructed with a bold external slope, or *talus*, only to be met with in the remains of ancient days, lend an air of beauty and strength. The vallation is estimated at three quarters of a coss, but I incline to think it not less than a mile and three quarters. The western face, which is the shortest, is about five hundred yards, running nearly north and south; the southern, or sea-face, not a straight line, but, for the last two hundred yards, bending to the north-east, is in all about seven hundred yards, and the eastern about eight hundred.* The height of the walls varies from twenty-five to thirty-five feet, and they are about sixteen

* By some mischance, I found no computation for the fourth, or north side, in my journal, but we may suppose it full six hundred.

sixteen thick at the base. A ditch, twenty-five feet broad, and about the same in depth (faced with masonry, and, like the walls, having a regular *talus*, or slope), which could be rendered wet or dry at pleasure, with an excellent *fausse-braye*, surrounds the whole. I did not count the towers, but they are sufficiently numerous to command and defend the curtains, and are pentagonal at the corners (at least at the S.E. angle), with the salient angle towards the country. Who was the Vauban to the kings of Nehrwalla, history deigns not to inform us. If these are not the individual ramparts and towers to which the ladders of Islam were applied, they must have risen from their ruins, the site and shape being similar. They are, however, only the defences of Somnat'h, not the circumvallation of the mortal dwellings of Deva-puttun, being far too circumscribed to contain either its wealth or population, the limits of which are pointed out at the distance of a mile. It does not, indeed, necessarily follow that the city was walled in. An important inscription (No. V.), found in the temple of Bhadri-Koli, sets this point at rest, and shews that whatever portion of the ancient barriers of Somnat'h escaped the pioneers of Mahmoud, the whole was rebuilt exactly two centuries after him by Komár-pál, king of Nehrwalla, and paramount sovereign of Saurashtra. The entrance to the city on the east side has, besides the external gateway, an internal court of defence, having another portal of noble dimensions, with the *pointed arch*, whose ribs spring from, and are supported on each side by, four richly-ornamented flat pilasters. The capitals of these represent a marine monster, from whose expanded jaws the arch springs, while into his mouth a human being is represented, in various attitudes, as entering unwillingly, and in others he is making his exit by the monster's throat, which he pierces with a javelin. There is a

unity

unity of design, proportion, and execution, in the whole, that would at once justify our deciding it to be Hindu. The mythological device and application are entirely so, for the *torun*, or inverted arch, in all ancient temples, Jain or Sivite, is represented springing from the jaws of this same marine monster. I have thus found it in the Sivite temples of Barolli on the Chumbul, and in the Jain temples of Aboo. The very utmost I would concede is, that *if* an Islamite architect gave the design of this arch, it was erected by a Rajpoot prince, *i. e.* Komár-pál and his architects.* As to the pilasters, they are beyond suspicion Hindu, and the superstructure being in perfect harmony therewith, we are *almost* within proof of the origin of the pointed arch. Its height is thirty feet, and the breadth proportional. At this gateway, I found the inscription (App. No. VI.) recording the good works of a fair votary, named Yamuni, daughter of a prince of Yadu race.

The main entrance, however, is on the north face, near its centre, and is at once the strongest and most modern, if we can apply this term to what is rebuilt from the *débris* of ancient temples. It is a *tripolia*, or triple portal, formed by a sort of double court. The first gate faces the north; the second is at right angles with the first, or to the east, and the third, in like manner, is at right angles with the last; on escaping from which, the grand temple appears in full view. The height of this fortified portal is full sixty feet. It is a noble place of arms, well calculated for resistance, and bears internal evidence that at this point was the main attack of the warriors of the Faith. A circular watch-tower, solid and symmetrical, surmounts the second gate, increasing its resemblance to the castellated style of the Normans, and rendering the whole an admirable subject for the pencil. There is much

* *Vide* Inscription.

much of sculptured ornament, the most pleasing portion of which is on the first gate, representing that favourite device in Sivite temples, man engaged in contest with the lion, on whose back he is seated, and while the animal's head is strained to seize, he plunges his javelin down its throat, probably allegorical of the force of reason and dexterity, over mere brute courage and strength.

Behold me in the vestibule of Somnat'h, the far-famed shrine of idolatry which lured "the star of Islam" from its orbit amidst the Paropamisan and Caucasus, to the sandy shores of the Indian ocean within the torrid zone; and though now but the shell of what it was, though denuded of its *sikra* (pinnacle), whose fragments strew the ground, divested of its majestic superstructure, and but the trunk of a once perfect form, yet from its wrecks we may judge of its pristine character. That so much has been spared, we owe to that excess of zeal, which made conquest incomplete without conversion; which transformed the *mindra* into the mosque, and the altar of the sun-god into a pulpit for the Moollah, whence, while yet reeking with blood, the song of victory resounded amid shouts of "*La Illah, Mahomed Rusool Illahi*," 'There is but one God, and Mahomed is his prophet.' But without is another symbol of conversion, the pinnacled minarets at the entrance of the temple, the handiwork of the Mooslem artificer, whence the Muezzin of Mahmoud called aloud on the soldiers of the Faith to give glory to God and his prophet, for the victory obtained over the infidel. Could we be assured that any spark of genuine taste and liberal feeling induced him to spare even this mutilated remnant of the days of old, we might try to veil the barbarities inflicted in the name of religion, under the spirit of chivalry which braved the varied perils encountered in her cause; for this, the twelfth expedi-

tion

tion of Mahmoud, must be ranked amongst the hardiest enterprizes which frenzied ambition, under the cloak of sanctity, ever undertook.

The construction of this temple differs not from that of Lakha Rana in Cheetore, (the sculpture the same, though far less ornate,) and other ancient temples to Siva in the remoter parts of India, which escaped the Islamites' domination. The ichnographic section* will give the best idea of the plan, while the picture will represent far better than the pen, the dimmed glories of him "who rules the moon" *(Soma)*. It is divided into four portions: the external vestibule; the *munduff*, or body; and an inner vestibule, leading to the *sanctum*. Colonnaded aisles surround the whole. The outer circumference is 336 feet, its length 117, and the extreme breadth seventy-four feet. Those who have formed their ideas of magnitude from St. Peter's or St. Paul's, the Cathedral of York or the Duomo of Milan, must remember that the idolaters of Asia did not worship in crowds, and should, moreover, call to mind the simple majesty of the Pantheon, to correct their standard of grandeur, which does not depend upon mere bulk. But we would recal another temple, familiar with our earliest impressions, and forming a far better object of analogy, being of the same antiquity, and taken perhaps from similar models, that of Sion, which, in length, was exactly that of Somnat'h, while the latter surpasses the temple of the "wise king" in breadth and height; and yet in those days, and in those countries, says the Jewish historian, "none such had ere been built." Nor should we exaggerate its claims to antiquity by assigning an earlier date to the temple of Balnat'h, in this Syria of India, than either to that on Gerazim or Balbec in the wilderness,

* See the end of the Chapter, p. 354.

ness, "when the children of Israel served Baalim and Ashtaroth, the gods of Syria, and the gods of the children of Ammon."

We should think little of a cathedral in Europe no larger than that of Somnat'h; but its cyclopean solidity, as if constructed in defiance of time and human malevolence, impresses the mind with a juster idea of grandeur. What then must it have been when its spire was the beacon of the mariner; when its colonnaded aisles were entire; before the vaulted roof of the portico was destroyed, and more than all, when its grand accessory, the *munduff* of Nanda, a temple in itself, with its columned dome, under which, and facing the emblem of Bal, knelt the brazen bull (the other chief type of the sun-divinity), was perfect. Let us, however, return to details; and first as to externals: the *beet'h*, or stylobate, is divided into bands or compartments, each of which takes its name from the character of the sculpture thereon. Immediately above the inferior beading, the first compartment is filled with heads of the *gras*, the griffin of Hindu mythics. A small cincture divides this from the next hood-fillet, or band, called the *guj-tur'h*, or elephant range, containing busts of this noble animal. Above this is the *aswa tur'h*, filled with horses in various attitudes, over which is a still broader fillet, with groups of Bacchanals (peculiar to the shrines of Iswara), in different positions, and bearing various instruments and emblematic devices. The sculptured figures above the plinth are of much larger size and in groups, but all so mutilated, that it would be impossible to describe them. A few fragments, at one place, discover the heavenly nymphs in the *Ras-mandola*, that mystic dance, typical of the harmonious movement of the spheres, and although the hammer of the Mooslem has deprived them of heads, arms, and legs, some of the trunks shew superior execution.

The

The dome of the central *munduff* is complete, but unfortunately too little in unison with the original design to sanction a belief that it is Hindu. The span of the arch is thirty-two feet, and as it is the section of an oblate spheroid, the height is greater than the radius, being, from the ground to the spring of the arch, about thirty feet.* The dome rests upon eight columns, (so placed as to form an octagon) whose capitals are connected by immensely ponderous architraves, of a marine conglomerate, of varied exuviæ, small pebbles, siliceous sand, and cement of shell-lime; its specific gravity is great, its texture remarkably close, and when struck, it is sonorous as metal. The position of these columns, and their architraves, forming an octagonal basis for a hemispherical superstructure, attest the Hindu design of an arch on the principle of horizontal pressure; but the present arch is on the more scientific or radiating principle, and moreover of brick, which compels us to come to the conclusion that, whether the work of Hindu or Toork, it was not a part of the original edifice. There is yet another strong proof to the same effect, and favouring the supposition that it was the work of the Mooslem. The intercolumniations, excepting at that face leading through the vestibule to the *sanctum*, are built up and arched, the arches being alternately pointed, or slightly elliptical. A spacious vaulted and colonnaded vestibule intervened between the main body just described, and the *sanctum*, which is now choked up with rubbish, precluding entrance. This devastation is of recent origin, and attributed to the reverberation of cannon, placed upon the roof of the temple to keep off French privateers, which frequented the coast during the war. I, however, made my way to the *cella*,

* There is a little obscurity in my journal on this point. I give the extract *verbatim*: "the span of the arch is thirty-two feet, its height nearly the same, and from the ground to the spring of the arch, thirty feet." I suppose I have put inadvertently the *spring* for the *vertex*.

cella, a plain dark chamber, twenty-three feet by twenty, having a small internal gallery to communicate with its aisle, probably for the priests of Bal to propound his oracles, through their brethren, to the votaries in the *munduff.* The spot where stood the symbolic lingam is deserted, and in the western wall, facing the holy city of Mecca, is excavated a pulpit for the Moollah. There is a range of massive columns between the main compartments of the temple and its external wall, from which project pilasters, flat or semicircular, on which rest the beams of the roof. The material is sandstone, of a very compact texture, from the Joonagurh hills, fashioned into immense square or oblong blocks, cemented with that calcareous concrete called *conker*, dug from the pits around Puttun.

But the temple of the Bal of the Sauras was only *primus inter pares,* superior to, yet deriving a great portion of its majesty from, the shrines of the *Dii minores* surrounding it; in this also resembling the temple of Solomon, which, as the annotators tell us, "was but a small edifice, though the many courts and offices about it made the whole a vast pile." The temple of Somnat'h stood in the centre of an immense quadrangular court, defended by its own lofty battlements. The subordinate shrines, which, like satellites, heightened the splendour of the 'Lord of the Moon,' are now levelled with the earth, and mosques, walls, and the habitations of mortals, have been raised from their *dêbris.* The extent of the court may be estimated by the simple fact, that the nearest of the reservoirs for the lustrations of Bal and his priests is full one hundred yards distant from the shrine. The great mosque, called the Joomma Musjid, must have absorbed the materials of at least five of these minor shrines; for its five vaulted cupolas, with all their appendages, are purely Hindu, and the enormous triple-colonnaded

colonnaded court, in which it stands, must have cost a dozen more.

Such was and such is the shrine of Somnat'h, even now a noble object, yet how much grander in the high and palmy days of Hinduism, with all its ministrant appendages! Mahmoud himself could scarcely have contemplated its present degradation. Even with the Hindu, all reverence for it is gone, nor do the minarets at the portal, or the pulpit pointing to Mecca, command the slightest homage from the Mooslem, whilst all the waters of the Ganges would not suffice to lustrate the now desecrated dwelling of the sun-god. Ahelia Bhae, the wife of the great Holcar, and whose munificence is conspicuous throughout India, from the glaciers of Cailas to the Land's End, has erected a shrine on the site of one of the minor abodes, to which the votaries of Somnat'h now repair. To this a spacious *dhermsala*, or pilgrim's hall, has been added by the Dewan of Baroda, already spoken of.

Nothing can surpass the beauty of the site chosen for the temple, which stands on a projecting rock, whose base is washed by the ocean. Here, resting on the skirt of the mighty waters, the vision lost in their boundless expanse, the votary would be lulled to a blissful state of repose by the monotonous roar of the waves. Before him is the bay, extending to Billawul, its golden sands kept in perpetual agitation by the surf, in bold and graceful curvature; it is unrivalled in India, and although I have since seen many noble bays, from that of Penzance to Salernum, perhaps the finest in the world, with all its accessories of back-ground, and in all the glory of a closing day, none ever struck my imagination more forcibly than that of Puttun. The port and headland of Billawul, with its dark walls raised as a defence against the

pirates

pirates of Europe, form a noble terminating point of view, and from which the land trends northwards to Dwarica. The peaks of Girnar, twenty coss distant (N. 7° E.), would raise the sublimest feelings, or if he choose more tranquil scenes, the country around presents objects of interest, the plains being well-wooded, and diversified both by nature and art.

Such is the chief temple of paganism, the destruction of which, in A.H. 416 (A.D. 1008), was deemed by the Sultan of Ghizni an act of religious duty. It might be supposed that the record of this war, a theme of glory for the Islamite historian, and in deeds of chivalry not surpassed by any in the annals of the Crusaders, would have been written with an adamantine pen on every stone of the temple; but it is no less true than unaccountable, that the earliest and direst scourge which ever inflicted misery on a nation, Mahmoud the Great, is unknown alike by Brahmin, Banya, or Byrajee, as well as by Mooslem, even in name, within the city of the god. With the aid of my friend Mr. Williams, and all the means he could command, I failed to discover a single traditionary legend, oral or graven, of him who had merited an eternity of infamy from the Hindu, and although the fragments of the once proud pinnacle of Bal are a book to those who know Ferishta, they are as Runes, illegible and unintelligible to those whom they most concern. Happy would it be for mankind, were the pall of oblivion ever thus cast over the head of ambition, instead of the tinsel crown which lures even the wisest to destruction. But would the pilgrim to Joppa, Acre, or even the Holy Hill itself, meet with more success at this day, if he asked tidings of Richard Cœur de Lion, or his more accomplished antagonist, Saladin?

On the last day of our halt, our unremitting search for MSS. was rewarded

rewarded, and one of my friend's officials obtained from the ignorant scion of an ancient Cazi, the fragment of a poem, "unknowing what it told," containing some account of the past. It has all the appearance of being a transmutation from an old original Persian poem, into the purest Hindee dialect, by some scald of the Rajpoots. I seized on it with avidity, and divesting it of its metrical character, have the pleasure to lay before the reader, in plain prose, the substance of the story of "The Fall of Puttun."

"The Hadji Mahmoud came from Mecca in a trading vessel, landing at Mangrole, a sea-port thirty miles N.W. of Puttun, whence he subsequently obtained the appellation of Mangroli Shah. Thence he came to Puttun, and sojourned at the house of a *Rebarri* (grazier). Here he learned that a Mooslem was daily devoted to the idol, Somnat'h, whose *tika* was made with the blood of the victim. Desirous of further information, he went into the town, and accosting the widow of an oilman, who was sending forth heart-rending lamentations, he learned the cause, in her only son being demanded by the priests as a sacrifice to Balnat'h. The Hadji told her to be of good cheer, for that he would offer himself to save her son; but, on its being reported to the prince that a stranger had volunteered his life to save the oilman's son, the idea was repudiated. The saint, however, was not to be repulsed. Repairing to the shrine, he sat himself down on the steps of the external temple, leading to the brazen bull, before whose images the sacrifices took place. Already the prince and the officiating priests were convened, and the victim at hand, when the Hadji asked the former if the bull ate the offerings placed before him. The prince replied in the negative, but said that it was always customary to bring gifts of *ladoos*, or comfit-balls. The Hadji called for water, and while

one

one of the votaries went to the fountain to fetch it, he seized the platter and held it up to the bull, who forthwith began to eat. All were struck with amazement, but when the Hadji gave the yell of 'Allah Akber!' the symbol of Somnat'h vanished, and an Ethiop started up in his place, who was commanded to bring water in the saint's own cup. He obeyed, and instantly after, it was reported that the reservoir was dried up, and that the sacred fishes were expiring. The cup of water was sent back, and again the reservoir was overflowing. The life of the oilman's son was spared; but the Hadji, not satisfied with his own miraculous ability to punish the idolaters of Puttun, despatched a messenger to Ghizni. The mandate of the holy man reached Mahmoud when his eyes were nearly blind from distemper; but he had no sooner reverentially carried the holy rescript to his forehead, than his sight was restored. The miraculous cure and the order of march were consentaneous."

Whatever faith we might have in the miracles of the Hadji, we can have none in his chronology, though, perhaps, the Hindu scald, who has intermingled his own *Bhakha* with the polished speech of Iran, may have to answer for the anachronisms. Mahmoud is made to cross the Sutledge near its confluence with the Indus, and to come through the desert by Jessulmér (not built till two centuries later) to Mangrole, against which the Shah bore a grudge. According to the MS., Mahmoud lost twenty-four thousand men ere Puttun capitulated. On his investing the city, fresh anachronisms occur. Komár-pál is made the prince of Puttun, while his brother, Jy Pal, is stated to govern at Mangrole. Now as Mahmoud's invasion took place in A.D. 1008 (or 1025), and Komár-pál died in A.D. 1166, the idea suggests itself that *this* may be the invasion (unnoticed in Mooslem history) described

cribed in the *Charitra*, which led to Komár-pál's dethronement, conversion, and death, followed by the succession of the 'mad' Ajipal.* The sole stumbling-block in the way is the name of Mahmoud; but this, or the similar one of Modud, was not uncommon amongst his successors at Ghizni. The *Charitra* further favours this suggestion, by mentioning that Komár-pál rebuilt the temple, gilded its dome, &c., and this would account for what I state regarding the reversed sculptures in its foundation.† But to the MS., which has evidently an authentic basis.

"The king took post at the great tank, and the Raja of Puttun at the Bhalca-coond,‡ and many severe battles were fought, with immense slaughter on each side, during one entire month. The Sultan then placed strong posts in their rear, and likewise at the sacred Triveni; but the Gohil brothers,§ Hamira and Begra, aiding the chief of Puttun, cut their detachments in pieces. Five months had fled, when another general battle took place, in which the army of the king lost nine thousand men, and the Hindus sixteen thousand. But the armies of the Faith pressed on; the Sultan gained the temple of Kankali, which he made his head-quarters, and soon he gave orders for a general assault on the works which defended Somnat'h. On that very day, when victory was about to crown his enterprise, the Hadji died. For three days the king tasted no food, and his grief was increased by his not having beheld the holy man for some time," (from which we may conclude that he was in the hands of the infidel). "At this period, although the Mooslem had lost more men than the Hindus, these sued for

* *Vide* page 184. † *Vide* page 351.

‡ *Vide* page 332.

§ The Gohil brothers had not settled in Saurashtra till long after Mahmoud.

for peace, and all its messengers, the Charuns and Bhats, and other heralds, were sent to Mahmoud to offer any terms, or any sums, if he would cease his persecution. But nothing short of reading prayers in the temple of Somnat'h could satisfy him. The sixth month was ushered in with another general engagement, in which the two Rajpoot champions being slain, the rest retired within the fortifications, and manning the *fausse-braye*, or Rani, they thence hurled defiance at their adversary. Unable to force these gigantic barriers, the king had recourse to stratagem to withdraw the defenders from their vantage-ground. He made a feint of retreat, surrendered all his advantages, and withdrawing his outposts, retired five coss from the walls. The besieged fell into the snare, and with shouts of joy for their deliverance, gave a loose to exultation.

" It was the *Jooma rat*, the Sunday of Islam. In the dead of the night, the green standard of the prophet was unfurled, and entrusted to a chosen band, led by two brothers, Jaffier and Mozuffur. They reached the gate almost unobserved. A huge elephant, whose mighty head generally served in ancient times, in lieu of a petard, to break open the portal, flinched from the projecting spikes, when a camel was made the *herole* (vanguard), the interposition of whose bulk saved the pioneer's head, and the gates were burst asunder. In rushed the tide of battle, and the advance, led by the brothers, was immediately followed by Mahmoud at the head of the main body. Indiscriminate massacre was the order of the day. For the glory of God and the faith of Islam, rivulets of blood ran through the streets of Puttun, and saving those who called for mercy in the name of the prophet, neither sex nor condition, helpless infancy or old age, was spared from the steel of the brutal Tatar. The language of supplication, in an unknown tongue,

tongue, would have found few listeners among the savage hordes from the north, infuriated by every bad passion. Revenge for the loss of relatives and friends in the long-protracted siege, the frenzy of religion, which made every infidel head a trophy of redemption to the zealot, and worthy of acceptance by the prophet; these, and the more gross stimuli of lust and spoil, were barriers of adamant against the flood of mercy. The Rajpoot defenders of Somnat'h fought in the spirit of despair, with all the hopes of *Vycoont* before their eyes, besides every incentive to the energies of manhood. They knew the only terms for safety were the destruction of their temples, the abandonment of their religion, and prostration before the altars of Mahmoud. Torrents of blood inundated the city; innumerable were the victims who fell on either side, in the cause of religion, ambition, or glory. The leaders of the chosen band, Jaffier and Mozuffur, were among the slain, and the mosque westward of the temple, dedicated to their memory, marks the spot of their martyrdom. The streets were choked with the dead, and thousands were strewed around the shrine of Somnat'h. Still, all the efforts of Mahmoud and the hardy myrmidons of the north were in vain, for on that day the banner of Islam was not destined to wave from the battlements which encircled the Palladium of the Hindus.

"Brief was the interval till the terminating conflict; seven hundred heroes, with their prince at their head, made their last stand at the threshold of the temple, to save the altar of their divinity from pollution. In the interim, the offer of forty lacs was made to obtain peace, which, whether from avarice or a more generous sentiment, was favourably received by Mahmoud; but his lagging zeal was stimulated by the reproaches of his advisers, and the cry of 'no terms with idolaters!

ters! destruction to the temple!' prepared them for their impending fate. The temple was stormed, and after an awful struggle, carried. Few of its defenders survived; the symbolic image was broken into fragments, and the name of the true God and his prophet resounded from the holy of holies, the altar of Somnat'h. The city was given up to plunder, and, together with the accumulated wealth of the temples, afforded an immense booty to the conquerors. Meeta Khan was left in charge of Puttun and its dependencies, and Mangrole, with its *chourassi*, or 'hundred,' was bestowed on a relative of the Hadji. After the king's departure, the Hindus rose on Meeta Khan, but the insurrection recoiled on themselves;" and thus ends the MS.

The fragment does not give the name of the princely defender, who, I suppose, was of the Chaora Rajpoots, the ancient lords of Saurashtra, and from this we may assume that Ferishta's authority is good, when he says he escaped on board a ship. The MS. further records the fable retained by this historian regarding the self-suspended image in the temple, which Mahmoud brought to the ground with a blow of his mace: it is only worthy of repetition as proving the MS. to be a fragment of original authority, perhaps the *Tarikh Mahmoud-i-Ghizni*, to obtain which, all my researches, even in the metropolis of Hindust'han, were vain, though several copies exist in Europe. An inspection of this can alone decide whether this conglomerate belongs to it, and we might at all events discover the name of the prince who thus bravely contended *pro aris et focis* with the Sultan of Ghizni.

Another point of yet greater consequence it would be satisfactory to ascertain; namely, if the existing remains are a portion of the identical temple devastated by Mahmoud, whether his religious fervour was appeased by the desecration of the shrine of Bal, and its conversion into

into a mosque of Islam. Could we be certain that the minarets of entrance, and the mambar, or pulpit for the Moollah, were left by him, we should see at once the extent of his destruction. Independently of there being no record of a second visitation of Islam, there is yet a stronger reason for this conclusion; *i. e.* no prince subsequent to Komár-pál (whose inscription shews that to him we are indebted for its repairs) had the means of raising so vast a pile; for the monarchy of Nehrwalla, after his death, went rapidly to ruin.

But if this inference be just, a still more perplexing question arises, and this is, who was the overturner prior to Mahmoud? Overturned it was beyond a doubt, for on a very minute inspection of the stylobate, I detected, at a spot where a portion of the facing had been withdrawn, a massive sculptured stone, still forming an integral portion of the foundation, with its figures reversed, and which could not by any possibility have been a repair, being a part never exposed to injury, and demonstrating that the existing foundation is formed of the *débris* of more ancient buildings. But we know of no invaders before Mahmoud, whose creed enjoined destruction (to idols), and none of the Indo-Getic invaders from Central Asia cared about such matters: at least, we are not told that they were iconoclasts, though they did pollute the Fountain of the Sun at Balabhi with blood, to compel the surrender of its defenders.

Although I have elsewhere touched upon the inscription which I discovered at Billawul (App. No. VII.), originally taken from the temple of Somnat'h, I cannot pass it without notice in this place, connected as it is with our subject. On its value as an historical document I have already descanted. It presents to us two entirely new eras, the Balabhi and the Seehoh; the first of which, corresponding with 375 of Vicrama,

relative

relative to the Surya princes of Balabhi, is most important. The discovery of the other inscription (App. No. IV) is a happy confirmation of this. It records Komár-pál's reign, not in the usual era of Vicrama, but in the Balabhi Samvat 850+375=S.V. 1225, being that following his eventful accession, and likely to be marked by an act of piety after all the dangers he had gone through before he grasped the sceptre of Anhulwarra.*

The destruction of Balabhi by the Indo-Getic invaders, is stated in the archive MSS. of Méwar to have occurred in the year 300, of course meaning its own era. Therefore, 300+375=675—56 (difference between the Christian and Vicrama eras) makes A.D. 619 for the sack of Balabhi and the overthrow of the dynasty of Keneksén from Lokote. This is the precise period to which Cosmas ascribes the invasion of the Abteteles, (Abteles) or White Huns, with a host of Getes, or Jits, who settled in the valley of the Indus at Minagara. This, we must repeat, was the second irruption of this race, the first being in the second century, as mentioned by the author of the *Periplus*, followed by D'Anville, Gibbon, De Guignes, &c. These tribes have left their stock in Saurashtra, but we should not expect from them the dilapidation of the shrines. We have but one conjecture left to account for this, yet one of great verisimilitude, *i. e.* that the power which drove the Chaora princes from Diu and Deva-puttun, in A.D. 746, on account of their piracies, and led to the foundation of Anhulwarra, was the Caliph Haroun, instead of Varuna, as recorded by the early traditions. So much for the ancient Deva-puttun.

The present town contains about nine hundred houses, of which two hundred

* [The Author appears here to have fallen into some mistake, in respect to the chronology, which it is impossible to explain or rectify. The date of the accession of Komár-pál (see p. 150) is S.V. 1189.]

hundred are Brahmins, four hundred Mahomedans, the same number of the mercantile or Banyah tribes, and the remainder of all classes. If this census be correct, the population must be under five thousand. The environs are interesting, presenting many objects connected with its past glory, especially fine reservoirs for the luxury and convenience of the people. The first of these tanks is about one thousand yards from the northern gateway. Its circumference is eighteen hundred yards; its figure a polygon of so many sides that it approaches a circle; it is lined throughout with solid blocks of close-grained free-stone, and has flights of steps all round, while at the cardinal points there are descents for cattle. Half a mile N.W. of it are the Bhalca and Padma-coondas, already noticed. These traces of the most remote periods of Hindu superstition are further interesting, from pointing out the positions of the invading armies of the north, as the MS. before-cited mentions that Mahmoud encamped near the Bhalca-coond. The innumerable graves around Puttun attest the myriads of martyrs to Islam; more are not to be seen about the largest cities of Hindust'han. On the beach is a large Eedgah; so that this nameless edifice may be said to have placed the fame of the founder on a sandy foundation.

Billawul, or correctly Velacula, is the port of Puttun, and had some pretensions to consequence in the flourishing days of Anhulwarra, when Noor-u-din of Ormuz served as admiral of its fleets, which have now dwindled down to a dozen commercial pattamars for the usual coasting trade, or the export of pilgrims to Mecca. It suffered, as did all the cities on this coast, from "the idolaters of Europe," whose rapacities and cruelties were not surpassed by those of the Tartars in the tenth, or of the Afghans led by Alla in the thirteenth century. I have already given a quotation from an ancient collection of voyages, relating to the conduct of Nuna da Cunha, and his worthy lieutenant, Antonio de Saldanha, in 1532. They were, in fact, licensed pirates, and fulfilled every function dependent on that character, such as were written in types of blood by their brethren of Spain, amongst the unhappy aborigines of the new world.

Ichnographic section of the Temple of Somnat'h.

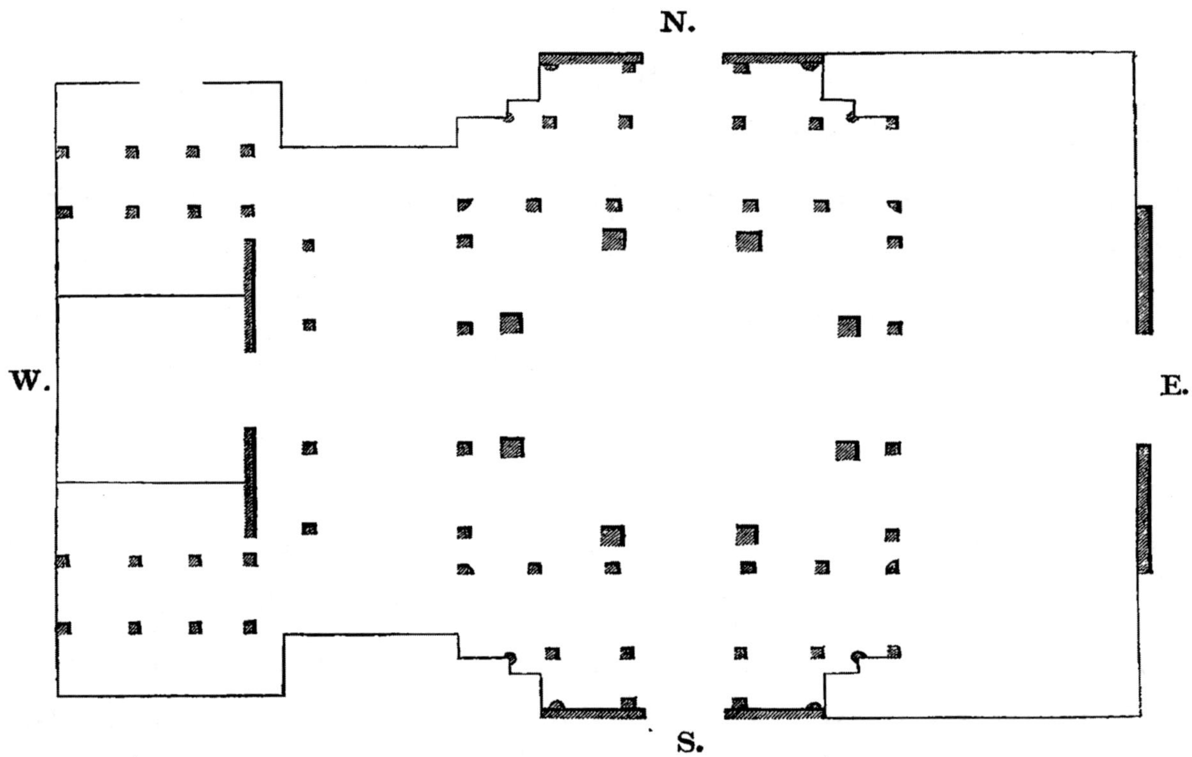

CHAPTER XVII.

Remnant of early civilization in the knowledge of distances.—Character of the soil.—Shrines and inscriptions.—Inhabitants.—Choorwaur.—Aheers.—Mallia.—Unyalla, or Ooniara.—Joonagurh.—Its ancient history and modern condition.—The "Ancient castle" described.—Reservoir of the Yadus.—The "Robber's cave."—Incognate characters.—Ancient inscribed rock of Girnar.—The characters.—Shrines.—Cryptographic inscriptions.—The "Leap of Bhiroo."—Isolated masses of rock.—Ancient palace of Khangar.

Choorwaur.—December 4th.—This day's march, according to the estimated measurement, was eight coss; it could not be less than sixteen miles, and about fourteen and a half of direct distance. Amongst the many points which present themselves to the reflection of a traveller in India, one which ought to strike him with surprise is, the general knowledge possessed by all classes of the distance of places within their immediate neighbourhood; and, however the standard may vary in different countries, yet within their own, a most singular uniformity and correctness prevail. To what can this be attributed? assuredly not to accident, nor to the mere report of the public *casids*, or runners. It is, in fact, a remnant of that ancient civilization, which we are accustomed to hold so cheap, embracing whatever related to the welfare, comfort, and intelligence of the community, and which, though buried under the ruins of ages of moral and political subjection, is not yet altogether obliterated, either from tradition or written record, both attesting that in remote times there were road-metres throughout India. This alone can account for the surprising facility which exists for laying down a champaign country from verbal estimation, with all the exactitude of the chain and theodolite. My

countrymen,

countrymen, who, in a march of one thousand or fifteen hundred miles, meet all the varieties of the coss, and who are apt to measure the pretensions of the natives to accuracy by their appetites for breakfast, will consign them *au diable* on finding the average Gangetic coss of two miles elongated by what the Scotch highlanders call "a wee bittie," or some four or five miles. But this variety merely denotes the numerous subdivisions of Rajaships, each of which had its own standard in currency, weights, and measures, the power to alter which is one of the marks and privileges of royalty.

The character of the country was like the preceding, and where the substratum was laid bare by the action of water, we saw that it was of that porous crumbling sandstone, which appears to run from the base of the central ridge, bisecting the peninsula, to the sea. Cultivation was restricted to the vicinage of the villages, where there was no want of young wheat, barley, and some fine patches of black sugar-cane. The sacred Girnar disclosed fresh peaks with our change of position, and from Choorwaur bore N. 26° E. twenty-five coss, or about forty-five miles of direct distance.

At the Aheer village of Dhab, about four miles from Puttun, are the ruins of two temples, one of which had been dedicated to the sun. There is also a fine old *baorie*, or reservoir, which I was told had an inscription, but unluckily it was below the water-line. We crossed several streams, and we heard that, at the embouchure of one with the sea, there was a temple to Choorwaur Mata, and also a large statue to Hanuman. Choorwaur would imply 'the city of thieves,'—a title not unmerited, for every harbour on the coast was a pirate's nest in past days. The present race of inhabitants pursue a very different occupation, being chiefly of the Rebarri and Aheer, or pastoral tribes. There

were

were likewise the tribes of Korea aud Raezada, the latter a branch of the ancient Chaurasima, once the princes *(Raes)* of the land. The chief of Choorwaur is a Jaitwa Rajpoot; all were fine, noble-looking fellows. There was nothing remarkable in the town; but I found an interesting inscription (App. No. VIII.), which had been brought from the ancient sun-temple of Koraussi. This I saw at a distance on my right. The inscription is not only valuable for its formula of invocation, but for its reference to the Gehlote tribe (that of the Ranas of Méwar), as having " conquered Saurashtra," which accounts for what otherwise appeared unaccountable, the declaration of Abulfazil, that in Akber's time " Circar *Sorat* (contraction for Saurashtra) was an independent territory; that the chief was of the Gehlote tribe, and commanded fifty thousand cavalry and one hundred thousand infantry." It may be remembered, that the great object of worship of this race, on settling in Méwar, was the sun, and it is still the most important, though not, as then, the sole object of devotion. I owed the discovery of this to a Jain priest of the Lonka sect *(gachá)*, a man of mild, unaffected manners, of some learning, and of considerable information in every thing relating to the shrines of his faith within the peninsula. He travelled much for amusement and instruction, and although he had never encountered a Frank before, I found him perfectly unreserved and communicative.

The Lonkas are deists; they worship the " One" alone, and " not in temples made by art," which they never enter. The mountain-top and sylvan solitude are deemed by them more fitting places to pour forth their homage. They credit the missions of the twenty-four *Tirthancars*, considering them as superior mortals, whose sanctity and purity of life gained them the divine favour, and the reward of *mookht*, or beatitude.

Accordingly,

Accordingly, they esteem them objects of reverence and intercession, but not of worship. My new friend has promised to accompany me to "the holy mount," and aid my researches. Happily, the "moon of intellect," my own revered Guru, is too enthusiastically bent on knowledge to be jealous of any one who can add to his stores.

CHOORWAUR is of considerable extent, being estimated at fifteen hundred houses, though it is far from fully peopled at present. The classes are Banya, Mooslem, but chiefly of the pastoral Aheer, and a tribe of which I never heard before, named *Hat'hi*; in appearance and occupation they resemble the Aheers, who form, perhaps, the most numerous part of the population of central Saurashtra. I have elsewhere described this singular and inoffensive community, who were in ancient times of some importance, and have every appearance of being the remains of the Palli race. In Central India, there is a large tract, designated after them, Aheerwarra, which is in the very heart of a region where every thing terminates in *pál*, as names of towns, &c., and a long dynasty of princes, whose capitals were Bhelsa and Bhopal, where are some of the finest remains of ancient Budhic architecture, and inscriptions in that peculiar character termed Palli, all denoting that this pastoral race professed the tenets of this heresy, of which every day adds strength to an hypothesis I was the first to start, namely, as to its not having originated in India Proper.

In Akber's reign, the Aheers were of political importance in the Saura peninsula, and Abulfazil tells us, that "on the banks of the river Doondy, there was a subdivision of them, having the local appellation of Poorunja, who mustered three thousand cavalry and the like number of infantry, and who were in a perpetual state of hostility with the tribe of Jam" (Jharéja). This intelligent cosmographer makes the

the Cat'hi a branch of the Aheer, but most erroneously observes, that "some people consider the tribe to be of Arabian origin," a mistake which sprung from their great attachment to horses. Doubtless, their manners may have assimilated, the Aheers, like the Cat'his, being divested of the prejudices belonging to the Brahminical hierarchy, and having all the freedom of their mixed predatory and pastoral occupations.

MALLIA.—DECEMBER 5th.—Seven coss. This is a place of high antiquity, of which, however, there are now few traces. It is prettily situated on a fine stream, which has its source in the upland beyond. Altogether, the condition of man in this morning's march was not very favourable: the villages were small, ragged, and depopulated; the cultivation was scanty and neglected. The population of Mallia was chiefly of the Banya and Rebarri tribes. Another village that we passed consisted entirely of Cat'his and Hat'his, but there were many Rajpoots of a tribe quite new to me, called Karya, said to be of Pramar origin, and several Koli families intermixed with the mass.

UNYALLA OR OONIARA.—DECEMBER 6th.—Nine coss. Our route was one continued but gradual ascent, over an expanded plain. From Shirgurh, a fortified post on a height near the end of our journey, we had a distinct view of the town of Mangrole, upon the coast. Ooniara signifies the abode of heat *(oon)*, a name referrible, I suppose, to its southern aspect and unsheltered position. The inhabitants were chiefly Mooslems, and the Lobana, a mercantile tribe, of Bhatti Rajpoot origin, very common in the valley of the Indus.

JOONAGURH.—DECEMBER 7th.—Nine coss. Throughout this morning's march, of nearly eighteen miles, we found the villages few and far between, in the heart of low jungle and brushwood. We might in

truth

truth have exclaimed, that from Ooniara to Joonagurh "all was barren;" yet there was no lack of interest, for each step brought us nearer to the sacred hill, the grand object of my pilgrimage. The villages were chiefly inhabited by Aheers, who raised some scanty crops around their habitations; but every thing denoted that the tyranny of man was the chief obstacle to prosperity; and here, unfortunately, the people have to contend against the double operation of political and religious antipathies, their governor being a Mahomedan.

The origin of Joonagurh is lost in the mists of time; tradition, or its living chroniclers, merely say it is *bhote joona*, 'very ancient,' and, in fact, its foundation having no date, it has been spoken of from distant ages as "the ancient castle." Recorded annals, however, state that it was the capital of princes of the Yadu race. It was so when the Rana of Méwar's ancestors were sovereigns of Balabhi; it was so when Mandalica, the last of his race, was vanquished by Mahomed Be-gacha: from which we have a right to infer that the line was unbroken, and consequently that a Yadu prince ruled on the invasion of Mahmoud, in the tenth century of the Christian era. Let us hear what Abulfazil says on this subject, in his statistical account of Saurashtra, which in Akber's time was "formed into nine divisions, each inhabited by a different tribe. The first division, commonly called *New Sorat*, had not been explored for a long time, on account of the thickness of the forests and intricacy of the mountains. A person was carried through by accident, who informed others of his discoveries. Here is a stone fort called Junagurh, which was conquered by Sultan Mahmood, who built another fortress at the foot of it."*

JOONAGURH,

* *Ayeen Akbery*, vol. ii. p. 66, Gladwin.—There is no language so ill-calculated to transmit proper names, and, of course, aught appertaining to geography, as the Arabic and Persian. Abulfazil's compendium

Joonagurh, although now inhabited, presents much the same character as described by Abulfazil centuries ago. It is encircled by a belt of deep forest, several miles in breadth, chiefly of the thorny babool *(mimosa Arabica)*, so closely interwoven as to admit of no ingress, but by two or three avenues cut through it, leading to the principal adjacent towns. Such belts accord with the injunctions of Menu, whose miscellaneous code includes the arts of war, as well as those belonging to civil society and religion. Whether or not this forest adds to security, it assuredly increases the insalubrity of all places so confined, whose inhabitants must constantly inhale impure air from the decomposed vegetation. Of this we had experience, for, although it was the most healthy period of the year, a few days' halt produced numerous cases of fever amongst our followers. In former times, the city was seven coss, or fourteen miles, in circuit, extending far beyond the limits of its present vallation, which is not above five miles; but even this reduced scale is far too large for the population, which does not exceed five thousand souls. The most numerous classes are the Nagar and Girnara Brahmins. In nearly equal numbers may be the Mooslems, and the rest is made up of the agricultural and artizan classes, as Aheers, Kolis, &c. &c., there being few, if any, Rajpoots. The present lord of "the ancient castle," is a Mooslem of the Babi race, with the title of nawab, who is tributary to the Guicowar. His revenues are scanty, and his views of ambition circumscribed as the belt which hems him in; he lives amidst ruin.

From

compendium of the statistics of this region, is deprived of much of its value from the mask borne by all the ancient towns and people. Chunagurh for Junagurh is a slight deviation; but who would ever discover the holy mounts of Satrunja and Girnar in Beranjy and Gowreener? (p. 67.) Again, in describing the third division, he says: "At the foot of the mountain of Sironj is a large city, now out of repair:" who would expect these to be Satrunja and Palit'hana? And so on.

From whichever side Joonagurh is viewed, the mind is immediately carried back to the earliest periods of history, and it must be pronounced coeval with the first line of Yadus who ruled Saurashtra, and probably the abode of Tessarioustus (*qu.* Teja Raja ?), the opponent of Menander and Apollodotus. It is venerable from its age, and romantic from position, while its numerous massive square towers, and crenellated parapet, give it an appearance of strength and dignity. Assuredly it had as much claim to the one, before the invention of gunpowder, as it still has to the other. The position, then judiciously chosen, is on a terminating elevation of the sandstone ridge, which forms the substratum of the whole country, from the base of the central range of Saurashtra to the sea, and which here rises into a plateau about thirty yards in height, at the N.E. angle of which is the citadel, in itself a gigantic work, and which is only separated from the granitic range by the interposition of the Sonarica river.

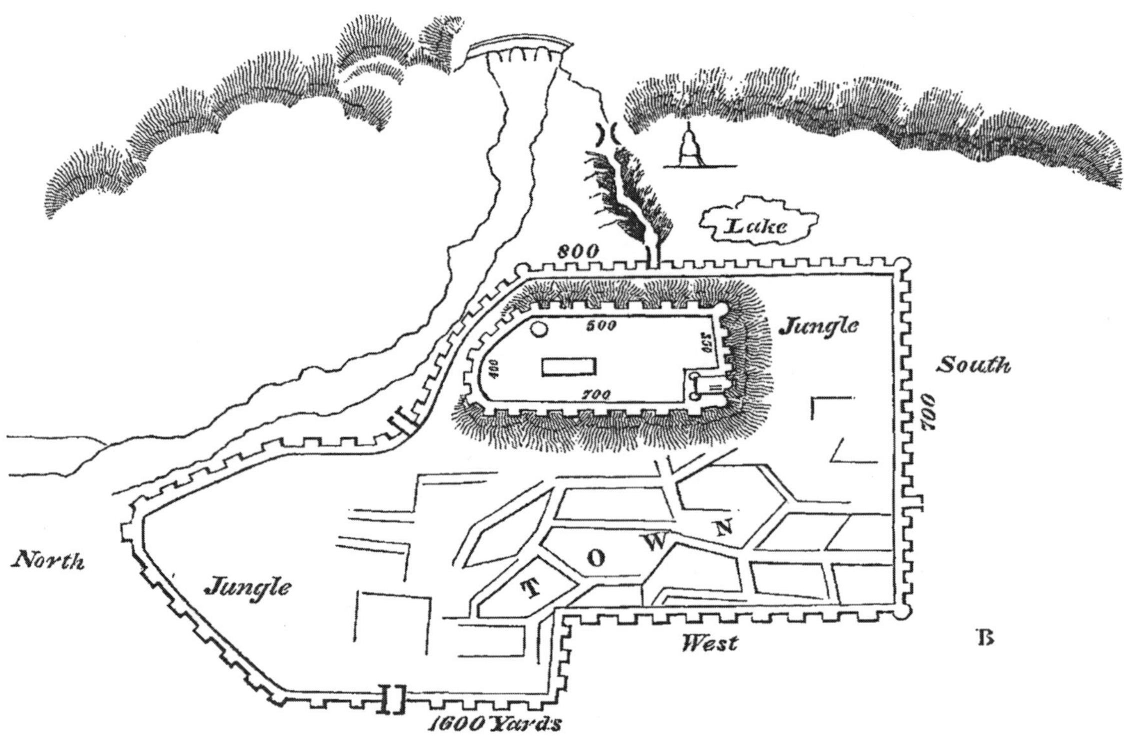

The ichnography of the "ancient castle" will admit of no specific classification. It is an irregular trapezium, the form of which may be best comprehended by the sketch, as I took its angles, and paced three sides of its circumvallation. The southern and shortest face, which is the chief entrance, is seven hundred yards; the eastern, which also has its gateway, is eight hundred, and nearly a straight line; and each of these has seventeen square towers, whose intervening curtains do not occupy greater space. The western and most extensive side is nearly two miles long; while the northern and most irregular is curvilinear, full another mile in length, having its portal at the head. Its huge rampart being carried along the edge of the Sonarica, whose deep precipices are hewn from the solid abutment of the rock, this forms the strongest side. A ditch has been chiselled out of the rock, varying from twenty to thirty feet in depth, and little less in breadth; and the ramparts, reared from the material, are placed on the very verge of the excavation: so that there is a vallation of from sixty to eighty feet, and, where it stands on the margin of the stream, of one hundred feet of perpendicular height, and there being a gradual slope from the external terre-pleine, the ditch could never be filled by the *débris* of the walls, even had there been cannon in those days. From the northern face the view is imposing. Girnar is seen towering in isolated grandeur through the opening of the range, one of whose natural portals bears the appropriate name of Doorga, the turreted Cybele, while the 'gold-flowing' Saronica is seen gliding through its gorge towards the castle-walls, which when she quits, her face is darkened by the shadows of the deep woods covering both sides of her ample margin.

The influence of Mr. Williams obtained us ingress to the citadel, a favour never, it was said, granted before to any European; and though

 abandoned

abandoned to all the luxuriance of nature within, it is guarded externally with a jealousy perfectly oriental. A guard of honour received us at the entrance, the number of which might imply respect or distrust; and as only half the huge portal grated on its hinges for our admission, we should not be wrong in imagining the operation of both sentiments. If there could be a doubt as to the antiquity of the city, the appearance of the citadel would remove it. Every stone carries us back to the days when the *Chapun cula Yadu*, 'the fifty-six Yadu tribes,' had paramount sovereignty in India. Whatever period may be assigned to the sway of Shamnath (afterwards deified) in Saurashtra, there is no doubt that a Yadu prince ruled here when Canac-shen, the Rana's ancestor from Lokote, in the Punjab, conquered Balcadés in the second century.

We entered through the two grand demi-lunes in the S.W. angle of the citadel, which defended the entrance. Having passed the first portals, we came upon a court, on the further side of which is another gateway of very antique design. The external faces of each gateway had the pointed arch, but internally there were architraves of huge blocks of granite, having a frieze in coarse marble of rude execution, resting on strong flat pilasters of the same material, four on each side. A more spacious court intervenes, bounded by a similar gateway, and over both are guard-rooms, of a bold and solid construction, for the defence of the court and entrance. The portals, made to shape the pointed arch, were of massive wood, covered with iron plates, of which patches were completely oxidized by atmospheric action. But what struck me as the greatest curiosities of this fortified entrance, were a sword and shield of stucco, in considerable relief, placed in the most conspicuous part of the guard-room overlooking the gate of entrance.

In

In such a position, no motto is required,—the thing speaks for itself; but whoever has perused the early history of the Varangian sovereigns of Russia, will find a pendant for this shield in that nailed on the portal of Byzantium by the son of Rurick, who, at the head of eighty thousand men, passed the Borysthenes, and even in the eighth century, imposed terms on that city, which yet is not theirs. Let us, however, recollect that the Varangians were Norman, and even at that time half Asiatic; and when we add to this that the parole treaty was confirmed by the Varangian guard, who swore "by their arms" for its maintenance, we might fancy them Rajpoots.

On quitting these defences, we ascended the terre-pleine of the castle by a flight of steps cut from the solid rock. Whatever buildings may have graced the interior, not one of Hindu construction now remains. An edifice has usurped the crest of the ancient castle—an enormous mosque, built with the *débris* of the shrines and palaces of the Yadus, as a memento of the success of Islam over the infidel Rajpoot. It is attributed to Sultan Mahomed Begácha, on his subjugation of Raja Mandalica. One uniform motive seems to have actuated each successive conqueror, and the greater the number of shrines sacrificed to "the true faith," the greater the glory, temporal and eternal. But even here, as far as regards the former, they have signally failed: for whether mosque, musjid, or eedga, the incongruous mass, though Mooslem in design, is Hindu in all its parts and materials. When I term it incongruous, I do not mean to deny it or its founders the merit justly due to it as a work of art: for, singular as its construction is, the architect has produced a fabric which, for uniformity, extent, solidity, and simplicity, deserves the epithet of magnificent. When I say that it is one hundred and forty feet in length and one hundred

in

in breadth, having its *plafonds*, vaulted and flat, supported by more than two hundred pillars and pilasters of granite, the reader will admit that, in respect to dimensions, the epithet is not misapplied. It is divided into three compartments, *viz.* a centre and wings. The centre consists of three octagons, each thirty feet in diameter, running longitudinally, with a colonnade round each, the intercolumniations of which are only eight feet. Domes were contemplated to cover these, in the usual Hindu style; for temporary columns, of rounded granite, thirty feet in height, each consisting of three portions, of equal dimensions, to answer the purpose of a centering until the vaults were completed, are still standing. The columns of the wings are square, all of granite, and about sixteen feet high, with plain capitals and pedestals. Immense architraves are placed over each pair of columns, which support a flat roof. Around the central domes, each pair of columns is connected by a pointed arch, which greatly relieves the somewhat heavy appearance of the mass. The north side (and the west, if my note is not incorrect,) is built up; the others are open, and have the pointed arch between each pair of columns. A pulpit, or screen, of a single block of variegated marble, about eighteen feet by ten, is a fine piece of sculpture.

Several reasons authorize a belief that this edifice was constructed from the wreck of other temples: chiefly the correspondence in size and shape between these columns and those yet left in several of the half-mutilated temples on the sacred hill above. The grand munduff of Komár-pál's temple had been carried off entirely, and likewise that of Nemnat'h, and their dimensions correspond with the intended domes of the Musjid. That of Somprit Raja, on the mount, which is of similar diameter, was, no doubt, destined for the third; but whether death

death or revolution arrested the founder's purpose, signifies not; this monument of one of the principal supporters of the Jain faith, who lived two hundred years before the Christian era, still stands intact on its granite foundations—itself of granite.

There is one indestructible monument of the Yadus,—a reservoir excavated in the solid rock, and not less than one hundred and twenty feet in depth. Its form is elliptical, the largest diameter being about seventy-five feet. The rock is faced with masonry. And we must not omit the grand defender of the castle, a tremendous piece of brass ordnance, placed on one of the western bastions. Its length is twenty-two feet, the diameter at the breach two feet two inches, and at the muzzle nineteen inches; calibre ten inches and a quarter. It had two inscriptions, indicating that it was cast in Turkey. It doubtless came in the fleet of Solyman the Magnificent, which attacked Diu in the fifteenth century, when that monarch obtained the crown-jewels of the sovereign of Guzzerat. Such are the few objects worthy of note within the "ancient castle," which is overgrown with jungle—the *sureefa*, or wild custard-apple, being predominant.

Descending by the north-west face, I visited the caves outside—one of the many objects of the pilgrim's attention. An elevated plateau of some extent has been entirely hollowed out into rude chambers of considerable size, to which fancy and tradition have assigned various occupants. One suite is designated after the Pandu brothers. Another belonged to Khopra Choor, the Robin Hood of past days in these regions, but whose exploits were far bolder than our hero's, for this is the individual who is represented ascending the pinnacle of the temple at Barolli, to steal the pieces of gold deposited in the *kullus*, or ball. Khopra's cave is divided into numerous compartments; one is termed

his

his hall, another his kitchen, a third his stable, and so on. It is a square of sixty feet, supported by sixteen massive square columns, about nine feet in height, disposed thus.

Khopra, the Robber's Cave.

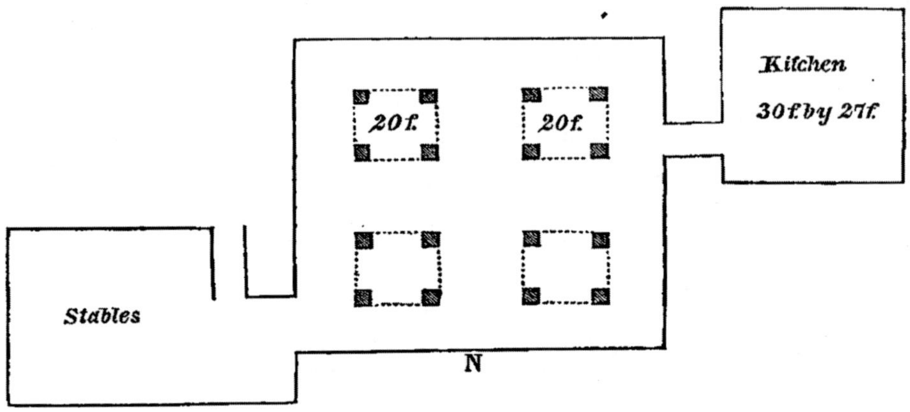

The process of transmutation is visible here, the Islamite having converted the unhallowed abode of Khopra into the Durgah of Shekh Ali Dervésh. The same incognate characters of which I have so frequently spoken, are inscribed on the walls. The following are specimens.

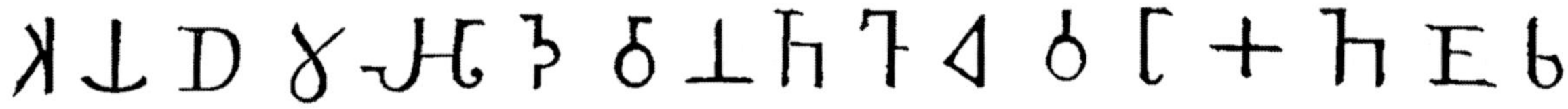

But it is time to put ourselves *en route* to *Avanti Gir*, the 'Hill of Safety,' one of the twenty-five classical appellations of the 'King of Hills,' *Gir-raj*, more familiarly known as Girnar, from *gir*, 'a hill,' and *nari*, which has the same import as *swami*, 'master.' Among others, are *Ujanti Gir*, or 'sin-destroying hill;' *Harsid-sikra*, the 'peak of Harsid,' or Siva, as lord of ascetics; *Suverna-gir*, the 'golden mount;' *Sri-dhank-gir*, or 'overshadowing all other hills;' *Sri-shesra-Comala*, or 'like the lotus of a thousand petals;' *Mordevi-parvati*, or 'the hill of Mordevi,' the mother of Adnat'h; *Bahabali-tert'ha*,' the 'place of pilgrimage of Bahabal, the second son of Adnat'h; &c. &c. Of all these, the

the most significant is *Suverna*, or ‘ golden,’ an epithet likewise attaching to the stream, which has numerous little feeders from the dark clefts and recesses of the mountain. I am convinced that the precious metal exists in this primitive mountain, not only from its name, in conjunction with the Sonarica, or ‘ golden-flowing,’ but from a tradition at the very head of the annals of the Rana’s family, which assigns as a reason for the powerful Yadu sovereign of Saurashtra giving his daughter to a refugee stranger, that “ he had the art of discovering the precious metals, and pointed out their existence in the hill of Girnar.”

But let us proceed, step by step, through the arched portal in the eastern face of the “ ancient castle.” The magnificent vanity of Soonderji, the horse-merchant, has commenced and proceeded far in a work, which will immortalize his name, while it secures the benedictions of the pilgrims, for making easy the road to the great object of adoration. From the walls of the city he has cut a noble avenue through the forest, planted on either side with mango, jamun, and other trees, which in due time will afford both shade and food to the wearied votary. At the point where the avenue meets the Sonarica, is an extensive paved causeway, running parallel with it, and terminating where the river runs directly across the gorge of the pass with a bridge of three arches, of great strength and in excellent taste, having an open casemated parapet. While it adds greatly to the picturesque effect of the scene, the utility of the work enhances its beauty; for not only does it give bread to a great body of poor people, but, when finished, it will entirely remove all danger from the devotee, formerly apt to be swept off by the sudden rise of the river. It is already carried over the most difficult part; and although Soonderji is dead, it does not languish under his son and successor, who, with religious zeal, is executing his father's commands to continue the causeway to the second ford of the stream, beyond which it would be more ornamental than useful. The views from the bridge are sublime: in front, seen through the range called the portal of Doorga, is the mighty cone of Girnar, towering in majesty, while behind, the "ancient castle" lowers "in proud decay," seeming as if erected as an outwork to defend the pass leading to the holy hill.

Leaving the bridge, let me describe what to the antiquary will appear the noblest monument of Saurashtra, a monument speaking in an unknown tongue of other times, and calling on the Frank *Vedyavan*, or *Savant*, to remove the spell of ignorance in which it has been enveloped for ages. Again, thanks to Soonderji, but for whose liberality it would still have remained embosomed in the pathless forest, covered with its tangled veil of the impervious babool. I should, however, previously notice two subordinate objects: the first, a fine piece of water, almost on quitting the gate of the city, called "the Goldsmith's Pool;" the other, a small shrine, at the base of Doorga's mount, dedicated to Bageswara Mata, the veritable Phrygian goddess, or at least her sister, and, like her, wearing an embattled crown, and whose steed is the tiger *(bag)* or lion, with both of which the forests of Saurashtra formerly abounded.

The memorial in question, and evidently of some great conqueror, is a huge hemispherical mass of dark granite, which, like a wart upon the body, has protruded through the crust of mother earth, without fissure or inequality, and which, by the aid of the "iron pen," has been converted into a book. The measurement of its arc is nearly ninety feet; its surface is divided into compartments or parallelograms, within which are inscriptions in the usual antique character. Two of these *cartouches* I had copied, by my old Guru, with the most scrupulous

scrupulous fidelity, and a portion of a third, where the character varied. The affinity of the former to the inscriptions on the triumphal pillars at Dehli, on "the column of victory" in the centre of the lake in Méwar, and in various of the most ancient cave-temples of India, is apparent. Each letter is about two inches long, most symmetrically formed, and in perfect preservation. The examples of a more modern character are, from the vertex and the west side of the mass, similar to those on the Indo-Getic medals I engraved for the *Transactions* of the Royal Asiatic Society, and of which I found several specimens in the ruins of Kali-kote and other ancient cities on the opposite side of the gulph. I here present them to the reader, that he may compare them with the rock-inscription. I may well call it a book; for the rock is covered with these characters, so uniform in execution, that we may safely pronounce all those of the most ancient class, which I designate the 'Pandu character,' to be the work of one man. But who was this man? They are of an age so evidently anterior to Menander and Apollodotus, the conqueror of the Suroi, that, despite the curious admixture of characters decidedly Grecian, we cannot suppose this to have been a land-mark of their visitations amongst the Rajpoots, or of their victory over Tessarioustus, or Teja Raja, in all probability the Yadu prince of Joonagurh. The philologist will remark the number of letters which resemble the more ancient Greek and Celto-Etruscan characters,—as follows:

Again, of Samaritan characters are the following:

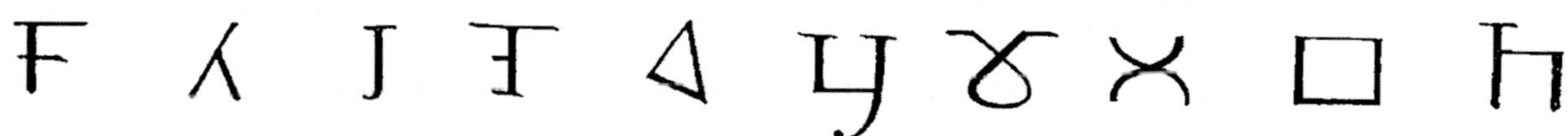

aleph *be* *pe* *he* *ain* *nún* *tau* *tau*

With

With each of these, as simple letters, there are various others compounded in the rock-inscription.

I am aware that by proving too much we prove nothing; but it has been no less pithily observed that, "*à force de scrupules sur la vérité, on reste étranger à la vérité même*," and I will risk an attempt at pioneer-philology. Endeavouring to facilitate the subject, I selected such characters as appeared simple, and from these traced their compounds. The first are limited to sixteen, but the compounds are innumerable. Of the simple O (Omicron) I found no less than seventeen compounds, and so of the rest. If the research yield no result, it is but the loss of my time; but when I state that two of these, *viz.* ƳΣ, concluding one of the *cartouches*, form the monogram on the *intaglio*, having the form and all the characteristics of the Greek Hercules,* I cannot but hope that a more rigid scrutiny and comparison of the ancient alphabets of Syria will yield some curious fruits. I do not pretend to be the first who has noticed the similitude between these characters and the Greek, and the old square character; for on our first intercourse with Northern India, more than half a century ago, the first Englishman who saw the pillar in the ancient palace of Feroz, pronounced it to be "a record of Alexander over Porus." I leave it to the *Vedya* to proceed with this, and to the Asiatic Society of Bombay to complete the subject, before time makes further inroad on the granite, whose upper surface has peeled off about the vertex of the mass, a very common occurrence with this material, and which renders it peculiarly unfit for the purpose of receiving inscriptions—a fact I have had often to lament amongst the shrines of Girnar. On this account, basalt, compact limestone, black and grey, and even slate schist, are selected by the Hindus for their records.

The

* See *Transactions* of the Royal Asiatic Society, vol. iii. p. 139.

The latter character is of a modern date, and modifications of it were in common use with the Jains, and them only, so late as the twelfth century. Of these I formed a large collection (the earliest, of the fifth century, recording the exploits of a prince of the Jit or Gete race), which were decyphered by the great assiduity of my Guru, through whose means I afterwards ascertained the important fact that the Sri-Pooj or Pontiff of his sect, with his librarians and favoured disciples, had a perfect knowledge of, and key to, the most complicated of this style of character; though he doubted as to the square kind, which has no analogy with the others.

Let us now cross the bridge, and entering the pass or opening in the range, proceed on our pilgrimage. The ever-fanciful Hindu has personified the two terminating points which form the portals to this narrow gorge. The Centaur Bhynasara guards the right, while Jogini Mata has taken post on the left, to prevent the ingress of the profane. From the gorge, the road winds along the left bank of the Sonarica, leaving a contracted path between her bed and the mountain, which is covered to the summit with foliage. The most conspicuous among this is the teak, gigantic only in its leaf, which scarcely seems to belong to its dwarfish, stunted stem. It, however, yields materials for husbandry and for house-building.

The first sacred edifice that attracts notice on the skirt of the hill, is dedicated to Damodra-Mahadeva, and is of considerable dimensions. Here the Sonarica is dammed up to form a reservoir, wherein the pilgrim purifies before he ascends the flight of steps leading to the temple, which is enclosed by a lofty wall, having *dhermsalas*, or places of repose, for the weary devotee. An upper flight conducts to another fountain, excavated from the rock, and faced with hewn-stone, its

compartments

compartments shewing the wrecks of sculptured figures, all mutilated by the Mahomedan. It is called the *Rewati-coonda*, and was dedicated, by the ancient Yadu lords of Joonagurh, to their great ancestor, Kanya. I was fortunate enough to discover an inscription (App. No. IX.) which had escaped the destroyers. From it we learn the impropriety of assigning this temple to Siva, as Damodra was also an infantine appellation of the deified Yadu leader, Kanya—most probably in the desperate sectarian warfare waged about the eighth century, between the Sivites and Vishnuvites, some votary of the former installed the image of his tutelary deity. A small temple, adjacent to the *coonda*, contains an image of Baldeva, the kinsman of Kanya, with the mace, discus, and war-shell. The ignorance of the Brahmins here is amazing; they do not even know the commonest symbols and attributes of the divinities they serve. There are several sepulchral *mindras* on the opposite side of the stream, of pilgrims who were happy enough to die on the skirt of the holy mount. This spot appears also to have been the Necropolis of the Yadu princes of Saurashtra, an opinion strengthened by the inscription. Vishnu (whose attributes are assigned to Kanya) has a double privilege to preside over this lustral fountain; first, as the great progenitor of the race, and secondly, in his quality of mediator and intercessor, and even conveyer of the souls of the dead to their destination. The inscription is valuable on several accounts. It records many of the names of the princes who ruled in this region, and are still well known to tradition, especially Mandalica and Khengar, with whom are numerous associations. Two bearing the former name are mentioned; the first lived in times 'of yore,' as the original has it, for it is very common in these stone records to mention some ancient land-mark, and pass over twenty generations to the more immediate

immediate ancestry of the person to be commemorated. This inscription appears to be a testimony of gratitude from Jey Sing to his chief warrior, Abhye Sing, of his own race, who fell in defending Jingir-kote against the "Javan," a term applied equally to the ancient Grecian, and to the Islamite 'barbarian.' Of Jingir-kote I have no knowledge, nor of its application to Joonagurh, though in its character of *tulaiti*, or lower town, it answers well enough to the description. It also furnishes an excellent example of cryptographic data, in which the Brahmin, like the Egyptian hierophant, delighted to hide every thing from profane understandings; but as I have elsewhere given a key to these, I will only briefly show how this is expounded. The *Samvat*, or era, is thus symbolically expressed: "*Rama, Toorunga, Sagur, Mahi;*" these must be read inversely, *i. e.* from right to left, when we have the date 1473. The *rationale* is this: there are *three* Ramas; Toorunga is *the* steed, Septaswur, the *seven*-headed courser of the sun; Sagur signifies the *four* seas which surround Mahi, or the earth, which is *Unity*.

Half a mile further, where the stream is once more crossed, in a most romantic dell, overshadowed by the noble foliage of the tamarind and peepul, are a temple and fountain sacred to Bhavanath Mahadeo. Here fresh ablutions are made, and the pilgrim receives the *tika* of *bhaboot*, or ashes, from the ministering priest, when he goes forth refreshed mentally and corporeally by a halt in this cool and delightful retreat. Another half-mile brings us to the place of rest of two Islamite saints, over whose tombs is raised a kind of altar, covered with cloth, upon and around which strutted with free license about a dozen cocks, of gaudy plumage, apparently conscious of their independence. Both Hindu and Islamite bowed the head to these memorials—one of the

many

many instances of the intuitive reverence of the Hindu for any object of a sacred character. Here we had the last view of the 'golden-flowing' stream, afterwards lost in the recesses of the forest, which became at each step more dense as we gradually attained the base of Gir-raj, where, in the S.E. angle, is her principal source. The path now became narrower, allowing space only for single passengers, and the deep over-arching foliage requiring to be put aside to protect the face. After a very short progress in this intricate pathway, the pilgrim is arrested by the *paduca* of one of the great sages *(moonis)* of yore, which exacts his prostration; and close by are five shrines, of the earliest and rudest style of architecture, having domes supported by columns of granite. These are ascribed to the Pandu brothers, and two more, in a still more ruinous condition, are given to their kinsman and companion, Kanya, and to Droopdevi, the common wife of the five Hindu-Scythic chiefs. To this point, the ascent from the gorge of the pass, a distance of three miles and a half, is gradual; from the *paduca* it becomes decided, and here the traveller discerns tremendous orbicular or columnar masses, severed by some convulsion from the pinnacles above, and hanging, as it were, suspended, ready for another fall. Such is the huge isolated fragment called the *Bhiroo Jamp*, about one hundred feet in height, and twice that in circumference, from whose summit those tired of this transitory world "leap the life to come," whence its name, the 'leap' or 'jump' of Bhiroo, the god of destruction. Ambition is generally the impelling motive to this suicide, the hope to better the victim's present condition—"to be a king in the *Nya-jenem*, or new birth." They are, therefore, never of the higher class, but consist of those who cannot be exalted by any ordinary effort of their own in this life. My friend Mr. Williams was here in 1812, when

From a sketch by Mrs. Col. Hervey Blair.

PALACE OF KHENGAR AND TEMPLES.

London, Published by W. H. Allen & Co.

when the *Sung*, or assembly of pilgrims, amounted to twelve thousand, yet only one made the leap to Bhiroo, and he was a poor wretched creature. Another of these dissevered masses is styled "the Elephant;" it is nearly half-way up the mountain, and on the very ledge of a cliff, fifteen hundred feet in perpendicular height. It is pyramidal in shape, from sixty to eighty feet high, and between it and the mountain there is just room for the pilgrim to pass. To this point the hill is covered with wood; but here vegetation ceases, and nothing meets the eye but bare granitic cliffs, which must be traversed with caution to attain the ruined palace of Khengar. The piety of the wealthy has rendered the path over these precipitous cliffs comparatively safe and easy, by means of low narrow steps, cut from the rock, and carried, according to the tortuous formation, in innumerable windings, and often on the extreme verge of the precipice. The preceding evening I had been seized with sudden lameness, and was compelled to be carried up in one of the mountain litters described at Aboo, and my sensations on passing these scarped ledges of rock, against which the car grated on the left, while on the right I looked down a perpendicular abyss of fifteen hundred feet, were not of the most agreeable nature. At eleven I entered the portals leading to the palace of the ancient kings of Saurashtra, whose black walls might defy the combined princes of the universe. Superstition could not have chosen a safer asylum to secure her shrines from profanation, nor could these have a more appropriate station from whence to elevate the soul to superior excellence. Here, on the very verge of the rock, in a small guard-room in the palace of Khengar, whose roof is supported by two pointed arches, I took my breakfast, at a height of nearly three thousand feet above the "ancient castle," on whose ruins, and from amidst ruins, I looked down. Casting a glance upwards, the temple of "the Mother of the Gods" appeared upon a peak full six hundred feet higher, with a crowning peak above, all inviting to enterprise.

CHAPTER XVIII.

Reflections of the Author.—Ascent to the peak of Goruknat'h.—The other peaks of Girnar.—Islamite saint.—Legend of the shrine of Kalka.—The Aghoris.—A wild ascetic.—Shrines.—Sects of the Jains.—Description of the shrines.—Inscriptions.—Temple of Nemi.—Resemblance between the statue of Nemi and that of Memnon.—The Khengar family.—Night spent in the ruined palace.—Descent of the mount.—Pilgrims to the shrine of Nemi.—Aged female Pilgrim.—The Elephant Rock.—Return to the tents.

In all ages, the mountain-top has been sought by the devotee, from whence to offer praise and homage to the Creator, and singularly moulded must be the mind which does not feel its conceptions of omnipotence enlarged by the contemplation of His works, when thus elevated above the jarring elements of the world. If reflection ever exert its power, it must be in such a position, where, as I sat in solitude amidst the ruins of ancient days, the deep silence only interrupted by the screaming of the kite, or the howling of the winds through the abode of desolation, I looked down upon man and his occupations with feelings of compassion. A distant view of that ocean, faintly illumined by the departing sun, on which, twenty-two years before, I was borne from home, and on which I was once more about to embark on my return thither, could not fail to kindle a host of associations, in which pain and pleasure were intermingled. At such a moment, and in such a scene, the mind reviewed in rapid succession the crowded actions of a life; and who, that has moved through so chequered a career, could do this without varied emotions? With me, the cycle of exile was complete; I was returning to the point whence I started, and vividly recalled the moment when I first bade a joyous

farewell

farewell to country and friends, to taste the "sparkling brim" of "life's enchanted cup," and calculated only the days which must intervene, ere I entered on the sphere of independent action. And this was destined to be of no scanty radius. From the snowy barriers which bound India on the north, to the mouths of the Ganges, Brahmaputra, and Indus, I had opportunities to observe much of man, his occupations, and varied habitudes; many friendships I had formed; many were dissolved by the hand of death; much of good and of evil had crossed my path; I had much to regret, yet more to remember; many bright scenes of exultation and hope, to balance against dark specks of grief and disappointment; and still clung to,—certainly was averse to quitting, perhaps for ever,—the country consecrated by early recollections; while the prospect of kindred and country before me was clouded with a sentiment of sadness at leaving those in whose companionship the joyous period of life had passed.

At sunrise I recommenced the ascent in the Indra-vahan, or celestial car, and reached the shrine of Amba-Mata, the Universal Mother, just as the sun had cleared the outer range of hills. I only waited to mark the height of this peak, and pushed on for the sikra of Goruknat'h. Elevated as we were, the air was yet close. The sun rose in clouds, and the thermometer, which was 66° at starting, mounted only one degree when he had been two hours above the horizon. To attain the peak of Goruknat'h, I had to make a considerable descent, and scale an intermediate elevation, and when I got to it, I found it so steep, as to compel me to abandon the car, and, with a pilgrim's zeal, clamber up the almost perpendicular cone on all-fours. On reaching the summit, I found myself on a small platform, not above ten feet in diameter, in the centre of which was a small monolithic shrine, sacred

to

to Goruknat'h. This fine peak is a truncated cone, about two hundred feet from its own immediate base, and about one hundred and fifty feet higher than that of the "Universal Mother." Satisfied with having attained the highest point of Gir-raj, I sat down by the *paduca* of the saint, covered by this miniature shrine, and took the bearings of the peaks, which my unseasonable lameness would not let me visit. Notwithstanding the weather was not altogether favourable for distant objects, the view was very grand. I did not obtain, as I had hoped, a bearing of Satrunja; but the sun lighted up the surface of the ocean, and though we could not discern the towns upon the coast, its direction, even at the distance of forty miles, was distinctly traced from Puttun to Poorbunder, while Dooragi, Jaitpoor, and other towns within the space of twenty-five miles, were clearly visible.

Girnar has six distinct peaks, although but four are prominently seen from the plains, and these only on diverging from either side his meridian; for, looking from the east or west, he appears one perfect cone. Majestic as these individually are when observed from Goruknat'h, and distinct as some are even at the distance of twenty-five miles, every mile beyond that, they gradually merge into the general mass. From Umrélie, the cone appears perfect, evincing the uniform direction of the peaks.

The following are the bearings from Goruknat'h :—

Peak of Mataji	West.
Ogur Sikra, or peak	N. 70° E.
Guru Dhatarie, do.	N. 70° E.
Kalka Mata, ... do.	East.
Raen Mata, ... do.	S. 73° E.

Other

Other objects.

Herimba's Swing .... S. 70° E.
Jumal Sah's Shrine .... S. 30° W.

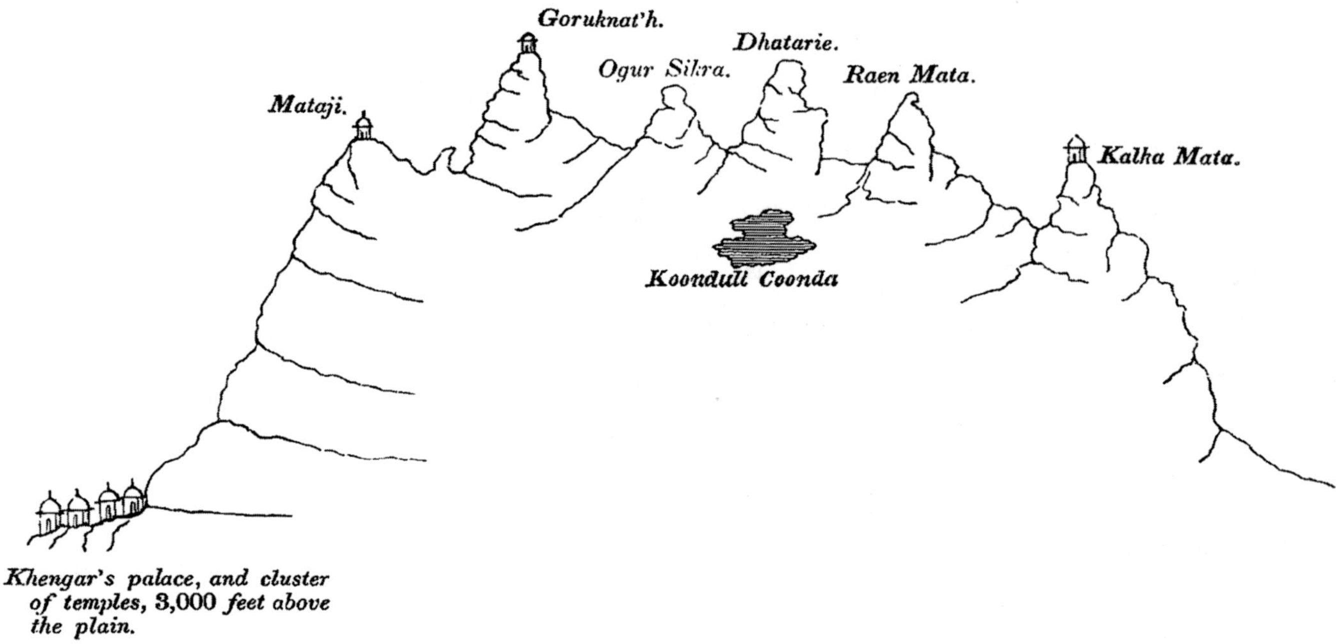

The distance between the shrines of the two "Mothers" of Production and Destruction may be about two miles in a direct line; the summit of the peak of the latter is not higher than the base of the former, while the intermediate peaks diverge just enough from the right line to be distinctly disclosed. From the shrine of Kalka, the descent to the opposite valley is abrupt and rapid.

From the pinnacle of Goruknat'h a just notion is obtained of the whole mass, fully justifying the epithet of *Meru Samun*, 'like Méru,' towering over the subordinate hills, which encircle it like a diadem, and forming between his base an immense amphitheatre, covered with impenetrable forest, through whose dark masses glide numerous streams, which have their sources in the fissures of the rock, each with a distinct appellation—as the *Sasu-vana*, or 'hare-wood;' the *Hanuman Bhara*,

Bhara, or 'monkey-streamlet,' &c. &c. Every wood and stream, as well as every peak in the surrounding range or on the mountain, is dedicated to some object of hope or terror, and tradition is eloquent with their legends. On one of the greatest elevations to the S.W., an Islamite saint, named Jumal Sah, has his station, and is an object of intercession with the faithful. "*Imam ca Khyr*," "the blessing of the Imam, and bodily health for himself and master," was the reply of an old Moslem servant, when I asked what he had sought there. One portion of the forest was pointed out as the "Swing of the daughter of Herimba," the forester-king in the days of the Pandus, and the rings are said yet to be seen by those with whom curiosity is more potent than fear, as the path leading to it is under the peak sacred to the infernal goddess. The legend tells, that the hand of the forest-king's daughter was to be his who could cause her gigantic frame to oscillate, and that Bhima was the happy man: the same legend exists in the Mokundra pass to this day. In another spot was pointed out a reservoir, called the *Kumundali* or *Koondull coonda*, where a hermit had passed a life prolonged far beyond the limits of mortality; his age was said to be one hundred and twenty years. He was almost worshipped, for the purity of his life and great beneficence, having, from the offerings of the devotees, established a *Sudda-birt*, or perennial charity, for the poorer pilgrim to Girnar. I could have wished to converse with him, but the will and the power went not together.

I was much more annoyed, however, at not being able to reach the shrine of Kalka, which tradition and universal report had clothed with something mysterious; and as I had signified to Lalla Joshea, the Guicowar's agent, my determination at all hazards to penetrate to this dread spot, in spite of his warnings, he and the rest very gravely imputed

imputed my sudden lameness to this profane resolution. To this awful *penetralium* the pilgrim never ventures, and the legend relates, that whoever has been so fool-hardy, has paid dearly for his temerity. A stranger was said always to join the sacrilegious visitor *en route*, who, on throwing aside her *incog.*, proved to be the dread Mother herself. Her rites are performed by the hideous Aghori, whose patroness she is, as *Aghoriswara Mata;* and it was a strong desire to unkennel some of these cannibals which tempted me to prolong my rugged pilgrimage to the Kalka Sikra, which in other respects has nothing attractive. At one time, they existed in these regions in some numbers; but, like brutes of the most noxious kind, they were only found in the wildest retreats, in the mountain-cave, or the dark recesses of the forest. Having elsewhere touched on the subject, I shall here only seek to establish the facts by some additional anecdotes.

The Ogur Sikra was called after one of these Murdi-khor, or man-eaters, who there established himself. Gazi was the name of one of these brutes, who used occasionally to quit his mountain-lair for the plain, to indulge his appetites. The last time he was seen, a live goat and an earthern vessel full of *shraub* were placed before him. He tore up the animal with teeth and nails, gorged, drank, slept amidst the offals, awoke, again gorged and drank, and then returned into the forest. In 1819, I appealed to my friend Mr. Williams (now with me) regarding these monsters. The following was his answer: "When I was in Cattiawar, there were three or four men who literally lived like wild beasts, realizing the story of Nebuchadnezzar, except that they also ate raw and human flesh. One of these devils came, I think in 1808, to Baroda, and actually ate the arm of a dead child. Another came into the camp of the Sirsohoh of Cattiawar, in 1811, but he was not

not suffered to remain, although they covered him with shawls, &c. At one of the Jatras at Girnar, one of these Aghoris came to the rock amongst the pilgrims, who made *pooja*, or worship, to him, and clad him with shawls, turbans, rings, &c. He sat for some time, and at length, with an idiotic laugh, sprung up, and darted into the forest." I was told that, not many months ago, one of the wretches issued from his retreat, and finding a Brahmin's boy who had strayed a little way from the temple, brought him down with a stone, but having only broken his leg, his cries summoned some one to his rescue. The Aghori fought for his prey, was mauled, and left for dead. Since this, they have kept still closer, and this last offender is said to have quitted the forest of Girnar altogether.

My reader will recollect, that although I have digressed into these details, he left me perched alone upon the pinnacle of Girnar, looking to the shrine of the "Great Mother" of these accursed images of man, and entirely absorbed in the chaos of ideas to which my singular position gave birth. My solitude was disturbed by a being whose approach I had not perceived, and who silently took his seat before the shrine of Goruknat'h. A rag of cloth was his sole covering; his loins were girded with a rope of hair, and his whole frame and matted locks were smeared with ashes. His features were fine, his figure manly and well-formed, but though not above twenty-two, he had already attained a low degree in the degradation of humanity. His eyes were inflamed, and he was in a state of stupefaction from drugs; yet he appeared to possess an instinctive sort of perception of the ceremonies he commenced. As soon as he was seated, facing the miniature shrine of the saint, he closed his eyes, and remained for some time in motionless abstraction. In a few minutes, there were certain indications of the spirit, expressed

 by

by contortions of the muscles of the face, writhings of the frame, and agitations of the neck and heart, as if the infernal divinity he worshipped had inspired him. When the fit was over, he rose, threw himself into attitudes, howling "*Aluc! Aluc!*" I allowed time for these ravings to subside, ere I disturbed him, for the speculation of his mind's eye was too cloudy to see me; but in vain did I endeavour to extort a sound from him. He heard, and even smiled, but this smile was the sole symptom of consciousness he evinced of my presence. He had a wallet, evidently containing provisions, a small coco-nut hookah to inhale his intoxicating drugs, and a pair of iron tongs, to help himself to fire. But what most surprised me, was a flute made of bamboo, which he carried in his hand. What effect the "concord of sweet sounds" could have on a creature who had banished every outward vestige of humanity, his impenetrable silence prevented me from ascertaining. Having made his final obeisance to Goruknat'h, howling "*Aluc!*" he departed, and clambered down the peak towards the interdicted shrine of Kalka, when intervening objects soon hid him from my sight. In vain I enquired who he might be; it was sufficient that he held no converse with his fellows, for those who beheld him to conclude that he must be more than man. Whether he was a Murdhikhor, I could not determine, although, as he went off direct to the Aghori peak, said to be frequented only by his sect, it is probable that he belonged to the fraternity.

I remained for some time upon the platform of the saint, musing upon the singularity of the encounter. There is always something awful in the absence of that god-like attribute, reason, and a certain feeling implanted in our nature makes us hasten from the contemplation of an object from whom the Almighty has hidden his face. But there

there was no mode of escape here from one who seemingly partook of the maniac and the demon, placed as I was upon a pinnacle between three and four thousand feet from the plain. Such speculation, however, never occurred to me, and my sole sensations were those of melancholy excitement and deep compassion for this outcast of Nature.

The sun soon began to warm, and at the same time to remind me that I had yet much to see; but it was not easy to resist the influence which enthralled the senses in such a scene. I pity the man who has never felt the luxurious languor of undisturbed cogitation, to which for a while I surrendered my entire energies. A cough, a hem, the lament of the wearied passing pilgrim, acted like a knell upon my nerves. I was jealous of my solitude, and felt as if the presence of others was an intrusion. But there must be an end to all things, and retracing my steps, I at length regained the temple of the more beautiful and more amiable "Universal Mother."

Taking a look at the goddess, who occupies an altar under the munduff, or vault, I passed to the western balcony, where, placing myself upon a block of granite, I feasted my eyes on the clusters of temples adjoining the ruined palace of Khengar below. The bird's-eye view of these monuments of Jainism is very grand, and affords a correct notion of their design and distribution. They are erected on the crest of the western extremity of the mountain, here forming a half-moon, on whose extreme edge, near a precipitous cliff full one thousand feet high, rises a lofty wall, like the rock it rests upon, of granite. The southern end is flanked by the palace of Khengar, surrounded by embattled walls, and defended by massive square towers, built of blocks of granite, and forming the sole entrance to this

 sacred

sacred *enceinte*, a fit abode for Doorga herself. As a fortress, Gir-raj would be unrivalled; for if well provisioned, having abundance of water from above, and being commanded by the peaks of Mata and Goruknat'h, no enemy could get possession of it. But let me conduct the reader *seriatim* through each of these shrines, of whose singular position the following sketch will present a correct idea.

Deo-kote, or Fortress of the Gods.

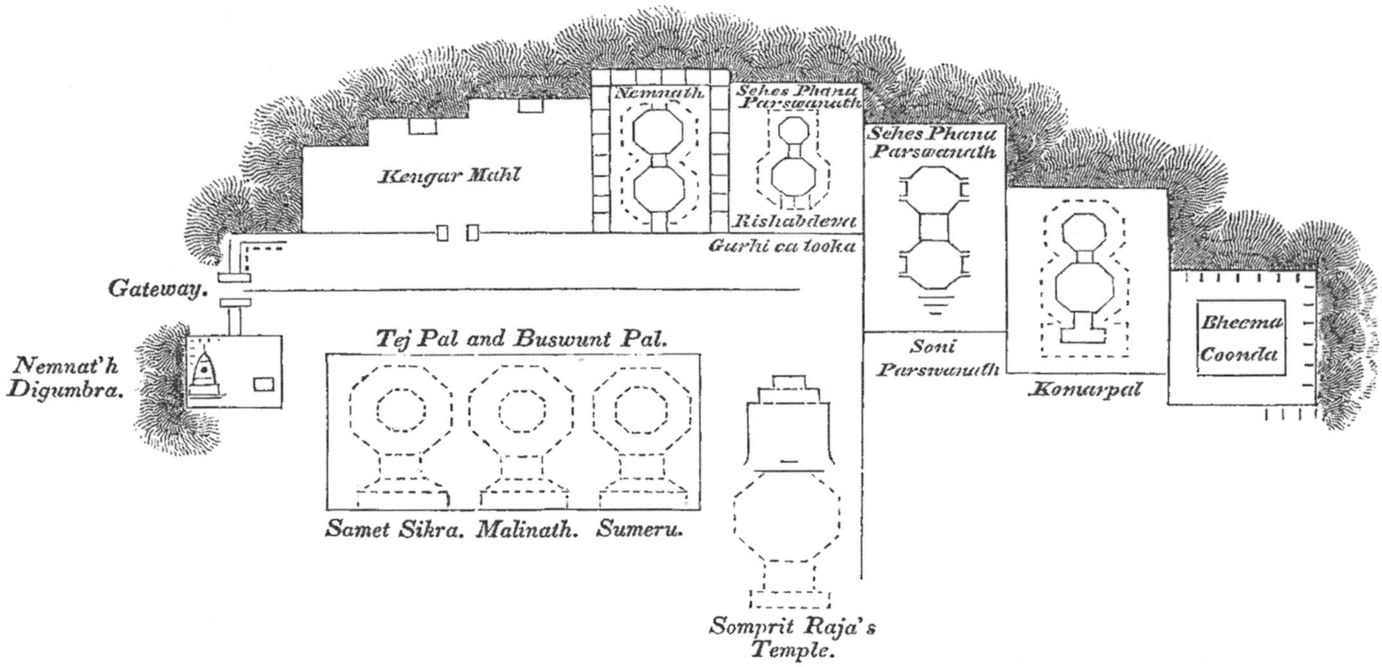

In descending from the peak of the "Great Mother," to whom there are divers manifestations of the Unitarian Jains' devotion, the reader will observe the numerous colonnaded cupolas placed upon the projecting eminences,* and imagine their picturesque effect in the general scene. He may likewise remark females gathering the white *béla*, and other favourite flowers, which are woven into chaplets, and sold to the pilgrims for offerings to the holy ones of Girnar.

The first temple adjoins the entrance-gate, and was erected by the Digumbra

* See plate of Khengar's palace.

Digumbra sect to Nemnat'h, the only one of the twenty-four Jinéswars whom they acknowledge, or who obtains their homage. I may here suggest to those who are ignorant of this religion, that the Jains have separated into two grand divisions, *viz.* Digumbra and Sweetumbra—the former signifying one who dispenses with all covering *(umbra)* but the canopy of heaven *(dig)*, in contradistinction to Sweetumbra, or one with "pure" raiment. Sid Sena Devaca Acharya was the founder of the former, in S. 400 (A.D. 344). The *Sri-pooj*, or Guru of the sect, accordingly, remains without vesture, not even covering his loins, except in the cold season, when he throws a loose quilt over him, as a protection from the weather; but few only (and one of these is now at Girnar) obtain this privilege, the reward of austerities and denial of all mundane feelings.* The colossal statues in the caves at Gwalior, some of which are fifty feet in height, and all of a similar description throughout India, belong to this sect. The present Guru has his head-quarters at Surat; his name is Vedyavandaboosen, and this 'ornament' *(boosen)* of 'science' *(Vedya)* has a high reputation for knowledge. He has but few disciples about his person, but there are several scattered over India. The votaries or laymen of this sect are *Banias*, or of the mercantile class, and chiefly Hoonibanas, one of the eighty-four great families. They calculate that there are forty thousand families of these lay votaries, many of whom are at Jeipoor, where there are several Digumbra temples. But even this sect is subdivided into *Kashta-Singis* and *Mura-Singis*, the former being merely an etymon for the parent stock, and the latter designated from carrying a feather of the pea-fowl *(Mura)*. These sectarians do not give eyes to their statues of Nemi

* I have seen one of these animals, to whom was assigned the place of honour at the Court of Dhalpoor, without even a fig-leaf.

Nemi (as do the other sects) of crystal, diamond, &c., and they deny beatitude to females, notwithstanding the homage the latter pay to the great unclad Sri-pooj, which he receives very imperturbably. Another peculiarity of this personage is, that he never feeds himself, the office being performed by one of the lay attendants. There is nothing particularly worthy of notice in this shrine.

The next is a group of three temples, erected or repaired by Tej Pál and Buswunt Pál, the princely brothers who devoted their immense wealth to the temples on Aboo. From an inscription (App. No. X.) found here, dated S. 1204 (A.D. 1148), it appears these were prior, by nearly half a century, to those of Aboo; but they do not compete with them either in extent or costliness. They are placed upon a large, elevated, paved terrace. The central shrine contains the statue of Malinat'h, the nineteenth deified Jain; that to the right is called Sumeru, and that to the left Samet-Sikra, two of the "Five *teerthas*," or holy mounts of pilgrimage of these Unitarians.* The shrine of Malinat'h, whose dark-blue colour often causes him to be mistaken for Nemnat'h, consists of four stories, diminishing to the apex, which is surmounted by a small image of Chandra Pribhu, the eighth Teert'hancar. There is besides an image to each cardinal point. At one is a miniature representation of *the* Hill, Méru, in yellow jasper, which also enters into the material of the roof.

The next temple, dedicated to Parswa-nat'h, the twenty-third deified pontiff, was erected by Raja Sompriti, a prince of great celebrity, of the Jain faith, whom I have often noticed, and who flourished

* Samet-Sikra is in Behar, part of the ancient kingdom of Magadha, sacred to Parswa, whose sect there flourished in former times, while to Méru, *the* Hill, they give a 'local habitation and a name' far west of the waters of Sinde, and, as I have already surmised, towards Balk-Bamian, whose colossal Jain figures, as described by Abulfazil, still exist.

flourished in the second century before Vicrama. This is the third temple it has been my good fortune to discover, attributed to this prince, and my reader has only to refer to the plates of my former work,* to see the two finest specimens of Jain, I might say of Hindu, architecture yet given to the western world. This memorial, if not so simple in design, is by far the finest specimen of architectural display on the hill of Girnar, or, indeed, in Saurashtra. Its situation is very fine, being on the verge of the rock, three stories from the ground, while its congregation of columns of dusky granite lend it a venerable aspect. The following ground-plan, which does not lay claim to perfect accuracy of measurement, will give a general idea of its construction.

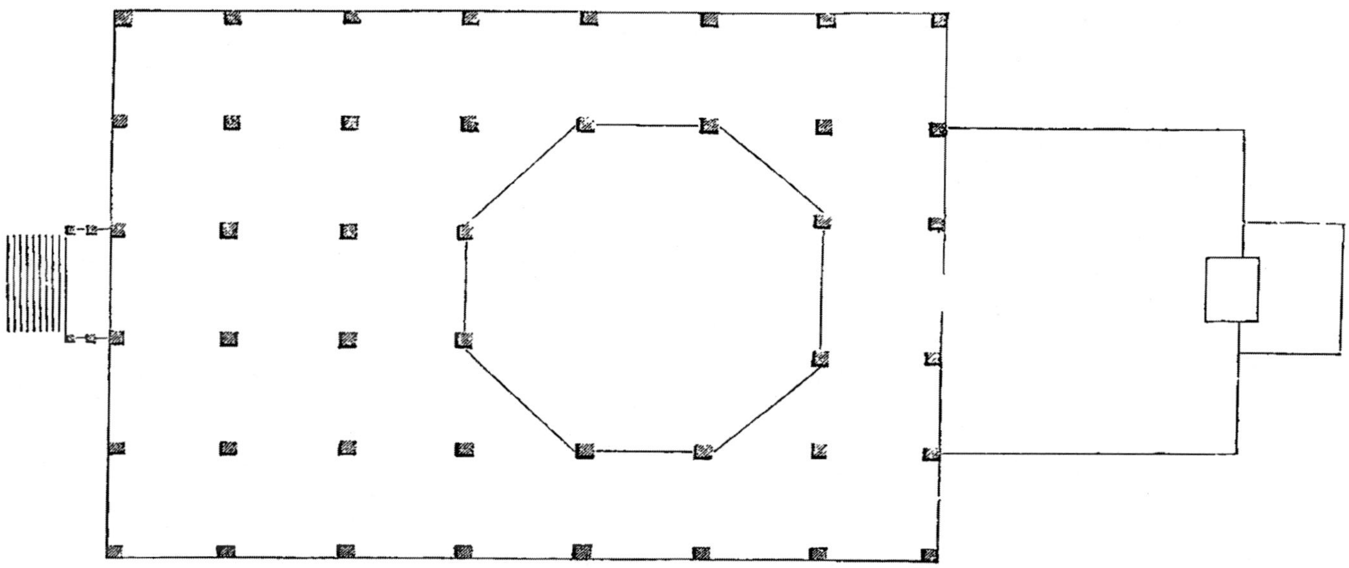

The entrance (now blocked up) to the west, was by a flight of steps to a small colonnaded portico, conducting to the body of the temple. Proceeding through a triple-colonnaded and vaulted hall, we reach the munduff, or central dome, about thirty feet square, and supported by pillars. Colonnaded aisles, with pilasters at the walls, connect this with a vestibule, and an interior munduff, also with a vaulted roof, beyond which

* *Annals of Rajast'han.*

which is the *Sompat*, or sanctuary, containing, upon a raised altar, the statue of Parswa. The columns are not above fourteen feet high; but on looking up and seeing a vaulted roof variously sculptured between every four columns, mere elevation is disregarded in the imposing and massive design. Both internally and externally, this work presents ample scope for the pencil. Near the western door, there is an opening in the floor, disclosing a subterranean retreat, by which Raja Mandalica made his escape, when his country and capital were subdued by Mahomed Begra.

From this shrine, I proceeded to the Bheema-coonda, excavated by Raja Bheemaca, one of the Yadu princes of the land, at the northern extremity of Devacuta. A flight of steps, cut, as well as the reservoir, in the living rock, leads to the water, which is confined within a space of seventy feet by fifty.

Adjoining this is a temple, said to have been founded by Komár-pál, of Anhulwarra. Its dilapidation renders this probable, as his successor is stated to have thrown down every temple that he raised, save that sacred to Ajit-nath, on the hill of Taringa. The superstructure is entirely destroyed down to the architraves covering the columns, some of which are also removed. I have already hinted, however, that Mahomed Begra, or whatever Mooslem conqueror erected the mosque at Joonagurh, probably applied the materials of this, among others, thereto. The plan of this is a complete copy of the temple of Parswa, and the extent about the same. The Committee of Jain laymen, who superintend the affairs of their churches, had commenced its restoration, and part of the sanctum was completed, when the bigotry of the great banker of these parts interposed, who determined to enshrine his own object of worship, the symbol of Siva. This was met by the only

kind

kind of opposition in the power of the Jains in charge, who threatened self-immolation on the threshold. Here the matter rests, and, between the two, Komár-pál has little chance of having his name perpetuated on Mount Girnar. This facility of changing one tabernacle into another, between the followers of Siva and Jaina, of Ad-eswara and Adnat'h, might throw some light upon their common origin.

The next, surrounded by a high-walled enclosure, is a temple to Sehes Phanu Parswanat'h, whose canopy is the thousand-hooded serpent, his *vahana*, or emblem. The familiar name of this shrine is Soni-Parswanath, from a goldsmith (*soni*) of Dehli, named Singram, who, in the reign of the emperor Akber, with whom he was a great favourite, rebuilt it at his own expense. Many tales are told of the vast wealth of this lay votary of the Jain faith, of his skill in magic, and in the transmutation of metals. Although this temple wants the externally antique appearance of that of Sompriti, it maintains a good character internally, having fine columns of syenite, of a dusky green. Its general shape is the same as that already detailed, and along the lateral wall of the court are cells, containing small statues of the Primates, according to the fancy of the various worshippers by whom they were enshrined.

The next portion is called *Gurhi-ca-tooka.* The shrine, sacred to Rishabdeva or Adnat'h, is very noble, possessing many fine columns; but it would be endless, as well as uninteresting, to give a minute description of it. There are miniature representations of the holy mounts of the Jains, Meru, Samet-sikra, &c., in white marble and yellow jasper; and also ranges of cells adjoining the area walls of the quadrangle, in which are enshrined the "Twenty-four."

 The

The last of the group, and which adjoins the palace of Khengar, is dedicated to Nemnat'h, the tutelary divinity of Girnar; but although the original shrine is of high antiquity, it is so disfigured by bad taste and modern repairs, that it may not compare in nobility of appearance with that of Sompriti. Like the temple of Adnat'h on Satrunja, its interior is bedecked with paintings and gaudy ornaments, more bespeaking the wealth than the taste of the votaries of the present day. In the Devachunda (*chunda*, 'choice'), or Gumbarra, as the penetralium is termed, the black statue (*Sham-moorut*) of Nemi is placed upon an altar, and adorned with golden chains and bracelets, wearing a crown of silver, and having crystal eyes. Lights in high brass candelabras, and incense, are kept perpetually burning, and here the offerings of the pilgrims are made. This shrine is lower in the rock than the others, and a passage is hewn for the votaries to reach it. There were many inscriptions in this passage, but the granite is so apt to exfoliate, that I could not find one perfect, and the two fragments I did find here are little more than five centuries old, and mere memoria of the pious repairers of the shrine. One, however, (App. No. XI.) contains a curious fact; besides a donation of two hundred mohurs, this recorder of his own munificence lent two thousand *on interest* for the purpose.

Another inscription (App. No. XII.), placed at the entrance of the palace of Khengar, also records its repairs by one of its own princes, Raja Mandalica; but whether the first or the third, we are left to conjecture; for, in the long line which for ages swayed in Joonagurh-Girnar, four princes are enumerated bearing this appellation. We must, therefore, dismiss it with the vague remark applied to the "ancient castle"

castle"—*bhote joona*, 'very old.' At all events, he was the fourth prince anterior to Khengar; but several of this name are also enumerated.*

I will not attempt the details of the shrine of Nemi. Let it suffice that it is an immense fabric, with a lofty spire; but plans of each would be required to satisfy curiosity. The most interesting object was the statue of the black Nemi himself, of basalt, or black marble. It is of colossal size, in a sitting posture, the hair crisped like a Negro's, and the countenance expresses benignity and repose. The striking resemblance between the Nemi of the Budhists of India, and the Egyptian Memnon in the British Museum, has often occurred to me, and the idea was more powerfully impressed upon me by the following passage from Burckhardt: "The heads of the Colossi at Ebsamboul, in Nubia, bear a great likeness to this, with this difference, that they are of sandstone. The expression of the face is the same; perhaps a little more gravity is expressed in those of Nubia, but the incomparable serenity and god-like mildness are remarkable in both." No better language could be selected to pourtray Neminat'h, whose crisped Ethiopic hair, lotos symbol, and black colour, cannot but suggest notions that a connection existed between the Indian Syria and the coasts of the Red Sea, in matters of religion as well as commerce, in ancient days.

It would be futile to enter into an elaborate description of the ruins of the palace—the pencil must speak instead of the pen. Still less would the reader thank me for detailing the interminable Yadu traditions

* It is very common in Rajpoot families to repeat names of celebrity in their lines. There were three Umras in the dynasty of Oodipoor; but, unfortunately, they do not, like us, attach numerals to distinguish one from the other, and the epithets which marked them when living, from some mental or physical peculiarity, are lost in after-generations.

tions respecting the root of its genealogical tree for the founder of the dynasty of Joonagurh. They do, however, trace it to Roodrapal, many generations after the War. The family carry their origin to Pridoman, son of Crishna, by his wife Rookmani. We have no check upon these traditionary accounts until we reach this Mandalica, and his son, Khengar, the rival of Sid-raj of Anhulwarra for the hand of the Deora Ranee; and as this prince reckons the peninsula amongst the eighteen kingdoms he conquered, probably Khengar's independence was sacrificed to his gallantry. According to a stanza familiar to all the bards of this region, and those of the Yadus in particular, there were *four* Mandalicas, *nine* Noguns, *seven* Khengars, *five* Soorujmals, and *eight* Roop-palas, in the genealogical chain of princes who ruled in Joonagurh-Girnar.

I quitted these relics of old with highly gratified feelings, and returned to the guard-room over the gateway of the palace to repose, after a day of unusual exertion—if repose it could be called, when I had to embody the host of objects that had come under review, which operation continued until light nearly failed.

The day was fast closing when I carried my chair to the parapet guarding the crest of the cliff, to take a last look at the sweeping prospect seen from Deva-cuta. Through the opening in the pass, the murky towers of Joonagurh were dimly visible, while our tents appeared like white specks in the distance. The intermediate space presented bold projections, sometimes crowned by slender cupolas, rising out of the forest, which the shades of evening blended into one indistinct tint.

The clouds, which had been floating about during the day, had congregated into a dense mass, obscuring the entire concave of heaven, excepting

excepting a narrow belt occupying a few degrees of the visible horizon. Behind this darkness, the sun had descended unobserved, and as I supposed, departed; when suddenly, like the lightning's flash, his fiery disk appeared, resting on the bosom of the ocean, illuminating its broad expanse as if by magic. The coast was rendered distinct from Puttun to Mangrole, though the cities which studded it remained wrapt in gloom. A momentary splendour flitted over some white objects, which were named as certain towns; but it was alike beautiful and brief, as was the dazzling effect of the sun's last ray slanting upon the Sonarica, and irradiating at intervals its serpentine course from the sea to the base of Girnar. In a few seconds, a tenfold gloom succeeded this "excess of brightness." I remained some time enjoying in perfect silence the remembrance of this evanescent vision; but the evening was cold, and I retired at length to the deserted guard-room.

The weather now became boisterous; the howl of the winds increasing till midnight, and I found the scanty bed-covering, though superabundant for the plains, far too slight here. The spirit of the blast yelled through the crannies and doorless halls of Khengar—a fitting lullaby for the scene, but for the coldness which accompanied it. I contrived, however, to diminish this, by filling up the opening to windward with bushes and straw, and, tired with the excitement of the day, soon fell asleep. How long I had reposed I know not, but all at once, my slumbers were rudely broken by some heavy mass rolling over me, and extinguishing the light. I started up, in doubt whether I was to attack a bear or an Aghori, or whether the "Dread Mother" herself had caught me in her rough embrace, when a sudden rush of air, from the space I had previously barricaded, revealed the quality of my nocturnal intruder. I presently got the barrier replaced by the aid of the

watchmen

watchmen of the Nawab, whom I roused from their bivouac in the court below, where they were chattering round their night-fire to beguile the time, and after this fitting *finale* to the drama of the last twenty-four hours, I once more, and not in vain, courted the "soft restorer."

Early next morning, I commenced my descent, and as I passed through the portals of the palace, the scene which in the evening had been dimly visible, opened in all its magnificence. The sun had risen in unclouded splendour, throwing his golden gleams on the dark masses of the mountain and forest, and cheering on their way crowds of pilgrims to the shrine of Nemi, and others of the many objects of adoration. Amongst the various groups, my attention was drawn to an aged female and her son, who, while she reclined against the rock, was engaged in the pious task of shampooing her enfeebled limbs, benumbed by the toil of the ascent. I entered into conversation with her, and found she had come from Gokul; had traversed on foot every spot sacred to the shepherd-god, from that, his own and her birth-place, to Dwarica and Peachee, the scene of his death, and was now returning to her pastoral land. As a model of content, the aged pilgrim was worthy the chisel of a sculptor, and the picture of mingled filial affection and devotion touched me sensibly; the feeling was perhaps heightened by the name of her country, Gokul, a scene which recalled many days of thoughtless happiness, and my earliest and dearest friends, but one of whom, alas! survives. Other pilgrims replied to my queries regarding their native land, that they had come from *Ganga-tit'h*, the 'banks of the Ganges,' from *Jamuna Cavari*, 'the skirts of the Jumna,' from *Casi-ji*, the sacred Benares, and as we passed on, the shout of *Ganga-ji-ca-jey!* 'victory to Ganga!' was responded to by numerous stragglers, who were clambering up the rock.

I halted

I halted at the point called 'the Elephant,' but though the sun had great power, it being now eight o'clock, the feathered Troglodytes of Girnar, the eagles and vultures, had not left their cells, which honeycomb this face of the mountain, where they were in full conclave. These crevices have a singular appearance, and unless carved out by the Monotheistic preservers of life, in whatever shape, for the purpose of sheltering the birds, I cannot account for them, many occurring in places not likely to be affected by the action of the atmosphere. Some of the larger perforations have smaller ones within, the resort of pigeons and lesser birds. Moreover, the surface is covered in many places with large black snails, so thickly studded, that, in some parts, not a particle of the rock can be seen. Whether the eagle, or more ignoble vulture, will condescend to touch such quarry, I know not; but, unless they feast with the Aghori, they must go abroad for their prey. The crow is not a denizen of Girnar, in which he shows his accustomed sagacity, wisely preferring association with the carnivorous Sivite, to the spare vegetable diet of the Jain.

High on this detached mass, cut in the living rock, in large, fair characters, appeared the name of "Rao Runingdeo, who, in S. 1215, performed the pilgrimage." Neither tribe nor country is mentioned, but I have no doubt that he was the chief of the tribe of Jhala, of Jhalawar, one of the subdivisions of Saurashtra, and the first vassal of Bhola Bheem, king of Anhulwarra. He is honourably named in the history of Pirthi Raj, the emperor of Dehli, who, in that year, first buckled on the sword to avenge the death of his father, Somesa, prince of Sambhur, slain in battle by this very king, Bhola Bheem. The name of Runingdeo is conspicuous amongst the feudal array that assembled to oppose Pirthi Raj, and it is conjecture equal to proof, that the Jhala chieftain

took

took the opportunity to visit this holy mount in progress from Jhalawar to the court of his sovereign.*

From the palace of Khengar to the Elephant Rock, all was bare; but here the foliage re-commenced, and I continued to feast upon every variety of prospect until I re-passed the lower portals of the "ancient city" to our tents in a nook of the forest, where I arrived fatigued, but delighted with the pilgrimage; for though Girnar may not compete with Arbudha, its pastoral plains (or *terre-pleine*), its lakes and rills, its varied vegetation, or the costly grandeur of its shrines, it has merits peculiarly its own. To many, as to me, the dusky syenite and ponderous granite columns may outweigh, in their antique magnificence, the more decorative marble and lighter workmanship of the other, while the eye, ranging over the expanse of ocean, conveys feelings to the mind which cannot arise in contemplating the sandy desert of Marust'hali.

Many a varied country have I since traversed; I have seen, from the summit of the Righi, the sun rise over the icy peaks of the Helvetian Alps, and beheld from the ruined Tortona his descent through a winter sky, crowning with roseate splendour the snow-clad Apennines; I have passed "the gathered winter of a thousand years" which nestles in the side of Mont Blanc; have watched, at the midnight hour, the moon clear the broken arches of the Coliseum, and between the Scirocco and sadness, have been excited into fever, as from the sable gondola I contemplated Venice in her humility, and wished the thunder of Jove could blast the bastard eagles perched on the palaces of her nobles; I have sat with the wild unscrupulous Calabrian amidst the ruins of Pæstum; these and many other sights, calculated to call forth heart-stirring emotions, have I witnessed; yet none produced such

* Vide p. 197.

such sentiments as I experienced on the summit of the seven-peaked Girnar, with the maniac Aghori heaving forth the outpourings of the spirit before the shrine of Goruka, in the presence of a solitary Frank; and on the precipitous verge of Deva-cuta, when, the shadows of night stealing around me, I saw the ocean lighted up by the sun's last rays, while silence ruled over the remains of fading glory. The only position which might compare with these, was a midnight descent from Mont Cenis, in the very heart of winter, when, clad with snow many feet deep from the summit to the valley, a brilliant moon illuminated the silvery surface of the mountain, throwing lengthened shadows from the clumps of dusky pine, which, as we rapidly whirled past, assumed an air of mysterious interest, heightened in no small degree by those grand appliances to the sublime, positive danger, and a stillness unbroken, save by the crackling of the horses' hoofs upon the frozen mass.

I found the barometer 10° higher than when we ascended, from the weather having cleared up. We halted a day to visit and receive the Nawab, the lord of Joonagurh.

CHAPTER XIX.

Dandoosir.—Jinjirrie.—Kattywauna.—Altered course of the Bhadra.—Tursye.—Old city of Kundornah.—Bhanwul.—Miserable appearance of the country.—Ruins of Goomlí.—Temple of the Jaitwas.—Temple of Ganpatí.—Jain temple.—The Portal of Rama.—Monumental *pallias* of the Jaitwas.—Inscriptions.—Historical account of the Jaitwas.—Destruction of Goomlí.—Chronology of Jaitwa history.—Migration of the Jaitwas.—Nugdeah.—Deolah.—Origin of the Aheers.—Mooktasirr.—Dwarica.—Desolate country.—Temple of Dwarica.—Shrines.—The *Mahatma*.—Legend of the Temple.

Dandoosir.—December 17th.—Four coss. Crossed a plain thickly strewed with the *babool*, and occasional scanty patches of cultivation, chiefly *gram*. The villages were poor, and inhabited by Aheers and Koolmbies, the pastoral and agricultural classes of these regions; but some contained wholly Sindies.

Jinjirrie.—December 18th.—Six coss. Cultivation as yesterday, but in addition to the usual classes, we had another western tribe, the Buloteh.

Kattywauna.—December 19th.—Eight coss. This place is entitled to be called a town, having three thousand houses, enclosed by a substantial wall; it is situated on the banks of the Bhadra, which has a volume of water larger than any of the peninsular streams I have yet seen. Abulfazil commends it for the excellency of its fish, but the only one we caught (by the hook) by no means justified the recommendation of the Indian Herodotus, tasting villainously of the tannin, which also discoloured the stream. The last two miles of our march were on the edge of the river, on whose bank we encamped. This town boasts of some antiquity, and in former ages was called Koontulpoor, and still possesses an interior castle dignified with the name of

Kali-kote.

Kali-kote. The "eighteen *burrun*," or castes, are said to have representatives in Kattywauna; but the population consists chiefly of the Bunya-Bhatti, from the valley of the Indus, and the Momun, or Mooslem cloth-weaver. The Bhadra has changed its course—a fact attested by a bridge now high and dry. The last famine had left marks of its ravages both in the town and country, and thinned the population of each. The villages were poor, consisting of from twenty to seventy huts, and the most useful classes so often named, Aheers and Koolmbies, were in a sad condition.

Tursye.—December 19th.—Eighteen coss. About five miles from the commencement of our march, we passed a considerable place called Esarioh, peopled by Aheers and Koolmbies, which had decided marks of improved cultivation, while on our left lay the old city of Kundornah,* belonging to the chief of the Jaitwa tribe. At Deolah, there is a small fortress on the bank of a stream which separates the Joonagurh territory from that of the Jam, while a third boundary lies a mile and a half to the left, that of the Jaitwa Rana, at Khulsuna. The hitherto scanty cultivation here becomes scantier still; the peasantry are of the same classes so often named. Tursye is close to the eastern line of the Burda hills.

Bhanwul

* From a small miscellaneous collection of mingled history and genealogical facts, belonging to a most intelligent Bhât, I extracted many notes on the old cities of Saurashtra; amongst others, the following on this place:—"The name of Kundornah, or Kundolah, was in very remote times *Visalanagri,* afterwards changed to *Sillânagri,* again to *Tillapoor,* and *Thun Kundole,* now *Kundolah.*" This is the order in which I copied from the Bard, but I think its name of *Tillapoor* should have preceded that of *Sillânagri,* if called after *Sil Comar* of the Jaitwa tribe. For many years I had vainly searched for Tillapoor-Puttun, one of the ancient capitals of the Ranas' (of Méwar) ancestry in Saurashtra, and cannot help conjecturing that this is the very place; nor is it at all improbable that its name of *Sillânagri* may be from *Silladitya,* of whom there were two, previous to the destruction of Balabhi, one in S. 477, the other, the last of the line who ruled them, in S. 56 A search for inscriptions might decide the question.

Bhanwul.—December 20th to 23d.—Seven coss. As we advance, the country becomes more miserable, a few patches only of cultivation appearing amidst extensive plains of rank grass and the thorny *mimosa*. We passed the village of Maepoor, in which are the remains of a fort destroyed some years back on account of its harbouring marauders; it is now inhabited by twenty-five families of miserable Aheers. Bhanwul belongs to the Jam of Nova-nagari, and contains about fifteen hundred houses, chiefly of the manufacturing Momun. The town stands upon the Bunwarri river, and what is not drained off in cultivation, falls into a large stream, the Vitodra, on the banks of which stands a temple dedicated to Indra.

Ruins of Goomli.—We halted at Bhanwul some days, and were joined by Major Barnewell, the Political Agent in this province, for the purpose of exploring the ruins of Goomlí, the ancient capital of the Jaitwa tribe, once distinguished in the peninsula.

Goomlí is situated at the northern face of the hills of Burrira, whose appellation in ancient Hindu geography was Puryata, famed as one of the retreats of the sage Brigu. This old city lies about three miles from Bhanwul, and from its sequestered position, takes the traveller by surprise, not even the spire of its famed shrine being visible till near; it may be said to be buried in a dell or valley, bounded to the south and east by the Burrira hills, rising about six hundred feet from their base, and the rest is concealed by a low ridge. The astonishment of the visitor is not diminished, when he learns that many centuries have elapsed since Goomlí ceased to be inhabited. Three faces of a most substantial circumvallation, built of masses of the calcareous concrete termed *conkra*, and strengthened with large square towers, enclose it to the east, north, and west, and unite it with the hills,

which

which form a material defence to the south. These walls had, moreover, been carried up the mountain, which presented the remains of a castle on the summit, now a den for wild beasts. A gateway is placed in the centre of each wall, nearly facing the cardinal points; the eastern and northern sides, about five hundred and eight hundred yards long, are the most perfect, the former, indeed, having its parapets and battlements complete. The western wall is most dilapidated—the remains of a spacious ditch are visible.

The first object that attracts notice, on entering this town, is the temple of the Jaitwas, near the palace, in the re-entering angle of the hills. This edifice is cruciform, a shape not uncommon in Hindu sacred architecture, and the entrance faces the rising sun. It stands on an elevated terrace one hundred and fifty-three feet in length, one hundred and twenty in breadth, and twelve in height, built of hewn stone, with a handsome enriched cornice. The shrine consists of an octagonal *munduff*, of twenty-three feet diameter, two stories high, surmounted by a dome, about thirty-five feet from the ground. The architectural and sculptured details of this are both uncommon, and differing from any thing I had ever seen. A series of columns placed octagonally, about twelve feet high, connected by sculptured stone architraves, formed the base. Above these is a second series of columns (having a stone gallery and railing in front), covered by a dome, embellished with sculptured figures, representing the *ras-mundala*, or heavenly dance, part of which has fallen in. The vestibules, projecting towards the east and west, like the nave of our cathedrals, are about fourteen feet by eight, having numerous columns, and a central vault, with a lotus ornament richly carved at the apex. Several smaller domes surround the large one, and like it, are

supported

supported by columns. The *devachna*, or penetralia to the west, is a small chamber about ten feet square; this is now empty, and a considerable portion of the *Sikra*, or pyramidal spire, which rose over it, has been thrown down. Although the extreme internal dimensions are only sixty-three feet by fifty-four, I have seen few edifices more calculated to excite admiration. The mythological sculptures of this temple of the Jaitwas are striking, especially the capitals of the columns supporting the main body, which exhibit a greater variety of singular devices than I have ever yet seen, representing lions, sphynxes, the *gras*, or griffin, monkeys, &c., and the never-failing substitute for the Grecian Caryatidæ, the distorted *Gatachuc*. These objects have every variety of posture, and are so well carved, that they would not be misplaced in some of our most ancient Saxon churches. There are no symbols within the temple, whence to infer the specific object of adoration; but the external sculpture of the *devachna* contains emblems of all-destroying Time, sufficient to authorize the conclusion, that it was dedicated either to Siva or to Hursid-Mâtâ, the tutelary goddess of the Jaitwas.

At a short distance to the S.W. stands the temple of Ganpatí, the chief of the *dii minores gentium* of the Hindu pantheon, his elephant-head, emblematic of wisdom, wanting the proboscis. The construction of this shrine is very singular; instead of columns around the *cella*, it has a wall with casemated windows, and a spherical roof. In an adjoining cell, carved upon the architrave, are personifications of the *No-grahas*, or nine planets, which rule the destinies of man.

Immediately to the north of this shrine of 'Wisdom,' are the ruins of the temple of 'Knowledge,' belonging to the heterodox followers of Budha. The construction of this, likewise, differs from any temple I have

have yet seen of this sect, having four contiguous *munduffs*, supported by columns, whose capitals, though somewhat dissimilar from those above described, and even repugnant to the tenets of the sect, are of the same whimsical character, and evidently of the same age, and by the same workmen, as the orthodox shrine of Hursid. Within was an image of Parswa, and a slab containing in relief the portraits of the twenty-four Jineswars, or deified Jain primates. The tree sacred to Time has been insidiously, but surely, operating upon these edifices, and will in a few years triumph over both.

From these ruins I passed to a *baoree*, or fountain, which affords some notion of the munificence of purse and spirit of the ancient Jaitwas; here my research for inscriptions was slightly rewarded by one bearing date S. 13– –, but merely attesting its repairs.

The most interesting, perhaps, as the most perfect, remnant of antiquity in Goomlí, is the *Rampol*, or portal of Rama, from whose generalissimo, Hanuman, as will be seen, the Jaitwas derive their origin. It is on the western face; but the pencil alone is competent to give a notion of its sculpture or its architecture. Three pilasters on each side support architraves composed of overlaying masses of stone, and on either side of this the most ancient form of arch, and in powerful contrast thereto, are two *pointed arches*, though evidently less ancient than the other; but as Goomlí, on indubitable evidence, has been utterly abandoned for nearly *eight hundred years*, how can we escape the conclusion that they must be Hindu? Sculptured designs of a most extraordinary character cover the whole; in some compartments, as in the ruins of Barolli and elsewhere, the noblest animal, man, is in conflict with the noblest beast; in another he is represented on his steed, and while the horse is rearing, the rider is loosing an arrow from his bow. Again, there are groups of male

and

and female figures, descriptive of some mythical episode; but, stranger still, satyrs like Pan occur, human to the waist, and goat below!

From the 'Gate of Rama,' I proceeded to the monumental *pallias* of the Jaitwas, overgrown with reeds and the thorny *mimosa;* many are thrown down, and the characters upon all are nearly obliterated. By diligent search, however, I obtained the memorials of five, for which, though brief, I felt highly grateful to the Destroyer, as they fully confirm the family legends regarding the destruction of Goomlí. These attest that the Rajpoot is no egotist, and that he was not in the habit of ascribing all the virtues under heaven to him who fell in his country's cause, the simple name and the date of self-devotion appearing to have sufficed for the eulogy of the deceased; thus:—

S. 1112, on the 7th of the month of *Pos* .... *Dhalota.*
S. 1112, on the 13th of *Cartica* .... *Bharug.*
S. ...., Vikut, Oomra and Venaji Jaiti, Huria-bunya Chohan, and Soonsirwa Jaitwa.
S. 1118, The full moon of *Phalgun* (Spring), on Monday, the Mahraja Harí Sing, Jaitwa.

S. 1119, The 6th of the month *Cartica* (December), *Veera Jaitwa.*

Thus the few of these remains, which presented any thing in the shape of a date, are as early as from A.D. 1056 to A.D. 1063, or thirty to forty years after the invasion of Mahmood of Ghizni; we shall see presently how far these dates accord with the destruction and fall of Goomlí.

On our return to camp at Bhanwul, we had the pleasure to find Major Barnewell, the Political Agent for this province (accompanied by Dr. Macadam), who had come from the capital of the Jam to meet us. To his courtesy I am indebted for the account I am enabled to draw

draw up of the Jaitwa princes of Goomlí. Already I had sketched an outline of their history from the oral traditions of an intelligent Charun, the living chronicle of these regions, who was likewise conversant with the general history of Saurashtra; but Major Barnewell sent to Poorbunder, on the coast, where the present chief of the Jaitwas resides, and his messenger returned accompanied by the family bard and the books of chronicles and kings.

The Jaitwa is one of the oldest Rajpoot families of the peninsula, and their power, about the period of the irruption from Ghizni, appears to have embraced the whole western nook, bounded by the Bhadra and the gulf of Cutch, and including the subdivisions of Hallour, Burrira (the Burda of the maps), and the western portion of Jhalawar. Although they boast of perfect independence at this period, it is evident from the annals of Anhulwarra, that they must have been under a feudal subjection to the Balharas. Since the destruction of Goomlí, the Jaitwa power has been on the wane, and the encroachments of his neighbour, the Jam, have confined him to a small tract south of the Burda hills, yielding not above one lac of annual revenue. Yet, despite this diminution of territory, the "Poonchería Ranas," or long-tailed princes, of Poorbunder, continue to hold up their heads amongst the smaller nobility of the land, and, proud of the ancient blood which circulates in their veins, look down with a sort of scorn upon their peasant suzerain, the Guicowar.

As I waded through the *Buhae vansa* (Book of Genealogies) of the Jaitwas, I felt the full force of St. Paul's advice to Timothy, "not to give heed to fables and endless genealogies." My two days of labour, however, were repaid by the consciousness that I, at least, knew as much as they did themselves of their origin. Names, with few facts, fewer dates, made the sum of this tradition. Yet I bore with exemplary patience the recital of a list of one hundred and forty-five princes, from the foundation to the destruction of Goomlí, with their intermarriages, the names of their wives and tribes,—hoping to be able by synchronisms to make something of this extensive chain of pedigree, which would be honoured even amongst the Cimbri of Wales. The book proved one of the greatest curiosities I had ever examined, and an excellent specimen of the craft.

As a curious instance of the distortion of mind that can record such absurdities, I will subjoin a single extract, which may vie with any ever concocted by a Scald or herald of the west. I have elsewhere had to remark on similar fables in the origin of tribes, invented to cover their barbarous origin. They pretend that the progenitor of these "long-tailed" chiefs came from Socotra, an island at the entrance of the Red Sea, (known to have been colonized at an early age by Greeks, Arabs, Egyptians, and Hindus, congregated for mercantile objects,*) which they classically term Sankhó-dwâra, 'the gate of the shell.' This personage was the generalissimo of Rama, the monkey-god Hanuman, who led his armies to Lanka, for the recovery of his wife, Síta. The maternal parent of the Jaitwas was no other than a *Macar*, (a marine animal, spoken of by Menu,) either a shark or an alligator. On the victorious return of Rama and his chivalry from Lanka, Macar-d'huraj ('standard of the Macars') was landed by his mother on the western coast of Saurashtra, there to establish a human race of sovereigns. But as distinction is transmitted *ex parte paternâ*, the mother, as the witty Gibbon remarks, going for nothing, the patriarchal Jaitwa bore one of the physical characteristics of his sire, in an elongation of the spine,

* Edin. Review, No. cxxiv.

spine, which, like that of the races described by Lord Monboddo and Dr. Plot, has gradually worn away in the succession of many generations, and the degeneracy of his posterity; so that the family bard found some difficulty in solving the question, whether the present incumbent had aught beyond the title of "*pooncheria*," though he stoutly contended for a superfluity of down in Prince Sontân, only four generations ago.*

Passing over the improbable period, and taking the more rational Charun as my assistant, we must endeavour to reduce these wild chronologies to something like reason and common sense. The first capital of this stranger race, the Macars, from Socotra, was erected on the spot where Macard'huraj was first landed, and named *Srinagara;* and the affix of *d'huraj*, or 'banner,' was borne by the princes until the time of Indrajeet. His son, Sil, changed both the name of the tribe and the capital. He founded Goomlí, and, by an obvious metonymy, assumed the name of *Camar* in lieu of *Macar*. Sil Camar went on a pilgrimage to the Ganges, and had the honour to receive the hand of the daughter of Anungpal, the Tüar prince of Dehli. Could we place any confidence in the records of the Jaitwas, (and in this they are supported by tradition,) we have at once a date for the foundation of Goomlí; for Anungpal was the regenerator of Dehli, whose era was S. 749, or A.D. 693. Even with this antiquity a Jaitwa might be satisfied, and a single glance at Goomlí confirms its truth. So much has been said of the northern tribes from central Asia, which have at various periods migrated into

* The credulous "father of history," who would have taken for gospel these chronicles of the Jaitwas, speaking of the Sileni, the companions of Dionysus or Osiris, the god of Nyssa, the first who reigned in that island, and who was so very ancient that none knew his origin, says, "forasmuch as he had a tail growing out of his rump, his posterity, partaking of his nature, had the same badge."

into these lands, that we shall merely remark, without disputing the Socotra origin, that the tribe of Camar is or was one of note in higher Asia; nor is it impossible that the legend of descent from the monkey-god has been invented to cover their "barbarian" origin. The Jaitwas have intermarried for ages with the Yadus of Joonagurh, the Ballas of Dhank, or Pra-puttun, with the Gohils of Mongy-puttun, the Sodas of Oomurkote; and last, not least, the Chaoras, who may dispute with the Yadus the ancient settlement in this peninsula. Nay, of this tribe (the Chaora) I learned, amongst their remains here, that they assert the same origin as the Jaitwas; "they came beyond sea from Socotra Bate, or 'the island of Socotra,' in the Red Sea, and first fixed in Okamundala, thence they went to Prachee Puttun, &c. &c."

The fourth prince from Sil, called Phool-Camar, erected the temple to the sun, still existing in Srinagar; and his successor, Bheem, constructed the castle on the summit of the Burda hills, overhanging the city of Goomlí, and called after him Bheemkote. My *compagnon de voyage*, Mr. Williams, who scrambled up, describes it as very extensive, and built of large hewn stones, closely fitted to each other without cement, though there are appearances of their having been clamped with iron or lead. There was a tank for water. But this strong-hold of the Jaitwas is now a receptacle for wild beasts, and my friend's spirit of research roused a boar from his lair.

The eighth prince is stated in the chronicle to have defeated Kurrun Bhagail; but an acquaintance with the annals of Anhulwarra detects this anachronism: for, instead of being victor over this celebrated prince of the Solankhi dynasty, Goomlí was actually destroyed during his reign.

The tenth prince, Bhanji, is made to invade Cutch, capture its then metropolis,

metropolis, Canthi-kote, and likewise the famed city of Bumunwarro,* in Sinde.

The fourteenth prince, Ramạ, is stated to have been cotemporary with Rao Choorchund Yadu, of Joonagurh, whose name appears in the Girnar inscriptions.

Mehap, the successor of Rama, married the daughter of the Cathi chief of Tullaye: a circumstance proving the "barbarian" origin of the Jaitwa.

There is nothing worthy of record until we reach Khemoo, the twenty-second prince of Goomlí; and his name is only worth preservation as being associated with that of his minister, Jaitoh, whose caste was the *cheepah*, or printers, to whose munificence is ascribed the noble reservoir in Goomlí before alluded to.

The twenty-fifth prince, Adit, had a son named Hurpal, who espoused the daughter of an Aheer, or of the pastoral tribe, and their issue are the Babrias of Dedan, occupying twelve villages, extending as far as Oona, Dailwarra.

Others succeed, some of whom intermarried with the aboriginal tribe of Mhér; and of this mixed issue, and bearing the maternal name, there are not less than two thousand, subject to the Jaitwa chief, capable of bearing arms.

At length, with the eighty-fifth prince, (who, being born under the Jeyt constellation, received this name,) the existing patronymic of Camari was exchanged for Jeytwa, or, as I write it, following custom, Jaitwa; and with this new appellation they assumed or received a new dignity, in the title of Maha-raja.

The

* Sheodadpoor is yet known as Kote-Bumun, and probably the Bumunwasso of my inscriptions, and the poems of Chund.

The ninetieth prince, Champ-sén, sheltered the celebrated Hamira, of the Soomra race, when expelled Sinde. This is the prince during whose reign the Caggar river (which, issuing from the grand northern chain, once watered the Indian desert) dried up, according to the traditional couplet still extant, but which was of little value until the name of Hamir synchronized with the annals of Anhulwarra. In this reign, the Jaitwa chronicle gives us a long account of royal nuptials at the court of Keneksén Çhohan. Amongst the sutiors are said to be Hamir of Méwar, and the Chaora king of Anhulwarra; but the "long-tailed" Jaitwa carried off the prize. Unfortunately for the chronicle, Hamir of Méwar lived four centuries after the destruction of Goomlí.

The hundredth prince of Goomlí, named Bhanji, took prisoner in battle prince Kurrun, the heir-apparent of Anhulwarra; and, as the price of his ransom, had the present title of Rana conferred on him by the Balharae. With the name of Bhanji, we reach something like a standing-place in the interminable ladder of Jaitwa genealogy. In this reign "the Ghorí Sûltân had his garrison *(thânêe)* at Mangrole;* he came to see Goomlí and Srinagara, and became the *adopted brother* of the Jaitwa queen." Bhanji was succeeded by Seoji, whose son, and heir to the sceptre of the Jaitwas, was named Salamun.

In a neighbouring state, the daughter of a Chohan chieftain had the gift of poesy, and her productions were the theme of universal admiration: nor did she put her light under a bushel, but, with that freedom granted to the Rajpoot fair in those chivalrous days (prior to the Islamite

* Mangrole is stated to have then been occupied, as it was centuries after, and I believe still is, by tne Macwhanas, said to be a branch of the Húns, and probably a colony of this race, while reigning at Minagara.

Islamite coming amongst them), she used to circulate her incomplete couplets, challenging the princely Komârs around to fill them up. One of these poetic circulars reached Goomlí, and in full durbar was placed by the itinerant bard of the Chohans in the hands of Salamun, who in an instant improvised a completion of the couplet, and in due time received the promised reward—the hand of this Sappho of the Chohans. But the king of the Jaitwas, instead of feeling pride in his son's successful talent, visited it with jealous wrath, sentencing him to *desvati*, or banishment. Salamun, with his bride, sought shelter in Sinde, from whose prince he received the lands of Doba and Dharaja for his support. There he remained, and had a numerous progeny, who, with himself, became converts to Islam; and, according to tradition, it was his son who brought an army from Sinde, and overturned Goomlí.

Without any apparent intention, the tale which occasionally adorns the dry genealogies of the Hindu bard has some moral or didactic tendency, and it is rarely that the overthrow of thrones is not ascribed to some act of impiety. The rape of a brazier's daughter, and its consequences, drove the princes of Goomlí from the throne, and in lieu of being lords of almost all the western peninsula, not a tithe of their ancient possessions was left them. The brazier's daughter was virtuous, and we may suppose beautiful; she rejected with indignation the base overtures of her sovereign, and feeling insecure against his power, sought the protection of the altar. But the mad passion of the prince rendered him blind to all consequences; he demanded that she should be delivered up, and this being refused, violated the sanctuary, and dragged his victim forth amidst the curses of the priests, who, imprecating vengeance on him and his race, slew themselves before the altar of the god. Soon after came the invader from Sinde, when Goomlí

was

was invested, and defended for six months. All that was precious to the people, their families and children, were placed in Bheemkote, whose defence was entrusted to the Mhérs, whilst the prince, his chiefs, and auxiliary Rajpoots, defended the *tulaîti*, or lower town. As the siege slackened at night, the defenders used to visit their families in Bheemkote, of which the besiegers took advantage, entered Goomlí, and, following up their success, scaled Bheemkote. An indiscriminate massacre followed, in which Seoji, the Tarquin of Goomlí, his kindred and friends, were cut to pieces: their names are enumerated, and amongst them are many of the ancient tribe of Dâby. The date of this catastrophe in the chronicle, as in the oral traditions of the bard, is S. 1109 (A.D. 1053), three years anterior to any date found on the monumental *pallias*. The *Asuras* (as the Islamites are generally styled by the Rajpoot bard) are distinctly stated to have worn long beards; and it is added, that, "having read the *Koran* in the temple," they forthwith returned to Sinde.

I have repeatedly drawn attention to those cities, as Cheetore, Goomlí, &c., on which the *tilâc*, or imprecation of the suttee, has been pronounced, reminding one of the curses of the Jewish prophets against Egypt, Edom, and Tyre; and of that denunciation, so powerfully and awfully, yet so simply, depicted in Holy Writ, that "they should be desolate in the midst of the countries that are desolate," so characteristic of the condition of Goomlí, which, in its lonely ruins, appears as if the wing of the angel of destruction had swept over it. It has all the marks of a city suddenly abandoned. The solemn vow extends even to the very stones, which accounts for the perfect state of the relics, seldom seen in any city gradually depopulated and deserted. Two awful warnings sufficed to perpetuate the suttee imprecation,

cation, and to protect the ruins of Goomlí. The first was in the example of Morewarra, built entirely from the ruins of the Jaitwa capital, and thrown to the ground by one of those visitations to which this region appears devoted, an earthquake, which was construed into a punishment for disregarding the anathema. So of Bhanwul, where several houses, constructed from its materials, so conveniently at hand, fell simultaneosly, burying their inmates in the fall. The remains have, therefore, little to fear from man, and may exist, as objects of curiosity, until some future throe of nature shall lay prostrate the ancient city of the Camari.

Thus we have two events in the history of the Jaitwas, the foundation of Goomlí in S. 749, and its destruction in S. 1109, each established on good grounds, the former by Sil Camar, the cotemporary of Anungpal of Dehli, (whose epoch we have established elsewhere by chronological tables, and proved by synchronisms with the annals of other states,) while its downfall is attested by the *pallias*, or monumental stones: a few years later, perhaps S.1119, might be adopted in preference to the chronicle. Between these two dates, including a period of three hundred and sixty years, we can admit only twenty crowned heads, and, in happy confirmation of this, my friend the Charun assured me that this was the number his list contained, and that the catastrophe happened "seven hundred and seventy years ago," an account in perfect accordance with the *pallias*. There is an intermediate period worthy of a passing observation, that of Singji, ten generations anterior to the fall of Goomlí, and who in the chronicle is said to have married a princess of Cheetore. Allowing the usual average of twenty-three years to a reign, this would place Singji in A.D. 823, which approximates sufficiently to that grand event recorded in the annals of Méwar, the first invasion of the Islamite, when all the Rajpoot chivalry assembled for the defence of Cheetore ; and amongst "the eighty-four princes whose cushions were spread within its walls," that of the Jaitwa chief is distinctly mentioned by the bard of Méwar. The circumstance recorded in the Jaitwa annals as having led to this intercourse, and carried its leader from "the land's-end" of Hinduism to protect its interests in the person of the king of Cheetore, though in itself puerile, becomes valuable as it shows that the story of *its* singular parentage is not of modern invention. An itinerant minstrel of Cheetore, in his vagabond journeyings, reached the court of the Jaitwa prince, by whom he was laden with gifts, and made the medium of a proposal of marriage ; to which the Rawul of Cheetore indignantly sent answer, that "he would bestow no daughter of his on the issue of a monkey-father and shark-mother." This refusal, coupled with the reproachful stigma, deeply affected the Jaitwa ; whereupon, the family Bhât repaired to the shrine of Hursid, on the summit of the Burda hills, and performed sacrifice and penance so severe, that the patroness of his order appeared, and *taught him the ancient genealogies of the Jaitwas*, with which he repaired to Cheetore, and conquered the scruples of its prince. In this curious admission, we can at once account for the "one-hundred and forty-five crowned heads" of the Pooncheria princes, who melt into thin air when tried by a synchronical process. Moreover, Hursid was no conjurer, and "the sun of the Hindus" not over bright, in allowing his fair daughter to be craftily transferred to the arms of the satyr-chief. Through these loose anecdotes we may, however, discern true historical facts, all appertaining to that dark, but interesting period, the few centuries preceding Islâm in India, when new tribes were pouring in, and amalgamating with the older Rajpoot.

It

It will be recollected by those who bestow a passing thought on Hindu chronology, that the Balabhi inscription, so often alluded to, contains no less than four distinct *samvats*, or eras, one, the latest, of which is styled *Seehoh*. Thus the Balabhi Samvat 945 = S. Vicrama 1320 = Seehoh S. 151, which — 1320, leaves S. 1169, or A.D. 1113, for its institution. At this period, the potent Sidrâj, king of Anhulwarra, was lord-paramount over all these regions. Is it likely that this, the greatest of all the Balharas, would have permitted the institution of a new era in a nook of Saurashtra, the nearest of his eighteen kingdoms? Yet to no other than the Seehoh of Goomlí can it be applicable. But Goomlí was destroyed, and its impious monarch gone to receive his reward. The Charun confirms the whole legend of the unhappy couplet, the banishment of Salamun, and "his protection by Jam Oonur of the Sinde-Summa dynasty, whose son, Bamunea, led the army to avenge and reinstate him; but Salamun, disgusted with a place where the blood of a father and of Brahmins had been shed, and which had been further desecrated by the anathemas of the suttee, abandoned altogether his native land and returned to Sinde, where he married two wives, one, the daughter of the Jhareja of Dhumarka; the other, from the Soomra of Oomurkote—thus his stock became Mooslem, and still holds the lands of Doba Dharajee, in Sinde.

The offspring of Salamun by the poetic Chohan returned to the peninsula, and established himself at Rampoor, where the family resided for many generations. Now as Goomlí was destroyed in S. 1109, and the Seehoh Samvat commenced in S. 1169, we have only to conclude that the son of Salamun and grandson of Seehoh commemorated his new era by the foundation of his new capital, very naturally naming it after the last lord of Goomlí.

To conclude this eventful story. The Jaitwas continued at Rampoor until dispossessed by the Jam, on which event they retired to the sea-coast, and erected temporary shelter *(chaya)*. The buildings gradually attained the dignity of a city, which yet bears the name of Chaya; and although they subsequently raised upon the site of Sudamapoor the present capital, Poorbunder, the installation of the Jaitwas continues to take place at Chaya. Eleven generations have elapsed since this last change. The present Rana of the Jaitwas is called Khémji, and is the *bhanaij*, or maternal nephew, of the Jam. He has two wives, one from the Bhalla of Dhank, the other from the Jhalla of Choara Rampoor. In this admixture of Cat'hi, Cunani, Mhér, Balla, Jhalla, and Jam, the Camari blood has not degenerated; and although they are enrolled by the chronicles of Saurashtra amongst the "*Chatees Rajcula*," or thirty-six royal races, we may assert that they have become Hindu only from locality and circumstance. The *Capit d'huraj*, or banner bearing the figure of Hanuman, still precedes his descendant in all processions, and the *pooncheria*, or tail, will continue to be the subject of *muzzak* or *badinage* amongst the kinsman of their wives while a Jaitwa remains in the land. Hursid is still their tutelary divinity, but his ancient shrine in the Burda is under the ban, and a new temple has been raised at Meannee. Bhalnat'h, Maha-deo, however, divides the homage with Hursid; but all are types of destruction and reproduction.

NUGDEAH.—DECEMBER 24th.—Seven coss, or fourteen miles. A dreary march through desolation; the three or four hamlets we passed were peopled by Aheers, who, here and there, in the midst of *babool* jungle and rank grass, had tilled a few fields, protected from wild beasts by hedges of impenetrable *cactus*. One of these villages, called Rajirio, possessed some interest, from having belonged to a family of Charuns,

who,

who, on the invasion of Mahmoud, committed *traga*, or suicide, the sole revenge of the bard against the oppressor. The *pallias*, or sacrificial pillars of these sons of song, confirm the tradition, and are still the objects of religious homage to their descendants. This day my eyes beheld the magnificent mount Girnar for the last time.

Deolah.—December 25th.—Six coss. About half-way we crossed the Lanni rivulet, also called the Okapât, near the village of Asiabhadra, the ancient boundary of Okamundala to the east. To the north is Hollur. Nearly the entire population is Aheer, but they are said to have no proprietary right in the soil, which belongs exclusively to the Rajpoots, who are very thinly scattered over this region. For the first time, I heard the Aheers speak of their origin; they claim to be of Yadu-vansa, and to have followed in the train of the shepherd-king, Kanya, from the pastoral Surasena, on the Jumna. At all events, their pretensions have a classical foundation; to the nomadic character their claim is indisputable. Take them altogether, the Aheers are not surpassed in personal qualifications by any class in the peninsula, and the *matériel* of agriculture, as ploughs, carts, and cattle, is unequalled throughout India; yet are the villages mean, averaging about thirty huts, and there is more of personal than domestic comfort. Meannee, whence we obtained some excellent fish, lay four coss on our left.

Mooktasirr.—December 26th.—Eight coss, full eighteen miles. But two hamlets, and these ten miles apart, *viz.* Sutteepoor, two miles from Deolah, consisting of twenty-five families of Aheers; and Bogant, of about fifty. Unequalled pastures cover these highlands, from which all the day we have been gradually descending, and herds of fine cattle were thriving on the luxuriant *dhoorba* and other grasses. The lake of beatitude,—such is the interpretation of 'Mooktasirr,'

tasirr,'—was covered with wild fowl, and in its bed is found that rich yellow mineral, of the jasper family, so much used in decorating the temples of these regions.

Dwarica.—December 27th.—Ten coss. From "the lake of bliss" to "the door *(dwara)* of the deity,"* a distance of full twenty miles, all was barren and desolate. There was, or rather had been, one village, called Maddi,† upon the brink of the ocean, but it had remained deserted since it was attacked by pirates some years ago. About four hundred yards west of this deserted village is the Khary rivulet, its *embouchure* closed by a bar of sand; which if removed, this nook *(coont)* of the world *(juggut)* would, as in the days of Crishna, be insular. We skirted the ocean rolling its breakers upon the sands, or hard concrete rock, the substratum of the island, barren of every thing but the *t'hoor*, or *cactus*, which thrives equally amidst barren rocks or sand. When about six miles distant, the spire of the temple of Dwarica became visible, and within a mile of it we forded another Khary, whose waters covered the saddle-flaps. Passing through the fortified town, we took a glance at the sacred fane, on our way to the camp, pitched at the 'Land's-end' of the Hindu.

Bar. 30° 4'.—Therm. at 6 a.m. 62°; noon 85°; sunset 79°.

The temple of Dwarica, the most celebrated of all the shrines raised to Crishna, is built upon an eminence rising from the sea-shore, and surrounded by a fortified wall, which likewise encircles the town, from which it is, however, separated by a lofty partition-wall, through which it is necessary to pass to see it to advantage. The architectural character of this temple is that to which we are accustomed to give the name

* *Dwarica-nat'h.*

† Maddi bearing S.E. dist. 1½ mile. I took the east bearing of the Goomlí hill, bearing S. 72° E., and thus these bearings will connect shore and shore

name of pagoda. It may be said to consist of three parts: the *munduff*, or hall of congregation; the *devachna*, or *penetralia* (also termed *gabarra*); and the *sikra*, or spire.

To begin with the *munduff*, which is here square, measuring twenty-one feet internally, and five distinct stories high. Each story is colonnaded, the lower being twenty feet in height, and of the same square form to the last, where the architraves are laid transversely to form a base for the surmounting dome, whose apex is seventy-five feet from the pavement. Four massive pillars on each face of the square form the foundation for this enormous weight; but these being inadequate to sustain it, intermediate pillars to each pair have been added, to the sacrifice of all symmetry. A colonnaded piazza surrounds the lowest story, of about ten feet in breadth, from which to the north, south, and west, portions are projected, likewise colonnaded. Each story of the *munduff* has an internal gallery, with a parapet of three feet in height, to prevent the incautious from falling. These parapets, divided into compartments, had been richly sculptured; but the chisel of Islâm had been also at work, and defaced every graven image, nor is there enough remaining to disclose the original design: nevertheless, this obliteration has been done with care, so as not to injure the edifice.

The basement, or square portion of the temple, from which springs the *sikra*, was the *sanctum* in former ages, when *Budha-trivicrama* was the object of adoration, anterior to the heresy of Crishna, who was himself a worshipper of Budha, whose miniature shrine is still the *sanctum-sanctorum* of Dwarica, while Crishna is installed in a *cella* beyond. The *sikra*, or spire, constructed in the most ancient style, consists of a series of pyramids, each representing a miniature temple, and each diminishing with the contracting spire, which terminates at

one

one hundred and forty feet from the ground. There are seven distinct stories before this pyramidal spire greatly diminishes in diameter; each face of each story is ornamented with open porches, surmounted by a pediment supported by small columns. Each of these stories internally consists of column placed on column, whose enormous architraves increase in bulk in the decreasing ratio of the superimposed mass, and although the majority at the summit are actually broken by their own weight, yet they are retained in their position by the aggregate unity. The capitals of these columns are quite plain, having four cross projections for the architraves to rest on; and by an obtuseness in the *Silpi* not to be accounted for, several of these architraves do not rest on the columns, but on the projections; and, strange to say, the lapse of centuries has proved their efficiency, though Vitruvius might have regarded the innovation with astonishment. The entire fabric, whose internal dimensions are seventy-eight feet by sixty-six, is built from the rock, which is a sandstone of various degrees of texture, forming the substratum of the island;—it has a greenish hue, either from its native bed, or from imbibing the saline atmosphere, which, when a strong light strikes upon it, gives the mass a vitreous transparent lustre. Internally it has a curious conker-like appearance. The architraves are, however, an exception, being of the same calcareous marine conglomerate, not unlike travertine, as already described in the temple of Somnat'h.

The foundation of this shrine must have been laid in the solstice, as its front varies ten points from the meridian line; and as the *Silpi*, or architect, in these matters, acts under the priest, we may infer that the *Surya Siddhaṇta* was little known to the Goorgoocha Brahmins, the ministrants of their times, who took the heliacal rising of those days

as

as the true east point; its breadth is, therefore, from N.N.W. to S.S.E. Contrary to custom, it has its back to the rising sun, and faces the west.

Crishna is here adored under his form of Rinchor, when he was driven from his patrimony, Surasena, by the Budhist king of Magadha. A covered colonnaded piazza connects the *cella* of Crishna with a miniature temple dedicated to Deoki, his mother; and, within the ample court are various other shrines, one of which, in the S.E. angle, contains the statue of Budha Tri-vicrama, or, as he is familiarly called, Tricam-Rae and Trimnat'h, which is always crowded with votaries. Opposite to this, or at the S.W. angle of the main temple, is a smaller one, dedicated to another form of Crishna, Madhu* Rae, and between these is a passage leading by a flight of steps to the Goomtee, a small rivulet, whose embouchure with the ocean is especially sacred, though it would not wet the instep to cross it. From the grand temple to the *sungum*, or point of confluence, where there is a small temple to Sungum-Narayn, the course of the Goomtee is studded with the cenotaphs of those pilgrims who were fortunate enough to surrender life at this "*dwara* of the deity." Amongst them are four of the five Pandu brothers, countenancing the tradition that the fifth proceeded across the Hemachil, where, being lost sight of, he is said to have perished in its snows, and whither he was accompanied by Baldeo, the Indian Hercules, whose statue is enshrined in the south-west corner of the great *munduff*, several steps under ground. Baldeo is represented on his ascent from *pâtâl*, or the infernal regions, after some monstrous combat.

* Madhú is one of the poetical names of Crishna, *viz.* the intoxicator, from *Madhwa,* 'strong drink;' and *Madhú,* 'the bee'—perhaps originating our *Mead.*

combat. At "the shrine of confluence" there was a very aged ministrant, called Byragi, said to have passed his hundredth year. He had been a great traveller, especially to all the *teeruts* of Vishnu, both in and out of India: but I found it difficult to extract from him any information. Not the least curious or interesting sight, were the hulls of two piratical ships, hauled high and dry upon the beach, close to the shrine of Sungum-Râe, the divinity under whose colours and protection they scoured these seas.

My search for inscriptions was unrewarded, for though I did obtain two, they were so designedly obliterated as to be perfectly illegible; and though the pilgrims and devotees of all ages and of all countries have covered the walls with their names, I could not, after much labour even amongst these humblest of records, obtain any thing worth noting in my journal. The ministers about the temple of "the god of thieves, as of harmony," are the most ignorant of their order, and the *Dwarica-Mahatma* is a dull prosaic ritual, without the redeeming admixture of profane events, which such works generally contain. The priests are expert enough in putting the *chaup* or seal of the god upon the arms of the votaries, and by a process similar to that employed by our sailors. The operation is performed at the *sungum;* the hair of the head being first cut off, as an offering to the deity of the waters, and the fees being paid, they can triumphantly appeal to this sign of their faith on return to their native land.

They ascribe the erection of this temple, over that of the more ancient fane of Tri-vicrama Budha, to Bujr-nâb, prince of Okamandala, and grandson of Crishna, whose posterity continued a century after the great international war and dispersion of the Yadus to various regions

regions upon and west of the Indus. Bujr-nâb himself eventually retired to Bhadri, in the mountains of the north, and his offspring, by intermarriage with the inhabitants of that region (called *danoos* in the tradition), returning to the "Land's End," took possession of Sankhodwara, and erected Kulore-kote, where they ruled a thousand years. At this juncture, two Yavanas appeared, called Raïb and Saïb, who slew these, and in their issue maintained it for one thousand five hundred years, when Mahomed Dhoonkra, in whose possession was the magic ring of Vicramaditya, came from Dehli, having already by it obtained Gor and Gujni. The descendants of Raïb and Saïb, who were of the Belem tribe,* were put to death by Mahomed, who seized upon Kulore-kote and Oka. Then came Keneksen Chaora from the east, whose descendants ruled during many generations, until Oméd Sing, of the Rahtore tribe, came from Marwar, slew the Chaoras and took possession of the "nook,"† since which it has been called *Wadail*, or *Badhail*, from *bad'ha*, 'massacre.' Bate, or '*the* island,' continued to be the capital, and the offspring of these Rahtores, by intermarriage with the pre-existing classes, were called Wagairs, and were famed for their daring piracies. It was during the time of Samla-Manik, Wagair, that Arungzebe came, destroying all the temples, on which occasion that of Dwarica had its *sikra*, or spire, thrown down; but Samla had previously removed the statue of Rinchor to Bate, where it still remains. The descendants of Samla-Manik continued to hold the lands of Oka, and pursue their piratical practices, until S. 1876 (A.D. 1820), when Mulloo Manik's atrocities drew upon him the vengeance of the English. Such is the pith of the story which connects

* Tradition assigns to this tribe and its chief, Gorí Belem, the destruction of Pali'thâna.

† This later portion of the traditional history of Okamandala is confirmed by the Rahtore annals.

connects the installation of Crishna at the 'Land's-End' of the Hindu, the expulsion of his successors by the Yavanas, or Greeks, the invasion of Mahomed (*qu.* bin Cassim ?), and the final extirpation of the pirates of Sungum-Râe, with the death of their leader, Mulloo Manik, by an army led by my friend and schoolfellow, the Hon. Colonel Lincoln Stanhope.

It would be a waste of time to erect hypotheses on such loose traditional tales of Asuras and Yavanas, of the Belem chiefs who succeeded, and who in turn were sacrificed by Mahomed, or Mahmood, followed by the Chaoras and Rahtores; but the three latter events are historical facts, and succeed in chronological order. Of the Belem we have already traditional notice in the destruction of Pali-t'hana, and we have full knowledge of the fact that the Yavanas, or Greeks, under Apollodotus and Menander, conquered these regions of the *Suroi,* at a period not very wide of the tradition. Their predecessors, the *danoos,* or Asuras, may have been Assyrians, which would account not only for the name of this peninsula of Sun-worshippers, but for its singular inscriptions.

CHAPTER XX.

Beerwalla.—Aramra.—Ancient Dwarica.—Goreja.—Graves of Yavanas.—*Pallias* of Pirates.—Bate, or Sankho-dwara.—Tradition of Crishna.—Shells of Bate.—The Rajpoot war-shells.—Pirates' Castle.—Shrines to the Hindu Apollo.—Meera Bae, the Rajpoot poetess.—Historical notices of the sea-kings.—Devotion of the Pirates.—The extent of their navigation.

December 30th and 31st.—Aramra and Bate. For eighteen miles we marched along the margin of the gulf, on an excellent road, passing the walled town of Beerwalla, and the little castle of Cutchgur'h. The ancient and interesting town of Aramra is separated from Bâte by the sea, but all was waste, and the *t'hoor*, or *cactus*, was the sole natural product throughout the morning's march. Some herds of fine buffaloes, tended by Rebarris, contrived to crop herbage enough to fatten them, and afforded the only symptoms of life. The piratical habits of ages have inflicted the vice of barrenness on their lands ; yet we found the industrious Loharra Bhatti, who may be met with wherever money can be made, mixed with the Kharwa mariner, and the piratical Waghair or Macwahana, the latter being the most numerous class. The Pâtel of Aramra, however, still vaunts his pure Rahtore blood, and if correct, he may indeed be vain of his descent. With several other sites, Aramra puts in its claim, and with good reason, to be considered as *mool* or 'ancient' Dwarica; its own appearance, and the many decayed shrines about it, furnishing strong evidence in favour of the boast. Here the pilgrim can receive the seal of Crishna, as well as at the greater shrine; but instead of the Brahmin, a Charun stamps the votary with the *chaup* : the fee is eleven rupees, from which not even the mendicant Byragi is exempted.

There

There is much that is interesting in the environs of Aramra, in which are several temples, but all bearing testimony to the rough usage of the Mahomedans. A colony of owls had found shelter in that dedicated to *Gordhun-nât'h*,* or 'lord of the mount of wealth,' one of the innumerable names of Crishna. At Goreja, or Goreecha, which we passed in the morning, and which they term Cacha Gujni, we saw the graves of two celebrated Yavanas, whose names of Assah and Purrah are still preserved, and the subject of wonderful narratives. They were upwards of twenty feet in length and of proportional breadth; but there are five others at Aramra said to be thirty-six cubits long and six broad, indicating that the Asuras, or Yavanas, who first dwelt in this "nook of the world," were veritable giants. Burckhardt, when descanting on the tomb of Neby Osha (the prophet Hosea), in Palestine, says, "It is in the form of a coffin, thirty-six feet long, three broad, and three and a half in height, constructed in conformity with the notion of the Turks, who thought all their forefathers were giants, especially the prophets before Mahomed;" and he adds, that "the tomb of Noah in Cœlo-Syria was still larger." If these Asuras of Aramra were of Aramean stock, the emigrants from the old Assyria, they would in all these practices be following the customs of their forefathers.

Let us quit the graves of the giants of Aramra for its more interesting memorials, the *pallias* of the pirates, which speak in a language not to be misunderstood, albeit a species of hieroglyphic, though one which will not admit of a double interpretation; for amidst the mouldering

* Gord'hun, a contraction of Goverd'hun, is a hill in the pastoral land of the Suraseni, where Crishna was born, and which first attested his miracles. It still attracts myriads, and is annually lustrated with milk.

mouldering cenotaphs and broken tomb-stones, there remain two, on which are sculptured in high relief "the ships of Tricam-râe" engaged in combat. One of these is a three-masted vessel, pierced for guns; the other is of a more antique form and character, having but one mast, and none of those modern inventions of war. Both are represented in the act of boarding the chase. One of the piratical sailors, with sword and shield, is depicted as springing from the shrouds; another from the bow of his ship; and it may be supposed they are the effigies of the heroes who lay here. Another *pallia* was inscribed to the memory of "Rana Raemul, who, in S. 1628 (A.D. 1572), "performed the *saka*, when attacked by the king; twenty-one of his "kindred were slain with him, and the Jaitwâní* became Suttee." *Pallias* are erected to each of the twenty-one. There was another, and the latest in date, erected to the memory of these buccaneers of Aramra, and sufficiently laconic: "S. 1819, (A.D. 1763), Jadroo Kharwa was slain on the seas." Kharwa is the most common epithet of the Hindu sailor.

January 1st 1823.—Crossed over to the Pirates' isle, emphatically called Bate, or '*the* island,' but in the classic traditions of the Hindu, Sankho-dwara, or 'the door of the shell,' one of the most sacred spots of his faith. It was here that Crishna, or Kanya,† acted the part of the Pythian Apollo, and redeemed the sacred books, slaying his Hydra foe, Takshac, who had purloined and concealed them in one of those gigantic shells, whence the island has its name. The whole history of Kanya, or Crishna, who assumed the form of Vishnu, is allegorical, but neither

* His wife, of the Jaitwa tribe.

† Kanya, or Vishnu, resembles the sun-god of the Egyptians in name as well as symbols. Kan was one name of the sun in Egypt, and his eagle-head is a well-known type.

neither devoid of interest nor incapable of solution. There is no part of their mythology more easy of illustration than this, which is allusive to the sectarian warfare carried on at this period between the new sect of Vishnuvites and the more ancient one of Budha. The races who supported the religion of Crishna are typified under his emblem, Garuda, or the eagle; while their wily adversary, the Budhist, is figured by the Tacshac, Naga, or serpent, a denomination given to the races of northern origin, which at various periods overran India, and of which were Taksiles (the friend of Alexander, the site of whose capital is still preserved in the Memoirs of Baber) and the still more famed Tacshac Salivahan, the foe of Vicrama.* In the legend of the Yadu prince, Crishna, (himself a seceder from the faith of Budha-Trivicrama to that of Vishnu, if not its founder) receiving the sacred volumes from his hydra-foe at this remote point of Hinduism, as well as his first combat with him in the Jumna, we have but the continuance of the same sectarian warfare, in which Crishna was in this instance successful, driving them before him both in the north of India and here: thus, his title of *Rinchor* was given on his defeat by Jarasindha, the king of Magadha, of the heretical faith, and at length these religious and civil conflicts led to his death, and the dispersion of the Yadu race, of which he was the chief support.†

Sankho-dwara

* On both these points I must refer the enquirer into such matters to the *Annals of Rajast'han*.

† These Yadus, I surmise to have been all originally Budhists, and of Indo-Getic origin, as their habits of polyandrism alone would almost demonstrate; and when we find the best-informed of the Jains assuring us that Nemnâth, the twenty-second Budha, was not only Yadu, but the near kinsman of Crishna, all doubt is at an end; and I am strongly inclined to pronounce decidedly, what I have before only suggested, that the Yadus are the Yute, or ancient Getes of the Jaxartes, amongst whom, according to Professor Neumann from Chinese authorities, one of the Shamanean sages sprung, eight hundred years before Christ. Both Nemnat'h and Sham-nat'h have the same personal epithets, derived from their dark complexions, the first being familiarly called Arishta-Nemi, 'the black

Sankho-dwara is still renowned for its shells, and one bank, uncovered at low water, whence they are obtained, is close to the landing-place; but as the *rin-sank'h*, or war-shell, with which he was wont to peal a blast, the onslaught to battle, no longer graces the hand of the Rajpoot in these degenerate days; its use is now restricted to the Brahmin, wherewith "to awake the gods in the morning;" to let the world know when he dines; or, what is of more importance, to form *chooris*, or bracelets, for the arms of the Hindu fair. Bengal is the best customer for the shells of Sankho-dwara; and I recollect an entire street occupied in the ancient city of Dacca by shell-cutters, all supplied from Bate. The banks are farmed of the Guicowar government by a Parsee merchant of Bombay, who contracts with the Kharwas, at the rate of twenty *korees* (from five to six rupees) per hundred, and loads them for Bombay, whence they are shipped for Bengal. The last exportation had taken place only two days before, and out of half-a-dozen, I obtained but one such as the heroes of old would have condescended to use. Perpetual allusion is made, in the martial poetry of the Rajpoot, to the "blast of the shell," which is as common as the charge of the brazen trump of our western chivalry. Of two of these, pre-eminent mention is made in the "Great War," *viz.* Crishna's own shell, named *Pan-chaên*, so ponderous that he alone could lift it; and that which belonged to his friend and brother in arms, Arjuna, called *Dacshinaverta*, from having its spiral reversed, and which fell a trophy to his rival, Bhisama, the leader of the Curus.

One

black Nemi,' the other Sham and Crishna, both also meaning 'dark-coloured;' and when this is not only confirmed by tradition, but the shrine of Budha itself is yet preserved within that of Crishna at Dwarica, we have no reason to question that his faith, prior to his own deification, was that of Budha.

One of this kind is said to be *ámaluc*, or 'without price;' and the sole one recorded besides this, belonged to the Balhara king, Sidrâj of Anhulwarra, and is said to be now in the possession of his descendant, the Solanki chief of Roopnagurh, one of the second class of nobles in Méwar: but although I have often questioned him touching his illustrious origin, I never thought of the war-shell heir-loom.

I have said that the pirates' castle was formerly called *Kullore-kote*. This castle, situated on the western side of the island, is compact and imposing, having lofty massive towers, on which there is no lack of iron ordnance, and very judiciously, the shortest and most efficient face is to the sea. It is fortunate for the lovers of the picturesque, that the determination of the last pirate chief to bury himself in its ruins was overruled; and there it will long stand as a memorial of a scourge, which from the earliest periods of history infested these waters, from the Sankho-dwara, at the entrance of the Red Sea, to the Gulf of Cutch, and the eradication of which is not the least of the benefits derived from British supremacy in the East.

As, amongst the Syro-Phœnician and Celtic people, the sun-god Belenus, or Apollo, was the patron of the mariner; so, in these lands, the sea-kings of Larice and Saurashtra almost monopolized this divinity, transferring their homage from Budha Trivicrama; nor is it less singular that with the Hindu as with the Greek mythics, the exchange of characteristics should take place between Apollo and Mercury. The arrows of Apollo, through whose influence he could hush the stormy wave, were purchased of his priestess by the Celtic mariner, who here bribes the god with a portion of his anticipated gains, whether his intents be lawful or unlawful. Accordingly, in no other region are there so many shrines to him (being almost as numerous

as

as his various forms) as at this Land's-end of the Hindu. Of these, the most ancient is that of Sankh-Narayn, and correctly the most legitimate object of worship; but the last form, Rinchor, has superseded it. His present dwelling, of the order styled *decah*, or tent-fashioned, is quite modern, having been erected about one hundred and fifty years ago by the Jam, on the invasion of Arungzebe; but the statue has been stolen, removed, and recovered, at least a dozen times. It is not a little singular, and attests better than any thing else his votaries' belief in his mortal mould, that wherever a shrine is raised to his honour, there is one to Deoki, his mother, the wife of the Yadu king, Basdeo of Mat'hura. "The divinity was asleep" when I visited the temple, and being on the point of embarkation for the opposite coast, I was obliged to decline the invitation "to wait until he awoke."

But the shrine which proved most attractive to me, was that raised by a princess of my own land, Méwar, the celebrated Meera Bâé, wife of Lakha Rana, to the pastoral divinity of the Surasení, in his genuine character as the lover of the Nine; and assuredly this Rajpoot queen was one of the most ardent of his votaries. The productions of her muse are said to have been unequalled by any of the bards of the day, and it is asserted that a *tíka*, or sequel to the *Gíta Govinda*, or canticles in honour of Kanya, will stand a comparison with the original by Jydeva. This and other odes, descriptive of the spiritual charms of her divine lover, and which still exist, are so fervidly Sapphic, as to have afforded themes for no small scandal—perhaps the malicious invention of the regular sons of rhyme, envious of her fame. But since the fact is attested, that she abandoned all the duties of her station, and that her life was passed in excursions to every land in which

Apollo was enshrined, where she danced before the god of her idolatry, in the character of one of the celestial nymphs in the mystic *rasmandala,* she afforded some ground for malice to build upon. Her lord and sovereign, however, never having entertained any jealousy or suspicion, notwithstanding, in one of these devotional ecstacies, Murali descended from his pedestal and embraced his devotee, it is but fair to infer that there was no just cause. Moreover, his son, Bikramajit, the opponent of the emperor Hemayoon, imbibed all the holy zeal of his mother, and "made offer of his own head, and the heads of one hundred thousand Rajpoots, to convey the deity from the polluted land of Vraja, daily desecrated by the blood of kine:" an undertaking which was executed by his gallant descendant, Rana Raj Sing, in the reign of the bigot Arungzebe.*

I had the satisfaction to encounter a most intelligent chieftain of the Jhala tribe, whose sister was wife to the last pirate chief of Bate, and who not only supplied me with some curious traditions regarding the origin of his own tribe, but of the *Badhails,* who had occupied the *mundala,* or region of Oka, for the last seven centuries. I had likewise the good fortune to fall in with one of the professional historians of the sacred 'nook,' from whose books of chronicles and kings I transcribed several pages.

Oméd Sing Rahtore was father to the first chief of this tribe who settled in Oka, and whose son obtained the epithet of *Badhail* from the treacherous massacre (*badha*) of the Chaoras, who then possessed this region. Aramra was the chief city of the Chaoras, and is still the *teelât,* or place of installation of the Badhails. Neither the Jhala chieftain,

* The reader who may desire to know more on the subject of this worship, may consult a paper of mine in Vol. II. of the *Transactions* of the Royal Asiatic Society.

chieftain, nor the chronicler, could give me the date of this event, or the number of generations elapsed; but the difficulty is cleared up by the annals of Marwar,* which state that a branch of the founder of this race in Maroost'hali, or the great Indian desert, settled in Oka. The unscrupulous Rahtore, who, in his extirpation of the Chaoras, merely obeyed the first impulse of the Rajpoot, which is "to get land," soon adapted himself and his hardy followers to their new mode of life, and that of their predecessors the Chaoras, whose piratical habits, as has been related in the annals of Anhulwarra, caused the destruction of Diu in the eighth century of Vicrama.†

Sungum-dharra, the *nom-de-guerre* of the sea-kings of Bate, was made the title of one who lived some generations after the first Badhail. He was the most notorious pirate who had swept the seas for ages; but his audacity at length led him into the toils—he was made prisoner, and conveyed to the king. But his spirit was as indomitable in the presence of Timoor, as on the deck of his own ship; they could not make him bow to the throne. He was not the first who experienced the clemency of these magnanimous princes. The pirate, instead of losing his head, returned to Bate with a title. He afterwards espoused the daughter of the Jhareja Rao of Cutch, and fell in an attack on Warasurra, a town belonging to the Jaitwas. Three generations after Sungum-dharra, was Rinna (the new title) Sowah, who was not inferior to him in daring intrepidity. To illustrate his gallantry we can desire no stronger terms than the language of the chronicle:—"he gave sanctuary *(sirna)* to Mozuffer, the king of Guzzerat," and not only

* *Annals of Rajast'han*, vol. ii. p. 14.

† In the additional fact, of this most remote corner of the peninsula being inhabited, even to the twelfth century, by the Chaoras, we have further confirmation of their being at one time the sovereigns of all Saurashtra; and perhaps the *Suroi* of Strabo, the opponents of Menander.

only refused to surrender him, but sent him safely in one of his own ships across the gulf, while he stood a siege in Aramra, and nobly fell in its defence. What a contrast does this pirate's conduct afford to that of Rao Bhara of Cutch (the son of Khengar, the founder of Bhooj, twelve generations ago), who bartered the person of his suppliant sovereign for the district of Morbee, in the peninsula! The emperor kept his word; he surrendered Morbee to the infamous Jhareja, but his head was the *nuzzerana*, or fine of relief for the gift, in this atrocious traffic of his allegiance;—and still further to mark his sense of the infamy of the Jhareja, and the honour of the pirate Badhail, he erected two *pallias* at the gates of Dehli, issuing an edict that whoever passed that of the Badhail should crown it with chaplets of flowers, while on that of the Jhareja the passer should bestow a blow with his slipper. Nor was the *pallia* of Jam Bhara exempt from this indignity until the period of Jam Jessa, who having by some service gained the royal favour, and being permitted to proffer any suit, intreated that the *pallia* might be taken down, or, at least, relieved from insults which affected the honour of every Jhareja.

Rinna Sowah, or Sowae, was only the title of this noble pirate, whose name was Raemul, and whose *pallia*, recording his death on the *saka* of Aramra, in S. 1628 (A.D. 1572), I had the satisfaction of discovering, as already mentioned. This date gives us the clue to this eventful epoch in the history not only of the sea-kings of Bate, but of their suzerains of Guzzerat.

The following collateral lists shew the descendants of the worthy and unworthy of that day, exhibiting nine chiefs from Raemul to Singram, a man of forty-five years of age; and eleven from the infamous Bhara to his descendant, who bears the same inauspicious name.

Rinna

Rinna Raemul,	Rae Bhara,
Akhirâj,	Meg,
Bheem,	Tumachee,
Singram,	Raedhan,
Bhajraj,	Prâg,
Dadoh,	Ghor,
Bahap,	Dessil,
Makha Bae,	Lakho,
Singram,	Ghor,
	Raedhan,
	Bhara and Desil, } brothers.

Rinna Bheem drew upon him the whole power of the Imaum of Muscat, who attacked him by land and water, in retaliation for the mischief done to his subjects by his piracies. Rao Dessil of Cutch was a partizan of the Muscat admiral on this occasion, and the small castle called Cutchgur'h was erected on the main by him to batter Kullore-kote. Several descents were made upon the pirates' isle, whose castle's strength laughed to scorn their united efforts; and the admiral having had several vessels stranded in the intricate navigation, and his ally of Bhooj being bribed by a promise of the lands around Cutchgur'h in *gros*, the fleet withdrew, and the admiral was compelled to rest satisfied with a single trophy of his success, the wooden portals of the shrine of Sankh-Narayn. These he converted forthwith into a bed; but to his horror was overturned in the night, and awoke with the infidel trophy laying over him, which, according to the legend, he forthwith sent back to Bate.

There is little of importance in the history of the pirates until

Singram,

Singram, the last of the Dharaêts of the *Sungum*, whose grandfather had been visited by an English frigate, which excited their astonishment (having never seen such a vessel before), destroying their vessels and soon reducing them to submission. The benevolent Colonel Walker, subsequently, by pacific measures, reclaimed them from their piratical habits, including them in his general arrangements for the peace of the peninsula. But his treaty, it is said, was not observed, and some ill-treatment received at the hands of the Guicowar officers, made the pirates rise upon his garrisons. At the same time, the priest of Tricum-Râe, who was prime-minister to Singram, had received a dispensation to violate his engagements, and once more to collect booty on the high seas. This sealed the fate of the lord of Sankhodwara, and the same blow which destroyed the Wagair pirates of Dwarica, annihilated the Badhails of Bate. The rapidity and severity of the vengeance, in the escalade of the strong-hold of the former by the British force under the Hon. Colonel Lincoln Stanhope, induced Singram to sue for terms, and he agreed to surrender Bate, and to live at Aramra on a stipend furnished by his suzerain, the Guicowar. It may be supposed that this surrender on his part was linked with a guarantee on ours; but, be this as it may, Aramra is no longer a place of *aram* (repose) for Singram; the last of the Badhails has been ejected, and is now a refugee in Cutch.

Of the Wagairs of Dwarica, who, with the Badhails of Aramra, were so long the terror of these seas, it is necessary to say something. They are a spurious branch of the Jhareja family of Bhooj, one of whom, called Abra, with the cognomen of *Moochwâl*, or 'the whiskered,' from a tremendous pair of these adjuncts to the face, came from Cutch in the time of Rinna Sowah, in whose family he intermarried, and from whom

whom he held in charge the *t'hânâ*, or garrison of the castle of Goomtee, or Dwarica. His son had offspring by a woman of impure caste, and they assumed the name of Wagair, with the distinctive affix of *Manik*, or 'gem.' The last four chieftains of this race were Mahap-Manik, Sadool-Manik, Sameah-Manik and Muloo-Manik, who, with all his kin and motley company of Wagairs, Badhails, Arabs, &c., after a desperate defence, was slain in the storm, or attempted retreat. Nor was this gallant feat achieved without loss to the assailants, amongst whom one daring spirit may be mentioned, who made his first and last essay in arms, on that day, against the pirates of Dwarica. Captain Mariott seems to have been born for the profession, and to have possessed in a high degree all the noble and chivalrous feelings, with which it ought ever to be associated. The spot where he fell, precipitated from the summit of the ladder, was appropriately selected for his tomb; but, not content with this memorial, his friends have raised upon the utmost projecting point of land a column in remembrance of this young hero, of whom it might well have been said, as of another high-minded soldier,—of Mariott as of Marçeau,—

> "Brief, brave, and glorious was his young career."

He obtained the fate he always wished, and while he yet lives in the remembrance of his brother officers, it may be soothing to his more distant friends to learn that the ground has become holy with the Hindu, and the abode of an ascetic; and when the navigator, no longer dreading to "hug the land," as he clears Cape Juggut, inquires why that pillar rose, he will learn the tale and the moral together.

Such is a brief outline of the pirates of the Land's End of more modern days. Could we fill it up with details, or go back to more remote times, and furnish an account of the sea-kings of Larice or

 Saurashtra,

Saurashtra, it might afford some interest; but we have only isolated facts, with intervals of centuries: from Alexander to the author of the *Periplus* in the second century; from the destruction of Deobunder, the capital of the Chaoras, in the eighth, to that of Dwarica and Bate in the nineteenth, the same depredators existed, and under the same appellation, for the Sangadians of Alexander are the Sungum-dharians of whom we speak, the robbers of the Sungum, the sanctified *embouchures* of the streams with the ocean, whence they sailed to scour the seas, and to which they returned for shelter and security under the protection of the divinity, patron of thieves, to whom all these creeks and points of confluence (*sungum*) were and are sacred. Various authors have descanted on the name of Sangadian, or Sangarian, as being that of a particular race, and at the head of them is D'Anville. He says: "Les Sanganes, dont Thévenot et Ovington font mention, occupent cette côte, et infestent cette mer de leurs pirateries. Le nom de cette nation est très ancien; car, on ne sauroit le meconnoître dans celui de Sangada, qui était propre à la contrée qui sort immédiatement de *l'embouchure du Sinde*, selon le Journal de Néarque, par qui la flotte d'Alexandre fut conduite."

On this we have to remark, that wherever there is an *embouchure*, there is a sungum; and wherever there is, or was, a sungum, there were Sangada, or Sungum-dhara, *i. e.* nests of pirates; and whether this *embouchure* was that at the Goomtee of Dwarica, or that of the Khary, one of the arms forming the delta of the Indus, in both is a shrine to Sungum-Narayn, the god of thieves, their protector; and this point Narayen-sirr, on the Khary, to which I am hastening, will be the "Turn-again" of my journey. Such is the etymology of a name immortalized by Arrian and D'Anville; not that of a nation, but a simple synonym for

'pirate,'

'pirate,' "the children of Tricum-rae," as they styled themselves. Whether those of Dwarica and Aramra ever formed a junction with their professional brethren of the Delta cannot be determined; but we distinctly recognize the same principle actuating each—religion and robbery conjoined. These corsairs never stretched their sails in quest of prey without first propitiating or bribing their deity, and never returned without offering a share of the spoil to this Mercury. Like the Pindarries, those scourges of India, "who prayed seven times a-day," these "seizers of rings" considered their hazardous occupation not only honourable, but sanctified: so indulgent is the human mind towards its own deformities. Whether the Sangarians of the Indus, or the Sauras of Saurashtra, ever boldly stretched the sail across the mighty deep to other lands, it is difficult to say; but so many names of Hindu divinities and heroes mark the line of coast from the Indus to Arabia, that there can be no question of its being familiar to them. The last of the Rover galleys which was laid high and dry, was a goodly and imposing-looking vessel, having a lofty poop and beaked *rostrum*.

But here is the *tindaêl* of my own good vessel, moored in view, with the sails all trimmed, to transport me across the *Canthi-colpus*, the gulf of Cutch, and eventually to the old haunts of the Sangada of Alexander.

CHAPTER XXI.

The author embarks.—Parting with companions.—The author's *Guru.*—The *Cant'hi,* or gulf of Cutch.—Description of the Gulf of Cutch by Ptolemy and Arrian.—The Rin.—Land at Mandavie —Description of the place.—Pilgrims.—Vessels of Arabia manned by Africans.—Effect of the abolition of the Slave Trade.—Historical notices of Mandavie.—Sepulchral monuments.—Coins.

JANUARY 1st, 1833.—We started with a fair wind, and so low is either coast, that we soon lost sight of both shores, and were o'er-canopied by the bright blue vault down to the dark line, which, as the Hindu bard would say, separates the domain of Indra from that of Varuna. I had not, however, much poetry in me, having parted with friends in whose society I had passed the last six months, enjoying that hospitality which is (or was) only known in the East. Moreover, whatever of interest these gleanings may possess, is chiefly owing to my friend, Mr. Williams,* through whose influence every facility was afforded to my inquiries, and whose knowledge of the tracts and the people materially guided my judgment in the selection of objects, and who furnished me much information upon all. It is with a grateful recollection of his prompt kindness that I extract from my journal this tribute of feeling, then warm from the heart, and still undiminished by the years which have intervened. Here also I parted with my friend and tutor, "the moon of intellect," the Yati Gyanchandra, who had been with me from my subaltern days, and who, during more than half the period of my sojourn in India, was one of the great comforts

* [The death of this gentleman, the Resident at Baroda, and political commissioner in Guzzerat, is announced whilst this sheet is passing through the press.]

comforts of my exile. He is often mentioned, in these pages and elsewhere, and being in fact identified with all my antiquarian labours, some description of him may not be unacceptable. He was a tall, spare figure, and though not more than threescore when we parted, had the first claim to veneration in his white locks; and when he entered the apartment, his long scarf flowing in the air, his head uncovered, and his staff in hand, he looked a true *vediavan*, or magician. He was a priest of Budha. He enjoyed as much as I did these ramblings in search of the relics of past days, and to his great historical knowledge, and patience in decyphering inscriptions, I am indebted for my chief discoveries. Along with him, I parted, too, with my gallant and favourite steed, Javadia, the gift of the Rana of Oodipoor, to whom I returned him after his pilgrimage, with a special request, that none but himself or my old equerry should ever cross his back; and, moreover, that he should enjoy the distinction of being the first *pooja'd* in the grand military festival, the *duserra.*

To dissipate painful reflections, I spread out the map, and with the "*Eclaircissemens de la carte de l'Inde*" before me, while the isles of Baraee were yet in sight, commenced my speculations on what change the *can'thi* of Cutch had undergone since the days of Ptolemy and the author of the *Periplus.* According to the latter authority, who in all probability visited it in his commercial speculations from Baroach, "Baraee est le nom d'un enfoncement du golphe, qui renferme des isles au nombre de sept:" and, from the Egyptian geographer, D'Anville says, "Un port nommé Balseti, ou Barseti, y paroît couvert de quelques isles, qui représentent celle de Baraee dans Ptolemée, *à la droite de l'entrée du Canthi-Colpus.*" No argument can be requisite to prove that Bate, the pirates' isle, is the same so circumstantially

stantially designated as the Balseti of D'Anville, and the Baraee of the second century; its nominal resemblance is the last of these tokens, the first being its position, to the right on entering the gulf of Canthí, (a term for this coast still recognized); the next, the number of islets about and further up the *enfoncement.* Bate is a name locally applied as *the* island, and one would be disposed to pronounce it a contraction of Balseti; but whence this derivation? All this land is sacred to Kanya, Crishna, or Narayen, whose infant appellation is Bala, Bala-nat'h, Balmokund, in his juvenile character as Murali or Murani, the shepherd-god, with his symbols, the reed (*murali*) and shepherd's staff. The resemblances are endless, and in the East deviated into grossness and monstrous inconsistency; while in the west, they are moulded and refined into those glowing and simple forms which disdain all association with the original.

Let us endeavour to clear up and reconcile another point at issue between these two great names:—"Le golphe, qui dans Ptolemée est appelé *Canthí-colpus*, paroît désigné sous le nom d'Irinus dans le *Periple.*" *Canthi* is not only the general designation for a coast, or margin, but is to this day especially applied to all that portion of Cutch lying between the hills and the sea; and the application of the term *Irinus* by Arrian must have been restricted to the fenny portion at the head of the gulf (*colpus*), familiarly known as the *Rin*, a corruption of the Sanscrit word *aranya*, or 'waste.' In like manner, the phrase *Erinos*, used by the first Arrian, must be understood to designate the greater Rin, which, uniting as it does with the smaller, actually makes Cutch insular. Further to silence cavil, the Looni river (whose course I have traced from its fountains,* and which flows through

* See map, *Annals of Rajast'han*

through, and may indeed be said to aid in the formation of, the greater Rin), is the same as that which, under the name of Khary, unites with the eastern arm of the delta of the Indus; *Looni* and *Khary* having the same meaning, the 'salt river.' If the Looni ever had a distinct exit or entry into the minor Rin, at the head of the Cutch gulf, we might account for the Orbadri of Ptolemy, which he makes there to fall in, and trace in this Sanscrit compound the same designation, confirming the attention paid to geography by the Hindus of past days, a fact already beyond dispute. *Bhadra* is a generic term for 'river,' and the prefix *or*, means a 'salt-marsh,' or 'salt-lake,' or where salt is deposited, the characteristic of the Looni, which every where, throughout its course, leaves a saline deposit. The town at the *embouchure* of the gulf, called Ari-sirr, would support this etymology, *sirr* being another term for a lake, and chiefly one of a saline nature; and if this river *(bhadra)* passed through it into the gulf, we should have a superfluity of characteristics, for the origin of its name. But as I have visited the Looni at its fountain-head, and crossed it in various parts of its course through Maroost'hali, or the desert, so I shall soon visit its *embouchure*, at Narayen-sirr, the last Hindu shrine within the Indus. Then may I say, what no individual can, that from Heri-dwara, where Ganga cleaves her course through the northern chain, to the conjoint *sungum* of the Brahmaputra and Ganges (the *Aurea Regia* of Ptolemy), also famed for its pirates, and to the *sungum* of the Indus with the sea of Onam, I shall have journied; but these earlier wanderings were never noted in a book, or at very irregular intervals—an omission now amongst my subjects of regret.

January 2d.—The high peak of Ninovee (the Ninoué of D'Anville), in the Bhooj range, bearing N.N.E., appeared in sight, as the wind died

died away, and left us rolling in the trough of the sea all night, to the infinite disquietude of the Gangaridæ in my train; and it was two P.M. of this day when we came to anchor in the Khary of Mandavie. But, worse than this, the wind had chopped round, and was now directly adverse to my further progress to the shrines of Koteswar and Narayen-sirr, the end of my pilgrimage: and the nakhoda talked of taking a week, instead of getting there in eighteen hours. The *Sarah* was to leave Bombay for England on the 15th of the month, and I had paid near £400 for my passage, and thus remained in no slight dilemma between my hopes and my fears. Having despatched an express to Mr. Gardiner, the resident at Cutch, descriptive of my wishes, I abided his reply, and the temper of the winds.

Early in the day I received a visit from the sons of the respectable and venerable Jaitaji, the governor of Mandavie, who accompanied me to the shore, under a salute of cannon, to a garden-house which he very kindly placed at my disposal; but I preferred my galley. Mandavie, or '*the mart*,' is the most celebrated on this coast, and generally termed *Musca-Mundee*, from the large village of Musca, separated from it only by the Rookmani river. The city is enclosed by a *seherpunna*, or circumvallation, having many towers, mounting cannon. It is the head of a district, but its importance arises from its wealth and position, having sometimes more than two hundred sail of vessels in its roadstead. Many are the property of its inhabitants, of whom the most wealthy are the Goséns, uniting, as already mentioned, commerce and religion, and who have branch establishments at Palli, Benares, &c. &c. There are upwards of fifty shroffs, or bankers, each of whom pays a tax of one hundred rupees to the state: it is a house-tax, from which none are exempt, and which is said to yield twenty-five thousand rupees per

per annum. The mercantile transactions of Mandavie are principally with Calikote (*qu.* Calicut?) and Muscat, in the Persian Gulf, though it trades with all the ports of Arabia and Africa. From the first it imports lead, *kaneh*, or green glass, copper, cardamums, pepper, ginger, bamboos, teak-wood for ship-building, *kustoori* (a medicine), ochres, dyes, drugs, &c.; from Muscat, the areca-nut, rice, coco-nut, dry dates (*kharik*) and fresh dates (*pind-kujoor*), silks, spices, &c. &c. The port duties are said to realize a lac of rupees annually.

I passed the day in perambulating the town and quays, all presenting new and interesting scenes, with groups of persons from all countries; the swarthy Ethiop, the Hindkí of the Caucasus, the dignified Arabian, the bland Hindu Banyan, or consequential Gosén, in his orange-coloured robes, half-priest half-merchant. I went from group to group, whether ship-owners or pilgrims, and put questions to all. The latter were to me far the most attractive. They came from Dehli, Peshawur, Mooltan, and various parts of Sinde, and were huddled together on the beach, or praying in columns, while their wives were preparing their meals, many having children about them. All were clad in the blue garb of the *Huj*, or pilgrimage to Mecca, which they are enabled to perform *gratis*, begging their food wherever they halt, and which it is meritorious to bestow. This explains the boast, that no Moslem power ever conquered or imposed tribute upon Cutch, and the act of liberality was at least as politic as it was charitable. There is a secret sympathy which unites strangers, of whatever class, or creed, or clime, when accidentally thrown together on a foreign strand, and I soon collected a considerable crowd around me. I pleased a group from Peshawur, who styled themselves the *Loag*, or 'multitude,' when I called them "the Hindkí," remembering the term from Mr. Elphin-

3 M stone's

stone's description. With others I conversed of Shah Shujah; of Runjeet's crusade against their native land, which they heard with perfect indifference, for in these despotic climes, love of country, and what we are accustomed to call patriotism, are by no means identical terms.

From these varied groups I passed to a yet more novel spectacle, the ships in the roadstead, which ply to "the golden coast of Sofala," or "spicy shores of Araby the blest;" nearly twenty sail were manned by the sable sons of Africa. Their average tonnage was six hundred candies, or one hundred and twenty-five tons, and each carried cannon, which, through the meritorious exertions of the Bombay Marine, in the extirpation of the Joasmees, are now only required for salutes. These pirates of the Arabian coasts were long the scourge of these seas, never sparing the lives of the captured, pleading a double motive for adding murder to piracy: "Without blood," they said, "it will be said we stole your property, but did not capture it, and *religion* forbids our eating the bread of infidels, whom we spared when in our power." The energetic measures of the Bombay Government have crushed, it is hoped for ever, this pest of commerce.

The construction of the Arabian vessels is, I suppose, the same as in the days of Hiram. They have an enormous quantity of canvas, stretched on yards large enough for the mainsail of a first-rate. Like the men, every thing was of sable hue, and their stems were hung with hundreds of earthen jars, the ventures of the sailors. Since human flesh has ceased to be an article of commerce, the grand markets of Swâl and Jungibar (the Sofala and Zinguebar of the maps) have ceased to be frequented; and although this illicit trade is not altogether extinguished, it exists but to small extent. The liberal opinions

opinions of the philanthropists have been largely imbibed by the African serf, who has, to use the words of my informant, "completely lost his habits of industry and fidelity," which, in the poor Sidi's vocabulary, perhaps means submission to stripes and toil: "they are not fit for us any longer," he added, "for when we tell them to work, they reply they will when they please; and if for this we punish them, they run away. Before, when the Rao's government was supreme, they were reclaimed; but now your power is there also. If compelled to short-commons ourselves, they will pilfer to make up for it, and some, if threatened with a blow, say they will return it; whereas, in former times, the only threat was, that *they would kill themselves* in revenge, saying, 'What is life to us? there is none to weep for us when we die, and we leave no unfriended mothers or offspring behind us.'" This is word for word the remark which was made to me by one who had derived profit from this unhallowed trade. I never saw merrier or more nimble and well-knit fellows than the Sidi sailors, whether the crews of the ships in the roads, or those belonging to the ports. The select of these, in the palmy days of slavery, fetched from two to three hundred korees, about eighty rupees, or ten pounds sterling. How the foregoing anecdote would have rejoiced the heart of Wilberforce!

January 3d.—The cruel wind still remains adverse; I have, therefore, modified my plan, and determined to make a run for the coast of Bhooj, and should any accounts there reach me of delay in the despatch of the *Sarah*, or the wind be propitious on return, I will risk every thing. I sent off a horseman last night to Mr. Gardiner, accepting his invitation to visit the court of Bhooj. To expedite my journey, he has placed a relay at Gujni, and I have sent off another

 from

from hence; and the old governor, the respected Jaitaji, has placed a saddle-horse and some troopers at my disposal for the first stage. I shall start at dusk this evening, and as the distance is under fifty miles, shall be there to breakfast to-morrow.

I filled up the time by prowling about the town and the quays, and making an excursion to some old sites in the neighbourhood. The town is large, having five thousand substantial houses, said to contain twenty thousand inhabitants. In the full tide of prosperity, not less than four hundred sail of shipping plied to and from this port, chiefly the property of its own wealthy merchants. But the universal stagnation of commercial enterprize has affected Mandavie, and with the exception of a few vessels to the ports of Arabia and Africa, the trade is mostly coasting, and confined to Malabar. Mandavie was at the height of her prosperity during the rule of Rao Ghor, who took a lively interest in maritime pursuits; and, in order to follow them to advantage, he erected a palace at this port, on the model of a Dutch factory; but the last earthquake, which left nothing untouched throughout Western India, shook to pieces this work of Rao Ghor, who also established a dock-yard, and personally superintended the building of his own ships. With all the zeal of the Great Peter, he determined that a ship constructed in his own yard, commanded and manned entirely by his own subjects, should navigate the seas to England. The voyage was performed, the good ship returned in safety, reaching the Malabar coast during the monsoon; but the nakhoda, like a genuine tar, sacrificed both ship and cargo at the shrine of a sable Venus; and, what is more astonishing, the Rao had the magnanimity to forgive him, in recompense for his skill and courage in the fulfilment of his project. Even now there are between two and three hundred

hundred vessels in the Khary and roadstead, one of them three-masted, belonging to the prince of Cutch. In Rao Ghor and the Gohil chief of Bhaonugger, we have two conspicuous instances of the pliancy of the human mind, and its adaptation to circumstances, for nothing in nature is more anomalous than the association of ships and trade with the Rajpoot. Hides of the rhinoceros, semi-transparent, resembling immense cakes of glue, were hanging up in the streets, prepared for being fashioned into shields; elephants' teeth for female bracelets and other ornaments; dates, dry and fresh, raisins, almonds, pistachios, all spoke the names of the lands with which Mandavie still maintained commercial intercourse. Cotton, however, is perhaps the staple article of trade; it is here packed in flat, circular, well-compressed bales; there were also cotton cloths of a coarse texture, sugar, oil, and ghee.

Mandavie, in the native records, is still designated by its more ancient name of *Raepoor-bunder*, or port of Raepoor, from the ancient site of Raen, three miles up the creek, or Khary, and to which I paid a visit. Two small hamlets are erected on its ruins, which offer no memorial of the past, but a small temple sacred to a divinity called Toorun-Nat'h, and he, they say, was a celebrated ascetic, who kept up a communication with the powers of darkness. It is related that, for neglecting some injunction to reform their lives, he caused Raen and all its subordinate towns to be overwhelmed. This Hindu tradition, like many others, affords an historical fact deeply imbued with fable; doubtless the ancient princes of Raen were not worse than their successors at Bhooj in the present day, who are still subject to earthquakes, and, in truth, they can hardly lay their heads on their pillows without the chance of being awakened by one.

The

The tide formerly admitted vessels up to Raen, but since its day of doom a bar of sand has choaked up the entrance, and the stream under it is no longer *khary* (salt), but fresh. I repaired to the remains of the ancient shrine of Toorun-Nat'h, and mounting the steps, found an ancient 'Jogi ascetic, of the class designated *Kanfarra* (from having his ears split), performing certain mysterious rites over the *churnpud*, or impress of the feet of Toorun, of whose school he was a disciple. I waited till he had "poured water," strewed green leaves, and waved the censer over each *tumulus* to the manes of his predecessors. These are the most singular sepulchral monuments I have yet seen in India, and evidently, from their allusions, belong to the priests of Bâl. They are very small, consisting of a series of concentric rings or steps, terminating in a little pillar at the centre, thus:—

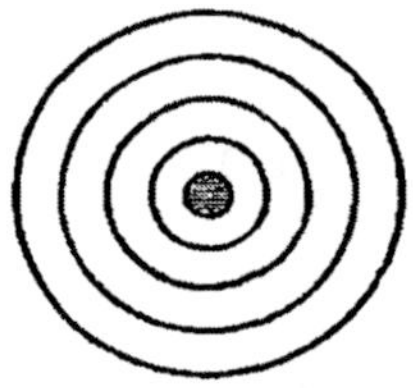

I entered into conversation with this solitary being, whose abode was amidst graves and ruins; but he either knew nothing beyond the ritual of his creed, or chose not to be communicative. I prowled about the fragments of desolation, amongst which I was told silver coins were frequently found; and my research was rewarded by two antiques, in excellent preservation, having the effigy of a helmed king on one side, and a pyramidal-shaped symbol on the reverse, with an epigraph in that incognate character found on the Girnar rock-inscriptions.* From the ruins of Raen to those of ancient Oojein, throughout the

* *Vide* p. 377.

the coasts and cities intervening, the same coins have occasionally been discovered, plainly denoting that some powerful dynasty possessed extensive sway—but whether the Balharas of Anhulwarra, or a race of kings still more ancient, is mere conjecture. Let us hope, from the impulse which this branch of investigation has received, that it may not always remain a mystery.

CHAPTER XXII.

Cath-kote, the ancient seat of the Cathi.—Necropolis of the Raos of Cutch.—The city of Bhooj.—The Jhareja chiefs visit the author.—Their costume.—Visit to the prince, Rao Desil.—The hall of mirrors.—The hall of audience.—Historical notice of the Jharejas.—The Yadu race.—Genealogical traits of the Rajpoots.—Extent of the Hindu affinities.—Union of the Budha faith with the Yadu race.—Yadu ancestry of the Jharejas.—Power of the Yadus.—The Yadus an Indo-Scythic race from Western Asia.—The Sind-Summa Jharejas.—Chronology.—Extract from the Jhareja chronicles.—Conversion of the Sind-Summa Jharejas to Islam.—Successors of Lakha the Proud.—Evils of Polygamy.—First settlement of the Summa race in Cutch.—Origin of the custom of infanticide amongst the Jharejas.—Catastrophe of Mohlutkote.—The practice still continued.—Lakha, the first *Jhareja*.—Raedhun, the founder of the Jhareja state, led a colony to the Great Rin.—Rao Khengar, founder of Bhooj.—The results of the genealogical history of the Jharejas.

January 4th.—To the steady-going occidentalist, who loves to loiter over and after a good dinner, it might appear a hardship to be summoned "to horse" instead of to coffee, and to pass the night on his saddle; but habit would soon reconcile him to such discipline, in which he would find abstract pleasure, independently of such objects as I had in view, to reward him. With the slightest dash of the romantic or love of adventure in his disposition, his own reflections would not only preserve his eyes from slumber, but would so kindle speculation, that the dawn would take him by surprise, and make him wish the night and his fancies prolonged. Certain associations and ideas would be awakened as he passed through the dark wood, or barren plain, in which he would find nothing to bear witness of humanity save in the group around him, or when the torches flared upon some ruined pile, such as the Cath-kote,* the ancient seat of the Cat'hi, where I scrambled

* There are various branches of this nomadic race, the most celebrated of which is the Coman-Cat'hi. Abulgazi describes a famous tribe in Khwarezm, the ancient Chorasmia, called Comani, the remains

I scrambled about the massive fragments of its temple, hunting for inscriptions. All around was silence, save my own and my guide's steps clambering amidst the ruins : even the gallant steeds appeared not insensible, as they turned their heads with inquisitive gestures to each other, as did their riders, when the flambeau's light glared upon their wild bearded faces, in which surprise was strongly depicted at the actions of the Frank. It was a scene for Gerard Dow or Schalken, and well worth a night on horseback in Cutch. Burckhardt tells us that, when visiting the Wady Moosa, and tomb of Haroon (Aaron), seeking amidst ruins for inscriptions, he was invariably distrusted, and regarded as a magician in search of treasures : and, throughout India, the same impression prevailed, even where I was well known, and they were few who credited the assertion of my research being prompted not by Mammon but Minerva. Nor is it wise to disregard altogether the expression of this feeling; for inhabitants of countries subject to eastern despotism, having no security for their riches beyond depositing them in the earth, naturally enough imagine that these tablets mark the spot where such hoards exist.

As the day broke, the hills of Bhooj appeared in sight, their wavy, barren summits covered with walls and towers, evincing little skill in the

remains of which were expelled by Jungeez Khan : and the royal author adds, "Urgens was not always the capital, and Abulfeda tells us Cat'h, also spelt *Kaht*, in 41° 45′ N. lat., was formerly the metropolis." What affinity there was between these, the people of Cat'hay, and Alexander's Cat'hi, it were vain to ask : it is sufficient for our purpose to trace them from "the Five Rivers," and to observe that the name of their first settlement in these regions was Cat'h-kote, from which, as stated, they were dislodged by the first Jhareja colony from Sinde. It is said of them, that they repeat couplets describing their migration from Mooltân, and temporary settlement in the tracts called Pawur, north of the Rin, and of Megum Rao, their leader conducting the first Cat'hi colony across the gulf into Saurashtra eight hundred years ago; and so predominant was their power, that it changed the ancient name of the peninsula to Cat'hi-wâr.

the Jhareja engineer, though they give a picturesque character to this otherwise desolate-looking valley. The last earthquake had been almost their only assailant, and had effected sundry breaches, which the present adminstration has had the sense not to repair. At sunrise, I reached the residence of the political agent, Mr. Gardiner, who was already seeking "health in the breeze;" and, in order to fill up the time, I steered my course to the *necropolis* of the Raos of Cutch. The monuments are placed to the westward, on the margin of the lake, which has a small island in the centre, and present objects of interest, both to the antiquary and the painter. The earthquake of 1818 had, however, committed sad havoc amidst the most splendid of these memorials of the Jharejas, while the humble *pallias* stood unhurt. Some, in fact, were masses of ruin, and even the mausoleum of Rao Lakha, the most recent as well as the most substantial, had suffered not a little. Their construction differs somewhat from those of Rajpootana, for, instead of being merely a cupola, sustained by open columns, resting on a terrace, these are enclosed by a stone screen or lattice, as if to keep out the profane. Through this I saw the *pallia* of Rao Lakha,* who is sculptured in relief upon it, on horseback, with lance in hand; subordinate *pallias* on each side correspond in number to the wives, or handmaids, who "seized the *sut*" (faith) on the occasion. Close to these *pallias*, or, as we should say, tomb-stones, is a small mace-shaped pillar, on whose head there is hollowed out a receptacle for a lamp, denoting the union of Mooslem with Rajpoot funereal rites; though, in fact, the Jhareja would now find it difficult to say what is his creed, so often has he changed it. All these cenotaphs shewed, in their

* For an admirable and correct drawing of this mausoleum, I refer the reader to Capt. Grindlay's "Scenery of Western India."

their sculptured effigies, that they were raised over the relics of warriors,—except that of one, who had fallen by his own hand. This figure was of a man kneeling, and, with a gesture of imprecation, pointing a dagger to his heart: in all probability, representing some remarkable *traga* of a Charun, or Bard, taking the only vengeance in his power against the oppressor.

As the city of Bhooj can only boast of three centuries of antiquity, my search for inscriptions pertaining to the Jharejas was fruitless; but there were some simple *pallias*, erected on plain altars, of ancient days, the inscriptions on which were effaced by time.

On my return, I found the Resident and his assistant, Lieut. Walter, and met with such a welcome, as afforded an ample recompense for the small inconveniences endured in excursions of this nature. To quiet my anxiety to reach the eastern arm of the Indus, Mr. Gardiner offered to lay a post instantly for me at Lukput; thus placing me, to use an eastern phrase, "between a well and a fountain;" for, if I accepted this offer, I had not a moment to lose, and must forego my search into the records and traditions of the Jharejas, which I had meditated. I therefore decided to make the most of *six-and-thirty hours at Bhooj*, and trust to the uncertain winds, on regaining my bark at Mandavie, for the completion of my enterprize. My intention was soon made known, and the zealous kindness of my host not only aided me with his own information, but soon furnished me with the bards and their books; while a long and interesting conversation with the respectable Ruttunji, the leading and most sagacious member of the Regency, gave me a thorough insight into the Jhareja form of government, and wherein it deviated from Rajpoot polity. He devoted, in fact, the whole of his time to me, in the most kind and gentlemanly

 manner,

manner, patiently allowing me to note down his reply to each question as I put it, and with the results I will conclude my sketch of Bhooj.

After breakfast, I was honoured by a visit of welcome from the minister, the members of the Regency, and all the Jhareja chieftains then at the capital. I was much gratified with the manly aspect and manners of this singular aristocracy, who are decidedly a fine race, though not tall, as I had understood them to be; nor does their complexion differ materially from the more eastern Rajpoot tribes, from whom they are chiefly distinguished in personal appearance by their long and inverted double-peaked beards, rendered so by their chin being shaved in the middle. Another difference consists in the superfluity of drapery which the Jhareja affects, with his huge trowsers, and loose but graceful turban. The next day, at noon, I attended the court of the minor prince, who is only seven years of age, having the family name of Desil, and being the fifth from the last who bore it. In this custom of recurring to distinguished family names, like the Rajpoots, they add, in order to distinguish them, the patronymic; thus the present is Desil Bharaní, or son of Bhara; in contradistinction to Desil Ghorani, or son of Ghor, &c. &c. These are the only two of this name, but the changes are repeatedly rung on those more celebrated, of Lakha and Raedhun, conspicuous links in their long genealogical chain. All that I had time to see of the town was in my route to the palace, and if it was a fair specimen of the whole, I lost nothing in not seeing more.

The young rao was seated upon a throne more elevated than is usual among the princes of Rajwarra, probably in order that he might at least be on a par with the *coorcis*, or chairs, of the *Saheb-loag*, which are never introduced in Rajpoot durbars. The long hall was crowded with the

the Jhareja vassalage, from the farther end of which the bards, as we entered, recited the names and deeds of the Jhareja heroes of old. Having sat the usual ceremonious time, the young rao gave us our *congé* in form, when we accompanied Ruttunji to inspect the *lion* of Bhooj, the *Sheesh-mahl*, or 'hall of mirrors,' of which there is one in every noble's palace in Rajwarra. This gorgeous bauble, on which were expended *eighty lakhs of korees* (more than three years' revenue of the crown-land of Cutch), implies neither taste nor judgment in the founder, Rao Lakha, who thus dissipated the treasure accumulated by the frugality of his predecessor. Its interior is of white marble, literally inlaid with mirrors, each separated by gilded ornaments. The ceiling, from which lustres are pendant, is painted in *fresco;* and the floor, which is laid with China tiles, was covered with Dutch and English chiming-clocks, which were all set a-going at once, forming a true Dutch chorus; while shelves about the centre of the wall were covered with all sorts of glass-ware, like a pawnbroker's shop, the resemblance being not a little increased by a variety of glass figures, which decorated the walls themselves. In the centre of this costliness, is placed the pallet of Rao Lakha, that in which he died, which stands on golden or gilded feet, and in front of which lights are perpetually burning. It is thus already enrolled amongst the *penates* of the Jharejas, and, if its perishable material will last long enough, may receive their homage as the substitute of Rao Lakha. A verandah surrounds this hall, the floor of which is also tiled, and a strange anomalous collection of portraits adorns its walls: Rana Juggut Sing of Méwar in contact with the Empress Catherine of Russia! Raja Bukt Sing of Marwar and Hogarth's Election, with other Flemish, English, and Indian subjects, intermingling with the princes of Cutch, from the

first

first rao, Khengar, to the present time. With all these incongruities, even the portrait gallery of a Jhareja affords some food for speculation ; and in contrasting the drapery and decoration of the past and present raos, we trace deviations from their primitive simplicity, in dress and in bearing.

Thence we proceeded to the newly-erected *durbar*, or hall of audience, not yet finished, whose simplicity of construction and decoration contrasted advantageously with the bauble we had quitted. Here solidity, utility, and comfort were studied. It is a place fit to receive the entire Jhareja *bhyâd* (frèrage), and is insulated by a canal, ornamented with *jets-d'eau*, to keep them cool, or make them fancy themselves so, in hot weather. The palace overlooks the lake, and may possess other objects of attraction, which my limited time would not permit me to see.

Let us now bestow a glance upon the past history of the Jharejas. I had entered the country full of hopes favourable to the old establishments of the family in these regions, trusting to recognize in them the descendants of Tessarioustus (Teja Raja ?), whose kingdom was over-run by Menander and Apollodotus two centuries before Christ ; and my surprise was great to find the Jhareja positions in Cutch within the limits of the Mooslem conquest, and their power as a substantive state not reaching beyond three hundred years. The genealogy of the Jharejas embraces a period of full three thousand years, in which, however, we cannot glean above three or four facts applicable to genuine history ; but these, though indirectly obtained, are of importance, and repay the investigator of Hindu antiquities for his wearisome and often unprofitable task.

The Jhareja is a branch of the great Yadu family, once the dominant

race

race in India. They claim an origin from Crishna, prince of the Suraseni, a country particularized by Menu for the warlike qualities of its inhabitants, as also by Arrian, the historian of Alexander. I consider the existence of Crishna, the son of Basdeo, son of Sursén, the prince of the Yadu race ruling on the Jumna, twelve hundred years before Christ, as much entitled to credence as any historical fact of the same age in any other country. By a singular piece of good fortune, or rather by unremitting research, I discovered the remains of Surpoora, the capital of the Suraseni, founded by the grandfather of Crishna ; and, as if to connect Hindu with Grecian history, it was amongst the ruins of this ancient site that my precious medal of Apollodotus was found.* The line of the Jumna, from where it bursts its rocky barrier, to Yoginipoor (modern Dehli), Mat'hura, Agra, Surpoora, to its confluence† with the Ganges at Prâg (the modern Allahabad), the capital of the Prasii of Megasthenes, was the bar of the ancient Yadu power; and not only is this clearly defined in the Puranic genealogies and old traditional couplets elsewhere given,‡ regarding the successive capitals of this race, but, in confirmation of this testimony, we have the evidence of the same unknown characters at Dehli, Allahabad, and Joonagur'h. Whatever be the origin of the Yadu race, whether descended, as their *vansanali* asserts, from Budha, prince of the Saca race of Western Asia, we shall not further inquire, but rest content with some material facts, gathered from their own and corroborated by other channels, which shew that Hinduism has been modified since those days of patriarchal sway.

Nothing

* *Vide* Transactions of the Royal Asiatic Society, vol. i. p. 314, for an account of this.

† *Sungum* is the point of confluence of *two* streams, and where a third joins, as at Prâg, *Triveni*: the Sarasvati is the name of the third stream.

‡ *Annals of Rajast'han,* vol. i.

Nothing is so repugnant to the ideas of the modern Rajpoot as intermarriage with the same tribe; he holds it to be strictly incestuous. Yet Crishna's own mother, Deoki, was cousin-germane to his father; nay, we even see amongst this race traces of the polyandry of the Getes of Transoxiana (the Yute, or Yuechi, of the Chinese historians), amongst whom, according to Neumann, from these authorities, a Budha was born eight hundred years before Christ. If the reader will consult my Essay on the Yadu princes of Jessulmér (who with the Jharejas alike claim from Crishna), and on the Jits, or Getic race,* he will observe that the latter claim kindred with the Yadus, whom we trace from Gujni (Gazni), migrating eastward to Salpoora in the Punjab, and eventually, with the progress of Islâm, across the Sutlej, to their present seats in the Indian desert.† While the Yadu-Bhatti family thus claim Gujni as their ancient capital, and the Chagitai as a renegade branch of their race, they at the same time ascribe their migration to Western Asia to the great civil war and death of their leaders, Crishna and the Pandus. But the fact is, as I have often stated, and will once more repeat, there was at that period a community of belief, and free intercommunication, from the Oxus to the Ganges. Every day is at length opening the eyes of those *savans* who dared not even look across the Indus for aught that was Hindu; but hermetically sealed it against all but the "barbarians." These contracted notions are renounced; Hindu cities and Hindu-Getic medals are discovered even in the Caucasus;‡ nor shall I be surprised at proof, that the Yadus, Pandus, and Curus of

* *Annals of Rajast'han*, vol. i. p. 106, and vol. ii. p. 179.

† See *Annals of Rajast'han*, vol. ii. p. 321.

‡ It would be well to bear these matters in mind, in our attempts to decypher these medals and inscriptions.

of the Great War were Yuechi, Yuti, or Getes; that Budha was their patriarchal leader and prophet, and that the mystic characters engraved on their triumphal columns at Dehli, at Prâg, and Girnar, belong to their race.

In proof of this intimate union of the faith of Budha with the Yadu, Yuti, or Gete race, let it be remembered that the apostle Nemi, the twenty-second Budha, was a Yadu, and of the family of Crishna, *i. e.* they were sons of two brothers; and as it is affirmed that Crishna, prior to his own deification, adored Budha-Trivicrama at Dwarica, it is evident that the act was then heretical. The chair of Budha is always filled by election, and in those days invariably from princely families; while, in the present, the elective right to the *sri-pooj*, or primacy, still obtains in the Oswal tribe, descended from the kings of Anhulwarra, but who have relinquished the sword for commerce. I mention this to account for the election of Nemi, the "Glory of Girnar," into the chair of Budha; and I will further add a tradition yet current amongst the Jains, in proof of the simultaneous bifurcation of these sects, to account for a deviation from Budhic ceremonials, in the erection of closed temples. The rites of Crishna, like those of Adonis, at first obtained chiefly amongst the Indian fair, and all flew to the shrine of the shepherd-god, to the neglect and abandonment of Budha. It was then that the Acharya of Budha transgressed a grand principle, not to worship "*The One within walls*;" and a statue of Nemi was enshrined, to bring back the fair to their own faith and their own gods. Although, however, from the traditions of the past and a knowledge of the present, we are satisfied that the unity of the divinity was the first principle of their belief, we at the same time observe that, like all early nations, they mixed up therewith adoration of the host of heaven, the sun, and his type the

 horse,

horse, which they annually sacrificed to him, as did the ancient Yuechi or Getes, who, we are told by Herodotus, held the immortality of the soul, on which doctrine nothing in paganism more sublime was ever penned than in the discourse of Crishna to his friend Arjuna.*

But these are not only uninteresting, but distasteful subjects to the many; we shall, therefore, descend another step from that period of Yadu tradition to the time of Alexander, and try whether we may not recognize in some of his opponents on the Indus the ancestors of these Jharejas. Let me once more repeat, that we are to treat of Crishna in his mere mortal capacity, as the prince of the Yadus, who was expelled from the land of the Suraseni, slain by the foresters of Saurashtra, and who left numerous issue by his eight wives. From one of these, named Jambavati, the Jharejas claim their origin; and of her issue, one son was named Samba.† After the death of Crishna, and the dispersion of the Yadu tribes, some, as the ancestry of the Jessulmér family, proceeded by the Punjab across the Indus, eventually establishing Gujni. Another branch continued to maintain itself in Saurashtra; while a third, that of Samba and his followers, gained a footing in the valley of the Indus, and erected a city, called after their leader Samba or Sama-nagara, at the bifurcation of the delta of the Indus, and on or near the site of modern Tat'ha. With the foundation of this capital, the name of Samba became titular to its princes and to his tribe, which has existed to modern days, and is described in the native annals, and recognised by Mooslem historians, as the Sinde-Summa dynasty. Saminagara, or 'the city of Samba,' is not only frequently mentioned by the Jhareja chronicles, but in the early annals

* See the *Bhagvat Gita*, translated by Sir Charles Wilkins.

† *Ba, ra, sa* are marks of the genitive case, or 'of' Sam, or Sham, the commonest epithet of Crishna, from his dark complexion.

annals of the collateral branch of Jessulmér, as Summa-kote.* I, therefore, here repeat what I stated elsewhere many years ago, there can be no doubt that the Saminagara of the Yadus is the Minagara of the author of the *Periplus*, who observes that it was the metropolis of an Indo-Scythic king, when he was at Baroach, that is, in the second century. Whether Arrian meant that a recent irruption from Higher Asia had supplanted the Summas, or that this race was considered by him entitled to the appellation of Scythic, it would be idle to enquire; but as the whole Balotch tribe, the most numerous of that region, is said to consist of proselytized Jits, claiming to be of Yadu stock, the suggestion is worth attending to by those whose inquiries are directed to the ethnography of the Hindu race.

Arrian, when touching on the genealogy of the family which enjoyed supreme dominion when Alexander was in India, states that their great ancestor was named Budæus (Βυδαιον), or Budha; thus attesting the intimate union of Budhism with Yadu genealogy, which is in strict conformity with the Yadu annals. For all the information possessed by Arrian and other writers on the subject of Hindu history, they are indebted to the now lost journal of Megasthenes, who was sent as ambassador by Seleucus to the king of the Prasii at Prâg, one of the chiefest and most ancient seats of Yadu power. Its king, Sandracottus, on whose name so many changes have been rung, is supposed to be the Chandragupta of the Puranic genealogies, a name belonging to each of the Yadu, Chohan, and Pramara races, at the earliest periods; but taking this coincidence of name, in conjunction with the incidental mention of *Budæus* by the Greek writer, as the patriarch of the then dominant race, we cannot hesitate to conclude that he was the Yadu prince

* *Kote, nagara,* are terms indifferently applied to a castle or fortified city.

prince of Prâg. A further proof of the continued existence of Yadu power, subsequent to the loss of universal dominion in India, is to be found in the frequent traditional notice of Sompriti Raja, prince of Bahar, in the second century, who was of the Budhic faith and Yadu race, and whose monuments at Ajmér, Komulmẹr and Girnar, are existing testimonies of his authority. But even in the peninsula of Saurashtra, ennobled by the death of their leader, the Yadu race was still powerful after the dispersion, of which we have a variety of proofs, and can appeal to inscriptions as well as to the *Mahatmas*, or rituals, of the sacred mounts, which repeatedly notice the pious munificence of the Yadu princes of Joonagur'h, in the repairs of the ancient shrines of the Budhist faith. The annals of other states also frequently allude to the Yadu princes as ruling in Joonagur'h at the earliest periods of their own establishment: thus, the annals of Méwar describe the Yadus* as lords of Joonagur'h, when they first settled in these regions, in the second century of Vicrama. So likewise do the chronicles of the Jaitwas and the Chaoras, which record their first matrimonial connections with them in the seventh and tenth centuries of Vicrama, periods long anterior to the migration of the Jharejas from Sinde to Cutch. The exuberance of tradition regarding the Yadu princes in this peninsula had indeed long been a subject of perplexity to me, as I confounded them and the Jhareja princes together, until from the chronicles of this family I found the latter in power in Saminagara on the Indus, even down to the twelfth century. In short, my opinion is, that the Yadu is *ab origine* an Indo-Scythic race from Western Asia; that under their patriarchal leader, Budha, (the

* Let it be remembered, that the celebrated tribes of Sarwegas and Chaurasimas, no longer known in Saurashtra, were branches of the Yadu.

(the Budæus of Arrian), they conquered all Gangetic India, which they apportioned into petty principalities, ruled by the branches into which they subdivided, known to history and tradition as the "*Chapun cula Yadu,*" or fifty-six Yadu tribes, *i. e.* Cúrú, Pandú, Aswa, Tacshac, Saca, Gete, &c., &c.; that, in their international wars, a dispersion took place, when some returned towards their original countries, approximating the regions on the Oxus and Jaxartes; that they founded Gujni in the Caucasus; Salpoora, or Salkote, in the Punjab; Saminagara, Sehwân, and other cities, on the Indus; that change of creeds and other causes drove some back on India; and that the Yadu-Bhattis of Jessulmér, and the Sinde-Summas, or Jharejas, of Cutch, are the representative branches, of which Crishna is the parent stock.

I return to the Sinde-Summa Jharejas. Referring to the annals of their neighbours, I shall endeavour to corroborate the authenticity of their own, and shew that they were still powerful upon the Indus in the earlier centuries of Vicrama. We will trace the Jhareja genealogy from the existing prince upwards, until we find a name mentioned in collateral dynasties. This is Choorchund, the fortieth prince anterior to the present, who in the Jaitwa annals is the cotemporary of Ram Camari, the fourteenth in descent from Sil, the founder of Goomlí. Now, 40 reigns × 23 (the estimated number of years in each reign*) = 920 — 1880 = S. 960 or A.D. 904, for the period of Choorchund Summa, king of Saminagara. Let us try this computation by the *pallia* inscriptions at Goomlí, whose prince Salamun, when banished, fled to Jam Oonur, who aided the refugee with an army to reinstate him. Jam Oonur, a name of celebrity in the Jhareja chronicles, being the first who changed the patronymic Summa

* For the *data* on which this average is founded, see *Annals of Rajast'han,* vol. i. p. 52.

Summa to Jam, was the eighth prince in descent from Choorchund, and 8 × 23 = 184 + 960 = S. 1144, differing but an inconsiderable number of years from the chronicle of the Jaitwas, which places the destruction of Goomlí, "by the Asuras of the Bamunea Summa race from Sinde, with long beards, and true Mooslems," in S. 1109; or, if we go by the inscriptions on the *pallias*, S. 1119. Thus we have two fixed dates of great value,—that of Jam Oonur, in A.D. 1053, shewing the conversion to Islâm and change of patronymic to be simultaneous; and that of Choorchund, the cotemporary of Ram Camar of Goomlí, in A.D. 904. It is stated also in the Jaitwa annals, that this prince married the daughter of Tullaji Cat'hi, of Cat'h-kote, which yields another important synchronism, *viz.*, the establishment of this Indo-Getic tribe in the peninsula at least a thousand years ago. But this is not all; for we deduce another important inference; namely, that the Yadu-Summas, Cat'his, Camari or Jaitwas, Chaoras, Jhallas, Ballas, Hoons, &c. &c., were all upon an equality as to *blood*, or pedigree, evincing none of the Rajpoot discriminations of these days in their intermixture by marriage; and, therefore, we may assume them to be of those tribes so often recorded by Arrian, Cosmas, &c., as migratory hordes, at various periods, from Higher Asia.

It is not worth while to recede further into the legends of this race, satisfied with tracing it as still holding dominion in Sinde in the year A.D. 904. The titular name of *Samba* was revived with the son of Choorchund, in whose reign the religion they professed (whether that of Budha or their deified ancestor, Crishna) was exchanged for that of Islâm, in connexion with which change, we have a singular piece of genealogical craft engrafted on the history of the tribe. Let me here recal the period of Choorchund of Sami-nagara, *viz.* S. 960, or A.D. 904.

His

His son, Sam-Yadu, had five sons, *viz.*, Aspati, Nirpati, Gujpati, Bhompati, and Sampati. Nearly two centuries prior to this epoch, the caliphs had made the conquest of Sinde;* and the singular story of Dahir, prince of Arore, and the Mooslem generalissimo, Mahomed-bin-Cassim, is familiar to every reader of Indian history. Conversion and conquest were conjoined, and the descendants of Samba, prince of Saminagara, when they subsequently alternated between Islâm and Hinduism, in order to conceal their forcible conversion, had recourse to the following invention. I give the passage *verbatim* as translated by the Purvoe, or English scribe, at the residency, from the chronicle of the Jharejas.—" Whoever came from Sham, in the country of Room, are called Summa. Sâd, the grandson of Sri-Crishna and Jambavati, dwelt in Sham, whence his descendants fled from fear of Nubee (the prophet), and arrived at the hill of Oossum ; but to their surprise, there they found Nubee at dinner. Perceiving that escape was impossible, they prostrated themselves before him, and Aspati accepted the invitation to dine with him, and drank water from his *kra*, or earthen jar. He became king of the Chagitais, and his brothers became tributary to him. Nirpati had Sinde, and inhabited Samai, whence the tribe was called Summa. Gujpati's descendants were called the Bhatti-Summa,† and held Jessulmér," &c. &c.

Thus, when dressed out in the trammels of Islâm, they find a birth-place in Syria, instead of the region of Sauras (in which is the hill of Oossum), and thus assume to be of the great Shemetic family ; yet in flying before this Nubee, if they mean Mahommed, they at once renounce all pretensions to antiquity. It is strange enough, however, that

* In A.H. 95, or A.D. 713. See *Annals of Rajast'han*, vol. i. p. 231 ; but the final conquest of Sinde was near half a century later, *ib.* p. 244.

† The Ashambhatty of Abulfazil.

that they should maintain, with the Yadu-Bhatti of Jessulmér, that the Tacshac, Turushca, or Turkish race of Chagitai (of Japhetic stock), belong to them, as well as that of Gor; and to this last some colour is given in the cognomen of *Sam*, which was held by Moezodín, the first conqueror of India. All this may be traced to a wish to conceal that blot in their genealogical history, their conversion to Islâm, which makes their alliance detested by the genuine Rajpoot; and as they vacillated between their more ancient or modern faith, they sacrificed the name of Samba, their great Hindu progenitor, for that of the Persian Jamshéd, and Sam became Jam; the epithet which now designates the branch residing at Noanagar.

We may pass over the seven princes intervening between Choorchund (the grandfather of the apostate Sam-Yadu), and Lakha, whose surname was Ghoraro, or the Proud, and who continued to rule in Saminagara. He had a numerous offspring, with a branch of which originated the Jhareja. By a lady of the Chaora tribe he had four sons, *viz.* Mor, Vera, Sand, and Hamir; and by another queen, whose birth-place was Canouj, four more, *viz.* Oonur, Munai, Jeya, and Phool.

Jam Oonur succeeded Lakha the Proud, and, as has been said, was the first Summa who assumed the name of Jam. It has been mentioned that Oonur was the son of Lakha by a princess of Canouj; and we can only account for his superseding his elder brothers, on the ground of her superior rank. Be this as it may, his assumption of the *gadi* of the Summas was fatal, and affords another instance of the mischievous effects of polygamy. Oonur, with his four elder brothers, was on a visit to Saerogur'h (now Lukput*), in the canton of Wagum, ruled

* Doubtless so called after Lakho Ghoraro. Besides Lukput, there are many other towns in Sinde, as Halla, &c., attesting the Summa sway.

ruled by the Chaora chieftain, brother to the elder queen of Saminagara. While here, he had private intelligence of the death of Rao Lakha, and giving them the slip, returned to the capital and received the royal unction. How long after this is uncertain; but his half-brothers, thus robbed of the right of primogeniture, conspired against him (his own brother, Munai, joining the confederacy) and slew him, during a festival, at Dhari-doond:—as Munai committed the act of assassination *(kair)*, he henceforth bore the name of *Kair-Munai*. The wife of Oonur, called "a daughter of the king," then pregnant, fled to her father for refuge; and he sent an army, which expelled Munai and his fratricidal brethren from Sinde, where they had remained twelve years after the murder. Kair-Munai, his brethren and retainers, fled to Cutch, attacked the Cat'hís, whom they expelled from Cat'h-kote, near to which Munai built a town, calling it Kaira. His elder brother, Mor, obtained Kunter-kote, and the others wrested lands from the Babrias, the Jaitwas, and other tribes.

Such was the first settlement of the Summa race of Sinde, in the province of Cutch, then parcelled out amongst numerous tribes, in which, from the delta of the Indus to the gulf of Cambay, that of Chaora was pre-eminent; and whence, we may repeat, the countries within these limits derived the name of Chaorashtra, or Saurashtra, which, though restricted by the Hindu geographer to the peninsula, was by the Greek and Roman, under the denomination *Syrastrene*, judiciously made to comprehend the enlarged limits just mentioned. It was not, however, till seven generations had passed away, that the ancient epithet of *Summa* was changed for that of *Jhareja*, when another colony from Saminagara almost obliterated the traces of this first conquest, which took place about A.D. 1075.

The descendants of Lakha the Proud, through Tumacha, the posthumous son of Jam Oonur, multiplied in Saminagara, until the time of Halla-Summa, the seventh from Jam Oonur, when an event occurred which at once caused a change in the patronymic, and originated the custom of infanticide amongst the Jharejas. It was with Halla (though others say with his brother, Vera) that the designation of Jhareja was introduced, proceeding from a trivial incident, which often suffices to give a name to a new dynasty amongst the Rajpoots. This prince had seven sons, six of whom died, one after another, from some epidemic disorder; the seventh was saved by the incantation of an ascetic. It is very common, in extreme illness, throughout these countries, to have recourse to the ceremony of *jhârnâ;* when the person (generally a Jogi recluse) who possesses the charm, waves his *jhar*, or brush of peacock-feathers, over the sick, as he recites a formula of prayer for his recovery. The son of the Summa chief, thus restored, ever after bore the name of *Jhareja*, which descended to his progeny, now a numerous tribe. The daughter of Halla* was given in marriage to a neighbouring prince, Oomur, lord of the Soomra tribe, whose residence was Mohbut-kote, afterwards named after him, Oomur-kote;* but a dispute having arisen, apparently during the nuptial festivities, the Soomra placed the Sinde prince in durance within his castle. So soon as the tidings of this disgraceful act reached Saminagara, the Summas assembled all their kin, and advanced to procure his liberation. The Soomras were not unprepared, and fifty thousand men of both tribes encountered in deadly strife under the walls of Mohbut-kote. The Summas conquered, though with the loss of ten thousand men,

* There is a town of Halla, north of Hydrabad, doubtless named after this prince; and for the name, position of Oomur-kote, and origin of the Soomra race, I refer the reader to the map and *Annals of Rajast'han.*

men, amongst whom was their prince; and the Soomras lost their capital, and seven thousand seven hundred of their tribe. On this catastrophe, which turned festivity into mourning, the bride joined the suttee victims of the Soomras, who, as they ascended the pyre, imprecated this anathema: "that wherever a Jhareja's daughter is espoused, she may prove barren and unhealthy;" since which occurrence, no one is ambitious to accept the coco-nut of this tribe. Such is the origin of the unnatural custom of infanticide practised to this day by the Jharejas, as taken from their own chronicles; yet to which not even the philanthropic Walker, who so earnestly laboured to extinguish the custom (and who erroneously believed he had been the saviour of the fair of Cutch), has alluded, though it is amply sufficient to account for its continuance through six centuries. Whether this explanation of its origin be genuine or not, it is now idle to inquire; and in defiance of such authority, I still incline to an opinion I have elsewhere expressed, that it was the conversion of the Summa race to Islâm, several generations prior to the assigned cause, and which excluded them from intermarriage with the pure Rajpoot, that originated the custom; and while this cause continues to operate, in conjunction with a belief in the suttee decree, it is vain to expect more than a mitigation of the barbarity. I was told, on good authority, that no relaxation had taken place, though more pains were taken to conceal the perpetration. But it is asserted, and may be credited, that not a few of the male offspring suffer the same fate as the female, having "*a little milk*" (in which opium is infused) administered to them upon their birth. We shall the more readily accord belief to this, by comparing the numbers of the Jharejas with the Rahtores, who cotemporaneously colonized Cutch and Marwar; for

 while

while the census of the Jharejas presents an aggregate of only twelve thousand of the tribe fit to bear arms, the Rahtores can now, and did a century ago, bring fifty thousand into the field to defend their prince and country against the tyrant Arungzeb—"all sons of one father" (*ĕke bâp cá bítâ*), to use their own impressive phraseology. Moreover, the Jharejas, in their remote and almost insular position, have been exempt from the scourge of war, which has perpetually thinned the ranks of the Rahtores, though the former plead, and justly, the depopulating influence of earthquakes and famine.

Lakha, the first Jhareja, succeeded Halla, who had no offspring. Lakha and Lakhyar were the sons of Vera, the younger brother of Halla; and it was the preservation of one or both of them from the epidemic that originated the new name of the tribe. It may likewise be assumed that it was Vera's, not Halla's, daughter who entailed the curse, which first fell on Lakha's own family. There were seven Jhareja daughters, says the chronicle, in the family of Lakha, who became the victims of this imprecation; but so unhallowed was the act deemed by the family priest, a Brahmin of the Sarsoti sect, that when he was commanded to sacrifice them, he not only refused obedience, but disdained to hold the office of Gúrú—in the words of the chronicle: "When the Sarsot father relinquished this duty, an Oudaieh Brahmin succeeded to his office, and executed the command; he burned the seven girls, and the issue of this Brahmin has ever since been the Râj-Gúrú of the Jharejas." It would have been well had the whole race remained Mooslem, nor attempted to regain a place within the pale of Hinduism; now, they are neither one nor the other. Perhaps, in this condition, they present better subjects for an experiment of conversion to Christianity than any other class or race (save the

Malabar

Malabar Helots) in India, and humanity would rejoice at any successful attempt to wean them from this savage trait in their manners.

RAEDHUN succeeded Lakha, and may be styled the founder of the Jhareja state in Cutch; for although the regicide colonists had already planted establishments, they were diminished and superseded by the sons of Jam Oonur, who drove them from Kaira, in prosecution of his revenge on the murderers of his father; so that, it is asserted, the immediate descendants of Kair-Munai mixed with the debased classes of Mérs and Meyanas, with which they were in time incorporated and lost. The descendants of Mor, however, who conquered Kunter-kote, held it for five generations, when his line perished in the person of the famous Lakha-Phoolaní, who is mentioned in the annals of every state of that period: thus Mor had Sarj, he Phool, he Lakha, with the surname Phoolaní, who was celebrated for his raids from the Sutlej to the ocean, when the Rahtores first established themselves in the Marust'hali, or Indian desert; and who, as recorded in the annals of Marwar,* was slain by Sehoji, in revenge for the death of his brother, Saitaram. This event, according to the Rahtore chronicle, immediately followed the Mooslem conquest of India, by Shabudin, in A.D. 1193; and as Raedhun was eight generations from Jam Oonur, whose period, from the synchronism in the Jaitwa annals, was A.D. 1053, we may safely assume the date of the final conquest and settlement in Cutch by the Jharejas to have been cotemporaneous with the Mooslem conquest of Northern India, *viz.* A.D. 1193.

Raedhun conducted a fresh colony from the banks of the Indus to the borders of the great Rin, where he fixed it first at Churrie, but soon again moved to Vend, or Oond, near to Butchâo. The four sons of

* See *Annals of Rajast'han*, vol. ii. p. 13.

of Raedhun accompanied him from Saminagara; but the chronicle says he had a "fifth son,"* named Poelo, by a handmaid; and that he had two sons, Zudub and Cootub, who remained in Sinde. No cause is assigned for the migration of Raedhun; neither is it mentioned whether these sons with Mooslem names held any authority in Sinde when their father abandoned it. The probability is, that Raedhun was driven thence. He had four sons—

1. Dedoh. Obtained Kunter-kote.
2. Gajun. Defeated the Jaitwas, and his son, Halla, gave the tract he conquered the name of Hallar, founding Noanuggur, and retaining the title of Jam.
3. Ot'ho. From whom is descended the reigning family of Bhooj.
4. Hot'hi. Had twelve villages in Burdah; his descendants are styled Hot'hi.

It is evident, from the third son, Ot'ho, succeeding to his father's allotment, that the rule of succession in the family was not exactly fixed, and that it was a mere scramble for whatever they could conquer and maintain. This it will be well to bear in mind, when we come to consider the existing political government of the Jharejas; nor, in doing so, must we forget the more ancient colonists from the time of Lakha the Proud, who, in all probability, but for these fresh colonies, would have shrunk into utter insignificance. Prior, however, to Choorchund, and the proselytism of the Summas to Islâm, there had been irruptions into Cutch, and the name of the tract termed Ubrassie bears testimony to the chronicle, which states it to be called after Ubra, son of the first Khengar.

There is nothing worth extracting from the chronicle until the time of

* Among the Rajpoots, the term of "*fifth son*" is used for one not born in wedlock.

of Hamir (the seventh in descent from Ot'ho), who was slain by the elder branch of his family, the Jam of Hallar, near the village of Tehra; but the motive for this assassination (to obtain the estates of Hamir) went unrewarded, for his own wife, of the Chaora tribe, and sister to the mother of Hamir's young offspring, determined to save them, and sent them to her brother, Kukul Chaora, who so faithfully fulfilled the trust, as to suffer his own son to be put to death rather than betray their concealment to the Jam. "Since that day," adds the chronicle, "the chieftains of Kukul have protection against being killed by the sword,"—rather a doubtful compensation for such a service. The young princes fled eastward from this concealment, and encountered Manik-Mér, one versed in the decrees of fate. Like all founders of royal lines, Khengar, the eldest of the brothers, bore the impress of sovereignty on his foot, which being espied by the astrologer as they were sleeping in a temple, he foretold his elevation, and bid him proceed in full confidence to Ahmedabad. As they sallied forth with renovated hope, *he found* a black horse in his path, an omen so propitious that they pressed on. The king was out hunting, and Khengar, joining in the chase, slew an enormous lion. With this chance introduction and his story, he was taken into favour, received the title of Rao, and a royal grant of Cutch and Morbee. By the aid of the royal forces, Jam Rawul was driven from his usurped power, and obliged to seek refuge in Hallar. Thus Rao Khengar, *Hamíraní* (son of Hamir), took possession in S. 1593 (A.D. 1537), and founded the city of Bhooj on Friday, the fifth of the month Megsir, in S. 1605, or A.D. 1549. Manik-Mér was not forgotten; he had the town and district of Veera (now Anjar) settled on him and his issue; but at present the English are the lords of Anjar. It must also be stated, that previous to the assassination of Hamir,

Hamir, he had bestowed several allotments on his kindred and minor children, whose descendants are still the *potawuts* or chieftains of Cutch; as Roha, Veejam, Maotaira, Nullia, Arrysirr, &c. &c.

Fourteen generations have elapsed from Rao Khengar, the founder of Bhooj, to the present minor incumbent; and their names, with the day of mounting the throne, and that of their descent into the tomb, are minutely recorded in the chronicle; but these would little interest the reader. The changes are rung on successive names, which stamp the different clans originating from them, forming the *bhyâd*, or frérage, of the Jharejas. But, however important it may be to those whose duty it is to be conversant with the political and family distinctions of these tribes and all their affiliations, the reader of the West would feel no interest in the detailed pedigrees of the Hamiranís, Khengaranís, Bharanís, Tumacheanís, Noghanís, Hallanís, Raedhunanís, Karanís, Ghoranís, &c., &c.; with their duplicate and triplicate epithets, to distinguish families descended from princes of the same name—as Khengar-Hamiraní, Khengar-Tumacheaní, Khengar-Noghaní; extending, perhaps, to half-a-dozen more patronymics in the collateral branches of the families descended from the different princes bearing the name of Khengar, and so on of the rest. All this is treasured up by the Jhareja genealogists; and, idle as it may at first sight appear, the utility of these pedigrees, in all that regards disputed successions, is incontrovertible.

It would have been an easy matter to amplify on this subject without going beyond the original chronicle; but my sole object is to mark out, as it were, a genealogical chart of the existing family, and to explain the peculiarities in the present form of government, from the many singular changes in the habits, positions, and religion of the jharejas.

Jharejas. Before I proceed to this part of my task, I will cast a retrospective glance at the prominent epochs of this race, and state two opinions, the result of much reflection on the subject.

Of the supreme dominion of the Yadu race in India, which was broken up at a period of about twelve hundred years before Christ, and their consequent dispersion, authority, analogous to history, in their chronicles, sacred and profane, their *mahatmas*, or rituals of holy places, traditions, inscriptions, &c. furnish superabundant evidence. From these sources we learn, that one of their tribes migrated to Western Asia, and established itself in Zabulist'han ; that another went to Sinde, and founded Saminagara, capital of the kingdom of Samba, even when Alexander sailed down the Indus ; that this patronymic of Samba, or Sam, was preserved to later times, when they changed their creed, and came under the dominion, moral and political, of the Mooslems, in whose history they are styled the Sinde-Summa dynasty, which name they retained until driven from Sinde, when the new patronymic of Jhareja threw a veil over the past. Thus we have the following epochs in the Sinde-Summa chronology. First, the establishment of Samba in Sinde, 1100 to 1200 B.C.; second, the existence of the race in the same position in the time of Alexander, 320 B.C. From this period to Choorchund, in A.D. 904, we have names but no dates. It was with his son, named Sam-Yadu, that the ancient name was revived, whose offspring, as has been related, preserved the distinctive epithet of the Summa princes of Saminagara, some of whom, if not all, changed their creed. At this point we pause. The author of the *Periplus* informs us that, in the second century, a Parthian or Indo-Scythic colony took possession of lower Sinde, whose king made *Minagara* (which is merely Saminagara deprived of its

initial

initial syllable) his capital. The question then presents itself: did this new race destroy or drive out the descendants of Samba; or is this race, called by Arrian Indo-Scythic, the ancestry of Choorchund and the present Jharejas, who, as they found themselves associated with a more exclusive system of religion and manners than they had been accustomed to in higher Asia, engrafted the annals of the race they supplanted, as an introduction to their own genealogies? There are traditions which savour of this, one of which, held by the Jams of Nuggur, runs as follows: "That their ancestor, Jusodur Morani, quitted Mooltân and the Punjâb, and came to Sinde." If the Summas are not of the Yuechi race, which conquered Sinde in the second century, then they were driven out by them; and as, in the first irruption of Islâm on the Indus, in the first century of the Hegira and eighth of Vicrama, we find the family of Dahir* on the throne of Upper Sinde, which race, according to Colonel Pottinger, was succeeded by the Tak or Takshac (one of the most celebrated of the Getic tribes), we are entitled to conclude that the Summa-Yadus were either lost in, or incorporated with, or became subservient to, the multitude of these new tribes and races from Western Asia. Prior to Choorchund, in A.D. 904, there are the names of thirty-six princes,—amply sufficient to connect him with the Indo-Scythic conquest of Sinde in the second century of Vicrama; and, indeed, as they furnish no more links to connect him with Samba, their founder, it might be assumed they had no other. These names are for the most part not uncommon to the Rajpoot, though several belong not to the Hindu within the Indus, but savour strongly of the Scythic and Hunnish breeds, which swarmed in these regions in the second and sixth centuries:

* It is a curious and even valuable fact, that Dahir "Díspati," or king Dahir of Sinde, assisted in the defence of Cheetore, on the first attack of Islâm. See *Annals of Rajast'han*, vol. i. p. 231.

ries: as, Osnica, Wisoobara, Ungud, Doorguc, Kayea, and even the celebrated and favourite family name Khengar. Whatever be the origin, the family was fixed in Saminagara many generations antecedent to Choorchund, a name familiar to his neighbours; and from whom, in A.D. 904, down to the present time, being certain of our thread, we need no longer attempt to follow it in the labyrinths of unprofitable speculation. With Sam-Yadu, the son of Choorchund, the name and dynasty of Summa was firmly established in Sinde; with Jam Oonur, still sovereign of that region, in A.D. 1053, is connected their first-recorded intercourse with Saurashtra; and with Raedhun, in A.D. 1193, the migration, settlement, and gradual conquest of Cutch, which, in A.D. 1537, assumed a fixed form of government under its first Rao, Khengar, being the fifth who held this name in the genealogies. With this disentanglement of a web, extending over a period of nearly a thousand years, I shall rest content, having wrested from Time some facts tending to history, if the controversialist will not admit them to be strictly historical.

Up to this period, every Jhareja claimed equality, and acknowledged no permanent authority in their *bhyâd*, or frèrage, until Khengar, being invested with the title of sovereign, and supported by the power of the kings of Ahmedabad, assumed, or had granted to him, that supremacy which was necessary to cement their disjointed acquisitions, and constitute a state. Twelve princes have succeeded, to each of whose offspring allotments were made; and these, with the older branches prior to Khengar, compose this singular confraternity, with a slight account of which, differing as it does from the feudal institutions of the more eastern Rajpoot states, I shall conclude my sketch of Cutch and the Jharejas.

CHAPTER XXIII.

Statistics and geography of Cutch.—Its political constitution.—The *Bhyâd,* or *Frèrage.*—Authority of the Rao.—Tenure of estates.—Case of disputed succession.—*Bhatna,* or sub-infeudation, carried to a destructive extent.—Cause of the differences between the political customs of the Western Rajpoot States and Cutch.—Consequences of contact with the British Government.—The British invited as mediators between the Rao and the *Bhyâd.*—A British subsidiary force introduced.—All within the grasp of British authority.—Mandavie.—On board the Pattamar.—Cross the Gulf —Appearance of a whale.—Characters of the nakhoda and crew of the Pattamar.—Arrival at Bombay.—Detention there.—Its alleviating results.—Conclusion.

Of the statistics of Cutch and its geography, political and even physical, there is sufficient before the public; I will merely, therefore, so far touch on the former as is essential to the few remarks I have to make on the internal policy of the Jharejas, and its variation from that of the other Rajpoot states. For this information I must again express my obligations to the intelligent Ruttunji, the most enlightened member of the Regency, from whose oral replies to a long list of questions, which I noted down in his presence, the following details are derived.

The Jhareja dominions extend over a tract of about one hundred and eighty miles in length, and sixty in breadth; the land is generally poor, indifferently cultivated, and thinly peopled; so much so, that, although it contains an area of upwards of ten thousand square miles, the number of inhabitants is only half-a-million, one-twentieth part of which is confined within the capital, Bhooj, and another twentieth within the sea-port of Mandavie. Except these two places, there is none which merits the name of city, though there are a few towns, as Anjar, Lukput, Moondia, &c., on the coast, which derive importance

importance from their position. Of this population, the number of the dominant race, the Jhareja, fit to bear arms, is estimated at only twelve thousand; the remainder are Mooslem and Hindu, of all sects and classes. The entire revenue of the state, feudal and fiscal, amounts to fifty lakhs of korees, or about sixteen lakhs of rupees. Of this, three-fifths appertain to the crown, the remaining two-fifths to the aristocracy. The feudal chiefs of note are about fifty, though, taking into account the smaller sub-infeudations and single villages, there may be two hundred.* But here, in Cutch, as in the more settled Rajpoot governments, there is a select body of the highest rank holding greater appanages; and as Méwar has its "sixteen," Ambér its "twelve," and Jodpoor its "eight," so Cutch has its "thirteen" chief nobles, the principal of whom are the descendants of chieftains established *prior* to Khengar, in whose line, as already stated, these incongruous elements first subsided into something like government. Previously, each chief exercised unlimited power within the lands which he or his ancestors obtained by casual conquest; and when the recognition of Khengar took place, in A.D. 1537, these great nobles retained all their ancient self-constituted privileges, paying to the head of the state no more service or homage than was essential to the integrity of the society. These are strictly the allodial vassalage of Cutch, and as they not only constitute a material element of its polity, but serve as models of imitation to all those branches of the royal family which obtained appanages subsequent to Khengar, the sovereign is invested with as little real authority as ever belonged to the chief of any state: the power being so nicely balanced

* Mr. Elphinstone, in his Report, states the latter number; but my inquiries limited the number possessing real consequence to fifty.

balanced between the monarch and the aristocracy, that the least misconduct on either side must precipitate great changes. Whether, when the disjointed Jhareja aristocraçy consented to receive Rao Khengar as their sovereign, they defined the extent of his authority and their own future privileges, I could not discover; but there was one stipulation made, and that material to the maintenance of their prerogative, namely, that no point of consequence, affecting the general weal, should be agitated without the advice of the assembled *bhyâd*, or band of brothers, the emphatic appellation of the nobles of Cutch. This council of state still exists, and includes every chieftain of note.

The Rao retains the right of calling out the *kher*, or *levy en masse* of all the vassal Jharejas; but there is a mark of independence attached to their obedience to supreme authority even in this point, a pecuniary sacrifice being exacted from the crown in return for this attendance, though on so moderate a scale, as to leave it a matter of doubt whether the right to summon, or power to disobey, be the stronger.

The smallness of this allowance, *viz.* one koree for a cavalier, and the same between two foot soldiers, indicates a sort of mutual compromise; for while it implies an acknowledgment on the part of the chief that this service is not compulsory (though, at the same time, it scarcely suffices to purchase rations), the tax is too slight to place the crown or the public weal in jeopardy.

On the demise of any of the vassal Jharejas, a sword and turban are sent by the Rao to the heir of the deceased; but he cannot influence the succession, nor does this imitation of investiture produce the incident of *nuzzerana*, or 'relief,' which marks the original emanation of the grant, and which in Méwar is fixed at one year's revenue of the

estate.

estate. In Cutch it is considered a mere acknowledgment of the succession, for which not even homage is paid. This is reserved only for the accession of the Raos, their marriage, or the birth of a prince; on which occasions every Jhareja attends at court, and makes his homage and *nuzzerana*.

The Jhareja princes, in making *puttas*, or grants, appear never to have had an idea of claiming any reversionary interest: there are no distinctions, as in Méwar, of "*Kala-puttas*," or "*Chur-ootar*" estates, that is, those for life, or resumable at pleasure, of which there was there a large class. Here, to use Ruttunji's own words, "*it is for ever, even if to a sweeper*," with power to do with it as he pleases: in short, the possession is as much freehold as any estate in England.

The sole instance in which the sovereign has any title to intermeddle with the lands or privileges of the aristocracy, is the right of decision in disputed cases of sub-infeudations; a right voluntarily acknowledged, though chiefly confined to those estates which emanated from the crown since Khengar was received as their head. But as no act of the Rao is independent of the great council of chiefs, so these appeals are, after all, but appeals to themselves, though individually yielded with reluctance. A case of disputed succession is now on the *tapis*, where the prince, or rather the council of regency governing in his minority, is opposed to the general council of chiefs. A petty chieftain, one of the older or allodial stock of the Jharejas, died, leaving no offspring or near kindred to inherit, but one illegitimate son by a woman of the Bhattia tribe. In this emergency, both parties appear to have lost sight of principles, the crown, in setting up, as heir-general, the novel claim to escheats of what it never granted; while the chiefs, in order to repudiate so unlawful a precedent, desire to confirm

the

the spurious issue in all the privileges of the *bhyâd*. The right course would be a compromise; *i. e.* to let the general council of chiefs adopt the nearest (no matter how remote) of the kin of the deceased, and for the crown to sanction the adoption. But it is evident that such compromise is not desired by one party; and though on abstract principles this party may be right, and might defend itself by appealing to the customs of other Rajpoot states, yet, as there is little or no analogy existing between these and the Jharejas, the argument is insufficient for such deviation from usage: at all events, the point ought to be adjusted upon Jhareja principles, and independent of British authority, further than as umpires.

The system of *bhatna*, or sub-infeudation, carried to the extent it is in Cutch, is a principle of destruction; for, according to the laws of Menu, where all the sons are co-heirs (though a kind of *majorat* is reserved for the eldest), as each must have his *bhat*, or portion, the rules of arithmetic would settle the point where all Jhareja subdivision should cease, when infinitely small quantities, such as, to use their own metaphor, "might be borne away on the point of their lance," would remain. A great moral crime is the sole corrective of this political error; and it is to prevent the destruction of families by following the supreme law of sub-infeudation, that the first law of nature and of God is violated, infanticide not being confined to female victims.* Were the British Government to negociate a statute of limitation, demonstrating how the general welfare is endangered by this *ad infinitum* division, and to effect by compromise a system of escheats, partly to the crown, partly to the *bhyâd*, the chain which holds

* Mr. Elphinstone, in his Report on Cutch, from which I extracted several notes, confirms this; adding that it accounts for the number of single heirs male in families

holds together this anomalous society would be strengthened, and such horrors avoided.

Thus we have briefly shown the singular picture of a prince, without any civil jurisdiction or control beyond his own personal domain, and exercising the smallest possible quantity of political power to keep the frame of society together; dispensing neither rewards nor punishments; in short, an armed federation, or *bhyâd*, of members of one great family, kept together by a sense of mutual danger and benefit: such was the constitution prior to Khengar, and, with the addition of this prominent feature, such did it until lately remain.

It is to the difference in the mode of colonization between the Western Rajpoot states and Cutch, that we must refer the different usages in their governments, and the policy which has preserved to this singular aristocracy all their ancient independent privileges. It was not until I paid this visit to Cutch, waded through its chronicles, and conversed with its wise men, that I could comprehend the existence of such a society; for while at a distance, on being made acquainted with some of its enactments, especially in respect to escheats, lapses, &c., I was persuaded that no government could go on where the aristocracy was independent of the crown. My reasoning was right, both abstractedly and from analogy; for such a government never could have survived a century, had it been subjected to the vicissitudes of Rajpootana. But the land of the Jharejas, being nearly insulated by the sea on one side, and the Grand Rin on the other, had little to dread from its Hindu neighbours; while, by a piece of admirable policy, that of undertaking to convey all Mahomedan pilgrims *gratis* to Mecca, they conciliated every Mahomedan power, and were never visited in wrath by the kings.

And

And thus, in all probability, the feudal system of the Jharejas might have held their *bhyâd* together for some centuries longer, had it not been destined that they should have, as neighbours, a state of high civilization, ambition, and ever-progressing power: I mean, of course, the British. The Mahratta wars placed the Guicowar court of Baroda under our influence, which soon entailed an interference with his feudatories in the Saurashtra peninsula; thence, though a gulf lay between us and Cutch, one step led inevitably to another, until we were brought into collision even with the remote people of Sinde.

In spite of the absence of those bonds of unity, and those symbolic evidences of supremacy, analogous to the incidents of European feudal polity, between the raos and the aristocracy of Cutch, there existed a division of the country which, with proper management, might have broken up the power of the aristocracy, and left the authority in the hands of its princes. The crown domain surpassed that of the whole body, and it engrossed the commercial revenues of several cities and towns. With the means this afforded, it could always command the services of a portion of the feudatories; for there are, and ever have been, adverse parties and rival principles at every court; and I was informed of instances wherein the entire *bhyâd* united to punish acts committed by one of their own body, which were held derogatory to their prince. With such influence, it was not difficult to call out the *khér*, or entire feudal array; and when the country was menaced by foreign invasion, the Jharejas have stood their ground against aggression. But the fashion, of late years, of introducing bands of Arabs, Sindies, or Rohillas amongst the retainers of these princes, has often produced great jealousy and heart-burnings in their nobles, whilst these mercenaries were the cause of no small embarrassment to their employers. They

were

were always ready to do their masters' bidding; but that mutual forbearance, that kind of politic balance, when there was no foreign interference, was lost. The fate of the last Rao, Bharmul, illustrates these deviations from ancient usage. His naturally intemperate disposition was aggravated by a love of strong drink; and, with these hireling foreigners at his command, he set at nought the ancient limitations of his power, for which he substituted his own will. But he had to deal with those who well knew their rights, and, rather than surrender them, they invited the British as mediators, which interference ended in an intimate alliance, and was followed by its invariable concomitant, a British Subsidiary Force! Rao Bharmul's intemperance increased to a state of madness, and he was deposed, confined, and his son Rao Desil put upon the *gadí*. Being an infant, a council of regency was formed, composed of some of the principal Jhareja chiefs, and the old civil officers, one of whom, my informant, Ruttunji, is entirely devoted to English interests. Moreover, the British Resident is considered as the head of the regency. As far as I could learn or observe, matters seemed to go on very smoothly; tranquillity was universal, and every one enjoyed the fruits of his industry, or his patrimony; nor is there any likelihood of this state of things being disturbed, so long as Rao Desil is a minor. The future will depend on his personal disposition, and the use that is made of the interim. The chiefs, while they preferred surrendering their independence to a foreign power, to seeing it wrested from them by their sovereign, have secured, by the guarantee of that power, the integrity of their possessions; and the little obedience they formerly acknowledged is now virtually annulled, though the mediator will be perpetually tormented by appeals from each, and most probably hated by both parties.

Such are the *mirabilia* and *memorabilia* of the ancient Syrastrene; a region, I repeat, superior to any in India for the diversity of tribes which have inhabited it, and for the architectural remains of past days which it still exhibits. All is now within the powerful grasp of British authority: the sovereign Guicowar, the lord of Anhulwarra, and his feudatories, Gohil, Chaora, the Cat'hi rover, the pirates of the Land's-end, and the Jhareja descendants of the Summas and Yadus, all have broken the charm of feudal confederacy which linked them to their own princes, and voluntarily submitted to the yoke of the foreigner. The inspired "preacher" of the Jews, and the last great bard of the Rajpoots, have, almost in the same words, proclaimed the dangers of a minority: "Woe to thee, O land, when thy king is a child!"* to which Chund adds, "and when women rule:" a position the consequences of which to the Rajpoot present a far greater subject of alarm, than the sequel to the stanza of the preacher, "and when thy princes eat in the morning." This would be a sign of regeneration devoutly to be wished with the Rajpoot, whose love of opiates and strong-drink leaves no desire to break his fast until the sun is high in his career. But neither the Jewish nor the Rajpoot bard was ever in a condition to judge of the superadded danger of that political monster, called "SUBSIDIARY ALLIANCE." It is hardly to be expected, that the Jharejas will be exempted from the invariable and inevitable sequence of such unions, which have established, as an axiom, the ultimate destruction of every semi-barbarous state, when thus connected with one of high civilization; and I may be permitted to say, that, however pure our intentions, yet with a British resident as chief of the regency; with the creature of our creation, Ruttunji, (worthy though

* Ecclesiastes, x. 16.

though he be) as the active agent of our influence; with chiefs who, having sinned beyond forgiveness in laying the Jhareja sceptre at our feet, now look to us alone for protection; it would be marvellous if this state should be the exception to the rule which has marked the past, and will mark the future, until, as the late Nestor of Rajpootana, Zalim Singh, foretold, "there will be but one emblem of power *(éki siccâ)* throughout India:" a prediction, the verification of which seems rapidly approximating. He well knew the short-sightedness of his countrymen, and that, to get rid of the collar when it pressed at the time, they would slip their necks into a yoke from which there was no extrication.

The baneful *uml-pâní* (opium) has too much benumbed the prophetic faculties of the Bhât, Charun Bardai, to point out these dangers to his *béndâ* chief, with whom, to use his own poetic phraseology, "as he sips his *imrita,*" his ambrosial draught, he bids the future take care of itself; and thus, left without a monitor, the Jhareja *bhyâd* has fraternized with a race, from whose embrace, hitherto, there has been no escape. The time cannot be remote, when the usual catalogue of British ministerialists, judges, collectors, adawlets, &c. will spread over the whole of Syrastrene; when some future D'Anville or Rennell may settle the yet unsettled point,* out of which arm of the Delta the Macedonian fleet sailed for Babylon; or some modern Lycurgus may solve the question, which is the most difficult task—to civilize the Jhareja; or put the harness of control on the Gorkhur, the wild-ass of the Rin?—to teach the former the inhumanity of infanticide, the

* Lieut. Pottinger, from minute and accurate survey, agrees with Dr. Vincent's theoretic deductions, preferring the eastern arm of the Delta; but the entire Potallina has undergone so much physical metamorphosis, that we find a difficulty in adopting any opinion, though the arguments of Lieut. P. are decidedly the most convincing.

the evils of polygamy, and the destructive policy of a too extended sub-infeudation? By the varied tribes of the Saurashtra peninsula, the transfer of mere feudal or tributary subjection from the Guicowar to our power would be received with satisfaction, for they have hitherto only known us as mediators for their good; and, greatly as I am averse to see a more extensive foreign influence or authority pervade these remains of such singular civilization in Rajpootana, yet, in the present moral and political condition of Cutch, any system would be better than that which violates the first principle of our nature, and places humanity below the brute creation.

Mandavie.—January 7th.—On board my pattamar. I retraced my steps in the same expeditious manner from the capital of the Jharejas, and reached "*the* mart" this morning. The wind being right in my teeth, I was reluctantly forced to resign my ulterior object, the *embouchure* of the Indus, and steer my bark over the ocean, of which I had to traverse five hundred miles to reach Bombay. The sails were unfurled, and, bidding adieu to my Mandavie friends, with a fine breeze we stood across the gulf, and, clearing the Finisterre of the Hindu, directed our course for Deobunder, the ancient capital of the Chaoras, where I had determined to land, in order to hunt for inscriptions relative to this race, the founders of Anhulwarra. But even to attain this was not my destiny, the determination being overruled by my nakhoda, who said I should never reach Bombay by the 14th if I loitered by the way, or lost any part of so fair a wind. I had only to obey, and the prow of my pattamar was turned from the land, or, as Ibrahim said, we were now to steer *lal* instead of *lîlâ*, 'red' in lieu of 'blue.' Unused to such nautical phraseology, I ascended the poop of my vessel to have a personal explanation in front of Ibrahim's binnacle. The

The mystery was soon solved, when I perceived that the subdivisions of his compass, instead of having each point lettered, had them coloured blue, red, green, yellow, &c., symbols more easily retained, where the march of intellect had not yet penetrated. But Ibrahim, though not lettered, was not uninformed; his wisdom was acquired in the best school, that of experience; and he could not only steer his bark without the use of letters, but call in the aid of the stars as his guide.

We pursued our course with a moderate breeze and an unclouded sky, making good progress until the shades of darkness began to close around us, when the wind rather lulled. The night was serene and beautiful: "Orion with all his bands" rode triumphant over our heads, and the deep silence was undisturbed, save by the gentle ripple of my bark as she glided slowly through the water. It was a night for meditation, and I gave myself up to "the sweet influences" of the past and the future.

> "Sleep, that knits up the ravell'd sleeve of care,
> The death of each day's life,"

had sealed the eyes of all about us, save Ibrahim, the nakhoda, and another of the crew, having a like patriarchal appellation, Ayoub, or Job. As we surveyed the heavenly host, I was much gratified to find Ibrahim familiar with the names of the principal groups: the *Hyades* he styled *Araní*, meaning, in Hinduví, the 'buffalo;' but as this animal is unknown to Arabia, the idea could not but suggest itself, that even for the name of the brilliant Aldebaran, 'the eye of the bull,' the Arabian is indebted to the Hindu astronomer, as well as for his algebra.

The

The succeeding day continued fair, with the same moderate breeze. As we were enjoying its freshness, about noon, no land in sight, a huge whale arose within musket-shot of the pattamar, followed by a shoal of porpoises extending many hundred yards. For at least an hour he retained his relative position, swimming in a parallel line, without heading us a yard, occasionally diving and rising, while his minor subjects were playing all sorts of gambols around him, leaping and splashing, as if it were a holiday. The Gangetic servants in my train, both Sipahis and domestics, were struck dumb with astonishment; the porpoise they had almost all seen in the Ganges, but even the name of this giant of the deep they had never heard. I could not resist the inclination to take a shot, either at the whale or lesser fry, and called for my gun; but yielded to Ibrahim's entreaties, not to follow the childish impulse: he used precisely the same language of dissuasion as the faithful Bedouin, Ayd, guide of the lamented Burckhardt, when he desired to shoot at a porpoise in the gulf of Akaba, "that it was unlawful to kill them, as they were the friends of man, and never hurt any body."

I have mentioned the patriarchal names of two of my crew, Ibrahim, "the lord of the boat" *(nâo khoda)*, and Ayoub; there was also an Ishmael. It is scarcely necessary to add, that the crew were entirely Mooslem. Ayoub was a garrulous, facetious sort of fellow, and though the types of wisdom had begun to diversify the honours of his beard, he preferred giving scope to his humours, to assuming a virtue he did not possess: he had a jest for every body and every thing, and generally required to be told twice what the nakhoda required of him. Moreover, in spite of the commands of the prophet, and though little

little better than a fresh-water sailor, he had acquired a taste for the "waters of life," regarding which he introduced his first knowledge with considerable *naïveté* and tact. While conversing with the nakhoda, Ayoub contrived every now and then to put in a word, and seizing his opportunity, he with great gravity observed, that he had heard wonderful stories regarding the *Valaiti-d'hood*, or 'milk of Europe,' as a kind of *axír*, or balm against all ills of mind or body; "did I know what it was?" and, as a smile of penetration passed over my face, "had I any of it?" quickly followed. I told him I not only knew and possessed it, but, to satisfy his inquisitiveness, would give him some; though he must first tell me how he became acquainted with the virtues of a thing which it was forbidden him to touch. He replied, that, having conveyed the baggage of an officer from Bombay to Poorbunder, and landed it during a heavy fall of rain, the officer gave him and his comrades a glass each of an *arac*, or essence, which he called by the name Ayoub used, when he propounded the question. I had forgotten him and this conversation, and was seated in my cabin reading by candle-light, when a voice called out for admittance: it was Ayoub, with his *cupra*, or coco-nut cup, come to claim the performance of my promise. I called a domestic to bring me the bottle, and had actually tilted it towards the *cupra*, when it struck me I was doing a very foolish thing, and might incapacitate our second in command, at this the first half of our voyage. The soldier, about to suffer death, could hardly have looked more stupified with surprise, when the word "recover arms," instead of "fire," was given, than Job, when I restored to the perpendicular attitude the bottle of elixir. He looked unutterable things;

not a word did he speak, but, with the still outstretched arm grasping the cup, he kept his eyes fixed on me for an explanation of the act. "Suppose, Ayoub," said I, "this should make you tipsy, and a storm should arise?" "Saheb!" was all the reply, but no change of attitude. "Supposing, Ayoub, I promised to give you a whole bottle on our arrival in the harbour of Bombay, would you not relinquish your cupful for to-night?" The hand and cup were withdrawn, and though the expression still was in correspondence with the old adage, of "a bird in the hand," &c., his features relaxed into a smile, and he brought himself to say, he thought I was right.

Nothing occurred in our smooth navigation during the five days of lovely weather, as we approached that magnificent scene, the entrance to Bombay, possessing, in every diversity and the grandest forms, all the accessories, mountain, wood, islands, and water.* But it was the 14th, the day previous to that fixed for the sailing of the *Sarah* to England; and the fore-topsails unfurled of two large ships withdrew my speculations from every other object. I pencilled a note and sent it by a small craft on board one of these, to know if either were my own ship, while I hastened to land my Sipahis and attendants, that I might be ready for the result. A few minutes ended my fears; though both were precursors of the *Sarah* for England. Making a present to my crew, and not forgetting the bottle of *Valaití-d'hood, alias* brandy, for Job, I landed my cargo of mutilated divinities, inscriptions, arms, manuscripts, to the number of forty boxes, on the beach, and soon had them sheltered under tents, which the kindness of friends had prepared for me. And here I was detained nearly three weeks before my

* Once more I refer the reader, for an adequate representation, to Capt. Grindlay's work, "Scenery of Western India."

my ship sailed, each day adding to my mortification at the non-accomplishment of my long-indulged scheme, for which half the time would have sufficed. But as there are few evils without some counterbalancing good, so, on the present occasion, my detention was productive of results far more important and gratifying than could, under any circumstances, have crowned my expectations from visiting the Indus. A few days before we sailed, I had a conversation with General Sir Charles Colville, then commander-in-chief, on the subject of my tour; on the beauties of Aboo, the ruins of Palit'hana, Somnath, Anhulwarra, Chandravati; and, at his request, drew up a detailed account of my route, inviting his attention to collateral objects, which I transmitted during the ship's delay at Cochin. His Excellency, taking this as his guide, soon after followed in my steps, visiting all these places of celebrity, the most of them known only to myself. Happily for me, and for architectural science, as well as for the lovers of the things of old, Colonel Hunter Blair was on his Excellency's staff, and to Mrs. Hunter Blair's enthusiastic taste for the arts, and the surpassing elegance of her pencil, the world stands indebted for the illustrations of the noblest specimens which the Hindu *silpi* has achieved: thus rescued from the oblivion in which they had lain for ages, and the destruction which soon followed. But we must not again mount the *cheval de bataille:* "Othello's occupation's gone," and henceforward I must look on the past as a dream, to which the present monotonies of life add the semblance of reality.

Here ends my story, or, in the concluding phraseology of the complete Hindí letter-writer, "what more need I say?" save that, as we continued our voyage, I kept my eyes upon the land, indulging my fancy in speculations on the future, of my return to my Rajpoots, as well as many a scheme for their welfare; and at length, when we ranged the last promontory of India, and, running through the gulf of Manar, dipped the pole-star in the wave, I parted with him as the last tie that bound me to the land where I had passed my best days, and had been the instrument of good to thousands. But as all my readers are not star-gazers, I should explain my attachment to that particular star, emblematic of constancy with the poets of the east as of the west. My principal walk at Oodipoor was on the terrace-roof of my *palazzo*, and there I often dined and slept, in those hot days when it was impossible to take exercise out of doors. The brilliancy in that country of the deep cerulean, spangled with its golden orbs, is indescribable, and with such a canopy over-head, I had almost become a Sabæan. A line drawn longitudinally across this terrace-roof, my quarter-deck, and prolonged through space, would have terminated at the polar-star, which hung over the gate of the city called the Dehli *Durwaza*; for years, therefore, this guided my steps in my nocturnal peregrinations, or received my salaam, when I took a lunar, or noted an eclipse of some one of Jupiter's moons. Whatever recalled these scenes in "the happy valley" and the small world around, which to me at least brought no satiety of interest, was a cherished object, and what object could more forcibly pourtray the past than "the star of the north," whose gradual departure I traced, as we ran down the latitude! When it was lost to me in the wave, I felt as though I had parted from a friend, and as we sailed through the North Atlantic Sea, I hailed his reappearance

appearance with delight. It but little concerns the reader, that I stopped at St. Helena, and concluded my pilgrimage at the tomb of

"The greatest, not the worst of men,"

the operations of whose gigantic mind I have since traced through many a land.

"Ill-weaved Ambition, how much art thou shrunk!
When that this body did contain a spirit,
A kingdom for it was too small a bound;
But now, two paces of the vilest earth
Is room enough!"

October 28th, 1835.

APPENDIX.

No. I. (p. 90).

Inscription on the Shrine of Kunkul-éswar, at Oreessa, now called Oreah.*

S. 1265. Bysak sood Poonum, Tuesday. Of Chaluc race, Purrum Bhuttarik Mahárájá Dheráj, Sremad Bheemdeo, in his paramount (Beejy Raj) reign and lifetime, and Srí Kurrun, minister, of all the princes of his time the mightiest, and while the umbrella of Dhárâburz Deo alone was spread over the land of Chandraoti Nuggri, Mandalakéswar, the fortune of the land. At this time, Preladun Deo, the prince, exercised the duties of government, and at this time the brave Kedaréswar repaired the temple of Kunkuléswar. The inscription written by the Pundit Lukmi Dhar.

No. II. (p. 88.)

[A copy of this inscription, notwithstanding diligent search, cannot be found amongst the Author's papers.]

No. III. (p. 186.)

Inscription concerning Komár-pál Solankhi, in Brimha's Temple, in Cheetore, called Lakhun's Mundur.

To him who takes delight in the abode of waters, from whose braided locks ambrosial drops continually descend,—even this Mahadéva, may he protect thee!

He

* Kunkul-éswar Mahadeo's shrine and fountain are at Bhadrinath. Those who bathe in this fountain have no second birth, kun-kul—*kul,* meaning 'tainted with errors and follies,' and *kun,* 'removing.'

He of the Chaluc tribe, having innumerable gems of ancestry, flowing from a sea of splendour, was Moolraj, sovereign of the earth. What did he resemble, whose renown was bright as a fair sparkling gem, diffusing happiness and ease amongst the sons of the earth? Many mighty princes there were of his line, but none before had made the Great Sacrifice.

Generations after him, in the lapse of years, was Sid-raj, a name known to the world, whose frame was encased in the rubies of victory, and whose deeds were sounded over the curtain of the earth, and, by the fire of his own frame and fortune, heaped up unconsumable wealth.

After him was Komár-pál Deo. What was he like, who, by the strength of his invincible mind, crushed all his foes; whose commands the other sovereigns of the earth placed on their foreheads; who compelled the Lord of Sacambhari to bow at his feet; who in person carried his arms to Sewaluc, making the mountain lords bow before him, even in the city of Salpoora?

On the mountain Chutturkote, - - - ar, the Lord of Men, in sport placed this [writing] amidst the Abode of the Gods, even on its pinnacle placed it. Why? That it might be beyond the reach of the hands of fools.

As does the Lord who rules the Night (*Nissanath*), looking on the faces of the fair Kamunis below, feel envious of their fairness, and ashamed of the dark spots in his own; even so does Chutturkote blush at seeing this (*prasishta*) on her pinnacle. S. 1207. (A.D. 1141.) [Month and day broken off.]*

No. IV. (p. 186.)

[A copy of this Inscription cannot be found.]

No. V. (pp. 336 and 352.)

Translation of an Inscription on a Slab found at the entrance of the Mundur of Bhadri-Koli, in Deo-Puttun, but originally belonging to Somnat'h.

Salutation to Him, from whose lock the Ganges flows; on whose thigh Parbutty reclines! Salutation to Vizeem Raj, the child of Parbutty! Salutation to Saruswuttee and

* [This inscription is given in the Appendix to vol. i. of the *Annals of Rajast'han.*]

and make my tongue his abode! By him, whom the sun and moon adore—by all may I be protected! [Remaining slocas omitted.]

Bháo Brisputée (Vrishpati), a Bramin of Kinoj (Canouj), left Benares on pilgrimage; he reached Awanti and Dharanuggur, then ruled by Jey Sing Deo. The Pramar prince and all his family elected him their Gooroo, and the prince called him brother.

Sid Rae Jey Sing was universal Lord when he went to heaven; Kunwar [Komar] Pál succeeded to his throne; Bháo Brisputee became the chief of his advisers. Kunwar [Komar] Pál was the Calp Vrich of the three worlds. He gave his seal, his wealth, and all under the command of Brisputee, and said, "Go and repair the fallen (*teerun*) temples of Deo-Puttun."* Bháo Brisputee made them resemble Kylas. He invited the Lord of the World to see his work. When he saw, he dwelt on the praise of the Gooroo, as he said, "My heart is rejoiced; to you and your sons I give the chief place in my kingdom."

Chundrama erected the first temple of gold; then Rawun of silver. After, Krishna Bheemdeo rebuilt it, and studded it with jewels; and then Kunwar [Komar] Pál made it once more resemble Meru. The Lord of Goorjen Mundali bestowed lands and wealth on Brimhpoora (the abode of Bramins). He raised fortifications from the south, the abode of Somnat'h, to the north, *including Brimhpoora.* The abodes of Sid-éswar, Bheem-éswar, were all repaired, and golden pinnacles raised on all. Wells and fountains, halls for travellers, reservoirs and silver conduits, through the temple of the god, for the water, with a throne for the god The temple of Pâp Mochun-éswar, erected by Rookmaun, and thrown down, was rebuilt. Balabhi Samvat, 850.†

No. VI. (p. 337.)

Inscription on a Gateway at Deva-puttun.

S. 1442. Assar-bood 8, Sanewar. After salutations to Saruswuttee. Of Yadu house was the Chetore Raja Bheem, his wife Manikdevi, his daughter Yamuni Bae; she was married to the chief of Rushtore, Bunee Brimohjee. They came to Prulias, and made gifts and charities, the virtues attending which still benefit the people (as in tanks, &c.) (On

* In the *Charitra,* it is said that the golden *kullus* was made by Vrishpati.

† B. S. 850+375=V. S. 1225, A.D. 1169, the year of the accession of Bhím Deo, of Puttun, next but one in succession to Komar-pál,

(*On the same stone.*)

S. 1273. Sambut Bikram Bysak bood Chouth. In Deo Puttun Raj Mooldeo. After whom Hamir, who repaired the temples and the munduff of Somnat'h.

No. VII. (p. 351.)

No. 1.—*Inscription found at Billawul, originally taken from the Temple at Somnat'h.*

Adoration to the Lord of all, to the *Light of the Universe!** Adoration to the form indescribable! to Him, at whose footsteps all kneel!

In the year of Mohummud 662, and in that of Bikram [Vicrama] 1320, and in that of Srimad Balabhi 945, and in the Seehoh [Siva-Singa] Sambut 151 (=A.D. 1264),† Assar bood, 13th, Sunday (Rubwar). Srimad Anhul (poor) Pât [either 'scarlet,' or mistaken for Patun], obeyed by numerous princes; Purn-éswar Bhuttarik, on whom the favour of the Lord of Oomia, of exalted fortune, fearing none, a thorn to his foe. Sri Chaluk Chakravarti Mahraja Dheraj Sremad Urgoon Deva, universally victorious! His minister, Sri Mal Deva, and the different officers of government, the five kulas, with Hoormuz of Belacool (Billawul), in the reign of Amira Rookn-oo-deen, walking in the path of virtue, and at the same time the Khoja Ibrahim, of Hormuz, son of the Admiral (*Nakhoda*) Noor-oo-deen Feeroz, with the Chaora Palook-deva, and Ranik Srí Soméswar Deva, and the Chaora Ramdeva, and the Chaora Bheemsing, and all the Chaora chiefs and other tribes assembled. Nansi Raja, Chaora, inhabiting Deo-Puttun, assembling the mahajuns (merchants), established and settled the offerings to the temples, and their repairs; that the flowers, oil, and water should be regularly supplied to Ruttun-éswar,‡ Choul-éswar,§ and the temple of Poolinda Dévi,‖ and various others, *erected a koti (wall) around the temple at Somnat'h, with a gateway to the north.* The Chaora son of Modula, Keelhandeo, with the son of Sohun, Loonsi, with the two baniahs (merchants), Balji and Kurrun, bestowed the profits of the weekly market on the temples. While the sun and moon

* This at once shews Somnat'h to be the *Sun,* or Lord of the Moon; in short, the Sun-God, Balnat'h, whose type was the phallus, or fructifier.

† V.S. 1320—945=375 of Vicrama (A.D. 319), for the commencement of the Balabhi era; and 1320—151=1169 of Vicrama (A.D. 1113), for that of the Siva-Singa era, established by the Gohils of Deo.

‡ Mahadeo's great temple at Somnat'h.

§ The tutelary divinity of the Chaluc race.

‖ The goddess of the Bheels.

moon endure, let it not be received! Feeroz is commanded to see this obeyed. Let the proper offerings on festivals be continued, and let the surplus offerings be placed in the treasury for the repairs of the st'han of faith. The Chaoras and the Nakhoda Noor-oo-deen are commanded to see these orders executed on all the population of merchants, Moosulmans, &c. Heaven will be the portion of him who obeys, and hell of him who breaks through these commands.*

No. 2.—*Another Inscription found in Billawul, but carried from Patun.*

Srimad Balabhi, 927. Phalgoon sood Beej Boodwár. Ad Srí, Deo-puttun, Mool Jog Gohil, and others, erected the temple to Gordhan Nath.

No. VIII. (p. 357.)

Inscription at Choorwar, from Sooraj Mudu Gate, Koraussi.

(After invocation to the Sun, to remove from the world all troubles of the mind). Thou, the Lord of a thousand rays, the remover of darkness, the Light of the Earth and Hills, causing the lotus to expand, to Thee, O Sun, I bow! Sprung of this Sun were princes, whose horse's hoof covered the proud with darkness. Of this was one of Bramin race, who attained sovereign power. Learned, brave, the thirty-six tribes of princes obeyed him. His residence was at the foot of Rabarri Achil (Aboo), in the mandala of Maroosthullee. After many generations of his race was the Lord of the Earth, Loonung; with a large army, and with the force of his arms and navy, he gained Saurashtra. His son was Bheem Sing, a mighty warrior. Lawin Pal was his son, who plundered his neighbours. His son, a mighty warrior, proud, and by the force of his own arms, fierce as the Sun; and splendid in renown was Bhomi Pal, and from him and his son, Lakshman Sing. From Panihul he came to Joonagurh; he was the Indra of this Indrapoora. His nephew was Raj-Sing; he cemented the nine regions into one kingdom. His son, Khem Raj, the Prince of Princes. His son was Som-Brimha, from whom Ben Guj, a mighty warrior.

In Saurashtra are sacred places removing sins—was Srimad Khengâr.

Srí

* [A copy of this inscription (with a few trifling variations), accompanied with explanatory notes by the Author, is given in the Appendix to Vol. I. of the *Annals of Rajast'han.*]

Srí Mohummud Brehunmud Padshah, even to Girnar, made his An and Deen respected by all but Khengâr, and his brother Bhimdeo, whose sister Rutnadévi was married to Raj Sing; whose son was Muldeo, who founded Koraussi. His son was Mooraj, like a mad elephant. His son was Seoraj, and his Maldeo. The Sun had foreknown his descendant would here found a temple to him; Maldeo erected it. His wife, Bunladevi, was faithful as Síta, of Pramar Cula. The fire sacrifice was prepared, and the Sun enshrined.

(Then follow several names of nephews and nieces, amongst them Moolraj Bhagaila.) S. 1445. Phalgoon-bood 5, Somwár.

No. IX. (p. 373.)

[This inscription is likewise wanting.]

No. X. (p. 374.)

Translation of an Inscription (on a small slab) at the Rewati-coonda, at Damadra-coondra.

Salutation to Ganésa; salutation to him, whom the chief of ascetics *(Jogiswara)* and sages *(mooni)* adore, in the hope of a glance from his eye: he, who plundered the churns of the *Gopis,** whose hands were pinioned to the *damuni* † by Yasooda,‡ even Vishnu Damadra, was here enshrined, he who created mankind!

Of yore, was Mandalica, the Lord of Men, of Yadu race. To his foe he was the *moodgil* § of the Athlete; blessed by Lacshmi, he was obeyed by the *lords of the land.* Descended from him was Mahé-pâla, from whom sprung the lord of the land, Khéngâr.‖ What did he resemble? an elephant, carrying destruction to his foe. He erected the abode *(st'han)* of Soméswara,¶ and to the Bramins he daily distributed silver gifts. He had a son, like Nanda, of antient times, named Jey Sing Deo. What did he resemble?

* *Gopis,* the shepherdesses of the pastoral Vroja, the birth-place of Crishna, or Kanyâ.

† *Damuni,* the churning-rod.

‡ *Yasoodá,* mother of Kanyâ.

§ Large blocks of wood, with handles, used by the *Calisthenic* professors.

‖ Khengâr is the name of the prince who erected the palace of which a view is given.

¶ Soméswar, or Somnât'h, 'Lord of the Moon,' a title of Siva; also applied to Suryâ, the Sun-God.

resemble? he, who fostered the four castes, and aterums? From him was Vicrama Sing; over the elephant-formed foe invariably victorious. Who was like unto him? Mighty heads, wearing crowns, have existed; many sons born of womankind, but none like him, the first amongst leaders *(samant)*. From him was Mandalíca,* from whom was Mélagâ, of exalted fortune, a sanctuary to the terrified. His son was Jey Sing, in whose reign was Abhye Sing, of Yadu race, the foremost of his warriors, who at the *t'halaiti* † of Jinjirkote slew the Javan ‡ foe, and walked in the path of virtue. §

Samvat|| Ram, Toorung, Sâgur, Mahi, in the month of Vysak *(soodi)* 5th, Brigúbasri, or Saturday, this spot was purified and consecrated, the edifices repaired, and this recording stone erected.

No. XI. (p. 390.)

No. 1.—*Inscription in the Temple of Chandra Pribhu, erected by the brothers, Tejpál and Busunt Pál.*

Of Yadu race, like the ocean in purity, was the Indu Neméswara,¶ ascending in the prints of whose lotus-footsteps unto the lofty Ujayanti,** multitudes of the Yadu race, generation after generation, touched with their foreheads the feet of Nemnat'h.††

In

* *Mandalica,* though a proper name, is also titular, *viz.* 'Lord of the Region;' this and Khéngâr are the two names best preserved by tradition, and to one or other many things at Joonargurh-Gírnar are attributed.

† *Thâlaiti,* or *tulaîtí,* is the term applied to the town at the foot of every hill-fortress; but I know no castle of this name, though Abulfazil mentions Jhanjír as a seaport in the eighth division of Saurashtra.

‡ The Javan, or Yavan, is applied by the Hindu both to Greek and Islamite.

§ "The path of virtue" of the Rajpoot is the same as the Roman, *viz.* manhood, and this metaphorical expression, as regards *Abhye Sing,* or, 'the fearless lion,' means, that he fell in battle.

|| Here is another of these cryptographic dates, explained in the *Annals of Rajast'han,* which without the key would be unknown, and thus all such inscriptions would become useless. The date is explained in the text.—S. 1473.

¶ The Yadu is one of the chief of the races of Indu, or Chandra, 'the moon.' Neméswar probably means the founder of this race; from *Nema,* 'foundation,' and *éswara,* 'lord.'

** Ujayanti, or Ujanti, one of the names of Girnar, explained p. 368.

†† This shows, beyond a doubt, that the Yadu races followed the faith of Budha, or Jaina; in fact, Nemnat'h, or, familiarly, Nemí (from his dark colour called *Arishta Nemi*), was of Yadu race, not only the cotemporary, but the very near kinsman of Crishna, being the sons of Basdeo and Samádru, the elder and younger of ten brothers.

In the Vicrama Samvat 1204,* on Wednesday *(Budhwar)*,† the sixth of the month of Phalgoon,‡ Srí Chandra Pribhu was enshrined during the sway of Srí Râj Thakoor Samanta Bhoj, his son, Asser Raj, and his wife, Srí Komar-deví, from whom was born Srí Looní Ram.

Of Srímâl tribe were the brothers Tejpál and Busunt Pál, with Lilítá-deví,§ and son.

No. 2.—*Second Inscription on the same stone as the foregoing, from the Temple of Chandra Pribhu.*

This place of devotion *(teertha)* of Neméswara, in Revachíl,|| *ornamented with various minerals,*¶ *brought from the distant shores of ocean by merchants of wealth,* S. 1227, Sri Sutroonjâ and Ujayantí, grand objects of worship, and frequented by hosts of pilgrims. This abode of the gods was repaired and embellished by the Chalúca warrior, Mahraja Raj Srí * * * * * * * [*Cætera desunt.*]

No. 3.—*Inscription in the Temple of Malinát'h.*

S. 1234.†† On the sixth of the month of Pos, on Srí Girnar the Gooroo, of places of religious resort, the merchants, Tejpâl and Busunt Pâl, with their father, Rajpâl, in the reign of Srí Komár-pâl, of Srí-Patun, erected on Ujayanti-Gir the gem amongst *teert'hás*, this similitude of Meru-mandala, together with the shrines of Srí Mulinát'h, Srí Chandra Pribhu, and Adéswara.

No.

* I have little doubt that the *zero* in this date, S. 1204, is erroneous, and that it should be S. 1234, which corresponds with the date on a succeeding inscription.

† *Budhwar*, or Wednesday, sacred to Budha, and named after him, is a day propitious to any new undertaking.

‡ *Phalgoon* is one of the chief months of spring, or *Vasant*.

§ Lilítá-deví was either the wife or daughter of one of these munificent merchants, or perhaps their mother.

|| *Revachíl* is the antient designation of this important range in the geography of Saurashtra.

¶ The chief mineral used in decorating this shrine has all the appearance of that marble called *jaune antique*, and may have been brought by these "merchants of wealth" from Myas Hormus, or some other port of the Red Sea, from the quarries afterwards so much resorted to by the Romans.

** The Chaluca prince, who repaired this shrine, must have been a subordinate branch of the then reigning family of Anhulwarra. It is a fresh proof that the worship of the Jain or Budha faith was common to the Rajpoot princes at this period.

†† S. 1234, or A.D. 1178. This date corrects the other, in the first inscription, which should be S. 1234, instead of S. 1204.

No. XII. (p. 394.)

Inscriptions at Girnar.

No. 1.—*On the great Nemnat'h, on a column of the Munduff.*

S. 1333. Bysak sood, 14. Somewar-Srí Jin Siroboda Sooree, by his order from Ooja Sroor, the Srawuk Gooroos, and his son, Beer Pál, and Heera Lakhu, on the great teerut of Ujayantí, repaired the temple of Neméswara; for which purpose he bestowed 200 mohrs from himself, and *lent* 2,000 *mohrs, to be repaid with interest.*

No. 2.—*Inscription in the Temple erected by Raja Sumpriti.*

S. 1215,* on the 8th of the month of Cheyt, Sunday, on the *teert'ha* (place of pilgrimage) Ujayanti-gír, this *devacúlí* (cells around the temple) was erected by Sacti Raja Comali Sindhérana,† in Saca Salivàhana - - - - - By Suryavansí, Jusohir and Thakoor Sodeva the gate of entrance was constructed. By Thakoor Bharat, and others, a *tanka*‡ was excavated.

No. 3.—*At the Gate of Khengár's Palace.*

(After praise of Girnar.) Of Yadu race was Srí Mandalica,§ the Lord of Men, who enlarged the temple of Nemnát'h. From him was Nogan; over the nine divisions *(No-Khanda)*|| his sway extended; he was munificent and bountiful. From him was Mahindra,¶ fosterer of the land *(Mahipala)*. In Pruhus-Puttun he repaired the temple of Somnat'h. From him was Khengar,** who plundered the fruit-tree of his foe. His son

* A.D. 1159, Komar-pál was at this time supreme monarch of Western India.

† This epithet would almost warrant the idea that this royal pilgrim, who constructed the *devacúlí*, or lateral cells, which were for places of rest, was a Rajpoot prince of Sinde. The Soda princes had regained much of their importance at this time; they also held the title of Rana.

‡ I have often had occasion to notice, that the word *tank*, or reservoir, is of pure Hindu origin.

§ The name of Mandalica was titular in this family, of whom there were four, and as he was four generations anterior to Khengar, the cotemporary of Sidraj, of Puttun, who ruled from S. 1150 to S. 1200, his era is easily calculated, as is that of the last of his name, subjugated by Mohamed Begra.

|| The *No-Khanda*, or nine divisions, into which the peninsula was divided.

¶ Mahindra, who repaired the shrine of Somnat'h, probably acted with the famed Sidraj in this work of piety, as lord paramount.

** Khengar, the most celebrated man of the Yadu line in Saurashtra, was the personal opponent and rival of the celebrated Sidraj, for the hand of the Deora princess.

son was Jey Sing-deva. His son was Mokul. His son was Molug, from whom was Mahípâla. He had Mandalica,* lord of the region *(mandala)* of Saurashtra, magnificent as Bhoj.

(The inscription concludes with the praise of Mandalica, addressing the pilgrims and mendicant races in a bold metaphorical strain: "Why want, when the *Calpa-vricsha*, or ever-fructifying Mandalica, is here? go to him, whom may happiness attend!")

No. 4.—*From the Shrine of Parswa, erected by the brothers Tej-Pál and Busunt-Pál.*

S. 1287, Phalgoon bodí teej, Rubiwâr (or Sunday, the third of the spring month, Phalgoon, A.D. 1231), the exalted of Chaluc race, in Anhulpoor-Patun, Comala-Raj-hansa-Srímant-Rajavalí Mahárájá dheráj Srí - - - - - - [here the most important part, the name of this paramount sovereign, *(Rajâvalí)*, has been obliterated; it recommences thus:] Ministers of Vira-dhuwal,† Samanta Sing, who was Lord of Guzerat, and Preladun, his son.‡

No. XIII.

Inscription on Mount Taringi.

[*Note by the Author.*—An inscription given me by a Yuti from this mount, sacred to Adnat'h and Aj'itnat'h, offered fresh subject] for astonishment at the boundless wealth of the brothers Busunt Pál and Tej Pál, the work of whose hands on Aboo are described, and on Mount Girnar.]

Svat Srí.—To the Omniscient! To the Almighty! S. 1284 (A.D, 1228), Phalgoon sood 2d, Sunday. The dweller in Anhulpoor, of Poorwur tribe, the son of Chand, Asso, his son Akhé Raj, and his wife Nokumar, was born Lunsár; his wife, Maldevi, and son, Buspál, on the mountain Taringi, erected the temples to Aj'itnat'h and Adnat'h, the first and second Teert'hancars.

No.

* Mandalica is here distinctly stated to be lord of Saurashtra, the enfeebled state of Anhulwarra having permitted their shaking off their subordinate character, established by Sidraj.

† "The banner of manhood."

‡ The inscription from Kunkul-éswar (No. 1) helps out this, and shews that Preladun, then having the epithet *Deva*, or 'god-like,' attached, was the son *regent* of Dhárâburz-deva, "whose umbrella alone was spread over *Chandrâvatí-Nuggrí*, the lord of the surrounding regions (*Mandalâcâ-éswara*)." This, I repeat, is the glorious opponent of Kootub-oo-deen, the viceroy and successor of Shab-oo-deen, the conqueror of India.

No. XIV.

Inscription on a Pillar at Puttun-Somnat'h.

[This inscription was copied, at the Author's request, by Pooranee Ramdut Krishna Dutt, of Puttun, and translated by Mr. Wathen, of Bombay, with the assistance of a learned Jain priest.]

I adore that Eternal Being, who is the source of the twenty-five principles!

The pulses of the five principles, Æther, Air, Fire, Water, and Earth, are the Sun and Moon; whoever contemplating these obtains abstraction, and thus discovers that which is perfection, such a one becomes concentrated in the Universal Spirit!

Praise be to Siva! The destroyers of the Daityas (demons), Lacshmi, Narayana, these are renowned throughout the Universe; they are deserving of worship!

This temple of Sri Somanat'ha is beautiful as a Rutnacanti (sparkling gem), and in magnificence brilliant as the splendour of the Sun and Moon. This Deity (Somanat'ha), consisting of an assemblage of virtues, containing in himself all descriptions of treasure, this God destroys and removes all kinds of pain and distress. Almighty Being! thou art victory! thou reignest on the shores of the ocean!

The Bramin Sompara is perfect, and well acquainted with the rights of sacrifice, and the rules of meditation, worship, and the ceremonies of making offerings.

There was a Prince of the Sandila race, and Raja Vera's family, who caused a great sacrifice to be performed. This Raja, Sovereign of Anhalapura Patana, such Mula Raja was as a Protector to the World. He caused the Ganga-ghata to be built on the river; many were the pious acts done by him. Mula Raja caused to be formed reservoirs of water, wells, tanks, temples, religious places, schools, and dharmasalas (caravanserays); hence these became as ensigns, displaying his good name; towns, villages, and hamlets were established by him, and governed happily. He became as a Chudamani gem (unexampled) in this universe; how can I describe his mighty feats? He conquered the whole world by his own power alone, and then protected his conquest. The son of Mula Raja, named Sri Madhu, then completed the subjection of this earth. He caused his kingdom to become populous, and well cultivated; he enjoyed his government, without fear (of his enemies). The son of this Prince was Dulabha Raja, who, as Siva reduced Camadeva to ashes, so did he also destroy the power of inimical kings. His younger brother was Vicrama Raja, in strength resembling a lion. Having assembled a

numerous

numerous army, he took possession of the throne, having subjected the Fairy Devangni; hence his fame became spread throughout the three worlds. This Prince, of high descent, governing with all the virtues required in a good King, rendered his people most happy. Having made his own the Goddess of Victory, she became his standard-bearer. Of this Purmar race, of Sri Vicrama's family, Sri Cumarapala Raja arose, a mighty Hero. He was a most renowned Warrior; he was a King, terrific and formidable as the waves of the ocean. The descent of Sri Cumarapala is now to be described:

The Chaluc race is most famous; in it have arisen Rajas generation after generation, forming a lofty tree of virtue; Rajas, who caused the forms of religion and the ways of justice to be observed; like Indra, inasmuch as they showered favours on their people as clouds by rain fertilize the earth. Of this family arose a king of high renown, a great hero, named Gulla Raja, who caused to be built the hall of the Temple of Someshvara, and a famous sacrifice, called *Méghadwanni*, was performed by his orders. His son was Lalackhia, whose son was Bhabhackhia; he was a great warrior. Bhima Raja was his friend; this Prince Lala, when seated on his throne, resembled the full moon in splendour. Whose son, Jayasinvha, having reigned with fame on this Earth, ascended to the realms of bliss; his son, Rajsinvah, caused Sanvat Cumarapala to be placed on the throne, but he himself conducted the affairs of th tate. The son of Cumarapala was Sri Rohini, a Great Sovereign, endued with all virtues, splendid as the sun. He became as Sridhar, bright as the moon. The Protector of the World, the mighty, the renowned, Raja Sri Bhima Bhupati, paid much attention and respect to the merchants.

Description of Sridhara Raja.

In the generations of the Chaluc family appeared this Prince, as a gem brilliant like the Moon, possessor of every valuable quality, famous as Sri Rama, beautiful as Camadeva; such was Sridhara Raja. In him was centered every virtue; by him was adoration shewn to the Deities,—respect to the priests: a Prince perfect in truth. As Iswara, superior to all the Deities of Vaicuntha, so was he to the Lords of this Earth, exalted as Indra. As the Cow Camadhenu, granting the desires of all, thus liberal was he, exceedingly compassionate, and possessed of great humility. Again, superior to other Rajas as a Rajahansa to other birds, his fame and splendour pervade this Globe as the rays of the Moon.

In Praise of Sri Somnat'ha.

Who can wash away sins as the waters of a torrent? Who can render his worshippers prosperous and successful? Such a Deity is Sri Somnat'ha.

This

This Temple is an unique place, in the three worlds; a fit spot for devotion; whoever has had an auspicious birth, such person meditates on this God; the virtues of this Deity are universally known, he is pure and undefiled! Such is that Siva, from hearing whose praise the mind becomes pure! He will bestow on his worshippers all good things, and will grant them entrance into Paradise. Resembling a gem, his place is central; he of his goodness will pardon the sins of those born in this Cali age. His majesty and might are as his virtues, spread throughout the world. May he always be predominant! Serpents are his ornaments! He is the Lord of the Universe! he is the sole asylum of mercy in the three worlds!

Description of Patana.

This is a city, called Devaca Pattana, possessing, by favour of Siva, lofty mansions magnificent temples, numerous gardens, and delightful groves.

Description of Sridhara.

As the sea by its waves can remove mountains of sin, so Sridhara by his army governs Somnat'ha Puri. There is in this city a beautiful Temple of Sri-Crishna; there is also a Minister of great prudence, who expels the evil-doers and vicious. This Sridhara having had several invocations recited, and sacrifices performed, has erected Temples for the sake of religion, and has enriched them with gardens, groves, and bowers. These Temples resemble the pinnacles of the Golden Méru in splendour and brilliancy; of these, that of Somnat'ha is most wonderful; there are cupolas of various forms, with a variety of flags, so that the place resembles the holy mountain.

Description of the High-Priest of the Temple.

The Priest is the most excellent of mankind, the abode of virtue, the compassionate Maheshvara. A constant worshipper of Shiva; one who possesses all the most estimable qualities of a priest, an unwearied performer of sacred rites and sacrifices. His mind is most pure, always engaged in the worship of Hari; he also pays adoration to Vishnu. Whose devotion is such as to secure to him the possession of whatever he may desire, which will ensure him the happiness of the immortals, as well as the blessings of this life and the comforts desired by mankind; which will obtain for him whatever object he may have fixed his inclination on, which is auspicious, which grants him all kind of bliss. By the virtues of this Sri Somnat'ha, good fortune is procured for men; he is Lord of the Moon! Sridhara Maharaja shines forth pre-eminent in his race; by this

Prince

Prince is great respect shewn to the Brahmins of this Deity. The King pays devoted regard to this Temple of Sri Somnat'ha; he bows to the renown of Siva. This Temple is the abode of saints; it is inhabited by Lacshmi; by worshipping this Siva's feet, all sin is removed. By sight of this Temple even the stain of evil deeds becomes effaced; pain and disease also disappear.

In Samvat of Sri Vicramaditya Raja 1272 (A.D. 1215), Vaisachha-vadu 4th (being Friday), this image was installed.

No. XV.

*Inscriptions at Joonagur, taken from Buildings on the Sacred Mountain Girinala (Girnar).***

[Translated by Mr. Wathen, of Bombay.]

No. 1.—(After invocation to Ganesa.) It is proper for me to describe the sacred mountain Girnala. In that Revtachala,† the Lord of mountains, devotees, ascetics, and holy men are engaged in the constant performance of the sacred rites of penance and devotion. On that holy Girnala exists a celebrated sacred spot, around which are thick forests, interspersed with various elegant temples, reservoirs of water, and many religious edifices, by which the mountain is ornamented and adorned. Wandering through these solitary regions, casting aside pride, covetousness, overcoming the passions, holy men worship the Almighty. Here, blessed with frequent visions, the virtuous finally attain (as the reward of their pains) happiness, prosperity, and wealth; their minds being intensely engaged in contemplation of the divine essence.

In very antient times, on this Girnala, famous sacrifices and magnificent festivals were celebrated by the illustrious Harivansa. Subsequently, many princes of the Yadu family secured to themselves mansions of bliss in Paradise by their munificent acts of piety on this mountain. Many generations having passed, there arose from the Yadu line a Raja, whose name was Mandalika, whose priest Hémacharya installed in a temple on this height the image of Srí Némnat'ha. Now will the virtues of this Raja be described; he was a great, valiant, and renowned heroic Prince, a protector of his subjects. His son was called Mahipala; in good qualities as God on earth, in generosity as

* [In dates and topics these inscriptions coincide with some of the preceding.]

† One of the many names of the mountain.

as the Calpavricsha. Then ruled Khéngara Raja; his reign was prosperous. Jayasinha Raja succeeded him; he was as a frontal ornament among princes, beautiful as the Rajhansa. Raja Mahipala then arose, as a protector to this earth, a destroyer of the unjust. His son, Mandalica, governed the country extending to the shores of the * Sindhu flood; his fame was spread abroad, he reigned virtuously; he was merciful and just, a protector of the weak and poor; thus did he rule the delightful territory of Soretha for successive years. Great and distinguished rajas paid obedience to this Mandalica, and the pride and arrogance of vicious princes he reduced and annihilated; long did this wise and virtuous prince reign.

Here is also a town, the abode of every blessing, the very form of prosperity; in it are many inhabitants, allured from all parts by its excellent government. Here reside many rajas wearing crowns, with their families; here are wells, reservoirs of water, various mansions, temples of the deities; for by the constant sight of this Revtachala the wealth of its inhabitants is greatly increased.

In latter times there appeared rajas of the Yadu race, who bowed their heads in adoration to the holy Jina, who thence enjoyed prosperity, and governed their people equitably.

In the year of Vicramaditya 1204 (A.D. 1148), Cartica Shuda 6th (of the light half of the moon of Cartica), Chandra Prasada became sovereign; then Samvatta Bhoja; Asha-raj Nanda, and Sri Kumara Devi; their son, Sri Lunirama; Sri Mala Kula; Sri Tejpála, who was succeeded by his elder brother's son, Vastupala; then reigned Sri Lalita Raja, who carries on an extensive commerce in S. 1277 (A.D. 1221). This Raja performed at Sitranji, Girnala, and other holy places, pilgrimages and festivals; he also erected a magnificent temple, dedicated to the Superior Devatas. Of the Chaluc tribe was Maharaja Lalita.

No. 2.—In praise of the Goddess Amba.

The destroyer of doubts and fears, the donor of all human desires and wishes; she who causes to be completed the designs of the devout; such Goddess Sri Mata Ambica is the sole power whereby the prayers of mankind are fulfilled. Be praise and glory unto her!

No. 3.—In 1339 (A.D. 1283), Jeshta Shuda 10th, being Thursday, the old ruined temples being removed from their sites on the mountain of Revtachala, new ones were erected.

No.

* The river Indus.

No. 4.—In 1333 (A.D. 1277), Vysack 4th, Monday, Sri-Jana Prabodha Acharya, being High-Priest at Ujain, by his directions the Sravaca Gunnesh, his son, Virapala, of the Srimali caste, Saha Hira Lack'ha expended 200 mohurs on Revtachala for the sake of installing Sri Nemnaṭ'ha in a temple, and distributed 2,000 mohurs daily for the worship of that deity.

No. 5.—By orders of Sri Pandita Devsena Sunga, in S. 1215 (A.D. 1159), Chytra shuda 8th, Sunday, the antient temples of the Devatas were removed, and new erected.

No. 6.—In Samvatsira Sindhiran reigned a raja named Shalivahana; his son was Suvara Thakoor; also Pati Shalivahana, his son Ruchyaparwa. These princes caused great sacrifices to be performed, and the reservoir called Bhimacunda to be made. Vastupala Tejpála caused the image of Sri Ambica to be placed on Girnala, and the well called Ruscumpica he caused to be formed.

No. 7.—In Samvata 1234 (A.D. 1178), Posh vuda 6th, Thursday, Saha Vastupala Tejpála caused to be built on Girnala a vast temple, in which was placed Sri Malinat'ha. At this period Cumarapala Raja* reigned at Patana, as a frontal ornament amongst princes.

* This would appear to antedate the reign of Komár-pal (whose accession is fixed S. 1189) by eleven years.

THE END.